SPORTS AND
RECREATIONAL
INJURIES

Jeffrey K. Riffer
Kadison, Pfaelzer, Woodard,
Quinn & Rossi
Los Angeles, California

SHEPARD'S/McGRAW-HILL
P.O. Box 1235
Colorado Springs, Colorado 80901

McGRAW-HILL BOOK COMPANY

New York • St. Louis • San Francisco • Colorado Springs
Auckland • Bogota • Hamburg • Johannesburg • London
Madrid • Mexico • Montreal • New Delhi • Panama • Paris
São Paulo • Singapore • Sydney • Tokyo • Toronto

12345678910 SHCU 894321098765

Library of Congress Cataloging in Publication Data

Riffer, Jeffrey K.
    Sports and recreational injuries.

    Bibliography: p.
    Includes index.
    1. Liability for sports accidents—United States.
I. Title.
KF 1290.S66R54   1985   346.7303'22   85-22324
ISBN 0-07-052828-4   347.306322

ISBN 0-07-052828-4

To Cathy, who is the best.

Acknowledgments

It would have been impossible to put together this book without the assistance of numerous individuals and entities and they deserve special acknowledgment. I owe a great debt to my law firm, Kadison, Pfaelzer, Woodard, Quinn & Rossi and its Executive Committee for allowing me to complete this project, a task which took several years. Alan Woodard, Esq. was especially helpful with his constant encouragement. Deans Ronald F. Phillips and James McGoldrick of Pepperdine University School of Law also deserve mention for their aid and also for allowing me to teach a Sports Law course at Pepperdine.

I also want to thank Steve Kotlowitz, Esq. who did some of the initial research and Cathy Conway, Esq. who assisted in the research and also acted as an additional editor. My assistant, Ms. Jackie Schwartz, performed in an outstanding manner and the book could not have been completed without her since she typed virtually every word of the text.

In addition, I gratefully acknowledge the following individuals and entities for allowing me to quote from their works: The American Law Institute for The Restatement (Second) of Torts; Dr. Frederick O. Mueller, Dr. Carl S. Blyth, and The National Collegiate Athletic Association for the Annual Survey of Catastrophic Football Injuries 1977-1982; Dr. Frederick O. Mueller, Mr. Richard D. Shindler, The National Collegiate Athletic Association, The National Federation of State High School Associations and the American Football Coaches Association for the Annual Survey of Football Injury Research 1931-1983.

Preface

Each year, millions of Americans are seriously injured, thousands fatally, while participating in sports and recreational activities. This book analyzes the legal aspects of those accidents.

The book is designed to help the reader find the applicable authority easily. Therefore, it is arranged in sections, primarily by the specific sport or recreational activity. In this manner, the reader can avoid, if he or she chooses, reading about sports or recreational activities which are not of concern. The unavoidable result of this arrangement is that the few readers who read the book from page one on will encounter some repetition in the basic legal principles because these do not vary signficantly from one sport or recreational activity to another and, therefore, are covered in most chapters.

The book is primarily organized in terms of potential defendants. For example, Chapter 1 discusses the liability of commercial recreational facilities; Chapter 2 deals with the liability of fellow sports participants; Chapter 3 analyzes government liability; Chapter 4 discusses the liability of schools; and Chapter 7 deals with sports and recreational products liability. Chapter 6 explains the common law liability of land occupiers and, therefore, also provides background reading for Chapters 1, 3, 4 and 8 (which discusses spectator injuries).

The legislatures in over 40 states have passed laws which reduce a landowner's liability for sports and recreational injuries when the plaintiff came on land of another without paying for that privilege. This major legislative exception to the trend in tort law of increasing liability is discussed in Chapter 5.

The traditional defenses of assumption of the risk and contributory and comparative negligence are analyzed in Chapter 9. The defenses that no duty of care was owed or breached or that causation was not present are discussed in the applicable sections dealing with the specific sport or recreational activity. Exculpatory agreements are discussed in Chapter 10.

The number of reported cases dealing with sports and recreational injuries is huge. I have attempted to include a representative sample of the decisions, from all jurisdictions, for each activity. Accordingly, the sections of the book which contain significantly more case citations than other sections are a result of the fact that I located significantly more cases dealing with those specific recreational injuries.

The reality of modern day tort practice is that federal and state statutes codify many of the significant rules. Accordingly, I have attempted to include citations to the relevant statutes regarding specific sports and recreational activities. Indeed, the statutory framework is so important in certain areas, e.g., claims against the government and claims against certain landowners, that I have included numerous sections which deal with the application of those statutes to sports injuries.

I sincerely hope that the reader finds this book helpful.

Jeffrey K. Riffer
Los Angeles, California

Contents

Liability of Commercial Recreational Establishments

1

§1.01   Introduction

This chapter deals principally with the liability of commercial recreational establishments for the injuries their patrons received while participating in a recreational activity.[1] In addition, it discusses the liability of certain other potential defendants, such as private not-for-profit organizations[2] and homeowners' associations,[3] because their responsibilities are similar to those of commercial recreational facilities. Most of the defendants in the cases analyzed in this chapter are landowners or occupiers, and a review of the applicable common law principles pertaining to those defendants may be warranted.[4]

General Duty of Care

It is clear that recreational establishments are not insurers.[5] Generally, they have a duty to exercise reasonable care under the circumstances.[6] This duty of care encompasses not only the area used for the sporting activity, but also extends to all other portions of the premises such as nurseries[7] or parking lots.[8]

It has been noted that a proprietor of a place of public amusement or entertainment is held to a stricter account for injuries on the premises than the owner of property not open to the public.[9] However, such statements really only mean that property open to the public is a *circumstance* which requires greater care by the owner than does property not open to the public.[10]

In some situations, recreational establishments have been held to a standard of care which is greater than *reasonable care*. Some establishments, e.g., ski

---

[1] Liability for spectator injuries is analyzed in **ch 8**. Products liability is discussed in **ch 7**.

[2] Hearl v Waterbury YMCA, 187 Conn 1, 444 A2d 211 (1982); Wells v YMCA, 150 So 2d 324 (La Ct App 1963); *see also* **§1.23**.

[3] Purvis v Holiday Hills Property Owners Assn, Inc, 163 Ga App 387, 294 SE2d 592 (1982); *see also* **§1.20**.

[4] *See* **ch 6**.

[5] Burgert v Tietjens, 499 F2d 1,4 (10th Cir 1974); Chapman v Foggy, 59 Ill App 3d 552, 375 NE2d 865, 868 (1978); Gatti v World Wide Health Studios, 323 So 2d 819, 822 (La Ct App 1975).

[6] Hooks v Washington Sheraton Corp, 578 F2d 313, 315 (DC Cir 1977); Taylor v Centennial Bowl, Inc, 65 Cal 2d 114, 416 P2d 793, 797, 52 Cal Rptr 561 (1966); Roll 'R' Way Rinks, Inc v Smith, 218 Va 321, 237 SE2d 157, 161 (1977).

[7] Georgia Bowling Enters, Inc v Robbins, 103 Ga App 286, 119 SE2d 52 (1961).

[8] Geraghty v Burr Oak Lanes, 5 Ill 2d 153, 125 NE2d 47 (1955).

[9] Parsons v National Dairy Cattle Congress, 277 NW2d 620, 623 (Iowa 1979).

[10] See **ch 5** for a discussion of state laws regulating the responsibilities of owners of property generally not open to the public.

resorts and amusement parks, have been held to be common carriers.[11] This requires the establishment to exercise the highest degree of care commensurate with the practical operation of the activity.[12] In addition, it has been held that establishments which allow children to use their premises must exercise the highest degree of care possible for their safety.[13]

Recreational establishments are not liable unless they breach a duty of care. For example, a horse racing facility had no duty to prevent an accident between a prospective patron and an automobile on a public street, over which the facility had no control, and, therefore, was not liable for the plaintiff's injuries.[14] In addition, an automobile racetrack does not owe a duty to the public to detain a motorist who enters its premises intoxicated.[15]

Some courts have held that recreational establishments owe no duty of care to patrons for *obvious* dangers,[16] notwithstanding the fact that such dangers were apparently not obvious to the plaintiffs. Furthermore, "what might be perfectly obvious to a person [under normal circumstances] is likely to be forgotten by a contestant in the excitement of a game."[17] Of course, analytically, the mere fact that a condition is *obvious* does not mean that it is not unreasonably dangerous.[18] Therefore, the better view is that the obvious character of the danger is only one factor to be considered in determining whether the recreational establishment breached its duty of care.[19]

A recreational establishment's compliance vel non with the custom of care prevalent in that industry is not dispositive of whether reasonable care was exercised in a particular situation.[20]

In some cases, a court's conclusion of no liability appears to be grounded on the defense that the participant assumed the risk of injury. However, some of those cases can also be read as holding that the recreational facility did

---

[11] Fisher v Mt Mansfield Co, Inc, 283 F2d 533, 534 (2d Cir 1960) (Vermont law) (ski lift); Lewis v Buckskin Joe's, Inc, 156 Colo 46, 396 P2d 933, 939 (1964) (amusement park). There are, however, cases to the contrary. *See* §§1.02, 1.20.

[12] Summit County Dev Corp v Bagnoli, 166 Colo 27, 441 P2d 658, 664 (1968).

[13] Burwell v Crist, 373 F2d 78, 81 (3d Cir 1967); Willis v YMCA, 28 NY2d 375, 270 NE2d 717, 321 NYS2d 895, 898 (1971).

[14] Laufenberg v Golab, 108 Ill App 3d 133, 438 NE2d 1238, 1240-41 (1982).

[15] Sports, Inc v Gilbert, 431 NE2d 534, 539-40 (Ind Ct App 1982); *see also* Restatement (Second) of Torts §315 (1965).

[16] Steele v Jekyll Island State Park Auth, 122 Ga App 159, 176 SE2d 514 (1970); Cronin v Northland Bowling Lanes Co, 389 SW2d 863, 866-67 (Mo Ct App 1965); Bluejacket v Carney, 550 P2d 494, 497 (Wyo 1976).

[17] Murphy v El Dorado Bowl, Inc, 2 Ariz App 341, 409 P2d 57, 59 (1965).

[18] *Id.*

[19] *Id.*

[20] Burgert v Tietjens, 499 F2d 1, 8 (10th Cir 1974); Westborough Country Club v Palmer, 204 F2d 143, 147 (8th Cir 1953); Marietta v Cliffs Ridge, Inc, 385 Mich 364, 189 NW2d 208, 209 (1971).

not breach a duty of care.[21] Accordingly, a review of the cases discussing the assumption of risk defense may be warranted.[22]

Although most injured participants have argued that the recreational establishment was negligent, other legal principles may also be applicable. For example, one injured participant successfully showed that he was a third-party beneficiary of a contract between a recreational establishment and the government which required the establishment to take certain safety precautions.[23]

Acts of Third Parties

A recreational facility is liable for its patrons' injuries which were caused by acts of third parties if the injury occurred because the facility failed to exercise reasonable care.[24] In several instances, for example, swimming facilities were liable for failing to stop *roughhousing* in the water before a patron was injured.[25] However, where an injury resulted from a sudden, isolated act of another patron, e.g., a golfer at a driving range moved out of a practice stall and into the path of another golfer, the facility had not acted unreasonably and, therefore, was not liable.[26]

Children

Reasonable care may require additional safety precautions when a recreational establishment is entrusted with the safety of children.[27] A golf facility may even be liable for allowing young children on the golf course because they may be hit by golf balls.[28]

In *Stafford v Catholic Youth Organization*,[29] the court held that an instructor had a duty to avoid inflicting injury upon the children because of his superior

---

21 *See* Wright v Mt Mansfield Lift, 96 F Supp 786, 791 (D Vt 1951); Lisman, *Ski Injury Liability*, 43 U Colo L Rev 307, 307 (1972).

22 *See generally* §§9.02, 9.03.

23 Baroco v Araserv, Inc, 621 F2d 189, 191 (5th Cir 1980).

24 Nance v Ball, 134 So 2d 35, 37 (Fla Dist Ct App 1961); Anderson v Clements, 284 So 2d 341, 345 (La Ct App 1973).

25 Gordon v Hotel Seville, 105 So 2d 175, 177 (Fla Dist Ct App 1958); Manganello v Permastone, Inc, 291 NC 666, 231 SE2d 678, 681 (1977); *see generally* Ky Rev Stat §231.110 (1982) (entertainment facility shall not allow disorderly or boisterous persons to remain on its premises).

26 Panoz v Gulf & Bay Corp, 208 So 2d 297 (Fla Dist Ct App 1968).

27 Lincoln v Wilcox, 111 Ga App 365, 141 SE2d 765, 768 (1965); Martin v Amusements of Am, Inc, 38 NC App 130, 247 SE2d 639, 643, *cert denied*, 296 NC 106, 249 SE2d 804 (1978).

28 Outlaw v Bituminous Ins Co, 357 So 2d 1350, 1353 (La Ct App), *writ ref*, 359 So 2d 1293 (La 1978).

29 202 So 2d 333, 336 (La Ct App), *writ ref*, 251 La 231, 203 So 2d 559 (1967).

strength and weight. However, when there was no breach of that duty, there was no liability because there is no per se liability for wrestling with children.[30]

Design

Recreational establishments must take reasonable care in the design of their premises. A country club was held liable for the negligent design of the golf course because an automobile driveway was located unreasonably close to where golf balls were known to land.[31] In addition, one court held that a pool builder which held itself out as an expert in pool design could be liable for the negligent design of a pool it built, but did not design, if it should have known of the dangers of the design yet failed to eliminate those dangers.[32]

Equipment

Recreational facilities which provide equipment to their patrons must furnish reasonably safe products.[33] This topic is also discussed in another chapter.[34]

Rescue

Recreational establishments must take reasonable steps to rescue patrons who are in danger.[35] However, there is generally no duty to rescue strangers, i.e., nonpatrons. In addition, a recreational establishment which commences to rescue a stranger may stop the attempt at any time without liability, as long as stopping the rescue does not place the stranger in a worse position than he or she was in before the rescue attempt was begun.[36]

One who intentionally or negligently prevents another person from giving aid necessary to prevent physical harm to a third person is subject to liability for physical harm caused to the third person due to the absence of aid.[37] This general rule requires three parties: an imperiled plaintiff, a rescuer and one who prevents or interferes with the rescuer.[38] In *Miller v Arnal Corp*,[39] the

---

30 *Id.*

31 Lexington Country Club v Stevenson, 390 SW2d 137, 141-42 (Ky Ct App 1965).

32 Shetter v Davis Bros, 163 Ga App 230, 293 SE2d 397, 399 (1982).

33 Gifford v Bogey Hills Golf & Country Club, Inc, 426 SW2d 98, 102 (Mo 1968).

34 *See* ch 7.

35 *See generally* Kopera v Moschella, 400 F Supp 131, 135 (SD Miss 1975) (Mississippi law); Smith v Jung, 241 So 2d 874, 876-77 (Fla Dist Ct App 1970).

36 Miller v Arnal Corp, 129 Ariz 484, 632 P2d 987 (1981).

37 Restatement (Second) of Torts §§326, 327 (1965).

38 Miller v Arnal Corp, 129 Ariz 484, 632 P2d 987, 994 (1981).

39 *Id.*

court held that a corporation cannot *interfere* with itself. Therefore, there was no liability where one corporate employee wished to pursue an attempt to rescue a hiker stranded in the mountains while another, more senior corporate employee, refused to allow this attempt—because there was not the requisite three parties.[40]

Causation

A recreational facility is not liable for a participant's injuries, even if it breaches its duty of care, unless the breach was a substantial factor in causing the injury or aggravating the damages.[41]

The courts have reached conflicting results regarding the applicability of the res ipsa loquitur doctrine in recreational accident cases. Although the doctrine has been applied in some cases,[42] several courts have not used it because the establishment did not have exclusive control of the dangerous instrumentality.[43]

State Statutes

There are state laws regulating recreational establishments involved in providing amusement rides,[44] firearms,[45] health spas,[46] horseback riding,[47] snow skiing,[48] and swimming facilities.[49]

§1.02   Amusement Parks and Rides

General Duty of Care

An amusement park[50] does not insure the safety of its patrons.[51] However,

---

40 *Id.*

41 Restatement (Second) of Torts §431 (1965).

42 Zimmer v Celebrities, Inc, 44 Colo App 515, 615 P2d 76, 79 (1980); Brown v Southern Ventures Corp, 331 So 2d 207, 210-11 (La Ct App 1976).

43 McKeever v Phoenix Jewish Community Center, 92 Ariz 121, 374 P2d 875, 877 (1962); Meyer v Whipple, 94 Idaho 260, 486 P2d 271, 273 (1971).

44 *See* §1.02.

45 *See* §1.07.

46 *See* §1.11.

47 *See* §1.12.

48 *See* §1.17.

49 *See* §1.24.

50 It is estimated that over 100 million people use amusement park rides each year. NY State Assembly Committee on Consumer Afairs and Protection, Amusement Parks: How Safe Are They? 1 (Apr 1982). There are about 8,000 amusement park ride accidents annually which require emergency room treatment. *See* US Consumer Prod Safety Commn, Natl Injury

in *Lewis v Buckskin Joe's, Inc*, the court held that these facilities owe their patrons the duty of care of a common carrier, viz., the highest degree of care commensurate with the practical operation of the ride.[52] The court imposed this high duty of care because the plaintiffs had completely given up their freedom of movement to the amusement park.[53]

Other jurisdictions have concluded that amusement park facilities are not common carriers.[54] In those states, the facility owes its patrons only a duty of reasonable care under the circumstances.[55] One court distinguished traditional common carriers, e.g., buses, railroads, and even elevators, from amusement rides because the former are used by people to travel from one place to another with the expectation that they will get to their destination without incident while the latter involve carriage which is incidental to the temporary sensation customers seek to obtain before they arrive back at their original location.[56]

Information Clearinghouse, Prod Summary Report (Mar 28, 1984). About seven of those accidents result in fatalities each year. *See* US Consumer Prod Safety Commn, An Overview of the US Consumer Prod Safety Commn's Involvement in Amusement Ride Safety, 1 (rev ed May 15, 1984).

One study concluded that the US Consumer Prod Safety Commn statistics on amusement park accidents significantly overstated the actual number of accidents. *See* E. Maasoumi, An Analysis of the Sampling Validity, the Estimation Procedure and the Estimates of Injuries Related to Amusement Park Rides Produced by the Consumer Prod Safety Commn (Sept 1980) (unpublished rep.).

51 Weisman v Herschend Enters, Inc, 509 SW2d 32, 38 (Mo 1974); Martin v Amusements of Am, Inc, 38 NC App 130, 247 SE2d 639, 643, *cert denied*, 296 NC 106, 249 SE2d 804 (1978); Wood v Conneaut Lake Park, Inc, 417 Pa 58, 209 A2d 268, 270 (1965). Plaintiff's counsel's argument to the jury that the facility had a duty to make its premises *safe* was error since safe is an absolute term; the facility's duty was only to make its premises reasonably safe. *See* Weisman v Herschend Enters, Inc, 509 SW2d 32, 38-39 (Mo 1974).

52 *See* 156 Colo 46, 396 P2d 933, 939 (1964).

53 *Id.*

54 *See* Harlan v Six Flags Over Georgia, Inc, 250 Ga 352, 297 SE2d 468, 469 (1982); Or Rev Stat §460.355 (1983); Wash Rev Code Ann §70.88.010 (1975).

55 Weisman v Herschend Enters, Inc, 509 SW2d 32, 38 (Mo 1974); Brown v Columbia Amusement Co, 91 Mont 174, 6 P2d 874, 877 (1931); Martin v Amusements of Am, Inc, 38 NC App 130, 247 SE2d 639, 643, *cert denied*, 296 NC 106, 249 SE2d 804 (1978); Wood v Conneaut Lake Park, Inc, 417 Pa 58, 209 A2d 268, 270 (1965); *See also* Or Rev Stat §460.355 (1983); *See generally* **§7.07.**

The American Society for Testing Materials has published several reports regarding a standard of care for amusement rides. *See* ASTM Standards F698-83; F770-82; F846-83; F853-83. In Great Britain, the Health and Safety Executive, the Association of Amusement Parks and Piers of Great Britain, the Showmen's Guild of Great Britain, and the British Amusement Catering Trades Assn have promulgated a Code of Safe Practice at Fairs (1984).

56 Harlan v Six Flags Over Georgia, Inc, 250 Ga 352, 297 SE2d 468, 469 (1982).

Children

An amusement park owner must take reasonable steps to protect children[57] using the rides.[58] It may be necessary to take precautions, in addition to those used for adults, to compensate for the youngsters' lack of understanding and appreciation of the dangers of the rides.[59] For example, if the gravitional forces from a ride pose a danger to children, the youngsters should not be allowed to use the ride unless they use a seat belt[60] or similar restraining device or are accompanied by an adult.[61]

Operation of Rides

Amusement parks must exercise reasonable care in operating the rides. A facility was negligent when it applied a brake without warning that this would cause a jolt and a patron was injured.[62] In addition, an amusement park employee may be negligent in failing to instruct a patron regarding the best manner to descend from a ride.[63]

Inspection and Maintenance of Rides

These facilities must reasonably inspect and maintain the rides.[64] In one case, where three of the four cables attached to a gondola broke, the amusement park was held negligent for not inspecting, maintaining, and replacing the equipment.[65]

Acts of Third Parties

A facility may be negligent if a customer was injured by the unlawful conduct of others and the facility failed to exercise reasonable care to prevent

---

[57] One source believes that young children account for over one half of all amusement park injuries. *See* US Consumer Prod Safety Commn, An Overview of the US Consumer Prod Safety Commn's Involvement in Amusement Ride Safety 2 (rev May 15, 1984).

[58] *See* Thomas v Pacheco, 163 Colo 170, 429 P2d 270, 273 (1967); Brown v Columbia Amusement Co, 91 Mont 174, 6 P2d 874 (1931).

[59] Martin v Amusements of Am, Inc, 38 NC App 130, 247 SE2d 639, 643, *cert denied*, 296 NC 106, 249 SE2d 804 (1978).

[60] Thomas v Pacheco, 163 Colo 170, 429 P2d 270, 274 (1967).

[61] *See id* 429 P2d at 273; Brown v Columbia Amusement Co, 91 Mont 174, 6 P2d 874 (1931).

[62] Statler v St Louis Arena Corp, 388 SW2d 833, 835 (Mo 1965). *But see* Murphy v Steeplechase Amusement Co, Inc, 250 NY 479, 166 NE 173, 174 (1929) (where the injury occurred as a result of the hazard which gave the participant the thrill he sought, there was no negligence).

[63] Schreiber v Walt Disney World Co, 389 So 2d 1040, 1041 (Fla Dist Ct App 1980).

[64] Martin v King Riding Device Co, 14 Mich App 480, 165 NW 2d 620, 622 (1968).

[65] *Id.*

the injury.[66] For example, in *Adamson v Hand*, the court held that it was a question of fact whether a tavern which had amusement devices on the premises was negligent in failing to stop a quarrel between patrons which resulted in another patron being shot.[67]

Rescue

A person injured in the attempted rescue of another passenger in an amusement ride, where the other passenger was placed in danger by the negligence of the facility, can recover from the facility for its negligence.[68] In *Brown v Columbia Amusement Co*,[69] a mother was injured while attempting to prevent her child from being forced out of an amusement ride by gravitional forces. She successfully sued the facility for its unreasonable conduct in failing to provide sufficient restraints to protect the child.[70]

Miscellaneous Duties of Care

It is not negligence for a *haunted* house to be dark; the amusement exhibit could not function otherwise.[71]

A facility's duty of care may be affected by the expected conduct of its patrons. For example, an amusement facility may be negligent in allowing inmates of a mental institution to use bumper cars.[72]

Causation

In *Jenkins v Ferguson*,[73] two women fell out of a carnival ride when the locking device failed. There was no direct proof of negligence by the facility. Indeed, there was evidence that the ride operator properly locked the device. Nevertheless, the court approved the use of the res ipsa loquitor doctrine and affirmed a verdict for the women.[74]

---

66 Adamson v Hand, 93 Ga App 5, 90 SE2d 669 (1955).

67 *Id.*

68 Brown v Columbia Amusement Co, 91 Mont 174, 6 P2d 874, 878 (1931); *see generally* Wagner v International Ry, 232 NY 176, 133 NE 437, 437-38 (1921) (Cardozo, J) ("danger invites rescue").

69 91 Mont 174, 6 P2d 874, 878 (1932).

70 *Id.*

71 Reech v Optimist Club, 408 So 2d 399, 402 (La Ct App 1981) (also held plaintiff assumed the risk).

72 Satcher v James H. Drew Shows, Inc, 122 Ga App 548, 177 SE2d 846, 847 (1970).

73 357 So 2d 39 (La Ct App 1978).

74 *Id* 41.

State Statutes

Several states have enacted safety legislation for amusement park rides.[75] In one state these laws explicitly apply to private, as well as publicly owned, rides.[76] However, the laws sometimes do not apply to slides or playground equipment.[77]

One very common state requirement is that the facility must carry liability insurance.[78] Some states have detailed safety laws, e.g., minors cannot operate the amusement devices[79] and braking procedures must be posted.[80] Other states have more general requirements, e.g., the facility must furnish and maintain safe equipment[81] and must maintain inspection records for each ride.[82] Obviously, counsel should review the inspection records to determine whether they contain useful evidence, and, if so, counsel should interview or depose the appropriate individuals.

It has been held that state safety laws preempt local ordinances regulating amusement parks.[83]

In one state the legislature provided that it will be guided by safety standards approved by the American Society of Testing Materials.[84] In investigating an accident in that state, or any other state, it should be determined whether those

---

[75] See Alaska Stat §05.20.010 (1984); Ark Stat Ann §§66-5901 to -5908 (Supp 1983); Cal Lab Code §§7900-7915 (West Supp 1984); Conn Gen Stat Ann §§29-129 to -143a (West Supp 1984); Iowa Code Ann §88A-.13 (1984); Me Rev Stat Ann tit 8, §502 (Supp 1984); Md Ann Code art 89, §§65-81 (Supp 1984); Mass Gen Laws Ann ch 140, §205A (West Supp 1984); Mich Comp Laws Ann §§408.651-408.667 (West Supp 1984); NH Rev Stat Ann §§321-A:1 to :9 (Supp 1983); NJ Stat Ann §§5:3-31 to -54 (West Supp 1984); NY Lab Law §§870-a to -m (McKinney Supp 1984); Ohio Rev Code Ann §1711.11 (Page 1984); Or Rev Stat §§460.310 -.990 (1983); Pa Act No 1984-81, SB No 298 (passed 1984); Tex Ins Code Ann §21.53 (Vernon Supp 1984); Wash Rev Code Ann §§70.88.010 to .100 (Supp 1984); see also Iowa Admin Code Labor 530, ch 61.1-62.19 (1984); Md Admin Reg tit 09.12.62 (1984); NJ Admin Code tit 12, §195 (1984); Wis Admin Code ch Ind 47 (1984).

[76] See Cal Lab Code §7901 (West Supp 1984).

[77] See Cal Lab Code §7901 (West Supp 1984).

[78] See, e.g., Ark Stat Ann §66-5903 (Supp 1983); Cal Lab Code §7912 (West Supp 1984); Conn Gen Stat Ann §29-139 (West Supp 1984); Iowa Code Ann §88A.9 (West 1972); Md Ann Code art 89, §78 (Supp 1984); Mass Gen Laws Ann ch 140, §205A (West Supp 1984); Mich Comp Laws Ann §408.666 (Supp 1984); Miss Code Ann §75-75-17 (1973); NH Rev Stat Ann §321-A:5 (Supp 1983); NJ Stat Ann §5:3-50 (West Supp 1984); Tex Ins Code Ann §21.53 (Vernon Supp 1984) ($1,000,000 per occurrence).

[79] See, e.g., Mass Gen Laws Ann ch 140, §205A (West Supp 1984).

[80] Id.

[81] See, e.g., Alaska Stat §05.20.010 (1983).

[82] See, e.g., NJ Stat Ann §5:3-46 (West Supp 1984).

[83] People v South Shore Amusements, Inc, 87 Misc 2d 256, 383 NYS2d 792, 793 (Sup Ct 1976).

[84] See Or Rev Stat §460.355 (1983).

safety standards were violated. This is because compliance with or violation of those safety standards may be evidence of whether reasonable care was provided.

§1.03   Billiards

Proprietors of billiard facilities are not insurers of their patrons' safety.[85] However, they owe their patrons a duty to exercise reasonable care to protect them from harm.[86] This includes the duty to use reasonable care in inspecting and maintaining the premises and equipment.[87]

An example of the length some courts will go to in enforcing the duty of maintaining the equipment is provided by *Archote v Travelers Insurance Co.*[88] The plaintiff in *Archote* was playing billiards in a pool room in a recreational facility which had a bar in an adjoining room. The pool room could not be observed from the bar and the bartender was the only employee on duty. The player, unaware that the cue stick he picked up was broken, took a hard shot. The stick broke and the splintered end lodged about 1 1/2 inches under the skin of his thumb. The court noted that this recreational business knew of the tendency of its clientele to break cue sticks. Therefore, the facility had a duty to have an attendant in the pool room, or at least make changes to the building to allow the bartender to have an unobstructed view of the pool room.[89] Either of those precautions would have resulted in the instant discovery of broken sticks which could then have been removed from play, reducing the risk of injury to patrons. The court held that the facility breached this duty of care and was therefore negligent.

Billiard facilities may be liable for injuries caused to patrons by dangerous individuals. For example, a billiard establishment may be negligent in failing to take any steps to stop a fight between four or five drunken patrons on its premises which ultimately resulted in an innocent patron's loss of an eye.[90]

The facility may be liable for failing to warn of expected violence. In

---

[85] Thompson v Cooles, 180 A 522, 526 (Del Super Ct 1935); Anderson v Clements, 284 So 2d 341, 344 (La Ct App 1973).

It is estimated that over 6,000 individuals each year require emergency room treatment for billiard injuries. *See* US Consumer Prod Safety Commn, Natl Injury Information Clearinghouse, Prod Summary Rep (Mar 28, 1984).

[86] Thompson v Cooles, 180 A 522, 526 (Del Super Ct 1935); Moone v Smith, 6 Ga App 649, 65 SE 712, 713 (1909); Anderson v Clements, 284 So 2d 341, 344 (La Ct App 1973).

[87] Archote v Travelers Ins Co, 179 So 2d 658, 660 (La Ct App 1965).

[88] 179 So 2d 658 (La Ct App 1965).

[89] *Id* 660.

[90] Moone v Smith, 6 Ga App 649, 65 SE 712 (1909).

Anderson v Clements,[91] a billiard player was injured by a bullet shot by the facility's employee in an attempt to prevent a battery by a disgruntled former patron wielding a butcher knife. The court held that the billiard facility was negligent in failing to warn its patrons of the danger of a shoot-out resulting from a dissatisfied customer who was known to be coming back to "cause trouble."[92]

The plaintiff's additional allegation in *Anderson* that the facility was negligent for failing to call the police was not accepted. The facility's behavior was not unreasonable for two reasons. First, a response by the police was unlikely in the short period of time between when the facility learned that *trouble* was coming and when it occurred.[93] Second, a private security guard was expected to arrive momentarily.[94]

Billiard facilities, like all businesses, have had problems with parts of the building falling and injuring customers. In one case, a billiard player injured by a piece of plaster which fell from the ceiling could not rely on the doctrine of res ipsa loquitur because it was not evident that the billiard facility was responsible for the accident.[95]

§1.04 Bowling

General Duty of Care

A bowling establishment is not an insurer of the safety[96] of its patrons.[97] However, it must exercise reasonable care in maintaining its premises,[98]

---

91 284 So 2d 341 (La Ct App 1973).

92 *Id* 345.

93 *Id.*

94 *Id.*

95 Thompson v Cooles, 180 A 522, 527 (Del Super Ct 1935).

96 It is presently estimated that there are more than 40 million bowlers in the United States. *See* Klein, *Fast Lanes: Bowling On TV*, Wall St J, Mar 23, 1983, at 19, col 1. Unfortunately, about 18,000 individuals each year require emergency room treatment for bowling injuries. *See* US Consumer Prod Safety Commn, Natl Injury Information Clearinghouse, Prod Summary Rep (Mar 28, 1984).

97 Taylor v Centennial Bowl, Inc, 65 Cal 2d 114, 416 P2d 793, 797, 52 Cal Rptr 561 (1966); Repka v Rentalent Inc, 477 P2d 470, 471 (Colo Ct App 1970); Kincaid v Lagen, 71 Ill App 2d 307, 218 NE2d 856, 859 (1966); True v Larimore, 255 Iowa 110, 123 NW2d 5, 10 (1963); Spiers v Lake Shore Enters, Inc, 210 So 2d 901, 903-04 (La Ct App 1968); Messina v Massachusetts Bonding & Ins Co, 171 So 2d 705, 707 (La Ct App 1965); Cronin v Northland Bowling Lanes Co, 389 SW2d 863, 867-68 (Mo Ct App 1965); Jones v Satterfield Dev Co, 16 NC App 80, 191 SE2d 435, 439 (1972).

98 Repka v Rentalent Inc, 477 P2d 470, 471 (Colo Ct App 1970); Schmidt v Bowl Am Florida, Inc, 358 So 2d 1385, 1386 (Fla Dist Ct App 1978); Elebash v Whitley, 114 Ga App 294, 151 SE2d 196, 198 (1966); Guidani v Cumerlato, 59 Ill App 2d 13, 207 NE2d

including the nursery[99] and the parking lot.[100] This would include the duty to remove or warn of dangerous conditions which it knows or should know exist.[101]

Some courts have held that bowling facilities are not liable for injuries resulting from dangers which are apparent or as well known to the bowler as to the bowling alley.[102] Nonetheless, the mere fact that a condition is open and obvious does not mean that it is not unreasonably dangerous.[103] For example, a bowling facility may be negligent for having a lowered floor adjacent to one of the bowling lanes.[104]

Dangerous Floor Conditions

Bowling establishments must take reasonable care in maintaining the condition of their floors and runways.[105] An untoward substance or condition on the approach to the lane which adversely affects the bowler's movement while the bowler is preparing to hurl the ball is very dangerous.[106] The runway must be smooth so that when a bowler slides his or her feet, as often happens when delivering the ball, the bowler will not fall.[107]

Bowling facilities have been held liable where a bowler was injured by

---

1, 6 (1965); Nelson v Midwest Mortg Co, 426 SW2d 149, 150 (Ky Ct App 1968); Spiers v Lake Shore Enters, Inc, 210 So 2d 901, 903-04 (La Ct App 1968); Miles v Ozark Bowl, 250 SW2d 849, 851 (Mo Ct App 1952); Belkin v Playdim, Inc, 194 Misc 950, 87 NYS2d 813, 815 (City Ct 1949); Jones v Satterfield Dev Co, 16 NC App 80, 191 SE2d 435, 439 (1972); Stelter v Cordes, 146 AD 300, 130 NYS 688, 688 (1911).

It may be negligent for a bowling facility to fail to cover the revolving blades of a ventilating fan located in the spectators' area. *See* Pittaluga v Diamond, 261 AD 850, 24 NYS2d 363, 364 (1941).

[99] *See* Georgia Bowling Enters, Inc v Robbins, 103 Ga App 286, 119 SE2d 52 (1961).

[100] *See* Geraghty v Burr Oak Lanes, 5 Ill 2d 153, 125 NE2d 47 (1955).

[101] *See* Cronin v Northland Bowling Lanes Co, 389 SW2d 863, 866-67 (Mo Ct App 1965) (sticky floors); Miles v Ozark Bowl, 250 SW2d 849, 855 (Mo Ct App 1952); Broome v Parkview, Inc, 49 Tenn App 725, 359 SW2d 566, 568 (1962); *see generally* **§7.10**.

[102] *See* Cronin v Northland Bowling Lanes Co, 389 SW2d 863, 866-67 (Mo Ct App 1965); Lenger v Modern Recreations, Inc, 203 SW2d 100, 105 (Mo Ct App 1947); Broome v Parkview, Inc, 49 Tenn App 725, 359 SW2d 566, 568 (1962).

[103] Murphy v El Dorado Bowl, Inc, 2 Ariz App 341, 409 P2d 57, 59 (1965) ("What might be perfectly obvious to a person walking normally is likely to be forgotten by a contestant in the excitement of a game.") *See also* 2 F. Harper & E. James, The Law of Torts §27.13, at 1491-93 (1956).

[104] Murphy v El Dorado Bowl, Inc, 2 Ariz App 341, 409 P2d 57 (1965).

[105] *See* Davanti v Hummell, 409 Pa 28, 185 A2d 554, 556 (1962).

[106] *Id.*

[107] *See id; see also* Nelson v Midwest Mortgage Co, 426 SW2d 149, 150-51 (Ky Ct App 1968).

slipping on a foreign substance[108] or a dangerous condition[109] on the approach to the lanes and the facility had or should have had[110] knowledge of the danger and the bowler did not have such knowledge.[111]

It is important to ascertain how long the danger existed. A bowling facility is negligent only where it failed to remove the danger in a reasonable period of time in light of all the circumstances. In *Burns v Goldammer*,[112] a bowler tripped on a piece of gum on the bowling lane. The court affirmed a jury verdict for the plaintiff because the facility should have known of the presence of the gum due to the extended length of time it remained on the floor, a conclusion supported by the fact that the gum was flattened and dirty.[113] In addition, a facility employee testified that gum on the alleys was a frequent problem.[114] Therefore, the facility should have taken additional care to eliminate the dangers posed by this recurring problem.

In most cases the appropriate length of time which must have elapsed before a facility will be considered to have acted unreasonably in not removing the foreign substance or dangerous condition from its floor is a question of fact.[115] Plaintiffs can argue that evidence that no inspection had been made during a particular period of time prior to an accident warrants an inference that the dangerous condition existed long enough so that the facility, had it exercised reasonable care, would have discovered the danger.[116] In *Schmidt v Bowl America Florida, Inc*,[117] a bowler slipped on a marking crayon while *moonlight bowling*[118] on a lane which had not been swept for more than five hours before the accident. The court held that there was a jury question concerning whether the dangerous condition had existed long enough that an owner exercising reasonable care should have learned of its existence.[119]

---

108 *See* Jones v Satterfield Dev Co, 16 NC App 80, 191 SE2d 435 (1972) (excess oil).

109 *See* Shipman v Foisy, 49 Wash 2d 406, 302 P2d 480 (1956) (small hole in approach to the lane); Spote v Aliota, 254 Wis 403, 37 NW2d 31 (1949) (loose floor boards).

110 This concept is sometimes referred to as having constructive knowledge of the condition. *See* Burns v Goldammer, 38 Ill App 2d 83, 186 NE2d 97, 99 (1962).

111 Jones v Satterfield Dev Co, 16 NC App 80, 191 SE2d 435, 439 (1972); *see generally* Corso v Knapp, 347 Ill App 556, 107 NE2d 59 (1952) (negligent to allow liquid substance to remain on steps).

112 38 Ill App 2d 83, 186 NE2d 97 (1962).

113 186 NE2d at 99.

114 *Id* at 98.

115 *See* Davanti v Hummell, 409 Pa 28, 185 A2d 554, 556 (1962) (sticky substance on approach 35 to 45 minutes).

116 Schmidt v Bowl Am Fl, Inc, 358 So 2d 1385, 1387 (Fla Dist Ct App 1978).

117 *Id.*

118 This is when the main lights over the bowling approachways and lanes are turned off. *See id* 1386.

119 *See id.*

It has been held that reasonable care of the approaches to the bowling lanes demands more frequent inspection and cleaning than that of common passageways in retail stores.[120] Such statements, of course, are of little practical significance since it is unclear how often retail store passageways should be cleaned and how much more is *more frequent*. In any event, a *sticky* spot on a floor which was in continual use by other bowlers for the preceding three hours without mishap was not so dangerous that the facility was negligent in having failed to remove it.[121]

There have been several cases in which bowlers were injured by splinters. In one instance a bowling facility was found negligent when it failed to plane the approach to the lanes and a splinter sticking up from the wood lodged in a bowler's finger.[122] However, where there was no showing that proper care by the facility would have removed or even discovered a small splinter, the plaintiff could not recover.[123]

It is not only foreseeable, but also predictable that an accident will occur when a bowler's shoes get wet.[124] Therefore, a facility must use reasonable care to prevent its patrons from encountering that situation.[125] In *Guidani v Cumerlato*,[126] an injured bowler contended he slipped because a liquid substance got on the bottom of his shoes while he was in the facility's restroom. The court held that the men's restroom in a bowling alley is one of the most likely places to encounter liquid on the floor.[127] The court concluded that the issue of whether dry-mopping the restroom floor only once in the morning and allowing liquid to accumulate under the steel matting in front of the urinals for a week at a time was negligent (as well as unsanitary) was for the jury.[128] However, in a different case, where there was no evidence that the bowling alley employees knew or should have known of the presence of water in a certain area, a directed verdict against a bowler who slipped on this water was proper.[129]

A recreational facility was not negligent for having waxed floors in a restroom.[130] The fact that a bowler slipped on the waxed floor while standing

---

120 Nelson v Midwest Mortgage Co, 426 SW2d 149, 150-51 (Ky Ct App 1968).

121 Fagan v Williamsport Lodge No 145, 361 Pa 446, 64 A2d 805, 807 (1949).

122 McGillivray v Eramian, 309 Mass 430, 35 NE2d 209, 210 (1941).

123 Stelter v Cordes, 146 AD 300, 130 NYS 688, 689 (1911).

124 Guidani v Cumerlato, 59 Ill App 2d 13, 207 NE2d 1, 7 (1965).

125 *Id.*

126 *Id.*

127 *Id.*

128 *Id.*

129 Nelson v Midwest Mortgage Co, 426 SW2d 149, 150-51 (Ky Ct App 1968).

130 Lenger v Modern Recreations, Inc, 203 SW2d 100, 106 (Mo Ct App 1947).

on one foot when she was changing from bowling shoes to street shoes is not evidence of negligence.[131]

§1.05 — Particular Situations

Placement of Facilities

In *Messina v Massachusetts Bonding & Insurance Co*,[132] a woman leaving the snack area was hit by a bowling ball swung by another patron who was standing near the ball rack, testing the weight of the ball. The court held that the placement of the ball rack near the snack bar was not a hidden danger which a bowling alley must remove or warn against.[133] Furthermore, a patron's testing of the weight of the ball or taking practice swings near the ball rack can be expected and, therefore, is a normal, obvious risk which the facility has no duty to remove or warn against.[134]

In *Miles v Ozark Bowl*,[135] a bowler tripped on steps which were beneath an information board. The lighting was dim and the board contained so much information that a bowler had to move to read all of it. The court reversed a verdict for the plaintiff because there should have been a jury instruction specifically addressed to whether the bowling alley knew or should have known that the placement of the board was dangerous.[136]

A bowling alley was not entitled to a directed verdict when a bowler attempted to lean against a plastic sheet which concealed the absence of a wall because it was for the jury to determine whether the facility's failure to warn of the dangers of leaning against the plastic was negligence.[137]

Nurseries

A bowling facility must exercise reasonable care over all of its premises, including a nursery it provides for the convenience of its patrons.[138] In *Georgia Bowling Enterprises, Inc v Robbins*,[139] a facility was found negligent when the wife of the manager of the bowling alley struck a baby staying in

---

131 *Id.*

132 171 So 2d 705 (La Ct App 1965).

133 *Id* 707.

134 *Id.*

135 250 SW2d 849 (Mo Ct App 1952).

136 *Id* 856.

137 Broome v Parkview, Inc, 49 Tenn App 725, 359 SW2d 566 (1962).

138 *See* Zimmer v Celebrities, Inc, 44 Colo App 515, 615 P2d 76 (1980); Georgia Bowling Enters, Inc v Robbins, 103 Ga App 286, 119 SE2d 52 (1961).

139 103 Ga App 286, 119 SE2d 52 (1961).

the facility's nursery. The court found that this woman was known to be of a *high tempered* nature and that she had previously been ordered to stay away from the nursery because of her prior assaults of the children. Therefore, the facility was negligent in allowing her access to the nursery.

In *Zimmer v Celebrities, Inc*,[140] a mother left her 25-month-old baby in the bowling alley's nursery while she bowled. An hour later the baby was crying and a medical examination revealed that the baby had a skull fracture.[141] There was no direct evidence of how the injury occurred. The plaintiff successfully recovered on a res ipsa loquitur theory.

The Zimmer court held that the four elements of the res ispa doctrine were properly applied.[142] First, this injury would not ordinarily occur in the absence of negligence. Second, there was no evidence of other causes of the injury; the baby was in no discomfort before being left in the nursery. Third, the apparent negligence was within the scope of the facility's duty to the baby. Fourth, there was no evidence that the child was in any way responsible for his injuries. The court specifically held that it was irrelevant that the injury could not be traced to a specific instrumentality in the exclusive control of the facility.[143]

Acts of Third Parties

A bowling alley is liable for injuries to patrons resulting from acts or conduct of other patrons or third parties which could have been reasonably anticipated and guarded against, but were not.[144] For example, summary judgment for the bowling alley should not have been granted where one bowler was assaulted by another bowler because there was some evidence that the bowling facility had prior knowledge of the violent propensities of the violent bowler and neglected to eliminate the danger.[145] However, where there was no evidence that a facility knew of the violent disposition of a bowler it was not liable for injuries resulting from that bowler's assault on another patron.[146]

---

140 44 Colo App 515, 615 P2d 76 (1980).

141 615 P2d at 79.

142 *Id.*

143 *Id. See also* Restatement (Second) of Torts §328D comment g (1965).

144 Nance v Ball, 134 So 2d 35, 37 (Fla Dist Ct App 1961); *see also* Taylor v Centennial Bowl, Inc, 65 Cal 2d 114, 416 P2d 793, 797, 52 Cal Rptr 561 (1966); Gustaveson v Gregg, 655 P2d 693, 695 (Utah 1982).

145 Nance v Ball, 134 So 2d 35, 37 (Fla Dist Ct App 1961).

146 Repka v Rentalent Inc, 477 P2d 470, 471 (Colo Ct. App 1970) (also held that it was not negligence to supply alcohol or to permit betting); Gustaveson v Gregg, 655 P2d 693, 695 (Utah 1982).

In *Taylor v Centennial Bowl, Inc*,[147] a female patron in a bowling alley's cocktail lounge was repeatedly propositioned by one man. When the lounge closed at 2:00 a.m., she prepared to leave and walk to her car which was in the parking lot. The facility bouncer told her not to go outside because that "goofball is out there." The woman left and was severely injured by knife wounds inflicted by the *goofball*.

The facility's defense was that it had fulfilled its duty of care because it had warned the plaintiff of the danger. The court rejected this argument for two reasons. First, it held that a warning is insufficient where it is apparent that because of lack of time or the character of the conduct to be expected, a warning will not give effective protection.[148] In this case, the lounge was closing and the plaintiff had to leave and go to her car. Second, the warning was insufficient because it did not inform the woman of the specific nature of the possible harm, viz., an assault with a knife.[149] The *goofball* had previously only propositioned the woman. Obviously, such behavior is offensive. Nevertheless, there is a significant difference between a verbal assault and a physical one. Therefore, to have fulfilled its duty, the facility should have warned her of the potential for physical danger.

In several cases a bowling alley was held not liable when one patron accidently hit another patron with a bowling ball while practicing a swing.[150] In one case the alley was not negligent because it was not reasonably anticipated that the accident would occur and, therefore, there was no duty to eliminate the risk.[151] In another case there was no duty to post signs that practice swings were allowed only in certain areas because bowlers had rarely taken practice swings in other areas.[152]

Causation

Some injured bowlers have had difficulty specifying what caused their injury. In some cases this has resulted in judgments adverse to those bowlers. For example, in *Houston v Canon Bowl, Inc*, a bowler was injured when her

---

[147] 65 Cal 2d 114, 416 P2d 793, 52 Cal Rptr 561 (1966).

[148] 416 P2d at 799. *See also* Restatement (Second) of Torts §344 (1965); James, *Tort Liability of Occupiers of Land*, 63 Yale LJ 605, 623, 628 (1954).

[149] 416 P2d at 799. The court also ruled that the plaintiff should have been allowed to elicit testimony from police officers that they had had to quell disturbances at this bowling alley numerous times in the recent past. This testimony would be some evidence of the facility's knowledge of the danger to its patrons. *See id* at 800.

[150] *See* Kincaid v Lagen, 71 Ill App 2d 307, 218 NE2d 856, 859 (1966); Messina v Massachusetts Bonding & Ins Co, 171 So 2d 705, 707 (La Ct App 1965).

[151] *See* Messina v Massachusetts Bonding & Ins Co, 171 So 2d 705, 707 (La Ct App 1965).

[152] *See* Kincaid v Lagen, 71 Ill App 2d 307, 218 NE2d 856, 859 (1966).

left foot unexpectedly stopped sliding when she was delivering the ball.[153] The court held that the circumstantial proof that the fall was caused by improper application of steel wool to the lanes was insufficient to allow the case to go to a jury.

Similarly, when a plaintiff could not prove that her fall on the approach to the lane was not due merely to losing her balance, a judgment in her favor was reversed.[154] A different court was more tolerant of the inferences which can be drawn from circumstantial proof, at least when the accident occurred right after the allegedly defective condition was encountered.[155] In any event, a plaintiff's failure to identify what caused him or her to fall may be insufficient, standing alone, to grant the bowling alley's summary judgment motion.[156]

A few injured bowlers have sued under the res ipsa loquitur doctrine when they were injured on the bowling lanes and could not specify what caused their injuries.[157] Although this doctrine was not applied because the lanes and approaches are not within the exclusive control of the facility,[158] there is authority to the contrary.[159]

§1.06 Camping

General Duty of Care

The owner of a camp is not an insurer of the safety of the campers.[160] Rather, it generally has a duty to guard against dangers which are foreseeable in the exercise of reasonable care.[161] This includes the duty to provide safe

---

[153] 443 Pa 383, 278 A2d 908, 911 (1971).

[154] Spiers v Lake Shore Enters, Inc, 210 So 2d 901, 906 (La Ct App 1968).

[155] See Guidani v Cumerlato, 59 Ill App 2d 13, 207 NE2d 1, 9-10 (1965) (bowler alleged he fell on his delivery of the ball after his shoes came into contact with a liquid in the facility's restroom; there was no direct proof that he stepped in the liquid while in the restroom).

[156] Akridge v Park Bowling Center, Inc, 401 SW2d 204, 206 (Ark 1966).

[157] See, e.g., Meyer v Whipple, 94 Idaho 260, 486 P2d 271 (1971); Zimmer v Celebrities, Inc, 44 Colo App 515, 615 P2d 76 (1980).

[158] See Meyer v Whipple, 94 Idaho 260, 486 P2d 271, 273 (1971).

[159] See Zimmer v Celebrities, Inc, 44 Colo App 515, 615 P2d 76, 79 (1980) (exclusive control is not a requirement).

[160] Sauer v Hebrew Institute, Inc, 17 AD2d 245, 233 NYS2d 1008, 1009 (1962), affd, 13 NY2d 913, 193 NE2d 642, 243 NYS2d 859 (1963); Klein v Hoffman, 15 AD2d 899, 225 NYS2d 628, 629 (1962).

[161] Sauer v Hebrew Institute, Inc, 17 AD2d 245, 233 NYS2d 1008, 1009 (1962), affd, 13 NY2d 913, 193 NE2d 642, 243 NYS2d 859 (1963); Klein v Hoffman, 15 AD2d 899, 225 NYS2d 628, 629 (1962).

premises and to supervise the campers adequately.[162]

The courts have not always agreed on the appropriate standard of care. One court held that a camp's duty of care is judged by the standard of the average reasonable parent.[163] Other courts have held that these organizations must exercise the highest degree of care because children are entrusted to them.[164]

In the leading case of *Sauer v Hebrew Institute, Inc*,[165] the court reversed a jury verdict for the plaintiff and held that the camp, as a matter of law, was not liable when a child involved in a water fight slipped and hit his head on a concrete walk near the grass area where the game was played. The court concluded that the camp's conduct was not unreasonable because this game was no more hazardous than any other ordinary camp activity which required physical exertion and it was inevitable that children would fall whether the grass was wet or dry.[166] Accordingly, the court ruled that: "To impose liability in this situation is to interdict the game itself, which in turn would so sterilize camping activity ... as to render it sedentary."[167]

Nevertheless, in *Greaves v Bronx YMCA*,[168] in a similar, although not identical, factual situation the plaintiff's $90,000 judgment against a camp was affirmed. In *Greaves*, the child was injured when he fell on wet grass during a game of ring-a-levio, a rougher version of run, hide, and seek, which was played on a sloping area near a swimming pool, an area where counselors previously had hosed off other campers after they left the pool.[169] The camp's fault was *where* it allowed the game to be played, viz., on a wet, sloping area, when a more appropriate place to play would have been on a nearby football field.[170]

When the camp did not act unreasonably, it was not liable. In *McClure v Suter*, a campground which posted a sign advising campers of its rule that adult supervision was required before a child was allowed to swim, and which,

---

162 Crohn v Congregation B'nai Zion, 22 Ill App 3d 625, 317 NE2d 637, 641 (1974); Soares v Lakeville Baseball Camp, Inc, 369 Mass 974, 343 NE2d 840, 841 (1976) (defendant not liable).

163 Weinstein v Tunis Lake Properties, Inc, 15 Misc 2d 432, 181 NYS2d 916, 918 (Sup Ct 1958), *affd*, 9 AD2d 960, 196 NYS2d 605 (1959).

164 Burwell v Crist, 373 F2d 78, 81 (3d Cir 1967); Willis v YMCA, 28 NY2d 375, 270 NE2d 717, 321 NYS2d 895, 898 (1971).

165 17 AD2d 245, 233 NYS2d 1008 (1962), *affd*, 13 NY2d 913, 193 NE2d 642, 243 NYS2d 859 (1963).

166 233 NYS2d at 1009.

167 *Id.*

168 87 AD2d 394, 452 NYS2d 27 (1982).

169 452 NYS2d at 28.

170 452 NYS2d at 29.

in addition, made periodic checks for children swimming unaccompanied by parents was held not negligent when a child drowned.[171]

Instruction

In *Weinstein v Tunis Lake Properties, Inc*,[172] a child attending a summer camp was directed to perform a standing broad jump and was injured. The court held that there was no negligence because the camp had no duty to instruct the child in the art of performing this activity and it was not unreasonable to fail to cushion the area to reduce the chance of injury.

Equipment

A scoutmaster who knew a child was compulsively adventuresome, required strict supervision, and frequently disregarded instructions may have been negligent in allowing the child access to climbing equipment because there were areas nearby in which it was dangerous to mountain climb.[173]

Counselors

A counselor does not have a duty to stay with the campers constantly since this is both physically impossible and pedagogically unwise because the campers should be allowed to develop a sense of responsibility.[174] Therefore, a counselor was not negligent in failing to watch campers during a rest hour.[175]

One court held that one counselor for each four children in a summer camp was, as a matter of law, an adequate number of counselors.[176]

§1.07   Firearms

Firearms dealers owe a duty of reasonable care to those individuals who are foreseeably endangered by the sale of firearms or ammunition.[177] The determination of which individuals are in the zone of foreseeable danger has been held to be a question of law to be decided by the court.[178]

---

171 63 Ill App 3d 378, 379 NE2d 1376, 1379 (1978).

172 15 Misc 2d 432, 181 NYS2d 916, 918 (Sup Ct 1958), *affd*, 9 AD2d 960, 196 NYS2d 605 (1959).

173 Coffey v Hilands, 42 Or App 193, 600 P2d 466, 469 (1979).

174 Goldberger v David Roberts Corp, 139 Conn 629, 96 A2d 309, 310-11 (1953).

175 *Id.*

176 *Id.*

177 Hulsman v Hemmeter Dev Corp, 68 Hawaii 58, 647 P2d 713, 720 (1982); *see generally* §7.12.

178 Hulsman v Hemmeter Dev Corp, 68 Hawaii 58, 647 P2d 713, 720 (1982).

Generally, a firearms dealer who sells dangerous instrumentalities to individuals whom it knows or should know are incapable of using them properly, e.g., young children, is liable for the resulting injuries.[179] However, the sale of shotgun shells to 14-year-old boys was not an unreasonably dangerous act because the children were not so young that the seller should have known that they were incapable of taking proper care of the shells.[180]

Statutes

Both the federal government and many state governments regulate firearms sales. Many of these statutes prohibit the sale of firearms to individuals below a specified age,[181] individuals of unsound mind,[182] or those who are intoxicated.[183]

These firearms statutes generally have not been given a broad construction.[184] For example, one court held that a statute prohibiting the sale of *pistols* did not proscribe the sale of *rifles*.[185] Another court held that a statute which prohibited the sale of firearms did not proscribe the sale of shotgun shells because ammunition is not a *firearm*.[186]

---

[179] Schmit v Guidry, 204 So 2d 646, 648 (La Ct App 1967).

[180] *Id.*

[181] *See, e.g.*, 18 USC §922 (illegal to sell shotgun, rifle, or ammunition to individual who knows or has reasonable cause to believe is less than 21 years old); Ala Code §13A-11-57 (1982); Ariz Rev Stat Ann §13-3109 (1978) (without written consent of parent); Ark Stat Ann §41-3109 (1977) (without consent of parent or guardian); Cal Penal Code §12551 (West 1982); Conn Gen Stat Ann §29-34 (1975); Del Code Ann tit 24, §901 (1981); DC Code Ann §22-3207 (1981); Fla Stat Ann §790.18 (West Supp 1984); Ga Code Ann §16-11-101 (1982); Hawaii Rev Stat §134-4 (1968) (unless child has hunting license); Idaho Code §18-3308 (1979) (without prior written consent of parent or guardian); Ill Ann Stat ch 38, §24-3 (Smith-Hurd 1977) (if the firearm can be concealed on the person); Ind Code Ann §35-47-2-7 (Burns Supp 1983); Iowa Code Ann §724.22 (West 1979) (without express consent of parent or guardian); Nev Rev Stat §202.310 (1983); NH Rev Stat Ann ch 159, §12 (1978); NJ Stat Ann §2C:58-3 (West Supp 1984); NC Gen Stat §14-315 (1981); ND Cent Code §62-01-11 (1960); Ohio Rev Code Ann §2923.21 (Page 1982); Okla Stat Ann tit 21, §2173 (West 1983); Or Rev Stat §166.470 (1983); Pa Cons Stat Ann tit 18, §6302 (Purdon 1983); RI Gen Laws §11-47-30 (1981) (without prior consent of parent or guardian); SC Code Ann §16-23-30 (Law Co-op Supp 1984); Tenn Code Ann §39-6-1705 (1982) (except for gun for hunting); *see also* Zamora v J. Korber & Co, 59 NM 33, 278 P2d 569, 570 (1955).

[182] *See, e.g.*, DC Code §22-3207 (1981); Fla Stat Ann §790.17 (Supp 1984); Ind Stat Ann §35-47-2-7 (Burns Supp 1983); Okla Stat Ann tit 21, §1289.10 (1983) ("idiot, moron or insane").

[183] *See, e.g.*, Del Code Ann tit 24, §901 (1981); NJ Stat Ann §2C:58-3 (West Supp 1984) (habitual drunkard).

[184] Criminal statutes are usually strictly construed. *See* Adamo Wrecking Co v United States, 434 US 275 (1978).

[185] Hulsebosch v Ramsey, 435 SW2d 161, 163 (Tex Civ App 1968).

[186] Schmit v Guidry, 204 So 2d 646, 647-48 (La Ct App 1967).

Negligence Per Se

When a firearms dealer did violate one of the applicable statutes and the party injured was in the class of people meant to be protected by the law, the courts have sometimes held that the dealer is negligent per se.[187] For example, one dealer was held liable for an underaged patron's injuries because it illegally sold him a .22 caliber rifle.[188]

However, all courts have not agreed that violation of such statutes is negligence per se. In *Olson v Ratzel*, the court held that a dealer's violation of the federal and state statutes prohibiting firearm sales to minors was not negligence per se.[189] The court based its conclusion that violation of the federal statute was not negligence per se on two major gounds. First, the federal legislation was concerned with the criminal use of firearms, not gun accidents.[190] Second, there was no reference to civil liability for violation of this portion of the statute, although in another portion of the statute, Congress expressly created a private cause of action.[191] The *Olson* court also held that the dealer's violation of state law was not negligence per se because the statute had such a broad scope and sought to deter so many hazards that imposition of negligence per se would be unreasonable.[192]

Minors

It has been held that where it is illegal to sell firearms to minors, the dealer is subject to strict liability regarding the minor's age.[193]

There have been several cases in which the dealer was not liable for selling a weapon directly or indirectly to a minor because of extenuating circumstances. In *Hulsebosch v Ramsey*, a retailer was not liable for selling a rifle to a child where it initially refused to make the sale, but later relented when the child returned to the store with his mother who stated the child was buying the rifle as a Christmas present for his father.[194] Tragically, one day before Christmas, the child misused the rifle and shot another child.[195] In a

---

187 Zamora v J. Korber & Co, 59 NM 33, 278 P2d 569, 570 (1955); Spires v Goldberg, 26 Ga App 530, 106 SE 585, 586 (1921) (minor); Restatement (Second) of Torts §286 (1965); *see generally* §1.21 (discussing negligence per se for violations of swimming safety laws).

188 Zamora v J. Korber & Co, 59 NM 33, 278 P2d 569, 570 (1955).

189 89 Wis 2d 227, 278 NW2d, 249 (1979).

190 *Id.*

191 *Id.*

192 278 NW2d at 246-47.

193 *See* Olson v Ratzel, 89 Wis 2d 227, 278 NW2d 238, 243 (1979).

194 435 SW2d 161, 163 (Tex Civ App 1968).

195 *Id.*

different case, the dealer was not liable when it sold a firearm to a parent, even though it knew a child would use the firearm, because the minor's age was not such as to indicate his inexperience with firearms.[196]

One court held that a dealer should not be entitled to summary judgment even when its sale to a minor may not have been illegal, a situation which would have been a defense to all of the allegations in the plaintiff's complaint, unless the dealer could also show that it was not guilty of common law negligence.[197]

Unsound Mind

Both federal law and some state statutes prohibit the sale of firearms to those who are mentally ill.[198] It has generally been held that there is no private cause of action for violation of the federal law.[199] In *Heist v Lock & Gunsmith, Inc*, a firearms dealer was held not liable where there was no evidence that the dealer knew or should have known that his customer was of unsound mind.[200]

Airguns, Gas Pellets, and BBs

Several states have statutes which prohibit the sale or disposition of airguns[201] or similar instruments to minors.[202] Where there is no specific statute banning such sales, it is probably not illegal to sell these items. One court held the sale of a BB gun is not a proscribed sale of a "weapon."[203]

A dealer's violation of a statute prohibiting the sale of airguns to minors may be negligence per se.[204] Of course, even if the sale does not violate a

---

196 Corey v Kaufman & Chernick, Inc, 70 RI 27, 36 A2d 103, 105 (1944) (the child was 16 year old); *but see* Semeniuk v Chentis, 1 Ill App 2d 508, 117 NE2d 883, 885-86 (1954); Sickles v Montgomery Ward & Co, 6 Misc 2d 1000, 167 NYS2d 977, 979 (Sup Ct 1957).

197 Pair v Blakley, 160 NJ Super 14, 388 A2d 1026, 1027 (1978) (open question whether BB pellet was a *blank cartridge* which should not have been sold to minor).

198 *See* 18 USC §922; 27 CFR §178; DC Code Ann §22-3207 (1981); Fla Stat Ann §790.17 (West Supp 1984); Ind Code Ann §35-47-2-7 (Burns Supp 1983); Okla Stat Ann tit 21, §1289.10 (West Supp 1983) (*idiot, moron or insane*).

199 *See* Hulsman v Hemmeter Dev Corp, 68 Hawaii 58, 647 P2d 713, 720 (1982); Olson v Ratzel, 89 Wis 2d 227, 278 NW2d 238, 249 (1979).

200 417 So 2d 1041, 1042 (Fla Dist Ct App 1982).

201 It is estimated that over 19,000 individuals injured each year from air guns require emergency room treatment. *See*, US Consumer Prod Safety Commn, Natl Injury Information Clearinghouse. Prod Summary Rep (Mar 28, 1984).

202 *See* Cal Penal Code §12551 (West 1982); NY Penal Law §265.10 (McKinney 1980) (illegal to "dispose of" airgun, spring gun or similar instrument to person under 16 years old).

203 Jimenez v Zayre Corp, 374 So 2d 28, 29 (Fla Dist Ct App 1979).

204 *See* Henningsen v Markowitz, 132 Misc 547, 230 NYS 313, 314 (Supp Ct 1928). Later courts have acted with the implicit assumption that a negligence claim by a person injured by

statute, it may still subject the firearms dealer to liability if the dealer knew or should have known of the unreasonable danger posed by selling the airgun to that particular customer.[205] Therefore, it is not surprising that it is difficult for a retailer who sold BB pellets[206] or similar items to minors to obtain summary judgment.[207] These products are dangerous and the retailer's conduct is rarely treated as being reasonable as a matter of law.[208]

A retailer is not liable, as a matter of law, for selling an air rifle to an adult if the dealer neither knew nor should have known that the rifle would be given to a child inexperienced in using it.[209] The fact that the customer's child was present in the store when the purchase was made and carried the air rifle from the store after the purchase is not enough to impose liability on the store.[210] However, in *Semeniuk v Chentis*, the court held that a retailer who sold an air rifle to an adult, but knew that the rifle was being purchased for a child and that the child was inexperienced in the use of such weapons, could be liable to a third party who was blinded by a BB pellet shot by the child.[211] The "naked legality"[212] of the sale to the parent does not relieve the retailer from liability.

A retailer has no duty to police its customers to ensure they are not purchasing carbon dioxide cartridges for a dangerous purpose, e.g., to power pellet guns, absent actual knowledge of the customer's intentions.[213] This is because such cartridges have a variety of relatively safe uses such as in airbrushes or seltzer bottles.[214] In fact, in *Holmes v J.C. Penney Co*, the court held that a retailer who sold carbon dioxide cartridges to minors in contravention of its policy not to do so did not, by that fact, breach a duty of care.[215] The court noted: "A policy established through the initiative of

---

the minor's use of the gun can be based on violation of this statute. *See* Collins v Caldor of Kingston, Inc, 73 AD2d 708, 422 NYS2d 524, 526 (1979).

205 Mautino v Piercedale Supply Co, 338 Pa 435, 13 A2d 51, 54 (1940) (retailer is liable even if clerk sold cartridges in contravention of store policy).

206 About 16,000 individuals injured each year from BBs or pellets require emergency room treatment. *See* US Consumer Prod Safety Commn, Natl Injury Information Clearinghouse, Prod Summary Rep (Mar 28, 1984).

207 *See* Pair v Blakly, 160 NJ Super 14, 388 A2d 1026, 1027 (1978).

208 *Id*; *but see* Jimenez v Zayre Corp, 374 So 2d 28, 29 & n 3 (Fla Dist Ct App 1979).

209 Masone v Unishops of Modell's, Inc, 73 AD2d 611, 422 NYS2d 450, 451 (1979), *affd*, 52 NY2d 855, 418 NE2d 671, 437 NYS2d 78 (1981).

210 *Id.*

211 1 Ill App 2d 508, 117 NE2d 883, 885-86 (1954).

212 Sickles v Montgomery Ward & Co, 6 Misc 2d 1000, 167 NYS2d 977, 979 (Sup Ct 1957).

213 Holmes v J.C. Penney Co, 133 Cal App 3d 216, 219-20, 183 Cal Rptr 777 (1982).

214 *Id.*

215 133 Cal App 3d 216, 220 n 1, 183 Cal Rptr 777 (1982).

the conscientious and safety minded should not automatically establish the existence of a legal standard of care, because otherwise such initiative would be discouraged."[216]

Causation

Some firearms dealers have argued that they are not liable for injuries to individuals harmed by their customers' use of firearms, even if the sale to the customer was an unreasonably dangerous act,[217] because the act causing the injury was performed by another individual. Generally, dealers have been successful with this argument when there was a superseding cause of injury, i.e., an independent act of another which was unforeseeable,[218] but liable in all other cases.[219] For example, a retailer who wrongfully sold firearm cartridges to minors was not relieved from liability because it was foreseeable that the minors would acquire a gun elsewhere and then use the ammunition.[220] Similarly, a firearms dealer may be liable for selling a pistol to a minor even though a different child misused the weapon because it was foreseeable that the pistol would be borrowed.[221] The dealer also may be liable for selling to a minor, although the child's mother later learned of the purchase but failed to take the pistol away from the child.[222]

Indeed, a firearms dealer could be held liable for the criminal act of a customer if that act were reasonably foreseeable.[223] In *Angell v F. Avanzini Lumber Co*,[224] the court held that injury was foreseeable when a dealer's employee sold a patron a rifle and ammunition after the patron repeatedly aimed and fired an unloaded rifle at the employee's head and sufficiently scared the employee that he called the police. The intervening act of the patron in later shooting the loaded rifle at someone else did not cut off the dealer's liability; its sale of the rifle and ammunition to her was a proximate cause of the plaintiff's death.[225] However, a dealer is not liable where a customer's criminal use of a firearm was reasonably unforeseeable.[226]

---

216 *Id.*

217 If the sale was not an unreasonably dangerous act, there is also no liability. Willigan v Sears, Roebuck & Co, 33 AD2d 1033, 308 NYS2d 74, 75 (1970), *affd*, 28 NY2d 680, 269 NE2d 399, 320 NYS2d 737 (1971) (sale of nondefective rifle to 17-year-old).

218 Ward v University of the South, 209 Tenn 412, 354 SW2d 246, 250-51 (1962).

219 Lundy v Hazen, 90 Idaho 323, 411 P2d 768, 774 (1966).

220 Mautino v Piercedale Supply Co, 338 Pa 435, 13 A2d 51, 54 (1940).

221 Spires v Goldberg, 26 Ga App 530, 106 SE 585, 588 (1921).

222 Lundy v Hazen, 90 Idaho 323, 411 P2d 768, 774 (1966).

223 Angell v. F. Avanzini Lumber Co, 363 So 2d 571, 572 (Fla Dist Ct App 1978).

224 *Id.*

225 *Id.*

226 Robinson v Howard Bros, 372 So 2d 1074, 1076 (Miss 1979).

§1.08   Fishing and Boating

General Duty of Care

A commercial fishing boat enterprise is not the insurer of its passengers' safety.[227] However, one court held that it owes its customers the highest degree of care in the operation of its vessels that is consistent with proper management of the boats.[228] Some commercial fishing and boating accidents will involve the law of admiralty and, therefore, a review of that subject matter is warranted.[229]

A ship operator must warn passengers of dangers which the vessel's employees may reasonably anticipate from weather conditions or other reasons and which are not readily apparent to the passengers.[230] However, a commercial fishing boat was not liable for failing to warn customers that sitting in the bow was unsafe when sitting there did not place the customers in an unreasonably dangerous position.[231] In fact, sitting in that area is common and is preferred by some customers to enhance their enjoyment of the open air.[232]

In addition, a customer on a commercial fishing boat could not recover for the recreational company's alleged negligence in taking the boat out to sea during adverse weather conditions when there was no proof that weather conditions were not normal.[233]

Vicarious Liability

A resort hotel which offers boats and fishing guides may be liable under the doctrine of respondeat superior for the negligent acts of a nonemployee, if that individual had apparent authority for his or her acts.[234] In *Seaboard Properties, Inc v Bunchman*,[235] the operator of a skiff was held to be an agent of

---

227 Summers v Motor Ship Big Ron Tom, 262 F Supp 400, 404 (DSC 1967).

Each year, over 60,000 individuals injured from fishing require emergency room treatment, although, obviously, not all of those injuries occurred on rented recreational fishing boats. *See* US Consumer Prod Safety Commn, Natl Injury Information Clearinghouse, Prod Summary Rep (Mar 28, 1984).

228 Summers v Motor Ship Big Ron Tom, 262 F Supp 400, 404 (DSC 1967). A fishing boat leased to others may be considered a demise or bareboat charter and be outside the scope of the owner's insurance coverage. *See* O'Donnell v Latham, 525 F2d 651, 653 (5th Cir 1976).

229 *See* §§2.05-2.06; *see generally* §3.12.

230 Summers v Motor Ship Big Ron Tom, 262 F Supp 400, 404 (DSC 1967).

231 *Id.*

232 *Id* 403.

233 *Id* 402-03.

234 Seaboard Properties, Inc, v Bunchman, 278 F2d 679 (5th Cir 1960).

235 *Id.*

a resort, even though he was not an employee of the resort, because the resort advertised fishing with guides as one of its services, the guide lived on the resort, his passengers were the resort's guests, the guests were usually billed by the resort for his services, and he had to pick up hotel guests whenever requested by the resort's dockmaster.[236]

Causation

In *Lockhart v Martin*,[237] a paying passenger on a commercial fishing boat slipped and injured himself when the boat moved suddenly. The fisherman was unable to explain the cause of the sudden movement. Therefore, he tried to rely on the doctrine of res ipsa loquitur to impose liability on the boat owner. The court held that this doctrine was inapplicable because the accident was no more likely to have been caused by the defendant's negligence than by other factors such as the movement of the waves.[238] Indeed, the bigger the wave, the more vigorous the impact on the boat and the more severe and sudden the movement on board.[239] This movement occurs even when the boat is not operated negligently.

Statutes

Individuals injured while employed to perform services on recreational boats have been able to recover[240] under the Longshoremen's and Harbor Workers' Compensation Act.[241] Indeed, it has been held that a plaintiff could recover even if he or she was not engaged in maritime employment at the precise moment of the injury.[242]

§1.09   Golf

General Duty of Care

A golf facility is not an insurer of its patrons' safety.[243] However, a golf

---

236 *Id* 681.

237 159 Cal App 2d 760, 324 P2d 340 (1958).

238 324 P2d at 341-42.

239 *Id.*

240 *See* Parker v Motor Boat Sales, Inc, 314 US 244 (1941); Schwabenland v Sanger Boats, 683 F2d 309 (9th Cir 1982); Mississippi Coast Marine, Inc v Bosarge, 637 F2d 665 (5th Cir), *modified on other grounds*, 657 F2d 665 (5th Cir 1981).

241 33 USC §901 *et seq.*

242 Schwabenland v Sanger Boats, 683 F2d 309, 312 n 4 (9th Cir 1982).

243 Westborough Country Club v Palmer, 204 F2d 143, 149 (8th Cir 1953); Steele v Jekyll Island State Park Auth, 122 Ga App 159, 176 SE2d 514, 514 (1970); Misenhamer v Pharr,

facility must exercise reasonable care to keep its premises in a reasonably safe condition and to warn of dangers which it knows or ought to know golfers may encounter while on the premises and which the golfers would not reasonably be expected to recognize.[244] One court has intimated that the golf facility should be held to a higher degree of care inside the clubhouse than on the course because a large number of patrons congregate in the relatively limited area of the clubhouse and the golf club has a greater ability to maintain this area.[245] In any event, a facility's compliance with the custom of care prevalent in the industry is not dispositive of whether reasonable care was exercised.[246]

Some golf facilities have been able to avoid liability for injuries arising from obvious dangers. In *Steele v Jekyll Island State Park Authority*,[247] a golfer's errant shot went into a drainage ditch. The golfer chose to go into the ditch to recover the ball. While doing so, he slipped on "something slick" and injured himself. The court held that the golf course had no duty to remove the moss and algae or warn of its presence because the accumulation of such growth in a wet place is a natural phenomenon which should be expected by both the proprietor and the golfer.[248] However, in a different case, a golf practice range facility was held negligent for allowing some "loose sand and gravel"[249] to remain on a dirt path.

Injuries from being hit by a golf ball can be serious and, therefore, golf facilities must take reasonable care to eliminate these dangers. One court held that a golf facility may be negligent in failing to screen an area to protect

---

99 Ga App 163, 107 SE2d 875, 879 (1959); Panoz v Gulf & Bay Corp, 208 So 2d 297, 301 (Fla Dist Ct App 1968); Foust v Kinley, 117 NW2d 843, 845-46 (Iowa 1962); Farfour v Mimosa Golf Club, 240 NC 159, 81 SE2d 375, 378 (1954); Taylor v Churchill Valley Country Club, 425 Pa 266, 228 A2d 768, 769 (1967).

It is estimated that about 23,000 individuals each year require emergency room treatment for golf injuries. *See* US Consumer Prod Safety Commn, Natl Injury Information Clearinghouse, Prod Summary Rep (Mar 28, 1984).

244 Panoz v Gulf & Bay Corp, 208 So 2d 297, 300 (Fla Dist Ct App 1968); Misenhamer v Pharr, 99 Ga App 163, 107 SE2d 875, 879 (1959); Foust v Kinley, 117 NW2d 843, 845-46 (Iowa 1962); Lexington Country Club v Stevenson, 390 SW2d 137, 140 (Ky Ct App 1965) (facility has duty of care toward individuals sitting in a car located on a driveway leading to the facility); Reardon v Country Club, 353 Mass 702, 234 NE2d 881, 883 (1968); Jones v New Mexico School of Mines, 75 NM 326, 404 P2d 289, 291 (1965); Farfour v Mimosa Golf Club, 240 NC 159, 81 SE2d 375, 378-79 (1954); Davis v Country Club, Inc, 53 Tenn App 130, 381 SW2d 308, 309 (1963); *See also* Sanders v Stutes, 400 So 2d 1159, 1161 (La Ct App 1981) (miniature golf).

245 *See* Panoz v Gulf & Bay Corp, 208 So 2d 297, 300 (Fla Dist Ct App 1968) (dicta).

246 Westborough Country Club v Palmer, 204 F2d 143, 147 (8th Cir 1953).

247 122 Ga App 159, 176 SE2d 514 (1970).

248 176 SE2d at 514. *See generally* Pais v City of Pontiac, 372 Mich 582, 127 NW2d 386, 387-88 (1964) (golf club not negligent in having an asphalt tile floor in the golf cart room)

249 Misenhamer v Pharr, 99 Ga App 163, 107 SE2d 875, 880 (1959).

golfers leaving one hole from being hit by golfers on another hole.[250] Similarly, a golf facility was found negligent for failing to warn boaters on a public waterway which traversed part of the golf course of the dangers from flying golf balls.[251]

A country club is not liable for failing to eliminate dangers which are not reasonably foreseeable. For example, a golf facility was entitled, as a matter of law, to a judgment in its favor where a golfer sat on a bench while waiting to tee off and was injured when the bench fell over.[252] The bench was movable and there was no evidence that the golf club knew that the bench had been placed on a slope and, therefore, there was no duty to warn of the risk of sitting on the bench.[253]

Course Design

A golf facility may be negligent for the design of the course.[254] In *Lexington Country Club v Stevenson*, a passenger in a car moving on the driveway to a country club was hit by an errant golf ball which came crashing through the car's window.[255] The court held that the placement of the driveway in an area which cut across a fairway was negligent.[256]

However, where the risk of injury to the plaintiff was too remote, e.g., an errant golf ball went through or over a natural barrier of 45 to 60-foot-high trees, the plaintiff could not recover under a negligent design theory.[257]

Correct Yardage

In *Cornell v Langland*, a country club was held negligent for failing to print the correct yardage on the scorecard.[258] In that case, a golfer teed off even though other golfers were on the green because, after consulting the scorecard for the yardage to the tee, he knew he could not hit the golf ball the distance

---

250 *See* Reardon v Country Club, 353 Mass 702, 234 NE2d 881, 883 (1968); *but see* Taylor v Churchill Valley Country Club, 425 Pa 266, 228 A2d 768, 770 (1967).

251 *See* Kirchoffner v Quam, 264 NW2d 203, 208 (ND 1978); *but see* Schlenger v Weinberg, 107 NJL 130, 150 A 434, 435 (1930) (no duty to warn of dangers of errant balls).

252 Foust v Kinley, 117 NW2d 843, 848 (Iowa 1962).

253 *Id.*

254 *See, e.g.*, Westborough Country Club v Palmer, 204 F2d 143, 148 (8th Cir 1953); Campion v Chicago Landscape Co, 295 Ill App 225, 14 NE2d 879 (1938). If an outside company designed the golf course, it may also be liable.

255 390 SW2d 137 (Ky Ct App 1965).

256 *Id* 141-42. One witness estimated that 20,000 golf balls would be hit over this driveway each year. *See id* 142.

257 Nussbaum v Lacopo, 27 NY2d 311, 265 NE2d 762, 317 NYS2d 347, 352 (1970).

258 109 Ill App 3d 472, 440 NE2d 985, 988 (1982).

indicated by the scorecard. Unfortunately, the green was almost 100 yards closer to the tee than the scorecard indicated and the ball hit one of the golfers standing on the green.

Golf Carts

A country club which provides golf carts must provide reasonably safe ones.[259] A golf establishment can be liable for injuries even if it did not have actual knowledge of a defective cart, as long as in the exercise of reasonable care it should have discovered the defect and fixed it.[260] In one case the defect in the cart had existed for several weeks, and the court held that this was enough time to warrant an inference that a routine inspection would have revealed the defect had the inspection been performed timely and properly.[261]

Acts of Third Parties

A golf facility can be negligent in failing to use reasonable care to protect patrons from the negligent acts of others.[262] For example, a golfer who was hit by a driverless car which rolled down a hill could sue the golf facility for allowing cars to be parked on a hill without adequate protection to keep the cars in a safe position.[263] However, in *Panoz v Gulf & Bay Corp*, a driving range facility was granted a directed verdict where a patron who apparently moved out of the practice stall was hit by a golf club swung by another patron.[264] The plaintiff was unable to produce evidence of prior, similar mishaps and the court concluded that the injury resulted from a sudden, isolated act which was not reasonably foreseeable.[265]

Children

Golf facilities, like all other recreational facilities, must be careful to reduce the risk of harm to children. A golf facility may even be liable for allowing

---

259 Gifford v Bogey Hills Golf & Country Club, Inc, 426 SW2d 98, 102 (Mo 1968); *See also* §7.14.

260 The cause of a defect in a golf cart can be shown by expert testimony given with a reasonable degree of engineering certainty. *See* Gifford v Bogey Hills Golf & Country Club, Inc, 426 SW2d 98, 101-02 (Mo 1968).

261 Gifford v Bogey Hills Golf & Country Club, Inc, 426 SWd 98, 102 (Mo 1968).

262 Gresser v Taylor, 276 Minn 440, 150 NW2d 869, 873 (1967).

263 *Id.*

264 208 So 2d 297 (Fla Dist Ct App 1968).

265 *Id.*

young children on the course because of the danger of their being hit by stray balls.[266]

Nuisance

Some property owners living near golf courses have argued that golf balls which landed on their property by mistake constituted a nuisance.[267] Most courts have held that these plaintiffs, individuals residing on very desirable lots which receive the advantages of country club surroundings, must accept these occasional, concomitant annoyances.[268] Accordingly, the errant golf balls which were found in the bushes and the fence area on a plaintiff's property once or twice a week were not a sufficient impairment of the plaintiff's rights to sustain a recovery for nuisance.[269]

In *Patton v Westwood Country Club Co*, the court did not enjoin the golf facility from creating or continuing the private nuisance of having its patrons' golf balls land on the plaintiff's property because the plaintiff purchased the property near the golf course knowing the risk of errant golf shots.[270] This court also noted that the golf club had made improvements to reduce the risk of the plaintiff's property being hit by golf balls and the plaintiff's proposed remedy would not decrease this hazard to neighboring property owners.[271]

§1.10 Gymnastics

General Duty of Care

Businesses which provide gymnastic equipment are not insurers of their patrons' safety.[272] However, they must exercise reasonable care.[273] Whether or

---

266 Outlaw v Bituminous Ins Co, 357 So 2d 1350, 1353 (La Ct App), *writ ref*, 359 So 2d 1293 (La 1978) (dicta).

267 A party commits a nuisance when its use of its property produces a tangible and appreciable injury to neighboring property or renders the enjoyment of the neighboring property uncomfortable or inconvenient. *See* J. Dooley, Modern Tort Law §31.01, at 207 (1982).

268 Nussbaum v Lacopo, 27 NY2d 311, 265 NE2d 762, 317 NYS2d 347, 351 (1970). *See also* Patton v Westwood Country Club Co, 18 Ohio App 2d 137, 247 NE2d 761 (1969).

269 Nussbaum v Lacopo, 27 NY2d 311, 265 NE2d 762, 317 NYS2d 347, 351 (1970).

270 18 Ohio App 2d 137, 247 NE2d 761, 764 (1969). The quantity of errant shots had not increased since she had purchased the property. *See id.*

271 *Id.*

272 It is estimated that over 50,000 individuals each year are injured while participating in gymnastics and require emergency room treatment. *See* US Consumer Prod Safety Commn, Natl Injury Information Clearinghouse, Prod Summary Rep (Mar 28, 1984). About 12,000 individuals injured each year on trampolines require emergency room treatment. *See id.* Those

not the conduct of a gymnastic business is reasonable may, in some instances, be evidenced by its conformance to the established customs of the industry. However, a gymnastic firm's compliance with the standard of care common in this industry is not dispositive of the absence of negligence in a particular case.[274]

When the facility acts reasonably, it is not liable for a patron's injuries. For example, in *Wells v YMCA*, a child could not recover for injuries incurred in jumping from a springboard because the YMCA organization did not provide faulty equipment and its protective regulations were followed.[275] In addition, a facility was not negligent for failing to warn a college-educated adult of the inherent dangers of trampolines when there were no hidden dangers and written instructions on the proper use of the trampoline were posted in different parts of the gym.[276]

Equipment

Gymnastic facilities may be liable for defective equipment, e.g., the improper attachment of pads to the edge of a trampoline.[277] In *Ragni v Lincoln-Devon Bounceland, Inc*,[278] an adult hit a padded steel frame of a trampoline, injuring himself. The plaintiff argued that the 1 1/2-inch thick pad over the trampoline frame misled him as to its strength and also that the gymnastics facility had breached a duty to warn him of the hard substance beneath the padding. The court rejected this argument, holding that the plaintiff did not need to be told that the only safe place to land on a trampoline was in the middle.[279] Therefore, there was no duty to warn the plaintiff that landing on the padded frame was unsafe.

Supervision

The injured plaintiff in *Ragni* also claimed that the facility negligently provided insufficient supervision of the equipment. The gymnast was unsuccessful on this claim because he failed to prove that the supervision given was not reasonably consistent with the practical operation of an outdoor trampoline park.[280]

---

figures, of course, are not limited to individuals injured at commercial gymnastic facilities.

273 Wells v YMCA, 150 So 2d 324, 326 (La Ct App 1963); *See generally* §7.15.

274 Kungle v Austin, 380 SW2d 354, 361 (Mo 1964).

275 150 So 2d 324, 326 (La Ct App 1963).

276 Daniel v S-Co Corp, 255 Iowa 869, 124 NW2d 522, 526 (1963).

277 Kungle v Austin, 380 SW2d 354, 358-59 (Mo 1964).

278 91 Ill App 2d 172, 234 NE2d 168, 170 (1968).

279 *Id.*

280 234 NE2d at 171.

In several cases, plaintiffs' claims that their accidents were caused by the facility's failure to provide sufficient, trained supervisory personnel were unsuccessful because they failed to prove causation, i.e., there was no showing that the accident would, more likely than not, not have occurred if trained supervisors had been present.[281]

An excellent illustration of this principle is provided by *Nabky v Jack Loeks Enterprises, Inc*,[282] where a woman lost her balance while using a trampoline and injured herself when she landed with all of her weight on one leg. She claimed that the gymnastics establishment was negligent for failing to provide an instructor. The court ruled against her because there was nothing an instructor could have said or done which was not readily apparent to her or would have removed the danger of her becoming unbalanced while using the trampoline.[283]

Instruction

Generally, a facility has no duty to give actual instruction on the use of the equipment to its patrons if the patrons have received instruction from others[284] or if instruction is available if requested.[285]

In *Kungle v Austin*,[286] a minor who hit the edge of a trampoline was not entitled to a jury instruction, regarding a facility's duty to instruct, for three reasons. First, she had received instructions on using the trampoline from a friend. Second, she did not ask an instructor for assistance because she "had nothing to ask her." Third, she was aware of the dangers of straying from the center of the trampoline.

Acts of Third Parties

A recreational facility is liable for a patron's injuries resulting from horse-play or other misconduct by other patrons provided it had sufficient notice of those acts to enable it to stop them in time.[287] The burden is on the plaintiff to show that the facility had or should have had such notice of the unreasonably

---

281 Daniel v S-Co Corp, 255 Iowa 869, 124 NW2d 522, 526 (1963); Nabky v Jack Loeks Enters, Inc, 376 Mich 397, 137 NW2d 132, 134 (1965).

282 376 Mich 397, 137 NW2d 132, 134 (1965).

283 *Id.*

284 Kungle v Austin, 380 SW2d 354, 359 (Mo 1964).

285 Daniel v S-Co Corp, 255 Iowa 869, 124 NW2d 522, 526 (1963). The facility had posted written notices that instruction was available, but the plaintiff, a college-educated adult, made no such request. *Id.*

286 380 SW2d (Mo 1964).

287 Ford v Brandan, 51 Tenn App 338, 367 SW2d 481, 483 (1962).

dangerous acts which might cause injury.[288] Accordingly, where there was virtually no evidence of horseplay which occurred before one teenager pushed another while they were both on a trampoline, the facility was not liable for the patron's injuries.[289]

§1.11   Health Clubs and Spas

General Duty of Care

A health club operator is not the insurer of the safety of its patrons.[290] However, the club owes its customers a duty to keep the premises reasonably safe for use in a manner consistent with the usual operations of the club.[291] Furthermore, the facility must make reasonable inspections of the premises to discover defects or hidden dangers.[292]

One plaintiff's lawyer listed most of the potential duties of health clubs:

1. To provide lifeguards at the pool

2. To provide instructions on the safe use of the facilities

3. To determine the physical impairments of the patrons

4. To determine the physical condition of the patrons

5. To provide a safe exercise program

6. To provide sufficient supervisory personnel

7. To provide adequate safety procedures

8. To provide first aid personnel

9. To provide first aid facilities[293]

---

288 *Id.*

289 *Id.*

290 Gatti v World Wide Health Studios, 323 So 2d 819, 822 (La Ct App 1975).

291 *Id; see also* Lubell v Roman Spa, Inc, 362 So 2d 922, 923 (Fla 1978). One court held that there is no distinction between the duties owed to patrons by health clubs and by swimming pool facilities. *See* Ely v Northumberland Gen Ins Co, 378 So 2d 1024, 1027 (La 1979).

Oregon regulates commercial spas. *See* Or Rev Stat §§448.005-.100 (1983).

The National Spa and Pool Institute in Washington DC and the US Dept of Health and Human Services have promulgated safety guidelines. *See* Appleson, *Shaping Up Has Many New Pitfalls*, Natl LJ, Oct 3, 1983, at 10, col 2; US Dept of Health & Human Servs, Centers for Disease Control, Suggested Health and Safety Guidelines for Public Spas and Hot Tubs (rev Jan 1985).

292 Gatti v World Wide Health Studios, 323 So 2d 819, 822 (La Ct App 1975).

293 Ely v Northumberland Gen Ins Co, 378 So 2d 1024, 1025-26 (La 1979).

Physical Examination

A club which requires it patrons to sign a statement stating that they are in good health, not pregnant, and able to undertake and complete a health program before they commence exercise has no additional duty to give a physical examination.[294] A requirement that a club conduct a physical examination before allowing customers to use the equipment would be unreasonably burdensome.[295]

Wet or Slippery Areas

Health clubs must use reasonable care to eliminate the dangers from water remaining on the floor.[296] However, the areas in and around swimming pools, whirlpools, steam rooms, and showers are slippery by nature and the danger of injury exists even if the facility has exercised due care.[297] Of course, where the plaintiff can show that he or she slipped because the club unreasonably failed to remove the water, the plaintiff can recover.[298] For example, a club may be negligent if it allows a slippery film, possibly from a detergent, to remain near a whirlpool.[299] In addition, the facility's posting of one small sign, not necessarily located in the pool area, stating *slippery when wet* may not be a sufficient warning.[300] Furthermore, such a sign may also be insufficient to warn of a latent danger, e.g., a slick detergent film near a whirlpool.[301]

It is unnecessary for the plaintiff to establish that the club knew of the specific wet area that caused the accident and unreasonably failed to attempt to eliminate it.[302] A plaintiff can recover if he or she can prove that the club realized that water was common in the general area, that the floor was dangerous when it was wet, and that the club did not take adequate steps to remove the danger.[303]

---

[294] McKinley v Slenderella Systems, 63 NJ Super 571, 165 A2d 207, 213 (1960).

[295] *Id.*

[296] *See* Bertrand v Palm Springs & European Health Spa, Inc, 257 Or 532, 480 P2d 424, 426 (1971).

[297] Sevin v Shape Spa for Health Beauty, Inc, 384 So 2d 1011, 1014 (La Ct App 1980).

[298] Bertrand v Palm Springs & European Health Spa, Inc, 257 Or 532, 480 P2d 424, 426 (1971).

[299] Adam Dante Corp v Sharpe, 483 SW2d 452, 455 (Tex 1972).

[300] *Id* 456.

[301] *Id.*

[302] *See* Bertrand v Palm Springs & European Health Spa, Inc, 257 Or 532, 480 P2d 424, 426 (1971).

[303] *See id.*

Safe Equipment

Clubs must provide reasonably safe exercise equipment.[304] However, the fact that an accident occurred does not necessarily show that the equipment was unsafe. In *Duncan v World Wide Health Studios, Inc*,[305] a health club was held not liable when one of the weights on a leg press came loose and injured an athlete. The plaintiff, an inexperienced athlete, had improperly used an advanced machine by placing tremendous weight on it, thereby losing some control over it. The club was not liable because it did not provide unreasonably unsafe equipment.[306] Other courts have also held that a facility was not liable for providing exercise machinery which was not dangerous when used properly.[307] Indeed, one club's evidence that a certain machine had been in use for years and had never previously malfunctioned was considered probative on whether the machine was used properly by the plaintiff.[308]

Miscellaneous Duties

A facility must provide reasonably safe facilities, e.g., a spa may be liable when a roof collapses on a patron in the steam room.[309] A club must also exercise care in giving medical advice.[310] It may be negligent to continue to recommend certain treatments when a patron's sore back may have been caused by those treatments.[311] In addition, a club must use reasonable care to maintain its hot tubs in a manner which precludes its patrons from contracting rashes or other diseases.[312]

Causation

A plaintiff cannot recover unless there is some negligent act or omission by the defendant which was a substantial factor in causing or aggravating the plaintiff's injury.[313] A member of a health club who was injured when she

---

304 *See generally* O'Pry v World Wide Health Studios, Inc, 268 So 2d 319, 321 (La Ct App 1972).

305 232 So 2d 835, 838 (La Ct App 1970).

306 *Id.*

307 O'Pry v World Wide Health Studios, Inc, 268 So 2d 319, 321 (La Ct App 1972).

308 *Id.*

309 Lubell v Roman Spa, Inc, 362 So 2d 922, 923 (Fla 1978).

310 McKinley v Slenderella Syss, 63 NJ Super 571, 165 A2d 207, 214 (1960).

311 *Id.*

312 *See* Appleson, *Shaping Up Has Many New Pitfalls*, Natl LJ, Oct 3, 1983, at 10, col 1, 2 & 3.

313 House v European Health Spa, 269 SC 644, 239 SE2d 653, 656 (1977) (concurring opinion).

slipped and fell on a slippery surface, i.e., the steps of a whirlpool or a steam room, could not recover from the club because she did not know what caused her to fall.[314] Losing one's balance on a wet surface does not, standing alone, show any negligence by the club.

If the plaintiff is unable to explain the cause of the injury, counsel must use imagination. In the cases where the plaintiff slipped near the whirlpool and steam room it may have been possible to show that the tiling in the pool was slippery, the club should have placed some type of tape or mat on the steps to reduce the risk of slipping, or there should have been a handrail to reduce the risk of falling. Of course, it must be shown that had these actions been taken, the accident probably would have been prevented.[315] It would be useful, although not dispositive, to learn whether these or similar devices are normally employed by spas to reduce the risk of slipping.[316]

§1.12   Horseback Riding

General Duty of Care

Horseback riding facilities are not insurers of the safety[317] of their patrons.[318] However, they generally have a duty to exercise reasonable

---

[314] Sevin v Shape Spa for Health & Beauty, Inc, 384 So 2d 1011, 1014 (La Ct App 1980) (whirlpool); Gatti v World Wide Health Studios, 323 So 2d 819, 822 (La Ct App 1975) (steam room).

[315] Gatti v World Wide Health Studios, 323 So 2d 819, 822 (La Ct App 1975).

[316] *Id.*

[317] It is estimated that as many as 80 million people will ride a horse at least once a year. Grossman, *Equestrian Injuries*, 240 J AMA 1881, 1881 (1978).

The annual number of equestrian injuries is unquantified. However, the risk of injury for the expert horseman is low. Barclay, *Equestrian Sports*, 240 J AMA 1893, 1894 (1978). One study showed that the age and riding skill of amateurs had little correlation with injuries. Grossman, *Equestrian Injuries*, 240 J AMA 1881, 1882 (1978).

The most common equestrian injury was to the head and this was associated with lack of headgear. *Id* 1881.

[318] Swann v Ashton, 327 F2d 105, 107 (10th Cir), *modified on other grounds*, 330 F2d 995 (10th Cir 1964); Koser v Hornback, 75 Idaho 24, 265 P2d 988, 991 (1954); Fredrickson v Mackey, 196 Kan 542, 413 P2d 86, 89 (1966); Alfonso v Market Facilities, Inc, 356 So 2d 86, 89 (La Ct App), *writ denied*, 357 So 2d 1169 (La 1978); Christian v Elden, 107 NH 229, 221 A2d 784, 789 (1966); Troop A Riding Academy v Steverding, 39 Ohio App 560, 177 NE 601, 602 (1931); Fortune v Holmes, 48 Tenn App 497, 348 SW2d 894, 898 (1960); Smith v Pabst, 233 Wis 489, 288 NW 780, 783 (1939).

A defendant's proposed jury instruction that it was not an insurer was refused when there was no suggestion to the contrary. *See* Vaningan v Mueller, 208 Wis 527, 243 NW 419, 423 (1932).

Where the facility did not act unreasonably, it is not liable. *See* Elias v Hess, 327 Mich 323, 41 NW2d 884 (1950).

care under the circumstances.[319] One court held that a camp which provided horseback riding for minors must exercise a greater degree of care, i.e., the highest degree of care possible, in selecting horses.[320]

A facility need not warn of the dangers which inhere in horseback riding, at least if the rider is aware of those risks.[321] Therefore, there is no duty to warn a rider of the dangers of thrusting a tree branch toward a horse's head.[322]

A plaintiff must introduce evidence of the standard of care which should have been met by the horseback riding facility. In *Hojem v Kelly*,[323] a patron at a riding stable was practicing riding in an enclosed, but supposedly empty, riding field when another horse appeared in the field and charged the patron's horse, causing the patron to fall. A judgment n.o.v. for the stable was affirmed because there was no evidence that the stable had exposed the patron, an experienced rider, to an unreasonable risk of harm by failing to warn her of and insulate her from another horse.[324] The court criticized the plaintiff's counsel for failing to introduce any testimony, expert or otherwise, regarding the standard of conduct for operators of riding stables.[325] In the absence of such evidence, the jury could only impermissibly speculate as to the basis for concluding the stable breached a duty of care to the patron.[326]

Implied Warranty of Care

There are numerous older decisions which have held that a riding stable impliedly warrants that the horses it provides are suitable for their intended purposes,[327] i.e., the facility impliedly warrants that it will not supply a

---

[319] Swann v Ashton, 327 F2d 105, 108 (10th Cir), *modified on other grounds*, 330 F2d 995 (10th Cir 1964); Alfonso v Market Facilities, Inc, 356 So 2d 86, 89 (La Ct App), *writ denied*, 357 So 2d 1169 (La 1978); Chanaki v Walker, 114 NH 660, 327 A2d 610, 611 (1974); Moore v Relish, 53 Wis 2d 634, 193 NW2d 691, 694 (1972); *see generally* §7.23.

A facility was not liable where its agents were not negligent. *See* Allen v Green Acres Farm, Inc, 396 F Supp 442, 446-47 (ND Ill 1975).

Some courts have held that a bailment relationship does not exist because the chattel, the horse, was on the facility's premises and both the horse and the rider were under the direct supervision of the facility's instructors. *See* Moore v Relish, 53 Wis 2d 634, 193 NW2d 691, 693-94 (1972).

[320] Burwell v Crist, 373 F2d 78, 81 (3d Cir 1967).

[321] *See generally* Fredrickson v Mackey, 196 Kan 542, 413 P2d 86, 89 (1966).

[322] *Id.*

[323] 93 Wash 2d 143, 606 P2d 275 (1980).

[324] 606 P2d at 277.

[325] *Id.*

[326] *Id.*

[327] *See* Estes v Smith, 132 Cal App 2d 529, 282 P2d 534, 536-37 (1955); Evans v Upmier, 235 Iowa 35, 16 NW2d 6, 9 (1944).

horse which it knows, or by the exercise of reasonable care should know, is dangerous to the rider.[328]

Generally, it does not require a long time for a facility to form an opinion of a horse's qualities.[329] Indeed, the facility usually attempts to ascertain this information before purchasing the horse.[330]

This so-called implied warranty of suitability is not a true warranty because it does not insure the suitableness of the horse. Rather, it is a contractual obligation that the facility will not negligently hire out an unsuitable horse.[331] Accordingly, proof of this cause of action is the same as proof of negligence.[332] Therefore, stables generally have not been liable for breach of this implied warranty where the horse had not previously exhibited dangerous characteristics.[333] This issue is discussed in greater detail at §1.14.

Rescue

Generally, a facility is liable for failing to exercise reasonable care to prevent injuries both to the person originally in danger and to all individuals injured while attempting to rescue that person.[334] In *Snyder v Kramer*,[335] an inexperienced rider, on a highstrung horse without a saddle, was instructed only to walk the horse. The horse went into an extended trot. A second rider concluded that the inexperienced rider had lost control and attempted to assist her in subduing the horse. Unfortunately, the second rider was injured when his own horse slipped. The court held that the horseback riding establishment was negligent in furnishing the inexperienced rider a horse with dangerous propensities and in failing to provide her with a saddle and, therefore, it was liable for the second rider's injuries.[336]

---

328 Palmquist v Mercer, 43 Cal 2d 92, 99, 272 P2d 26 (1954); Kersten v Young, 52 Cal App 2d 1, 125 P2d 501, 503-04 (1942); Evans v Upmier, 235 Iowa 35, 16 NW2d 6, 9 (1944); Smith v Pabst, 233 Wis 489, 288 NW 780, 783 (1939); Vaningan v Mueller, 208 Wis 527, 243 NW 419, 421 (1932).

329 Evans v Upmier, 235 Iowa 35, 16 NW2d 6, 10 (1944).

330 16 NW2d at 10.

331 Dam v Lake Aliso Riding School, 6 Cal 2d 395, 57 P2d 1315, 1318 (1936).

332 Koser v Hornback, 75 Idaho 24, 265 P2d 988, 991 (1954).

333 Troop A Riding Academy v Steverding, 39 Ohio App 560, 177 NE 601, 601-02 (1931).

334 *See generally* Wagner v International Ry, 232 NY 176, 133 NE 437 (1921) ("danger invites rescue").

335 94 AD2d 860, 463 NYS2d 591 (1983).

336 463 NYS2d at 593-94. The court also held that the connection between the facility's negligence and the rider's injuries was not so attenuated as to preclude a finding of proximate cause. *See* 463 NYS2d at 594.

Tightening the Girth, Saddling the Horse, and Selecting the Bit

A facility has a duty to exercise reasonable care to ascertain if the girth needs tightening in order to be reasonably safe and if tightening is found necessary to make it reasonably safe, to tighten it.[337] One court held that when a child allegedly tightened the saddle girth of a horse negligently, the child was held to the standard of a child of like age, intelligence, and experience.[338]

In *Douglas v Holzhouser*,[339] a riding academy was exonerated in a suit brought by a rider who claimed that the academy had negligently failed to tighten the girth causing the saddle to slip during a ride. The court found that the academy's standard procedure was to check the girth of the saddle at least three times and that this procedure was followed here. Furthermore, the saddle remained secure until the plaintiff began to gallop, an action which was prohibited on this ride. The academy had not acted unreasonably in failing to tighten the girth to withstand stresses which were not expected. However, a riding facility was held liable when a rider fell from an improperly saddled horse even though the rider had, after leaving the stable, traded horses with another patron, because the facility knew riders exchanged horses and yet failed to instruct the riders not to make such exchanges.[340]

A facility must use reasonable care in selecting the proper bit, considering, for example, the horse's temperament and the experience of the rider.[341]

Instructors, Trail Guides, and Wranglers

A riding establishment's instructors, trail guides, and wranglers must exercise reasonable care to avoid danger[342] and also to avoid exacerbating the situation once a patron is in trouble.[343] Accordingly, facilities may be held liable in situations where their instructors allowed a horse to go

---

337 Ogan v Perkins, 191 SW2d 666, 667 (1945); *see generally* Gober v Nolan, 81 Ga App 16, 57 SE2d 700, 702 (1950); Lanzilli v Smith, 341 Mass 732, 170 NE2d 340, 341 (1960); Lackey v Perry, 366 SW2d 91, 95 (Tex Civ App 1963).

It is clearly inferable that the failure to tighten the saddle properly caused a plaintiff to be thrown from the horse. See Gober v Nolan, 81 Ga App 16, 57 SE2d 700, 702 (1950).

338 Heath v Madsen, 273 Wis 628, 79 NW2d 73, 74 (1956).

339 94 Misc 2d 204, 404 NYS2d 528 (Sup Ct 1978).

340 Lackey v Perry, 366 SW2d 91, 95 (Tex Civ App 1963).

341 Fortune v Holmes, 48 Tenn App 497, 348 SW2d 894, 897 (1960).

342 Moore v Relish, 53 Wis 2d 634, 193 NW2d 691, 694 (1972).

343 *Id.*

too fast for an inexperienced rider,[344] told a minor to ride a horse acting skittish and difficult to manage,[345] or caused a stampede on a walking horse ride.[346]

Where the riding establishment's employees did not act unreasonably, the establishment was not negligent.[347] In *Moore v Drummet*,[348] the court held that a ranch was not negligent when one of its wranglers approached a guest's horse from behind, possibly causing the guest's horse to bolt. There was no negligence because it was reasonable for the wrangler to ride principally in the rear so he could observe all the riders.[349] Furthermore, he did not breach a duty to the guest by approaching from behind because the guest's horse had no known tendency to run if approached in that manner.[350]

It is not necessary for the plaintiff to introduce expert testimony regarding the standard of care of instructors.[351]

§1.13 —Additional Issues

Acts of Third Parties

A riding facility is liable for injuries caused by the acts of third parties if those acts were reasonably foreseeable;[352] the test is foreseeability and it is immaterial whether the acts by the third person were innocent, negligent, intentional, or criminal.[353]

Causation

A plaintiff cannot recover against a horseback riding facility unless his or

---

344 Harris v Breezy Point Lodge, 238 Minn 322, 56 NW2d 655, 659 (1953).

345 Christian v Elden, 107 NH 229, 221 A2d 784, 787 (1966).

346 O'Connell v Walt Disney World Co, 413 So 2d 444 (Fla Dist Ct App 1982).

347 Roots v Claremont Riding Academy, 20 AD2d 536, 245 NYS2d 172, 173 (1963), *affd without opinion*, 14 NY2d 827, 200 NE2d 457, 251 NYS2d 475 (1964) (urged plaintiff to remount after she fell). *But see* Fortune v Holmes, 48 Tenn App 497, 348 SW2d 894, 899 (1960) (may be negligent to fail to have a rider dismount after the horse reared up).

348 478 SW2d 177 (Tex Civ App 1972).

349 *Id* 180-81.

350 *Id.*

351 Christian v Elden, 107 N 229, 221 A2d 784, 787 (1966). *But cf* Hojem v Kelly, 93 Wash 2d 143, 606 P2d 275, 277 (1980) (plaintiff must introduce some evidence of the proper standard of care).

352 Cooper v Eberly, 211 Kan 657, 508 P2d 943, 950 (1973) (opened a gate permitting horses to escape).

353 *Id.*

her injuries were caused or exacerbated by the facility's unreasonable acts or omissions.[354]

A plaintiff does not have to disprove the existence of all other possible causes of the accident. The burden is only to make it appear more likely than not that the injury resulted from the defendant's negligence.[355] For example, in *Chanaki v Walker*, the court held that a trail guide's negligence in leaving some patrons alone may have been a cause of one patron falling off his horse after the horse reared for the third time, because had the guide stayed he might have been able to calm the horse.[356]

The courts have reached different conclusions regarding the applicability of the res ipsa loquitur doctrine when a patron fell from a horse after the saddle turned.[357] In *Tezon v Perkins*, the court held the doctrine inapplicable because the rider, rather than the facility, had control of the saddle.[358] In addition, the slipping of the saddle may have been caused by factors other than the facility's negligence, e.g., the manner in which the plaintiff was riding the horse.[359]

However, the court in *Rafter v Dubrock's Riding Academy*[360] reached the opposite conclusion. It held that in the ordinary course of events a saddle does not slip and fall if proper care has been used in cinching it on the horse.[361] The fact that the saddle became loose in some way, causing it to fall and carrying the plaintiff with it, gives rise to the inference that the saddling was done in an improper manner or the equipment was defective.[362] The court held that the riding establishment had exclusive control at the time of the alleged negligent act, i.e., at the time the horse was saddled. This was sufficient to allow the res ipsa loquitur doctrine to be used, even if there was no exclusive control at the time of the accident, as long as the plaintiff proves

---

[354] Ennis v Bridger, 41 F Supp 672, 674 (MD Pa 1941), *affd*, 129 F2d 1019 (3d Cir 1942).
One court allowed a policeman to testify about what defendant's employee told him was the cause of the accident. *See* Burwell v Crist, 373 F2d 78, 80-81 (3d Cir 1967).

[355] Chanaki v Walker, 114 NH 660, 327 A2d 610, 612 (1974).

[356] *Id.*

[357] *Compare* Tezon v Perkins, 240 Mo App 696, 214 SW2d 732, 734 (1948) *with* Rafter v Dubrock's Riding Academy, 75 Cal App 2d 621, 171 P2d 459, 462-63 (1946); *see generally* McComas v Al G Barnes Shows Co, 215 Cal 685, 12 P2d 630, 635 (1932) (res ipsa loquitur applied when plaintiff fell off elephant because howdah slipped).

[358] 240 Mo App 696, 214 SW2d 732, 734 (1948).

[359] *Id.*

[360] 75 Cal App 2d 621, 171 P2d 459 (1946).

[361] 171 P2d at 462-63; *see generally* McComas v Al G Barnes Shows Co, 215 Cal 685, 12 P2d 630, 635 (1932) (res ipsa loquitur applied when plaintiff fell off elephant because howdah slipped).

[362] Rafter v Dubrock's Riding Academy, 75 Cal App 2d 621, 171 P2d 459, 462-63 (1946).

that the condition of the instrumentality had not been changed after it left the defendant's possession.[363]

Ownership

The general rule is that an employer is not vicariously liable for the negligence of an independent contractor where the contractor is employed to perform work which is legal and not intrinsically dangerous.[364] The two major exceptions to the rule are cases in which the job is inherently dangerous unless proper precautions are taken; or in which there is a special relationship between the employer and the public.[365] Horseback riding generally does not involve those two situations.[366] Accordingly, a land developer was not vicariously liable for its guests' injuries caused by the alleged negligence of a horseback riding facility.[367]

In some cases, individuals and entities are vicariously liable as owners for the negligence of others who reasonably appear to be their employees, even when there is no employment relationship in fact. For example, in *Christian v Elden*,[368] two individuals were held vicariously responsible for the negligence of a riding instructor when it reasonably appeared that they owned the riding facility and that the instructor worked for them, even though those were not the actual facts. Similarly, an owner of a lodge was held to be estopped to deny ownership of an adjacent riding stable when the lodge's promotional literature indicated the availability of riding facilities at the resort, guests charged their horseback riding expenses to their lodge bill, and the stable issued receipts in the name of the lodge.[369] However, a landlord was not a joint adventurer with a tenant who rented out horses where there was no sharing of profits and losses.[370]

Jury Instructions

When there are various theories of liability, e.g., negligence, breach of implied warranty, and strict liability for damages by a dangerous animal,

---

363 171 P2d at 462.

364 Reeves v John A. Cooper Co, 304 F Supp 828, 832 (WD Ark 1969).

365 *Id.*

366 *Id.*

367 *Id.* The developer was also not negligent in selecting the riding establishment because it acted reasonably in conducting an investigation of the facility and learning that the facility's reputation was unimpeachable. *Id.*

368 107 NH 229, 221 A2d 784, 788 (1966).

369 Walsh v Pheasant Run, Inc, 25 Ill App 3d 769, 323 NE2d 855, 858 (1975).

370 Swann v Ashton, 327 F2d 105 (10th Cir), *modified on other grounds*, 330 F2d 995, 996-97 (10th Cir 1964).

care must be taken that the jury instructions do not confuse the elements of liability under each discrete theory.[371]

State Statutes

Several states have passed laws regarding horses which may be applicable when a person is injured by a horse from a horseback riding facility.[372] In Louisiana, although the statute appears to impose strict liability, it is not applicable where the plaintiff was injured while riding a horse.[373]

§1.14 —Providing a Suitable Horse

Horseback riding establishments must exercise reasonable care to furnish a horse whose qualities are commensurate with the rider's experience, ability and purposes.[374] They must ascertain the habits and disposition of the horses for hire which are kept in their stables, and if they know that the horses are dangerous or unsuitable, or by the exercise of reasonable care could ascertain that fact, they will be liable for any injuries to a customer resulting from the horses' vicious propensities,[375] at least if they failed to warn of them.[376]

---

371 *See* Estes v Smith, 132 Cal App 2d 529, 282 P2d 534, 537 (1955).

372 *See, e.g.,* La Civ Code Ann art 2321 (West 1979); *see also* Ga Code §51-2-7 (1982); Kan Stat Ann §§47-122, 47-123 (1981). In Georgia, the facility is not liable unless it knew or should have known of the horse's dangerous characteristics. *See* Pearce v Shanks, 153 Ga App 693, 266 SE2d 353, 354 (1980). In Kansas, the statute was interpreted only to prohibit an owner from negligently allowing a horse to wander at will; the statute does not impose strict liability. *See* Cooper v Eberly, 211 Kan 657, 508 P2d 943, 952 (1973).

373 Alfonso v Market Facilities, Inc, 356 So 2d 86, 89 (La Ct App), *writ denied,* 357 So 2d 1169 (La 1978); Fontenot v Soileau, 336 So 2d 1006, 1008 (La Ct App 1976).

374 Hargrave v Wellman, 276 F2d 948, 951 (9th Cir 1960); *see also* Shandy v Sombrero Ranches, Inc, 525 P2d 487, 487 (Colo Ct App 1974); Fredrickson v Mackey, 196 Kan 542, 413 P2d 86, 89 (1966); Nisbet v Wells, 76 SW 120, 120 (Ky Ct App 1903) (horse and buggy); Herbert v Ziegler, 216 Md 212, 139 A2d 699, 701-02 (1958); Hodge v Montclair Riding Club, 133 NJ Eq 331, 32 A2d 840 (1943); Troop A Riding Academy v Miller, 127 Ohio St 545, 189 NE 647, 649 (1934); Moore v Relish, 53 Wis 2d 634, 193 NW2d 691, 694 (1972).

It must be remembered that customers generally have little knowledge of the qualities of the horse they are renting. *See* Evans v Upmier, 235 Iowa 35, 16 NW2d 6, 10 (1944).

375 Palmquist v Mercer, 43 Cal 2d 92, 99, 272 P2d 26 (1954); Johnson v Hurt, 120 Ga App 761, 172 SE2d 201, 202 (1969) (plaintiff was on a test ride before purchasing the horse); Herbert v Ziegler, 216 Md 212, 139 A2d 699, 702 (1958); Elias v Hess, 327 Mich 323, 41 NW2d 884 (1950); Verriale v Sunnybrook Acres, Inc, 37 AD2d 603, 322 NYS2d 904, 904 (1971); Troop A Riding Academy v Miller, 127 Ohio St 545, 189 NE 647, 649 (1934); *see generally* Allen v Green Acres Farm, Inc, 396 F Supp 442, 447 (ND Ill 1975); Reeves v John A. Cooper Co, 304 F Supp 828, 833 (WD Ark 1969); Walter v Southern Ariz School For Boys, Inc, 77 Ariz 141, 267 P2d 1076, 1078 (1954).

A seller of a horse is not liable to a buyer if he or she neither knew nor should have known

An employee's knowledge of a horse's propensities is imputed to the facility if the care and control of the animal is within the scope of the employee's job.[377] However, in all cases, the plaintiff must prove that the exact horse which caused his or her injuries possessed the dangerous propensities which were known or should have been known to the riding establishment.[378]

There are numerous cases where the facility was held liable for giving an inexperienced rider an unsuitable horse;[379] a gentle *walker* type of horse should have been provided to such riders.[380] A facility also should not place a partially blind horse in the hands of a patron.[381]

The fact that a horse threw a rider is insufficient, standing alone, to show negligence by the horse's owner.[382] Indeed, there are numerous cases which have held that the owner is not negligent where the horse had not previously caused a problem or acted particularly spirited or dangerous.[383] For example, where a horse had never indicated a disposition to pitch, run away, or engage in any other equine vice, but rather had been kind and docile it was not negligent to allow someone to ride the horse.[384] Similarly, an owner of a show horse, accustomed to noise and crowds and with no prior history of being skittish during a parade, was not liable when the horse struck a participant in a parade after its bit was pulled.[385] In addition, an actor did not recover against a riding academy for injuries he incurred when the horse stepped on his hand while he was crawling under the horse for a television production because there was no evidence that the horse's owner should have known of any vicious or unruly propensities of the horse.[386] A facility was held not negligent when two horses bucked, injuring their riders, after a sudden bolt of lightning and a clap of thunder because

---

of the horse's dangerous propensities. *See* Gabe v Forbes, 141 Colo 419, 348 P2d 377, 378 (1960).

376 O'Brien v Gateway Stables, 104 Cal App 2d 317, 231 P2d 524, 526 (1951).

377 Walter v Southern Ariz School For Boys, Inc, 77 Ariz 141, 267 P2d 1076, 1078 (1954); Herbert v Ziegler, 216 Md 212, 139 A2d 699, 702 (1958).

378 Varriale v Sunnybrook Acres, Inc, 37 AD2d 603, 322 NYS2d 904, 904 (1971).

379 Dickie & Goelzer v Henderson, 95 Ark 78, 128 SW 561 (1910); Harris v Breezy Point Lodge, 238 Minn 322, 56 NW2d 655, 658 (1953).

380 *See generally* Shandy v Sombrero Ranches, Inc, 525 P2d 487, 487 (Colo Ct App 1974).

381 Shanklin v Rogers, 213 SW2d 730, 732 (Tex Civ App 1948).

382 Wolfe v Wilkins, 491 P2d 595, 597 (Colo Ct App 1971).

383 Reeves v John A. Cooper Co, 304 F Supp 828, 833 (WD Ark 1969); Wolfe v Wilkins, 491 P2d 595, 596-97 (Colo Ct App 1971); Cooper v Layson Bros, 14 Ga App 134, 80 SE 666, 667 (1914); Moore v Drummet, 478 SW2d 177, 180 (Tex Civ App 1972).

384 O'Brien v Gateway Stables, 104 Cal App 2d 317, 231 P2d 524, 525 (1951).

385 Moore v Drummet, 478 SW2d 177 (Tex Civ App 1972).

386 Baum v New York Cent RR, 12 Misc 2d 622, 175 NYS2d 628, 630 (Sup Ct 1958).

the horses were normally gentle and the ride had begun before the rain started.[387]

Even the most tranquil horse may kick on occasion.[388] Accordingly, a horse which was a little *high spirited*, *nervous*, and *touchy* to the extent the animal would shy away from sudden noises and would become startled upon being approached from behind was not considered mean, fractious, or as having an unruly disposition. Indeed, the horse could still be considered "gentle."[389] For the same reason, a horse's tossing of its head would not alert the facility that this horse intended to bolt.[390] In addition, a horse which reared and showed some spirit is not necessarily *vicious*, especially when the plaintiff, an experienced rider, was told that the horse was to be used by experienced riders.[391]

It has sometimes been stated that a facility's knowledge of a horse's vicious propensities is a question of fact.[392] Although this is generally true, there are cases where the facts are undisputed and one party may be entitled to judgment as a matter of law.[393]

The courts have reached conflicting results regarding whether the horseback riding establishment was entitled to judgment as a matter of law where the horse had not previously exhibited dangerous propensities. One court held that the facility was entitled to a directed verdict where the horse ran and threw the plaintiff because there was no evidence of prior acts of a similar nature of which the facility knew or should have known.[394] The fact that this horse subsequently also threw an attendant was evidence of the character of the horse at that later time and was not probative of the facility's knowledge of the horse's propensities at an earlier point in time.[395] A different court

---

387 Alfonso v Market Facilities, Inc, 356 So 2d 86, 89-90 (La Ct App), *writ denied*, 357 So 2d 1169 (La 1978).

388 Cohen v Rodenbaugh, 162 F Supp 748, 748 (ED Pa 1957).

389 Willis v Schuster, 28 So 2d 518, 520 (La Ct App 1946).

390 Troop A Riding Academy v Miller, 127 Ohio St 545, 189 NE 647, 649 (1934).

391 O'Donnell v Holdorf, 304 Ill App 442, 26 NE2d 653, 659 (1940).

392 Davis v Roberts, 155 Colo 387, 395 P2d 13, 15 (1964).

393 *See* Chandler v Gately, 119 Ga App 513, 167 SE2d 697, 702 (1969) (summary judgment granted to defendant; plaintiff's statements in her affidavit that owner had such knowledge were not given any weight because they were not based on personal knowledge; when plaintiff's affidavit opposing summary judgment motion contradicted her deposition testimony, the affidavit was construed against her); Fontenot v Soileau, 336 So 2d 1006, 1011 (La Ct App 1976) (affidavit which asserted that defendant knew of horse's dangerous characteristics but gave no factual support for that conclusion was insufficient to oppose summary judgment motion).

394 Gober v Nolan, 81 Ga App 16, 57 SE2d 700, 702 (1950).

395 *Id.* One court, in a questionable ruling, held that testimony as to the subsequent sales price and subsequent bad acts of the horse was admissible evidence because the low price and poor behavior indicated that the horse had dangerous characteristics. *See* Hodge v Montclair Riding Club, 133 NJ Eq 331, 32 A2d 840, 842 (1943).

held that the one unfortunate act by the horse which caused the plaintiff's injury was sufficient evidence of the facility's lack of care that the issue was for the jury.[396]

There are at least two situations in which a facility can be liable for allowing a patron to ride a horse even if the horse has not exhibited prior bad behavior. First, if an expert rider could tell by proper observation of the horse that it would be dangerous to ride, the facility should not allow patrons to use that horse because the facility is held to the standard of care of an expert.[397] Second, if a prior owner of the horse had told the defendant that the horse was not suitable for riding, that information should have put the facility on notice of the potential danger.[398]

The fact that the horse has previously been involved in an accident is not dispositive, sometimes not even probative, of the facility's negligence in allowing a patron to ride that horse. One court ruled that a facility was entitled to a directed verdict even though the day before the accident the plaintiff's horse had thrown a woman because the plaintiff failed to produce any evidence that the horse, rather than the rider, was responsible for that previous accident.[399] However, a different court held that if a facility knew that a horse had previously bucked, this may be sufficient evidence to go to the jury regarding whether the facility was negligent in allowing a patron to ride this horse.[400] In addition, where the horse had been involved in prior accidents, even though they were not of the same type as that involved in the instant case, it was a jury question whether or not the cumulative effect of the previous mishaps was sufficient to indicate that the horse was unsuitable.[401]

A horse may be suitable for a patron while used under supervision, but unsuitable without supervision.[402] In *Dee v Parish*, the court held that a facility should not have directed an inexperienced rider to leave a supervised area where she would probably be injured as a result of either the dangers encountered or the manner in which she handled her mount.[403] Similarly, it was negligent for a camp to allow a 10-year-old child who had only been on

---

Evidence of complaints to the facility about the horse which occurred after the injury are hearsay and should not have been admitted. *See* Vaningan v Mueller, 208 Wis 527, 243 NW 419, 423 (1932). Complaints before the injury are admissible to show that the facility was, or should have been, on notice of the horse's dangerous propensities. *See id.*

396 Koser v Hornback, 75 Idaho 24, 265 P2d 988, 992 (1954).

397 Dorobek v Ride-A-While Stables, 262 Cal App 2d 554, 68 Cal Rptr 774, 778 (1968).

398 Cowan v Sullivan, 199 So 2d 500, 500 (Fla Dist Ct App 1967).

399 Cohen v Rodenbaugh, 162 F Supp 748, 748 (ED Pa 1957).

400 Walter v Southern Ariz School For Boys, Inc, 77 Ariz 141, 267 P2d 1076, 1080 (1954).

401 Bocker v Miller, 213 Cal App 2d 345, 28 Cal Rptr 818, 821 (1963).

402 Dee v Parish, 160 Tex 171, 327 SW2d 449, 452 (1959).

403 *Id.*

a horse once before, to ride an unattended horse when her mother did not want her to ride at all.[404]

§1.15   Ice Skating

Ice skating facilities have a duty to keep their rinks in a reasonably safe[405] condition.[406] If they have actual or constructive notice of an unsafe condition and fail to take the reasonably necessary steps to remedy the situation, they can be held liable for negligence.[407] In addition, where the attendants at a skating rink created a dangerous situation, viz., an irregular ice ridge made up of dirt, paper, and cigarette butts at the rink's edge, the facility was liable when an accident occurred at the ridge because the attendants' knowledge of the existence of the danger was imputed to the owner.[408]

It is not necessary that the ice skating establishment have prior knowledge of the exact cause of the injury. In *Sauro v Arena Co*,[409] a minor was injured when his skate became caught in a rut in soft ice. It was clear that the facility did not have actual prior notice of the existence of the particular rut which caused the injury. However, a jury could have found that it had constructive notice of the existing dangerous condition of the rink because it failed to follow its usual practice of clearing off the slush at an afternoon break.[410] Accordingly, the judgment for the skater was affirmed.

Liability cannot be imposed unless the plaintiff can prove that he or she was injured because of the establishment's negligence. In *O'Brien v Midtown Skating Club*,[411] an ice skater who fell on the ice a few seconds after the rink was reopened after resurfacing received a $25,000 jury verdict. The court set the verdict aside because there was no evidence that the skating establishment acted unreasonably, i.e., there was no showing that the establishment failed to remove a dangerous condition which existed so soon after resurfacing. There was a strong dissent which argued that the establishment was negligent in

---

404 Bulkin v Camp Nockamixon, 367 Pa 15, 79 A2d 234, 235 (1951).

405 It is estimated that over 19,000 individuals injured while ice skating are admitted each year to an emergency room. *See* US Consumer Prod Safety Commn, Natl Injury Information Clearinghouse, Prod Summary Rep (Mar 28, 1984).

406 Sauro v Arena Co, 171 Conn 168, 368 A2d 58, 59 (1976).

407 *Id*; Nierman v Casino Arena Attractions, Inc, 46 NJ Super 566, 135 A2d 210, 212 (1957) (negligence found when skater fell into a hole in the ice). One court held that the rink owner was negligent where it departed from its usual procedure in preparing the ice and the ice became too slippery. Mesitrich v Casino Arena Attractions, Inc, 31 NJ 44, 155 A2d 90, 92 (1959).

408 Oberheim v Pennsylvania Sports & Enters, 358 Pa 62, 55 A2d 766, 768 (1947).

409 177 Conn 168, 368 A2d 58, 59 (1976).

410 368 A2d at 60.

411 77 AD2d 829, 430 NYS2d 621, 621 (1980).

allowing skaters to use the rink before ascertaining whether the rink was in a condition to be used safely.[412]

§1.16   Roller Skating

General Duty of Care

A roller skating facility is not an insurer of the safety[413] of its patrons.[414] It has, however, a duty to exercise reasonable care in maintaining its premises.[415] It must take reasonable steps to discover dangerous conditions which exist on its premises and to correct them or warn of their presence.[416] Where a boy fell while roller skating, through no act or omission of the facility other than allowing him to skate, the facility was not negligent and, therefore, not liable.[417]

Skates

A roller skating business has a duty to see that its patrons are furnished reasonably safe skates.[418]

Facilities

A roller skating establishment must provide reasonably safe facilities.[419] A patron who fell while he was stepping from one area to another with a different elevation could state a claim for negligence.[420] The establishment's

---

412 430 NYS2d at 623.

413 Over 100,000 individuals injured each year while roller skating are admitted to hospital emergency rooms. *See* US Consumer Prod Safety Commn, Natl Injury Information Clearinghouse, Prod Summary Rep (Mar 28, 1984).

414 Thomas v Studio Amusement, Inc, 50 Cal App 2d 538, 123 P2d 552, 555 (1942); Chapman v Foggy, 59 Ill App 3d 552, 375 NE2d 865, 868 (1978); Humbyrd v Spurlock, 345 SW2d 499, 502 (Mo Ct App 1961); Roll 'R' Way Rinks, Inc v Smith, 218 Va 321, 237 SE2d 157, 161 (1977); *see also* Johnson v Amphitheatre Corp, 206 Minn 282, 288 NW 386, 387 (1939).

415 Chapman v Foggy, 59 Ill App 3d 552, 375 NE2d 865, 868 (1978); *see also* Holley v Funtime Skateland S, Inc, 392 So 2d 1135, 1136 (Miss 1981); Benoit v Marvin, 120 Vt 201, 138 A2d 312, 315 (1958); Roll 'R' Way Rinks, Inc v Smith, 218 VA 321, 237 SE2d 157, 161 (1977). *See generally* Johnson v Amphitheatre Corp, 206 Minn 282, 288 NW 386, 387 (1939).

416 *See* Holley v Funtime Skateland S, Inc, 392 So 2d 1135, 1136 (Miss 1981).

417 Damer v State of New York, 34 Misc 2d 363, 228 NYS2d 997, 999 (Ct Cl 1962).

418 Humbyrd v Spurlock, 345 SW2d 499, 502 (Mo Ct App 1961).

419 *See* Zambito v Southland Recreation Enters, Inc, 383 So 2d 989, 991 (Fla Dist Ct App 1980).

420 *Id.*

argument that the defect was obvious, i.e., the plaintiff's knowledge of the change in floor elevations was equal to the establishment's, does not totally bar the plaintiff's complaint, although it is a factor for the jury to consider in determining whether the establishment was negligent.[421]

Roller skating businesses are negligent if they have actual knowledge of a dangerous condition and fail to act.[422] Where there was abundant evidence that a roller skating facility was aware of the fact that a railing which skaters used for support was splintering, it was negligent for the facility not to repair it before a skater was injured by a splinter.[423]

However, a plaintiff can recover for injuries, in appropriate circumstances, even where the establishment did not have actual notice of the dangerous conditions.[424] The establishment is responsible if, by the exercise of reasonable care, it should have discovered the dangerous condition.[425] Generally, if a plaintiff is relying on this theory, sometimes call constructive notice, he or she must establish that the dangerous condition existed for a sufficient amount of time so that the business should have discovered it had it exercised reasonable care.[426] For example, a roller skating establishment was found negligent when it failed to warn of wet areas on the skating floor which it should have known existed because it had been raining and the roof had a tendency to leak.[427] Indeed, if the establishment knew of a defect which had a history of causing a dangerous condition to recur, it had a duty to patrons who were unaware of such a condition to issue an appropriate warning and a duty to take the steps reasonably necessary to remedy the defect which caused that condition;[428] the fact that such a condition may have been dormant for a period of time before the accident was immaterial.[429]

Acts of Third Parties

A roller skating facility has a duty to guard patrons from the dangers of other skaters, if it has reasonable notice, actual or constructive, of those

---

421 *Id.*

422 Chapman v Foggy, 59 Ill App 3d 552, 375 NE2d 865, 868-69 (1978).

423 *Id.*

424 *Id.*

425 *Id*; Roll 'R' Way Rinks, Inc v Smith, 218 Va 321, 237 SE2d 157, 161 (1977).

426 Chapman v Foggy, 59 Ill App 3d 552, 375 NE2d 865, 868 (1978); *see also* Restatement (Second) of Torts §343 (1965).

427 Benoit v Marvin, 120 Vt 201, 138 A2d 312, 316 (1958).

428 Roll 'R' Way Rinks, Inc v Smith, 218 Va 321, 237 SE2d 157, 162 (1977).

429 *Id.*

dangers.[430] Accordingly, a facility which knew of the dangers of patrons skating in the lobby and which had a sign prohibiting such activity could be held liable for negligence in failing to stop a group of boys from skating in that area before they fell and struck the plaintiff.[431] In addition, a facility was negligent when one patron was hit by a second patron who had been skating, for some time, at a speed violative of rink safety regulations in the presence of a guard who should have seen the second skater.[432] However, when a facility did not breach that duty, there was no liability.[433]

Skating Ability

A roller skating establishment generally has no duty to ascertain whether its patrons can skate before allowing them on the rink.[434] In *Blizzard v Fitzsimmons*, the court held that the proprietor of a roller skating rink in a large municipality, where paved sidewalks abound, is entitled to assume when a healthy nine-year-old child requests to skate that the child knows how to skate and is reasonably able to take care of him or herself in that respect.[435] The proprietor is not liable unless it is informed that the patron is wholly without experience as a skater.[436]

Evidence

Evidence of prior, substantially similar, accidents is admissible to show the facility's knowledge of a dangerous condition.[437] However, the facility is entitled to a cautionary instruction that this evidence is not to be considered to prove negligence or causation in the case at hand.[438]

§1.17   Snow Skiing

Skiing is one of the more popular recreational activities in this country.[439]

---

430 Reay v Reorganization Inv Co, 224 SW2d 580, 582 (Mo Ct App 1949); *see generally* Thomas v Studio Amusements, Inc, 50 Cal App 2d 538, 123 P2d 552, 555 (1942); Agans v Showalter, 92 Ill App 3d 939, 416 NE2d 397, 399 (1981).

431 Johnson v Amphitheatre Corp, 206 Minn 282, 288 NW 386, 387-88 (1939).

432 Schamel v St Louis Arena Corp, 324 SW2d 375, 377 (Mo Ct App 1959).

433 Agans v Showalter, 92 Ill App 3d 939, 416 NE2d 397, 399 (1981).

434 *See* Blizzard v Fitzsimmons, 193 Miss 484, 10 So 2d 343, 344 (1942).

435 *Id.*

436 *Id.*

437 Roll 'R' Way Rinks, Inc v Smith, 218 Va 321, 237 SE2d 157, 160-61 (1977).

438 *Id* 161.

439 It is also a popular topic for law journal articles. *See, e.g.,* Fagen, *Ski Area Liability for Downhill Injuries,* 49 Ins Couns J 36 (1982); Hagglund, *Ski Liability,* 32 Fedn Ins Q 223 (1982), Lisman, *Ski Injury Liability,* 43 U Colo L Rev 307 (1972); Wells, *Liability of Ski Area*

It is estimated that there are approximately 14 million skiers.[440] This is more than quadruple the number of skiers in 1971.[441]

Unfortunately, skiing is a hazardous activity and numerous participants have been injured, some fatally.[442] One study concluded that skiing injuries occur with greater comparative frequency than football injuries.[443] It is, therefore, not totally surprising that there are reported decisions which affirm verdicts of six[444] and seven[445] figures. There are, of course, other cases where the skier suffers serious, even fatal, injuries through no fault of the ski facility.[446]

General Duty of Care

A ski facility is not an insurer of the safety of its patrons.[447] However, it must conduct itself in a reasonably prudent manner to prevent injuries.[448] In addition, ski facilities must also exercise reasonable care not to aggravate a skier's injuries once an accident has occurred.[449] The

Operators, 41 Den LJ 1 (1964); Comment, *Negligence*, 1 Washburn LJ 316 (1961); Note, *Ski Operators and Skiers*, 14 New Eng L Rev 260 (1978); Note, *Utah's Inherent Risks of Skiing Act*, 1980 Utah L Rev 355 (1980); Note, *Assumption of Risk After Sunday v Stratton Corp*, 3 Vt L Rev 129 (1978).

440 *See* Fagen, *Ski Area Liability for Downhill Injuries*, 49 Ins Couns J 36, 36 (1982).

441 *See* Note, *Ski Operators and Skiers*, 14 New Eng L Rev 260, 260 (1978).

442 It was estimated that there were over 210,000 skiing injuries in 1980. *See* Fagen, *Ski Area Liability for Downhill Injuries*, 49 Ins Couns J 36, 36 (1982). Over 40,000 individuals injured snow skiing each year are admitted to a hospital emergency room. *See* US Consumer Prod Safety Commn, Natl Injury Information Clearinghouse, Prod Summary Rep (Mar 28, 1984).

443 *See* Note, *Ski Operators and Skiers*, 14 New Eng L Rev 260, 260 (1978).

444 Rosen v LTV Recreational Dev, Inc, 569 F2d 117 (10th Cir 1978).

445 Sunday v Stratton Corp, 136 Vt 293, 390 A2d 398 (1978). This decision was criticized in Fagen, *Ski Area Liability For Downhill Injuries*, 49 Ins Couns J 36, 41-42, 49 (1982).

446 Leopold v Okemo Mt, Inc, 420 F Supp 781 (D Vt 1976).

447 Albert v State, 80 Misc 2d 105, 362 NYS2d 341 (Ct Cl 1974), *affd*, 51 AD2d 611, 378 NYS2d 125 (1976). *See also* Note, *Assumption of Risk After Sunday v Stratton Corp*, 3 Vt L Rev 129, 139 (1978).

448 Marietta v Cliffs Ridge, Inc, 385 Mich 364, 189 NW2d 208, 209 (1971); *see generally* §7.20 A former member of a ski club was not barred from suing the club for its negligence regarding a defective ski tow merely because he was a member when the tow was installed. *See* Winn v Ski Club, 207 F Supp 448, 450 (D Minn 1962).

One commentator has written that it is difficult to determine whether a ski facility met its standard of care because of three factors. First, the combination of challenge, risk, and natural setting provides the enjoyment of the sport as well as the danger. Second, skiers possess a wide range of abilities which are difficult, if not impossible, for the operator to ascertain. Third, natural conditions, including the weather and changes in terrain, are difficult, if not impossible, to control. Fagen, *Ski Area Liability for Downhill Injuries*, 49 Ins Couns J 36, 46 (1982).

449 Elliot v Taos Ski Valley, Inc, 83 NM 575, 494 P2d 1392, 1394-95, *affd*, 83 NM 763, 497 P2d 974 (1972).

customary usage or practice of the skiing industry is relevant evidence which can be used in determining whether the standard of care has been met in a particular case. However, industry practice is not dispositive[450] because this industry, like all others, cannot set its own standard of care.[451]

There is generally no duty to warn of the inherent dangers[452] in the sport of skiing.[453] Similarly, there is generally no duty to extinguish those dangers.[454] One court has held that unpadded utility poles may be included in those dangers.[455] However, considering the cost of padding, the better view may be to the contrary.

Many of the ski cases which hold that the skier assumed the risk of injury can also be read as holding that the ski facility did not act unreasonably, i.e., that it was not negligent.[456] For example, the often cited decision of *Wright v Mt Mansfield Lift*, is generally considered to have held that a skier assumed the risk of hitting a snow-covered stump on the slopes.[457] However, the court also used language consistent with a finding that the ski facility did not act unreasonably. The court stated:

> To hold that the terrain of a ski trail down a mighty mountain, with fluctuation in weather and snow conditions that constantly change its appearance and slipperiness, should be kept level and smooth, free from holes or depressions, equally safe for the adult or the child, would be to demand the impossible. It cannot be that there is any duty imposed on the owner and operator of a ski slope that charges it with the knowledge of these mutations of nature and requires it to warn the public against such.[458]

---

450 Marietta v Cliffs Ridge, Inc, 385 Mich 364, 189 NW2d 208, 209 (1971).

451 *Id.*

452 One commentator argued that the word *inhere* refers to those dangers that are the sport, the challenges without which the activity would not be sport at all, and the intrinsic risks that the participants would not dispense with even if they could. *See* Note, *Assumption of Risk After Sunday v Stratton Corp*, 3 Vt L Rev 129, 141 (1978). *See also* the cases analyzed in **§9.21** regarding assumption of risk in skiing accidents.

453 Green v Sherburne Corp, 137 Vt 310, 403 A2d 278, 279 (1979).

454 *Id.*

455 *Id.*

456 *See* Lisman, *Ski Injury Liability*, 43 U Colo L Rev 307, 307 (1972).

457 96 F Supp 786, 791 (D Vt 1951).

458 *Id.* At another point on the same page, the court concluded: "In this skiing case, there is no evidence of any dangers existing which reasonable prudence on the part of the [ski facility] would have foreseen and corrected." *See id.*

What was once an inherent risk of the sport may not remain as such over time.[459] The *Wright* decision was handed down in 1951. By 1978, in *Sunday v Stratton Corp*, the court affirmed a judgment of over one million dollars when a skier hit a concealed bush.[460] In both *Wright* and *Sunday* skiers were injured by concealed objects. However, new technology had so changed the ski industry that an inherent risk in 1951 was no longer considered such a risk 27 years later.[461]

Some portions of a ski facility, e.g., approaches to the slopes, are inherently slippery. Accordingly, a ski facility would not have breached its duty of care by failing to maintain those areas in a nonslippery condition.[462] Of course, the fact that snow or ice is present is a factor to measure the reasonableness of the facility's protective measures, but it does not, standing alone, indicate that a facility owed no duty of care to patrons injured by those conditions.[463] For example, a ski facility may be liable if it fails to clear hazardous conditions near a public restroom.[464]

In *Vogel v West Mountain Corp*, the court held that mere sponsorship of a ski race, without control of the event, does not impose a duty of care on the sponsor.[465] Accordingly, Miller Brewing Co was not liable for a skiing accident since it neither owned nor controlled the operation of the ski slope and was not realistically in a position to assume such control.[466] It was held irrelevant that the company financially benefited from its promotion of the event.[467]

Smooth Slopes

The technology simply does not exist which would allow a facility to have perfectly smooth slopes. Accordingly, a facility is not negligent for having conditions which are not perfect.[468] Skiers can observe the

---

[459] *Compare* Rosen v LTV Recreational Dev, Inc, 569 F2d 1117 (10th Cir 1978) (a patron's collision with a lift tower was the result of the facility's negligence) *with* Leopold v Okemo Mt, Inc, 420 F Supp 781 (D Vt 1976) (a collision with a lift tower is an inherent risk of the sport).

[460] 136 Vt 293, 390 A2d 398 (1978). The *Sunday* court noted that the facility had advertised its meticulously manicured slopes. It does not appear, however, that plaintiff pursued a remedy for misrepresentation.

[461] Note, *Utah's Inherent Risks of Skiing Act*, 1980 L Rev 355, 360.

[462] Jung v State, 12 NY2d 778, 186 NE2d 569, 569 234 NYS2d 722 (1962).

[463] Stearns v Sugarbush Valley Corp, 130 Vt 472, 296 A2d 220, 222 (1972).

[464] Eisenhart v Loveland Skiing Corp, 33 Colo App 120, 517 P2d 466, 468 (1973).

[465] 97 AD2d 46, 470 NYS2d 475, 476 (1983).

[466] 470 NYS2d at 478.

[467] *Id* at 477-478.

[468] Kaufman v State, 11 Misc 2d 56, 172 NYS2d 276, 282 (Ct Cl 1958).

prevailing conditions regarding the presence and amount of snow on the terrain. Furthermore, when a facility made a reasonable inspection of the slopes to remove debris, it was not negligent when a skier tripped on a rock. It would be prohibitively expensive, if not physically impossible, to remove all of these natural conditions.[469]

Collisions

Ski facilities must exercise reasonable care to avoid collisions between skiers[470] and to minimize the injuries resulting from a skier's collision with manmade objects on the trails.[471] One ski facility attempted to escape liability for a collision, which unfortunately catapulted one of the skiers into a steel pole, by arguing that there is no liability for injuries from a *second impact*. However, in *Rosen v LTV Recreational Development, Inc*,[472] the court properly ruled that there are no special rules for *second impact* cases. The only legitimate factor in determining causation is whether the injury was foreseeable.[473] In that case, the facility could have been held negligent in its placement of the steel pole and its failure to place padding around the pole.[474] In a different case, a court held that it was a question of fact whether a ski facility was negligent in using 1 1/2-inch sapling poles as slalom gate markers rather than bamboo or fiberglass poles.[475]

There are additional hazards of skiing at night and a ski facility must take additional precautions if it allows this activity. However, a ski facility was found not negligent when it adequately illuminated a traffic control device which a night skier hit.[476]

Instructors

Ski facilities may be liable if an instructor's conduct falls below that of a reasonable person under the circumstances.[477] Therefore, a facility may be liable for its instructor's negligence in giving ski lessons on a hill crowded with other skiers.[478] The facility could not escape liability by arguing that the

---

469 *Id.*

470 Davis v Erickson, 53 Cal 2d 860, 350 P2d 535, 537, 3 Cal Rptr 567 (1960).

471 *See* Marietta v Cliffs Ridge, Inc, 385 Mich 364, 189 NW2d 208, 211 (1971).

472 569 F2d 1117 (10th Cir 1978).

473 *Id* 1120-21.

474 *Id.*

475 Marietta v Cliffs Ridge, Inc, 385 Mich 364, 189 NW2d 208, 211 (1971).

476 Rowett v Kelly Canyon Ski Hill, Inc, 102 Idaho 708, 639 P2d 6 (1981).

477 *See generally* Davis v Erickson, 53 Cal 2d 860, 350 P2d 535, 3 Cal Rptr 567 (1960); Seidl v Trollhaugen, Inc, 305 Minn 506, 232 NW2d 236, 240 (1975).

478 Davis v Erickson, 53 Cal 2d 860, 350 P2d 535, 537, 3 Cal Rptr 567 (1960).

accident was caused by the intervening act of the skier who collided with the student because that intervening act was reasonably foreseeable.[479]

Causation

A ski facility is not liable, even if it breaches its duty of care, unless that breach was a substantial factor in causing the injury or aggravating the damages.[480] For example, even if the towers at a ski facility should have been padded, there was no negligence if the accident and resulting injury from hitting the unpadded towers would not have been prevented by the padding.[481] The same principle applies to the placement of ladders on the ski facility towers.[482]

§1.18 — Chairlifts

Ski establishments owe their skiers the duty of maintaining the chairlifts, gondolas, and other, similar devices in a reasonably safe operating condition.[483] In addition, ski establishments which allow sightseeing activities on their premises during the off-season owe nonskiers who use their chairlifts a duty of care.[484]

Plaintiffs injured on the lifts cannot recover unless they can prove that the ski facility breached a duty of care. The facility is not negligent merely because a patron's clothes became caught in the chair and the individual was injured while being dragged along the ground.[485] Indeed, a facility has been held to be entitled to a jury instruction stating that the mere fact that an accident occurred does not prove that it was the result of negligence.[486]

At one ski lift an attendant was stationed at the loading platform to instruct the passengers where to look and where to stand and was also expected to grasp the approaching chair and guide it to the passenger so that the passenger

---

479 *Id.*

480 Restatement (Second) of Torts §431 (1965).

481 Leopold v Okemo Mt, Inc, 420 F Supp 781, 787 (D Vt 1976).

482 *Id* 788.

483 Albert v State, 80 Misc 2d 105, 362 NYS2d 341, 343 (Ct Cl 1974), *affd*, 51 AD2d 611, 378 NYS2d 125 (1976); Friedman v State, 54 Misc 2d 448, 282 NYS2d 858, 860 (1967), *modified*, 31 AD2d 992, 297 NYS2d 850 (1969); *see generally* §7.20.

484 *See* Albert v State, 80 Misc 2d 105, 362 NYS2d 341, 343 (Ct Cl 1974), *affd*, 51 AD2d 611, 378 NYS2d 125 (1976); Friedman v State, 54 Misc 2d 448, 282 NYS2d 858 (Ct Cl 1967), *modified*, 31 AD2d 992, 297 NYS2d 850 (1969).

485 Math v State, 37 Misc 2d 1023, 237 NYS2d 478, 480 (Ct Cl 1962).

486 Houser v Floyd, 220 Cal App 2d 778, 786, 34 Cal Rptr 96 (1963). The California Supreme Court had previously held that this type of instruction should not be given. *See* Butigan v Yellow Cab Co, 49 Cal 2d 652, 659, 320 P2d 500 (1958).

could sit down safely. When the attendant failed to fulfill his duties and a passenger was injured, the ski establishment was found negligent.[487]

In *Friedman v State*,[488] a very religious 16-year-old girl was stranded with her date on a chairlift when the lift closed for the night before it had finished taking them to the bottom of the mountain. The girl became terribly frightened. She had the obvious fear of spending a night suspended in air. Furthermore, she was a member of an orthodox religion which considered it a mortal sin to stay with a man, not her husband, without a third person present. The court heard testimony that a girl in that situation may have preferred to jump to her death rather than violate her religious convictions. In this case, the girl did jump, and was severely injured, although not fatally.

The court in *Friedman* held that the ski facility had acted unreasonably when it closed the lift for the night in sole reliance on one passenger's statement that he did not see anyone else on the mountain. The dangers of stranding patrons on the lift required the facility to exercise more care to ascertain whether additional skiers remained on the mountain, e.g., a loudspeaker system could have been utilized to give notice that the lift was closing.[489]

The ski establishment may not be negligent for causing a ski lift accident if adequate safety equipment was provided. In *Lawrence v Davos, Inc*,[490] a skier was aware of the safety chains on the lift, but failed to use them and was injured when the lift jolted. The court held that in the absence of any evidence that the safety chains were not usable or that the injuries would have been sustained even if the chains were used, the defendant was not negligent.[491] However, when the ski facility failed to utilize the safety equipment properly, e.g., by not closing the bar of a chairlift, and a nine-year-old girl became frightened that she would fall out of the chairlift on her trip down the mountain, the facility was liable for the injuries resulting from her emotional trauma.[492]

As a general rule, a facility is not required to anticipate careless conduct on the part of others. Therefore, a ski facility was entitled to a jury instruction that it had a right to assume that "passengers using the ski lift would do so in a reasonable and careful manner."[493] Of course, if there are circumstances

---

487 Graver v State, 9 AD2d 829, 192 NYS2d 647, 649 (1959).

488 54 Misc 2d 448, 282 NYS2d 858 (Ct Cl 1967), *modified*, 31 AD2d 992, 297 NYS2d 850 (1969).

489 *Id*.

490 46 AD2d 41, 360 NYS2d 730 (1974).

491 360 NYS2d at 732.

492 Battalia v State, 26 AD2d 203, 272 NYS2d 28, 30 (1966), *aff'd without opinion*, 24 NY2d 980, 250 NE2d 224, 302 NYS2d 813 (1969).

493 Allen v State, 110 NH 42, 260 A2d 454, 457 (1969).

which would cause a reasonable person to anticipate and guard against careless conduct, then it is negligence not to do so.

Some states have safety codes[494] and administrative regulations[495] for aerial tramways.

Causation

Several ski lift accident cases have involved the application of the res ipsa loquitur doctrine. This doctrine, which usually creates a presumption of negligence, has been held to have three elements:

1. The accident must have been caused by an instrumentality under the exclusive control of the defendant

2. The accident must be of a kind which ordinarily does not occur in the absence of the defendant's negligence

3. The accident must not have been due to any voluntary act or contribution by the plaintiff[496]

A different, but more concise, statement of the res ipsa loquitur doctrine is that it applies where the accident is of such a nature that it can be said, in the light of past experience, that it probably was the result of negligence by someone and that the defendant is probably the person who is responsible.[497] Where no *balance of probabilities* in favor of negligence can be found, the doctrine does not apply.[498]

The doctrine of res ipsa loquitur has usually not been sufficient to prove the facility's negligence for ski lift accidents. In *Jordan v Loveland Skiing Corp*,[499] the plaintiff's clothing became entangled with a ski lift chair, resulting in her inability to alight properly, and she fell to the ground. The court did not apply the res ipsa loquitur doctrine because the accident could have occurred absent the defendant's negligence.[500]

---

494 *See* Friedman v State, 54 Misc 2d 448, 282 NYS2d 858, 865 (Ct Cl 1967), *modified on other grounds*, 31 AD2d 992, 297 NYS2d 850 (1969).

495 *Id.*

496 Jordan v Loveland Skiing Corp, 503 P2d 1034, 1035 (Colo Ct App 1972). The third element of this three-pronged test is not synonymous with contributory negligence. *Id.* This doctrine may be inapplicable when plaintiff has been able to prove a prima facie case by other means. *Id.*

497 Houser v Floyd, 220 Cal App 2d 778, 34 Cal Rptr 96, 99 (1963).

498 34 Cal Rptr at 99.

499 503 P2d 1034 (Colo Ct App 1972).

500 *Id.*

Similarly, in *Albert v State*,[501] individuals were injured when the gondola car they were riding in fell from its support cable and struck the ground. The plaintiffs relied on the res ipsa loquitur doctrine to prove their prima facie case. However, the ski facility produced evidence that the accident occurred because of atmospheric conditions and the overtightening of a bolt beyond specifications. More importantly, there was uncontroverted evidence that the possibility of this type of failure was not known when the lift was designed and there was additional evidence that accepted testing procedures and inspections would not have uncovered the problem. Therefore, the court held that this was an unfortunate accident which could not have been reasonably anticipated and the defendant was exonerated.[502]

§1.19   —Permits and Accident Reports

Many ski facilities are operated pursuant to special use permits issued by the United States.[503] These permits require the ski facilities to operate in a certain manner. It has been held that these permits do not set a standard of due care for the facilities, at least where they are worded imprecisely.[504] Nonetheless, counsel should obtain a copy of the relevant permit to ascertain whether the facility met the standard and if this had a bearing on how or why the accident occurred.

There may be accident reports submitted to the federal government, as well as state tramway boards. These reports may not be admissible evidence because they are hearsay.[505] However, counsel should review them to see whether they could lead to admissible evidence.

§1.20   —Common Carrier

A few courts have held that a ski lift operator is to be treated as a common carrier.[506] This requires the operator to exercise the highest degree

---

501 80 Misc 2d 105, 362 NYS2d 341 (Ct Cl 1974), *affd*, 51 AD2d 611, 378 NYS2d 125 (1976).

502 *Id.*

503 *See, e.g.*, Summit County Dev Corp v Bagnoli, 166 Colo 27, 441 P2d 658 (1968); Pessl v Bridger Bowl, 164 Mont 389, 524 P2d 1101 (1974); Elliot v Taos Ski Valley, Inc, 83 NM 575, 494 P2d 1392, *affd*, 83 NM 763, 497 P2d 974 (1972).

504 Summit County Dev Corp Bagnoli, 166 Colo 27, 441 P2d 658, 662-65 (1968).

505 Pessl v Bridger Bowl, 164 Mont 389, 524 P2d 1101, 1106 (1974).

506 Fisher v Mt Mansfield Co, Inc, 283 F2d 533, 534 (2d Cir 1960) (Vermont law); Summit County Dev Corp v Bagnoli, 166 Colo 27, 441 P2d 658, 664 (1968). The *Fisher* case is analyzed in Comment, *Negligence*, 1 Washburn LJ 316 (1961).

of care commensurate with the practical operation of the lift.[507] However, even common carriers are not liable for undiscoverable latent defects in their equipment.[508]

Even if a ski lift operator is considered a common carrier, this does not impose absolute liability. In fact, it is not negligence, as a matter of law, for a facility to fail to assist and instruct passengers on a ski lift.[509] There is also no need to state specifically in the jury instructions that a ski lift operator was a *common carrier* as long as the appropriate standard of care was explained.[510]

One court distinguished ski tow ropes from chair lifts in determining whether a facility which provided lifts was a common carrier.[511] A tow rope does not physically carry skiers; the skiers' feet are in contact with the ground and their bodies remain under their own control. In contrast, skiers using chair lifts are under the complete control of the ski facility. The more a skier surrenders control of his or her body to the lift, the greater the chances that the lift facility will be considered a common carrier.[512]

Some states have passed laws which specifically exempt ski operators from common carrier status,[513] and several courts have held that ski lifts are not common carriers.[514]

§1.21 — State Statutes

Several states have enacted legislation regulating ski facilities and skiers.[515]

---

[507] Summit County Dev Corp v Bagnoli, 166 Colo 27, 441 P2d 658, 664 (1968).

[508] Albert v State, 80 Misc 2d 105, 362 NYS2d 341, 344 (Ct Cl 1974), *affd*, 51 AD2d 611, 378 NYS2d 125 (1976).

[509] Allen v State, 110 NH 42, 260 A2d 454, 457 (1969).

[510] Hunt v Sun Valley Co, Inc, 561 F2d 744, 746 (9th Cir 1977).

[511] McDaniel v Dowell, 210 Cal App 2d 26, 31, 26 Cal Rptr 140 (1962).

[512] Hagglund, *Ski Liability*, 32 Fedn Ins Q 223, 224-25 (1982).

[513] *See, e.g.,* Cal Pub Util Code §212(c) (West Supp 1984); Mont Code Ann §23-2-703 (1983); NM Stat Ann §24-15-6 (1983); NY Transp Law §2.7 (McKinney Supp 1984); Utah Code Ann §63-11-51 (Supp 1983); Wash Rev Code Ann §70.88.010 (1975).

[514] Hunt v Sun Valley Co, Inc, 561 F2d 744, 746 (9th Cir 1977) ("We have no reason to believe that Idaho would deem a ski lift a common carrier. ...."); Pessl v Bridger Bowl, 164 Mont 389, 524 P2d 1101 (1974); Boldoc v Herbert Scheider Corp, 117 NH 566, 374 A2d 1187, 1189 (1977); Albert v State, 80 Misc 2d 105, 362 NYS2d 341, 344 (1974), *affd*, 51 AD2d 611, 378 NYS2d 125 (1976).

[515] Alaska Stat §09.65.135 (1983); Colo Rev Stat §§33-44-101 to -111 (Supp 1983); Idaho Code §§6-1101 to -1109 (Supp 1983); Me Rev Stat Ann tit 26, §§488, 489 (Supp 1984); Mass Gen Laws Ann ch 143, §71H-71S (West Supp 1983); Mich Comp Laws Ann §§408.321 to .344 (West Supp 1983); Mont Code Ann §§23-2-731 to -737 (1983); NH Rev Stat Ann §§225-A:1 to :26 (Supp 1984); NJ Admin Code tit 12, §175 (1984); NM Stat Ann §§24-15-1 to 24-15-14 (1983); NY Lab Law §§865-868 (McKinney Supp 1984); Or Rev Stat §§30.970-.990 (1981); RI Gen Laws §§41-8-1 to -4 (Supp 1983); Utah Code Ann §§63-11-37 to -53, 78-27-51 to -54 (Supp 1983); Vt Stat Ann tit 12, §1037 (Supp 1983); Va

One relatively common characteristic of these statutes is the formation of ski safety or tramway boards.[516]

Many of the states require ski facilities to mark the difficulty of slopes and the location of certain manmade objects.[517] A few states also require the facility to carry specified amounts of insurance.[518]

Some statutes specify the skiers' duty of care.[519] For example, skiers are presumed, unless shown to the contrary by a preponderance of the evidence, responsible for a collision with marked manmade objects on the trails.[520] Other statutes make that presumption conclusive and apply it to collisions with individuals as well.[521] Some *rules of the slopes*, e.g., yielding to other skiers when starting downhill, have also been enacted.[522]

Several states appear to limit, with only a few specified exceptions, an injured skier's potential causes of action against a facility to violations of these statutes.[523] However, when the statutes do not regulate ski instruction,

---

Code §§40.1-128 to -134 (1981); Wash Rev Code Ann §§70.117.010-.117.040 (Supp 1983).

These ski statutes, specifically Utah's, are criticized in Note, *Utah's Inherent Risks of Skiing Act*, 1980 Utah L Rev 355; *see also* Fagen, *Ski Area Liability for Downhill Injuries*, 49 Ins Couns J 36 (1982). The Vermont statute is anlayzed in Note, *Assumption of Risk After Sunday v Stratton Corp*, 3 Vt L Rev 129, 140-45 (1978).

One commentator has recommended modifications to these statutes. *See* Note, *Ski Operators and Skiers*, 14 New Eng L Rev 260, 277 (1978).

516 *See, e.g.*, Mich Comp Laws Ann §408.323 (West Supp 1983); NH Rev Stat Ann §225-A:3 (Supp 1984); NY Lab Law §867 (McKinney Supp 1983); Utah Code Ann §63-11-39 (Supp 1983).

The Utah statute requires the tramways to meet the United States of America Standard Institute Safety Code for Aerial Passenger Tramways. *See* Utah Code Ann §63-11-37 (Supp 1983). *See also* Va Code §40.1-131 (1981).

517 Colo Rev Stat §§33-44-106 to -107 (Supp 1983); Idaho Code §6-1103 (Supp 1983); Mich Comp Laws Ann §408.326a (West Supp 1983); NH Rev Stat Ann §255-A:23 (Supp 1984); NM Stat Ann §24-15-7 (1983); RI Gen Laws §41-8-1 (Supp 1983); Utah Code Ann §78-27-54 (Supp 1983); Wash Rev Code Ann §70.117.010 (Supp 1983).

Some ski facilities are also required to place shock-absorbent material on manmade structures located on the slopes. *See* Colo Rev Stat §33-44-107(7) (Supp 1983).

518 *See, e.g.*, NH Rev Stat Ann §225-A:25(II) (Supp 1984) ($300,000 per accident); NM Stat Ann §24-15-4 (1983); Wash Rev Code Ann §70.117.040 (Supp 1983).

519 *See* Mich Comp Law Ann §§408.341, .342 (West Supp 1983); NM Stat Ann §§24-15-10, -11 (1983); RI Gen Laws §41-8-2 (Supp 1983); Wash Rev Code Ann §70.117.020 (Supp 1983).

520 *See* Colo Rev Stat §33-44-109(2) (Supp 1983); NM Stat Ann §24-15-10 (1983); RI Gen Laws §41-8-2 (Supp 1983).

521 *See* Me Rev Stat Ann tit 26, §488 (Supp 1984); Mass Gen Law Ann ch 143, §710 (West Supp 1983).

522 *See, e.g.*, Or Rev Stat §30.985 (1981).

523 *See, e.g.*, Alaska Stat §09.65.135 (1983); NH Rev Stat Ann §§225-A:24(II), 225-A:25 (Supp 1984); NM Stat Ann §24-15-14 (1983). *But see* Ford v Black Mt Tramways, Inc, 110 NH 20, 259 A2d 129, 130 (1969) (statute does not preempt common law claims).

they do not bar claims for negligent instructions.[524] Similarly, the statutes do not preclude a recovery against a facility under product liability law or for negligent acts which are not otherwise prohibited by these statutes.[525] One commentator has implicitly criticized those decisions by arguing that one purpose of those statutes was to enable ski facilities to gauge the full extent of their legal responsibilities prior to litigation and, therefore, compliance with the statute should bar all claims based on breach of common law duties.[526]

A few states also require an injured skier to give notice of the accident to the facility in a very short period of time, usually 90 days, and several states also have short statutes of limitations for ski injuries.[527] The short notice requirements may have been an attempt to aid ski facilities which, as employers of transient seasonal workers, may otherwise have difficulty in locating witnesses.[528] Nevertheless, the quick notice requirements and short statutes of limitations have not been strictly construed. One notice provision was construed to mean only notice of injuries caused by violations of the statute; common law claims were not barred by the failure to give this notice.[529] Another court held that the short statute of limitations did not apply to injuries arising out of defects in a ski rope tow since that type of injury was not part of the *sport* of skiing.[530]

Many states prohibit skiers from recovering for injuries resulting from the inherent risks of skiing and in most of those states these risks are specifically identified, e.g., variations in terrain, changes in the weather.[531]

§1.22 Swimming

General Duty of Care

A swimming facility is not an insurer of the safety[532] of its patrons.[533]

---

524 Adie v Temple Mt Ski Area, Inc, 108 NH 480, 238 A2d 738, 741 (1968).

525 Bolduc v Herbert Schneider Corp, 117 NH 566, 374 A2d 1187, 1189 (1977) (dicta).

526 Note, *Ski Operators and Skiers*, 14 New Eng L Rev 260, 281 (1978).

527 *See, e.g.*, NH Rev Stat Ann §225-A:25 (Supp 1984); Or Rev Stat §30.980 (1981). One state also gives favorable venue to the ski facility. *See* NH Rev Stat Ann §225-A:25 (Supp 1984).

528 Note, *Utah's Inherent Risks of Skiing Act*, 1980 Utah L Rev 355, 362 n 39.

529 *See* Ford v Black Mt Tramways, Inc, 110 NH 20, 259 A2d 129, 131 (1969).

530 *See* Marshall v Town of Brattleboro, 121 Vt 417, 160 A2d 762, 764-65 (1960); *see generally* Adie v Temple Mt Ski Area, Inc, 108 NH 480, 238 A2d 738 (1968).

531 *See, e.g.*, NH Rev Stat Ann §225-A:24(I) (Supp 1984); NM Stat Ann §24-15-10 (1983); Or Rev Stat §§30.970, .975 (1981); Utah Code Ann §§78-27-52, -53 (Supp 1983); Vt Stat Ann tit 12, §1037 (Supp 1983).

532 It is estimated that over 125,000 individuals injured while swimming each year require emergency room treatment. However, not all of those injuries occur at commercial swimming

Generally, its obligation is to exercise reasonable care for the safety of its customers.[534] The swimming facility must make reasonable provisions to warn or guard against those accidents which common knowledge and experience indicate are likely to befall those engaged in swimming and other aquatic sports.[535]

The swimming establishment is expected to keep the pool in a safe condition, to have certain safety devices available for use, and to inspect the premises with sufficient qualified personnel.[536] It is also responsible for properly maintaining

---

facilities. *See* US Consumer Prod Safety Commn, Natl Injury Information Commn, Prod Summary Rep (Mar 28, 1984).

More people become quadriplegics from diving accidents than from all other recreational accidents combined. *See* Gabrielsen & Olenn, *Swimming Pool Litigation*, 18 Trial 39 (Feb 1982).

[533] Burgert v Tietjens, 499 F2d 1, 4 (10th Cir 1974) (Kansas law); McKeever v Phoenix Jewish Community Center, 92 Ariz 121, 374 P2d 875, 877 (1962); Brody v Westmoor Beach & Blade Club, Inc, 524 P2d 1087, 1090 (Colo Ct App 1974); Ward v City of Millen, 162 Ga App 148, 290 SE2d 342, 343 (1982); Rigdon v Springdale Park, Inc, 551 SW2d 860, 862 (Mo Ct App 1977); Swan v Riverside Bathing Beach Co, 132 Kan 61, 294 P 902 (1931); Manganello v Permastone, Inc, 291 NC 666, 231 SE2d 678, 680 (1977); Smith v American Flyers, Inc, 540 P2d 1212, 1215 (Okla Ct App 1975); Blacka v James, 205 Va 646, 139 SE2d 47, 50 (1964).

[534] *See* Hooks v Washington Sheraton Corp, 578 F2d 313, 315 (DC Cir 1977); Kopera v Moschella, 400 F Supp 131, 134 (SD Miss 1975) (Mississippi law); Webb v Thomas, 133 Colo 458, 296 P2d 1036, 1039 (1956); Gordon v Hotel Seville, 105 So 2d 175, 176 (Fla Dist Ct App 1958); Lincoln v Wilcox, 111 Ga App 365, 141 SE2d 765, 768 (1965); Kavanaugh v Daniels, 549 SW2d 526, 528 (Ky Ct App 1977); Lefort v Ponchatoula Beach Dev Corp, 292 So 2d 354, 356 (La Ct App 1974); Hanson v Christensen, 275 Minn 204, 145 NW2d 868, 872 (1966); Boll v Spring Lake Park, Inc, 358 SW2d 859, 862 (Mo 1962); Bristol v Ernst, 261 AD 713, 27 NYS2d 119, 120 (1941); Manganello v Permastone, Inc, 291 NC 666, 231 SE2d 678, 680 (1977); Butler v Sports Haven Intl, 563 P2d 1245, 1247 (Utah 1977) (nonprofit corporation). *See also* Cal Health & Safety Code §24101.2 (West 1984); *see generally* §7.21.

A jury instruction which stated that a facility is not required to maintain a pool which is "accident proof" was held erroneous. *See* Dunlap v Goldwin, 425 NE2d 724, 726 (Ind Ct App 1981).

Some counsel have attempted to use swimming and diving manuals issued by the American Red Cross and the Boy Scouts of America as setting a standard of due care. *See* McLaughlin v Rova Farms, Inc, 56 NJ 288, 266 A2d 284, 291 (1970).

One court held that plaintiff's counsel could be limited in his use of the Red Cross life saving and water safety manual in cross-examining the facility's owner because this was repetitious of plaintiff's expert who testified what safety equipment and personnel should be provided at a reasonably maintained swimming pool. *See* Kavanaugh v Daniels, 549 SW2d 526, 528 (Ky Ct App 1977).

[535] Rigdon v Springdale Park, Inc, 551 SW2d 860, 862 (Mo Ct App 1977); Blacka v James, 205 Va 646, 139 SE2d 47, 50 (1964).

[536] McKeever v Phoenix Jewish Community Center, 92 Ariz 121, 374 P2d 875, 877 (1962); *see generally* US Dept of Health & Human Servs, Center of Disease Control, Suggested Health and Safety Guidelines for Recreational Water Slide Flumes (July 1981).

the facilities.[537] These same rules apply to owners of apartment complexes[538] and motels and hotels[539] that provide pools for their patrons.

It has sometimes been said that swimming facilities have a high duty of care. One state court, for example, has held that reasonable care for swimming pool facilities requires a higher degree of diligence than that applied to other places of business.[540] However, it was not error for the court to give jury instructions which did not include the phrase *high degree of care* since the instructions stated "the greater the risk, the greater the degree of diligence that must be exercised."[541]

Reasonable care may require additional safety precautions when a swimming facility is entrusted with the safety of children,[542] especially if they cannot swim.[543]

If a swimmer has as much knowledge of a dangerous condition or hazard as the pool owner, the owner generally has no duty to warn the swimmer of that condition.[544] For example, when a homeowner, a regular user of a pool, had as much knowledge of the condition of the steps leading from the pool as the homeowners' association, she could not recover from the association when she fell on those steps.[545]

The common practice of an industry is a factor to consider in determining whether sufficient care has been exercised in a particular case, at least where the conduct in question is not inherently dangerous; but the compliance vel

---

537 Burgert v Tietjens, 499 F2d 1, 4 (10th Cir 1974) (Kansas law); Ward v City of Millen, 162 Ga App 148, 290 SE2d 342, 343 (1982); Ridgon v Springdale Park, Inc, 551 SW2d 860, 862 (Mo Ct App 1977); Swan v Riverside Bathing Beach Co, 132 Kan 61, 294 P 902 (1931).

538 Kopera v Moschella, 400 F Supp 131, 134-35 (SD Miss 1975); Smith v Jung, 241 So 2d 874, 876 (Fla Dist Ct App 1970); Raponotti v Burnt-Mill Arms, Inc, 113 NJ Super 173, 273 A2d 372, 376 (1971); S&C Co v Horne, 218 Va 124, 235 SE2d 456, 459 (1977).

539 Hooks v Washington Sheraton Corp, 578 F2d 313 (DC Cir 1977) (affirmed a $4,500,000 verdict for plaintiff); Kalm, Inc v Hawley, 406 SW2d 394 (Ky Ct App 1966); Brown v Southern Ventures Corp, 331 So 2d 207, 209 (La Ct App 1976); Kandrach v Chrisman, 63 Tenn App 393, 473 SW2d 193 (1971); Harris v Laquinta-Redbird Joint Venture, 522 SW2d 232 (Tex Civ App 1975).

This duty of reasonable care extends to a guest of a hotel patron. *See* Kandrach v Chrisman, 63 Tenn App 393, 473 SW2d 193, 195 (1971); *but see* Andrews v Taylor, 34 NC App 706, 239 SE2d 630, 632 (1977) (duty only to avoid wilful or wanton acts).

540 Hanson v Christensen, 275 Minn 204, 145 NW2d 868, 873 (1966).

541 Yogerst v Janish, 303 Minn 33, 226 NW2d 291, 292-93 (1975).

542 Lincoln v Wilcox, 111 Ga App 365, 141 SE2d 765, 768 (1965).

543 YMCA v Bailey, 107 Ga App 417, 130 SE2d 242, 245 (1963).

544 Purvis v Holiday Hills Property Owners Assn, Inc, 163 Ga App 387, 294 SE2d 592, 594 (1982); Smith v American Flyers, Inc, 540 P2d 1212, 1216 (Okla Ct App 1975) (danger presented by diving through an inner tube was obvious to an adult).

545 Purvis v Holiday Hills Property Owners Assn, Inc, 163 Ga App 387, 294 SE2d 592, 594 (1982).

non with the customary conduct in the industry is not dispositive of whether reasonable care was exercised in a particular instance.[546] Murky water in a public pool, even if it is *cleaner* than water in other pools in the area, was held to be evidence of negligence notwithstanding the conditions at other pools.[547]

Unfortunately, some swimming accidents have involved very serious injuries. It is, therefore, not surprising that in some cases there have been large verdicts for the plaintiff.[548] However, in other cases, the defendant was found not liable.[549]

Lessors

Generally, lessors are not liable for injuries arising from dangerous conditions on the leased premises.[550] However, lessors who lease property to which the public is admitted can be liable if they should have known of the dangerous condition on the leased premises, had reason to know that the public would be admitted before the danger was removed, and failed to use reasonable care to remove the danger.[551] One court held that the lessor could be liable for a diver's accident only if it had *actual knowledge* that the swimming pool was unreasonably dangerous.[552]

Dangerous Conditions Off the Premises

A recreational facility has, under some circumstances, a duty to warn of dangerous conditions in a nearby swimming area. For example, a hotel had a duty to warn of dangerous conditions in the ocean along its beach frontage which were neither known nor ought to have been known by a guest swimming in the area.[553] Indeed, in *Montes v Betcher*, the court held that a resort owner which availed itself of the advantages of riparian

---

546 *See* Burgert v Tietjens, 499 F2d 1, 8 (10th Cir 1974) (Kansas law).

547 *Id.*

548 *See, e.g.,* Chrisler v Holiday Valley, Inc, 580 SW2d 309, 312 (Mo Ct App 1979) ($2,300,000 verdict upheld); Baroco v Araserv, Inc, 621 F2d 189 (5th Cir 1980) ($500,000 verdict).

549 *See, e.g.,* Townes v Hawaii Properties, Inc, 708 F2d 333 (8th Cir 1983) (apartment owner not liable for the drowning of a child in the apartment swimming pool).

550 Utesch v Atlas Motor Inns, Inc, 687 F2d 20, 23 (3rd Cir 1982) (court reversed a $6,000,000 judgment for plaintiff).

551 Restatement (Second) of Torts §359 (1965).

552 Utesch v Atlas Motor Inns, Inc, 687 F2d 20, 23 (3d Cir 1982).

553 Tarshis v Lahaina Inv Corp, 480 F2d 1019, 1020 (9th Cir 1973) (plaintiff, while in the ocean, was thrown onto the beach by a powerful wave); *see also* Kaczmarczyk v City & County of Honolulu, 65 Hawaii 612, 656 P2d 89, 92 (1982) (city has same duty); *but cf* Jones v Halekulani Hotel, Inc, 557 F2d 1308, 1310 (9th Cir 1977) (hotel had no duty to warn users of seawall of shallowness of water because the hotel had no right to control the users of this public seawall).

ownership owed its patrons a duty of reasonable care which included *active vigilance* in protecting them from foreseeable risks in the water, even though it did not own the body of water and the land beneath it.[554] In *Montes*, the resort was found negligent for failing to warn of the dangers of diving off a boat dock, failing to *rake* the lake periodically in search of dangerous obstructions, and failing to segregate swimming areas from boating areas.[555] The practical effect of this ruling is that a plaintiff can recover even if he or she does not show the recreational facility's actual knowledge of the existence of the dangerous condition off its premises.[556]

Personal Liability of Corporate Officers

The officers of an organization which had a pool open to the public were not liable as a matter of law when there was no showing of their personal negligence.[557]

Breach of Contract

A swimming establishment may, under appropriate circumstances, be liable for breach of contract when a swimmer drowns. In *Baroco v Araserv, Inc*,[558] a facility failed to follow the safety precautions it had agreed to take in its contract with the government. The court held the facility's patrons to be third-party beneficiaries of this contract and, therefore, allowed them to sue for breach of contract.[559]

Diving

A recreational facility is under a duty to use reasonable care to see that the water beneath the diving board is of a sufficient depth to be reasonably safe for diving,[560] or if it is not reasonably safe to dive, to warn of the hazards.[561] One court held that the presence of a diving board at a swimming pool is an

---

554 480 F2d 1128, 1131 (8th Cir 1973) (Minnesota law).

555 *Id.*

556 *Id.*

557 Ward v City of Millen, 162 Ga App 148, 290 SE2d 342, 345 (1982); *see generally* Andrews v Taylor, 34 NC App 706, 239 SE2d 630, 632 (1977) (only owners or operators of a facility are liable).

558 621 F2d 189, 191 (5th Cir 1980).

559 *Id.*

560 Pleasant v Blue Mound Swim Club, 128 Ill App 2d 277, 262 NE2d 107, 112 (1970); McLaughlin v Rova Farms, Inc, 56 NJ 288, 266 A2d 284, 292 (1970).

561 Boll v Spring Lake Park, Inc, 358 SW2d 859 (Mo 1962); *see also* Waddel's Adminr v Brashear, 257 Ky 390, 78 SW2d 31, 32 (Ky Ct 1934).

invitation to patrons to use it and by its presence the facility has impliedly represented that it generally may be used safely.[562]

In *Pleasant v Blue Mound Swim Club*, the court held that a facility which knew of a diver's presence, and also knew that the water depth had been lowered to a dangerous degree because of the backflushing of the filters, owed the diver a duty to warn him of the dangers posed by the lowered water level.[563] However, the owners of a recreational beach were not liable for failure to warn of the dangers of diving when they posted warning signs and employed a lifeguard who orally told the plaintiff of the dangers of diving.[564]

A facility which wants to prohibit diving must do so explicitly. A sign stating *swimming and diving at your own risk* may he held insufficient for that purpose because those words could be construed to mean that swimming and diving were authorized activities, although the participant would assume the inherent risks of the sport.[565]

A facility generally does not have to warn of the dangers which would have been perceived by a person exercising reasonable prudence under the same or similar circumstances.[566] This standard is objective and, therefore, it is not important whether the plaintiff actually perceived the danger.[567] Accordingly, it can be argued that the dangers presented by shallow water in the pool are obvious and, therefore, a facility had no duty to warn or remove these dangers.[568] It is, however, generally a question of fact whether the dangers were obvious,[569] and in one case the jury was taken to the pool to view it.[570]

One court held that proof of the absence of prior diving accidents at the swimming establishment was irrelevant and therefore inadmissible.[571]

---

[562] Pleasant v Blue Mound Swim Club, 128 Ill App 2d 277, 262 NE2d 107, 112 (1970).

[563] 262 NE2d at 113.

[564] Lefort v Ponchatoula Beach Dev Corp, 292 So 2d 354, 356-57 (La Ct App 1974).

[565] McLaughlin v Rova Farms, Inc, 56 NJ 288, 266 A2d 284, 288 (1970).

[566] Atkins v Bisigier, 16 Cal App 3d 414, 94 Cal Rptr 49, 56 (1971). Even if the risk of danger is obvious, it may also be unreasonable for the facility not to reduce the risk of injury. *See* §1.01.

[567] Atkins v Bisigier, 16 Cal App 3d 414, 94 Cal Rptr 49, 56 (1971). If plaintiff did perceive the danger, he may have assumed the risk or been contributorily negligent. *See* §§9.01, 9.02, 9.03, 9.04.

[568] Atkins v Bisigier, 16 Cal App 3d 414, 94 Cal Rptr 49, 56 (1971); *see generally* Webb v Thomas, 133 Colo 458, 296 P2d 1036, 1040 (1956).

[569] Atkins v Bisigier, 16 Cal App 3d 414, 94 Cal Rptr 49, 56 (1971).

[570] *Id.*

[571] *See generally id*, 94 Cal Rptr at 57.

§1.23 — Additional Duties

Lifeguards and Proper Supervision

A swimming establishment must provide sufficient, qualified lifeguards at the pool to supervise patrons and rescue those in peril.[572] Indeed, more than one lifeguard may be necessary depending on the size of the pool and the number of swimmers.[573]

A lifeguard is required to use the care reasonably exercised in similar circumstances by a qualified lifeguard,[574] e.g., to keep a proper lookout,[575] to detect signs of distress,[576] and to attempt a rescue.[577] In *S&C Co v Horne*, the court held that a lifeguard was negligent in failing to detect a swimmer's distress when the pool was small, only five other people were in the water, no lifeguard duties called him from his post, and he failed to sit in a guard chair at the edge of the deep end of the pool as required by city regulations.[578] The pool owner is liable for the negligence of lifeguards in the performance of their duties.[579]

It is rather easy to allege that an establishment should have had more lifeguards on duty. Accordingly, the courts have not been particularly receptive to this argument, especially when no one else in the pool saw the swimming accident occur. In those situations it is difficult for the plaintiff to prove that additional lifeguards would have been able to prevent an accident that no one else observed.[580]

Acts of Third Parties

A swimming establishment must take reasonable care to prevent injury to

---

[572] Kopera v Moschella, 400 F Supp 131, 135 (SD Miss 1975) (Mississippi law); Smith v Jung, 241 So 2d 874, 876-77 (Fla Dist Ct App 1970); Manganello v Permastone, Inc, 291 NC 666, 231 SE2d 678, 681 (1977); Larkin v Saltair Beach Co, 30 Utah 86, 83 P 686 (1905); S&C Co v Horne, 218 Va 124, 235 SE2d 456, 459 (1977); *but see* Andrews v Taylor, 34 NC App 706, 239 SE2d 630, 632 (1977).

[573] *See generally* YMCA v Bailey, 107 Ga App 417, 130 SE2d 242, 245 (1963).

[574] *See* Kaczmarczyk v City & County of Honolulu, 65 Hawaii 612, 656 P2d 89, 93 (1982).

[575] Carter v Boys' Club, 552 SW2d 327, 330-31 (Mo Ct App 1977).

[576] S&C Co v Horne, 218 Va 124, 235 SE2d 456, 460 (1977).

[577] *Id.*

[578] *Id.*

[579] Lipton v Dreamland Park Co, 121 NJL 554, 3 A2d 571, 571-72 (1939); S&C Co v Horne, 218 Va 124, 235 SE2d 456, 459 (1977).

[580] *See, e.g.*, Kaczmarczyk v City & County of Hawaii, 65 Hawaii 612, 656 P2d 89, 94 (1982); Carreira v Territory, 40 Hawaii 513 (1954); *see generally* §1.25.

patrons by third parties.[581] However, where the accident occurred without any warning and the facility could not have discovered or prevented it by the use of reasonable care, it was not liable.[582] In *Lincoln v Wilcox*, a public swimming pool facility was held to be not negligent when a child swimming in the water was seriously injured after being hit by a diver because it would have been unreasonable, if not impossible, to have required the facility's lifeguard to anticipate every possible negligent act by other patrons and to eliminate the danger.[583]

A facility owed a duty to all of its patrons either to prohibit *rough-housing* or to supervise it closely.[584] If rough or boisterous play is to be permitted at all, it should be confined to a restricted area or, at a minimum, closely guarded.[585] Accordingly, a facility may be negligent in not eliminating horseplay if that horseplay could have been prevented by the lifeguards but was not, resulting in a patron being injured.[586] For example, a woman who was injured while swimming when she was struck by a man who had been thrown into the pool by others may be able to recover against the owner of the pool.[587] Similarly, a swimming establishment may be liable when a swimmer was injured by other swimmers doing backflips from each other's shoulders.[588] The establishment's argument, that the backflipping activity did not become dangerous until the participants moved to within striking range of the plaintiff and did not last long enough to put the establishment on notice of the danger, was rejected.[589] Participants in such a rough activity could reasonably be expected to change direction and move to different locations relatively quickly, posing a danger to other swimmers, and the facility, therefore, should have removed the danger earlier.[590]

Quality of Water

A facility may be negligent for allowing water to remain murky if the

---

[581] Lincoln v Wilcox, 111 Ga App 365, 141 SE2d 765 (1965).

[582] *Id.*

[583] 141 SE2d at 767-68.

[584] Manganello v Permastone, Inc, 291 NC 666, 231 SE2d 678, 681 (1977); *see generally* Ky Rev Stat §231.110 (1982) (entertainment facility shall not allow disorderly or boisterous persons to congregate around the premises).

[585] 231 SE2d at 682.

[586] Gordon v Hotel Seville, 105 So 2d 175, 177 (Fla Dist Ct App 1958).

[587] *Id.*

[588] Manganello v Permastone, Inc, 291 NC 666, 231 SE2d 678, 681 (1977).

[589] *Id.*

[590] *Id.*

condition of the water bears a substantial relationship to the injury, e.g., if the condition impeded a rescue.[591]

Rescue

Swimming facilities generally must take reasonable steps to rescue their patrons.[592] In *Yania v Bigan*,[593] a 30-year-old man drowned after jumping into a body of water at a strip mining operation. The property owner saw this happen, but failed to extricate the man. The court held that although the owner saw the man in the water he had no legal[594] obligation to rescue him unless he was responsible for placing the man in the dangerous situation. In this case, the court held that there was no such responsibility and the complaint alleging failure to rescue was dismissed.[595]

Rescue Equipment

Some courts have held that swimming facilities should provide adequate life saving equipment.[596]

Pool Design

Engineers who designed a motel swimming pool could be found negligent for failing to provide a covering for the main drain outlet which could not be removed easily, a violation of state law.[597] Unfortunately, in that case, a minor's arm became lodged in the drain, and the child ultimately drowned.[598] In addition, in *Shetter v Davis Brothers*, the court held that a pool builder may be liable for the negligent design of the pool, even where the builder did not prepare the design but merely complied with the plans furnished by the owner's architect.[599] A builder which has held itself out as an expert in the design of pools is liable if it can be shown that the builder knew or should

---

[591] Ward v City of Millen, 162 Ga App 148, 290 SE2d 342, 344 (1982).

[592] *See generally* Kopera v Moschella, 400 F Supp 131, 135 (SD Miss 1975) (Mississippi law); Smith v Jung, 241 So 2d 874, 876-77 (Fla Dist Ct App 1970).

[593] 397 Pa 316, 155 A2d 343 (1959).

[594] There was a moral duty. *See* 155 A2d at 346.

[595] *See id.*

[596] Kopera v Moschella, 400 F Supp 131, 135 (SD Miss 1975) (Mississippi law); Smith v Jung, 241 So 2d 874, 876-77 (Fla Dist Ct App 1970).

[597] Henry v Britt, 220 So 2d 917, 918 (Fla Dist Ct App), *cert denied*, 229 So 2d 867 (Fla 1969).

[598] *Id.*

[599] 163 Ga App 230, 293 SE2d 397, 399 (1982) (the case was decided by a 5-4 vote); *but see* Andrews v Taylor, 34 NC App 706, 239 SE2d 630, 633 (1977).

have known that the pool would be dangerous if constructed in accordance with the plans it was given, but failed to take action to eliminate the danger.[600]

§1.24 —Violation of Statutes, Ordinances, and Regulations

Many localities and state administrative agencies have enacted safety regulations for public swimming pools.[601] For example, some ordinances require swimming pools which are open to the public[602] to provide adequate, trained personnel,[603] proper rescue equipment,[604] and self-closing gates.[605]

The construction of these regulations has been held to be a question of law for the court to determine.[606] One court held that a city ordinance which required a pool owner to have at least one employee watch the pool all day was not violated when such an employee left the pool for 10 minutes on an errand because the ordinance was construed only to require the owner to hire employees on an all-day basis and not to require the employees never leave the premises.[607] A Dallas ordinance requiring a *life pole or shepherd's crook type of pole* was construed to require a pole with a hook or pulling device which could be used to retrieve unconscious persons.[608]

---

600 293 SE2d at 399.

601 *See, e.g.,* Townes v Hawaii Properties, Inc, 708 F2d 333, 334 (8th Cir 1983); Hooks v Washington Sheraton Corp, 578 F2d 313, 315 (DC Cir 1977); Raponotti v Burnt-Mill Arms, Inc, 113 NJ Super 173, 273 A2d 372, 377 (1971); Coleman v Shaw, 314 SE2d 154, 155 (SC Ct App 1984); Harris v Laquinta-Redbird Joint Venture, 522 SW2d 232, 233 (Tex Civ App 1975) (Dallas ordinance). *See* Cal Admin Code tit 17, §§7774-7833 (West 1984); Mich Stat Ann §18.1287(192) (Callaghan 1980); NJ Stat Ann §26:4A-1 (West Supp 1984); Okla Stat Ann tit 63, §§1-1013 to -1015 (West 1984); Or Rev Stat §§448.005-.100 (1983); RI Gen Laws §23-22-15 (Supp 1983); SC Dept of Health & Environmental Control Reg 61-51 (1983 Supp).
In California, the *public* swimming pool statute applies to all pools other than private pools maintained for the use of family or friends. *See* Lucas v Hesperia Golf & Country Club, 255 Cal App 2d 241, 63 Cal Rptr 189, 194 (1967).

602 *See* Raponotti v Burnt-Mill Arms, Inc, 113 NJ Super 173, 273 A2d 372, 376 (1971) (apartment complex pools are included).

603 Cal Health & Safety Code §§24101.1, .4 (West 1983); NJ Stat Ann §§26:4A-1, -1.1 (West 1983).

604 NJ Stat Ann §26:4A-1 (West 1983).

605 Gordon v Strawther Enters, Inc, 273 Cal App 2d 504, 78 Cal Rptr 417, 424 (1969).

606 *See, e.g.,* Harris v Laquinta-Redbird Jt Venture, 522 SW2d 232, 234 (Tex Civ App 1975) (Dallas ordinance); *see also* Kavanaugh v Daniels, 549 SW2d 526, 528 (Ky Ct App 1977) (administrative regulations only apply to artificial structures such as swimming pools; they do not apply to natural bodies of water such as lakes).

607 Bell v Page, 2 NC App 132, 162 SE2d 693, 696 (1968).

608 *See, e.g.,* Harris v Laquinta-Redbird Joint Venture, 522 SW2d 232, 235 (Tex Civ App 1975) (Dallas ordinance).

It is ordinarily a question of fact whether these ordinances were violated.[609] However, when a violation occurred, the swimming establishment may be liable for negligence per se if the injured swimmer is in the class of individuals for whose benefit the law was enacted.[610]

It is important, therefore, to ascertain the conduct intended to be prevented by the ordinance in order to determine whether the establishment's violation shows a breach of the duty of care in a particular situation. In *Gordon v Strawther Enterprises, Inc*, the court held the underlying reason for the ordinance requiring a self-closing device was to guard against the possibility that the gate would be opened by someone who would neglect to close it.[611] When that unfortunate situation happened, and a young child fell into the pool and was severely injured, the plaintiff was entitled to judgment as a matter of law for the establishment's violation of the ordinance.[612]

Many of the local ordinances serve multiple functions. For example, the prevention of horseplay reduces the risk of injury and also makes it easier to discover swimmers in danger.[613] Similarly, a divider rope may serve as both a lifeline and a warning device,[614] and the presence of lifeguards helps keep swimmers from getting into danger and allows for their rescue when danger occurs.[615] When a drowning has occurred and several of those requirements were not met, e.g., horseplay was allowed, no divider rope was provided, and an insufficient number of lifeguards were on duty, an inference of negligence arises

---

609 *See* Coleman v Shaw, 314 SE2d 154, 156 (SC Ct App 1984).

610 *See, e.g.*, Haft v Lone Palm Hotel, 3 Cal 3d 756, 478 P2d 465, 468, 91 Cal Rptr 745 (1970); Raponotti v Burnt-Mill Arms, Inc, 113 NJ Super 173, 273 A2d 372, 376 (1971); Coleman v Shaw, 314 SE2d 154, 156 (SC App 1984); Harris v Laquinta-Redbird Joint Venture, 522 SW2d 232, 234 (Tex Civ App 1975); Bell v Page, 271 NC 396, 156 SE2d 711, 715 (1967) (violation of municipal ordinance imposing a public duty and designed for the protection of life and limb is negligence per se).

Some states have codified the elements of the negligence per se doctrine. *See, e.g.*, Cal Evid Code §669 (West Supp 1984). The four elements are:

1. Violation of a statute, ordinance or regulation of a public entity
2. The violation proximately caused injury
3. The injury resulted from an occurrence of the nature which the statute, ordinance, or regulation was designed to prevent
4. The person suffering injury was in the class of persons for whose protection the statute, ordinance, or regulation was adopted.

611 273 Cal App 2d 504, 78 Cal Rptr 417, 423 (1969).

612 78 Cal Rptr at 425.

613 Bartley v Childers, 433 SW2d 130, 132 (Ky Ct App 1968).

614 *Id*.

615 *Id*.

and a directed verdict for the swimming establishment is inappropriate.[616]

However, if the regulation was not intended to prevent the accident which occurred, an instruction on negligence per se is inappropriate.[617] One court held that a local regulation requiring the placement of a rope and buoys in swimming pools was designed to prevent drowning accidents, not diving accidents, because the divider was intended to warn poor swimmers of deeper water, to afford support for swimmers who may find themselves in need of it, and to serve as a barrier between the shallow water and the deep water.[618] Accordingly, it held that a woman who dived into relatively shallow water without realizing its depth could not rely on the doctrine of negligence per se even though the owner of the pool had not complied with this rope and buoy regulation because this regulation was not designed to prevent diving accidents.[619]

In addition, in *Hooks v Washington Sheraton Corp*, the court held that a jury instruction on negligence per se for violations of local ordinances is proper only when the defendant failed to introduce evidence explaining why noncompliance was still consistent with the exercise of due care.[620] The defendant argued that the pool's deviation from the requirements of an ordinance was not evidence of unreasonable conduct because the city had approved the changes.[621] However, there was no admissible evidence of this approval and, therefore, the negligence per se instruction was proper. In a different case an apartment complex's excuse for failing to have a self-closing gate was that the gate was "on order."[622] This excuse was labeled *paltry and trifling* by the court and the apartment complex was not considered to have acted with reasonable care.[623]

Safety codes are generally admissible evidence at trial as long as the proper

---

616 *Id* 133.

617 Smith v American Flyers, Inc, 540 P2d 1212, 1215 (Okla Ct App 1975) (statutes and regulations did not require the swimming facility to protect plaintiff from diving through an inner tube); *see also* Brody v Westmoor Beach & Blade Club, Inc, 524 P2d 1087, 1090-91 (Colo Ct App 1974); Kelly v Koppers Co, 293 So 2d 763, 764 (Fla Dist Ct App), *cert denied*, 302 So 2d 415 (Fla 1974).

618 Atkins v Bisigier, 16 Cal App 3d 414, 94 Cal Rptr 49, 54 (1971).

619 94 Cal Rptr at 54.

620 578 F2d 313, 315-16 (DC Cir 1977).

621 *Id.*

622 Gordon v Strawther Enters, Inc, 273 Cal App 2d 504, 78 Cal Rptr 417, 425 (1969).

623 *Id.*

foundation is laid.[624] Administrative rules, even if not mandatory, may also be admissible.[625]

If a state administrative agency's rules regarding swimming pool maintenance exceeded the power granted to that body, evidence of the rule violation is erroneous.[626] However, this issue does not involve fundamental error and if it was not raised in the lower court, it cannot be raised on appeal.[627]

Even if the defendant's acts were negligent per se, this only establishes the defendant's breach of duty. The plaintiff must still prove that the accident was caused by this breach of duty.[628] Nonetheless, several courts have held that breach of a statutory duty may give rise to an inference that the injury resulted from violation of the statute.[629] However, when there was no evidence that violation of a building code caused a diver's injury, the diver's multi-million dollar judgment was reversed.[630]

§1.25   —Causation

General Principles

The mere fact that a swimming accident occurred, even when the swimming establishment failed to use reasonable care to protect its patrons, does not,

---

624 *See* Raponotti v Burnt-Mill Arms Inc, 113 NJ Super 173, 273 A2d 372, 378 (1971). *See also* Comment, *Admissibility of Safety Codes, Rules and Standards in Negligence Cases*, 37 Tenn L Rev 581 (1970).

Health inspection reports indicating that the defendant was apprised of the safety laws over an extended period of time are admissible to show that the defendant's continued violation of the laws was wilful and wanton. *See* Haft v Lone Palm Hotel, 3 Cal 3d 756, 478 P2d 465, 479-80, 91 Cal Rptr 745 (1970).

625 *See* Smith v Jung, 241 So 2d 874, 875-76 (Fla Dist Ct App 1970).

626 Atlas Properties, Inc v Didich, 226 So 2d 684, 691 (Fla 1969).

627 *Id.*

628 Haft v Lone Palm Hotel, 3 Cal 3d 756, 478 P2d 465, 469, 91 Cal Rptr 745 (1970); Coleman v Shaw, 314 SE2d 154, 156 (SC Ct App 1984); Townes v Hawaii Properties, Inc, 708 F2d 333, 335 (8th Cir 1983) (violation of state regulations was not the proximate cause of the fatality). *See generally* §1.25.

A California statute required either lifeguards or a warning that no lifeguards were present. When neither alternative was provided, the pool owner's liability was measured from the failure to provide lifeguards. *See* Haft v Lone Palm Hotel, 3 Cal 3d 756, 478 P2d 465, 472, 91 Cal Rptr 745 (1970). To calculate liability from failing to provide the warning would undermine the statute. *See id.*

629 Haft v Lone Palm Hotel, 3 Cal 3d 756, 478 P2d 465, 469, 91 Cal Rptr 745 (1970); Lucas v Hesperia Golf & Country Club, 255 Cal App 2d 241, 63 Cal Rptr 189, 196 (1967).

630 Utesch v Atlas Motor Inns, Inc, 687 F2d 20, 25 (3d Cir 1982); *see generally* §1.25.

without more, establish liability.[631] The defendant's negligence must have been the proximate cause of injury before liability can be found.[632]

Causation is generally proved by inference.[633] As a result, there is almost always a measure of uncertainty regarding whether the facility's act or omission caused the accident.[634]

It is not necessary at trial that the plaintiff exclude all possible causes of the injury other than the one that he or she advances.[635] All the plaintiff must prove is that the injuries were the natural, although not the necessary and inevitable, result of the defendant's negligence, i.e., that the injuries were more likely than not, under ordinary circumstances, the result of the defendant's negligent acts.[636]

Proof of causation must be based on reasonable inferences drawn from the facts, not conjecture.[637] When reasonable minds could infer that there was a causal relationship between the facility's negligent acts and the injury, this question must be submitted to the jury; the court should not decide this issue as a matter of law unless a plaintiff's verdict would have to be based on speculation or conjecture.[638]

In unwitnessed drowning cases it is impossible to produce direct evidence that the accident victim would not have been injured, or that the injury would have been less severe, had the swimming facility acted properly.[639] Therefore, a jury is allowed broader latitude to infer proximate causation.[640] Where a swimming facility did not have proper life-saving equipment and there was testimony that had the appropriate equipment been available, the rescue of a boy who drowned would have been quicker and, therefore, possibly successful, a prima facie showing of proximate causation was made.[641] Similar conclusions were drawn in cases where there was a failure to provide lifeguards,[642] where a lifeguard failed to keep a proper lookout for an

---

631 Blacka v James, 205 Va 646, 139 SE2d 47, 50 (1964).

632 *Id.*

633 Hill v State, 121 RI 353, 398 A2d 1130, 1132 (1979).

634 *Id* 1132; Coleman v Shaw, 314 SE2d 154 (SC Ct App 1984).

635 Hill v State, 121 RI 353, 398 A2d 1130, 1131 (1979).

636 Carter v Boys' Club, 552 SW2d 327, 331 (Mo Ct App 1977); McFarland v Grau, 305 SW2d 91, 96-97 (Mo Ct App 1957).

637 Carter v Boys' Club, 552 SW2d 327, 331 (Mo Ct App 1977); Hill v State, 121 RI 353, 398 A2d 1130, 1131 (1979).

638 Carter v Boys' Club, 552 SW2d 327, 331 (Mo Ct App 1977); Hill v State, 121 RI 353, 398 A2d 1130, 1131 (1979).

639 Carter v Boys' Club, 552 SW2d 327, 331 (Mo Ct App 1977); Harris v Laquinta-Redbird Joint Venture, 522 SW2d 232, 236 (Tex Civ App 1975).

640 *Id.*

641 *Id.*

642 McFarland v Grau, 305 SW2d 91, 98, 100-01 (Mo Ct App 1957).

inexperienced swimmer,[643] and where there were no warnings of a steep drop-off.[644]

Indeed, the court in *Coleman v Shaw*, noted: "To require direct evidence here that had an employee trained in first aid been on hand and emergency equipment provided, the drowning would not have occurred, would amount to requiring evidence made impossible to obtain due to the very negligence of which [the defendant] is guilty."[645]

One court held that the burden of proof on this issue shifts to the defense under these circumstances.[646]

Lifeguards

A jury cannot be allowed to speculate regarding the relationship between a swimming establishment's lack of sufficient lifeguards and the drowning of a patron. In *Hahn v Perkins*,[647] a boy disappeared one afternoon near a refreshment stand at a public swimming facility and his body was found the next day in the water. The court held for the defendant because there was no evidence of how, when, or where the boy died.[648] The plaintiff's claim that the facility should have had more lifeguards was rejected because no one in the crowd of people in the pool saw the child in difficulty or even in the pool and, therefore, there was no relationship between the proper number of lifeguards and the fatality.[649] Similarly, in *Blacka v James*, a swimming establishment was not liable for a drowning, even though it failed to provide any lifeguards, when the swimmer disappeared without a trace in front of hundreds of people in and around the lake.[650]

Rescue

The court in *Hahn v Perkins*, held that a facility was not negligent in failing timely to locate a child who drowned, when the child's mother did not state that the child was last seen in or near the pool and where there was no evidence that immediate action would have successfully rescued the child.[651]

---

643 Carter v Boys' Club, 552 SW2d 327, 330-31 (Mo Ct App 1977).

644 Hill v State, 121 RI 353, 398 A2d 1130, 1132 (1979).

645 314 SE2d 154, 158 (SC Ct App 1984); *see also* Haft v Lone Palm Hotel, 3 Cal 3d 756, 478 P2d 465, 474-75, 91 Cal Rptr 745 (1970).

646 Haft v Lone Palm Hotel, 3 Cal 3d 756, 478 P2d 465, 475-77, 91 Cal Rptr 745 (1970).

647 228 NC 727, 46 SE2d 854 (1948).

648 46 SE2d at 858.

649 *Id* 857.

650 205 Va 646, 139 SE2d 47, 51 (1964).

651 228 NC 727, 46 SE2d 854, 857 (1948).

Warning of Water Depth

One court ruled that a swimming establishment's failure to mark the varying depths of the water was not negligence when there was no showing that this act bore any relation to a drowning.[652]

Quality of Water

The murkiness of water in which a drowning victim has been swimming may show negligence by the swimming facility if there is a relationship between the condition of the water and the injury.[653] For example, if the water had been clear, a lifeguard might have been able to rescue the swimmer quicker, thus saving his or her life.[654] Evidence that the pool water was dirty 30 days after the accident was held not admissible because it was not sufficiently probative of the condition of the water on the day of the injury.[655]

Multiple Causes

In some situations the swimming accident is the unfortunate result of the negligence of more than one party and each defendant may attempt to argue that it did not *cause* the accident. For example, in *Tucker v Dixon*,[656] a minor hit the hard surface of a detached portion of some cleaning equipment as she surfaced from a dive. The facility argued that it was not liable because the injuries were caused by the intervening acts of third parties who detached the object from the cleaning equipment and left it in the water. The court rejected this argument, holding that the facility was negligent in leaving the cleaning equipment near the pool and that this negligence was a concurrent cause of the injury (along with the third party's negligence), subjecting the facility to liability.[657]

Res Ipsa Loquitur

Res ipsa loquitur is a rule of circumstantial evidence where an inference of negligence is drawn against a defendant because the facts indicate this to be the more probable cause of injury in the absence of other plausible explanations by credible witnesses.[658]

---

652 *Id.*

653 Ward v City of Millen, 162 Ga App 148, 290 SE2d 342, 345 (1982).

654 *Id.*

655 Atkins v Bisigier, 16 Cal App 3d 414, 94 Cal Rptr 49, 57 (1971).

656 144 Colo 79, 355 P2d 79 (1960).

657 *Id* 355 P2d at 82-83.

658 Brown v Southern Ventures Corp, 331 So 2d 207, 210 (La Ct App 1976).

Some courts have been reticent about applying the res ipsa loquitur doctrine in drowning cases.[659] For example, in *McKeever v Phoenix Jewish Community Center*,[660] a 10-year-old girl drowned and there was no evidence of the cause of the accident. The court did not apply the res ipsa loquitur doctrine for two reasons.[661] First, the plaintiff failed to prove that the accident was a result of someone's negligence.[662] The child may simply have lost her balance and fallen. Second, the defendant did not have exclusive control of an instrumentality, viz., the pool, causing the injury.[663] The defendant's control was shared with all who were using the facility, in this case, about 40 other people.

However, in *Brown v Southern Ventures Corp*, the court applied this doctrine to find a motel liable for negligence when a patron was found drowned in its pool and there were no witnesses to the accident.[664] It noted that the coping at the edge of the pool was loose and there was some evidence that the decedent had fallen since there was a tear in his pants and a scratch on his new watch.[665] This was sufficient for the court to conclude that the res ipsa loquitur doctrine was applicable.

In cases where a swimming facility does not appear to have failed to exercise ordinary care, it may be entitled to a jury instruction that an unavoidable accident is one which ordinary care could not have prevented.[666]

§1.26   Miscellaneous Recreational Activities

Go-Carts

A go-cart facility is not an insurer of the safety[667] of its patrons.[668] However,

---

659 *See* McKeever v Phoenix Jewish Community Center, 92 Ariz 121, 374 P2d 875, 877 (1962); Blacka v James, 205 Va 646, 139 SE2d 47, 50-51 (1964).

660 92 Ariz 121, 374 P2d 875, 877 (1962).

661 *Id.*

662 *Id.*

663 *Id.*

664 331 So 2d 207, 210-11 (La Ct App 1976).

665 *Id.*

666 McKeever v Phoenix Jewish Community Center, 92 Ariz 121, 374 P2d 875, 878 (1962).

667 It is estimated that each year there are about 9,500 individuals injured severely enough, while using go-carts, to require emergency room treatment. *See* US Consumer Prod Safety Commn, Natl Injury Information Clearinghouse, Prod Summary Rep (Mar 28, 1984).

668 Balart v Michel's Kartway, Inc, 364 So 2d 90, 92 (Fla Dist Ct App 1978).

it must exercise reasonable care for its patrons' safety.[669]

In *Balart v Michael's Kartway, Inc*, a 10-year-old girl lost control of a go-cart on a curve and was injured when the cart ran into a chain-link fence.[670] The court took judicial notice of the distance per second that a motor-driven vehicle travels and of a driver's reaction time.[671] However, it ruled that it was a jury question whether the facility was negligent in placing a fence so close to a curve on the trace.

Mountain Lodges

Mountain lodges must take reasonable care of their facilities.[672] However, in *Bluejacket v Carney*,[673] a mountain lodge was entitled to summary judgment where a patron, an experienced outdoorsman, slipped and fell on a path at night. The court held that the plaintiff produced no evidence that the lodge's alleged breaches of duty, e.g., the failure to shovel, sand, or salt the path and the failure to erect a warning sign, caused the accident.[674] In addition, the court ruled that the lodge was not liable for injuries from dangers which were obvious or, if not obvious, at least as well known to the person injured as to the lodge.[675]

Pleasure Cruises

The owner and operator of a pleasure cruise ship must exercise the highest degree of care for its patrons consistent with the safe transportation and practical operation of the ship.[676] In *O'Connor v Chandris Lines*,[677] a married couple was injured when the husband's bunk collapsed, falling on the wife. The court held that the ship's owner had a continuing legal duty to provide bunks that were soundly constructed, securely held in place, and strong enough to sustain a 200-pound man with a reasonable margin of safety.[678] In that case, the court applied the res ipsa loquitur doctrine, holding that a bunk does not normally collapse in the absence of negligence, and the most

---

669 *Id.* In New Jersey, the minimum safety conditions for a go-cart track are specified. *See* NJ Admin Code tit 13, §22-9 (1984).

670 364 So 2d 90, 92 (Fla Dist Ct App 1978).

671 At 25 miles per hour, the go-cart would travel approximately 37 feet per second. The reaction time of an able adult driver is generally 2/3 to 3/4 of a second. Obviously, an inexperienced child driver's reaction time would be slower. *See id.*

672 *See* Bluejacket v Carney, 550 P2d 494 (Wyo 1976).

673 *Id.*

674 *Id* 497.

675 *Id.*

676 O'Connor v Chandris Lines, 566 F Supp 1275, 1279 (D Mass 1983).

677 *Id.*

678 *Id.*

probable cause of the negligence was the ship's employees' failure to remove the defective bunk.[679]

In *Kuntz v Windjammer "Barefoot" Cruises, Ltd*, the court held a cruise company was ultimately liable for over $100,000 for the death of a woman passenger who drowned while scuba diving.[680] The cruise diving instructor was negligent in failing to maintain proper supervision of the students by staying close to the spot where the dive occurred and also in failing to establish a surface support station.[681] However, the plaintiff's actual damages were reduced by 50 per cent because the woman's motor functions were significantly diminished by drinking alcohol and smoking marijuana the night before the dive.[682]

Rodeos

A rodeo must maintain its premises in a reasonably safe condition.[683] In *Rosenberger v Central Louisiana District Livestock Show, Inc*,[684] a bronco rider was injured when his bucking horse attempted to go through a partially opened gate. The court held that such horses have a propensity to go through partially opened gates and, therefore, a rodeo facility should inspect the gates to insure that they are secured before commencing a bronco riding contest.[685]

Tennis

A tennis establishment was entitled to a directed verdict where the plaintiff failed to prove that the establishment had notice, actual or constructive, of the raised seam on the court.[686] Without such notice there can be no liability for negligence because the failure to remedy the situation was not unreasonable.[687] In addition, in that case the plaintiff failed to prove that his injuries were caused by tripping on the raised seam.[688]

---

679 *Id* 1279-80.

680 573 F Supp 1277 (WD Pa 1983). The court applied federal admiralty law even though the accident occurred on the seas near the Bahamas because all the important parties were United States citizens and the cruise contract was executed in America. *See id* 1280-81. The court also allowed a state survival action to be prosecuted with a wrongful death action under the Death on the High Seas Act. *See id* 1285-86.

681 *See id* 1282. In addition, he did not provide for a *buddy* system, a requirement of the National Association of Underwater Instruction. *See id* 1281-82.

682 *See id* 1282-83.

683 Rosenberger v Central La Dist Livestock Show, Inc, 312 So 2d 300, 305 (La 1975).

684 *Id.*

685 *Id* 305.

686 Katcher v Ideal Tennis, Inc, 65 AD2d 751 , 409 NYS2d 756, 757 (1978).

687 *See generally id.*

688 *Id.*

Volleyball

Organizations providing facilities for volleyball must act reasonably.[689] In *Hearl v Waterbury YMCA*,[690] the court set aside a $75,000 jury verdict to a plaintiff who suffered permanent injuries when he collided with another volleyball player in midair. The court ruled that the organization was not negligent in failing to provide supervision of the volleyball game because there was no showing of causation, i.e., even if supervisors were provided they would not have eliminated, or substantially reduced, the risk of this accident.[691] The players were all adults and there was no testimony of wrongdoing, rule violations, or consumption of alcohol. It was considered irrelevant that the game was intensely competitive.[692]

---

689 Hearl v Waterbury YMCA, 187 Conn 1, 444 A2d 211 (1982).

690 444 A2d at 212.

691 *Id.*

692 *Id.*

Liability of Fellow Participants

2

§2.01 Introduction

This chapter is principally concerned with the liability of fellow participants for sports and recreational accidents.[1] In addition, it discusses the liability, both vicarious and independent, of other individuals and entities who may also be responsible for those injuries, for example, employers of participants[2] and

---

[1] However, injuries during professional games are also discussed. *See* §§2.02, 2.17.

[2] Employers may be vicariously liable under the doctrine or respondeat superior for their employees' negligence and may also be liable for an independent act of negligence.

parents of child participants.[3] The chapter also discusses issues of insurance coverage, including an injured participant's own insurance, for sports and recreational accidents.[4]

Duty of Care

Generally, individuals must use reasonable care while engaging in recreational activities.[5] There is, however, at least one aberrational case which held that there is a common law duty to social guests, viz., passengers on a pleasure craft, only to refrain from wilfully or wantonly injuring them.[6]

Several state legislatures have passed guest statutes which limit the duty of care an individual has in transporting guests.[7] For example, one guest statute allowed an injured motorcycle passenger to recover from the motorcycle driver only if the driver acted wilfully or wantonly.[8] However, courts have not applied motor vehicle guest statutes to boating[9] or golf-cart accidents.[10]

Whether one participant's conduct causing injury to another constitutes actionable negligence hinges upon the facts of the case.[11] Material factors to be considered include, among others, the specific game involved, the ages and physical attributes of the participants, their respective skills at the game and their knowledge of its rules and customs, their status as amateurs or professionals, the type of risks which are inherent in the game and those which are outside the realm of reasonable anticipation, the presence or

---

3 Parents may be vicariously liable for their child's actions under the family purpose doctrine or state statutes. In addition, they may be liable for their own negligence, e.g., negligently entrusting a dangerous product to an inexperienced minor. *See, e.g.*, §2.09.

4 There may be insurance benefits under an accidental death policy, a homeowners' policy, or an automobile policy.

5 Jackson v Livingston Country Club, Inc, 55 AD2d 1045, 391 NYS2d 234, 235 (1977); *see generally* Lambert, *Tort Law And Participant Sports: The Line Between Vigor And Violence*, 4 J Contemp L 211 (1978).

However, several courts have held that a participant may recover from a fellow participant in contact sports only for conduct which goes beyond negligence. *See, e.g.*, Oswald v Township High School Dist, 84 Ill App 3d 723, 406 NE2d 159, 159–60 (1980); McAdams v Windham, 208 Ala 492, 94 So 742, 743 (1922).

6 *See* McDonnell v Flaharty, 636 F2d 184 (7th Cir 1980) (Indiana law).

7 *See, e.g.*, Hately v Hamilton, 81 NM 774, 473 P2d 913, 914 (App), *cert denied*, 81 NM 773, 473 P2d 912 (1970); Hankins v Bates, 271 Or 676, 534 P2d 170, 172 (1975) (statute specifically applied to watercraft).

8 *See* Hately v Hamilton, 81 NM 774, 473 P2d 913, 914 (App), *cert denied*, 81 NM 773, 473 P2d 912 (1970).

9 *See* Clipp v Weaver, 451 NE2d 1092, 1094 (Ind 1983); Reed v Reed, 182 Neb 136, 153 NW2d 356, 358 (1967).

10 *See* Nepstad v Randall, 82 SD 615, 152 NW2d 383, 386 (1967).

11 Niemczyk v Burleson, 538 SW2d 737, 741–42 (Mo Ct App 1976).

absence of protective uniforms or equipment, and the degree of zest with which the game is being played.[12]

Several courts have grappled with the issue of whether a participant's violation of the rules of the sport is negligence. In *Nabozny v Barnhill*,[13] where a soccer player was kicked in the head, and more recently in *Duke's GMC, Inc v Erskine*,[14] a case involving two experienced golfers who were both aware of the golfing rules, the courts indicated that violation of the rules may be negligence.[15]

However, it also has been held that what the scorekeeper may record as an "error" is not the equivalent, in law, of negligence.[16] Indeed, the court in *Segoviano v Housing Authority* noted:

> A player is not negligent simply because he violates a playing rule; even an inference of negligence does not automatically arise [under the negligence per se doctrine]. Many rules are violated under the heat of competition as evidenced by the numerous penalties called in organized football, basketball and baseball games. The defendant's conduct like the plaintiff's conduct is to be adjudged under the particular facts by the standard of an ordinary person.[17]

One commentator assumed that a participant has no duty to refrain from conduct which is permitted by the rules and customs of the game.[18]

Children

The courts have reached conflicting conclusions regarding the proper standard of conduct for children participating in recreational accidents. Children have been held to an adult standard of reasonable care while engaged in golf,[19] motorboating,[20] motorcycling[21] and snowmobiling.[22] However, child

---

12 *Id.*

13 31 Ill App 3d 212, 334 NE2d 258, 260–61 (1975).

14 447 NE2d 1118, 1124 (Ind Ct App 1983).

15 *See also* Page v Unterreiner, 106 SW2d 528, 533 (Mo Ct App 1937).

16 McGee v Board of Educ, 16 AD2d 99, 226 NYS2d 329, 332 (1962).

17 143 Cal App 3d 162, 175 n 5, 191 Cal Rptr 578 (1983).

18 *See* Lambert, *Tort Law and Participant Sports*, 4 J Contemp L 211, 216 (1978).

19 Neumann v Shlansky, 58 Misc 2d 128, 294 NYS2d 628, 635 (County Ct 1968), *affd*, 63 Misc 2d 587, 312 NYS2d 951 (Sup Ct 1970), *affd without opinion*, 36 AD2d 540, 318 NYS2d 925 (1971); *but see* Gremillion v State Farm Mut Ins Co, 331 So 2d 130, 132–33 (La Ct App 1976).

20 Dellwo v Pearson, 259 Minn 452, 107 NW2d 859, 863 (1961).

21 *See, e.g.*, Harrelson v Whitehead, 236 Ark 325, 365 SW2d 868, 869 (1963); Prichard v Veterans Cab Co, 66 Cal 2d 727, 408 P2d 360, 47 Cal Rptr 904, 907 (1965).

22 Robinson v Lindsay, 92 Wash 2d 410, 598 P2d 392, 393 (1979).

defendants have been held to the standard of care of a similar child of the same age and experience[23] while using firearms[24] or engaging in snow skiing.[25]

The idea that children should be held to the standard of a reasonable child was originally grounded upon the belief that a child's development and learning of new skills could be retarded if the child were liable for failing to act like an adult.[26] However, with the availability of comprehensive insurance,[27] a cost not usually borne by the child,[28] an adult standard is probably appropriate, especially in dangerous recreational activities.

Parents

The parental immunity doctrine, which extinguished parents' liability to their injured children, originated in America, not England.[29] This doctrine, like most other common law immunities, has been on the decline for a number of years.[30] However, some American jurisdictions still hold that a child has no cause of action against his or her parents for negligent supervision in general[31] or for negligently entrusting him or her with a dangerous instrumentality in particular.[32]

---

23 *See* Daniels v Evans, 107 NH 407, 224 A2d 63, 64 (1966) (where the activities are appropriate for a child).

24 *See, e.g.*, Stephan v Marlin Firearms Co, 353 F2d 819, 825 (2d Cir 1965), *cert denied*, 384 US 959 (1966); Townsend v Moore, 165 Ga App 606, 302 SW2d 398, 400 (1983); Kuhns v Brugger, 390 Pa 331, 135 A2d 395, 401 (1957).

25 Goss v Allen, 70 NJ 442, 360 A2d 388, 391 (1976).

26 *See* James, *Accident Liability Reconsidered: The Impact Of Liability Insurance*, 57 Yale LJ 549, 554–55 (1948).

27 *See* Goss v Allen, 70 NJ 442, 360 A2d 388, 395 (Schreiber, J dissenting).

28 *See* James, *Accident Liability Reconsidered: The Impact Of Liability Insurance*, 57 Yale LJ 549, 554–55 (1948).

29 *See* Note, *The "Reasonable Parent" Standard*, 47 U Colo L Rev 795, 796 (1976). The doctrine seems first to have been articulated in Hewlett v George, 68 Miss 703, 9 So 885, 887 (1891).

30 *See* Hollister, *Parent-Child Immunity: A Doctrine In Search of Justification*, 50 Fordham L Rev 489 (1982); McCurdy, *Torts Between Parent And Child*, 5 Vill L Rev 521 (1960); McCurdy, *Torts Between Persons in Domestic Relations*, 43 Harv L Rev 1030, 1078–80 (1930); Thuillez, *Parental Nonsupervision*, 40 Alb L Rev 336 (1976); Note, *Torts*, 42 Brooklyn L Rev 125 (1975); Note, *The "Reasonable Parent" Standard*, 47 U Colo L Rev 795 (1976); Note, *Parental Immunity: California's Answer*, 8 Idaho L Rev 179 (1971); Note, *The Demise Of The Parent-Child Tort Immunity*, 12 Willamette LJ 605 (1976).

A summary of the status of the parent-child immunity doctrine in each state is given in Hollister, *Parent-Child Immunity*, 50 Fordham L Rev 489, 528–32 (1982).

31 *See* McCallister v Sun Valley Pools, Inc, 100 Mich App 131, 298 NW2d 687, 691 (1980).

32 *See* Nolechek v Gesuale, 46 NY2d 332, 385 NE2d 1268, 413 NYS2d 340, 343 (1978) (child blind in one eye and with impaired vision in other eye allowed to ride a motorcycle).

Under the common law, parents are generally not liable to third parties for the torts of their children merely because of the family relationship.[33] However, parents are liable for their own acts of negligence, e.g., entrusting a dangerous instrumentality such as a boat[34] or a firearm[35] to a child incapable of using it properly.

Parents may be vicariously liable to third parties for their child's acts under two situations. First, in many states, parents are liable by statute for their child's wilful acts.[36] Second, there is vicarious liability under the common law family purpose doctrine.[37] This doctrine, which is not uniformly followed,[38] imposes liability upon the owner or person with ultimate control of a vehicle for its negligent operation by another when:

1. The operator was a member of the family

2. The vehicle was provided for the general use and pleasure of the family

3. The vehicle was being so used with the owner's consent at the time of injury[39]

The doctrine has been applied in boating[40] and motorcycle accidents.[41]

Where the plaintiff is a child, a defendant may sue the plaintiff's parents for indemnity or contribution for the parents' acts or omissions in allowing the child to be put in danger.[42] Several courts have not allowed these actions,

---

33 *See* LeSauvage v Freedman, 100 Misc 2d 857, 419 NYS2d 1018, 1020 (Civ Ct 1979); Hopkins v Droppers, 184 Wis 400, 198 NW 738, 739 (1924); Harbison, *Family Responsibility in Tort*, 9 Vand L Rev 809, 813 (1956).

34 LeSauvage v Freedman, 100 Misc 2d 857, 419 NYS2d 1018, 1020 (Civ Ct 1979).

35 *See* §2.09.

36 *See, e.g.*, Colo Rev Stat §13-2-107(2) (Supp 1984); Conn Gen Stat Ann §52–572 (West Supp 1984); Ill Ann Stat ch 70, §53 (Smith-Hurd 1984); La Civ Code Ann §§237, 2318 (West 1979); NM Stat Ann §32-1-46 (Supp 1984); Ohio Rev Code Ann §3109.09 (Page 1984); Tex Fam Code Ann §33.02 (Vernon Supp 1984).

37 This doctrine was purportedly grounded on the law of agency. However, it is clear that agency theory is stretched beyond all recognition and the doctrine really rests on social policy. *See* Comment, *Survey of Developments In North Carolina Law, 1977*, 56 NCL Rev 843, 1145 (1978); Comment, *Automobiles - Family Purpose Doctrine*, 3 Vand L Rev 644, 644–45 (1950); *see generally* Note, *Automobiles-Agency-Family Purpose Doctrine*, 38 NCL Rev 249 (1960).

38 *See* Comment, *Survey of Developments in North Carolina Law, 1977*, 56 NCL Rev 843, 1145 (1978).

39 Williams v Wachovia Bank & Trust Co, 292 NC 416, 233 SE2d 589, 592 (1977).

40 Sanders v Griffin, 134 Ga App 689, 215 SE2d 720 (1975); *but see* Felcyn v Gamble, 185 Minn 357, 241 NW 37, 38 (1932).

41 Williams v Wachovia Bank & Trust Co, 292 NC 416, 233 SE2d 589, 592 (1977); *see generally* §2.12.

42 American Motorcycle Assn v Superior Court, 20 Cal 3d 578, 578 P2d 899, 146 Cal Rptr 182, 200 (1978); Nolechek v Gesuale, 46 NY2d 332, 385 NE2d 1268, 413 NYS2d

reasoning that if the plaintiff-child cannot sue a parent under the parent-child immunity doctrine, defendants cannot sue the plaintiff's parents.[43]

Employer Liability

An employer of an athlete is vicariously liable for the acts of the athlete when those acts are within the scope of employment.[44] One court held that a player's act of throwing a ball out of a stadium, where the baseball hit and injured a pedestrian, was within the scope of employment and the employer was liable for those injuries.[45] However, a different court held that an employer was not liable for the acts of a catcher who struck a batter from behind because such an act was outside the scope of employment.[46]

Employers may also be liable for their negligence, e.g., in acting unreasonably in supervising, selecting, training, or retaining a professional athlete.[47]

Insurance

It is important to ascertain whether a recreational accident is covered by insurance. Where the language in an insurance contract is ambiguous, the courts have construed the ambiguity against the insurance company, the party that created the ambiguity, because it drafted the policy.[48] However, this does not mean that courts should engage in a strained construction of the terms of the policy.[49]

340, 343 (1978) (minor, blind in one eye and with impaired vision in the other eye, was killed while riding a motorcycle when he rode into suspended steel cable).

43 Pedigo v Rowley, 101 Idaho 201, 610 P2d 560, 564 (1980); Seeberger v LeGare, 48 AD2d 994, 370 NYS2d 210, 212 (1975); *but see* Larson v Buschkamp, 105 Ill App 3d 965, 435 NE2d 221, 226, (1982) (not a recreational accident case).

44 *See* Bonetti v Double Play Tavern, 126 Cal App 2d Supp 848, 274 P2d 751, 754 (1954); *see also* §8.01 *see generally* Note, *Tort Liability In Professional Sports*, 44 Alb L Rev 696, 706–11 (1980) (discusses employer liability); Note, *Professional Sports And Tort Liability: A Victory For The Intentionally Injured Player*, 1980 Det CL Rev 687, 704–06; Note, *Assumption Of Risk And Vicarious Liability In Personal Injury Actions Brought By Professional Athletes*, 1980 Duke LJ 742, 759–60; Note, *Torts In Sports—Deterring Violence In Professional Athletics*, 48 Fordham L Rev 764, 777–90 (1980).

45 Bonetti v Double Play Tavern, 126 Cal App 2d Supp 848, 274 P2d 751, 754 (1954).

46 Averill v Luttrell, 49 Tenn App 56, 311 SW2d 812, 814 (1957); *see generally* Palestina v Fernandez, 701 F2d 438, 440 (5th Cir 1983) (part-time employee, without permission, took a boat for a pleasure ride and caused a collision; employer was not liable).

47 *See* Note, *Tort Liability In Professional Sports*, 44 Alb L Rev 696, 707–09 (1980). Note, *Torts In Sports—Deterring Violence In Professional Athletics*, 48 Fordham L Rev 764, 787 (1980).

48 *See* Hidalgo v Allstate Ins Co, 374 So 2d 1261, 1263–64 (La Ct App 1979); Agricultural Workers Mut Auto Ins Co v Baty, 517 SW2d 901, 904 (Tex Civ App 1974).

49 Safeco Ins Co v Gilstrap, 141 Cal App 3d 524, 190 Cal Rptr 425, 431 (1983).

Coverage clauses are interpreted broadly to afford the greatest possible protection to the insured,[50] and exclusionary clauses are interpreted narrowly against the insurer.[51] Therefore, even when there were two different policies which used similar language for mutually exclusive purposes, e.g., one defining coverage and the other defining an exclusion, when the words used were ambiguous, there was coverage under both policies.[52]

Some courts have held that an insurance policy covers a recreational accident as long as one cause of the accident is covered.[53] For example, an insurance policy which excluded coverage for injuries arising out of the use of an automobile was held, by one court, to cover a hunting accident where the gun discharged in the automobile, injuring a passenger.[54] In that case, the insured had previously filed down the trigger of a handgun.[55] The court reasoned that this accident was caused both by an excluded risk, viz., driving the car, and also by a nonexcluded risk, viz., filing down the trigger.[56] It concluded that since one cause of the accident was a risk covered by the policy, the policy covered the accident.[57]

The courts have reached conflicting results regarding whether there is uninsured motorist coverage for recreational accidents. Coverage was found for a motorcycle accident,[58] but not for a golf-cart accident.[59]

Some new homeowners' insurance policies restrict coverage for risks which commonly occur in recreational accidents, e.g., liability for negligent entrustment of instrumentalities and liability for a coinsured's acts or omissions.[60]

---

[50] State Farm Mut Auto Ins Co v Partridge, 10 Cal 3d 94, 514 P2d 123, 109 Cal Rptr 811, 816 (1973).

[51] Id.

[52] Id.

[53] See, e.g., State Farm Mut Auto Ins Co v Partridge, 10 Cal 3d 94, 514 P2d 123, 109 Cal Rptr 811, 813 (1973); Ohio Casualty Ins Co v Hartford Accident & Indem Co, 148 Cal App 3d 641, 196 Cal Rptr 164, 168 (1983).

[54] See State Farm Mut Auto Ins Co v Partridge, 10 Cal 3d 94, 514 P2d 123, 109 Cal Rptr 811, 813 (1973).

[55] Id.

[56] Id.

[57] Id.

[58] See Griffin v Armond, 358 So 2d 647, 648–49 (La Ct App 1978).

[59] See Chase v State Farm Mut Auto Ins Co, 131 Ariz 461, 641 P2d 1305, 1310 (App 1982).

[60] See Sloane, *Homeowners' Insurance Is Revised*, New York Times, Dec 26, 1984, at 28, col 3.

Statutes

There are statutes which regulate boating,[61] firearms,[62] snowmobiling,[63] and water skiing.[64]

§2.02   Baseball

Baseball players must use reasonable care.[65] However, one court held that child players are held to the standard of care of children of the same age, intelligence, and experience.[66]

The fact that the potential for injury for some acts is open and obvious is not dispositive of whether the baseball player acted with reasonable care.[67] For example, a batter may breach a duty of care and be negligent when he or she hits another player, even though it is obvious that it is dangerous for anyone to stand near the batter.[68]

There have been several professional baseball players who have sued other players for injuries they received on the field.[69] However, none

---

61 *See* §2.04; *see also* §2.07 (Federal Limitation of Liability Act).

62 *See* §§2.08, 2.09.

63 *See* §2.14.

64 *See* §2.16.

65 Bourque v Duplechin, 331 So 2d 40, 42 (La Ct App 1976); Ceplina v South Milwaukee School Bd, 73 Wis 2d 338, 243 NW2d 183, 185 (1976).

Over 450,000 baseball players injured each year receive emergency room treatment. *See* US Consumer Prod Safety Commn, Natl Injury Information Clearinghouse, Prod Summary Report (Mar 28, 1984).

One baseball player who played in the major leagues, Roy Chapman, was killed when he was hit by a fastball during a game in 1920. Gibson, *Violence In Professional Sports: A Proposal For Self-Regulation*, 3 COMM/ENT 425, 427 n 25 (1981).

In Kurowsky v Green, No 77–385 (RI May 23, 1979) an amateur softball player received over $90,000 in damages from an opponent who hit her. *See* Comment, *Torts: Athlete States Cause Of Action For Injury During Professional Football Game*, 19 Washburn LJ 646, 651 (1980).

66 Gaspard v Grain Dealers Mut Ins Co, 131 So 2d 831 (La Ct App 1961); *See generally* §2.01.

67 Ceplina v South Milwaukee School Bd, 73 Wis 2d 338, 243 NW2d 183, 186 (1976). If the potential for danger was obvious, plaintiff may have assumed the risk or been contributorily negligent. *See id.*

68 *Id.*

69 John Roseboro sued Juan Marichal and his employer, the San Francisco Giants, for injuries when Marichal hit Roseboro over the head with a bat during a professional game in 1965. The case was reportedly settled for $7,500. *See* Note, *Tort Liability In Professional Sports*, 44 Alb L Rev 696, 702 n 34 (1980); Comment, *Violence In Professional Sports*, 1975 Wis L Rev 771, 775 n 28.

Jim Brewer sued Billy Martin after he was hit by Martin. The case was settled for an undisclosed sum. *See* Note, *Torts In Sports—Deterring Violence In Professional Athletics*, 48 Fordham L Rev 764, 764 n 4 (1980).

of those cases has resulted in a published opinion.

Base Running

Baseball players who fail to take reasonable care on the base paths are liable for their negligence.[70] A base runner, who left the base path and ran, standing up, into a second baseman who had just tagged second base and was attempting a double play by throwing to first base, breached his duty of care to the second baseman and was negligent.[71] In addition, an infielder who blocked the baseline, when the base runner had the right-of-way on the base path, thereby causing a collision, also breached a duty of care.[72]

Batting

Batters must exercise reasonable care in choosing and swinging the bat.[73] In *Gaspard v Grain Dealers Mutual Insurance Co*,[74] a batter, playing baseball on a hot summer day, realized his hands were sweaty and wiped them on his blue jeans. However, when he swung at the ball, he missed, and the bat, which was heavy and had a chipped knob at its end, slipped out of his hands and injured another player. The court ruled that the batter was not negligent.[75] The bat was the favorite of these players and one of only three bats available. The court rhetorically asked "what more could he have done, other than refrain from batting entirely?"[76]

The answer, of course, is that the batter should have refrained from batting if it was unreasonably dangerous to proceed, i.e., if it was so hot and the available bats were in such poor condition that a batter could not safely grip them. Indeed, a batter who swung a bat, between innings, with a batting ring which was too large, resulting in the ring flying off the bat and hitting an umpire, may be liable for the resulting injury.[77]

The batter is not liable where he or she did not act negligently. In *Richmond v Employers' Fire Insurance Co*,[78] a baseball player standing near third base was hit by a bat which slipped out of the hands of a batter standing

---

70 *See* Bourque v Duplechin, 331 So 2d 40, 42 (La Ct App 1976); Niemczyk v Burleson, 538 SW2d 737, 739 (Mo Ct App 1976).

71 Bourque v Duplechin, 331 So 2d 40, 42 (La Ct App 1976).

72 Niemczyk v Burleson, 538 SW2d 737, 739 (Mo Ct App 1976).

73 Richmond v Employers' Fire Ins Co, 298 So 2d 118 (La Ct App 1974).

74 131 So 2d 831 (La Ct App 1961).

75 *Id* 833.

76 *Id*.

77 Stewart v D&R Welding Supply Co, 51 Ill App 3d 597, 366 NE2d 1107, 1110 (1977).

78 298 So 2d 118 (La Ct App 1974).

near him who was hitting practice balls. The injured player argued that the batter was negligent in telling him to move to the location where he was ultimately hit by the bat. The court held that there was no negligence because the batter did not act unreasonably in giving that instruction.[79] The move protected the player from being hit by a ball batted by a different batter, practicing at the same time, who was standing at home plate.[80]

Throwing

A baseball must be thrown with reasonable care.[81] However, there is no negligence when a baseball player's errant throw in warming up for a game did not expose anyone to an unreasonable risk of harm.[82] It is well known that during a warm-up period there is much activity, e.g., balls are batted and thrown about and several balls may be in use at the same time. Inevitably, during this period, balls will not follow the path the thrower intended; however, that fact, standing alone, is not negligence.[83] Accordingly, in *McGee v Board of Education*,[84] the court held that a first baseman's throw across the field to third base during practice, which, unfortunately, hit an inattentive assistant coach standing behind the pitcher, was not negligent. In contrast, a ballplayer, angry at himself for committing an error, could be held liable for negligence when he threw a baseball out of the park where it hit a pedestrian.[85]

Parents

The parents of a child playing baseball generally owe no duty of care to other players.[86] Accordingly, a child injured when a whiffle ball bat slipped out of the hands of another child could not recover against the parents of the batter because they owed no duty to the plaintiff.[87] Furthermore, even if there was a duty of care, there was no breach of that duty because the parents could not have prevented the accident.[88]

---

79 *Id* 121.

80 *Id.*

81 Mann v Nutrilite, Inc, 136 Cal App 2d 729, 289 P2d 282 (1955).

82 *Id.*

83 289 P2d at 285.

84 16 AD2d 99, 226 NYS2d 329, 332–33 (1962).

85 *See generally* Bonetti v Double Play Tavern, 126 Cal App 2d Supp 848, 274 P2d 751 (1954) (case turned on whether the business sponsoring the ball player's team was liable).

86 Schuh v Hickis, 37 Misc 2d 477, 236 NYS2d 214, 215 (Sup Ct 1962).

87 *Id.*

88 *Id.*

Vicarious Liability

A professional baseball team is generally not liable for an employee's battery of another player if the act was neither incident to nor in furtherance of the employer's business.[89] In *Averill v Luttrell*,[90] the batter in a professional baseball game had three balls in a row thrown so close to him that he had to move to avoid being hit. The fourth pitch did hit him and he threw his bat in the direction of the pitcher. At that point the catcher, without warning, struck the batter from behind. The batter was hit with such force that he was rendered unconscious and his jaw was fractured when his face hit the ground. The court held, as a matter of law, that the catcher's employer was not liable because the catcher's act was a wilful, independent act outside the scope of the catcher's duties.[91] However, a sponsor of a baseball team was liable when a player, in anger after committing an error that cost his team the championship, threw a ball out of the stadium where it hit a pedestrian because the player's conduct was within the general scope of his responsibilities.[92]

Leagues

In *Dillard v Little League Baseball, Inc*,[93] an injured umpire sued a baseball league, alleging that it was negligent for failing to provide him with an athletic supporter or protective cup. The court held that the league was not negligent in failing to provide that item, even though it provided other safety equipment such as masks and chest protectors because the equipment it provided, in contrast to an athletic supporter, was not personal to one umpire.[94]

Insurance

In *Bourque v Duplechin*,[95] the court held that a baseball player's insurance policy covered a situation in which he ran, head on, into a second baseman standing five feet from the base in an attempt to break up a double play. The insurance company's argument that there was no coverage for this intentional act was rejected. The court held that the act was not intentional, even if it

89 Averill v Luttrell, 44 Tenn App 56, 311 SW2d 812, 814 (1957); *but see* Bonetti v Double Play Tavern, 126 Cal App 2d Supp 848, 274 P2d 751, 754 (1954).

90 *Id.*

91 *Id.*

92 Bonetti v Double Play Tavern, 126 Cal App 2d Supp 848, 274 P2d 751, 754 (1954).

93 55 AD2d 477, 390 NYS2d 735 (1977) (held that umpire assumed risk of injury).

94 390 NYS2d at 738.

95 331 So 2d 40 (La Ct App 1976).

was reckless, because the runner had no desire to injure the second baseman and there was no substantial certainty that injury would result.[96]

§2.03   Boating

Boating is a particularly dangerous recreational activity. In recent years there have been over 1200 fatalities annually.[97]

Duty of Care

Generally, the operator of a boat must exercise reasonable care,[98] i.e., the operator must take such precautions as would be required by a prudent person to avoid an accident.[99] There is no need for special jury instructions that a boat operator should exercise due diligence and maritime skill to avoid injury; instructions which state that an operator should act as a reasonably careful person under the circumstances suffice.[100]

---

[96] *Id* 43. It is questionable whether there really was no intent. In this case, plaintiff's jaw was fractured, his chin required plastic surgery, seven teeth were broken and one other tooth was replaced with a bridge. *See id.*

[97] Boating Statistics 1983, US Dept of Transp 11 (June 1984); Bearak, *New Laws Combat An Old Problem: Drunk Boaters*, LA Times, July 30, 1984, at 6, col 1. This is a fatality rate of about 8 per 100,000 boats. *See* Boating Statistics 1983, US Dept of Transp 11 (June 1984). The fatality rate has decreased significantly in recent years. As late as 1975, the annual fatality rate was over 19 per 100,000 boats. *See* Boating Statistics 1983, US Dept of Transp 11 (June 1984).

It is estimated that there are between 70,000 and 140,000 vessels involved in accidents annually. *See* Boating Statistics 1983, US Dept of Transp 11 (June 1984).

[98] Engle v Stull, 377 F2d 930, 933 n 1 (DC Cir 1967) (must act like a reasonable boat operator); Bremmer v Shedd, 467 F Supp 261, 266 (WD Pa 1979); Cashell v Hart, 143 So 2d 559, 561 (Fla Dist Ct App 1962); Clipp v Weaver, 439 NE2d 1189, 1193 (Ind Ct App 1982); Holman v Reliance Ins Co, 414 So 2d 1298, 1303 (La Ct App 1982); Johnson v State Farm Fire & Casualty Co, 303 So 2d 779, 785 (La Ct App 1974) (boat operator was negligent when he accidentally accelerated when he tried to turn the boat). *But see* McDonnell v Flaharty, 636 F2d 184 (7th Cir 1980) (Indiana law) (boat owner only owes social guest the duty to refrain from wilful or wanton acts).

The Coast Guard has estimated that half of all boating accidents are caused, in part, by alcohol. *See* Schmalz, *Increasing Problem Of Drunken Boating Spurring New Laws*, NY Times, Sept 2, 1984, at 23, col 1; *see also* National Transp Safety Bd, Recreational Boating Safety & Alcohol 15, 17 (1983).

The United States Coast Guard has published Rules of the Road for Boating. *See* Bremmer v Shedd, 467 F Supp 261, 265 (WD Pa 1979). These rules may establish the appropriate standard of care.

The failure to act appropriately has resulted in large settlements as well as large verdicts. *See* Eben v State, 130 Cal App 3d 416, 181 Cal Rptr 714, 715 n 1 (1982) (boat driver settled for $300,000 in a case where waterskier hit a submerged rock and was rendered a quadriplegic).

[99] Bremmer v Shedd, 467 F Supp 261, 266 (WD Pa 1979).

[100] Parker v Parker, 241 Ark 940, 411 SW2d 12, 13 (1967).

Boat operators must maintain a careful lookout[101] and drive at a safe speed.[102] Boat operators must also use reasonable care in passing other watercraft, e.g., by keeping a safe distance, moving at a reasonable speed,[103] and avoiding creating wakes.[104] One court awarded over $500,000 damages to a plaintiff when she fell because her boat was rocked by the wakes of passing vessels.[105]

In addition, boat operators may be negligent in failing to turn their boat to avoid a collision with a boat rapidly approaching from behind[106] or in attempting to "jump" a sandbar.[107]

A boat operator is not negligent when he or she did not act unreasonably, even if an accident occurred. In *Burton v Varmer*,[108] the boater was not negligent when a water skier he was towing collided with a metal pipe because as soon as he saw the pipe, he pulled the throttle. Similarly, in *Branch v Schumann*,[109] the operator of a boat was not negligent, as a matter of law, when he restarted an engine without ventilating the engine compartments because the boat was adrift in a channel bordered by a jagged, rocky coastline and there was no time to do the ventilation. Unfortunately, however, the failure to ventilate, termed a *suicidal* act by one expert, resulted in an explosion which injured a guest passenger. The court drew additional support for its ruling that there was no negligence by noting that the plaintiff testified that the defendant's attempt to restart the engine without performing the ventilation was a *natural* reaction to the situation.[110]

Social Guests

In one aberrational case, *McDonnell v Flaharty*,[111] the court held that the owner of a boat only owed his passengers the duty to refrain from wilfully, wantonly, or intentionally injuring them. In that case, the plaintiff's husband, a social guest on a pontoon boat, drowned after the boat capsized. The court

---

101 Bremmer v Shedd, 467 F Supp 261, 266 (WD Pa 1979); *see also* Chute v United States, 610 F2d 7, 15 (1st Cir 1979).

102 Chute v United States, 610 F2d 7, 16 (1st Cir 1979).

103 Moran v The M/V Georgie May, 164 F Supp 881, 884–85 (SD Fla 1958).

104 Anthony v International Paper Co, 289 F2d 574, 579 (4th Cir 1961); Sweeney v Car/Puter Intl Corp, 521 F Supp 276, 286 (DSC 1981); Moran v The M/V Georgie May, 164 F Supp 881, 884–85 (SD Fla 1958).

105 *See* Sweeney v Car/Puter Intl Corp, 521 F Supp 276 (DSC 1981).

106 Reed v Reed, 182 Neb 136, 153 NW2d 356, 358 (1967).

107 Gasquet v Commercial Union Ins Co, 391 So 2d 466, 473 (La Ct App 1980).

108 296 So 2d 641, 643 (Fla Dist Ct App 1974).

109 445 F2d 175, 177 (5th Cir 1971).

110 *Id.*

111 636 F2d 184 (7th Cir 1980) (Indiana law).

held that pleasure boat owners owed their guests only that limited duty of care and since there was no evidence of such wilful misconduct here, the defendant was entitled to summary judgment.

This decision appears to be analytically flawed. The low standard of care the court applied, although consistent with the low standard of care sometimes owed to social guests, applies a legal principle which is on the wane.[112] More significantly, that low duty of care generally only applies to landowners and occupiers.[113] Individuals involved in activities, and boating would certainly be so categorized, usually have been held liable for their negligence.[114] Furthermore, the court's statement that its holding promotes Indiana's policy of "fostering hospitality"[115] must sound like a twisted attempt at humor to an injured plaintiff who will find nothing hospitable about being denied a recovery for his or her host's negligence.

Guest Statutes

Boaters sued by injured passengers have argued that state guest statutes lower their duty of care to refrain only from gross negligence. In *Hankins v Bates*,[116] the court held that a state's guest statute, which was specifically applicable to watercraft, reduced the duty of care a boater owed to a passenger who left the boat and entered the water. The court held that it was irrelevant that the plaintiff was in the water and not being transported at the time of the injury.[117] It reasoned that the statute should be broadly construed and, therefore, was applicable when the host began performance of the gratuitous undertaking.[118]

Some boat owners have argued that they owed their social guests the duty only to refrain from gross negligence under state motor vehicle statutes. The courts have not been receptive to this argument.[119] In *Clipp v Weaver*,[120] the court held that the motor vehicle guest statute did not apply to motorboat

---

112 *See* §§6.01, 6.04.

113 *See* §6.01. A subsequent Indiana case held to the contrary. *See* Martin v Shea, 463 NE2d 1092 (Ind 1984). However, a different Indiana court held that the duty of reasonable care applied to boat operators. *See* Clipp v Weaver, 451 NE2d 1092 (Ind 1983).

114 *See* §6.01.

115 636 F2d at 187.

116 271 Or 676, 534 P2d 170 (1975).

117 534 P2d at 172.

118 *Id.*

119 *See* Reed v Reed, 182 Neb 136, 153 NW2d 356, 358 (1967); Hanson v Lewis, 11 Ohio Ops 42, 44, 26 Ohio L Abs 105 (1937); *see generally* Annot, 98 ALR2d 543 (1964).

120 439 NE2d 1189 (Ind Ct App 1982). This decision was later vacated by the Indiana Supreme Court. *See* 451 NE2d 1092 (Ind 1983). However, the Supreme Court concurred with the appellate court's conclusion. *See* 451 NE2d 1092 (Ind 1983).

accidents for two reasons. First, the motor vehicle statute applies to vehicles operated on public highways, and boats do not qualify except under a strained construction of that act.[121] Second, there is a state statute requiring persons operating boats to do so in a careful and prudent manner.[122] The court concluded that the boat statute requiring reasonable care should be applied because it is more closely applicable to the facts than the motor vehicle statute.[123]

Children

Certain activities engaged in by minors, e.g., operating a motorboat, are so potentially hazardous as to require that the minor be held to an adult standard of care.[124] In the leading case of *Dellwo v Pearson*,[125] a 12-year-old boy crossed his motorboat behind the boat of the plaintiff. The motor got caught in the plaintiff's fishing line, the fishing reel came apart, and part of it flew into the plaintiff's eye. The Minnesota Supreme Court held that a minor operating a motorboat is held to the same standard of care as an adult and not the lower standard of a similar child acting under similar circumstances.[126] The court reasoned that the standard of care of a reasonable adult was necessary because motorboats are readily available to minors and frequently operated by them and, therefore, it would be dangerous to the public to allow these boats to be operated with less than an adult standard of reasonable care.[127]

Spousal Tort Immunity

In recent years the courts have not been receptive to claims of spousal tort immunity.[128] The courts have rejected arguments by a husband that he is immune from a suit alleging that he negligently[129] or intentionally[130] injured his wife in a boating accident.

---

121 439 NE2d 1189 (Ind Ct App 1982).

122 *Id.*

123 *Id* 1193.

124 Goss v Allen, 70 NJ 442, 360 A2d 388, 390 (1976) (dicta). This conclusion appears to be questioned in Demeri v Morris, 194 NJ Super 554, 477 A2d 426, 428–29 n 6 (1983).

125 259 Minn 452, 107 NW2d 859 (1961). This case is analyzed in Comment, *Torts*, 47 Minn L Rev 317 (1962).

126 107 NW2d at 863.

127 *Id.*

128 *See generally* Annot, 92 ALR3d 901 (1979).

129 Klein v Klein, 58 Cal 2d 692, 376 P2d 70, 26 Cal Rptr 102, 105 (1962).

130 Small v Rockfeld, 66 NJ 231, 330 A2d 335, 344 (1974).

Boat Owners

An owner of a boat who negligently entrusts the boat to an incompetent operator may be liable for the damages which proximately result from that act.[131] This principle has been applied to parents who negligently entrust their boats to their children.[132]

In *Palestina v Fernandez*,[133] the Fifth Circuit ruled that a boat owner was not liable, as a matter of law, for leaving the keys to a boat in the ignition so that an unauthorized person was able to take the boat. Boat owners owe no duty of care to third parties who are injured by the negligent operation of the boat by unauthorized users.[134] Therefore, since there is no duty of care, there can be no breach of that duty and the owner is not liable under any circumstances.[135]

Parents

Under the common law, a parent incurred no vicarious liability for a child's negligence merely because there was a parent-child relationship.[136] Parents could not be held liable unless they were negligent, e.g., if they negligently entrusted a boat to a child who was incapable of properly operating it.[137]

In light of the relatively impecunious situation of many children, courts were faced with an uncomfortable situation where the negligent individual was a child and could not compensate the plaintiff, but the defendant's parents had that ability. Accordingly, some courts created the *family purpose* doctrine, purportedly an extension of agency principles, although really just a fiction, which expanded a parent's vicarious liability to include acts within the scope of family purposes. This doctrine holds that parents are financially responsible for the negligence of their child when the child's negligence arises out of the use of a product that the parents provided for the child's general use, convenience, and pleasure.[138]

---

131 Jawanowitch v Florida Power & Light Co, 277 So 2d 799, 800 (Fla Dist Ct App 1973).

132 Sanders v Griffin, 134 Ga App 689, 215 SE2d 720, 722 (1975).

133 701 F2d 438 (5th Cir 1983).

134 *Id* 440.

135 *Id.*

136 LeSauvage v Freedman, 100 Misc 2d 857, 419 NYS2d 1018, 1020 (Civ Ct 1979); Grindstaff v Watts, 254 NC 568, 119 SE2d 784, 786 (1961).

A parent could, theoretically, be liable under traditional agency principles, but these rules would not apply, almost by definition, to recreational accidents since the activity was not commercial.

137 LeSauvage v Freedman, 100 Misc 2d 857, 419 NYS2d 1018, 1020 (Civ Ct 1979).

138 *See generally* §2.01.

The family purpose doctrine has been applied, although not uniformly,[139] to boating accidents.[140] For example, in *Stewart v Stephens*,[141] the Georgia Supreme Court held that a father was liable for his 13-year-old daughter's negligence in operating a pleasure boat when she ran into and killed a swimmer. The court noted that the father provided this boat for the convenience and pleasure of his family and his daughter was operating the boat with his permission.[142]

This doctrine has been applied even if the child was married and living apart from the owner's household.[143] However, it was not applied when a third party was operating the motorboat without the owner-father's consent, even though the owner's son was a passenger.[144]

Causation

A plaintiff cannot recover from a defendant, even if the defendant was negligent, if there was a superseding cause of the injury.[145] In *Wagner v Owens*,[146] the plaintiff was injured when he was trying to start an outboard motor. The plaintiff wrapped the starting rope around his hand and when the motor misfired, the rope recoiled, pulling the plaintiff against the motor. The court held that even if the defendant's failure to warn the plaintiff of the defective motor were a negligent act, there would be no recovery because there was an independent, efficient cause of the injury—the plaintiff's wrapping of the starting rope around his hand.[147]

The res ipsa loquitur doctrine may be applied where an accident does not ordinarily occur in the absence of negligence, the injury was caused by an instrumentality within the defendant's control, and evidence of the real cause

---

The doctrine was originally applied to automobile accidents, but it has not been uniformly followed even in cases involving that product. *See* 60A CJS *Motor Vehicles* §433 (1), at n 72 (1969).

139 *See* Felcyn v Gamble, 185 Minn 357, 241 NW 37, 38 (1932); Grindstaff v Watts, 254 NC 568, 119 SE2d 784 (1961); *Cf* Florenzie v Fey, 26 Misc 2d 295, 205 NYS2d 91 (1960) (in the absence of legislation to the contrary, boat owners are not liable for the negligent acts of others). The North Carolina legislature overruled *Grindstaff*. *See* NC Gen Stat §75A-10.1 (1981); Williams v Wachovia Bank & Trust Co, 292 NC 416, 233 SE2d 589, 592 (1977).

140 *See* Sanders v Griffin, 134 Ga App 689, 215 SE2d 720 (1975). *See also* Peck, *The Role of the Courts and Legislatures in the Reform of Tort Law*, 48 Minn L Rev 265, 303 (1963) (the family purpose doctrine should be extended to powerboats).

141 225 Ga 185, 166 SE2d 890, 892 (1969).

142 *Id.*

143 Sanders v Griffin, 134 Ga App 689, 215 SE2d 720, 722 (1975).

144 Wallace v Lessard, 248 Ga 575, 285 SE2d 14 (1981).

145 Wagner v Owens, 155 So 2d 181, 182 (Fla Dist Ct App 1963).

146 *Id.*

147 *Id* 182.

of the accident is more readily accessible to the defendants.[148] In *Holman v Reliance Insurance Co*,[149] gravitational forces from a boat that was turning and stopping threw a passenger out of her seat, injuring her. The court held that such accidents ordinarily are caused by someone's negligence, that the defendant controlled the boat, and that the defendant's negligence in operating the boat was the most plausible cause of the abnormal behavior of the boat.[150] Therefore, the res ipsa doctrine was applied.

Indemnity

Where the plaintiff is a child, a defendant may attempt to bring an indemnity or contribution action against the plaintiff's parents for their negligence in allowing the plaintiff to be placed in a dangerous situation. In *Pedigo v Rowley*,[151] a girl was struck by a speedboat while she was floating on an air mattress on a lake. She sued the boat's operator and its owner for negligence. They, in turn, sought to join the plaintiff's father in an action for contribution, alleging that he negligently failed to supervise his daughter properly. The court held that there is no cause of action against parents for negligently supervising their children[152] and that this parental immunity bars third parties from seeking contribution.[153] The court explained that, except in cases of great wealth, the parent and child are one economic entity. Therefore, allowing contribution in such cases would effectively reduce the child's actual recovery.[154]

In some situations, a defendant is entitled to indemnification only where the defendant is passively or vicariously negligent.[155] For example, in *Degen v Bayman*,[156] the court held that an operator of a boat was not entitled to be indemnified by a boat manufacturer for its negligence because the operator was actively negligent in starting the engine when a boy was nearby.

Insurance

In *Ohio Casualty Insurance Co v Hartford Accident & Indemnity Co*,[157] a homeowners' insurance policy was held applicable to a boating accident. In

---

148 Holman v Reliance Ins Co, 414 So 2d 1298, 1305 (La Ct App 1982).

149 *Id.*

150 *Id* 1306–07.

151 101 Idaho 201, 610 P2d 560 (1980).

152 *See generally* Annot, 19 ALR2d 423 (1951).

153 610 P2d at 564; *see generally* §2.09 (indemnity).

154 610 P2d at 564–65.

155 Degan v Bayman, 86 SD 598, 200 NW2d 134, 138 (1972).

156 *Id.*

157 148 Cal App 3d 641, 196 Cal Rptr 164 (1983).

that case the boat owner, along with several students, took the boat to the middle of the lake and set it adrift, its engine turned off. One student asked to go for a swim and the boat owner gave the student permission to do so. Unfortunately, when the student surfaced she was hit by another boat which was operating nearby.

The boat owner's homeowners' insurance policy excluded coverage for injuries arising from the "ownership, maintenance, operation, use, loading or unloading"[158] of watercraft. The court held that this exclusion was not applicable and, therefore, there was coverage because one cause of the accident was an act or omission which was not excluded, viz., the owner's negligent supervision of the swimmer. This negligence was not dependent on the use of the boat; indeed, that it occurred on a boat was merely fortuitous.[159]

However, homeowners' policies do not cover all watercraft accidents. In *International Insurance Co v Mason*,[160] the court held that a homeowners' insurance policy did not cover an accident in which a boy was injured while taking his father's motorboat from the davit where it was sitting into the water. Watercraft injuries generally were excluded from coverage under that homeowners' policy; however, the exclusion did not apply while the watercraft was stored. The court held that *stored* denotes a certain degree of permanency and in this case, the boat's attachment to the davit was neither permanent nor long-term.[161] Therefore, the exclusion was applicable.

§2.04   —State Statutes

Background

Most states have passed statutes which regulate boating.[162] However, judging

---

158 196 Cal Rptr at 168.

159 *Id.*

160 442 So 2d 379 (Fla Dist Ct App 1983).

161 *Id* 380.

162 *See* Ariz Rev Stat Ann §§5–301 to –391 (Supp 1983); Colo Rev Stat §§33–13–101 to–115 (Supp 1984); Conn Gen Stat §§15–121 to–157 (Supp 1983); Fla Stat Ann §§327.01 –.72 (West Supp 1983); Ga Code Ann §§17–601 to–623 (Supp 1982); Ill Ann Stat ch 95½, §§315–1 to–13, 316–1 to–3 (Smith-Hurd Supp 1983); Ind Code Ann §§14–1–1–1 to–64 (Burns 1983); Iowa Code Ann §§106.1 to 106.34 (West Supp 1983); Kan Stat Ann §§82a–801 to–828 (1977); Ky Rev Stat Ann §§235.010–.990 (Bobbs-Merrill 1982); La Rev Stat Ann §§850.1–851.18 (West Supp 1984); Me Rev Stat Ann tit 12, §§7791 to 7801; tit 38, §§281 to 285 (Supp 1984); Md Nat Res Code Ann §§8–701 to–738 (Supp 1983); Mass Gen Laws Ann ch 90B, §1–35 (West Supp 1983); Mich Stat Ann §§18.1287(1)–(199) (Callaghan 1983); Minn Stat Ann §§361.01–.29 (West Supp 1984); Miss Code Ann §§59–21–1 to–163 (1983); Neb Rev Stat §§37–1201 to–1274 (1978); Nev Rev Stat §§488.015–.365 (1983); NC Gen Stat §§75A–1 to–26 (1983); Okla Stat Ann tit 63, §§801 to 837 (West Supp 1984); Or Rev Stat §§488.005–.995 (1983); RI Gen Laws §§46–22–1 to–24 (1983); SC Code Ann

from the limited number of decisions which cite these statutes, it is possible that many counsel are unaware of them.

Several states have codified navigational "rules of the water."[163] These rules include, for example, who has the right of way, the rules for passing other watercraft, and the direction of normal traffic flow.[164] In addition, some states specify the required safety equipment, e.g., personal flotation devices.[165] Other states require vessels to carry safety equipment in accordance with current United States Coast Guard rules[166] or federal law.[167]

Age Requirements

Many states have minimum age requirements for operators of motorboats.[168] In some states this requirement is waived if the individual obtains a boat safety certificate[169] or there is a responsible adult in the boat.[170]

---

§§50–21–10 to–160 (Law Co-Op Supp 1983); SD Codified Laws Ann §§42–8–1 to–67 (Supp 1983); Tex Parks & Wild Code Ann §§31.001 to 142 (Vernon Supp 1982); Vt Stat Ann tit 25, §301–322 (Supp 1983); Va Code §§62.1–166 to–186 (1982); Wis Stat Ann §§30.50–.99 (West Supp 1983); Wyo Stat §§41–13–101 to–218 (1977).

163 *See* Ariz Rev Stat Ann §5–345 (1974); Conn Gen Stat Ann §15–131 (West Supp 1983); Ga Code Ann §17–615.1 (West Supp 1982); Ill Ann Stat, ch 95½, §315–8 (Smith-Hurd 1983); Ind Code Ann §14–1–1–26 (Burns 1981); Iowa Code Ann §106.26 (West Supp 1983); Mich Stat Ann §18.1287 (71) (Callaghan 1980); Or Rev Stat §488.110 (1983); Tex Parks & Wild Code Ann §31.093 (Vernon 1976); Vt Stat Ann tit 25, §312 (1975); Wis Stat Ann §30.65 (West 1973).

164 *See* statutes cited in the preceding footnote.

165 *See* Ariz Rev Stat Ann §5–331 (A) (Supp 1983) (must be United States Coast Guard approved); Colo Rev Stat §33–31–105 (Supp 1984); Conn Gen Stat Ann §15–129 (West Supp 1983); Ind Code Ann §14–1–1–7 (1983); Iowa Code Ann §106.9 (West Supp 1983); Mass Gen Laws Ann ch 90B, §5A (West Supp 1983); Minn Stat Ann §361.141 (West 1984); Neb Rev Stat §37–1241 (1978); Nev Rev Stat §488.193 (1983); SD Codified Laws Ann §42–8–34 (1977).

166 *See* Fla Stat Ann §327.50 (West Supp 1983); Or Rev Stat §488.031 (1983); Tex Parks & Wild Code Ann §31.066 (Vernon Supp 1982); Wyo Stat §41–13–213 (1977).

167 *See* Me Rev Stat Ann tit 12, §7801(16) (1981); Wis Stat Ann §30.62(3) (West Supp 1983).

168 *See* Conn Gen Stat Ann §15–133b (Smith-Hurd Supp 1983); Ill Ann Stat, ch 95½, §315–13 (West 1983); Ind Code Ann §14–1–1–18 (Burns 1981); Iowa Code Ann §106.12 (West Supp 1983); Kan Stat Ann §82a–810 (1977); Me Rev Stat Ann tit 12, §7801(13) (1981); Mich Stat Ann §18.1287(62) (Callaghan 1980); Minn Stat Ann §361.055 (West 1984) ("except in case of emergency"); Miss Code Ann §59–21–85 (1983); Wis Stat Ann §30.68 (West Supp 1983).

169 *See* Conn Gen Stat Ann §15–133b (West Supp 1983); Mich Stat Ann §18.1287(62) (Callaghan 1980).

170 *See* Ill Ann Stat, ch 95½, §315–13 (Smith-Hurd 1983); Ind Code Ann §14–1–1–18 (Burns 1981); Iowa Code Ann §106.12 (West Supp 1983); Kan Stat Ann §82a–810 (1977); Me Rev Stat Ann tit 12, §7801(13) (1981); Mich Stat Ann §18.1287(62) (Callaghan 1980); Minn Stat Ann §361.055 (West 1984); Miss Code Ann §59–21–85 (1983).

Duty of Care of Boat Operator

These statutes typically provide that no person shall operate a watercraft in a negligent manner.[171] In one state, the ascertainment of fault is determined according to the United States Coast Guard Navigation rules.[172] In addition, most states also prohibit persons under the influence of alcohol or controlled substances from operating watercraft.[173]

Several statutes give examples of certain other proscribed behavior, e.g., operating the watercraft with a passenger riding on the bow or gunwale[174] or operating a vessel while pulling a water skier in a manner which may result in a collision.[175]

---

171 *See* Ariz Rev Stat Ann §5–341 (1974); Colo Rev Stat §33–31–107 (Supp 1984); Conn Gen Stat Ann §15–133 (West Supp 1983) ("reckless manner"); Fla Stat Ann §§327.32, 327.33 (West Supp 1983); Ga Code Ann §17–611 (Supp 1982); Ill Ann Stat, ch 95½, §§315–1, –2 (Smith-Hurd Supp 1983); Ind Code Ann §14–1–1–16 (Burns 1981); Iowa Code Ann §106.12 (West Supp 1983); Kan Stat Ann §82a–810 (1977); Ky Rev Stat Ann §235.240 (Bobbs-Merrill 1982); La Rev Stat Ann §§850.4, 851.9 (West 1964); Me Rev Stat Ann tit 12, §7801(8) (1981); Mass Gen Laws Ann ch 90B, §8 (West Supp 1983); Mich Stat Ann §18.1287(74) (Callaghan 1980); Minn Stat Ann §361.05 (West 1984); Miss Code Ann §59–21–83 (1973); Neb Rev Stat §37–1254 (1978); Nev Rev Stat §488.205 (1983); NC Gen Stat §75A–10 (1981); Okla Stat Ann tit 63, §809 (West 1973); Or Rev Stat §§488.099, .100, .101 (1983); RI Gen Laws §46–22–9 (1980); SC Code Ann §50–21–110 (Law Co-op 1977); SD Codified Laws Ann §42–8–46 (Supp 1983); Tex Parks & Wild Code Ann §31.094 (Vernon 1976); Vt Stat Ann tit 25, §311 (1975); Va Code §62.1 –176 (1982); Wis Stat Ann §30.68 (West Supp 1983); Wyo Stat §41–13–203 (1977).

172 Fla Stat Ann §327.33 (West Supp 1983).

173 *See* Ariz Rev Stat Ann §5–342 (Supp 1983); Colo Rev Stat §33–31–107 (Supp 1984); Conn Gen Stat Ann §15–133 (West Supp 1983); Fla Stat Ann §327.35 (West Supp 1983); Ga Code Ann §17–611 (Supp 1982); Ill Ann Stat ch 95½, §315–11 (West Supp 1983); Ind Code Ann §14–1–1–21 (Burns 1981); Iowa Code Ann §106.12 (West Supp 1983); Kan Stat Ann §82a–810 (1977); Ky Rev Stat Ann §235.240 (Bobbs-Merrill 1982); La Rev Stat Ann §§850.8, 851.9 (West 1964); Me Rev Stat Ann tit 12, §7801(9) (1981); Minn Stat Ann §361.12 (West 1984); Neb Rev Stat §37–1254 (1978); Nev Rev Stat §488.205 (1983); NC Gen Stat §75A–10 (1981); Okla Stat Ann tit 63, §809 (West 1973); Or Rev Stat §488.160 (1983); RI Gen Laws §46–22–9 (1980); SC Code Ann §50–21–110 (Law Co-op 1977); Tex Parks & Wild Code Ann §31.097 (Vernon 1976); Va Code §62.1 –176 (1982); Wis Stat Ann §30.68 (West Supp 1983); Wyo Stat §41–13–206 (1977).

There is a noticeable trend in the state legislatures to strengthen laws prohibiting boaters from drinking alcohol. *See* Bearak, *New Laws Combat An Old Problem: Drunk Boaters,* LA Times, July 30, 1984, at 6, col 1.

174 *See* Ariz Rev Stat Ann §5–341 (1974); Ga Code Ann §17–615 (Supp 1983); Ind Code Ann §14–1–1–36 (Burns 1983); La Rev Stat Ann §850.13 (West 1964); Minn Stat Ann §361.11 (West 1984); Or Rev Stat §488.140 (1983); Wis Stat Ann §30.68 (West Supp 1983); Wyo Stat §41–13–210 (1977).

175 *See* Colo Rev Stat §33–13–109 (Supp 1984); Fla Stat Ann §327.37 (West Supp 1983); Ill Ann Stat ch 95½, §315–9 (Smith-Hurd 1983); Miss Code Ann §59–21–87 (1973); Neb Rev Stat §37–1261 (1978); NC Gen Stat §75A–13 (1983); Okla Stat Ann tit 63, §812 (West Supp 1984); Or Rev Stat §488.144 (1983); Va Code §62.1–179 (1982); Wyo Stat §41–13–212 (1977).

Liability of Boat Owner

Several statutes have modified the liability of boat owners. In some states an owner of a boat is not liable for the negligent operation of the boat unless he or she was the operator or was present in the boat when the accident occurred.[176] In other states, greater liability is imposed on the owner.[177] However, even in those states, a boat owner is usually not liable unless the boat is being used with the owner's express or implied consent.[178]

Many of these statutes presume[179] that the boat is being operated with the knowledge and consent of the owner if, at the time of the injury or damage, the boat is under the control of the owner's spouse, father, mother, brother, sister, son, daughter, or other immediate family member.[180] Two states have expressly codified the *family purpose* doctrine.[181]

The definition of *owner* is not necessarily restricted to the holder of record title. Where a parent has record title, a child may be the beneficial owner when the child has the control and use of the boat.[182]

---

176 *See* Fla Stat Ann §327.32 (West Supp 1983); *but see* Ky Rev Stat Ann §235.300 (Bobbs-Merrill 1982) (family purpose doctrine applies).

177 *See* Iowa Code Ann §106.18 (West Supp 1983); Minn Stat Ann §361.13 (West 1984) (owner and operator are jointly and severally liable); Miss Code Ann §59–21–157 (1973); Neb Rev Stat §37–1267 (1978); NC Gen Stat §75A–10.2 (1981); Okla Stat Ann tit 63, §815 (West 1973); RI Gen Laws §46–22–15 (1983).

178 *See* Ga Code Ann §17–611.2 (Supp 1982); La Rev Stat Ann §850.24 (West 1964); Mich Stat Ann §18.1287(131) (Callaghan 1980); Minn Stat Ann §361.13 (West 1984); Neb Rev Stat §37–1267 (1978); Okla Stat Ann tit 63, §815 (West 1973); RI Gen Laws §46–22–15 (1983). These statutory provisions are similar to the family purpose doctrine. *See* Wallace v Lessard, 248 Ga 575, 285 SE2d 14, 15 (1981).

The owner of a boat was not liable where he gave permission to one person to operate the boat and that person allowed a third party to drive the boat and while this third person was in control of the boat, it collided with another boat. *See* Wallace v Lessard, 248 Ga 575, 285 SE2d 14, 15–16 (1981).

179 It is unclear whether this presumption: (1) is conclusive or rebuttable; and (2) affects the burden of proof or the burden of going forward.

180 *See* Ga Code Ann §17–611.2 (Supp 1982); La Rev Stat Ann §850.24 (West 1964); Mich Stat Ann §18.1287(131) (Callaghan 1980); Minn Stat Ann §361.13 (West 1984); Neb Rev Stat §37–1267 (1978); Okla Stat Ann tit 63, §815 (West 1973); RI Gen Laws §46–22–15 (1983).

181 *See* NC Gen Stat §75A–10.1 (1981); Or Rev Stat §488.178 (1983) (except where there is admiralty jurisdiction).

The North Carolina statute overruled Grindstaff v Watts, 254 NC 568, 119 SE2d 784 (1961), which held that the family purpose doctrine did not apply to boating accidents. *See* Williams v Wachovia Bank & Trust Co, 292 NC 416, 233 SE2d 589, 592 (1977); Comment, *Survey of Developments in North Carolina Law, 1977*, 56 NCL Rev 1145, 1147 (1978).

182 *See* Stirrup v Reiss, 410 So 2d 537, 539 (Fla Dist Ct App 1982).

Rescue

The state boating statutes typically provide that the operator of a watercraft involved in a collision or accident must, to the extent he or she can do so without serious danger to the watercraft or persons aboard the watercraft, render all practical and necessary assistance to persons injured or put in danger by the accident.[183] One state provides that failure to comply with this statute, unless reasonable cause for the failure is shown, is prima facie evidence that the collision was caused by a wrongful act of that party.[184]

A few states have good Samaritan statutes which preclude a person who gratuitously and in good faith rendered assistance at an accident, without objection from the person being assisted, from being held liable for damages as long as the person giving assistance acted in a reasonably prudent fashion.[185]

Report of Accidents

Most states require a written report to be submitted in a very short period of time whenever there is personal injury or property damage resulting from a watercraft accident.[186] A few states will not allow

---

183 *See* Ariz Rev Stat Ann §5–349 (Supp 1983); Colo Rev Stat §33–31–108 (Supp 1984); Conn Gen Stat Ann §15–132 (West Supp 1983); Fla Stat Ann §327.30 (West Supp 1983); Ga Code Ann §17–612 (Supp 1982); Ill Ann Stat, ch 95½, §316–1 (Smith-Hurd 1983); Ind Code Ann §14–1–1–42 (Burns 1981); Iowa Code Ann §106.7 (West Supp 1983); Kan Stat Ann §82a–811 (1977); Ky Rev Stat Ann §235.250 (Bobbs-Merrill 1982); La Rev Stat Ann §§850.10, 851.10 (West 1964); Me Rev Stat Ann tit 12, §7801(17) (1981); Md Nat Res Code Ann §8–724 (1983); Mass Gen Laws Ann ch 90B, §9 (West 1969); Mich Stat Ann §18.1287(51) (Callaghan 1980); Minn Stat Ann §361.13 (West 1984); Miss Code Ann §59–21–55 (1983); Neb Rev Stat §37–1255 (1978); Nev Rev Stat §488.215 (1983); NC Gen Stat §75A–11 (1983); Okla Stat Ann tit 63, §810 (West 1973); Or Rev Stat §488.164 (1983); RI Gen Laws §46–22–10 (1980); SC Code Ann §50–21–130 (Law Co-op 1977); Tex Parks & Wild Code Ann §31.104 (Vernon 1976); Vt Stat Ann tit 25, §313 (1975); Va Code §62.1–177 (1982); Wis Stat Ann §30.67 (West 1973); Wyo Stat §41–13–105 (1977).

184 *See* Conn Gen Stat Ann §15–132 (West Supp 1983).

185 *See* Ga Code Ann §17–612 (Supp 1982); Mich Stat Ann §18.1287(51) (Callaghan 1980); Miss Code Ann §59–21–55 (1983); SC Code Ann §50–21–130 (Law Co-op 1977); Va Code §62.1–177 (1982).

186 *See* Ariz Rev Stat Ann §5–349 (Supp 1983); Colo Rev Stat §33–31–108 (Supp 1984); Fla Stat Ann §327.30 (Supp 1983); Ga Code Ann §17–612 (Supp 1982); Ill Ann Stat, ch 95½, §316–1 (Smith-Hurd 1983); Ind Code Ann §14–1–1–43 (Burns 1983); Iowa Code Ann §106.7 (West Supp 1983); Kan Stat Ann §82a–811 (1977); Ky Rev Stat Ann §235.250 (Bobbs-Merrill 1982); La Rev Stat Ann §851.10 (West 1964); Me Rev Stat Ann tit 12, §7801(19) (1981); Md Nat Res Code Ann §8–724 (1983); Mass Gen Laws Ann ch 90B, §9 (West 1969); Mich Stat Ann §18.1287(53) (Callaghan 1980) (oral report may be sufficient); Miss Code Ann §59–21–51 (1983); Neb Rev Stat §37–1256 (1978); Nev Rev Stat §488.215 (1983); NC Gen Stat §75A–11 (1983); Okla Stat Ann tit 63, §810 (West 1973); Or Rev Stat §488.168 (1983); SC Code Ann §50–21–130 (Law Co-op 1977); SD Codified Laws Ann §42–8–58 (Supp 1983); Tex Parks & Wild Code Ann §31.105 (Vernon 1976); Vt Stat Ann

those reports to be used as evidence in a trial.[187]

Sanctions

There are sanctions, albeit usually mild ones, for violating these boating laws.[188] In one state, a violation of these laws is prima facie evidence of negligence, but not negligence per se.[189] Furthermore, in that state the conviction of violating these laws is not admissible in a civil action.[190]

Preemption

One court held that the Federal Boat Safety Act[191] preempts virtually all state laws which establish safety standards except where the state law implements and supplements the act.[192]

§2.05 — Admiralty Jurisdiction

This section and the following two sections discuss the law of admiralty as applied to recreational boating accidents. Although the discussion primarily discusses admiralty in the context of the liability of fellow boaters, at times it also discusses its application to commercial boating vessels involved in recreational accidents.[193] There is a separate discussion of admiralty in chapter 3.[194]

---

tit 25, §313 (1975); Va Code §62.1–177 (1982); Wis Stat Ann §30.67 (West Supp 1983); Wyo Stat §41–13–105 (1977).

187 *See* Ariz Rev Stat Ann §5–349 (1983); Colo Rev Stat §33–31–108 (Supp 1984); Fla Stat Ann §327.30 (West Supp 1983); Ill Ann Stat, ch 95½, §316–1 (Smith-Hurd 1983); Iowa Code Ann §106.7 (West Supp 1983); Ky Rev Stat Ann §235.260 (Bobbs-Merrill 1982); Md Nat Res Code Ann §8–724 (1983); Mass Gen Laws Ann ch 90B, §9 (West 1969); Mich Stat Ann §18.1287(56) (Callaghan 1983); Miss Code Ann §59–21–53 (1983); Or Rev Stat §488.176 (1983); SC Code Ann §50–21–130 (Law Co-op 1977); Tex Parks & Wild Code Ann §31.105 (Vernon 1976); Va Code §62.1 –177 (1982); Wyo Stat §41–13–105 (1977).

188 *See* Ariz Rev Stat Ann §5–391 (Supp 1983); Colo Rev Stat §33–13–115 (Supp 1984); Conn Gen Stat Ann §15–139 (West Supp 1983); Fla Stat Ann §327.72 (West Supp 1983); Ind Code Ann §14–1–1–59 (Burns 1983); Iowa Code Ann §106.13 (West Supp 1983); Ky Rev Stat Ann §235.990 (Bobbs-Merrill 1982); La Rev Stat Ann §851.15 (West Supp 1984); Mass Gen Laws Ann ch 90B, §14 (West Supp 1983); Minn Stat Ann §361.22 (West 1984); Wyo Stat §41–13–216 (1977).

189 *See* Minn Stat Ann §361.23 (West 1984).

190 *See id.*

191 46 USC §1451 *et seq.*

192 Sanders v Richmond, 579 SW2d 401, 404 (Mo Ct App 1979).

193 E.g., an accident involving a cruise ship.

194 *See* §3.12.

Background

At one time it was reasonably clear that admiralty jurisdiction applied whenever an accident occurred on navigable waters.[195] Indeed, the Supreme Court had assumed, although the issue was never squarely presented, that admiralty jurisdiction existed over pleasure craft accidents occurring on navigable waters.[196]

In a landmark decision, *Executive Jet Aviation v City of Cleveland*,[197] an airplane struck a flock of seagulls on takeoff, then lost power and crashed in navigable waters. The Supreme Court held in that case that admiralty jurisdiction did not exist, even though the accident occurred on navigable waters, because the accident did not bear a significant relationship to traditional maritime activity.[198]

In 1982, in *Foremost Insurance Co v Richardson*,[199] the Supreme Court applied the two-part test set out in *Executive Jet* to an accident caused by the collision of two pleasure boats on navigable waters. The Court held that admiralty law applied because: (1) the accident occurred on navigable waters, and (2) there was a relationship to traditional maritime activity. It specifically held that the requirement of a relationship to traditional maritime activity can be satisfied by noncommercial vessels.[200] In this case, a link to such traditional activity was present for two reasons. First, an accident involving noncommercial vessels may have a disruptive effect on commercial vessels attempting to navigate in that area.[201] Second, admiralty has traditionally

---

195 *See* Levinson v Deupree, 345 US 648, (1953). This was called the *locality test*.

One commentator has argued that locality should not be a necessary prerequisite to admiralty jurisdiction. *See* George, *Maritime Tort Jurisdiction: A Survey of Developments From Executive Jet To Foremost Insurance Co v Richardson*, 24 S Tex LJ 495, 511 (1983).

196 *See* Levinson v Deupree, 345 US 648, (1953); Coryll v Phipps, 317 US 406, (1943); Just v Chambers, 312 US 383, (1941).

197 409 US 249 (1972). The case did not involve a sports or recreational activity.

198 Id 268.

199 457 US 668 (1982). This decision has been praised by some commentators. *See* Note, *Admiralty Jurisdiction*, 13 J Mar L & Commerce 537, 538 (1982) ("the court has taken a long-needed step in fashioning a less mechanical definition of the scope of federal admiralty jurisdiction which should help serve the needs of the maritime community"). However, other commentators have criticized it. *See* Carnilla & Drzal, *Foremost Insurance Co v Richardson: If This is Water, It Must be Admiralty*, 59 Wash L Rev 1 (1983); Note, *Pleasure Boating Under Admiralty Jurisdiction: An Unwarranted Expansion of Federal Authority*, 12 Cap UL Rev 545, 558–63 (1983).

200 457 US at 674–75. Many commentators had previously argued that admiralty jurisdiction should be limited to commercial cases. *See* Black, *Admiralty Jurisdiction: Critique and Suggestions*, 50 Colum L Rev 259, 280 (1950); Stolz, *Pleasure Boating and Admiralty*, 51 Cal L Rev 661, 718 (1963); Note, *Admiralty Jurisdiction and the FMLA: The Maritime Lien on Houseboats*, 14 USFL Rev 641, 642 (1980).

201 457 US at 668–69.

been concerned with applying uniform *rules of the road,* which govern the manner and direction in which a vessel may correctly move upon the water. The failure to follow those rules was the cause of the boating accident.[202]

Navigable Water

Unfortunately, there is no one omnibus legal definition of *navigable* waters. This creates a situation which is rife for producing error because there are four different uses of the term.[203] Waters are navigable, for purposes of determining admiralty jurisdiction, when they are susceptible of being used,[204] in their ordinary condition, as highways for commerce.[205] One court held that the type of craft used in accomplishing trade or travel over the waters is of no particular significance.[206]

Even where a body of water is not passable in its natural and ordinary condition, if by reasonable improvements it may be rendered navigable, then the body of water is navigable without the improvements.[207] In addition, artificial bodies of water, e.g., man-made reservoirs, are also considered navigable if they are used or are capable of being used as an interstate highway for commerce over which trade or travel is presently being conducted or may be conducted in the future.[208]

Some courts have not followed the broad language declaring that water

---

202 *See id.* It is not self-evident why this requires uniform federal law to be applied in a federal court. Federal jurisdiction is not required to prevent chaos in automobile traffic. *See id* 682 (Powell, J dissenting); Carnilla & Drzal, *Foremost Insurance Co v Richardson: If This is Water, It Must be Admiralty,* 59 Wash L Rev 1, 6–7 (1983). Indeed, according to the dissent, the *Richardson* decision extended admiralty jurisdiction to the edge of absurdity. *See* 457 US at 678 (Powell J dissenting).

203 *Navigable* has been used in four distinct ways: (1) the limit of jurisdiction over admiralty and maritime cases under the United States Constitution; (2) the boundaries of navigational servitudes; (3) the scope of Congress' regulatory authority under the Interstate Commerce Clause; and (4) the extent of authority of the Army Corps of Engineers under the Rivers and Harbors Appropriation Act of 1899. *See* Kaiser Aetna v United States, 444 US 164, (1979). Although decisions defining navigable waters in one of those areas should not be blindly followed in determining whether waters are navigable in the other areas, they are "not without significance." *See* Finneseth v Carter, 712 F2d 1041, 1043–44 n 2 & 1045 n 4 (6th Cir 1983).

204 The Montello, 87 US (20 Wall) 430 (1874).

205 The Daniel Ball, 77 US (10 Wall) 557, 563 (1870); Votava v Material Serv Corp, 74 Ill App 3d 208, 392 NE2d 768, (1979); Johnson v State Farm Fire & Casualty Co, 303 So 2d 779, 784 (La Ct App 1974).

206 Wreyford v Arnold, 82 NM 156, 477 P2d 332, 336 (1970); *but cf* Edwards v Hurtel, 717 F2d 1204 (8th Cir 1983), *affd on reh,* 724 F2d 689 (8th Cir 1984).

207 United States v Appalachian Elec Power, 311 US 337 (1940).

208 Finneseth v Carter, 712 F2d 1041, 1044 (6th Cir 1983); Wreyford v Arnold, 82 NM 156, 477 P2d 332, 336 (1970).

is navigable as long as it may be used for trade in the future.[209] In *Edwards v Hurtel*,[210] the court held that there must be "contemporary navigability in fact",[211] i.e., the water must be presently used for commercial purposes or there must be a reasonable likelihood that it will be so used in the near future. In that case, the plaintiff, a recreational boater, could not sue under admiralty law because the lake where the accident occurred was used exclusively for recreational purposes and there was no reasonable likelihood that it would be used for commercial shipping in the near future.[212]

Water on private land has been held to be not navigable.[213] In *Votava v Material Service Corp*, the court held that the accident did not occur on navigable waters because the lake in question was on private land used for the defendant's business and the public was prohibited by *no trespassing* signs and by the defendant's employees.[214]

In one case testing the physical limits of admiralty jurisdiction, the court held that an individual who slipped and fell on a boat launching ramp could not recover in admiralty for his injury because he was not injured in navigable waters even though his feet were in the water at the time of the injury.[215]

The determination of whether water is navigable is a question of fact.[216] There is no presumption that water is navigable.[217] Furthermore, the determination by the United States Coast Guard that water is navigable is not binding on a court, although such a determination is probative evidence of that fact.[218] In any event, a court can take judicial notice that water is navigable.[219]

---

[209] Edwards v Hurtel, 717 F2d 1204 (8th Cir 1983), *aff'd on reh*, 724 F2d 689 (8th Cir 1984); Motley v Hale, 567 F Supp 39, 40 (WD Va 1983).

[210] 717 F2d 1204 (8th Cir 1983), *aff'd on reh*, 724 F2d 689 (8th Cir 1984).

[211] *Id* 1205; *see also* Chapman v United States, 575 F2d 147, 149–50 (7th Cir 1978); Adams v Montana Power Co, 528 F2d 437, 440 (9th Cir 1975); *but see* St Hilaire Moye v Henderson, 496 F2d 973, 979 (8th Cir), *cert denied*, 419 US 884 (1974).

[212] 717 F2d at 1205.

[213] Votava v Material Serv Corp, 74 Ill App 3d 208, 392 NE2d 768, (1979).

[214] *Id.*

[215] Hastings v Mann, 340 F2d 910, 912 (4th Cir), *cert denied*, 380 US 963 (1965).

[216] Wreyford v Arnold, 82 NM 156, 477 P2d 332, 335 (1970).

[217] Johnson v State Farm Fire & Casualty Co, 303 So 2d 779, 785 (La Ct App 1974). The mere fact that the water was deep enough to float a fishing boat is not sufficient to prove navigability. *See id.*

[218] Wreyford v Arnold, 82 NM 156, 477 P2d 332, 335–36 (1970).

[219] *See, e.g.*, Edwards v Hurtel, 717 F2d 1204 (8th Cir 1983), *aff'd on reh*, 724 F2d 689 (8th Cir 1984); Smith v Hustler, Inc, 514 F Supp 1265, 1268 (WD La 1981); Wreyford v Arnold, 82 NM 156, 477 P2d 332, 335 (1970).

Traditional Maritime Activity

The determination of whether a boating accident bears a relationship to *traditional maritime activity* is, unfortunately, sometimes difficult to make. The courts have not given guidance which is simple to follow and, as a result, the cases are partially irreconcilable.

Courts in the following instances have held that the accident bore a relationship to traditional maritime activity: a skindiver was run over by a speedboat;[220] an individual involved in noncommercial *crabbing* was hit by a pleasure craft;[221] two racing yachts collided;[222] a pleasure boat exploded;[223] a defect in a pleasure boat injured a boater;[224] and a seaplane crashed in the water.[225]

In the following situations, courts have concluded that there was no relationship to traditional maritime activity: swimmers were injured by other swimmers;[226] a swimmer was hit by a surfboard rider;[227] a swimmer was struck by a pleasure motorboat;[228] swimmers were injured by an unidentified object protruding from the sand;[229] a waterskier was hit by a towboat;[230] pleasure divers were injured other than by boats;[231] there was an accident on a boat which did not leave the dock;[232] there were injuries from an unsecured flotation platform of a showboat;[233] and there was a float-fishing accident.[234] One court held that finding admiralty jurisdiction in such cases

---

220 Green v Ross, 338 F Supp 365, 366 (SD Fla 1972).

221 Scholl v Town of Babylon, 95 AD2d 475, 466 NYS2d 976 (1983).

222 Kayfetz v Walker, 404 F Supp 75, 77 (D Conn 1975).

223 Richards v Blake Builders Supply, Inc, 528 F2d 745, 749 (4th Cir 1975).

224 *See* Smith v Hustler, Inc, 514 F Supp 1265, 1267 (WD La 1981) (dicta).

225 Hark v Antilles Airboats, Inc, 355 F Supp 683, 686 (DVI 1973).

226 Executive Jet Aviation, Inc v City of Cleveland, 409 US 249 (1972) (dicta).

227 Executive Jet Aviation, Inc v City of Cleveland, 409 US 249, 256 n 6 (1972) (dicta). The court severely criticized Davis v City of Jacksonville, 251 F Supp 327, 328 (MD Fla 1965) which held to the contrary.

228 Medina v Perez, 575 F Supp 168, 171 (DPR 1983); *cf* Motley v Hale, 567 F Supp 39 (WD Va 1983) (towed on inner tube).

229 McGuire v City of New York, 192 F Supp 866, 870–71 (SDNY 1961).

230 Crosson v Vance, 484 F2d 840, 842 (4th Cir 1973); Webster v Roberts, 417 F Supp 346, 347 (ED Tenn 1976). The above cases overruled King v Testerman, 214 F Supp 335 (ED Tenn 1963).

231 Onley v South Car Elec & Gas Co, 488 F2d 758, 760 (4th Cir 1973); Chapman v City of Grosse Pointe, 385 F2d 962 (6th Cir 1967); Rubin v Power Auth, 356 F Supp 1169, 1171–72 (WDNY 1973).

232 Montgomery v Harrold, 473 F Supp 61, 64 (ED Mich 1979).

233 Clinton Bd of Park Commnrs v Claussen, 410 F Supp 320, 326 (SD Iowa 1976).

234 Estate of Fitzpatrick v Brehm, 580 F Supp 731, 734 (WD Ark 1984).

would usurp state sovereignty, frustrate state tort law, and burden the federal courts.[235]

There have been several cases in which the accident occurred on a pontoon or ferry. One court held that there was no relationship to traditional maritime activity where the plaintiff was injured in a rear-end automobile collision which occurred on a floating pontoon at a ferry landing while he was waiting in line to obtain a ticket to board the ferry.[236] A similar result was reached where a motorcyclist was injured while crossing a pontoon bridge on a highway.[237] However, a different court held that such a relationship existed where passengers aboard a commercial ferry boat sued the boat operator for injuries when their car careened off the ferry, across a floating pontoon barge and into the river.[238]

A traditional maritime activity has been found where the cause of the injury was on land, as long as the injury occurred at sea, e.g., where a pilot of a pleasure boat moving on navigable waters was injured by rifle fire coming from an individual on land.[239] Similarly, the court in *Duluth Superior Excursions, Inc v Makela*[240] held that an individual hit, on dry land, by a car driven by an intoxicated person just minutes after both individuals disembarked from a chartered cruise ship, advertised as a "booze cruise," could sue the cruise operators in admiralty. The plaintiff claimed the cruise operators inadequately supervised the passengers who became illegally intoxicated, and also failed to provide a safe means of exit for the passengers. The court held that carrying passengers for hire is a traditional maritime activity and tort suits for injuries to passengers are covered by admiralty law.[241] In this case, the sequence of causal events which culminated in the accident started on board the vessel, therefore, pursuant to the Admiralty Extension Act,[242] admiralty jurisdiction existed.[243]

§2.06 — The Effects of Admiralty Law

This section, although not a comprehensive analysis of all of the substantive

---

235 *See* Medina v Perez, 575 F Supp 168, 171 (DPR 1983).

236 Peytavin v Government Employees Ins Co, 453 F2d 1121, 1127 (5th Cir 1972).

237 Cookmeyer v Louisiana Dept of Highways, 433 F2d 386, 386 (5th Cir), *affg*, 309 F Supp 881 (ED La 1970).

238 Byrd v Napolean Ave Ferry, 125 F Supp 573 (ED La 1954), *affd per curiam*, 227 F2d 958 (5th Cir 1955).

239 Kelly v Smith, 485 F2d 520, 526 (5th Cir 1973).

240 623 F2d 1251 (8th Cir 1980).

241 *Id* 1253.

242 *See* the Admiralty Extension Act, 46 USC §740.

243 Duluth Superior Excursions, Inc v Makela, 623 F2d 1251, 1253 (8th Cir 1980).

and procedural effects that result from a finding of admiralty jurisdiction,[244] summarizes the most important areas of admiralty law which are involved in recreational boating accident cases.

Those important aspects are: the claims are cognizable in federal court;[245] there is no minimum jurisdictional amount;[246] the right to a jury trial is limited;[247] the doctrine of laches applies rather than a strict statute of limitations;[248] a defendant's duty of care does not differ depending on whether the plaintiff was a licensee or invitee;[249] the rules of comparative negligence are applied;[250] and there is contribution among tortfeasors.[251]

State courts have concurrent jurisdiction over most maritime torts with federal courts.[252] However, admiralty suits are governed by federal law[253] wherever the action is brought.[254] State law may be applied by reference only when the federal law of admiralty is incomplete.[255] State law may not be applied if it would defeat or narrow any substantial admiralty rights of recovery.[256]

At one time, maritime law provided no recovery for wrongful death within

---

[244] Several leading commentators have discussed this subject. *See, e.g.*, 1 Benedict on Admiralty §112 (7th ed 1983); 7A J. Moore, Federal Practice ¶.325[1] (1972).

[245] *See* US Const art III, §2; 28 USC §1331(1).

The filing of a lawsuit in federal court, without simultaneously filing a state court suit, can have disastrous consequences if there is no admiralty jurisdiction. This is because if there is no admiralty jurisdiction, the federal court may have no subject matter jurisdiction. Accordingly, since a motion to dismiss for lack of subject matter jurisdiction can be raised at any time, *see* Smith v Hustler, Inc, 514 F Supp 1265, 1272-73 n 13 (WD L 1981), defense counsel may choose to raise this defense after the state statute of limitations has run. *See generally id* 1271 (filing of federal action does not toll running of state statute of limitations).

[246] *See* 1 Benedict on Admiralty §106, at 7-17 (7th ed 1983).

[247] Gilmore v Witschorek, 411 F Supp 491, 496 (Ed Ill 1976); Green v Ross, 338 F Supp 365, 367 (SD Fla 1972).

[248] *See* 1 Benedict on Admiralty §112, 7-41 (7th ed 1983).

[249] Kermarec v Compagnie Generale Transatlantique, 358 US 625, 630-32 (1959).

[250] Faust v South Carolina State Hwy Dept, 721 F2d 934, 940 (4th Cir 1983); Sanders v Richmond, 579 SW2d 401, 408 (Mo Ct App 1979); Scholl v Town of Babylon, 95 AD2d 475, 466 NYS2d 976, 977 (1983).

[251] Kennedy Engine Co v Dog River Marina & Boatworks, Inc, 432 So 2d 1214, 1215 (Ala 1983).

[252] *See* 28 USC §1333(1).

[253] Kermarec v Compagnie Generale Transatlantique, 358 US 625, 628 (1959).

[254] *See* Carlisle Packing Co v Sandanger, 259 US 255 (1922).

[255] Palestina v Fernandez, 701 F2d 438, 439 (5th Cir 1983); St Hilaire Moye v Henderson, 496 F2d 973, 980 (8th Cir), *cert denied*, 419 US 884 (1974). The *St Hilaire* court also stated, in dicta, that state law could be applied to broaden the scope of liability. *See id.* However, this dictum was rejected in Branch v Schumann, 445 F2d 175, 178 (5th Cir 1971).

[256] St Hilaire Moye v Henderson, 496 F2d 973, 980 (8th Cir), *cert denied*, 419 US 884 (1974).

a state's territorial waters.[257] However, in the landmark decision of *Moragne v States Marine Lines*,[258] the United States Supreme Court overruled prior decisions in that regard and held that there was a wrongful death action for violation of maritime duties on navigable waters within a state as well as on the high seas. When a *Moragne* action is brought in state court pursuant to the saving-to-suitors clause,[259] federal maritime law applies.[260]

Several state laws have been held to have been preempted by admiralty law. For example, a state law which imposed the highest degree of care on boat operators was not applied since the appropriate admiralty standard of care is only that of a reasonable person under the circumstances.[261] In addition, state guest statutes which limit a social guest's right to recover damages, from the operator of a boat, to injuries caused when the boat was operated wilfully and wantonly have also been preempted.[262] One court also held that admiralty law preempted state notice laws enacted to apprise local governments quickly of claims for injuries.[263]

In *Byrd v Byrd*, apparently the only case ever decided on this issue, the court held that federal admiralty jurisdiction does not recognize interspousal immunity and, therefore, one spouse could sue the other spouse for negligent operation of a boat.[264]

§2.07 — The Federal Limitation of Liability Act

The Federal Limitation of Liability Act, originally passed in 1851, states that the liability of a boat owner[265] "without privity or knowledge"[266] of the

---

257 Sanders v Richmond, 579 SW2d 401, 406 (Mo Ct App 1979).

258 398 US 375 (1970).

259 28 USC §1333.

260 Sanders v Richmond, 579 SW2d 401, 408 (Mo Ct App 1979).

261 Branch v Schumann, 445 F2d 175, 178 (5th Cir 1971).

262 St Hilaire Moye v Henderson, 496 F2d 973, 980 (8th Cir), *cert denied*, 419 US 884 (1974); *see also* Blevens v Sfetku, 259 Cal App 2d 527, 66 Cal Rptr 486 (1968).

263 *See* Scholl v Town of Babylon, 95 AD2d 475, 466 NYS2d 976, 982 (1983).

264 657 F2d 615 (4th Cir 1981) (wife sued husband for his negligence in failing to affix a deck chair on a pleasure boat to the deck).

265 It is sometimes difficult to determine whether a party is an *owner*. See Pelaez, *Ownership At Sea: Identifying Those Entitled To Limit Liability In The Admiralty*, 22 Duq L Rev 397 (1984).

A fishing boat leased to others may be considered a demise or bareboat charter and be outside the scope of the owner's insurance coverage. *See* O'Donnell v Latham, 525 F2d 651, 653 (5th Cir 1976). Accordingly, in those cases, the owner may have significant personal financial exposure if the Limitation Act is not applicable.

266 *Privity* means some fault or neglect in which the owner personally participates and *knowledge* means personal cognizance or means of knowledge, of which the owner is bound to avail himself. *See* 3 Benedict on Admiralty §41, at 5-4 (7th ed 1982).

act causing loss or damage is limited to the value of the owner's interest in the vessel as of the termination of the voyage in which the damage was incurred.[267] Therefore, where a vessel is a total loss this limitation of liability is really an extinguishment of liability.[268]

The determination of whether a ship owner is entitled to this limitation of liability is a two-step process.[269] First, it must be determined what acts of negligence or conditions of unseaworthiness caused the accident.[270] Second, it must be determined if the owner had knowledge or privity of those negligent acts or unseaworthy conditions.[271]

As a practical matter, most courts have found knowledge or privity when the owner was on board the ship when the accident occurred.[272] For example, in *Armour v Gradler*, the court held that an owner-operator of a boat who knew that it was dangerous to ride in the boat in rough waters because of deficiencies in the ship's hull, a condition which ultimately led to the death of a passenger, had *knowledge* of the condition causing injury and the act was inapplicable.[273] One court found privity in a corporate context where a manager failed to train his employees properly and one of them, while operating a pontoon, failed to modify his course or signal an oncoming boat and the two vessels collided.[274]

The failure of the owner to comply with federal law is a basis for denying the petition for limitation on liability. In *Rowe v Brooks*,[275] a young boy was operating a motorboat and demonstrating the boat's capabilities to prospective purchasers when a collision occurred causing fatal injuries. The court noted that an applicable federal law required the boat to be operated by a licensed individual over 18 years old and since that law was violated, there was knowledge or privity, and the petition for limitation of liability should be denied.[276]

---

267 46 USC §183(a). *See generally* Pelaez, *Ownership At Sea: Identifying Those Entitled To Limit Liability In The Admiralty*, 22 Duq L Rev 397 (1984).

268 Armour v Gradler, 448 F Supp 741, 749 (WD Pa 1978).

269 Farrell Lines v Jones, 530 F2d 7, 10 (5th Cir 1976). The burden of proof is on the party claiming lack of knowledge of privity. *See id.*

270 *Id.*

271 *Id.*

272 *See* Title v Aldacosta, 544 F2d 752, 756 (5th Cir 1977); Bremmer v Shedd, 467 F Supp 261, 267 (WD Pa 1979); Armour v Gradler, 448 F Supp 741, 749 (WD Pa 1978).

273 448 F Supp 741, 749 (WD Pa 1978).

274 Baldassano v Larsen, 580 F Supp 415, 420 (D Minn 1984).

275 329 F2d 35 (4th Cir 1964).

276 *Id* 44-45.

Pleasure Craft

The courts have repeatedly held that the Limitation Act applies to owners of pleasure crafts.[277] This interpretation is consistent with a literal reading of the law since the act applies to "vessels,"[278] and pleasure craft[279] are vessels. However, some cases, in dicta,[280] and virtually all commentators[281] have criticized these rulings because the purpose behind the passing of the act in 1851, viz., to encourage shipbuilding and the employment of ships in commerce so this country could compete with the British maritime industry,[282] bears no relationship to limiting the liability of owners of small pleasure cruisers. Indeed, there seems to be no legitimate reason to encourage pleasure boating at the expense of individuals injured by the improper operation of those boats.[283]

Finally, in *Baldassano v Larsen*, a case where a pontoon and a speed boat collided, the court noted that it was making a "precedent breaking" ruling and held that the act was not applicable to owners of pleasure boats.[284] It reasoned that recreational boating was not the type of activity which was intended to be encouraged by the act.[285] Accordingly, it held that to "limit liability in a case such as this would be as outrageous as allowing an automobile owner to limit his liability to the value of his car should he crash while out on a Sunday drive."[286]

Some courts have held that the Limitation Act only applies when there is

---

[277] Title v Aldacosta, 544 F2d 752, 756 (5th Cir 1977); Gibboney v Wright, 517 F2d 1054, 1057 (5th Cir 1975); Feige v Hurley, 89 F2d 575 (6th Cir 1937); *In re* Brown, 536 F Supp 750, 752 (ND Ohio 1982); *In re* Rowley, 425 F Supp 116, 119 (D Idaho 1977); *In re* Porter, 272 F Supp 282, 285 (SD Tex 1967). *See also* the plethora of cases cited in Stolz, *Pleasure Boating and Admiralty*, 51 Cal L Rev 661, 709 n 202 (1963). The Supreme Court has assumed that the act applies to pleasure crafts. *See, e.g.*, Coryll v Phipps, 317 US 406 (1943).

[278] *See* 46 USC §§183(a), 188.

[279] *See* 1 USC §3.

[280] *See* Richards v Blake Builders Supply, Inc, 528 F2d 745, 748 (4th Cir 1975); Armour v Gradler, 448 F Supp 741, 749 (WD Pa 1978).

[281] *See* G. Gilmore & C. Black, The Law of Admiralty §10-23, at 700 (1957); Harolds, *Limitation of Liability and Its Application to Pleasure Boats*, 37 Temple LQ 423, 444-45 (1964); Comment, *Limitation of Liability in Admiralty*, 19 Vill L Rev 721 (1965).

[282] *See* Harolds, *Limitation of Liability and its Application to Pleasure Boats*, 37 Temple LQ 423, 426 (1964).

[283] Stolz, *Pleasure Boating and Admiralty*, 51 Cal L Rev 661, 710 (1963). *See also* Richards v Blake Builders Supply, Inc, 528 F2d 745, 748 (4th Cir 1975) ("we can perceive no reason to extend that protection to the relatively affluent owners of pleasure boats and their insurers at the expense of those injured or killed and their familites").

[284] 580 F Supp 415, 419-20 (D Minn 1984).

[285] *Id* 419.

[286] *Id.*

admiralty jurisdiction[287] or when the accident occurred on navigable waters.[288] However, this construction of the act has also been rejected.[289]

Procedure

Although generally the owner must petition a federal district court for this limitation of liability within six months after being given written notice of the claim of liability against him or her,[290] this defense can also be asserted by an answer in federal court where the plaintiff sues the owner for damages.[291] When a plaintiff sues in state court, the owner's raising of this defense by answer is effective only when the owner's claim is uncontested; if the plaintiff challenges the owner's claim the issue must be resolved in federal court because there is exclusive federal jurisdiction of this issue.[292]

§2.08   Firearms

A possessor of a loaded firearm is not an insurer for all injuries resulting from the use of the firearm.[293] However, the possessor must, at a minimum, exercise reasonable care,[294] and many courts have held that the standard is extraordinary care.[295] The obvious reason why some courts have

---

[287] Clinton Bd of Park Commnrs v Claussen, 410 F Supp 320 (SD Iowa 1976).

[288] See Marroni v Matey, 492 F Supp 340, 343 (WD Pa 1980); In re Stephens, 341 F Supp 1404, 1407 (ND Ga 1965); In re Madsen, 187 F Supp 411 (NDNY 1960); See generally G. Gilmore & C. Black, The Law of Admiralty 843-44 (2d ed 1975).

[289] See 1 Benedict on Admiralty §248, at 15-56 (7th ed 1982).

[290] 46 USC §185.

[291] Deep Sea Tankers, Ltd v The Long Branch, 258 F2d 757 (2d Cir 1958), cert denied, 358 US 933 (1959).

[292] Cincinnati Gas & Elec Co v Abel, 533 F2d 1001 (6th Cir), cert denied, 429 US 858 (1976). This decision was criticized in Volk & Cobbs, Limitations of Liability, 51 Tul L Rev 953, 977 (1977).

[293] Kuhns v Brugger, 390 Pa 331, 135 A2d 395, 403 (1957).

[294] Pundt v McNeill, 500 SW2d 559, 563 (Tex Civ App 1973). However, a firearm is a highly dangerous instrumentality and, since its possession is attended by extraordinary danger, it can be argued that reasonable care requires that the possessor exercise care consistent with that extraordinary danger. Kuhns v Brugger, 390 Pa 331, 135 A2d 395, 400 (1957).
Early common law held that a person injured by a firearm had an action for trespass vi et armis and the only defense was that the defendant was without fault. See Winborn v Mayo, 434 SW2d 207, 208 (Tex Civ App 1968) (citing other sources).

[295] Woodward v First Ins Co, 333 So 2d 709, 710 (La Ct App), writ denied, 338 So 2d 295 (La 1976); Kuhns v Brugger, 390 Pa 331, 135 A2d 395, 403 (1957). See also Reida v Lund, 18 Cal App 3d 704, 96 Cal Rptr 102, 105 (1971) ("highest standard of due care"); Stoelting v Hauck, 56 NJ super 386, 153 A2d 339, 348 (1959) ("a duty of higher than ordinary care"). The duty of care is proportionate to the probability of injury. See Winborn v Mayo, 434 SW2d 207, 208 (Tex Civ App 1968).

imposed a high standard of care is that these weapons frequently cause tragic accidents.[296]

Several courts have held that it was not error to reject a proposed jury instruction which stated that a high degree of care is necessary in the use of loaded weapons; the proper jury instruction was that the defendant must exercise reasonable care under the circumstances.[297] These courts reasoned that the decision of whether *the circumstances* of using a firearm require a high degree of caution is a question of fact to be resolved by a jury.[298]

The use of firearms is not an ultrahazardous activity resulting in absolute liability to the owner.[299] When terrible accidents have occurred in the absence of fault, no recovery has been allowed.[300]

Absent unusual circumstances,[301] an owner of a firearm is not vicariously liable for the negligence of others.[302] However, the owner of a firearm must exercise reasonable care in safeguarding the weapon from reasonably anticipated use by others.[303] In addition, reasonable care must be taken in entrusting the gun to others.[304]

Combat

Where the parties engage in mutual combat using firearms, each is liable to the other for injury inflicted during the fight.[305] The fact that the parties voluntarily engaged in combat is no defense.[306]

One commentator noted that it is highly speculative whether a jury's verdict is significantly affected when the appropriate standard of care is *highest care* rather than only *reasonable care*. *See* Sherman, *Torts*, U Pitt L Rev 451, 455 (1966).

296 One state study revealed that almost 40% of all hunting accidents resulted in a fatality. *See* Seabolt v Cheeseborough, 127 Ga App 254, 193 SE2d 238, 240 n 2 (1972).

297 *See* Purtle v Shelton, 251 Ark 519, 474 SW2d 123, 126 (1971); Seabolt v Cheeseborough, 127 Ga App 254, 193 SE2d 238, 241 (1972).

298 *See* Purtle v Shelton, 251 Ark 519, 474 SW2d 123, 126 (1971); Seabolt v Cheeseborough, 127 Ga app 254, 193 SE2d 238, 241 (1972).

299 Orser v Vierra, 252 Cal App 2d 660, 60 Cal Rptr 708, 717 (1967). *See also* Restatement (Second) of Torts §519 (1965).

300 *See, e.g.*, Stephan v Marlin Firearms Co, 353 F2d 819 (2d Cir 1965), *cert denied*, 384 US 959 (1966) (child, while walking single file, was shot in back when a companion's hand slipped and a gun discharged); Winborn v Mayo, 434 SW2d 207 (Tex Civ App 1968) (hunter died when gun went off accidentally).

301 E.g., the family purpose doctrine, *see* §2.01; or state statutes, *see* §2.11.

302 Mercier v Meade, 384 So 2d 262, 263 (Fla Dist Ct App 1980).

303 Garguilo, *Liability for Leaving a Firearm Accessible to Children*, 17 Clev-Mar L Rev 472, 472 (1968); *see also* §2.09.

304 Mercier v Meade, 384 So 2d 262, 263 (Fla Dist Ct App 1980); *see also* §2.09.

305 Colby v McClendon, 85 Okla 293, 206 P 207, 208 (1922).

306 *Id.*

Hunting

Hunters must exercise reasonable care.[307] For example, a hunter was held liable for failing to have the safety on when he approached another individual.[308]

A hunter, before shooting, must first ascertain that no one is in the line of fire[309] and then ascertain that he or she is shooting at game.[310] If a hunter, through the use of reasonable care, could have detected that the plaintiff was a human, not a deer, then there was a duty to refrain from shooting.[311] It is only when a hunter reasonably believes that no one is close enough to the line of fire to be in danger that he or she is not negligent in firing a weapon.[312]

In *Mileur v Briggerman*,[313] a hunter, wearing camouflage, shook both of this feet in an attempt to stop mosquitoes from biting him. Unfortunately, another hunter standing behind him thought that the movement was that of a turkey and he shot, injuring the plaintiff. The court held that the defendant in this case was negligent, as a matter of law, in failing to observe whether his target was a man or another animal.[314]

Members of a hunting club may be liable for each other's torts, but this liability cannot extend past traditional principles of agency law.[315] For example, members of a duck hunting club are not liable for other members' negligent shooting of frogs and mudhens which resulted in a human fatality.[316] However, a party is liable, even where he or she did not shoot the bullet causing injury, if he or she knew the person who was shooting breached a duty of care and was nonetheless giving that person substantial assistance and encouragement.[317]

Insanity

One court rejected, as a matter of law, the defense of insanity when it was asserted in a civil case involving a firearm.[318]

---

307 Breithaupt v Sellers, 390 So 2d 870, 873 (La 1980); Houk v Pennington, 550 SW2d 584, 588 (Mo Ct App 1977); Pundt v McNeill, 500 SW2d 559, 563 (Tex Civ App 1973).

308 Gross v State, 242 Ark 181, 412 SW2d 278, 279 (1967) (also evidence that defendant intentionally shot the decedent).

309 Summers v Tice, 33 Cal 2d 80, 83, 199 P2d 1 (1948).

310 Pundt v McNeill, 500 SW2d 559, 563 (Tex Civ App 1973).

311 Breithaupt v Sellers, 390 So 2d 870, 873 (La 1980).

312 *See* Houk v Pennington, 550 SW2d 584, 588 (Mo Ct App 1977).

313 110 Ill App 3d 721, 442 NE2d 1356, 1359 (1982).

314 442 NE2d at 1359.

315 Orser v Vierra, 252 Cal App 2d 660, 60 Cal Rptr 708, 716 (1967).

316 *Id.*

317 60 Cal Rptr at 714. *See also* Restatement (Second) of Torts §876 (1965).

318 Vosnos v Perry, 43 Ill App 3d 834, 357 NE2d 614, 616 (1976).

Pointing Firearm at Another Person

In some states, pointing a pistol at another is illegal.[319] Violation of these statutes may be regarded as negligence per se.[320]

Even where it is not negligence per se, a prima facie case of negligence can be established where a person picks up a firearm, points it at another person, and squeezes the firing mechanism.[321] Any reasonable person should know that even with blank ammunition it is dangerous to place the muzzle of a .22 caliber pistol directly against someone; when that act caused damage, the defendant may have committed assault and battery. [322]

The courts have held that a possessor of a firearm has acted unreasonably dangerously in pointing a gun at another person where the possessor was a minor,[323] the possessor did not know that the firearm was loaded,[324] and the possessor's actions were unintentional.[325]

Minors

Under the Restatement (Second) of Torts, a minor is held to an adult standard of care when: (1) he or she engages in an activity for which adult qualifications are required; and (2) the activity is normally engaged in only by adults.[326] Several courts have concluded that minors are not held to an adult standard of care in using firearms because hunting and other recreational activities involving firearms are not activities normally engaged in only by adults.[327] Other courts have come to the same conclusion although their reasoning differed.[328]

---

319 *See, e.g.,* Colo Rev Stat §18-12-106 (1978); Idaho Code §18-3304 (1979); Minn Stat Ann §609.66 (West Supp 1984); Nev Rev Stat §202.290 (1983); NY Penal Law §265.35 (McKinney 1980); Or Rev Stat §166.190 (1983); Vt Stat Ann tit 13, §4011 (1974); Va Code §18.2-282 (1982); Wis Stat Ann §941.20 (1982).

320 Kuhns v Brugger, 390 Pa 331, 135 A2d 395, 402 (1957).

321 Kuhns v Brugger, 390 Pa 331, 135 A2d 395, 400-01 (1957).

322 Sigler v Ralph, 417 SW2d 239, 424 (Ky Ct App 1967).

323 Woodward v First Ins Co, 333 So 2d 709, 710 (La Ct App), *writ denied,* 338 So 2d 295 (La 1976).

324 Kuhns v Brugger, 390 Pa 331, 135 A2d 395, 401 (1957).

325 Palmer v Decker, 253 Ind 593, 255 NE2d 797, 800 (1970).

326 *See* Restatement (Second) of Torts §283A comment c (1965).
Where the child standard of conduct is applied, there should be a jury instruction that the defendant child is held to the standard of conduct of a similar child of the same age, ability, intelligence, training, and experience. *See generally* Prater v Burns, 525 SW2d 846, 852 (Tenn Ct App 1975).

327 *See, e.g.,* Purtle v Shelton, 251 Ark 519, 474 SW2d 123, 125 (1971); Thomas v Inman, 282 Or 279, 578 P2d 399, 403 (1978).

328 *See, e.g.,* Stephan v Marlin Firearms Co, 353 F2d 819, 825 (2d Cir 1965), *cert denied,*

Those decisions which hold that children using firearms are only held to the standard of care of other children seem wrong.[329] The danger in the use of firearms is not only self-evident, but probably greater than in the use of any other recreational product for which an adult standard of care has been applied.[330] Firearms are also more dangerous than cars, and children using the latter are generally held to an adult standard of care.[331] There is no reason, other than a blind following of stare decisis, to hold minors to a lower standard of care here.

In contrast, the standard for judging a child's use of a toy rifle should be that of a reasonably prudent child of the defendant's age, experience, and intelligence.[332]

Wilful and Wanton Acts

A party is guilty of wilful or wanton behavior where he or she consciously performs an act or fails to perform an act with knowledge that the behavior is likely to cause injury.[333] Such behavior is also shown where there is a reckless indifference to the consequences of the party's acts or omissions.[334]

In *Barnes v Haney*,[335] two experienced bird hunters were hunting when one of them, unknown to the other, approached the other hunter, without giving notice, from behind. When a bird was flushed in front of the first hunter and flew to his rear, that hunter turned and fired, not knowing the second hunter was in that vicinity, and the second hunter was injured.[336] The court held that there was no evidence of wilful or wanton behavior.[337]

---

384 US 959 (1966); Townsend v Moore, 165 Ga App 606, 302 SE2d 398, 400 (1983); LaBarge v Stewart, 84 NM 222, 501 P2d 666, 670 (App), *cert denied*, 84 NM 219, 501 P2d 663 (1972); Kuhns v Brugger, 390 Pa 331, 135 A2d 395, 401 (1957); Prater v Burns, 525 SW2d 846, 851 (Tenn Ct App 1975); *see generally* Palmer v Decker, 253 Ind 593, 255 NE2d 797 (1970).

329 *See* Purtle v Shelton, 251 Ark 519, 474 SW2d 123, 130 (1971) (Byrd, J dissenting): Because a bullet fired from a gun by a minor is just as deadly as a bullet fired by an adult, I'm at a loss to understand why one with "buck fever" because of his minority is entitled to exercise any less care than anyone else deer hunting. One killed by a bullet so fired would be just as dead in one instance as the other and without any more warning.

330 *See, e.g.*, Prichard v Veterans Cab Co, 66 Cal 2d 727, 408 P2d 360, 47 Cal Rptr 904, 907 (1965) (motorcycle); Dellwo v Pearson, 259 Minn 452, 107 NW2d 859 (1961) (boat); Robinson v Lindsay, 92 Wash 2d 410, 598 P2d 392 (1979) (snowmobile).

331 *See, e.g.*, Harrelson v Whitehead, 236 Ark 325, 365 SW2d 868 (1963) (citing cases); Nielsen v Brown, 232 Or 426, 374 P2d 896 (1962).

332 Gordon v Harris, 86 AD2d 948, 448 NYS2d 598, 560 (1982).

333 Barnes v Haney, 280 Ala 39, 189 So 779, 782 (1966).

334 *Id.*

335 *Id.*

336 *Id.*

337 *Id.*

One jury concluded that a person who shot a rifle into an abandoned mine tunnel where the bullet hit a person who was exploring there did not act with a wilful disregard of the rights of others.[338]

Causation

In the landmark case of *Summers v Tice*,[339] the California Supreme Court held that two hunters could be held liable for an injury even though only one of them caused the accident. In *Summers*, the plaintiff, part of a hunting threesome, was on a hill and the two other hunters were standing beneath him on opposite sides of the hill when both of them shot at a quail. The plaintiff was hit by the bird shot fired by one of his hunting companions, but he could not determine which hunter fired the shot which hit him. The court held that both defendants were negligent in shooting in an area where a person was located, and since the plaintiff could not ascertain whose shot injured him, each defendant had the burden to absolve himself.[340] The court reasoned that the plaintiff was put in the predicament of being unable to determine which defendant's shot hit him, when neither defendant should have fired in his direction, by the defendants' negligent actions and, therefore, each defendant had to show his shot did not cause the plaintiff's injury.[341] *Summers* was followed in other hunting accident cases where the exact identity of the shooter was not known.[342]

Circumstantial proof of causation can be sufficient to impose liability. In *Pundt v McNeill*, a hunter hit by a bullet was entitled to recover from the only other hunter in the area where only one shot was fired and the other hunter admitted making that one shot.[343]

The doctrine of res ipsa loquitur has been applied in firearm injury cases.[344] This doctrine may apply where the occurrence which resulted in an injury does not ordinarily happen in the absence of negligence, the instrumentality involved was under the management and control of the defendant, and the defendant possesses superior knowledge or information as to the cause of the

---

[338] Harman v Chase, 160 Colo 449, 417 P2d 784, 786 (1966).

[339] 33 Cal 2d 80, 199 P2d 1 (1948).

[340] 33 Cal 2d at 86.

[341] *Id.*

[342] *See* Orser v Vierra, 252 Cal App 2d 660, 60 Cal Rptr 708 (1967).

[343] 500 SW2d 559, 562-63 (Tex Civ App 1973).

[344] *See, e.g.,* Vosnos v Perry, 43 Ill App 3d 834, 357 NE2d 614, 616 (1976); Koclanes v Hertenstein, 130 Ill App 916, 266 NE2d 119, 120-21 (1971) (hunter was injured by a pellet from a shotgun fired by another hunter).

occurrence.[345] It puts the burden on the defendant to show he or she was not negligent.[346]

The pleading of res ipsa loquitur is sufficient where the plaintiff did not have sufficient knowledge of why the firearm accident occurred to prove a specific act of negligence.[347] In addition, this doctrine has been allowed even where the plaintiff made specific allegations of negligence, e.g., a hunter's failure to keep a proper lookout.[348]

Indemnity

In some instances, an individual being sued for causing a firearm accident has asserted a claim for indemnity or contribution against the firearm manufacturer or the retailer who sold the firearm or ammunition.[349] Such claims were not successful where the original defendant failed to read the safety instructions and took the gun into a public place, where it was dropped and the gun discharged,[350] or where the original defendant was convicted of manslaughter in a collateral criminal proceeding arising out of the same incident.[351]

Insurance

Individuals injured in a firearm accident may be insured for such accidents under a homeowners' or automobile insurance policy. In addition, the person who caused the firearm accident may also have insurance coverage for such an accident.

In *State Farm Mutual Automobile Insurance Co v Partridge*,[352] the California Supreme Court held that a homeowners' insurance policy which excluded injuries arising out of the use of an automobile does not preclude coverage where a firearm accident resulted from the concurrence of a nonautomobile-related cause and an automobile-related cause. In that case, the insured had filed the trigger mechanism of his .357 magnum pistol to give it hair-trigger action. On the day of the accident, the insured was hunting jackrabbits in a four-wheel drive vehicle with two friends. He drove the car off the paved

---

345 Parker v Roszell, 617 SW2d 597, 600 (Mo Ct App 1981).

346 Vosnos v Perry, 43 Ill App 3d 834, 357 NE2d 614, 616 (1976).

347 Gates v Tauchen, 497 SW2d 183, 185 (Mo 1973).

348 *Id* 600-01.

349 *See* Pair v Blakly, 160 NJ Super 14, 388 A2d 1026 (1978) (ammunition should not have been sold to minor).

350 Colt Indus Operating Corp v Coleman, 246 Ga 559, 272 SE2d 251, 252-53 (1980).

351 Adkinson v Rossi Arms Co, 659 P2d 1236, 1240 (Alaska 1983).

352 10 Cal 3d 94, 514 P2d 123, 109 Cal Rptr 811 (1973).

road to keep a rabbit within the car's headlights. The vehicle hit a bump and the pistol discharged injuring one of the passengers.

The court held that the accident was caused, in part, by the insured's negligent driving, an excluded risk. However, the accident was also caused, in part, by the insured's negligent filing of the pistol, a nonexcluded risk. The court concluded that there was coverage under the policy because the accident was partly caused by a nonautomobile, i.e., a nonexcluded risk; coverage cannot be defeated because there is also a separate excluded risk which is an additional cause of the injury.[353]

Similarly, a homeowners' insurance policy, which excluded coverage for damages arising out of the operation of an automobile, covered an accident where a passenger in an automobile was injured by a 12-gauge shotgun which fired accidentally.[354] The court held that one cause of the injury was the placing of a loaded gun under the front seat of an automobile and that risk was not excluded because it was not an excluded *use* of a vehicle.[355] As long as one cause of the accident is not excluded, the policy covers the accident.[356]

However, a homeowners' policy which excluded coverage for damages from loading or unloading an automobile did not cover a situation where the insured, while his pickup truck was stopped, stepped outside and reached back into the car for his gun, and the gun discharged.[357]

Several courts have held that an automobile insurance policy does not supply coverage for firearm injuries which occurred in an automobile unless there is some causal connection between the use of the automobile and the accident.[358] There is no such relationship when a firearm accidentally discharges in a stationary automobile.[359] In contrast, there is a connection when a party, while unloading camping materials from a camper truck, throws a sleeping bag to the ground causing a concealed, loaded gun in the bag to discharge because the *use* of an automobile includes its loading and unloading.[360]

---

353 109 Cal Rptr at 813.

354 Glen Falls Ins Co v Rich, 49 Cal App 3d 390, 122 Cal Rptr 696 (1975).

355 122 Cal Rptr at 699.

356 *Id* 701.

357 Morari v Atlantic Mut Fire Ins Co, 105 Ariz 537, 468 P2d 564, 566 (1970).

358 *See* Brenner v Aetna Ins Co, 8 Ariz App 272, 445 P2d 474, 478 (1968); Aetna Casualty & Sur Co v Safeco, 103 Cal App 3d 694, 163 Cal Rptr 219, 223 (1980); Azar v Employers Casualty Co, 178 Colo 58, 95 P2d 554 (1972); United States Fidelity & Guar Co v Western Fire Ins Co, 450 SW2d 491 (Ky 1970).

359 Aetna Casualty & Sur Co v Safeco, 103 Cal App 3d 694, 163 Cal Rptr 219, 223 (1980).

360 Viani v Aetna Ins Co, 95 Idaho 22, 501 P2d 706 (1972).

Statutes

Several states have laws which prohibit the negligent use of firearms.[361] It is also common to prohibit the use of firearms by individuals under the influence of alcohol or drugs.[362]

It is usually illegal for a child below a certain age[363] (the specific age varies by state), to possess a firearm, at least in the absence of consent by the child's parent or guardian,[364] or another adult.[365]

In one state, it is illegal to possess a concealed weapon unless the possessor is engaged in certain lawful recreational activities.[366]

§2.09 —Parental Liability

Parents of a child who caused a firearm accident may be liable to injured parties if the parents were negligent. Parents may act unreasonably in entrusting a firearm to their child, safeguarding the firearm in the house, or in training their child in the proper use of the weapon. However, unless there is vicarious liability,[367] where the parents are not negligent, they are not liable.[368]

Entrustment

Parents may be liable to injured third parties for their negligent entrustment

---

[361] *See, e.g.*, Idaho Code §18-3312 (1979); Mich Comp Laws Ann §752.861 (West 1968); Minn Stat Ann §609.66 (West Supp 1984) ("recklessly"); Nev Rev Stat §202.280 (1983); NH Rev Stat Ann §207:37a (1978); Okla Stat Ann tit 21, §1289.11 (West 1983) ("recklessly"); Or Rev Stat §166.180 (1983); SD Codified Laws Ann §22-14-7(1) (1978) ("recklessly"); Vt Stat Ann tit 13, §4009 (1974); W Va Code §61-7-11 (1977); Wis Stat Ann §941.20 (West 1982) ("recklessly"). *See also* Colo Rev Stat §18-12-106 (1978) (bow and arrow); Mich Comp Laws Ann §752.881 (West 1968) (bow and arrow).

[362] *See, e.g.*, Alaska Stat §11.61.210 (1983); Ohio Rev Code Ann §2923.15 (Page 1982); Va Code §18.2-285 (1982).

[363] *See, e.g.*, Ill Ann Stat ch 38, §24-3.1 (Smith-Hurd 1977); RI Gen Laws §11-47-33 (1981).

[364] *See, e.g.*, Alaska Stat §11.61.220 (1983); NY Penal Law §265.05 (McKinney 1980) (airgun); Utah Code Ann §§23-20-20, 76-10-509 (1976); Vt Stat Ann tit 13, §4008 (1974); *see generally* Iowa Code Ann §724.22 (1979).

[365] *See, e.g.*, Fla Stat Ann §790.22 (West Supp 1984); Mass Gen Laws Ann ch 131, §14 (West Supp 1984); Mich Comp Laws Ann §752.891 (West Supp 1984); Nev Rev Stat §202.300 (1983); NJ Stat Ann §2C:58-6.1 (West Supp 1984).

[366] *See* Alaska Stat §11.61.220 (1983).

[367] *See, e.g.*, Ortega v Montoya, 97 NM 159, 637 P2d 841, 843 (1981); Cal Civ Code §1714.3 (West Supp 1984).

[368] Hutcherson v Amen, 98 Idaho 776, 572 P2d 879, 880 (1977).

of a firearm, i.e., permitting a child to possess a weapon where it is reasonably understood that the child is incapable of using it properly.[369]

A father who had knowledge of his son's prior carelessness with a BB gun was held negligent in allowing him access to a gun.[370] The father argued that a BB gun or air rifle is merely a toy and that he was not negligent for allowing his child to use a toy. The argument was rejected because such guns can be deadly weapons.[371] In addition, a party acted negligently when he pumped a BB gun for a seven-year-old child immediately after seeing the child point the gun at another person.[372]

Similarly, in *Stoelting v Hauck*, a parent was negligent when a daughter with virtually no training or instruction in using small arms was allowed to wear and play with automatic revolvers and allowed to sleep in a room with a loaded gun kept in an unlocked desk.[373] Although the specific accident which occurred, viz., a house guest was shot, was probably unforeseeable, there was liability because some harm could have been reasonably foreseen.[374]

In several older cases, parents were held not liable as a matter of law because the child was thoroughly familiar with the use of firearms and had a history of safely handling them.[375] Nevertheless, one court held that even where there is some evidence of the child's experience in handling weapons, where an accident occurred because the child did not know that a shotgun was loaded, that fact alone may be evidence of the child's lack of adequate training and a directed verdict for the parent would be improper.[376]

Parents are not liable for negligent entrustment as a matter of law when there is no evidence that they knew their child possessed a dangerous firearm.[377]

Safeguarding

Parents may be liable for negligent safeguarding of a firearm, i.e.,

---

[369] Whalen v Bennett, 4 Mich App 81, 143 NW2d 797, 800 (1966); Prater v Burns, 525 SW2d 846, 849 (Tenn Ct App 1975).

[370] Williams v Davidson, 241 Ark 699, 409 SW2d 311, 313 (1966).

[371] *Id.*

[372] Rodriguez v Esquijarosa, 391 So 2d 334, 335 (Fla Dist Ct App 1980) (the opinion is unclear whether the defendant was related to the child whose gun he cocked).

[373] Stoelting v Hauck, 56 NJ Super 386, 153 A2d 339, 347-48 (1957), *revd on other grounds*, 32 NJ 87, 159 A2d 385 (1960).

[374] 153 A2d at 338-39.

[375] *See, e.g.*, Palm v Ivorson, 117 Ill App 535 (1905); Klop v Vanden Bros, 263 Mich 27, 248 NW 538 (1933); Herndobler v Rippen, 75 Or 22, 146 P 140 (1915).

[376] Prater v Burns, 525 SW2d 846, 850 (Tenn Ct App 1975).

[377] Gordon v Harris, 86 AD2d 948, 448 NYS2d 598, 600 (1982).

leaving a weapon in a place accessible to children.[378]

In *Kuhns v Brugger*,[379] a grandfather was held liable when he kept a pistol with a clip of cartridges in its handle in an unlocked drawer in his unlocked bedroom and his grandchild knew where the firearm was located. The court held that the grandfather should have foreseen the danger of leaving a loaded weapon in a place so accessible to children.[380] Indeed, the court stated:

> It is contrary to every human experience to expect that children, particularly boys, would not want to touch and handle a pistol. There is something magnetic about highly engined firearms with their harmonious lines and graceful proportions which attracts both young and old.... When [the grandchild] came upon this pistol his first impulse—common to all boys—was to see if he could operate it. He ... was simply overwhelmed by an impulse the existence of which is known to adults and against which [the grandfather] should have taken precautions.[381]

A parent may not be negligent where he attempted to conceal the gun from his children, instructed the children that they were not to enter the room where the gun was kept and provided for a relative to stay at the house on a day he was not home.[382]

Training

Parents may also be liable to injured plaintiffs for their negligent failure to train, control, and supervise their child.[383] However, there was no such liability where a child took a rifle and intentionally shot at strangers because the child had not previously intentionally injured anything.[384]

Causation

Some parents have argued that their negligence was not the proximate cause of a plaintiff's injury because, after all, they did not fire the weapon

---

378 Reida v Lund, 18 Cal App 3d 698, 707, 96 Cal Rptr 102, 107-08 (1971).

379 390 Pa 331, 135 A2d 395 (1957).

380 135 A2d at 403.

381 *Id* 403-04. *See also* Stoelting v Hauck, 32 NJ 87, 159 A2d 385, 389 (1960):
> Firearms are so inherently dangerous and so magnetic to the young that a person of ordinary prudence in the exercise of reasonable care will take cautious preventive measures commensurate with the great harm that may ensue from the use of the gun by someone unfit to be entrusted with it.

382 Thomas v Inman, 282 Or 279, 578 P2d 399, 404 (1978).

383 Reida v Lund, 18 Cal App 3d 698, 701, 96 Cal Rptr 102, 103-04 (1971).

384 *Id.*

which injured the plaintiff. Generally, this argument is successful only when the intervening event which caused the injury was not, in the natural and ordinary course of things, reasonably anticipated as a result of the parent's negligence.[385] For example, a mother who furnished an airgun to her 10-year-old child without directly supervising him created a dangerous situation and, therefore, was liable when one of the child's friends took the gun and injured another child because the subsequent taking of the weapon by another child was a reasonably foreseeable result of the mother's action.[386]

Indemnity

In *Seeberger v LeGare*,[387] one minor, while hunting, accidentally shot his friend. The plaintiff sued both the minor who caused the accident and his mother for her negligence in supervising her son. The defendant-parent counterclaimed, alleging that the plaintiff's parents failed to supervise their son properly and, therefore, should be liable for contribution. The court dismissed the counterclaim on the ground that, because an infant has no claim for negligent supervision by his or her parents, there can be no action for contribution against a parent.[388]

The court's reasoning is weak and results in an anomalous situation. A child is precluded, at least in some states, from suing his or her parents for negligent supervision because of a policy decision to avoid parent-child litigation. However, allowing the counterclaim in this case would not inject that evil here.

Furthermore, the practical result of the court's decision is that everyone, with the sole exception of a plaintiff's parents, is responsible for his or her acts. Under comparative negligence, the plaintiff's own negligence would reduce his or her recoverable damages. In addition, the child who negligently shot the rifle, and that child's parent, may be liable for their negligence. However, the plaintiff's parents' negligence would be totally ignored, under this ruling, even if they were the most culpable parties in causing the accident. This is a strange result.

---

[385] Taylor v Webster, 12 Ohio St 2d 53, 231 NE2d 870, 873 (1967); Kuhns v Brugger, 390 Pa 331, 135 A2d 395, 404 (1957); Prater v Burns, 525 SW2d 846, 850 (Tenn Ct App 1975).

[386] Taylor v Webster, 12 Ohio St 2d 53, 231 NE2d 870, 873 (1967).

[387] 48 AD2d 994, 370 NYS2d 210 (1975).

[388] 370 NYS2d at 212. *But cf* Nolechek v Gesuale, 46 NY2d 332, 385 NE2d 1268, 413 NYS2d 340, 343 (1978) (counterclaim allowed when dangerous instrumentality, a motorcycle, was involved).

Statutes

Most states regulate the possession and use of firearms.[389] Some states specifically prohibit parents from allowing their children to possess firearms.[390] In addition, unless there is an exception for parents,[391] the broad prohibition against furnishing firearms to a child[392] would be applicable to parents.

The violation of such statutes has been held to be negligence per se.[393] Accordingly, a mother who gave her 10-year-old boy an airgun, which was used by a friend of the boy to injure another child, was negligent.[394]

Vicarious Liability

In one state, parents are vicariously liable for their children's acts regarding firearms if the parent permitted the child to have the firearm or left it in a place which was accessible to the child.[395] In other states, parents are vicariously liable for the child's wilful acts.[396] The wilful shooting of firearms, including BBs, is covered by such statutes.[397]

§2.10 Fishing

Anglers have a duty to use reasonable care under the circumstances.[398]

---

389 *See generally* §2.10.

390 *See, e.g.,* Miss Code §97-37-13 (1973); Mont Code Ann §45-8-344 (1983) (except where the child is accompanied by a parent); NC Gen Stat §14-316 (1981) (except where there is parental supervision); ND Cent Code §62-04-03 (Supp 1984) (except where there is an adult present).

391 *See e.g.,* Ind Code Ann §35-47-7 (Burns Supp 1983); Mass Gen Laws Ann ch 140, §130 (West 1974); NH Rev Stat Ann §159:12 (1978); Vt Stat Ann tit 13, §407 (1974).

392 *See, e.g.,* Ala Code §13A-11-57 (1982); Conn Gen Stat §29-34 (1975); Ga Code Ann §16-11-101 (1982); Hawaii Rev Stat, tit 10, §134-4 (1968); Me Rev Stat Ann §17A:554 (1983); Miss Code §97-37-13 (1973); NJ Stat Ann §2C:58-3 (West Supp 1984); NC Gen Stat §14-316 (1981); ND Cent Code §62-01-11 (1960); Va Code §18.2-284 (1982) (toy firearm).

393 *See* Taylor v Webster, 12 Ohio St 2d 53, 231 NE2d 870, 872 (1967).

394 231 NE2d at 872.

395 Cal Civ Code §1714.3 (West Supp 1984) (liability for injury caused by discharge of firearm by person under 18 years imputed to parent if parent either permitted minor to have firearm or left firearm in a place accessible to child; however, maximum liability is $15,000 per person, $30,000 per occurrence).

396 *See, e.g.,* Colo Rev Stat §13-21-107(2) (Supp 1984); Conn Gen Stat Ann §52-572 (West Supp 1984); Ill Ann Stat ch 70, §53 (Smith-Hurd 1984); La Civ Code Ann art 237, 2318 (West 1979); NM Stat Ann §32-1-46 (Supp 1984); Ohio Rev Code Ann §3109.09 (1984); Tex Fam Code Ann §33.02 (Vernon Supp 1984).

397 Ortega v Montoya, 97 NM 159, 637 P2d 841, 843 (1981).

398 Rabiner v Rosenberg, 176 Misc 885, 28 NYS2d 533, 534 (1941).

When such care has been used, there is no liability.[399] For example, in *Rabiner v Rosenberg*,[400] as a fisherman was pulling a fish out of the water, the fish slipped off the hook causing the hook and line to which it was attached to snap back and the hook imbedded itself in the eye of a girl standing nearby. The court held that the fisherman was not negligent because there was no evidence that he committed an unreasonably dangerous act.[401] The risk of a fish hook going astray when suddenly pulled free cannot be eliminated in this sport.[402]

Several cases have discussed the applicability of the res ipsa loquitur doctrine.[403] In *Carrick v Pound*,[404] a fisherman fell and was injured when the driver of a boat pulled the throttle from fully open to closed because a swell appeared without warning creating a large trough. The court correctly refused to give a res ipsa loquitur jury instruction because such an accident can ordinarily occur in the absence of negligence.[405] The sea can move in sudden and unpredictable ways. Therefore, it was not more likely that the accident was caused by negligence than by the driver's reasonable reaction to changing conditions of the sea.[406]

In contrast, in *Hawayek v Simmons*,[407] the court held that the res ipsa loquitur doctrine was applicable. In that case a fisherman, while looking at the water, was struck in the eye with a fish hook from another fisherman in the boat. The plaintiff was unable to specify how the other fisherman had acted negligently because he was not looking at the defendant when the accident occurred. The court held that the res ipsa doctrine was applicable because it would not be expected in the case of an angler making an overhead-forward cast that the lure would take a lateral and horizontal tangent and strike another person, absent some negligence on his or her part.[408]

The federal government estimates that over 60,000 individuals each year who are injured while fishing require emergency room treatment. *See* US Consumer Prod Safety Commn, Natl Injury Information Clearinghouse, Prod Summary Report (Mar 28, 1984).

399 Rabiner v Rosenberg, 176 Misc 885, 28 NYS2d 533, 534 (1941).

400 *Id.*

401 *Id.*

402 *Id.*

403 Carrick v Pound, 276 Cal App 2d 689, 81 Cal Rptr 234 (1969); Hawayek v Simmons, 91 So 2d 49 (La Ct App 1956).

404 276 Cal App 2d 689, 81 Cal Rptr 234 (1969).

405 81 Cal Rptr at 236-37.

406 *Id.*

407 91 So 2d 49 (La Ct App 1956).

408 *Id* 52.

§2.11   Golf

General Duty of Care

Golfers, modern participants in the ancient game of Scottish kings, must exercise reasonable care under the circumstances for the safety of others.[409] A golfer must give adequate and timely notice to all persons, including caddies,[410] who appear to be unaware of his or her intention to hit the ball when he or she knows, or by the exercise of reasonable care should know, that such persons are sufficiently close to the reasonably foreseeable path of the ball that danger can reasonably be anticipated.[411] In addition, a golfer must use reasonable care to avoid having his or her club hit a person standing nearby.[412]

A player's violation of golfing rules may be evidence of negligence.[413] In *Duke's GMC, Inc v Erskine*,[414] a golfer was blinded in one eye after being struck by a golf ball hit by a golfer playing behind him. The trial court gave an instruction[415] which dealt with the assumption that people playing golf would observe the rules of that game. The appellate court found no error with this instruction, holding:

---

[409] Thomas v Shaw, 217 Ga 688, 124 SE2d 396, 397 (1962); Schmidt v Orton, 190 Neb 257, 207 NW2d 390, 392 (1973); Jackson v Livingston Country Club, Inc, 55 AD2d 1045, 391 NYS2d 234, 235 (1977); Wood v Postelthwaite, 6 Wash App 885, 496 P2d 988, 990 (1972). *See generally* Scalf & Robinson, *Injuries Arising Out Of Amateur And Professional Sports: Viability Of the Assumption Of Risk Defense*, 27 Def LJ 419, 433-34 (1978).

Children may be held to a lower standard of care than adults. *See* Gremillion v State Farm Mut Ins Co, 331 So 2d 130, 132-33 (La Ct App 1976); *but see* Neumann v Shlansky, 58 Misc 2d 128, 294 NYS2d 628, 635 (1968), *affd*, 63 Misc 2d 587, 312 NYS2d 951 (1970), *affd without opinion*, 36 AD2d 540, 318 NYS2d 925 (1971).

It is estimated that over 20,000 individuals injured each year playing golf require emergency room treatment. *See* US Consumer Prod Safety Commn, Natl Injury Information Clearinghouse, Prod Summary Report (Mar 28, 1984).

[410] Page v Unterreiner, 106 SW2d 528, 534 (Mo Ct App 1937); Toohey v Webster, 97 NJL 545, 117 A 838, 839 (1922).

[411] Boynton v Ryan, 257 F2d 70, 72 (3d Cir 1958); Miller v Rollings, 56 So 2d 137, 138 (Fla 1951); Schmidt v Orton, 190 Neb 257, 207 NW2d 390, 392 (1973); Page v Unterreiner, 106 SW2d 528, 534 (Mo Ct App 1937); Take v Orth, 395 SW2d 270, 274 (Mo Ct App 1965); Jackson v Livingston Country Club, Inc, 55 AD2d 1045, 391 NYS2d 234, 235 (1977); Jenks v McGranaghan, 30 NY2d 475, 285 NE2d 876, 334 NYS2d 641, 643 (1972); Wood v Postelthwaite, 6 Wash App 885, 496 P2d 988, 990 (1972).

A well-hit golf ball travels over 160 miles per hour at impact and can, therefore, cause significant damage. *See* Scalf & Robinson, *Injuries Arising Out Of Amateur And Professional Sports: Viability Of the Assumption Of Risk Defense*, 27 Def LJ 419, 433 (1978).

[412] Tannehill v Terry, 11 Utah 2d 368, 359 P2d 911, 912 (1961).

[413] *See generally* §2.01. A standard of care may also be supplied by golf organizations. *See generally* Take v Orth, 395 SW2d 270, 273 (Mo Ct App 1965).

[414] 447 NE2d 1118 (Ind Ct App 1983).

[415] Unfortunately, the court did not state the text of the instruction in its opinion.

The recognized rules of a sport are at least an indicia of the standard of care which the players owe each other. While a violation of those rules may not be negligence per se, it may well be evidence of negligence. Neither player in this instance was a novice golfer and both parties were aware of the rules and etiquette of the game. Yet there was evidence presented that [the defendant] violated one or more of those rules; the result of which was [the plaintiff's] injury. Therefore, [the plaintiff] was entitled to such an instruction. The instruction did not elevate the rules of golf to the level of law and neither does this court.[416]

Duty to Warn

A golfer's duty to warn extends only to those individuals who are located in an area where he or she will swing the club or where it is reasonably foreseeable that the ball will land; a golfer does not have a duty to warn everyone in the entire area of his or her play before making each shot.[417] In *Hoffman v Polsky*,[418] a golfer was entitled to a directed verdict when her errant ball hit another golfer who was standing in the rough and was not in the general direction of the drive or within the intended line of flight of the ball. The defendant did not see the plaintiff prior to taking this shot and, therefore, did not see anyone to warn. Furthermore, a reasonable person would not expect to see a golfer standing in the rough because golfers are not expected to remain there.[419] In contrast, a golfer intending to strike the ball would certainly have a duty to warn another golfer who was standing with his or her back toward the person addressing the ball.[420]

There are no fixed rules regarding the distance and angle which are considered within the ambit of foreseeable danger.[421] Of course, the poorer the player, the greater the zone of danger. However, at some point the plaintiff's location on the course is not within the danger zone, even if the golf ball ultimately hits him or her.[422] For example, a deviation of 90 degrees from

---

416 447 NE2d at 1124.

417 Walsh v Machlin, 128 Conn 412, 23 A2d 156, 157 (1941); Hoffman v Polsky, 386 SW2d 376, 378 (Mo 1965).

418 386 SW2d 376, 378 (Mo 1965).

419 *Id* 377; *see also* Mazzuchelli v Nissenbaum, 244 NE2d 729, 730 (Mass 1969).

420 Allen v Pinewood Country Club, Inc, 292 So 2d 786, 789 (La Ct App 1974); Take v Orth, 395 SW2d 270, 274-76 (Mo Ct App 1965); *see also* Brady v Kane, 111 So 2d 472, 474 (Fla Dist Ct App 1959) (negligent to take a practice swing when another golfer was addressing the ball).

421 *See* Hollinbeck v Downey, 261 Minn 481, 113 NW2d 9, 12 (1962).

422 Jenks v McGranaghan, 30 NY2d 475, 285 NE2d 876, 334 NYS2d 641, 644 (1972) (holding there was no negligence as a matter of law). When there was no undisputed evidence

the intended direction of the ball has been characterized as a *near impossibility* and, therefore, a golfer addressing the ball has no duty to warn a player standing at that angle from him or her.[423]

The duty to warn is not limited to the time before the shot is made. There may also be a duty to warn after the ball is hit when a golfer sees or should see another golfer in an area where the errant shot may land.[424]

The duty to warn is also not limited to shots on the course. If a player on a driving range knew, or in the exercise of reasonable care should have known, that the person *shagging* the balls was in a zone of danger and was unaware of the player's intention to drive the ball, the golfer should have given a warning or not driven the ball until the other person was in a safe place.[425]

The appropriate warning is usually the shouting of *fore* and then affording sufficient time for the individuals in the potential range of the golf ball to step aside far enough to avoid danger.[426] Yelling *fore* is inadequate if it does not provide sufficient time for the other golfers to avoid being hit.[427]

A golfer is not required to give a warning to another player known to have the golfer in view and known to be aware of the intention to drive the ball.[428] In that situation, the warning would be superfluous because the plaintiff would already have knowledge of the danger.[429]

In *Schmidt v Orton*,[430] the court had to determine liability when a plaintiff

---

of the relative angles between the golfer who hit the shot and the golfer who was injured, summary judgment was inappropriate. Boozer v Arizona Country Club, 102 Ariz 544, 434 P2d 630, 634 (1968).

[423] Boozer v Arizona Country Club, 102 Ariz 544, 434 P2d 630, 633 (1968) (the court further stated in dicta that in such a case a directed verdict would be justified and if the facts were undisputed, even a summary judgment might be proper); *see also* Oakes v Chapman, 158 Cal 2d 178, 322 P2d 241 (1958); Walsh v Machlin, 128 Conn 412, 23 A2d 156, 156 (1941).

The fact that there are several reported cases involving golf balls which landed 90 degrees from their intended location is some evidence that this degree of deviation is not so rare as to preclude a duty to warn.

[424] *See* Thomas v Shaw, 217 Ga 688, 124 SE2d 396, 397-98 (1962).

[425] Hollinbeck v Downey, 261 Minn 481, 113 NW2d 9, 12-13 (1962).

[426] Allen v Pinewood Country Club, Inc, 292 So 2d 786, 789 (La Ct App 1974); Jackson v Livingston Country Club, Inc, 55 AD2d 1045, 391 NYS2d 234, 235 (1977); Jenks v McGranaghan, 30 NY2d 475, 285 NE2d 876, 334 NYS2d 641, 643 (1972).

[427] Schmidt v Orton, 190 Neb 257, 207 NW2d 390, 391 (1973).

[428] Boynton v Ryan, 257 F2d 70, 72 (3d Cir 1958); Allen v Pinewood Country Club, Inc, 292 So 2d 786, 789 (La Ct App 1974) (dicta).

[429] Oakes v Chapman, 158 Cal 2d 178, 322 P2d 241, 244-45 (1958); Walsh v Machlin, 128 Conn 412, 23 A2d 156, 157 (1941); Stober v Embry, 243 Ky 117, 47 SW2d 921, 922 (1932).

[430] 190 Neb 257, 207 NW2d 390, 391-92 (1973).

was injured by a golfer in a foursome who played through his party of golfers. A golfer in the plaintiff's foursome was found negligent for telling a foursome behind his party to play through and then failing to warn the plaintiff that he was doing so, with the result that the plaintiff was hit in the eye by a ball driven by a golfer in the second foursome.[431] In addition, the golfer playing through a hole was found negligent in failing to warn a golfer in the party allowing him to play through of his intention to drive the ball.[432]

Other Duties of Care

The mere fact that a golf ball did not travel in its intended course is not proof that the golfer was negligent.[433] Even the best players cannot avoid an occasional hook or slice.[434] The court in *Page v Unterreiner* correctly noted:

> Golf is a game of exact precision, requiring perfect coordination of mind and body. It does not require an intimate knowledge of geometry to know that a slight deviation of the club head may send the ball from the tee at an unintended angle ... [Accordingly] to hold that golf player was negligent merely because the ball did not travel in a straight line ... would be imposing upon him a greater duty of care than the creator endowed him with faculties to carry out.[435]

Nonetheless, although there are no cases on point, it is certainly imaginable that a golfer would take so little preparation before hitting the ball, or address the ball so improperly, that his or her actions would be negligent.

A golfer may also be negligent for failing to watch the flight of the ball, but the fact that a golfer temporarily lost sight of the ball is not, standing alone, enough to prove he or she failed to keep a proper lookout.[436] Furthermore, a golfer cannot be expected to break his or her concentration while addressing

---

431 207 NW2d at 391-92.

432 *Id* 391.

433 Page v Unterreiner, 106 SW2d 528, 533 (Mo Ct App 1937). Jenks v McGranaghan, 30 NY2d 475, 285 NE2d 876, 334 NYS2d 641, 643 (1972).

434 *See* Boynton v Ryan, 257 F2d 70, 71 (3d Cir 1958) ("Even the best of golfers is sometimes painfully surprised to see a hoped for straight shot slice into the woods"); Jenks v McGranaghan, 30 NY2d 475, 285 NE2d 876, 334 NYS2d 641, 643 (1972); Nussbaum v Lacopo, 27 NY2d 311, 319, 265 NE2d 762, 317 NYS2d 347 (1970).

435 Page v Unterreiner, 106 SW2d 528, 533 (Mo Ct App 1937).

436 Barrett v Fritz, 98 Ill App 2d 75, 240 NE2d 366, 369 (1968). *affd on other grounds*, 92 Ill 2d 529, 248 NE2d 111 (1969).

the ball the instant before hitting in order to look up and see if someone has just stepped into the danger zone and, therefore, has no duty to do so.[437] However, a golfer may be negligent in taking a practice swing behind a fellow golfer without his or her knowledge at a time when it was not expected, e.g., when a third golfer was in the process of driving his ball from the tee.[438]

Children

An adult golfer owes a duty to a child golfer not to drive the ball in his or her direction.[439] This is because young children possess limited judgment and are likely at times to behave without thinking, oblivious to danger.[440] This is particularly true where the child is sufficiently close to the path of the ball so that after the ball is hit a warning to return to safety cannot be voiced and acted upon quickly enough to prevent an injury.[441] In one case, a child's crouching behind his own golf bag for protection was not sufficient protective behavior to allow the adult to drive the ball in that general area because it could be reasonably anticipated that the child would raise his head above the golf bag, an act which, unfortunately, happened.[442]

In *Neumann v Shlansky*, the court held an 11-year-old golfer whose shot injured another player to the same standard of care as a reasonable adult, and not the lower standard of care of a reasonable person of the same age, intelligence, and experience as the child.[443] Golf is an adult activity which involves the risk of serious injury, and an application of a lower standard of care "ignores the realities of the game."[444] Furthermore, it obviously makes little difference to the maimed plaintiff whether the defendant was an adult.[445] However, a different court held that the lower standard of care of a reasonable child should be applied.[446] In any

---

437 Jenks v McGranaghan, 30 NY2d 475, 285 NE2d 876, 334 NYS2d 641, 644 (1972).

438 Brady v Kane, 111 So 2d 472, 474 (Fla Dist Ct App 1959).

439 Outlaw v Bituminous Ins Co, 357 So 2d 1350, 1352 (La Ct App), *writ ref*, 359 So 2d 1293 (La 1978) (affirmed a $150,000 judgment for the minor).

440 *Id.*

441 *Id.*

442 *Id.*

443 58 Misc 2d 128, 294 NYS2d 628, 635 (County Ct 1968), *affd*, 63 Misc 2d 587, 312 NYS2d 951 (Sup Ct 1970), *affd without opinion*, 36 AD2d 540, 318 NYS2d 925 (1971). This case is analyzed in Comment, *Torts*, 20 Syracuse L Rev 823 (1969).

444 294 NYS2d at 634-35.

445 294 NYS2d at 633.

446 Gremillion v State Farm Mut Ins Co, 331 So 2d 130, 132-33 (La Ct App 1976) (plaintiff hit by golf club in back yard of residence; court held the child defendant was not liable as a matter of law).

event, if this issue is not raised in the trial court, it may not be raised on appeal.[447]

Parents

A parent who is aware, or by the exercise of reasonable care should be aware, of the danger of allowing a child to use a golf club and who fails to restrict or supervise the child in the use thereof may be liable for negligence to a person injured by the child's use of the golf club.[448] However, where a parent has no reason to anticipate that a child, through known dangerous proclivities or possession of a dangerous instrumentality, may cause harm, there is no parental liability even when the child acts negligently.[449] In one case, parents were granted summary judgment where their child took a golf club out of an unlocked storage building behind the house, swung it, and hit another child standing behind him. The court held that the parents were not liable because their son previously had not shown a dangerous proclivity to swing golf clubs in the presence of others and he was not given possession of a dangerous instrumentality.[450] In another case, there was no liability where a child used a golf putter to hit a deflated volleyball and the end of the putter broke and flew off, injuring a child standing nearby, because the parents had not acted negligently.[451]

A parent may also be liable to a young child for allowing him or her to play on a golf course and exposing the child to the risk of injury from the nonnegligent actions of other golfers.[452]

Golf Carts

Golf carts must be driven with reasonable care.[453] A passenger who fell out of a golf cart driven by another golfer could not recover when the driver was not negligent.[454] The plaintiff's description of the allegedly negligent turn

---

[447] *See* Kirchoffner v Quam, 264 NW2d 203, 207 (ND 1978).

[448] Patterson v Weatherspoon, 17 NC App 236, 193 SE2d 585, 587 (1972) (father gave son a golf putter and then left; son used the putter as a driver and during his follow-through the putter hit another child in the eye). Parents may also be vicariously liable for their children's torts under the family purpose doctrine. *See generally* **§2.01.**

[449] Muse v Ozment, 152 Ga App 896, 264 SE2d 328, 329 (1980); Poythress v Walls, 151 Ga App 176, 259 SE2d 177, 178 (1979).

[450] Muse v Ozment, 152 Ga App 896, 264 SW2d 328, 329 (1980).

[451] Poythress v Walls, 151 Ga App 176, 259 SE2d 177, 178 (1979).

[452] Outlaw v Bituminous Ins Co, 357 So 2d 1350, 1353 (La Ct App), *writ ref*, 359 So 2d 1293 (La 1978).

[453] *See generally* Miller v Robinson, 241 Md 335, 216 A2d 743 (1966).

[454] *Id.*

of the cart using the words *sharp* and *suddenly* was held to be weak evidence since it did not describe the accident with sufficient facts.[455]

In *Nepstad v Randall*, the court held that a motor-driven golf cart operated on a golf course was not a *motor vehicle* within the meaning of the motor vehicle guest statute.[456] The court held that the guest statute only applied to vehicles primarily designed for transportation on public highways.[457] Therefore, the driver of the golf cart was not given the benefit of the lower standard of care applicable under the guest statute.

Insurance

One court held that a golf cart is a motor vehicle designed for use principally off public roads and, therefore, is not a vehicle covered by an uninsured motorist provision of an automobile policy.[458] In addition, it held that such an exclusion did not violate any public policy.[459]

Miscellaneous

A golfer may be injured by a negligent act committed outside the golf course. For example, a motorist who carelessly parks a car on a hill while attending a golf tournament may be negligent when the car rolls down the hill and strikes a golfer.[460]

§2.12   Motorcycling

Motorcyclists must exercise that degree of care which a reasonable person would exercise under similar conditions.[461] For example, a motorcyclist who weaved his vehicle around automobiles stopped in the travel lanes and violated city and state traffic regulations was negligent when an accident occurred.[462]

---

455 216 A2d at 745. This analysis is questionable since it is common for individuals to describe turns as *sharp* and *sudden* rather than by stating the degree of the turn or the seconds of time which elapsed. Furthermore, a defendant is not unduly prejudiced by such a description of events by the plaintiff because cross-examination could test the plaintiff's memory of the details and the fact-finder could assess the plaintiff's credibility.

456 82 SD 615, 152 NW2d 383, 386 (1967).

457 152 NW2d at 385.

458 Chase v State Farm Mut Auto Ins Co, 131 Ariz 461, 641 P2d 1305, 1310 (Ct App 1982).

459 641 P2d at 1312.

460 Greeser v Taylor, 276 Minn 440, 150 NW2d 869, 874 (1967).

461 Williams v Wachovia Bank & Trust Co, 292 NC 416, 233 SE2d 589, 593 (1977).

It is estimated that over 35,000 individuals injured on mopeds each year require emergency room treatment. *See* US Consumer Prod Safety Commn, Natl Injury Information Clearinghouse, Prod Summary Report (Mar 28, 1984).

462 White v Nicosia, 351 So 2d 234, 236 (La Ct App 1977).

Where small children are present the motorcyclist must take additional care because children have less capacity to avoid danger than adults.[463] This is true whether the children are on a public street or private property.[464] In one case,[465] a motorcyclist hit a three-year-old child who ran out in front of him while he was riding on the property of the child's parents. The cyclist was found negligent for failing to keep a proper lookout and for driving faster than reasonable when children could be expected to be present.[466]

Minors

Numerous courts have held that minors who operate motorcycles,[467] motorbikes or motorscooters,[468] or dirt bikes[469] are held to the adult standard of care of a reasonable person, not the lower standard of care of a minor of a similar age in similar circumstances. Minors are entitled to be judged by a standard commensurate with their age, experience, and wisdom only when they are engaged in activities appropriate for their age, experience, and wisdom; and riding a motorcycle is not such an activity.[470]

When a minor causes a motorcycle accident, there is an increased risk that the injured plaintiff may not be fairly compensated because the minor does not possess sufficient financial strength. Some courts have attempted to remedy this problem by invoking the family purpose doctrine.[471] This doctrine

---

463 Williams v Wachovia Bank & Trust Co, 292 NC 416, 233 SE2d 589, 593 (1977).

464 *Id.*

465 *Id.*

466 *Id.*

467 Harrelson v Whitehead, 236 Ark 325, 365 SW2d 868, 869 (1963); Prichard v Veterans Cab Co, 66 Cal 2d 727, 408 P2d 360, 47 Cal Rptr 904, 907 (1965); McNaill v Farmers Ins Group, 181 Ind App 501, 392 NE2d 520, 527 (1979), *transfer denied*, 423 NE2d 593 (Ind 1981); Williams v Esaw, 214 Kan 658, 522 P2d 950, 959 (1974); Daniels v Evans, 107 NH 407, 224 A2d 63, 66 (1966). *See also* Restatement (Second) of Torts §283A comment c (1965) (a child who engages in an activity normally undertaken only by adults and for which adult qualifications are needed may be held to the standard of an adult).

468 Medina v McAllister, 202 So 2d 755, 757 (Fla 1967); Sheetz v Welch, 89 Ga App 749, 81 SE2d 319, 324 (1954); Perricone v DiBartolo, 14 Ill App 3d 514, 302 NE2d 637, 641 (1973); Adams v Lopez, 75 NM 503, 407 P2d 50, 52 (1965); Powell v Hartford Accident & Indem Co, 217 Tenn 503, 398 SW2d 727, 733 (1966). *But see* Hemmelgarn v Bailey, 61 Ohio L Abs 179, 104 NE2d 50, 52 (1950).

469 Demeri v Morris, 194 NJ Super 554, 477 A2d 426, 429 (1983) (driven on public road).

470 Daniels v Evans, 107 NH 407, 224 A2d 63, 64 (1966).

471 Williams v Wachovia Bank & Trust Co, 292 NC 416, 233 SE2d 589, 592 (1977); Meinhardt v Vaughn, 159 Tenn 272, 17 SW2d 5, 6-7 (1929). *See also* Peck, *The Role Of The Courts And Legislatures In The Reform Of Tort Law*, 48 Minn L Rev 265, 303 (1963) (family purpose doctrine should be extended to include motorcycles).

imposes liability upon the owner or person with ultimate control of a vehicle for its negligent operation by another when:

1. The operator was a member of the family or household and was living in his or her home
2. The vehicle was owned, provided, and maintained for the general use, pleasure, and convenience of the family
3. The vehicle was being so used by a member of the family at the time of the accident and with the owner's express or implied consent[472]

Although this doctrine originally applied only to automobile accidents, several courts have now also applied it in motorcycle accident cases.[473] It has been applied where the motorcycle accident occurred on private property.[474]

Guest Statutes

Passengers injured on a motorcycle may have their recovery against the operator of the motorcycle limited by state motor vehicle guest statutes.[475] In addition, in *Hately v Hamilton*, the court held that the parent of the operator of the motorcycle is not liable to an injured party under the family purpose doctrine if the operator would not be liable under the state guest statute.[476]

Causation

The plaintiff cannot recover from the defendant unless the defendant's negligence was the proximate cause of injury.[477] For example, when a motorcyclist exchanged motorcycles with a friend and was killed shortly thereafter, the decedent's estate could not recover against the other cyclist who was a party to the motorcycle exchange because the fatal injury would have occurred on either motorcycle. The other party's actions in making the exchange bore no causal relationship to the accident.[478]

One court held that the parents of a motorcyclist were not liable, as a

---

[472] Williams v Wachovia Bank & Trust Co, 292 NC 416, 233 SE2d 589, 592 (1977).

[473] *See id*; Menhardt v Vaughn, 159 Tenn 272, 17 SW2d 5, 6-7 (1929). *See also* Peck, *The Role Of The Courts And Legislatures In The Reform Of Tort Law*, 48 Minn L Rev 265, 303 (1963) (family purpose doctrine should be extended to include motorcycles).

[474] *See* Williams v Wachovia Bank & Trust Co, 292 NC 416, 233 SE2d 589, 593 (1977).

[475] *See* Hately v Hamilton, 81 NM 774, 473 P2d 913, 914 (App), *cert denied*, 81 NM 773, 473 P2d 912 (1970).

[476] 81 NM 774, 473 P2d 913, 916 (Ct App), *cert denied*, 81 NM 773, 473 P2d 912 (1970).

[477] *See* Restatement (Second) of Torts §430 (1965).

[478] Nolechek v Gesuale, 46 NY2d 332, 385 NE2d 1268, 413 NYS2d 340, 346 (1978).

matter of law, to a passenger injured on their son's motorcycle, for their negligent entrustment of the motorcycle to their son.[479] In that case, the motorcycle the parents gave to their child had more horsepower than was allowed by statute. The court reasoned that the parents could be liable only if two inferences were accepted, viz., (1) the child's failure to exercise control of the motorcycle could be inferred from the skid marks on the road, and (2) the parents' knowledge of the risk that their child would be unable to control the motorcycle could be inferred from the cycle's illegal horsepower. The court concluded that basing an inference on an inference is incorrect and affirmed a summary judgment in favor of the parents.[480] The court's conclusion that the parents were not negligent may have been correct, although this is certainly not obvious. However, its reasoning is flawed. There is nothing wrong with basing an inference on an inference.

§2.13   —Insurance

Both automobile and homeowners' insurance policies may provide coverage for motorcycle accidents. Several courts have held that a motorcycle is not an *automobile*, for purposes of such insurance policies,[481] although there is authority to the contrary.[482] Indeed, one court held that a moped was an automobile under the terms of an insurance policy.[483]

It is important to distinguish the cases which hold that a motorcycle accident is a covered automobile risk under an insurance policy, a construction which affords more insurance, and cases in which a motorcycle is not an automobile for purposes of interpreting an exclusion of coverage, a construction which also affords more insurance. If an insurance policy ambiguously defines automobile, both interpretations are possible because ambiguities in an insurance policy are generally construed against the insurance company,[484] the party which drafted the policy and created the ambiguity. For example, in one case an automobile policy provided that it did not cover an insured while the insured was driving an automobile other than the insured automobile. The court

---

479 Hately v Hamilton, 81 NM 774, 473 P2d 913, 916 (Ct App), *cert denied*, 81 NM 773, 473 P2d 912 (1970).

480 *Id.*

481 State Farm Mut Auto Ins Co v Christian, 555 SW2d 571, 572 (Ky 1977); Agricultural Workers Mut Auto Ins Co v Baty, 517 SW2d 901, 903 (Tex Civ App 1974).

It is not illegal to exclude motorcycles from insurance coverage. *See* State Farm Mut Auto Ins Co v Christian, 555 SW2d 571, 573 (Ky 1977).

482 State Farm Mut Auto Ins Co v Drysdale, 81 AD2d 1011, 440 NYS2d 94, 95 (1981).

483 *See* Royal-Globe Ins Co v Schultz, 385 Mass 1013, 434 NE2d 213, 214 (1982).

484 State Farm Mut Auto Ins Co v Partridge, 10 Cal 3d 94, 514 P2d 123, 109 Cal Rptr 811, 816 (1973).

construed this provision strictly and held that although there was no coverage while the insured was driving another automobile, he was covered when he was injured on a motorcycle.[485]

A motorcyclist injured by an uninsured automobile may recover under an insurance policy on his or her automobile which provides for uninsured motorist coverage.[486] Indeed, several courts have held that there was insurance coverage for a motorcycle accident where the claimant was injured on a motorcycle, a vehicle that was not insured, when the accident was with an uninsured motorist and there was uninsured motorist coverage on an automobile.[487] These courts reasoned that the injured party was an *insured* under an automobile policy because the policy defined insured as the named insured and all residents of the named insured's household. As long as the plaintiff lived with the named insured and the named insured had an automobile policy with an uninsured motorist provision, the injured party was an insured and could recover under the uninsured motorist provision of such policies.

Some courts have held that there is coverage for motorcycle accidents even where no such coverage was provided in the policy. One court held that where an automobile policy did not explicitly contain an uninsured motorist provision, such a provision would be read into the policy because state law required such coverage.[488] A different court held that an exclusion for coverage for uninsured motorists for motorcycle accidents is contrary to public policy and, therefore, would not be applicable.[489]

Of course, under no circumstances can an injured cyclist recover under an uninsured motorist provision where the vehicle causing the accident was insured.[490]

A motorcyclist hit by an uninsured party should ascertain whether *stacking* of coverage is possible.[491] Stacking occurs when the injured party is an insured,

---

485 St Charles v Allstate Ins Co, 115 Ariz 407, 565 P2d 913, 915 (Ct App 1977); *but cf* Summit Ins Co v Beach, 80 Misc 2d 382, 363 NYS2d 210, 212-13 (1974) (a policy defined insured as the named insured and also other individuals driving the named insured's automobile; this policy was construed not to cover individuals who drove the named insured's motorcycle).

486 Boucher v Employers Mut Casualty Co, 121 NH 524, 431 A2d 137, 138 (1981).

487 Bradley v Mid-Century Co, 78 Mich App 67, 259 NW2d 378, 381 (1977), *affd*, 409 Mich 1, 294 NW2d 141 (1980); *see also* Griffin v Armond, 358 So 2d 647, 648-49 (La Ct App 1978); Agricultural Workers Mut Auto Ins Co v Baty, 517 SW2d 901, 904 (Tex Civ App 1974); *see generally* Annot, 28 ALR4th 362 (1984).

488 Citrano v Berkshire Mut Ins Co, 171 Conn 248, 368 A2d 54, 57 (1976). *But see* Boucher v Employers Mut Casualty Co, 121 NH 524, 431 A2d 137, 138 (1981) (partial exclusion for accidents caused by uninsured motorists is not invalid).

489 Clarke v Sharshan, 355 So 2d 1333, 1334-35 (La Ct App 1977).

490 Turcotte v Foremost Ins Co, 460 A2d 1369, 1370-71 (Me 1983).

491 *See generally* Hoffman, *Stacking Uninsured Motorist Coverage*, 26 For Def 3 (Nov 1984).

for purposes of uninsured motorist coverage, for two or more vehicles and the uninsured motorist coverage for both vehicles is considered available for compensation.[492]

Several courts have held that a passenger on a motorcycle hit by an uninsured vehicle could stack uninsured motorist benefits under the automobile insurance policy covering multiple vehicles.[493] This is true even if the claimant did not pay any of the premiums of the insurance policy on the vehicles, as long as he or she is an insured under the policy,[494] a result which can occur if the claimant resides with the named insured. For example, an insured who paid premiums for coverage on two automobiles, each with uninsured motorist coverage of $15,000, was entitled to coverage of $30,000 when he was injured on a motorcycle by an uninsured motorist.[495]

Several injured motorcyclists have argued that an insurance policy provision which excluded coverage for injuries arising out of a motorcycle accident were not applicable because there were multiple causes of the accident, one of which was not excluded from coverage. In *Daggs v Foremost Insurance Co*,[496] the plaintiff, while participating in a motocross motorcycle race, collided with a chain-link barrier fence and was injured. He sued the operator of the race course and as part of the settlement of that claim received an assignment of the operator's claim against its insurance carrier for coverage. The insurance policy specifically excluded liability for injuries arising out of a race. The plaintiff argued that there was an act of negligence which was not excluded, viz., the negligent design and construction of the chain-link fence. The court, however, rejected this argument, holding that the injury solely arose out of an excluded risk, the race.[497]

Similarly, in *Safeco Insurance Co v Gilstrap*,[498] the court held that a home-owners' insurance policy which excluded coverage for damages arising out of the *ownership, maintenance, operation, use, loading or unloading... of any motor vehicle* excluded coverage for a motorcycle accident. The plaintiff, a passenger injured on a motorcycle driven by a minor, argued that the exclusion was not applicable because he sued the driver's parents for their negligent entrustment

---

492 Federated Am Ins Co v Raynes, 88 Wash 2d 439, 563 P2d 815, 820 (1977).

493 *See*, e.g., Brister v American Indem Co, 313 So 2d 355, 337-38 (La Ct App 1975); Estate of Rosato v Harleysville Mut Ins Co, 328 Pa Sup 278, 476 A2d 1328, 1331 (1984); Federated Am Ins Co v Raynes, 88 Wash 2d 439, 563 P2d 815, 820 (1977); *but see* Providence Wash Ins Co v Rosato, 328 Pa Super 290, 476 A2d 1334, 1339 (1984) (cannot stack under garage fleet insurance policy).

494 Estate of Rosato v Harleysville Mut Ins Co, 328 Pa Super 278, 476 A2d 1328, 1333 (1984).

495 Federated Am Ins Co v Raynes, 88 Was 2d 439, 563 P2d 815, 820 (1977).

496 148 Cal App 3d 726, 196 Cal Rptr 193 (1983).

497 196 Cal Rptr at 196.

498 141 Cal App 3d 524, 190 Cal Rptr 425 (1983).

of the motorcycle to their child, a nonexcluded risk. The court held, however, that where there was a specific exclusion in the policy regarding an instrumentality, viz., a motor vehicle, there was no coverage on any claim based on negligent entrustment of that instrumentality.[499]

In some situations, a motorcycle injury is caused, in part, by a nonexcluded risk and, in those cases, there is insurance coverage. One homeowners' insurance policy excluded coverage for injuries arising out of an automobile accident. This policy was held to cover an accident where a motorcycle was hit by a car and, after the accident, the motorist dragged the cyclist from the street in a manner which aggravated her injuries.[500] The dragging of a cyclist was an independent act unrelated to the use of the vehicle and, therefore, it was covered under the motorist's homeowners' policy.[501]

A father's insurance policy can be *excess* when a son is injured on a motorcycle covered by a policy which has an uninsured motorist provision.[502] In one case, an automobile insurance policy which stated that it was *excess insurance*, and provided coverage only in the amount by which the liability limit in the policy exceeded the liability limit in the primary policy, did not provide coverage where the liability limits in the two policies were the same.[503]

In one case an insurance company was not liable when it was notified by the insured of the motorcycle accident over 200 days after the accident occurred because such notice was not "as soon as practicable."[504]

§2.14 Snowmobiling

There are over two million snowmobiles in operation in the United States.[505] Tragically, it is estimated that there are over 10,000 snowmobile accidents,[506]

---

499 190 Cal Rptr at 431.

500 State Farm Fire & Casualty Co v Kohl, 131 Cal App 3d 1031, 182 Cal Rptr 720 (1982).

501 182 Cal Rptr at 723.

502 Country-Wide Ins Co v Wagoner, 45 NY2d 581, 384 NE2d 653, 412 NYS2d 106, 108-09 (1978).

503 State Farm Mut Auto Ins Co v Drysdale, 81 AD2d 1011, 440 NYS2d 94, 95 (1981).

504 Summit Ins Co v Beach, 80 Misc 2d 382, 363 NYS2d 210, 213 (1974).

505 Robinson v Lindsay, 20 Wash App 207, 579 P2d 398 (1978), *affd*, 92 Wash 2d 410, 598 P2d 392, 394 (1979); *see generally* Reel, *Dashing Through The Snow: Oregon And The Open Sleigh*, 3 Env L 74 (1973) (discusses the growth of the snowmobile industry); *see generally* Bardenwerper, *Snowmobile Litigation And Insurance Coverage*, 13 For Def 29 (1972).

506 US Consumer Prod Safety Commn, Natl Injury Information Clearinghouse, Product Summary Report (Mar 28, 1984).

One commentator concluded, apparently without any empirical support, that many snowmobile accidents are caused by an operator's prior drinking of alcohol. *See* Comment, *Snowmobiles — A Legislative Program*, 1972 Wis L Rev 477, 490.

One study showed that many snowmobiles failed to absorb a significant percentage of

resulting in hundreds of casualties,[507] each year. The incidence of accidents is particularly high among inexperienced operators.[508]

Snowmobilers must act with reasonable care.[509] For example, a snowmobile operator who jumped an artificial snowbank or hump, causing an injury, rather than avoiding the obstacle, was negligent.[510] One court, however, assumed that a state motor vehicle guest statute applied to snowmobiles and, therefore, there was liability only for gross negligence.[511]

Children who operate snowmobiles are not entitled to be judged by the lower standard of care of a similar child of the same age and experience; the adult standard of care applies.[512] In *Robinson v Lindsay*,[513] a child's thumb was severed[514] when it was caught in a tow rope between an inner tube and a snowmobile. The court held that a child's actions in operating a snowmobile should be judged by the adult standard of reasonable care, and not the lower standard of a child of the same age, intelligence, and experience, because snowmobiling is an inherently dangerous activity and an adult standard of care is necessary for anyone who operates a snowmobile.[515] Application of a child standard to children engaging in childlike acts protects them from liability where the danger of injury to others is not great. However, where the risk of injury is great because the activity is inherently dangerous, it is important to protect individuals who may be harmed and, therefore, an adult standard of care is appropriate.[516]

Insurance

The courts are not in agreement regarding whether a snowmobile is an

---

the gravitational forces which result from a four-foot drop. *See* Comment, *Snowmobiles—A Legislative Program*, 1972 Wis L Rev 477, 486-87.

507 598 P2d at 394.

One study concluded that the major cause of death in snowmobile accidents was from head injuries. *See* Comment, *Snowmobiles—A Legislative Program*, 1972 Wis L Rev 477, 484 & n 30. Indeed, wearing a helmet significantly reduces the probability of sustaining a head injury. *See id & n 31.*

508 598 P2d at 394.

509 *See* Robinson v Lindsay, 92 Wash 2d 410, 598 P2d 392, 393-94 (1979).

510 Ujifusa v National Housewares, Inc, 24 Utah 2d 219, 469 P2d 7, 8 (1970) (plaintiff was a business invitee of defendant).

511 Shockey v Shields, 272 Or 226, 536 P2d 424, 425 (1975).

512 Robinson v Lindsay, 92 Wash 2d 410, 598 P2d 392, 393 (1979); *see generally* §2.01.

513 Robinson v Lindsay, 92 Wash 2d 410, 598 P2d 392, 393 (1979).

514 Fortunately, the thumb was reattached, but the plaintiff did not regain full use of it. *See* 20 Wash App 207, 579 P2d 398, 399 (1978), *affd*, 92 Wash 2d 410, 598 P2d 392, 392 (1979).

515 598 P2d at 393. The giving of an erroneous standard of care jury instruction is inherently prejudicial. *See* 579 P2d at 401.

516 598 P2d at 394.

automobile under an automobile insurance policy. When a plaintiff is struck by an uninsured person operating a snowmobile on a highway, the plaintiff's uninsured motorist provision in his or her automobile coverage is sometimes applicable,[517] although there is authority to the contrary.[518] One court held that a passenger on a snowmobile who was injured in a collision with another snowmobile off the road was not entitled to recover under the uninsured motorist provision of an automobile policy.[519]

Statutes

Many states have enacted legislation regulating snowmobiles and snow vehicles.[520] A common requirement is that snowmobiles be registered.[521] It is also not unusual to find that snowmobiles must contain certain specified equipment,[522] e.g., brakes, at least one head lamp, a hand throttle,[523] and red

---

[517] *See* Rooney v Detroit Auto Inter-insurance Exch, 94 Mich App 448, 288 NW2d 445, 447 (1979); Oberstar v State Farm Mut Auto Ins Co, 222 NW2d 557, 559 (Minn 1974); *see generally* Gallo v JC Penney Casualty Co 328 Pa Super 267, 476 A2d 1322, 1325 (1984).

One court held that a snowmobile was a *motor vehicle* for purposes of a criminal statute making it illegal to operate a motor vehicle without proper safety equipment. *See* State v Carkhuff, 26 Ohio Misc 216, 270 NE2d 379, 380 (1971).

[518] Stepec v Farmers Ins Co, 301 Minn 434, 222 NW2d 796, 798 (1974).

[519] Detroit Auto Inter-insurance Exch v Spafford, 76 Mich App 85, 255 NW2d 780, 782 (1977).

[520] *See* Alaska Stat §§05.30.010-.020 (1983); Colo Rev Stat §33-7-101 to -120 (Supp 1984); Conn Gen Stat Ann §§14-379 to -390 (West Supp 1984); Idaho Code §§49-2601 to -2615 (Supp 1983); Ill Ann Stat ch 95½, §603-1 to -611 (Smith-Hurd Supp 1983); Ind Stat Ann §§14-1-3-1 to -18 (Burns Supp 1983); Mass Gen Laws Ann ch 90B, §§20-35 (West Supp 1983); Mich Comp Laws Ann §§257.1501 to -.1518 (West Supp 1983); Mont Code Ann §§23-2-601 to -644 (1983); Neb Rev Stat Ann §§60-2001 to -2023 (1977); NM Stat Ann §§66-9-1 to -7 (Supp 1983); NY Parks, Rec & Hist Pres Law §§21.01-25.29 (McKinney 1984); ND Cent Code §§39-24-01 to -11 (Supp 1983); Or Rev Stat §§481.770-.810, 483.710-.775 (1981); Pa Cons Stat Ann ch 77, §§770-7753 (Purdon 1977); Vt Stat Ann tit 31, §§801-813 (Supp 1983); Wash Rev Code Ann §§46.10.010-.910 (Supp 1983); Wis Stat Ann §§350.01-.13 (West Supp 1983); *see also* 36 CFR §2.34 (in national parks).

One commentator suggested a model snowmobile statute. *See* Comment, *Snowmobiles—A Legislative Program,* 1972 Wis L Rev 477, 505.

[521] *See* Alaska Stat §05.30.010 (1983); Colo Rev Stat §33-7-102 (Supp 1984); Conn Gen Stat Ann §14-380 (West Supp 1984); Idaho Code §49-2604 (1980); Ill Stat Ann ch 95½, §603-1 (Smith-Hurd Supp 1983); Ind Stat Ann §14-1-3-2 (Burns Supp 1983); Mich Comp Law Ann §257.1503 (West Supp 1983); Mont Code Ann §23-2-611 (1983); Neb Rev Stat Ann §60-2002 (1977); NM Stat Ann §66-9-3 (Supp 1983); ND Cent Code §39-24-03 (Supp 1983); Or Rev Stat §481.775 (1981); Pa Cons Stat Ann §7713 (Purdon 1977); Vt Stat Ann tit 31, §802 (Supp 1983); Wash Rev Code Ann §46.10.020 (Supp 1983); Wis Stat Ann §350.12 (1971). *See also* 36 CFR §2.34(b) (in national parks).

[522] *See* Alaska Stat §05.30.080 (1983); Colo Rev Stat §33-7-113 (1974); Idaho Code §49-2611 (1980); Ill Stat Ann ch 95½, §604-1 (Smith-Hurd Supp 1983); Ind Code Ann §§14-1-3.5-13 (Burns Supp 1983); Mass Gen Laws Ann ch 90B, §24 (West Supp 1983); Mich Comp Laws Ann §257.1513 (West Supp 1983); NM Stat Ann §66-9-9 (Supp 1983);

rear reflectors.[524] In at least one state everyone riding in a snowmobile must wear protective headgear.[525]

It is illegal to operate a snowmobile in a manner which endangers persons or property[526] or in a careless or negligent manner.[527] It is also illegal to operate a snowmobile while under the influence of liquor or drugs.[528] In some states, an owner or any other person having control of a snowmobile is prohibited from allowing a person to operate the snowmobile unless the operator is capable of doing so.[529] In addition, there are usually minimum age requirements to operate a snowmobile,[530] although one state does not have such a requirement except for driving in certain areas.[531]

NY Parks, Rec & Hist Pres Law §25.17 (McKinney 1984); ND Cent Code §39-24-09 (1972); Or Rev Stat §483.730 (1981); Pa Cons Stat Ann §7741 (Purdon 1977); Vt Stat Ann tit 31, §805 (Supp 1983); Wash Rev Code Ann §46.10.090 (Supp 1983); Wis Stat Ann §350.09 (1971).

[523] See Alaska Stat §05.30.080 (1983).

[524] See Mass Gen Laws Ann ch 90B, §24 (West Supp 1983).

[525] See Mass Gen Laws Ann ch 90B, §26 (West Supp 1983); see also NJ Admin Code tit 13, §22-8.2 (1984).

[526] See Mass Gen Laws Ann ch 90B, §26 (West Supp 1983).

[527] See Colo Rev Stat §33-7-115; Conn Gen Stat Ann §14-386a (West Supp 1984); Idaho Code §49-2611 (1980); Ill Stat Ann ch 95½, §605-1 (Smith-Hurd Supp 1983); Mont Code Ann §23-2-632 (1983); Neb Rev Stat Ann §60-2015 (1977); NM Stat Ann §66-9-9 (Supp 1983); ND Cent Code §39-24-09 (1972); Or Rev Stat §483.730 (1981); Pa Cons Stat Ann §7726 (Purdon 1977); Wis Stat Ann §350.10 (1971). See generally Mich Comp Laws Ann §257.1515 (West Supp 1983) (at an unreasonable speed); Wash Rev Code Ann §46.10.090 (Supp 1983) (at an unreasonable speed); 36 CFR §2.34(g) (in national parks).

[528] See Colo Rev Stat §33-7-115 (Supp 1974); Conn Gen Stat Ann §14-386a (West Supp 1984); Idaho Code §49-2611 (1980); Ill Stat Ann ch 95½, §605-1 (Smith-Hurd Supp 1983); Ind Code Ann §14-1-3.5-15 (Burns Supp 1983); Mass Gen Laws Ann ch 90B, §26 (West Supp 1983); Mich Comp Laws Ann §257.1515 (West Supp 1983); Mont Code Ann §23-2-632 (1983); Neb Rev Stat §60-2015 (1977); NM Stat Ann §66-9-8 (Supp 1983); NY Parks, Rec & Hist Pres Law §25.03 (McKinney 1984); Pa Cons Stat Ann §7726 (Purdon 1977); Wis Stat Ann §350.10 (West 1981).

[529] See Or Rev Stat §483.710 (1981); Pa Cons Stat Ann §7726 (Purdon 1977); Wis Stat Ann §350.08 (West 1971).

[530] See Colo Rev Stat §33-7-108 (1974) (10 years unless accompanied by an older person); Ill Stat Ann ch 95½, §605-3 (Smith-Hurd Supp 1983) (10 years); Ind Code Ann §14-1-3.5-12 (Burns Supp 1983) (14 years unless supervised by an adult); Mass Gen Laws Ann ch 90B, §26 (West Supp 1983) (14 years); Mich Comp Laws Ann §257.1512a (West Supp 1983) (12 years unless accompanied by adult); Neb Rev Stat Ann §60-2018 (1977) (12 years unless accompanied by an adult); NY Parks, Rec & His Pres Law §25.19 (McKinney 1984) (10 years unless accompanied by an older person or child-operator has obtained a safety certificate); ND Cent Code §39-24-09.1 (Supp 1983) (12 years); Or Rev Stat §483.725 (1981) (has an operator's license or has a certificate); Pa Cons Stat Ann §7725 (Purdon 1977) (10 years); Wash Rev Code Ann §46.10.120 (Supp 1983) (12 years); see also 36 CFR §2.34(e) (in national parks).

[531] See Wis Stat Ann §350.05 (West Supp 1984).

An operator of a snowmobile involved in an accident must render as much assistance to the injured parties as may be practicable to minimize their injuries.[532] In addition, a snowmobiler involved in an accident resulting in personal or property damage must quickly report the accident to the proper authorities.[533] In a few states the accident must be reported by the "quickest means of communication".[534] In at lease one state, these accident reports are not admissible at trial.[535]

In some states the snowmobile owner is liable for the operator's negligence when the snowmobile was operated with the owner's permission, whether the permission was express or implied.[536] In one state the owner and operator are jointly and severally liable for any damage caused by the operation of a snowmobile.[537] In another state the owner of a snowmobile must have insurance or comply with the applicable self-insurance provisions.[538]

Many states restrict the use of snowmobiles on public streets.[539]

§2.15 Snow Skiing

A skier must exercise reasonable care to avoid injuring fellow skiers.[540]

---

532 *See* Ill Stat Ann ch 95½, §606-1 (Smith-Hurd Supp 1983); Vt Stat Ann tit 31, §811 (Supp 1983).

533 *See* Alaska Stat §05.30.100 (1983); Idaho Code §49-2613 (1980); Ill Stat Ann ch 95½, §606-1 (Smith-Hurd Supp 1983); Mass Gen Laws Ann ch 90B, §27 (West Supp 1983); Mont Code Ann §23-2-635 (1983); Neb Rev Stat Ann §60-2023 (1977); NM Stat Ann §66-9-11 (Supp 1983); NY Parks, Rec & Hist Pres Law §25.25 (McKinney 1984); Or Rev Stat §483.745 (1981); Pa Cons Stat Ann §7728 (Purdon 1977); Vt Stat Ann tit 31, §811 (Supp 1983); Wash Rev Code Ann §46.10.140 (Supp 1983).

534 *See* Alaska Stat §05.30.100 (1983); Colo Rev Stat §33-7-114 (1974); Ind Code Ann §14-1-3.5-16 (Burns Supp 1983); Mich Comp Laws Ann §257.1516 (West 1977).

535 *See* Ill Stat Ann ch 95½, §606-1 (Smith-Hurd Supp 1983).

536 *See* NY Parks, Rec & His Pres Law §25.23 (McKinney 1984); Pa Cons Stat Ann §7729 (Purdon 1977).

537 *See* Ill Stat Ann ch 95½, §606-2 (Smith-Hurd Supp 1983).

538 *See* NY Parks, Rec & Hist Pres Law §25.13 (McKinney 1984).

539 *See* Colo Rev Stat §33-7-109 (1974); Conn Gen Stat Ann §14-387 (West Supp 1984); Idaho Code §49-2610 (1980); Ill Stat Ann ch 95½, §605-2 (Smith-Hurd Supp 1983); Ind Code Ann §§14-1-3-11, 14-1-3.5-12 (Burns Supp 1983); Mass Gen Laws Ann ch 90B, §25 (West Supp 1983); Mont Code Ann §23-2-631 (1983); Neb Rev Stat Ann §60-2013 (1977); NM Stat Ann §66-9-9 (Supp 1983); ND Cent Code §39-24-09 (1972); NY Parks, Rec & Hist Pres Law §25.05 (McKinney 1984); Or Rev Stat §483.740 (1981); Pa Cons Stat Ann §7721 (Purdon 1977); Vt Stat Ann tit 31, §806 (Supp 1983); Wash Rev Code Ann §46.10.110 (Supp 1983); Wis Stat Ann §§350.02, .03 (West Supp 1983).

540 *See generally* Ninio v Hight, 385 F2d 350, 352 (10th Cir 1967) (Colorado law).

It is estimated that over 40,000 individuals injured while skiing require emergency room treatment each year. US Consumer Prod Safety Commn, Natl Injury Information Clearinghouse, Prod Summary Report (Mar 28, 1984).

For example, a skier has a duty to look for dangerous conditions and will be presumed, in case of an accident, to have looked where he or she was supposed to look and to have seen what one could reasonably be expected to see; failure to look and to see what reasonably could and should have been seen is negligence.[541] Indeed, a beginning skier who was hit by an experienced skier was entitled to such a *rule of the road* jury instruction, even though general negligence instructions were also given.[542]

The United States Ski Association and the National Ski Patrol have set standards of proper conduct on the slopes.[543] Although violation of these standards is not negligence per se, it is evidence of negligence.[544] Documentary proof of these associations' standards may be admissible evidence, but in some cases it may not be reversible error if they are not admitted.[545]

An expert skier must act in accordance with his or her advanced knowledge of skiing.[546] This is consistent with the general principle that a person having special knowledge must exercise a quantum of care which is commensurate with that special skill and training.[547] However, one court held that the failure to give a jury instruction on this issue in a skiing collision case when the defendant was an expert skier was not prejudicial error.[548]

Child skiers are held to the standard of care of a reasonably prudent person of their age and experience.[549] In *Goss v Allen*,[550] the defendant, a 17-year-old beginning skier who had never attempted a downhill run, was successfully completing a short run until he came to an abrupt left turn at the end of the slope. He lost control while attempting to negotiate the turn and then noticed two girls ahead of him. The girls attempted to get out of the way, but one of them was unable to do so.

The *Goss* court held that the standard of care of a similar child was appropriate because skiing is enjoyed by children as well as adults. Furthermore, in this case, the defendant's attempt to negotiate the lower end of the beginners' slope could not be characterized, as a matter of law, as hazardous to others and, therefore, there was not a need to impose a high standard of conduct.[551]

---

541 Ninio v Hight, 385 F2d 350, 352 (10th Cir 1967).

542 *Id.*

543 LaVine v Clear Creek Skiing Corp, 557 F2d 730, 733 (10th Cir 1977).

544 *See id* 733-74.

545 *See id.*

546 *Id* 734.

547 Restatement (Second) of Torts §289(b) (1965).

548 LaVine v Clear Creek Skiing Corp, 557 F2d 730, 735 (10th Cir 1977) (Colorado law).

549 Goss v Allen, 70 NJ 442, 360 A2d 388, 391 (1976); *see generally* **§2.01**.

550 Goss v Allen, 70 NJ 442, 360 A2d 388, 391 (1976).

551 *Id.*

The *Goss* court stated that the cut-off age for invoking the similar child standard of care is 18 years old, the age of legal maturity.[552] It noted the obviously arbitrary nature of a rigid cutoff.[553] There is, after all, no substantive difference in the actions of a child one day before and one day after his or her eighteenth birthday. However, a line has to be drawn somewhere and it is arbitrary wherever it is drawn.[554]

§2.16 Water Skiing and Towing

Negligence

The operators of a boat must exercise reasonable care while the boat is being used by water skiers.[555] For example, they can be liable where they fail to keep a proper lookout and, as a result, an accident occurs.[556]

However, boat operators are not liable unless they act negligently. There was no liability in *Tompkins v Gering*,[557] a case where a water skier was injured when he was jerked out of his skis and his head struck the bottom of the lake, because there was no credible evidence that the boat operator acted unreasonably. The plaintiff's contention that the operator's sharp turn of the boat created a jerk which caused the accident could not be substantiated by an expert water skier.[558]

In addition, an operator is not liable unless there is a causal connection between the negligent act and the injury. In *Strickland v Roberts*,[559] a boat operator was not liable for failing to have a required ski watcher on board because there was no causal relationship between the failure to have a watcher on the boat and the skier's injury. In that case, the skier intentionally skied as close as possible to a dock to spray water on sunbathers and, unfortunately, came too close and hit the dock.[560] The boat operator had observed the skier but he was still unable to avoid an accident because of the skier's conduct. An additional watcher on the boat would have been superfluous because

---

552 *Id.*

553 *Id.*

554 *Id.*

555 Harrop v Beckman, 15 Utah 2d 78, 387 P2d 554, 554 (1963); *see generally* §2.04. Each year, approximately 30,000 water skiers require emergency room treatment for their injuries. *See* US Consumer Prod Safety Commn, Natl Injury Information Clearinghouse, Prod Summary Report (Mar 28, 1984).

556 Harrop v Beckman, 15 Utah 2d 78, 387 P2d 554, 554 (1963).

557 64 Wash 2d 389, 391 P2d 957 (1964).

558 *Id.*

559 382 So 2d 1338, 1339 (Fla Dist Ct App), *review denied*, 389 So 2d 1115 (1980).

560 382 So 2d at 1339-40.

the watcher, like the operator, would also have been powerless to avoid the collision.[561]

Insurance

In *Deschler v Fireman's Fund American Life Insurance Co*, the Utah Supreme Court held that an accidental death insurance policy which excluded coverage for fatal injuries from the use of a *device for aerial navigation* did not cover a person who died while operating a waterski kite, a vehicle which stays in the air while it is towed by a motorboat.[562] The court concluded that the waterski kite was a device for aerial navigation because (1) aerodynamic principles affect the kite's ability to become and stay airborne; and (2) the operator has some degree of control over the landing.[563]

State Statutes

Many states regulate water skiing and similar towing activities. A common requirement is that a watercraft which has a person in tow must have, in addition to the operator of the boat, an observer.[564] In one state the observer must display a brightly colored flag when the person in tow falls into the water.[565] A few states dispense with the requirement of an observer if the boat is equipped with a wide-angle rear-view mirror which allows the operator to observe the person being towed[566] or if the skier wears a life preserver.[567] One state requires both an observer and a rear-view mirror.[568] A different jurisdiction requires only a rear-view mirror.[569]

The timing of towing activities has also been specified. For example, in some states it is illegal to have a person in tow on water skis or a similar contrivance

---

561 *Id.*

562 663 P2d 97 (Utah 1983).

563 *Id* 99.

564 *See* Ariz Rev Stat Ann §5-346 (1974); Conn Gen Stat §15-134 (West Supp 1983) (observer must be at least 12 years old); Ill Ann Stat, ch 95½, §315-9 (1983); Ind Code Ann §14-1-1-32 (Burns 1983); Iowa Code Ann §106.15 (West Supp 1983); La Rev Stat Ann §850.15 (West 1964); Md Nat Res Code Ann §8-725 (1983); Miss Code Ann §59-21-87 (1973); Nev Rev Stat §488.235 (1983); Or Rev Stat §488.144 (1983); RI Gen Laws §46-22-12 (1980); Va Code §62.1-179 (1982); Wis Stat Ann §30.69 (West Supp 1983).

565 *See* Ariz Rev Stat Ann §5-346 (1974).

566 *See* Fla Stat Ann §327.37 (West Supp 1983); Ga Code Ann §17-614 (Supp 1982); Kan Stat Ann §82a-813 (1977); Minn Stat Ann §361.09 (West 1984); Neb Rev Stat §37-1258 (1978); Okla Stat Ann tit 63, §812 (West Supp 1984); SD Codified Laws Ann §42-8-49 (1977); Wyo Stat §41-13-212 (1977).

567 *See* NC Gen Stat §75A-13 (1983); Vt Stat Ann tit 25, §315 (1975).

568 *See* Mich Stat Ann §18.1287(78) (Callaghan 1980).

569 *See* Tex Parks & Wild Code §31.071 (Vernon 1976).

between sunset and sunrise,[570] one-half hour after sunset to one-half hour before sunrise,[571] one hour after sunset to one hour prior to sunrise,[572] or one hour after sunset to sunrise of the following day.[573]

§2.17   Miscellaneous Recreational Activities

Automobile Racing

In one case, the court held that a husband who died while racing a Formula F race car was killed in an *automobile* and, therefore, his wife could recover under their automobile policy.[574]

Basketball

It is estimated that over 400,000 basketball players each year require emergency room treatment for their injuries.[575]

The courts, as early as 1927, have held that a basketball player injured by another player cannot recover for negligently inflicted harm, but only for intentional torts.[576] For example, in *Griggas v Clauson*,[577] a plaintiff's verdict was affirmed where one basketball player pushed another player, then hit him in the face, and, as the injured player fell to the floor, the other player struck him again, rendering him unconscious.

---

570 *See* Ariz Rev Stat Ann §5-346 (1974); Conn Gen Stat §15-134 (West Supp 1983); Ga Code Ann §17-614 (1982); Kan Stat Ann §82a-813 (1977); Md Nat Res Code Ann §8-725 (1983); Wis Stat Ann §30.69 (West Supp 1983).

571 *See* Fla Stat Ann §327.37 (West Supp 1983); Ill Ann Stat, ch 95½, §315-9 (1983); RI Gen Laws §46-22-12 (1980). *See also* Okla Stat Ann tit 63, §812 (West Supp 1984) (one-half hour after sunset to sunrise).

572 *See* La Rev Stat Ann §850.15 (West 1964); Mich Stat Ann §18.1287(77) (Callaghan 1980); Neb Rev Stat §37-1259 (1978); Neb Rev Stat §488.235 (1983); NC Gen Stat §75A-13 (1983); Or Rev Stat §488.144 (1983); SD Codified Laws Ann §42-8-48 (Supp 1983); Tex Parks & Wild Code Ann §31.003 (Vernon 1976); Va Code §62.1-179 (1982); Wyo Stat §41-13-212 (1977).

573 *See* Minn Stat Ann §361.09 (West 1984).

574 Carney v American Fire & Indem Co, 371 So 2d 815, 817 (La 1979); *but see* Williams v Cimarron Ins Co, 406 SW2d 173, 175 (Tex Civ App 1966); Beagle v Automobile Club Ins Co, 18 Ohio Ops 2d 280, 176 NW2d 542, 544 (1960); *see also* **§8.02**.

575 US Consumer Prod Safety Commn, Natl Injury Information Clearinghouse, Prod Summary Report (Mar 28, 1984).

576 Thomas v Barlow, 5 NJ Misc 764, 138 A 208, 209 (1927); Oswald v Township High School Dist, 84 Ill App 3d 723, 406 NE2d 159 (1980); Griggas v Clauson, 6 Ill App 2d 412, 128 NE2d 363 (1955). The *Thomas* case is discussed in *Assault And Battery—Liability For Injuries Received in Athletic Contests*, 26 Mich L Rev 322 (1927).

577 6 Ill App 2d 412, 128 NE2d 363, 365-66 (1955).

In *Oswald v Township High School District*,[578] the court affirmed the dismissal of a plaintiff's claim that a fellow basketball player was negligent when he kicked the plaintiff during a game. The court addressed the issue of whether there is liability for a negligent breach of a safety rule and held that the negligent violation of rules was not actionable; rule infractions are virtually inevitable in contact sports[579] and, therefore, they are actionable only when the offending player's conduct is deliberate, wilful, or done with a reckless disregard for the safety of others, a situation which did not occur there.[580]

There have been at least two cases where injured professional basketball players sued other players and their teams.[581] In *Tomjanovich v California Sports, Inc*,[582] a jury awarded over $3 million to a professional basketball player who was struck in the face during a game by another player who had been involved in several previous fights during his professional career.

Bicycling

One study estimated that there are over 500 fatalities and about 500,000 individuals who are permanently crippled each year from bicycle accidents.[583]

Bicyclists may be injured by dogs in the neighborhood. In *Henkel v Jordan*,[584] a bicyclist who was injured when he attempted to avoid a menacing dog recovered against the dog's owners. The court held that the owners were liable for allowing their dog to roam at will in the neighborhood when he had a history of menacing behavior.[585]

When a child bicyclist causes an accident, the injured party may attempt to impose liability on the child's parents for their negligence. Where the

---

578 84 Ill App 3d 723, 406 NE2d 159 (1980).

579 The court specifically drew a distinction between contact and noncontact sports. 406 NE2d at 160.

580 406 NE2d at 159-60.

581 Tomjanovich v California Sports, Inc, No H-78-243 (SD Tex 1979); *see also* Ranii, *Sports Violence Lawsuits Erupt*, Natl LJ, Feb 9, 1981 at 30, col 3 (Richard Rhodes received over $125,000 in damages for injuries received during a game which were caused by Lucius Allan and the Kansas City Kings).

582 No H-78-243 (SD Tex 1979), discussed in D. Merrihugh, The Esoteric Torts 53-54 (1980); *see* Note, *Tort Liability In Professional Sports*, 44 Alb L Rec 696, 710 (1980); Comment, *Assumption Of Risk And Vicarious Liability In Personal Injury Actions Brought By Professional Athletes*, 1980 Duke LJ 742.

The case was finally settled out of court for $750,000. Note, *Liability In Professional Sports: An Alternative To Violence*, 22 Ariz L Rev 919, 920 n 15 (1980).

583 *See* Goss v Allen, 70 NJ 442, 360 A2d 388, 394 n 2 (1976) (Schreiber, J dissenting); *see also* US Consumer Prod Safety Commn, Natl Injury Information Clearinghouse, Prod Summary Report (Mar 28, 1984) (over 570,000 bicyclists and 30,000 individuals on trail bikes or minibikes require emergency room treatment each year).

584 7 Kan App 2d 561, 644 P2d 1248 (1982).

585 644 P2d at 1352.

parents are not negligent, the plaintiff may try to argue that the family purpose doctrine applies and that the parents are therefore vicariously liable for the child's negligence.[586] The Georgia courts, however, have repeatedly held that parents are not responsible under the family purpose doctrine for accidents caused by their children while riding bicycles.[587]

In some cases, an injured bicyclist may be covered by an insurance policy. One court held that a homeowners' insurance policy covered the damages inflicted on a third party by a child's negligent use of a bicycle.[588] In a different case a passenger on a dirt bike who was injured in a collision could recover from an insurance company because he was considered to be a *pedestrian*.[589] There is also authority that a trail bike, not equipped with a head lamp, tail lamp, or horn, was not a *motor vehicle* under an insurance policy.[590]

Boxing

The courts have consistently held that where two parties engage in a friendly boxing match and one party, without intending to do so, accidentally hurts the other, the injured party cannot recover from the other boxer.[591] Play between two people, even if it is rough or dangerous, is not a basis for recovery if the defendant had no intent to harm the other party.[592] However, if the boxing match is illegal, an injured participant can recover from the other party.[593]

Dune Buggy

The driver of a dune buggy must use reasonable care in operating that

---

586 *See* §2.01.

587 Carter v Kearse, 142 Ga App 251, 235 SE2d 755, 756 (1977); *see also* Calhoun v Pair, 197 Ga 703, 30 SE2d 180 (1944).

588 *See* United States Fire Ins Co v Schnackenberg, 89 Ill App 3d 431, 411 NE2d 1057, 1059 (1980).

589 Tomei v Insurance Co of N Am, 194 NJ Super 400, 476 A2d 1283, 1285-86 (1984); *but see* McKenna v Wiskowski, 181 NJ Super 482, 438 A2d 355 (1981) (passenger on moped was not a *pedestrian*).

590 Siefert v Nationwide Ins, 289 Pa Super 160, 432 A2d 1101 (1981).

591 McAdams v Windham, 208 Ala 492, 94 So 742, 743 (1922) (the court also held that the plaintiff assumed the risk); Gibeline v Smith, 106 Mo App 545, 80 SW 961, 962 (1904); Colby v McClendon, 85 Okla 293, 206 P 207, 209 (1922) (dicta); *see generally* Note, *Compensating Injured Professional Athletes: The Mystique of Sports Versus Traditional Tort Principles*, 55 NYUL Rev 971, 978-79 (1980).

592 Gibeline v Smith, 106 Mo App 545, 80 SW 961, 962 (1904).

593 Stout v Wren, 8 NC (1 Hawks) 420 (1821).

vehicle.[594] Indeed, where a plaintiff driving a car on a highway entered an intersection on a green light, pursuant to a policeman's signal, and then collided in the intersection with a dune buggy, there was evidence that the operator of the dune buggy was negligent.[595] In addition, under respondeat superior an employer may be liable for its employee's negligence in driving a dune buggy.[596]

The courts have consistently held that individuals injured by uninsured operators of dune buggies could not recover under the uninsured motorist provision of their automobile policies.[597] In *Kansas Farm Bureau Insurance Co v Cool*,[598] the Kansas Supreme Court held, for three principal reasons, that a dune buggy was not an *automobile* and that an insured plaintiff could not collect when he was injured under the uninsured motorist provision. First, the dune buggy was not treated as an automobile by its owners because it was sold without a certificate of title.[599] Second, it was not safe for use on public highways.[600] Third, the risk of injury in a dune buggy was much greater than in an automobile.[601] One court held that it was not against public policy for an insurance company to fail to include insurance for accidents caused by uninsured dune buggies.[602]

Homeowners' insurance policies which exclude coverage for injuries arising out of *motor vehicle* accidents do not cover dune buggy accidents.[603] One

---

[594] Wagner v Hazelquist, 347 So 2d 1265, 1268 (La Ct App 1977) (defendant did not disput this).

In Tollison v Dyal, 263 So 2d 290, 290 (Fla Dist Ct App), *cert denied*, 268 So 2d 906 (Fla 1972), the defendant was granted a summary judgment because he was not grossly negligent, the applicable standard of care because of a guest statute then in effect, in driving a dune buggy off a drop in the sand dunes).

[595] Stephens v McClain, 129 Ga App 634, 200 SE2d 511, 512 (1973).

[596] Uris v Gurney's Inn Corp, 405 F Supp 744, 745 (EDNY 1975) ($300,000 damages allowed).

[597] Kansas Farm Bureau Ins Co v Cool, 205 Kan 567, 471 P2d 352 (1970); Meeks v Berkbuegler, 632 SW2d 24, 26 (Mo Ct App 1982) (dune buggy is not a *motor vehicle* because it was designed mainly for use off public roads). An uninsured provision in an insurance policy is not applicable where, at the time of the accident, plaintiff was injured by a dune buggy owned by her minor son because the policy does not cover vehicles owned by the insureds or their family. The son's attempted disaffirmance of the purchase of the vehicle after the fact was held irrelevant. Wise v Truck Ins Exc, 11 Wash App 405, 523 P2d 431, 433 (1974).

[598] 205 Kan 567, 471 P2d 352 (1970).

[599] 471 P2d at 358.

[600] *Id.*

[601] *Id.*

[602] Meeks v Berkbuegler, 632 SW2d 24, 27 (Mo Ct App 1982).

[603] *See* State Farm Fire & Casualty Co v Camara, 63 Cal App 3d 48, 133 Cal Rptr 600 (1976); *see also* Bills v National Mut Ins Co, 317 Pa Super 188, 463 A2d 1148, 1151-52 (1983) (a dune buggy which was unregistered, and not equipped with a rear lighting system, turn signals, hazard warning lights, a muffler, or rear wheel shields was not a "motor vehicle").

plaintiff's attempt to argue that there was coverage because the accident resulted partly from a nonexcluded risk was rejected.[604] The court held that the transformation of a car into a dune buggy and the negligent driving of the dune buggy both arose out of the maintenance and operation of a vehicle and, therefore, both were excluded risks.[605]

Football

It is unquestioned that football is a violent sport.[606] However, there are limits to what one player can do to another player during a game.[607]

In *Hackbart v Cincinnati Bengals, Inc*,[608] a professional football player was intentionally hit from the rear by another player during a game. The defendant, an offensive back, had just run a pass pattern. The pass was intercepted and the plaintiff, a defensive back, then attempted to block the defendant by throwing his body in front of him. After that, the plaintiff

---

604 State Farm Fire & Casualty Co v Camara, 63 Cal App 3d 48, 133 Cal Rptr 600 (1976).

605 133 Cal Rptr 603-04.

606 President Theodore Roosevelt once threatened to abolish football if the game could not be made less violent. R. Horrow, Sport Violence: The Interaction Between Private Law Making And The Criminal Law 7 (1980); Note, *Injuries Resulting From Nonintentional Acts In Organized Contact Sports: The Theories Of Recovery Available To The Injured Athlete*, 12 Ind L Rev 687, 688 (1979).
Over 400,000 football players each year receive emergency room treatment for their injuries. *See* US Consumer Prod Safety Comm'n, Nat'l Injury Information Clearinghouse, Prod Summary Report (Mar 28, 1984).

607 In People v Freer, 86 Misc 2d 280, 381 NYS2d 976 (Dist Ct 1976), the defendant was convicted of criminal assault for his acts during a football game.

608 601 F2d 516 (10th Cir), *cert denied*, 444 US 931 (1979). The case has been extensively discussed in the law journals. *See, e.g.*, Note, *Tort Liability In Professional Sports*, 44 Alb L Rev 696 (1980); Note, *Liability In Professional Sports: An Alternative To Violence*, 22 Ariz L Rev 919 (1980); Note, *Judicial Scrutiny of Tortious Conduct In Professional Sports: Do Professional Athletes Assume The Risk Of Injuries Resulting From Rule Violations? Hackbart v Cincinnati Bengals*, 17 Cal W L Rev 149 (1980); Note, *The "Booby" Trap: Does The Violent Nature Of Professional Football Vitiate The Doctrine Of Due Care In Participant Tort Litigation?*, 10 Conn L Rev 365 (1978); Note, *Professional Sports And Tort Liability: A Victory For The Intentionally Injured Player*, 1980 Det CL Rev 687; *Torts—Civil Lribility Of Athletes*, 84 Dick L Rev 753 (1980); Comment, *Assumption Of Risk And Vicarious Liability In Personal Injury Actions Brought By Professional Athletes*, 1980 Duke LJ 742; *Tort Law—Reckless Misconduct In Sports*, 19 Duq L Rev 191 (1980); *Torts—Assumption of Risk*, 12 Ga L Rev 380 (1978); *Torts*, 15 Gonz L Rev 867 (1980); Note, *Injuries Resulting From Nonintentional Acts In Organized Contact Sports: The Theories of Recovery Available To The Injured Athlete*, 12 Ind L Rev 687, 704-10 (1979); Note, *Tort Liability In Professional Sports: Battle In The Sports Arena*, 57 Neb L Rev 1128 (1978); *On Finding Civil Liability Between Professional Football Players: Hackbart v Cincinnati Bengals, Inc*, 15 New Eng L Rev 741 (1980); Note, *Compensating Injured Professional Athletes: The Mystique Of Sport Versus Traditional Tort Principles*, 55 NYU L Rev 971 (1980; Comment, *Federal Jurisdiction—Torts*, 11 Rut-Cam LJ 497 (1980); Note, *Torts: Athlete States Cause Of Action For Injury During Professional Football Game*, 19 Washburn LJ 646 (1980).

turned, with one knee on the ground, to watch the rest of the play. The defendant, angry and frustrated, then used his right forearm to strike the back of the plaintiff's head, and both players fell to the ground as a result of the force of the blow. No foul was called because the officials failed to see this incident. The court held that the aggressor may have been guilty of reckless misconduct and, therefore, the plaintiff was entitled to a trial on this issue.[609]

Go-Cart

There are about 10,000 individuals injured by go-carts annually who require emergency room treatment.[610]

In one recent case a child hit by an uninsured person operating a go-cart was able to recover under an automobile uninsured motorist provision.[611] The policy did not explicitly define *automobile* and the court held that a go-cart was an automobile for purposes of interpreting this insurance policy.[612]

Hang Gliding

Several courts have held that an operator of a hang glider was engaged in "aerial navigation"[613] or travel in an "aircraft"[614] and, therefore, the applicable exclusions in insurance policies precluded the beneficiary from receiving insurance benefits when the insured was injured while engaged in this activity.

Hockey

Each year, about 25,000 individuals require emergency room treatment for injuries received while playing hockey.[615] Although there have been several

---

609 601 F2d at 524-25.

610 US Consumer Prod Safety Commn, Natl Injury Information Clearinghouse, Prod Summary Report (Mar 28, 1984).

611 Hidalgo v Allstate Ins Co, 374 So 2d 1261, 1264 (La Ct App 1979).

612 *Id.*

613 Fireman's Fund Am Life Ins Co v Long, 148 Ga App 216, 251 SE2d 133, 134 (1978); *see also* Wilson v Insurance Co of N Am, 453 F Supp 732, 734-35 (ND Cal 1978) (hang kite).

614 Fielder v Farmers New World Life Ins Co, 435 F Supp 912 (CD Cal 1977).

615 US Consumer Prod Safety Commn, Natl Injury Information Clearinghouse, Prod Summary Report (Mar 28, 1984); Yeager, *The Savage State Of Sports*, Physician & Sportsmedicine 94, 96 (May 1977).

Owen McCourt was killed in 1907 by a hockey stick. Hallowell & Meshbesher, *Sports Violence And The Criminal Law*, 13 Trial 29 (Jan 1977).

criminal cases brought against hockey players,[616] there is a dearth of civil suits.[617]

Horseback Riding

In many cases where an individual is injured riding a horse on the land of another, it is unclear whether the law of premises liability[618] or animal law should be applied.[619] In *Mercer v Fritts*, the court held that such a determination should be based on which factor was more significant in causing the injury.[620] In that case, a woman was injured while riding a stallion at the home of her in-laws. She alleged that the host was negligent in furnishing her with a saddle which was inadequate and also in riding a mare near her horse which made her horse act unruly. The court reasoned that the alleged negligence related to the horse, not the premises, so animal law should be applied.[621] Accordingly, citing Restatement (Second) of Torts §518, it held that the host could be liable for its negligence for harm done by domestic animals.[622]

It is generally held that a person is not liable for providing an unsuitable horse unless the horse had dangerous propensities and the provider of the horse knew or should have known of those propensities.[623] The fact that a horse was *high strung* or *skittish* is not enough to impose liability because

---

616 *See, e.g.*, Regina v Maki, 14 DLR3d 164 (1970); Regina v Green, 16 DLR3d 137 (1970); Regina v Maloney, 28 CCC2d 323 (1976); Regina v Watson, 26 CCC2d 150 (1975); *see generally* Gibson, *Violence In Professional Sports: A Proposal For Self-Regulation*, 3 COMM/ENT 425, 425, 428-29 (1981); Hechter, *The Criminal. Law And Violence In Sports*, 19 Crim LQ 425 (1976); *see* Note, *Torts In Sports—Deterring Violence In Professional Athletics*, 48 Fordham L Rev 764, 771 n 55 (1980) (noting several convictions).

The American criminal case against Dave Forbes for his actions during a professional hockey game is discussed in R. Horrow, Sports Violence: The Interaction Between Private Law Making and the Criminal Law 162 (1980); *See generally* Note, *Liability In Professional Sports: An Alternative To Violence*, 22 Ariz L Rev 919, 925 (1980); Note, *Consent In Criminal Law: Violence In Sports*, 75 Mich L Rev 148 (1976); Comment, *Violence In Professional Sports*, 1975 Wis L Rev 771.

617 *See* Agar v Canning, 54 WWR 302 (1965), *aff'd*, 55 WWR 384 (1966).

One professional hockey player, Dennis Polonich, received a jury verdict of $850,000 in 1982 for injuries from being hit by another player in the rink. Mortisugu, *Should Courts Be Refereeing Sports Fights?*, Wall St J, Sept 1, 1982 at 19, col 3. Another hockey player, Henry Boucha, reportedly received over $1,000,000 in an out of court settlement of his civil action against Dave Forbes, the Boston Bruins team and the National Hockey League. *See* Ranii, *Sports Violence Lawsuits Erupt*, Natl LJ, Feb 9, 1981, at 1, col 1.

618 *See* §6.13.

619 Mercer v Fritts, 9 Kan App 2d 232, 676 P2d 150, 154 (1984).

620 *Id.*

621 *Id.*

622 676 P2d at 153-54.

623 Williams v Hawkins, 304 So 2d 75, 77 (La Ct App 1974), *writ denied*, 307 So 2d 373 (La 1975); *see generally* §§1.12, 1.13, 1.14.

many horses exhibit such behavior.[624] In *Williams v Hawkins*,[625] a plaintiff did not recover where the horse had never thrown a rider before and there was no other evidence of the horse's dangerous characteristics or its owner's knowledge of those characteristics.

The doctrine of res ipsa loquitur was not applied where a rider was thrown from a horse because such accidents do not ordinarily occur because of a defendant's negligence.[626] The most mild-mannered horse can become frightened and throw a rider in the absence of negligence.[627]

Some states have enacted statutes regulating liability for injuries by animals.[628]

Parachuting

Several courts have held that a person who died while sport parachuting was engaged in a "device for aerial navigation"[629] or "participating in aeronautics,"[630] and, therefore, under the applicable exclusion, there was no insurance coverage for those injuries. However, there is authority to the contrary.[631]

Playground Activities

About 200,000 individuals injured annually on playground equipment receive emergency room treatment.[632]

In *Holodook v Graney*,[633] the court held that a child who fell from the third or fourth step of a school playground slide could not sue his father

---

624 Williams v Hawkins, 304 So 2d 75, 77 (La Ct App 1974), *writ denied*, 307 So 2d 373 (La 1975). However, if the owner knew the horse was unusually skittish and that plaintiff was incapable of riding the horse properly, the owner may still be negligent.

625 304 So 2d 75, 77 (La Ct App 1974), *writ denied*, 307 So 2d 373 (La 1975).

626 *Id; see generally* §§1.12, 1.13, 1.14.

627 304 So 2d 75, 77 (La Ct App 1974), *writ denied*, 307 So 2d 373 (La 1975).

628 *See, e.g.*, La Civ Code Ann art 2321 (West 1979); Ill Rev Stat ch 8 §366 (Smith-Hurd 1975). The Louisiana statute is construed in Daniel v Cambridge Mut Fire Ins Co, 368 So 2d 810, 815 (La Ct App), *writ denied*, 369 So 2d 1063 (La 1979).

629 *See* Edison v Reliable Life Ins Co, 664 F2d 1130, 1132 (9th Cir 1981); Cabell v World Serv Life Ins Co, 599 SW2d 652, 653-54 (Tex Civ App 1980);

630 Smith v Mutual Beneficial Health & Accident Assn, 175 Kan 68, 258 P2d 993, 995-96 (1953).

631 *See* Childress v Continental Casualty Co, 461 F Supp 704, 707 (ED La 1978), *affd per curiam*, 587 F2d 809 (5th Cir 1979); *see also* Clark v Lone Star Life Ins Co, 347 SW2d 291, 293 (Tex Civ App 1961) (parachute is not a "species of aircraft").

632 US Consumer Prod Safety Commn, Natl Injury Information Clearinghouse, Prod Summary Report (Mar 28, 1984).

633 36 NY2d 35, 324 NE2d 338, 364 NYS2d 859, 863 (1974). This case is criticized in Note, *Torts*, 42 Brooklyn L Rev 125 (1975).

for negligently supervising him because a child has no such cause of action against his or her parents. However, an infant injured on a swing set can recover against an uncle and aunt for their failure to use reasonable care in protecting him or her, even where they were not being compensated by the mother for their efforts.[634]

Roller Skating

Each year, over 100,000 people injured while roller skating receive emergency room treatment.[635] In one case, a 16-year-old roller skater who was involved in a collision with another skater was held to be not negligent because his conduct did not fall below the standard of care of a similar child of his age, mental capacity, and experience.[636]

Soccer

In *Nabozny v Barnhill*,[637] a soccer player kicked the head of the crouched, opposing goalkeeper, the plaintiff, while he was in the penalty area. This was a direct violation of the applicable soccer rules which prohibited any contact with the goalkeeper while the goalkeeper was in a penalty area. Indeed, the rules prohibit kicking at all times.

The *Nabozny* court stated that "a player is . . . charged with a legal duty to every other player on the field to refrain from conduct proscribed by a safety rule."[638] This sounds like, and the facts of the case are consistent with, a holding that violation of a safety rule is negligence. Unfortunately, the court created confusion by remarking in the next sentence: "A reckless disregard for the safety of other players cannot be excused."[639] Accordingly, it is unclear whether *Nabozny* made negligent violations of safety rules actionable or only reckless violations. A later court held that only intentional violations were actionable.[640]

---

634 Zalak v Carroll, 15 NY2d 753, 205 NE2d 313, 257 NYS2d 177, 178 (1965).

635 US Consumer Prod Safety Commn, Natl Injury Information Clearinghouse, Prod Summary Report (Mar 28, 1984).

636 Agans v Showalter, 92 Ill App 3d 939, 416 NE2d 397, 399 (1981).

637 31 Ill App 3d 212, 334 NE2d 258 (1975). This case is analyzed in Note, *Participant's Liability For Injury To A Fellow Participant In An Organized Athletic Event*, 53 Chi-Kent L Rev 97 (1976); Note, *Injuries Resulting From Nonintentional Acts In Organized Contact Sports: The Theories Of Recovery Available To The Injured Athlete*, 12 Ind L Rev 687, 697-704 (1979); *Torts—Participant In Athletic Competition States Cause Of Action For Injuries Against Other Participant*, 42 Mo L Rev 347 (1977); *Tort Liability For Players In Contact Sports*, 45 UMKC L Rev 119 (1976).

638 334 NE2d at 260-61.

639 334 NE2d at 261.

640 *See* Oswald v Township High School Dist, 84 Ill App 3d 723, 406 NE2d 159, 159-60 (1980).

One court held that a soccer player was not entitled to summary judgment where there was evidence that he committed wilful misconduct, even though the plaintiff had not alleged those facts.[641]

Swimming

Over 125,000 swimmers require emergency room treatment for their injuries each year.[642]

In *McCallister v Sun Valley Pools, Inc,*[643] a child who suffered permanent paralysis as a result of a diving accident in a family swimming pool sued his parents for negligence in failing to warn him of the dangers of diving. The court held that the doctrine of parental immunity was still applicable where the alleged negligent act involved an exercise of reasonable parental authority over the child.[644] It concluded that the negligence alleged here involved such issues and, therefore, the plaintiff's claim was barred.[645]

The court rejected the plaintiff's argument that his parents' $100,000 liability insurance policy would pay for the damages and, therefore, since the reason for the immunity doctrine, viz., to minimize judicial interference with the parent-child relationship, did not apply, the immunity should be eliminated.[646] The court noted that the availability of insurance, a fact which did not exist when the parent-child immunity doctrine was first created, has provided a reason, in other jurisdictions, to abrogate most parental immunity.[647] However, the exception for parental discretion should remain because it would be too difficult to fashion the appropriate standard of care in light of the cultural, educational, or financial conditions of each family.[648] Finally, the court noted that the insurance in this case may be inadequate since the ad damnum clause prayed for five million dollars in damages, a sum far in excess of the policy limits.[649]

---

641 *See* Moore v Jones, 120 Ga App 521, 171 SE2d 390, 391 (1969).

642 US Consumer Prod Safety Commn, Natl Injury Information Clearinghouse, Prod Summary Report (Mar 28, 1984).

643 100 Mich App 131, 298 NW2d 687 (1980).

644 298 NW2d at 691.

645 *Id.*

646 *Id.*

647 *Id.* Future insurance policies generally may not cover actions between two insureds under the same policy. *See* Sloane, *Homeowners' Insurance Is Revised*, New York Times, Dec 26, 1984, at 28, col3.

648 298 NW2d at 693.

649 *Id* at 694. In light of the fact that most cases settle and in the few that do not, the jury is not bound by the ad damnum clause, a court's reliance on the plaintiff's prayer seems misplaced.

Liability of Governments

3

§3.01 Introduction

Federal, state, and local governments now provide significant recreational facilities.[1] In so doing, governmental entities may create dangerous conditions for recreational enthusiasts.[2]

Individuals injured by acts of sovereigns such as federal and state governments were traditionally denied recovery under the common law doctrine of sovereign immunity.[3] At one point the related doctrine of governmental immunity shielded public employees and other governmental entities from liability.[4]

Those common law doctrines have now been limited in most jurisdictions. The United States waived its immunity in many areas with the passage of the Federal Tort Claims Act.[5] Similarly, most states have now modified their immunity and the immunity of cities and counties through the enactment of state tort claims acts[6] and other statutes.[7]

In no event is the government an insurer of the safety of the public.[8] A school board which owns a basketball court is not liable for injuries that occurred on the court where no defect in the building caused the accident.[9] However, where there is no immunity, the government has a duty to exercise reasonable care for the safety of users of its recreational facilities.[10] For example, a city which shared responsibility with a hockey league for supervising ice hockey players using a city-owned skating rink must take steps to provide adequate supervision of the game.[11]

Governmental units are landowners and land occupiers. Therefore, a review of the common law liabilities of such defendants is warranted.[12] In addition, the government may be entitled to the same limited tort immunity as that given to owners of land who are sued by individuals who used their land for recreational purposes.[13]

---

1 See §§3.14-3.18.

2 See §§3.12, 3.13.

3 See §3.02.

4 See §3.02.

5 See §3.11.

6 See §§3.03-3.09.

7 See §3.10.

8 Johnson v Salt Lake City Corp, 629 P2d 432, 434 (Utah 1981); see also Adamczyk v Zambelli, 25 Ill App 2d 121, 166 NE2d 93, 97 (1960).

9 Morris v City of Jersey City, 179 NJ Super 460, 432 A2d 553, 554 (1981).

10 See Santangelo v City of New York, 66 AD2d 880, 411 NYS2d 666, 667 (1978).

11 Id.

12 See ch 6.

13 See McCarver v Manson Park & Recreation Dist, 92 Wash 2d 370, 597 P2d 1362, 1366 (1979); see also §5.06.

Vicarious Liability

A governmental entity is vicariously liable under the doctrine of respondeat superior for the torts of its agents where the agent was acting at the instance of or under the direction and control of the government.[14] However, a person who went to a neighboring cabin to check on the safety of a conservation officer was not by that act alone an agent of the conservation officer.[15] Accordingly, the state was not liable when that person shot an occupant of the conservation officer's cabin.[16]

A governmental entity is not necessarily liable for the negligence of a different governmental unit. In *Hedman v City of Rochester*,[17] the court held that a city was not liable to a girl who was injured at a city-owned tennis court. The tennis court was under the exclusive control of the school district, a separate legal entity, and at the time of the injury she was participating in a recreational program supervised by the school district.[18]

Eleventh Amendment

The Eleventh Amendment to the United States Constitution states: "The Judicial power of the United States shall not be construed to extend to any suit in law or equity, commenced or prosecuted against one of the United States by Citizens of another State, or by Citizens or Subjects of any Foreign State."[19]

The Eleventh Amendment has not been interpreted in a manner consistent with its text. For example, it has been clear for almost 100 years that the amendment prohibits a citizen from suing his or her own state in federal court,[20] although there are no words to that effect, and a conventional tool of construction would lead to the opposite result.[21] Moreover, notwithstanding

---

14 Wheeler v Smith, 96 Idaho 421, 529 P2d 1293, 1295 (1974).

15 *Id.*

16 *Id.*

17 64 AD2d 817, 407 NYS2d 300, 300 (1978), *affd*, 47 NY2d 933, 393 NE2d 1041, 419 NYS2d 969 (1979).

18 *Id.*

19 There has been a large amount of scholarly commentary in this area in recent years. *See, e.g.*, Baker, *Federalism and the Eleventh Amendment*, 48 U Colo L Rev 139 (1977); Field, *The Eleventh Amendment and Other Sovereign Immunity Doctrines: Part One*, 126 U Pa L Rev 515 (1978); Gibbons, *The Eleventh Amendment and State Sovereign Immunity: A Reinterpretation*, 83 Colum L Rev 1889 (1983); Thornton, *The Eleventh Amendment: An Endangered Species*, 55 Ind LJ 293 (1980).

20 Hans v Louisiana, 134 US 1 (1890).

21 The principle of construction is expresio unis est exclusio alterius: when certain exceptions to a general rule are stated, other exceptions are necessarily excluded.

the amendment's broad language, it has been held inapplicable to injunctions prohibiting a state official from violating federal law.[22]

The Eleventh Amendment bars actions in federal court in which a state would be required to pay damages if liability were found.[23] In *Rutledge v Arizona Board of Regents*, a college football player at a state university alleged, among other things, that in retaliation for a poor punt his coach grabbed him, shook his head from side to side, and struck him in the mouth. The *Rutledge* court held that the football player's claims against the state university and the state board of regents for the battery were not cognizable in federal court because the damages would be paid from state funds.[24] The fact that the damages may have been paid directly from an insurance policy did not change the result because the insurance premiums were paid with state funds.[25]

The Eleventh Amendment does more than preclude actions against the state or state entities in federal court; it also prohibits suits nominally against state officials if public funds would be used to pay the damages.[26] The state university athletic director in *Rutledge* who was sued for his alleged vicarious liability for the acts of the school's football coaches was entitled to have those claims dismissed because actions for vicarious liability are really actions against the state.[27]

In contrast, the plaintiff's claims in *Rutledge*, that university coaches and the athletic director personally committed common law torts, were not barred because the state would not pay those damages.[28] Those individuals were liable for their own acts. The fact that the wrongs were committed by public

---

[22] Pennhurst State School & Hosp v Halderman, 465 US 89 (1984); *Ex parte* Young, 209 US 123 (1908); *see also* Edelman v Jordan, 415 US 651 (1974).

[23] Rutledge v Arizona Bd of Regents, 660 F2d 1345, 1349 (9th Cir 1981), *aff'd on other grounds*, 460 US 719 (1983).

[24] *Id*; *See also* Hemphill v Sayers, 552 F Supp 685, 688 (SD Ill 1982) (claims against the state resulting from a college football injury are not allowed in federal court).

[25] Rutledge v Arizona Bd of Regents, 660 F2d 1345, 1349 (9th Cir 1981), *aff'd on other grounds*, 460 US 719 (1983). *But see generally* §3.03 (governmental immunity in many states is waived if the governmental entity has insurance).

[26] Rutledge v Arizona Bd of Regents, 660 F2d 1345, 1349 (9th Cir 1981), *aff'd on other grounds*, 460 US 719 (1983); *see also* Pennhurst State School & Hosp v Halderman, 465 US 89 (1984); Ford Motor Co v Department of Treasury, 323 US 459 (1945) (refund of state taxes).

[27] Rutledge v Arizona Bd of Regents, 660 F2d 1345, 1350 (9th Cir 1981), *aff'd on other grounds*, 460 US 719 (1983).

[28] *Id*; *see also* Hemphill v Sayers, 552 F Supp 685, 688 (SD Ill 1982). *See generally* Hopkins v Clemson Agricultural College, 221 US 636, 642-43 (1911) ("The Eleventh Amendment was not intended to afford [public officials] freedom from liability ... [where] they have injured one of the state's citizens.").

employees in the scope of their employment was held to be irrelevant.[29] The
court's distinction was that these defendants were sued for their own wrongful
acts and not under a theory of vicarious liability. In addition, the plaintiff's
actions against those defendants were not barred, even though the state could
indemnify them, because indemnification was not assured.[30]

Under some circumstances, the Eleventh Amendment defense can be
waived.[31] However, there is no implied waiver when a state conducts an
activity regulated by the federal government unless the governing statute
requires a waiver.[32] One court held that a state's operation of a ferry in
navigable waters did not cause a waiver of its Eleventh Amendment defense.[33]
Some jurisdictions have statutes which provide that Eleventh Amendment
immunity is not to be waived.[34]

The Eleventh Amendment does not protect political subdivisions of a state
such as cities or counties.[35] In addition, it is only a defense in federal actions;
it does not apply in state lawsuits. However, where it does apply it is similar
to a jurisdictional defense and may be raised at any time in the proceedings.[36]

Indemnity

Indemnity provisions which purport to protect the federal government
from its own negligence are generally not enforced unless there is clear and
unequivocal support that such protection was intended.[37] This is particularly
true where there is a vast disparity in bargaining power between the parties
to the indemnity clause.[38] Accordingly, in *Price v United States*,[39] a county, in
a state of emergency because of damage by a hurricane, that agreed to hold
the United States *free from damages due to the approved work* in restoring a
seawall, was not barred from enforcing claims against the federal government.

---

29 Rutledge v Arizona Bd of Regents, 660 F2d 1345, 1350 (9th Cir 1981), *aff'd on other
grounds*, 460 US 719 (1983).

30 Hemphill v Sayers, 552 F Supp 685, 688-89 (SD Ill 1982).

31 Pennhurst State School & Hosp v Halderman, 465 US 89 (1984); Parden v Terminal
RR Co, 377 US 184 (1964); *see generally* Note, *Eleventh Amendment Immunity and State-Owned
Vessels*, 57 Tul L Rev 1523, 1527 (1983).

32 Edelman v Jordan, 415 US 651, 673 (1974); *see also* Employees v Missouri Pub Health
Dept, 411 US 279 (1973).

33 Faust v South Carolina State Highway Dept, 721 F2d 934, 941 (4th Cir 1983).

34 *See, e.g.*, Nev Rev Stat §41.031 (1979); Pa Cons Stat Ann tit 42, §8521 (Purdon 1982).

35 *See* Edelman v Jordan, 415 US 651, 667 (1974).

36 Faust v South Carolina State Highway Dept, 721 F2d 934, 940 (4th Cir 1983); *see also*
Edelman v Jordan, 415 US 651, 677-78 (1974).

37 Price v United States, 530 F Supp 1010, 1017 (SD Miss 1981).

38 *Id*; *see also* United States v Seckinger, 397 US 203 (1970).

39 530 F Supp 1010, 1017 (SD Miss 1981).

The court held that this indemnity provision did not apply to damages from a dredging operation.[40]

An indemnity provision in a lease which states that the government is not liable for injuries cannot be enforced against an injured person who was not a party to the contract.[41]

Civil Rights

In *Rutledge v Arizona Board of Regents*,[42] a college football player sued his coach in federal court alleging that the coach assaulted and battered him after a poor punt and that that action violated his civil rights under 42 USC §1983. The court held that such allegations do not state a civil rights claim because there was no deprivation of due process i.e., the plaintiff had a sufficient state tort law remedy.[43]

Conspiracy to Intimidate Witnesses

In *Kush v Rutledge*,[44] the United States Supreme Court held that a college football student could sue state university athletic officials for conspiracy to intimidate potential witnesses in a federal lawsuit under 42 USC §1985(2) without the necessity of proving that the conspiracy was motivated by racial or other class-based animus. The Supreme Court held that the racial or class-based animus requirement of §1985 only pertains to conspiracies to intimidate witnesses in state proceedings.[45]

General Principles of Liability

§3.02   Common Law Sovereign and Governmental Immunity

Sovereign Immunity

The actual origins of the sovereign immunity doctrine are obscure.[46]

---

40 *Id.*

41 Ward v United States, 208 F Supp 118, 124 (D Colo 1962).

42 660 F2d 1345 (9th Cir 1981), *aff'd,* 460 US 719 (1983).

43 660 F2d 1345, 1352 (9th Cir 1981), *aff'd on other grounds,* 460 US 719 (1983).

44 460 US 719, 726-27 (1983).

45 *Id.*

46 *See* Civil Actions Against State Government §2.3, at 14 (1982).

However, some commentators have reported that authority for this doctrine existed 700 years ago.[47]

It was at times believed that this doctrine was the divine right of kings, i.e., that "the king can do no wrong."[48] However, this thinking flourished over only a rather brief period of time, and even then it was always coupled with the qualification that for every act of the king some minister who was without immunity was responsible.[49] The original meaning was that the king must not be allowed to do wrong and that an injured individual could proceed by petition of right.[50] Accordingly, the expression *the king can do no wrong* originally meant precisely the contrary to what it later came to mean.[51]

Although the original British doctrine of sovereign immunity rarely had the effect of completely denying compensation,[52] the *doctrine* of sovereign immunity was adopted, for reasons which are unclear,[53] in America in a way which generally precluded suits against governmental units.[54] The common law rule was that the state, being sovereign, was not amenable to suit in its own courts absent its consent.[55] In some states, sovereign immunity was provided for in the state constitution.[56] Accordingly, after the American Revolution the citizens of the United States lost rights against the new government which they previously had against the British sovereign.[57]

---

47 *See* 1 E. Pollock & F. Maitland, The History of English Law 516 (2d ed 1968). *See generally* Restatement (Second) of Torts ch 45A, Special Note on Governmental Immunity (1977) (doctrine goes back to *ancient times*).

48 Blackstone penned that felicitious phrase. *See* Blackstone, Commentaries (10th ed 1887).

49 Restatement (Second) of Torts ch 45A, Special Note on Governmental Immunity (1977). *See also* Pennhurst State School & Hosp v Halderman, 465 US 89 (1984) (Stevens, J, dissenting).

50 Jaffe, *Suits Against Governments and Officers: Sovereign Immunity*, 77 Harv L Rev 1, 4 (1963). The so-called doctrine of sovereign immunity was largely an abstract idea without determinative impact on the subject's right to relief against governmental illegality. *Id* 18.

51 Jaffe, *Suits Against Governments and Officers: Sovereign Immunity*, 77 Harv L Rev 1, 4 (1963); *see also* Hall, *Sovereign Immunity and Reemergence of the Governmental/Proprietary Distinction: A Setback in Idaho's Governmental Liability Law*, 20 Idaho L Rev 197, 200 (1984).

52 *See* Muskopf v Corning Hosp Dist, 55 Cal 2d 211, 359 P2d 457, 458-59, 11 Cal Rptr 89 (1961).

53 K. Davis, Administrative Law Treatise §25.01, at 436 (1958).

54 *See* Muskopf v Corning Hosp Dist, 55 Cal 2d 211, 359 P2d 457, 458-59, 11 Cal Rptr 89 (1961).

55 Schenkolewski v Cleveland Metroparks Sys, 67 Ohio St 2d 31, 426 NE2d 784, 785 (1981), *overruled on other grounds sub nom* Haverlack v Portage Homes, Inc, 2 Ohio St 3d 26, 442 NE2d 749 (1982); *see generally* Restatement (Second) of Torts §895B (1977).

56 *See, e.g.,* Ala Const art 1, §14 (1977); Ark Const art 5, §20 (1947); W Va Const art VI, §35 (1982).

57 Jaffe, *Suits Against Governments and Officers: Sovereign Immunity*, 77 Harv L Rev 1, 19 (1963).

It is ironic that the American courts would have embraced the concept that the sovereign is above error after America had revolted against the British king. *See* Hall, *Sovereign Immunity*

The sovereign immunity doctrine has been justified at various times, and with varying degrees of support, in this country primarily on five different grounds. One historical justification, perhaps the main one,[58] for this doctrine was the fear that absent such protection there would be unexpected and unplanned claims on the public fisc.[59]

A second justification, closely related to the first, was that public policy required such a defense. A government that could be held liable for damages would eliminate or reduce public recreational areas and this would, on balance, be a greater loss to society.[60]

A third justification, and one once embraced by the United States Supreme Court, was that a sovereign was exempt from suit on the *logical and practical ground* that there can be no legal right against the authority that makes the law on which the right depends.[61]

A fourth justification was that governmental units are not liable for the torts of their employees.[62]

A final justification was that under the concept of separation of powers a judicial branch's decision should not triumph over a decision made by the executive branch, a coequal branch of government.[63]

Sovereign immunity, when it applies, protects all acts or omissions of the government. Most courts have refused to adopt the distinction that sovereign immunity applies only to governmental functions, not proprietary functions,[64] a distinction which at one time was almost uniformly applied to decide the immunity of lower governmental units.[65]

---

and *Reemergence of the Governmental/Proprietary Distinction: A Setback in Idaho's Governmental Liability Law*, 20 Idaho L Rev 197, 201 (1984).

[58] Jaffe, *Suits Against Governments and Officers: Sovereign Immunity*, 77 Harv L Rev 1, 19 (1963) (perhaps the prime reason for sovereign immunity in the United States was the powerful resistance of the states to being sued on their debts).

[59] Standiford v Salt Lake City Corp, 605 P2d 1230, 1235 (Utah 1980). The wide availability of insurance in twentieth century America has now significantly reduced the basis for this fear.

[60] List v O'Connor, 21 Ill App 2d 399, 158 NE2d 103, 107 (1959), *aff'd*, 19 Ill 2d 337, 167 NE2d 188 (1960).

[61] Kawananakoa v Polyblank, 205 US 349, 353 (1907) (Holmes, J); *see also* Torres v State, 476 SW2d 846, 847 (Tex Civ App 1972).

[62] *See* Greenhill & Murto, *Governmental Immunity*, 49 Tex L Rev 462, 462 (1971).

[63] Ralph v City of Daytona Beach, 412 So 2d 875, 877 (Fla Dist Ct App 1982); Willis v Department of Conservation & Economic Dev, 55 NJ 534, 264 A2d 34, 35 (1970); *see generally* Note, *Local Government Sovereign Immunity: The Need for Reform*, 18 Wake Forest L Rev 43, 54 (1982).

[64] Williams v West Chester State College, 29 Pa Commw 240, 370 A2d 774, 776 (1977). *See also* Green v Commonwealth, 13 Mass App 524, 435 NE2d 362, 365 (1982). *But see* Smith v State, 93 Idaho 795, 473 P2d 937, 944 (1970).

[65] *See* §3.03.

The Congress and numerous state legislatures have now significantly modified the sovereign immunity doctrine by passing tort claims acts and other liability statutes.[66] Nonetheless, there is some authority that sovereign immunity cannot be waived by the legislature.[67]

Immunity of State Agencies and other State Entities

Generally, the tort immunity of a state extends to all subordinate bodies of the state, such as boards, commissions, and other agencies.[68] For example, the courts have consistently held that state universities are entitled to claim the benefits of sovereign immunity.[69]

In at least one state, the determination of whether a state agency is entitled to the protection of sovereign immunity depends on whether the agency's revenues are derived from the state treasury or, if they are partially received from other sources, whether the money is channeled back into the state treasury.[70] A state racing commission which obtains such state funding and returns the revenue it receives from other sources to the state is entitled to sovereign immunity.[71]

It has recently been held that a state board which was given the power by the legislature *to sue and be sued* was entitled to the defense of sovereign immunity.[72] The court held that that legislative provision was not a waiver of immunity.[73]

Immunity of State Officials

Generally, state employees enjoy at least some of the benefits of sovereign

---

66 *See* §§3.03–3.11.

67 *See* Santiago v Clark, 444 F Supp 1077, 1079 (ND W Va 1978).

68 Santiago v Clark, 444 F Supp 1077, 1078 (ND W Va 1978); *see also* Restatement (Second) of Torts §895B comment g (1977); *see generally* Note, *The Applicability of Sovereign Immunity to Independent Public Authorities*, 74 Harv L Rev 714 (1961).

A handful of states have held that there is no immunity for proprietary activities. *See* Carroll v Kittle, 203 Kan 841, 457 P2d 21, 27 (1969); Biello v Pennsylvania Liquor Control Bd, 454 Pa 179, 301 A2d 849, 851-52 (1973).

State agencies may be immune for claims alleging that injuries resulted from the exercise of official judgment or discretion. *See* Willis v Department of Conservation & Economic Dev, 55 NJ 534, 264 A2d 34, 37 (1970).

69 Cantwell v University of Mass, 551 F2d 879, 880 (1st Cir 1977); Williams v West Chester State College, 29 Pa Commw 240, 370 A2d 774, 775 (1977); Lowe v Texas Tech Univ, 540 SW2d 297, 298 (Tex 1976).

70 Santiago v Clark, 444 F Supp 1077, 1079 (ND W Va 1978) (West Virginia law).

71 *Id.*

72 Kringen v Shea, 333 NW2d 445, 446 (SD 1983).

73 *Id.*

immunity.[74] This is certainly true where the officials are sued in their individual capacities in order to circumvent the rule against suing the state.[75] However, state officials cannot claim sovereign immunity where the plaintiff's claim is not, in essence, a suit against the state.[76] For example, an aide to a state day care center who was allegedly negligent in supervising a minor using playground equipment could not claim sovereign immunity.[77]

There is authority that a state employee is immune for nonfeasance but liable for misfeasance,[78] a distinction which is rather difficult to apply with precision. One court construed those rules to mean that an assistant coach would be immune for the *mere* failure to spot a gymnast, even if it was his duty to do so. However, if he had, by affirmative conduct, reasonably led the gymnast to believe he would spot her and she reasonably relied on those acts, he would be liable if he failed to do so.[79]

It has sometimes been held that state employees are entitled to sovereign immunity only for discretionary acts and not for ministerial ones.[80]

§3.03 Immunity of Local Governmental Units

The national and state governments are the only true sovereigns.[81] However, since the early English case of *Russell v Men of Devon*,[82] some courts have applied the doctrine of sovereign immunity to local governmental units.[83] Since local governmental units are not sovereigns, this immunity has been called by another name: governmental immunity.

---

[74] Santiago v Clark, 444 F Supp 1077, 1078 (ND W Va 1978); Lowe v Texas Tech Univ, 540 SW2d 297, 298 (Tex 1976). *See generally* Restatement (Second) of Torts §895D (1977).

[75] DeStafney v University of Ala, 413 So 2d 391, 393 (Ala 1982).

[76] *Id* 395.

[77] *Id.*

[78] *See* Cantwell v University of Mass, 551 F2d 879, 880 (1st Cir 1977) (Massachusetts law).

[79] *Id* 881.

[80] *See* Kringen v Shea, 333 NW2d 445, 446 (SD 1983); *but see* Merrill v Birhanzel, 310 NW2d 522 (SD 1981).

[81] *See generally* Schenkolewski v Cleveland Metroparks Sys, 67 Ohio St 2d 31, 426 NE2d 784, 785 (1981), *overruled on other grounds*, Haverlack v Portage Homes, Inc, 2 Ohio St 3d 26, 442 NE2d 749 (1982).

[82] 100 Eng Rep 359 (KB 1788).

[83] *See* Wright v City of N Charleston, 271 SC 515, 248 SE2d 480, 481 (1978). *See generally* Restatement (Second) of Torts §895C (1977).

This immunity has been criticized by numerous commentators. *See* Fuller & Casner, *Municipal Tort Liability in Operation*, 54 Harv L Rev 437 (1941); Liebman, *Assault on the Citadel*, 4 Suffolk UL Rev 832 (1970); Seasongood, *Municipal Corporations*, 22 Va L Rev 910 (1936).

Most courts have not allowed local governmental units to assert complete immunity.[84] At one time the prevailing rule was that such governmental entities were immune only for torts which arose out of activities of a governmental nature; torts arising out of proprietary activities of the government were not protected.[85]

The purported distinction between governmental functions and proprietary functions has been heavily and correctly criticized as difficult, if not impossible, to apply properly.[86] Not surprisingly, the cases are truly irreconcilable.[87] A few recent examples of how this distinction has been applied to sports and recreational accidents follow.

The athletic activities provided by a school have generally been considered an exercise of a governmental function.[88] Accordingly, plaintiffs injured in extracurricular football programs cannot recover from the school district.[89] The fact that admission was charged for admittance to the games

---

84 In some states there is no immunity for municipalities. *See, e.g.*, State v Jennings, 555 P2d 248 (Alaska 1976).

85 *See generally* Standiford v Salt Lake City Corp, 605 P2d 1230, 1233 (Utah 1980). The first case which applied this distinction in the United States was Bailey v City of New York, 3 Hill 531 (NY 1842).

At one point, every state other than Florida, Ohio, and South Carolina applied the governmental/proprietary distinction. *See* Hall, *Sovereign Immunity and Reemergence of the Governmental/Proprietary Distinction: A Setback in Idaho's Governmental Liability Law*, 20 Idaho L Rev 197, 212 (1984).

86 *See, e.g.*, Indian Towing Co, Inc v United States, 350 US 61, 65 (1955) (*quagmire*); Johnson v Salt Lake City Corp, 629 P2d 432, 433 (Utah 1981) (distinction was *inherently unsound and unworkable*). *See also* K. Davis, Administrative Law of the Seventies §25.07, at 559 (1976); W. Prosser, The Law of Torts §131, at 982 (4th ed 1971); Hall, *Sovereign Immunity and Reemergence of the Governmental/Proprietary Distinction: A Setback in Idaho's Governmental Liability Law*, 20 Idaho L Rev 197, 221 (1984); Olson, *Governmental Immunity From Tort Liability—Two Decades of Decline: 1959-1979*, 31 Baylor L Rev 485, 486-87 (1979); Roberts & Thronson, *A New Perspective—Has Utah Entered the Twentieth Century In Tort Law?*, 1981 Utah L Rev 495, 511-12.

87 *Compare* City of Terre Haute v Webster, 112 Ind App 101, 40 NE2d 972 (1942) (public parks are proprietary activities) *with* Collision v City of Saginaw, 84 Mich App 325, 269 NW2d 586 (1978), *revd on other grounds*, 406 Mich 944, 277 NW2d 643 (1979) (public parks are governmental activities); *compare* Sarmiento v City of Corpus Christi, 465 SW2d 813 (Tex Civ App 1971) (swimming pools are proprietary activities) *with* Scott v City of Millen, 153 Ga App 231, 265 SE2d 30, 31 (1980) and Virovatz v City of Cudahy, 211 Wis 357, 190 NW 843 (1933) (swimming pools are governmental activities); *compare* Boyer v Iowa High School Athletic Assn, 256 Iowa 337, 127 NW2d 606, 608 (1964) (school was engaged in governmental function where it charged spectators for admission) *with* Sawaya v Tucson High School Dist.No 1, 78 Ariz 389, 281 P2d 105 (1955) (leasing of football stadium was proprietary activity).

88 Cody v Southfield-Lathrup School Dist, 25 Mich App 33, 181 NW2d 81, 83 (1970); Hall v Columbus Bd of Educ, 32 Ohio App 2d 297, 290 NE2d 580, 583 (1972); Real v School Dist No 211, 7 Wash 2d 502, 110 P2d 179, 181 (1941).

89 Lovitt v Concord School Dist, 58 Mich App 593, 228 NW2d 479, 481 (1975).

does not convert the governmental function into a proprietary function.[90] A school was held immune from liability where a student was injured while using a swing because the furnishing of swings was a governmental function.[91] A city-run day camp was a protected governmental function because the activities were solely for the public benefit, there was no profit made on the activity, and it improved the public health and welfare.[92]

In some states, actions for nuisance were an exception to the common law of governmental immunity.[93] A municipality may create a nuisance through wrongful acts that produce a situation where injury is probable;[94] it is conduct beyond mere negligence.[95] For example, a city's failure to keep a chain blocking an access road brightly painted was not a nuisance, and a motorcyclist who ran into the chain could not recover.[96] Similarly, toboggan runs, at least ones which are safely constructed and maintained, are not nuisances per se.[97]

Some courts have not allowed an exception for nuisance claims because there are only *highly technical* distinctions between negligence and nuisance and the reasons behind the immunity doctrine are equally valid whatever the label of the claim.[98] One court held that the nuisance exception could not apply where this general area of immunity had been codified and this exception was not specified.[99]

In Texas, there is governmental immunity for claims of attractive nuisance.[100] Accordingly, a city was immune when a boy drowned in a garbage

---

90 *Id.* The school's net operating loss for the past five years was further evidence of this. *Id.*

91 Duson v Midland County Indep School Dist, 627 SW2d 428, 429 (Tex Civ App 1981).

92 Austin v Mayor & City Council, 286 Md 51, 405 A2d 255, 262 (1979); *see also* Porter v City of Gainesville, 147 Ga App 274, 248 SE2d 501, 503 (1978) (park is a governmental function).

93 *See* Scott v City of Millen, 153 Ga App 231, 265 SE2d 30, 31 (1980); Collision v City of Saginaw, 84 Mich App 325, 269 NW2d 586, 588 (1978), *revd on other grounds*, 406 Mich 944, 277 NW2d 643 (1979); Dean v Bays Mt Park Assn, 551 SW2d 702, 704 (Tenn Ct App 1977).

94 Dean v Bays Mt Park Assn, 551 SW2d 702, 704 (Tenn Ct App 1977).

95 *Id.*

96 *Id* 705. In Tennessee, a municipality is liable for a nuisance, but not for negligence. *See id* 704-05.

97 Buddy v State, 59 Mich App 598, 229 NW2d 865, 867 (1975). *But see* Collison v City of Saginaw, 406 Mich 944, 277 NW2d 643, 643 (1979).

98 Walker v Forest Preserve Dist, 27 Ill 2d 538, 190 NE2d 296, 297-98 (1963).

99 *See* Collision v City of Saginaw, 84 Mich App 325, 269 NW2d 586, 588 (1978), *revd on other grounds*, 406 Mich 944, 277 NW2d 643 (Mich 1979).

100 *See* Tex Rev Civ Stat Ann art 6252-19, §14(11) (Vernon 1970).

disposal area.[101] However, there are also decisions holding that claims of attractive nuisance are not barred by governmental immunity.[102]

There is authority that local governmental units are immune only for injuries resulting from their discretionary acts. The Ohio Supreme Court, in *Marrek v Cleveland Metroparks Board of Commissioners*,[103] recently held that a park district board of commissioners had no immunity except for acts or omissions involving the exercise of an executive or planning function, i.e., the making of a basic policy decision that was characterized by the exercise of a high degree of official judgment or discretion. However, once the board's decision to engage in a certain activity has been made, it is liable for the negligence of its employees in the performance of those activities, absent a statute to the contrary.[104] Accordingly, the board's failure to supervise a sledding area was not given immunity.[105]

A governmental unit's liability may turn on the name of the plaintiff's cause of action. In *Sims v Etowah County Board of Education*, the Alabama Supreme Court held that a county board of education can be sued for breach of an implied contract to furnish a safe place for a spectator to watch a football game, but the board of education has immunity from tort liability for injuries arising out of the same accident.[106]

In any event, common law immunity is now the exception, rather than the rule, for local government units.[107]

Immunity of Local Governmental Officials

Many local government employees have not been entitled to claim governmental immunity when they were sued for athletic injuries.[108] For example, it has sometimes been held that even if a school has immunity, this immunity does not cover teachers or coaches.[109] Indeed, one court stated that "no matter how highly we regard the profession of teaching, we cannot conclude that the

---

101 City of Houston v George, 479 SW2d 257, 258 (Tex 1972).

102 Metropolitan Govt v Counts, 541 SW2d 133, 137 (Tenn 1976).

103 9 Ohio St 3d 194, 459 NE2d 873, 875 (1984).

104 *Id.*

105 *Id.*

106 337 So 2d 1310, 1314 (Ala 1976) (spectator injured when viewing stand on which she was sitting collapsed).

107 Restatement (Second) of Torts §895C comment e (1977). Only a handful of jurisdictions do not have statutes limiting the immunity of local governmental units. *See* Note, *Local Government Sovereign Immunity: The Need for Reform*, 18 Wake Forest L Rev 43, 46 (1982).

108 *See generally* Restatement (Second) of Torts §895D (1977).

109 Baird v Hosmer, 46 Ohio St 2d 273, 347 NE2d 533, 536 (1976); *see also* Proehl, *Tort Liability of Teachers*, 12 Vand L Rev 723, 740 (1959); *see generally* Kersey v Harbin, 591 SW2d 745, 749 (Mo Ct App 1979) (school superintendent, principal, and teacher were not immune); Lovitt v Concord School Dist, 58 Mich App 593, 228 NW2d 479, 483 (1975).

teacher is exercising some of the sovereign powers of the state in performing duties of his profession."[110] In *Short v Griffitts*, the court held that the
athletic director, the baseball coach and the buildings and ground supervisor,
all employees of a county school board, were not entitled to claim immunity
when they were sued for their negligence in failing to warn of or remove
broken glass from a track.[111]

The courts have reached different results regarding the immunity of school
principals and superintendents. One court concluded that they should be given
immunity,[112] but there is contrary authority.[113]

Insurance

Several jurisdictions have held that the purchase of insurance does not, by
itself, waive governmental immunity[114] or sovereign immunity.[115] However,
in many states, the applicable tort claims act provides that if insurance is
provided there is no immunity.[116]

Decline of Sovereign and Governmental Immunity Doctrine

Many state courts, beginning primarily in the 1960s, judicially abolished or
modified sovereign and governmental immunity.[117] Although one court held
that any contraction of immunity is a task for the legislature,[118] the judicial
trend towards reduction of immunity is unmistakable.[119]

Numerous legislatures have passed tort claims acts and other liability statutes
limiting sovereign and governmental immunity.[120] Indeed, the overwhelming

---

110 Baird v Hosmer, 46 Ohio St 2d 273, 347 NE2d 533, 536 (1976) (quoting Leymel v
Johnson, 105 Cal App 694, 288 P 858, 860 (1930)).

111 220 Va 53, 255 SE2d 479, 481 (1979).

112 Lovitt v Concord School Dist, 58 Mich App 593, 228 NW2d 479, 482 (1975).

113 Kersey v Harbin, 591 SW2d 745, 749 (Mo Ct App 1979).

114 *See, e.g.*, Cody v Southfield-Lathrup School Dist, 25 Mich App 33, 181 NW2d 81, 85
(1970); *see generally* Annot, 68 ALR2d 1473 (1959).

115 Strong v Curators of the Univ of Mo, 575 SW2d 812, 813 (Mo Ct App 1978).

116 *See* §3.04.

117 Brown v Wichita State Univ, 219 Kan 2, 547 P2d 1015, 1019-20 (1976) (citing cases).
One commentator stated that the doctrines of sovereign and governmental immunity may have
been subjected to a more protracted and caustic challenge than any other rule of law. *See*
Olson, *Governmental Immunity From Tort Liability—Two Decades of Decline: 1959-1979*, 31
Baylor L Rev 485, 485 (1979). Indeed, the governmental immunity doctrine was criticized as
early as 1924. *See* Borchard, *Governmental Liability in Tort*, 34 Yale LJ 1 (1924).

118 *See, e.g.*, Austin v Mayor & City Council, 286 Md 51, 405 A2d 255, 258 (1979).

119 *See generally* Restatement (Second) of Torts ch 45A, Special Note on Governmental
Immunity (1977).

120 *See* Brown v Wichita State Univ, 219 Kan 2, 547 P2d 1015, 1021-22 (1976) (giving
examples); *see also* §§3.03-3.11.
A county's waiver of immunity has been held to apply only to accidents which occurred

majority of states have now eliminated or limited this doctrine either by judicial decision or by legislative enactment.[121]

§3.04 State Tort Immunity Statutes

A significant number of states have now enacted statutory provisions which specify to what extent public entities and public employees can be sued for their torts.[122] These statutes generally provide that public entities[123] are not liable

---

after the waiver legislation became effective. Berg v Merricks, 20 Md App 666, 318 A2d 220, 230 (1974).

[121] Austin v Mayor & City Council, 286 Md 51, 405 A2d 255, 270 n 1 (1979) (Cole, J, dissenting) (citing cases); Ohio Valley Contractors v Board of Educ, 293 SE2d 437 (W Va 1982) (nonrecreational accident case). One commentator concluded that only six states have not substantially modified this doctrine. *See* Note, *The King Can Do Wrong - Maybe: Abolition of Court - Imposed Sovereign Immunity for Nondiscretionary Negligent Acts,* 3 Miss CL Rev 103, 106 (1982).

A summary of the current status of governmental and sovereign immunity in the various states is given in Harley & Wasinger, *Governmental Immunity,* 16 Washburn LJ 12, 33 (1976).

[122] *See, e.g.,* Ala Code §§11-47-190 to -192, 11-93-1 to -3, 31-9-16 (Supp 1984); Alaska Stat §§09.50.250 -.300 (1983); Cal Govt Code §815-840.6 (West Supp 1984); Fla Stat Ann §768.28 (West Supp 1983); Ga Code §36-33-1 (Supp 1983); Hawaii Rev Stat §§661-1 to -11, 662-1 to -16 (1983); Idaho Code §§6-901 to -928 (Supp 1983); Ill Ann Stat ch 37, §439.8, ch 85, §§1-101 to 9-107 (Smith-Hurd Supp 1983); Ind Code Ann §34-4-16-1 to -7, 34-4-16.5-1 to -19 (Supp 1983); Iowa Code Ann §§25A.1 -.22, 613A.1-.13 (West Supp 1984); Kan Stat Ann §§75-6101 to -6118 (Supp 1983); Mass Gen Laws Ann ch 258, §1-13 (West Supp 1983); Mich Stat Ann §3.996 (107) (Callaghan 1977); Minn Stat Ann §§3.736, 466.01-.15 (West 1977); Mo Ann Stat §537.600 (Vernon Supp 1984); Neb Rev Stat §§23-2401 to -2420 (1977); Nev Rev Stat §§41.0305-.039 (1979); NJ Stat Ann §§59:2-1 to -10, 59:3-1 to -14 (West 1982); NY Ct of Cl Act §8 (McKinney 1963); NC Gen Stat §§143-291, 153A-435, 160A-485 (1983); Ohio Rev Code Ann §2743.02 (Baldwin 1984); Okla Stat Ann tit 51, §§151-170 (West Supp 1984); Or Rev Stat §§30.260 -.400 (1981); Pa Cons Stat Ann tit 42, §§8521-8528, 8541-8564 (Purdon 1982); SC Code Ann §5-7-70 (Law Co-op 1977); Tenn Code Ann §§29-20-101 to -407 (Supp 1983); Tex Rev Civil Stat Ann art 6252-19 (Vernon Supp 1982); Utah Code Ann §§63-30-1 to -38 (1983); Vt Stat Ann tit 12, §§5601-5605 (1973); Wash Rev Code Ann §§4.92.010-.090 (Supp 1983); Wyo Stat §§1-39-101 to -119 (Supp 1984).

One court held that such statutes were not to be given retroactive application. *See* Larson v Independent School Dist No 314, 289 NW2d 112, 122-23 (Minn 1979).

The Idaho Tort Claims Act is analyzed in Hall, *Sovereign Immunity and Reemergence of the Governmental/Proprietary Distinction: A Setback in Idaho's Governmental Liability Law,* 20 Idaho L Rev 197 (1984).

One commentator concluded that only Delaware, the District of Columbia, Hawaii, Louisiana, South Dakota, and Virginia do not have statutes specifying the liability of local governmental units. *See* Note, *Local Government Sovereign Immunity: The Need For Reform,* 18 Wake Forest L Rev 43, 46 n 37 (1982).

The requirements of the tort claims act must be followed strictly because neither the state nor one of its agencies may waive some requirements such as venue. *See* Catania v University of Neb, 204 Neb 304, 282 NW2d 27, 33 (1979).

In some states there is a different tort claims act for the state than for other governmental

for the torts of their employees except to the extent specified in the statute.[124] However, the statutes generally impose liability, with specified exceptions,[125] on the government for the negligent acts or omissions of its employees if a private individual under similar circumstances would be liable.[126] In some states the government is only liable for the negligence of its employees; it is not liable for their wilful or malicious acts.[127] For example, the government was not vicariously liable for the injuries caused by a physical education teacher who assaulted and battered a student.[128]

Care must be taken when pleading a cause of action under these statutes. Several courts have required plaintiffs to state their claim against the government with great specificity.[129]

As alluded to earlier, many state legislatures have created or retained immunity in certain specified areas, many of which are applicable to recreational accidents. The five most important areas where immunity has been retained are for injuries resulting from:

1. Dangerous natural conditions of unimproved public property[130]

2. The exercise of discretionary acts[131]

3. The exercise of governmental functions[132]

---

entities. A state university is an agency of the state, and, therefore, the state tort claims act should be used, not the tort claims act for political subdivisions. *See* Catania v University of Neb, 204 Neb 304, 282 NW2d 27, 32 (1979).

Not all jurisdictions have limited immunity. *See, e.g.,* Ark Stat Ann §12-2901 (1979) (all counties and municipal corporations are immune from tort liability).

123 Some tort claims acts apply to all governmental entities, including counties, municipalities, and the state itself. *See, e.g.,* Fla Stat Ann §768.28 (West Supp 1982).

124 *See, e.g.,* Pa Cons Stat Ann tit 42, §8541 (Purdon 1982).

125 *See* §§3.05-3.09.

126 *See, e.g.,* Fla Stat Ann §768.28 (West Supp 1983); Mass Gen Laws Ann ch 258, §2 (West Supp 1983). Accordingly, if a private individual would not be liable because there was no negligence or the negligent act or omission would not subject the actor to liability under an applicable state statute, the government also would not be liable. *See* Watson v City of Omaha, 209 Neb 835, 312 NW2d 256 (1981) (government is entitled to benefits of state recreational user statute); *see also* §5.07.

127 NJ Stat Ann §59:2-10 (West 1982); Mass Gen Laws Ann ch 258, §10 (West Supp 1983).

128 Willis v Dade County School Bd, 411 So 2d 245, 246 (Fla Dist Ct App 1982).

129 *See* Mittenhuber v Herrera, 142 Cal App 3d 1, 190 Cal Rptr 694, 696-97 (1983); ("plaintiff must set forth facts in his complaint sufficiently detailed and specific to support an inference that each of the statutory elements of liability is satisfied. General allegations are regarded as inadequate."); Keyes v Santa Clara Valley Water Dist, 128 Cal App 3d 888, 180 Cal Rptr 586, 590 (1982).

130 *See* §3.05.

131 *See* §3.06.

132 *See* §3.07.

4. Recreational accidents[133]

5. School activities[134]

Insurance

A government's purchase of insurance can have important ramifications. In some states, but not all,[135] if the government has obtained insurance, immunity[136] is waived up to the limits of the insurance policy[137] or to the extent stated in policy.[138] Where there was no evidence that the board of education had purchased liability insurance thereby waiving its immunity, the plaintiff could not prevail.[139]

The courts have held that damages for governmental acts that are not covered by the insurance policy are not recoverable. For example, if the insurance policy were limited to liabilities in excess of $1 million and a plaintiff only claimed $50,000 damages, there would be no waiver of immunity.[140] Similarly, there is no waiver of immunity for the deductible amount of the insurance policy.[141]

The waiver of immunity for acts covered by an insurance policy is usually explicitly provided for in the tort claims statute.[142] In *Beach v City of Springfield*, the court held that even where there was no statute on point an insurance company that accepted public funds to provide insurance was estopped to argue that the governmental unit was immune from liability.[143]

The government's purchase of insurance does not waive the requirement that the injured party must give notice of the accident to the government prior to commencing suit.[144]

---

[133] *See* §3.08.

[134] *See* §3.09.

[135] *See, e.g.,* Mich Comp Laws §691.1409 (Supp 1984).

[136] This has been construed to waive only the immunity provided in the same statute and not immunity created by other laws. *See* Kobylanski v Chicago Bd of Educ, 63 Ill 2d 165, 347 NE2d 705, 709-10 (1976).

[137] Ill Ann Stat Ch 85, §9-103 (Smith-Hurd Supp 1983); Minn Stat Ann §466-06 (West 1977); Mo Ann Stat §537.610 (Veron Supp 1983) (policy limit is $100,000 per person, $800,000 per occurrence); NC Gen Stat §§153A-435, 160A-485 (1983); Tenn Code Ann §29-20-404 (1980); Vt Stat Ann tit 29, §1403 (Supp 1984); Wyo Stat §1-39-118 (Supp 1984).

[138] *See. e.g.,* Neb Rev Stat §23-2413 (1977).

[139] Clary v Alexander County Bd of Educ, 285 NC 188, 203 SE2d 820, 825 (1974).

[140] Beckus v Chicago Bd of Educ, 78 Ill App 3d 558, 397 NE2d 175, 178, 33 Ill Dec 842 (1979).

[141] Beach v City of Springfield, 32 Ill App 2d 256, 177 NE2d 436, 440 (1961).

[142] *See* Beckus v Chicago Bd of Educ, 78 Ill App 3d 558, 397 NE2d 175, 178 (1979); Clary v Alexander County Bd of Educ, 285 NC 188, 203 SE2d 820, 825 (1974).

[143] 32 Ill App 2d 256, 177 NE2d 436, 439 (1961).

[144] Roberts v City of Boulder, 197 Colo 97, 589 P2d 934, 935 (1979).

Notice of Claim

In many jurisdictions, notice of the accident must be given to the government, usually in a short period of time.[145] The purpose of requiring notice is to provide the government with an adequate opportunity to investigate the accident while the facts are still fresh.[146] There are usually no serious consequences if the details of the accident are not perfectly accurate.[147] A claim was not defective merely because it erroneously described the location of the accident by 500 feet.[148]

A plaintiff's failure to file notice within the requisite time period, sometimes as short as 90 days after the injury, has been held to be a complete defense for the government.[149] However, in some states if the injured person is incompetent[150] or a minor,[151] the notice requirement is tolled. In addition, some state laws provide that failure to comply in a timely fashion with the notice requirement does not preclude a plaintiff's lawsuit if the government had actual notice of the accident[152] or if the government should have reasonably apprised itself of the occurrence of the incident or could have done so with the exercise of proper diligence.[153]

Maximum Recoveries

Many jurisdictions have set a maximum amount which can be recovered

---

145 *See, e.g.,* Ala Code §11-47-192 (1977); Fla Stat Ann §768.28 (West Supp 1983); Idaho Code §§6-905, 6-906 (1978); Ill Ann Stat ch 85, §8-102 (Smith-Hurd Supp 1983); Ind Code Ann §34-4-16.5-6 (Burns Supp 1983); Iowa Code Ann §25A.13 (West 1978); Mass Gen Laws Ann ch 258, §4 (West Supp 1983); Minn Stat Ann §466.05 (West 1977); Neb Rev Stat §23-2416 (1977); Nev Rev Stat §41.036 (1979) (not a condition precedent to suit); NJ Stat Ann §59:8-3 (West 1982); Okla Stat Ann tit 51, §156 (West Supp 1984); Or Rev Stat §30.275 (1981); Tenn Code Ann §29-20-302 (Supp 1983); Tex Rev Civ Stat Ann art 6252-19 (Vernon Supp 1982) (not apply if government has actual notice); Wash Rev Code §§4.92.100, 4.96.020 (Supp 1984). *See also* Mills v American Playground Device Co, 405 NE2d 621, 624 (Ind Ct App 1980).

146 Leone v City of Utica, 66 AD2d 463, 414 NYS2d 412, 416 (1979), *affd,* 49 NY2d 811, 403 NE2d 964, 426 NYS2d 980 (1980).

147 *See* Mills v American Playground Device Co, 405 NE2d 621, 624 (Ind Ct App 1980).

148 Leone v City of Utica, 66 AD2d 463, 414 NYS2d 412, 416 (1979), *affd,* 49 NY2d 811, 403 NE2d 964, 426 NYS2d 980 (1980).

149 Roberts v City of Boulder, 197 Colo 97, 589 P2d 934, 935 (1979) (bike accident); Besette v Enderlin School Dist No 22, 288 NW2d 67, 70 (SD 1980) (citing cases). *But see* Wis Stat Ann §893.80 (West 1983).

150 Ind Code Ann §34-4-16.5-8 (Supp 1983).

151 Hunter v North Mason High School, 12 Wash App 304, 529 P2d 898, 900 (1974).

152 Tex Rev Civ Stat Ann art 6252-19 (Vernon Supp 1982).

153 Tenn Code Ann §29-20-302 (Supp 1983).

from the government.[154] In addition, most states prohibit claims for punitive damages.[155]

Indemnification

Generally, public employees will be provided a defense and indemnified by the government for acts within the course and scope of their employment.[156] However, several states will not provide these benefits if the employee acted wilfully or wantonly,[157] fraudulently,[158] or with criminal intent.[159]

Constitutionality

State tort immunity acts have been upheld as constitutional.[160]

---

154 *See, e.g.*, Ala Code §11-93-2 (Supp 1983) ($100,000 per occurrence); Fla Stat Ann §768.28 (West Supp 1983) ($100,000 per person, $200,000 per occurrence); Idaho Code §6-926 (1978) ($100,000 per person, $300,000 per occurrence, plus insurance); Ind Code Ann §34-4-16.5-4 (Supp 1983) ($300,000 per person, $5,000,000 per occurrence); Kan Stat Ann §§75-6105 to 75-6111 (Supp 1983) ($500,000 per occurrence or insurance policy limits, whichever is higher); Mass Gen Laws Ann ch 258, §2 (West Supp 1983) ($100,000 maximum); Minn Stat Ann §§3.736, 466.04 (West Supp 1984) ($200,000 per person, $600,000 per occurrence); Mo Ann Stat §537.610 (Vernon Supp 1984) ($100,000 per person, $800,000 per occurrence); Nev Rev Stat §41.035 (1979) ($50,000); Okla Stat Ann tit 51, §154 (West Supp 1984) ($25,000 per person for property damage, $100,000 per person for personal injury, $1,000,000 per occurrence); Or Rev Stat §30.270 (1981) ($50,000 per person for property damage, $100,000 per person for personal injury; $300,000 per occurrence); Pa Cons Stat Ann tit 42, §8553 (Purdon 1982) ($500,000); Tex Rev Civ Stat Ann art 6252-19b (Vernon Supp 1982) ($100,000 per person, $300,000 per occurrence); Utah Code Ann §63-30-34 (Supp 1983) ($250,000 per person, $500,000 per occurrence); Vt Stat Ann tit 12, §5601 (1973); Wis Stat Ann §893.80 (West 1983) ($50,000); Wyo Stat §1-39-118 (Supp 1984) ($500,000 per occurrence).

155 *See, e.g.*, Cal Govt Code §818 (West 1980); Fla Stat Ann §768.28 (West Supp 1983); Idaho Code §6-918 (1978); Ill Ann Stat ch 85, §2-102 (Smith-Hurd Supp 1984); Ind Code Ann §34-4-16.5-4 (Supp 1983); Iowa Code Ann §25A.4 (West Supp 1983); Kan Stat Ann §75-6105 (Supp 1983); Mass Gen Laws Ann ch 258, §2 (West Supp 1983); Minn Stat Ann §466.04 (West 1977); Mo Ann Stat §537.610 (Vernon Supp 1984); Nev Rev Stat §41.035 (1979); Okla Stat Ann tit 51, §154 (West Supp 1984); Or Rev Stat §30.270 (1981).

156 Cal Govt Code §825 (West 1980); Conn Gen Stat Ann §10-235 (West Supp 1984) (applies to schools); Ind Code Ann §34-4-16.5-5 (Supp 1983) (governing body must determine that payment of damages is in the best interests of the governmental entity); Wis Stat Ann §895.46 (West 1983).

157 Fla Stat Ann §768.28 (West Supp 1983); Iowa Code Ann §25A.21 (West 1978); Minn Stat Ann §466.07 (West 1977); Or Rev Stat §§30.285, 30.287 (1981); Tex Rev Civ Stat Ann art 6252-19b (Vernon Supp 1982) (or gross negligence); *see generally* ND Cent Code §§32-12.1-.04 (Purdon Supp 1983) (indemnification for all acts within the scope of employment).

158 Kan Stat Ann §§75-6108, -6109 (Supp 1983); NC Gen Stat §160A-167 (Supp 1983); Okla Stat Ann tit 51, §161 (West Supp 1984); Utah Code Ann §63-30-37 (Supp 1983).

159 Idaho Code §6-903 (1983); Minn Stat Ann §3.736 (West Supp 1984); Nev Rev Stat §§41.0339, 41.0349 (1979).

160 Roberts v City of Boulder, 197 Colo 97, 589 P2d 934, 935 (1979); Brown v Wichita State Univ, 219 Kan 2, 547 P2d 1015, 1025-26 (1976) (did not violate equal protection);

§3.05   —Dangerous Natural Conditions of Unimproved Public Property

Several states have eliminated governmental liability for accidents arising out of the natural conditions of any unimproved public property.[161] These laws were enacted because it was perceived that the burden and expense of transforming public property from its natural condition into a safe condition would be so great that many public entities would refuse to perform that undertaking and would instead close those areas to public use.[162] In effect, the legislatures have made the *price* to use this type of property the forfeiture of a civil remedy for injuries which result from the use of the property.[163]

The government is generally not liable for injuries arising from the natural topography of the land, because that would make it an insurer of the safety of the public.[164] Indeed, natural topographical conditions are not considered dangerous conditions unless they constitute a deceptive trap for individuals who exercise due care.[165] In *Mittenhuber v Herrera*,[166] a child riding a bicycle on a hill approached an intersection and was unable to stop quickly enough to avoid having an accident. The court held that was no governmental liability because a city is not required either to grade all its streets in hilly areas or to forgo development in those areas.[167]

This statutory tort immunity for injuries resulting from natural conditions of unimproved public property has been given a broad construction.[168] Public property has been considered by some courts to be unimproved until there is a physical change in the condition of the property at the location of the

---

see generally Winston v Reorganized School Dist R-2, 636 SW2d 324 (Mo 1982) (statute substantially reestablishing sovereign immunity is constitutional).

161 Cal Govt Code §831.2 (West 1980); Ind Code Ann §34-4-16.5-3 (Burns Supp 1984); Kan Stat Ann §75-6104(o) (Supp 1983); Okla Stat Ann tit 51, §155 (West Supp 1984).

162 *See* Senate Legislative Committee Comment to Cal Govt Code §831.2 (West 1980). Certain types of physical hazards, such as steep and slippery banks along a lake or stream, may be difficult, if not impossible, to modify. Therefore, some immunity from tort liability arising out of those dangerous conditions of public property may be advisable in order to keep those areas open to the public. *See* Van Alstyne, *A Study Relating To Sovereign Immunity*, 5 Cal L Revision Comm Rep 494 (1963). *But see* Gonzales v City of San Diego, 130 Cal App 3d 882, 182 Cal Rptr 73, 76 (1982) (there would be an inevitable public outcry if public property was closed from use).

163 *See generally* Senate Legislative Committee Comment to Cal Govt Code §831.2 (1980).

164 Mittenhuber v Herrera, 142 Cal App 3d 9, 190 Cal Rptr 694, 698 (1983).

165 *Id.*

166 *Id.*

167 *Id.*

168 Fuller v State, 51 Cal App 3d 926, 125 Cal Rptr 586, 592 (1975).

injury.[169] A government's raising and lowering of the water level of a lake was held not to be an *improvement* where the plaintiff, while water skiing, hit a submerged rock near the shoreline.[170] Similarly, there was no liability where a boy drowned because the floatation device he was using to go down a river hit a *snag*, several uprooted trees held together by mud in the center of the river, and he became trapped under water. The fatal injury was caused by natural conditions.[171] It was not enough that the flow of water could be controlled by artificial means several miles upstream.[172]

In *Fuller v State*, the court held that although a governmental unit had placed portable lifeguard towers, restroom facilities, and concrete fire rings on a beach, the beach was not converted from unimproved property, which is protected with immunity, into improved property, which is not immune. The accident, viz., diving into shallow water, had no relationship to those improvements.[173]

However, other courts have not been so reticent to find an improvement. In *McKenna v City of Fort Wayne*,[174] a city was not immune when a person in a public park was injured by a limb which fell from a tree. The immunity for injuries arising out of natural conditions of unimproved property did not apply because the property was held to have been improved, viz., there was a picnic table placed under the tree, the grass beneath the tree was mowed, and there was a playground close by.[175]

Governments cannot rely on immunity regarding injuries caused by natural conditions of unimproved public property where the injury was caused by natural conditions and other factors. A city which negligently performed lifeguard services at a beach could be held liable for an injury which resulted because of a combination of a natural condition and another cause, viz., a riptide and the city's failure to warn of a known hazardous condition.[176] In addition, a city may be liable when a beach becomes an exceedingly dangerous place to surf because of the effects of the construction of a jetty and the deposit of dredged sand.[177]

---

169 Eben v State, 130 Cal App 3d 416, 181 Cal Rptr 714, 717-18 (1982). *See also* Keyes v Santa Clara Valley Water Dist, 128 Cal App 3d 888, 180 Cal Rptr 586, 589 (1982) (the fact the injury occurred on manmade lake is not enough to show a change).

170 Eben v State, 130 Cal App 3d 416, 181 Cal Rptr 714, 718-19 (1982).

171 County of Sacramento v Superior Court, 89 Cal App 3d 216, 152 Cal Rptr 391 (1979).

172 152 Cal Rptr 391, 392-93.

173 Fuller v State, 51 Cal App 3d 926, 125 Cal Rptr 586, 592 (1975); *see also* Rendak v State, 18 Cal App 3d 289, 95 Cal Rptr 665, 667 (1971).

174 429 NE2d 662, 666 (Ind Ct App 1981).

175 *Id.*

176 Gonzales v City of San Diego, 130 Cal App 3d 882, 182 Cal Rptr 73, 75 (1982).

177 Buchanan v City of Newport Beach, 50 Cal App 3d 228, 123 Cal Rptr 338, 342 (1975).

A city may be liable for not prohibiting or warning swimmers of the dangers of other individuals who are body surfing in the area.[178] The statutory immunity for unimproved property does not apply because the danger resulted from the conduct of third parties as well as from a condition of the property.[179]

§3.06 —Discretionary Acts

Many state statutes provide, in one of the most significant changes from the common law, that the government is not liable for a public official's failure to exercise or perform a discretionary act, whether or not the discretion is abused.[180] The justification for these provisions has been that it should not be a tort for the government to govern.[181]

However, virtually all acts are the result of someone's exercise of some discretion. Therefore, to avoid transforming these statutes into a wholesale enactment of governmental immunity, many courts have construed these provisions to protect only planning functions, and not to immunize operational decisions.[182] The distinction between acts at the planning level and those at an operational level has not been definitively adopted, and there may still be

---

[178] Kleinke v City of Ocean City, 163 NJ Super 424, 394 A2d 1257, 1261 (1978).

[179] Id.

[180] See Alaska Stat §09.50.250 (1983); Cal Govt Code §820.2 (West 1980); Ga Code §36-33-2 (Supp 1983); Hawaii Rev Stat §662-15 (1968); Idaho Code §6-904 (1978); Ill Ann Stat ch 85, §2-201 (Smith-Hurd Supp 1983); Ind Code Ann §34-4-16.5-3 (Supp 1983) (does not state whether it applies if the discretion is abused); Iowa Code Ann §25A.14 (West 1978); Kan Stat Ann §75-6104 (Supp 1983); Mass Gen Laws Ann ch 258, §10 (West Supp 1983); Minn Stat Ann §§3.736, 466.03 (West 1977); Neb Rev Stat §23-2409 (1977); Nev Rev Stat §41.032 (1979); NJ Stat Ann §§59:2-3, 59:3-2 (West 1982) (does not state whether it applies if the discretion is abused); Okla Stat Ann tit 51, §155 (West Supp 1984) (does not state whether it applies if the discretion is abused); Or Rev Stat Ann §30.265 (1983); Tenn Stat Ann §29-20-205 (1980); Tex Rev Civ Stat Ann art 6252-19 (1970); Utah Code Ann §63-30-10 (Supp 1983); Vt Stat Ann tit 12, §5602 (1973). See also The Federal Tort Claims Act, 28 USC §2680(a).

A few courts, without legislative prodding, have also immunized discretionary acts. See, e.g., Loger v Washington Timber Prod, Inc, 8 Wash App 921, 509 P2d 1009 (1973).

One court held that discretionary immunity should be narrowly construed because it is an exception to the general rule of imposing liability for wrongful acts. See Larson v Independent School Dist No 314, 289 NW2d 112, 121 (Minn 1979).

In Michigan, it is unclear whether public employees are immune for all acts within the scope of their employment or only for discretionary acts. See Grames v King, 123 Mich App 573, 332 NW2d 615, 619 (1983).

[181] Dalehite v United States, 346 US 15, 57 (1953) (Jackson, J, dissenting); Ralph v City of Daytona Beach, 412 So 2d 875, 878-79 (Fla Dist Ct App 1982); Brown v Wichita State Univ, 219 Kan 2, 547 P2d 1015, 1030 (1976).

[182] Willis v Dade County School Bd, 411 So 2d 245, 246 (Fla Dist Ct App 1982); cf §3.11 (Federal Tort Claims Act has been interpreted in a similar fashion).

immune discretionary acts below the planning level.[183] Indeed, other courts have stated that these statutes immunize high-level policy decisions[184] and nonministerial acts.[185]

It is no easy task to decide whether an official's acts are entitled to immunity under these statutes. Therefore, several examples of cases involving sports and recreational accidents follow.

A city's decision to allow, restrict, or regulate vehicular traffic at a beach required the exercise of basic policy evaluations by the government. Therefore, a claim against the city by a sunbather at a public beach who was run over by an automobile was denied because the city's negligence was the result of a protected discretionary act.[186]

A decision to establish and equip a public park is a discretionary function which is immune from suit.[187] A negligent failure to construct a safety fence or barrier near a creek has also been given immunity.[188] However, the failure to maintain existing recreational facilities in a safe condition or to warn of dangers is not a protected discretionary function.[189] Therefore, a city's defective installation and maintenance of a slide[190] or a water fountain[191] is actionable. Similarly, a city may be liable for failing to remove sharp objects on the bottom of a lake.[192]

The government's decision to provide no supervision at night in a recreational area is a protected discretionary decision.[193] Similarly, the decision of where to deploy lifeguards has been held to be discretionary.[194] However, where a city voluntarily assumes a protective duty toward the public by providing lifeguard and police protection at such an area, it must act reasonably.[195]

A school's failure to supervise teachers and students, either in class or in an evening recreational program,[196] is generally not given immunity. [197] For

---

183 See Restatement (Second) of Torts §895A comment b (1977).

184 See, e.g., Larson v Independent School Dist No 314, 289 NW2d 112, 120 (Minn 1979); Sutphen v Benthian, 165 NJ Super 79, 397 A2d 709, 711 (1979).

185 Vargo v Svitchan, 100 Mich App 809, 301 NW2d 1, 4-5 (1980); Cook v Bennett, 94 Mich App 93, 288 NW2d 609, 611-12 (1979).

186 Ralph v City of Daytona Beach, 412 So 2d 875, 878 (Fla Dist Ct App 1982).

187 Mills v American Playground Device Co, 405 NE2d 621, 626 (Ind Ct App 1980).

188 Tamas v Columbus, 244 Ga 200, 259 SE2d 457, 458 (1979).

189 Mills v American Playground Device Co, 405 NE2d 621, 626 (Ind Ct App 1980); see also Baker v State Bd of Higher Educ, 20 Or App 277, 531 P2d 716, 723 (1975).

190 Mills v American Playground Device Co, 405 NE2d 621, 626 (Ind Ct App 1980).

191 Jenkins v City of Miami Beach, 389 So 2d 1195, 1196 (Fla Dist Ct App 1980).

192 Marlow v City of Columbia Heights, 284 NW2d 389, 392 (Minn 1979).

193 Jenkins v City of Miami Beach, 389 So 2d 1195, 1196 (Fla Dist Ct App 1980).

194 Fuller v State, 51 Cal App 3d 926, 125 Cal Rptr 586, 600 (1975).

195 Gonzales v City of San Diego, 130 Cal App 3d 882, 182 Cal Rptr 73, 76 (1982).

196 Law v Newark Bd of Educ, 175 NJ Super 26, 417 A2d 560, 564 (1980).

example, in *Sutphen v Benthian*, a teacher and a board of education were not immune for failing to require protective hockey equipment, failing to give adequate instruction, and negligently allowing a hockey game to be played in an area too small for safe play, since none of those acts or omissions were high-level policy decisions.[198]

Similarly, a physical education teacher who negligently spotted a gymnastic headspring and improperly attempted to teach a student to perform this activity without the proper background skills was not given immunity.[199] A principal who failed to supervise the physical education curriculum properly also was not protected.[200]

A school board's negligent hiring or retention of a physical education teacher with dangerous propensities was held to be an operational, not a planning, function and, therefore, there was no governmental immunity.[201]

§3.07   —Governmental Functions

In Michigan, the government is immune from tort liability for all governmental actions which involve the exercise of "a governmental function."[202] This has been construed to mean that the government is immune for torts arising out of activities that can be effectively accomplished only by the government.[203] The operation of a beach,[204] roller-skating rink,[205] or a general recreational area[206] is not so characterized, and, therefore, there is no immunity. Nonetheless, the operation of a toboggan slide in a city park[207] and the teaching of a physical education course[208] were immune activities.

197 Cook v Bennett, 94 Mich App 93, 288 NW2d 609, 611-12 (1979) (there may be liability for failing to stop a dangerous recreational game called *kill* in which students attempt to obtain a ball from other students by tackling and jumping).

198 165 NJ Super 79, 397 A2d 709, 710-11 (1979).

199 Larson v Independent School Dist No 314, 289 NW2d 112, 120-21 (Minn 1979).

200 *Id* 121.

201 Willis v Dade County School Bd, 411 So 2d 245, 246 (Fla Dist Ct App 1982). The duty to supervise high school students is generally ministerial. *See* Rupp v Bryant, 417 So 2d 658, 665 (Fla 1982).

202 Mich Stat Ann §3.996(107) (Callaghan Supp 1984); Mich Comp Laws §691.1407 (Supp 1984).

203 Feliciano v State, 97 Mich App 101, 293 NW2d 732, 735 (1980).

204 *Id.*

205 Cronin v Hazel Park, 88 Mich App 488, 276 NW2d 922, 923 (1979).

206 Daugherty v State, 91 Mich App 658, 283 NW2d 825, 828 (1979).

207 Collision v City of Saginaw, 84 Mich App 325, 269 NW2d 586, 587-88 (1978), *revd on other grounds*, 406 Mich 944, 277 NW2d 643 (1979).

208 Cody v Southfield-Lathrup School Dist, 25 Mich App 33, 181 NW2d 81, 83 (1970). Other Michigan cases have given the government immunity for virtually all school sports accidents. *See* §3.09.

In Idaho, the tort claims act has been interpreted to exclude liability for acts which have no *parallel* in the private sector.[209]

§3.08   —Recreational Activities

Several states have specifically reduced or eliminated governmental liability for recreational accidents.

In a few states, the government is not liable, unless it acted wilfully and wantonly,[210] for an injury where the liability is based on the existence of a condition of any public property intended or permitted to be used as a park, playground, or open area for recreational purposes.[211] These statutes were designed to encourage the development and maintenance of public parks, playgrounds, and similar recreational areas.[212] Accordingly, in *Jackson v Board of Education*, the court held that allegations that a school board negligently supervised a playground and negligently maintained playground equipment did not state a claim for relief.[213] In addition, these statutes bar claims under the attractive nuisance doctrine.[214]

In New Jersey there is no liability for a failure to provide supervision of public recreational facilities.[215] However, this immunity does not protect

---

209 Dunbar v United Steelworkers of Am, 100 Idaho 523, 602 P2d 21, 44 (1979); *see also* Hall, *Sovereign Immunity and Reemergence of the Governmental/Proprietary Distinction: A Setback In Idaho's Governmental Liability Law,* 20 Idaho L Rev 197, 200 (1984).

210 Plaintiffs must allege facts in their complaint which show wilful or wanton acts; allegations of negligence followed with a conclusory allegation of wilful conduct are insufficient to state a claim for relief. *See* Jarvis v Herrin City Park Dist, 6 Ill App 3d 516, 285 NE2d 564, 570 (1972).

211 *See* Ill Ann Stat ch 85, §3-106 (Smith-Hurd Supp 1984); Kan Stat Ann §75-6104 (Supp 1983); *see also* Keller v Board of Educ, 68 Ill App 3d 7, 385 NE2d 785, 787 (1978) (landowners cannot recover for damage to their property from errant baseballs); Yeater v Decatur Park Dist, 8 Ill App 3d 957, 290 NE2d 283 (1972).
The Illinois statute has been held constitutional. *See* Maloney v Elmhurst Park Dist, 47 Ill 2d 367, 265 NE2d 654, 655 (1971);

212 Jackson v Board of Educ, 109 Ill App 3d 716, 441 NE2d 120, 121 (1982).

213 *Id.*

214 441 NE2d at 122 (dicta).

215 NJ Stat Ann §59:2-7 (West 1982). It is not significant that the accident occurred away from the recreational facility if the negligent act occurred at the facility. *See* Law v Newark Bd of Educ, 175 NJ Super 26, 417 A2d 560, 564 (1980) (student who was negligently supervised climbed on fire truck and later fell off).
A New Jersey statute also provides that no one maintaining or operating a playground for public use acquired or maintained for philanthropic purposes and not for profit shall be liable in damages for accidents happening within the bounds of such playground. *See* NJ Stat Ann §5:3-30 (West 1973). However, this statute has been construed not to apply to municipalities, but only to individuals. *See* Primo v City of Bridgeton, 162 NJ Super 394, 392 A2d 1252, 1253-54 (1978).

negligent acts once supervision is provided.[216]

A public entity in California is not liable for an injury caused by a condition of any trail or unpaved road that provides access to fishing, hunting, camping, hiking, riding, water sports, or recreational areas.[217]

California also recently enacted a law which provides that public entities and public employees are not liable to a person who participated[218] in a hazardous recreational activity on public property and who knew or reasonably should have known that the activity created a substantial risk of injury.[219] However, this statute does not apply where there was:

1. A failure to warn of a known dangerous condition that was not reasonably assumed by the participant as an inherent part of the activity

2. A specific fee charged for the activity[220]

3. A negligent failure to construct or maintain the recreational equipment

4. Gross negligence by the government[221]

§3.09 —Schools

In several jurisdictions, school districts and teachers generally have been granted immunity for their acts.[222] This immunity also has been applied to

---

216 NJ Stat Ann §59:3-11 (West 1982). A city was not liable where it had an employee at a gymnasium because the employee was not supervising the basketball game, but only keeping out older children. *See* Morris v City of Jersey City, 179 NJ Super 460, 432 A2d 553, 555 (1981).

217 Cal Govt Code §831.4 (West 1980).

218 This includes spectators. *See* Cal Govt Code §831.7 (West Supp 1983).

219 Cal Govt Code §831.7 (West Supp 1983).

220 *See also* §5.18.

221 Eben v State, 130 Cal App 3d 416, 181 Cal Rptr 714, 717-18 (1982).

222 *See* Ark Stat Ann §12-2901 (1979); Ill Ann Stat ch 122, §§24-24, 34-84a (Smith-Hurd Supp 1984); Tex Rev Civ Stat Ann art 6252-19(19A) (Vernon 1970), Tex Educ Code Ann §21.912 (Vernon Supp 1982). *See also* Kobylanski v Chicago Bd of Educ, 63 Ill 2d 165, 347 NE2d 705 (1976); Fustin v Board of Educ, 101 Ill App 2d 113, 242 NE2d 308, 312 (1968); Winston v Reorganized School Dist R-2, 636 SW2d 324, 327 (Mo 1982) (schools are immune for all torts except those arising out of motor vehicle accidents or those caused by the condition of property); *see generally* Md Educ Code Ann §6-109 (1978).

In Texas, school districts are virtually immune from liability for negligence. *See* Tex Rev Civ Stat Ann art 6252-19 (19a) (Vernon Supp 1984). *See also* Duson v Midland County Indep School Dist, 627 SW2d 428, 429 (Tex Civ App 1981); Calhoun v Pasadena Indep School Dist, 496 SW2d 131, 132 (Tex Civ App 1973); *see generally* Greenhill & Murto, *Governmental Immunity*, 49 Tex L Rev 462, 468 (1971). Tex Educ Code Ann §21.912 (Vernon Supp 1982) grants immunity for discretionary acts. However, this statute is ambiguously worded. One court has interpreted this immunity provision to apply to all discretionary acts, except disciplinary ones. *See* Schumate v Thompson, 580 SW2d 47, 48 (Tex Civ App 1979).

In Michigan, school districts have repeatedly been given immunity for athletic injuries. *See*

other defendants, e.g., the state and a state educational agency, who were sued in an attempt to circumvent those statutes.[223] The doctrine of in loco parentis does not allow a student to sue a school where a tort claims act provides immunity.[224]

However, some courts have held that these statutes do not bar claims brought by spectators against schools[225] or teachers who sue their students for causing an athletic accident.[226] The Illinois Supreme Court held that these immunity provisions did not protect educators who were sued for providing defective athletic equipment to their students.[227] In California, schools are not liable for injuries which occur during a school field trip or excursion.[228]

These statutes granting immunity to schools have been held constitutional.[229]

§3.10   State Tort Liability Statutes

Some legislatures have passed specific laws imposing liability on the government. Three such statutes, all of which have been construed by courts in deciding athletic injury cases, are considered here.

Dangerous Conditions of Public Property

In some states, the government is liable, absent a specific statute to the contrary, for injuries caused by dangerous conditions of public property.[230] There is no liability if the injury did not result from a dangerous *condition* of

---

Grames v King, 123 Mich App 573, 332 NW2d 615, 619 (1983); Churilla v School Dist, 105 Mich App 32, 306 NW2d 381, 382 (1981); Deaner v Utica Community School Dist, 99 Mich App 103, 297 NW2d 625, 628 (1980). The courts are in conflict over whether individual school personnel are immune when they act within the scope of their employment or only when they perform a discretionary act. *See* Grames v King, 123 Mich App 573, 332 NW2d 615, 619 (1983) (citing cases for both propositions).

One court held that a school district was not a *municipality* for purposes of a statute which waived the sovereign immunity of a municipality. *See* Kuhn v Ladue School Dist, 598 SW2d 281, 282 (Mo 1979).

223 *See* Torres v State, 476 SW2d 846, 849 (Tex Civ App 1972).

224 Duson v Midland County Indep School Dist, 627 SW2d 428, 429 (Tex Civ App 1981).

225 Tanari v School Directors of Dist 502, 69 Ill 2d 630, 373 NE2d 5, 8 (1977).

226 American States Ins Co v Flynn, 102 Ill App 3d 201, 429 NE2d 587, 587 (1981).

227 *See* Thomas v Chicago Bd of Educ, 77 Ill 2d 165, 395 NE2d 538 (1979).

228 *See* Cal Educ Code §§35330, 72640 (West 1978). *But see* Castro v Los Angeles Bd of Educ, 54 Cal App 3d 232, 126 Cal Rptr 537, 540 (1976) (statute only applies to nonrequired field trips).

229 *See* Schumate v Thompson, 580 SW2d 47, 48-49 (Tex Civ App 1979) (Tex Educ Code Ann §21.912 (Vernon Supp 1984)).

230 Cal Govt Code §835 (West 1980); NJ Stat Ann §59:4-2 (West 1982).

public property. In *Gonzales v City of San Diego*,[231] a spectator at a football game who was injured by another spectator alleged that the city was negligent because it failed to take reasonable steps to remove the danger from tailgate parties in a public stadium's parking lot. The court held that there was no liability under this statute unless, at a minimum, some physical condition in the property, if not a defect, was a contributing cause of the injury.[232] Since there was no physical condition in the parking lot property which increased the risk of injury from other spectators, the government was immune from suit.[233]

Where an injury results from the conduct of a plaintiff or third parties, and not from a condition of public property, the government is not liable.[234] The government was not liable for leaving a gate unlocked which allowed children to play a dangerous skateboard game, because the injury was caused by the dangerous conduct of the children and not a dangerous condition of the property.[235]

The California statute only applies where the plaintiff exercised due care.[236] Obviously, a plaintiff who dove in an inappropriate place did not exercise due care. Therefore, the statute was not applied, and the government was held immune from suit.[237]

Defective Tangible Property

In Texas, the government is liable for injuries caused by some condition or use of tangible property under circumstances where the government, if it were a private person, would be liable.[238] This provision eliminated immunity for a state university where it furnished defective football equipment to an athlete and where it failed to furnish proper protective equipment for the athlete's injured knee.[239]

Safe Buildings

In Michigan, the government is liable for injuries resulting from dangerous

---

[231] 156 Cal App 3d 256, 202 Cal Rptr 634 (1984).

[232] 156 Cal App 3d at 258.

[233] *Id.*

[234] Bartell v Palos Verdes Peninsula School Dist, 83 Cal App 3d 492, 147 Cal Rptr 898, 900 (1978).

[235] *Id.*

[236] *See* Cal Govt Code §830 (West 1970).

[237] Fuller v State, 51 Cal App 3d 926, 125 Cal Rptr 586, 594 (1975).

[238] Tex Rev Civ Stat Ann art 6252-3 (Vernon 1970); *see also* Lowe v Texas Tech Univ, 540 SW2d 297, 299 (Tex 1976).

[239] Lowe v Texas Tech Univ, 540 SW2d 297, 300 (Tex 1976); *see generally* Thomas v Chicago Bd of Educ, 77 Ill 2d 165, 395 NE2d 538 (1979).

or defective conditions in public buildings.[240] This statute was not applied where the injury resulted from equipment or the absence of equipment inside a building, rather than from defects in the physical structure of the building itself.[241] Accordingly, the government was not liable for failing to place nets or other safety devices between two indoor tennis courts to protect against injury caused by errant tennis balls,[242] or in failing to have sufficient weight-lifting safety machines or floor mats.[243]

This statute was not applied where an injury resulted from a school's negligent supervision of athletic activities, viz., negligently compelling a girl to perform gymnastic exercises on a minitrampoline,[244] negligently failing to provide a separate locker room and facilities for a visiting basketball team,[245] or negligently allowing students to use a gymnasium which was inadequately ventilated.[246]

§3.11 Federal Tort Claims Act

The United States is a sovereign entity and no action lies against it unless the action has been authorized by Congress.[247] Indeed, unless the relinquishment of sovereign immunity is clear, the courts do not have jurisdiction to decide tort actions against the United States.[248]

In 1946, Congress passed the Federal Tort Claims Act (FTCA),[249] a comprehensive statute that waived, under some circumstances, the sovereign immunity of the United States. The FTCA was the culmination of a long effort to mitigate the unjust consequences of sovereign immunity. As the federal government had expanded its activities over the years, its agents had caused an increasing number of torts, and the injured parties were remediless unless Congress passed a private bill for that specific party, solely because the wrongs were committed by government employees.[250] The FTCA eliminated both the problems involved in passing a private bill for each injured plaintiff

---

240 *See* Mich Comp Laws Ann §§691.1406, 691.1407 (West Supp 1984); Mich Stat Ann §§3.996, 3.996(106) (Callaghan Supp 1984); Schmit v City of Detroit, 88 Mich App 22, 276 NW2d 506, 507 (1979).

241 Zawadzki v Taylor, 70 Mich App 545, 246 NW2d 161, 164 (1976).

242 *Id.*

243 *See* Vargo v Svitchan, 100 Mich App 809, 301 NW2d 1, 7 (1980).

244 Cody v Southfield-Lathrup School Dist, 25 Mich App 33, 181 NW2d 81, 84-85 (1970).

245 Grames v King, 123 Mich App 573, 332 NW2d 615, 617 (1983).

246 *See* Vargo v Svitchan, 100 Mich App 809, 301 NW2d 1, 7 (1980).

247 Thompson v United States, 592 F2d 1104, 1107 (9th Cir 1979).

248 *Id.*

249 28 USC §§1346(b), 2671-2680.

250 *See* Fischer v United States, 451 F Supp 918, 919 (EDNY 1978).

and the unfairness to the victims who were unable to obtain the benefits of that procedure.[251]

The FTCA generally allows plaintiffs to recover damages against the federal government for injuries caused by the negligent act or omission of a federal employee acting within the scope of his or her employment, under circumstances where the United States, if it were a private person, would be liable to the claimant in accordance with the law of the place where the act or omission[252] occurred.[253] Accordingly, where private individuals have been granted partial tort immunity, e.g., state recreational statutes which have reduced the liability of landowners to individuals injured on the landowner's property while engaged in a recreational activity, the federal government has been allowed to obtain the benefit of such laws.[254] However, the federal government has not been entitled to claim the immunity of other governments, such as municipalities.[255]

If the federal government is not liable under the FTCA, the court lacks subject matter jurisdiction over the claim, and the complaint must be dismissed.[256]

Discretionary Acts

The FTCA did not waive the sovereign immunity of the United States in all respects. One of the most important exceptions is that the federal government is not liable for injuries that result from a federal employee's performance or failure to perform a discretionary function, whether or not the discretion involved is abused.[257]

---

251 *See generally id*; L. Jayson, Handling Federal Tort Claims §52 (1984); Mikva, *Sovereign Immunity: In A Democracy the Emperor Has No Clothes*, 1966 U Ill LF 828, 831; Harris & Schnepper, *Federal Tort Claims Act: Discretionary Function Exception Revisited*, 31 U Miami L Rev 161, 164-65 (1976).

252 It may be difficult to ascertain where the omission occurred. Accordingly, one court held that the law to be applied is that of the place where the act necessary to avoid the negligence should have occurred. *See* Ducey v United States, 713 F2d 504, 508 n 2 (9th Cir 1983).

253 28 USC §§1346(b), 2674; Davis v United States, 716 F2d 418, 423 (7th Cir 1983) (state law applies). In some cases it is difficult to ascertain whether the statute of limitations has run. *See* Annot, 29 ALR Fed 482 (1976).

254 *See, e.g.*, Gard v United States, 594 F2d 1230, 1233 (9th Cir), *cert denied*, 444 US 866 (1979); *see also* §5.06.

255 Ward v United States, 208 F Supp 118, 121 (D Colo 1962).

256 Smith v United States, 546 F2d 872, 876 (10th Cir 1976); Henretig v United States, 490 F Supp 398, 403 (SD Fla 1980).

257 28 USC §2680(a). This section marks the boundary between Congress's willingness to impose tort liability upon the United States and its desire to protect certain governmental activities from exposure to suit by private individuals. *See* United States v SA Empresa De Viaco Aerea Rio Grandense, 104 S Ct 2755, 2762 (1984). The major Supreme Court case interpreting this provision is Dalehite v United States, 346 US 15 (1953).

However, *Dalehite* has been modified by subsequent Supreme Court decisions. *See, e.g.*,

Even though the FTCA was passed almost 40 years ago, the limits of this exception for discretionary acts are still not clear.[258] Some, although not all, courts have interpreted this exception to immunize only decisions made on a policy or planning level, as opposed to those made on an operational level.[259]

The government's decision to encourage recreation at a specific place is usually considered to involve the exercise of discretion.[260] For example, the government's decision to issue a permit to a racing association to allow the association to conduct a motorcycle race on government land is a discretionary act that, even if it were done negligently, would not subject the government to liability.[261] Nonetheless, the government usually has a duty to warn of or guard against hazards resulting from its decision to encourage recreation, at least if it did more than merely allow a recreational activity to occur.[262] This is because the decisions made in the actual management of a recreational area usually do not involve the broad policy decisions that are protected by this exemption.[263]

Many of the policy decisions regarding the management of national parks have been held to be protected discretionary decisions.[264] Courts have held, for example, that a park's policy for the handling of bears is protected.[265] In addition, one court held that a park's failure to place boardwalks and handrails in its recreational areas was a discretionary act and there was no liability.[266] However, a different court ruled that the government's decision not to warn of the known dangers of thermal pools or provide safeguards such

---

Rayonier, Inc v United States, 352 US 315 (1957); Indian Towing Co v United States, 350 US 61 (1955).

For a more detailed discussion of this exception, *see* Civil Actions Against the United States §§6.16, 6.17, 6.18 (1982); L. Jayson, Handling Federal Tort Claims §§245-249 (1984); *see generally* United States v SA Empresa De Viaco Aerea Rio Grandense, 104 S Ct 2755, 2762-65 (1984).

[258] *See* United States v SA Empresa De Viaco Aerea Rio Grandense, 104 S Ct 2755, 2762-65 (1984).

[259] *See* Ducey v United States, 713 F2d 504, 515 (9th Cir 1983); Lindgren v United States, 665 F2d 978, 980 (9th Cir 1982); *cf* §3.06.

[260] *See* Ducey v United States, 713 F2d 504, 515 (9th Cir 1983).

[261] Thompson v United States, 592 F2d 1104, 1111 (9th Cir 1979).

[262] *See* Ducey v United States, 713 F2d 504, 515 (9th Cir 1983); *see also* Davidow v United States, 583 F Supp 1170, 1173-74 (WD Pa 1984) (failure of park rangers to maintain a danger buoy off the tip of a peninsula was not a discretionary act).

[263] Ducey v United States, 713 F2d 504, 515 (9th Cir 1983).

[264] *But cf* Stanton v United States, 685 F2d 117 (4th Cir 1982) (park ranger's shooting at plaintiff's dogs was not a discretionary act).

[265] Martin v United States, 546 F2d 1355, 1360 (9th Cir 1976), *cert denied*, 432 US 906 (1977); Ashley v United States, 215 F Supp 39, 45-46 (D Neb 1963), *aff'd on other grounds*, 326 F2d 499 (8th Cir 1964).

[266] Henretig v United States, 490 F Supp 398, 403 (SD Fla 1980) (woman fell while walking on a trail at Yellowstone National Park).

as guardrails and boardwalks in those dangerous areas in a national park was not a discretionary act.[267] The government's argument that its failure to add those safeguards was really a discretionary decision to keep the park undeveloped was rejected because it proved too much: all failures to act could be justified, after the fact, by the argument that the intention was for the property to be left alone.[268]

The decision to draw down the water level of a reservoir was a protected discretionary decision.[269] However, the government's failure to warn that it was causing the water level of a river to fluctuate without notice may be a nonprotected operational decision.[270]

The supervising, contracting, and actual performance of a contract to repair a seawall involve operational decisions, and if the decisions are negligently carried out, the injured party can recover from the government.[271] Therefore, the government was liable where it contracted for the repair of a seawall, knowing that large amounts of sand were required for this job and that the removal of the sand near a public beach created a dangerous depression in which several people later drowned.[272]

The courts have consistently held that the setting of a *coyote getter* which ejected poison when tripped was not a protected discretionary act.[273] Indeed, one court rejected this argument "out of hand."[274]

Military Personnel

Generally, injured military personnel are barred from recovery under the FTCA.[275] However, one court held that a former air force cadet who was no longer subject to military discipline could bring an action alleging that government doctors negligently prescribed an anti-inflammatory

---

267 Smith v United States, 546 F2d 872, 877 (10th Cir 1976) (the ground near a thermal pool gave way and a child fell into the pool severely burning himself).

268 *Id.*

269 Spillway Marina, Inc v United States, 445 F2d 876, 878 (10th Cir 1971) (property damage only); Graves v United States Coast Guard, 692 F2d 71, 75 (9th Cir 1982) (operation of dam was a protected activity).

270 Lindgren v United States, 665 F2d 978, 982 (9th Cir 1982) (water skier injured when his ski struck the riverbed); *see also* Graves v United States Coast Guard, 692 F2d 71, 75 (9th Cir 1982).

271 Price v United States, 530 F Supp 1010, 1017 (SD Miss 1981).

272 *Id.*

273 Worley v United States, 119 F Supp 719, 721 (D Or 1952); Fritz v United States, 216 F Supp 156, 159 (DND), *appeal dismissed*, 324 F2d 959 (8th Cir 1963).

274 Fritz v United States, 216 F Supp 156, 159 (DND), *appeal dismissed*, 324 F2d 959 (8th Cir 1963).

275 Feres v United States, 340 US 135 (1950).

drug so he could play varsity football at the academy even though he was injured.[276]

Acts of Independent Contractors and Agents

The United States is not liable under the FTCA for the negligence of its independent contractors,[277] although it is liable for acts or omissions of its agents. The test for distinguishing an independent contractor from an agent is the existence of federal authority to control the detailed, daily operations of the third party.[278] If there is no such authority, the third party is an independent contractor. The ability of the government to compel compliance with federal standards, standing alone, does not transform the party into an agent.[279] Accordingly, a concessionaire at a national park who maintained boat slips and boat service facilities was not an agent of the United States because the government did not have the power to regulate the detailed physical performance of that concession business.[280]

The federal government is not responsible for the negligence of nonfederal employees, even if they are working under a federal contract, maintaining property owned by the federal government, or working on projects funded by the federal government.[281] Accordingly, the government is not liable for the negligence of a racing association's employees who conducted a motorcycle race on federal land.[282]

Procedural Requirements

Before suit is commenced, the injured party must submit an administrative claim.[283] However, the failure to comply completely with this requirement is not a jurisdictional defect. For example, an administrative claim made by an attorney on behalf of his client was accepted even though the attorney failed to submit evidence of authority to present the claim.[284]

---

[276] Fischer v United States, 451 F Supp 918, 921 (EDNY 1978).

[277] Ducey v United States, 713 F2d 504, 516 (9th Cir 1983); *see also* 28 USC §2671.

[278] Ducey v United States, 713 F2d 504, 516 (9th Cir 1983). *See generally* Civil Actions Against the United States §6.4, at 335-36 (1982).

[279] Ducey v United States, 713 F2d 504, 516 (9th Cir 1983).

[280] *Id.*

[281] Thompson v United States, 592 F2d 1104, 1107 (9th Cir 1979).

[282] *Id.*

[283] *See generally* Civil Actions Against the United States §§6.1, 6.11, at 332-33, 344-46 (1982); L. Jayson, Handling Federal Tort Claims §§315-326 (1984).

[284] Graves v United States Coast Guard, 692 F2d 71, 74-75 (9th Cir 1982).

Limits on Recovery and Attorneys' Fees

The FTCA does not allow a successful plaintiff to recover prejudgment interest or punitive damages.[285] In addition, it is illegal for an attorney to receive over 25 per cent of the judgment in fees.[286]

§3.12   Federal Suits in Admiralty Act

Where the plaintiff's action against the United States is within the admiralty court's jurisdiction, the plaintiff must sue under the federal Suits in Admiralty Act.[287] The act, like the Federal Tort Claims Act, provides that the United States is liable to the same extent as a private person would be under similar circumstances.[288]

There must be strict compliance with the Suits in Admiralty Act. The act requires, for example, that the plaintiff shall *forthwith* serve a copy of his or her libel on the United States Attorney for the district and mail a copy thereof by registered mail to the Attorney General of the United States.[289] In *Brown v United States*, the court dismissed a wrongful death action because the United States Attorney was not served with a copy of the complaint until eight months after it was filed.[290]

At one time it was difficult to state the test used in determining whether an action was governed under admiralty law.[291] However, in 1982, the United States Supreme Court, in *Richardson v Foremost Insurance Co*, held that admiralty jurisdiction exists over recreational boating accidents where the

---

285 28 USC §2674.

286 28 USC §2678.

287 Respess v United States, 586 F Supp 861, 862 (ED La 1984); Hartman v United States, 522 F Supp 114, 120 (DSC 1981). The Suits in Admiralty Act is codified at 46 USC §§741-752.

If admiralty jurisdiction is not present, the action must be brought under the Federal Tort Claims Act. Respess v United States, 586 F Supp 861, 862 (ED La 1984). The Federal Tort Claims Act is discussed in §3.11.

Those two federal acts are mutually exclusive. 28 USC §2680(d). *See also* Kelly v United States, 531 F2d 1144, 1149 (2d Cir 1976) (this conclusion is mandated from the 1960 amendment of 42 USC §742); Respess v United States, 586 F Supp 861, 963 n 1 (ED La 1984); Brown v United States, 403 F Supp 472, 473-74 (CD Cal 1975).

One of the most important practical differences between the two laws is that the Suits in Admiralty Act does not provide immunity for discretionary acts. Lane v United States, 529 F2d 175, 179 (4th Cir 1975).

288 *See* 46 USC §742; *see generally* Faust v South Carolina State Highway Dept, 721 F2d 934, 937 (4th Cir 1983).

289 46 USC §742.

290 403 F Supp 472, 474-75 (CD Cal 1975).

291 *See* §2.05.

tort occurred on navigable waters and the tort bore a significant relationship to traditional maritime activity.[292]

The United States Supreme Court in *The Daniel Ball* stated the test used in determining whether waters are navigable:

> Those rivers must be regarded as public navigable rivers in law which are navigable in fact. And they are navigable in fact when they are used, or are susceptible of being used, in their ordinary condition, as highways for commerce, over which trade and travel are or may be conducted in the customary modes of trade and travel on water. And they constitute navigable waters of the United States within the meaning of the acts of Congress, in contradistinction from the navigable waters of the States, when they form in their ordinary condition by themselves, or by uniting with other waters, a continued highway over which commerce is or may be carried on with other states or foreign countries in the customary modes in which such commerce is conducted by water.[293]

In essence, water is navigable if it is part of an interstate highway[294] and it is used or capable of being used for commercial activity.[295]

Although a dispositive determination of whether water is navigable can only be made by the courts, a determination of navigability made by federal agencies may be persuasive.[296] Lists of administrative determinations of navigability are kept in the district office of the Corps of Engineers.[297]

The second major test is whether the accident bore a significant relationship to traditional maritime activity.[298] In *Kelly v Smith*, the court articulated four factors to be considered in determining whether such a relationship existed:

---

292 457 US 668 (1982). This case is also discussed in **§2.05**.

293 77 US (10 Wall) 557, 563 (1871).

294 Finneseth v Carter, 712 F2d 1041, 1044 (6th Cir 1983) (a reservoir that straddles two states meets this test); *see* Calamari, *The Wake of Executive Jet - A Major Wave Or a Minor Ripple*, 4 Mar Law 52, 62 (1979) (landlocked lake within a state does not qualify).

295 Finneseth v Carter, 712 F2d 1041, 1044 (6th Cir 1983); Hartman v United States, 522 F Supp 114, 116 (DSC 1981). However, the Eighth Circuit has repeatedly held that the test is whether there is *contemporary navigability in fact*. *See* Edwards v Hurtel, 717 F2d 1204, 1205 (8th Cir 1983); Livingston v United States, 627 F2d 165, 170 (8th Cir 1980), *cert denied*, 450 US 914 (1981). Where a lake's navigability was permanently altered when a dam was constructed and "there is no reasonable likelihood that the lake will be rendered susceptible of use for commercial shipping in the foreseeable future," the lake is not navigable. *See* Smith v Hustler, Inc, 514 F Supp 1265, 1269 (WD La 1981).

296 *See* Hartman v United States, 522 F Supp 114, 117 (DSC 1981).

297 *See* 33 CFR §329.16.

298 *Cf* **§2.05** (there is a discussion of cases interpreting this provision in cases against recreational boaters).

1. The functions and roles of the parties
2. The types of vehicles and instrumentalities involved
3. The causation and type of injury
4. Traditional concepts of the role of admiralty law[299]

The *Kelly* four-factor analysis was applied in *Respess v United States*.[300] The *Respess* court concluded that there was admiralty jurisdiction where passengers in a recreational boat were injured when the boat collided with a tree branch hanging over a canal, because the accident involved vessel passengers in contrast to water skiers or swimmers, involved a vessel,[301] and was caused by a navigational obstruction, a traditional concern of admiralty law.[302]

In other cases which did not apply the *Kelly* four-factor analysis, courts have held that there was a relationship to traditional maritime activity where the government negligently placed low-hanging power lines over a river and a man sailing a catamaran was killed when the vessel's aluminum mast hit the lines,[303] where a speedboat hit a concrete piling or bridge support of an old bridge,[304] where there was a collision between a cabin cruiser and the submerged hulks of wrecked vessels,[305] where a pleasure craft was shelled by a United States ship,[306] and where there was a negligent rescue operation by the United States Coast Guard.[307] Indeed, even if the negligent act originated on land, if the damage occurred on water there was admiralty jurisdiction.[308]

§3.13   —Marking Sunken Vessels or Other Obstructions

Some recreational boaters have been injured when their boats collided with sunken vessels or other obstructions in the water. In those situations, one potential defendant is the United States.

---

299 485 F2d 520, 525 (5th Cir 1973).

300 586 F Supp 861 (ED La 1984).

301 The court did not explain what would not be covered. *See id* 865.

302 586 F Supp 861, 865 (ED La 1984).

303 Brown v United States, 403 F Supp 472, 474 (CD Cal 1975) (dicta).

304 Hartman v United States, 522 F Supp 114, 119-20 (DSC 1981).

305 Lane v United States, 529 F2d 175, 180 (4th Cir 1975).

306 Szyka v United States Secretary of Defense, 525 F2d 62, 64 (2d Cir 1975).

307 Kelly v United States, 531 F2d 1144, 1147 (2d Cir 1976).

308 *Id* 1146 (allegation that Coast Guard negligently failed to rescue a person after he fell from his sailboat).

The owner of a sunken vessel is required to mark the vessel with a buoy or beacon and to commence its removal.[309] This law applies to vessels owned by the federal government.[310] However, in *Chute v United States*, the court held that the government was not required to mark a vessel that was deliberately put on a shoal as a bombing target by the Navy.[311]

The federal government may also be required to mark sunken vessels which it does not own, as well as other obstructions in the water. Congress has declared that the Secretary of Transportation may mark for the protection of navigation any sunken vessel or other obstruction existing on any navigable waters of the United States in such manner and for so long as, *in his judgment*, the needs of maritime navigation require.[312]

It is unclear how the phrase *in his judgment* should be construed. In *Chute v United States*, the court held that the phrase "entrusts these matters to the Secretary, not the courts,"[313] and, therefore, the federal government is not liable for its failure to mark the obstructions except in the most egregious cases. However, a different court appeared to apply a negligence standard to determine the propriety of the government's actions.[314]

The federal government's duty to mark sunken barges requires a physical marking at the location of the barge.[315] Markings by the National Oceanic and Atmospheric Administration on a chart are not sufficient to discharge this duty.[316]

Several courts have held that the federal government does not have a duty to mark objects placed in the water as an aid to navigation, e.g., a dike[317] or a cable.[318]

The United States has no general duty to maintain safe conditions on navigable water.[319] Nonetheless, the federal government can be liable if it

---

309 33 USC §409. This is true whether the vessel was sunk accidently or not. *Id.*

310 Chute v United States, 610 F2d 7, 10 (1st Cir 1979).

311 *Id* 11.

312 14 USC §86. Prior to 1965, this section was phrased in mandatory terms. *See* Faust v South Carolina State Highway Dept, 721 F2d 934, 938 (4th Cir 1983).

313 610 F2d 7, 12 (1st Cir 1979); *see also* Faust v South Carolina State Highway Dept, 721 F2d 934, 939 (4th Cir 1983) (the executive branch should have the power to determine how best to allocate scarce resources).

314 *See* Lane v United States, 529 F2d 175, 179 (4th Cir 1975) (government could be liable for damage to a pleasure boat caused by a collision with a sunken barge).

315 Lane v United States, 529 F2d 175, 180 (4th Cir 1975); *see also* 14 USC §86 (duty is discretionary).

316 *See* Lane v United States, 529 F2d 175, 180 (4th Cir 1975).

317 Magno v Corros, 630 F2d 224, 228 (4th Cir 1980).

318 Faust v South Carolina State Highway Dept, 721 F2d 934, 938 (4th Cir 1983) (reversing a $500,000 judgment for the plaintiff).

319 *Id* 939.

undertakes to warn the public of danger, thereby inducing the public to rely on its acts, but then fails to act properly.[320] However, this theory of recovery was not applied in a case where the government marked a wreck with a buoy rather than a tall daymark, an allegedly superior marking,[321] or where the United States was not directly responsible for safety devices on a ferry.[322]

Specific Activities and Facilities

§3.14 Local Parks, Playgrounds, and Recreational Centers

General Duty of Care

A municipality is not an insurer of the safety of those who use its parks, playgrounds, and recreational facilities.[323] However, it must exercise reasonable care to make and keep those facilities safe[324] and to provide a safe means of ingress and egress to the facilities.[325] This includes taking reasonable precautions to minimize the risk of injury to children who will use these areas to roam, climb, and play.[326]

A city is not negligent for failing to reduce the risks of danger that are not reasonably foreseeable. For example, a city did not negligently maintain a water fountain by allowing a copper coil to be torn from it by a boy who then threw it at a girl, because the boy's acts were not reasonably foreseeable.[327]

---

320 *See* Indian Towing Co, Inc v United States, 350 US 61 (1955); Magno v Corros, 630 F2d 224 (4th Cir 1980); De Bardeleben Marine Corp v United States, 451 F2d 140 (5th Cir 1971); Donily v United States, 381 F Supp 901 (D Or 1974).

321 Chute v United States, 610 F2d 7, 15 (1st Cir 1979).

322 Faust v South Carolina State Highway Dept, 721 F2d 934, 940 (4th Cir 1983).

323 Lisk v City of West Palm Beach, 160 Fla 632, 36 So 2d 197, 199 (1948); Kaczmarczyk v City & County of Honolulu, 65 Hawaii 612, 656 P2d 89, 91 (1982); Mills v American Playground Device Co, 405 NE2d 621, 627 (Ind Ct App 1980).

324 Lisk v City of West Palm Beach, 160 Fla 632, 36 So 2d 197, 198 (1948); Kaczmarczyk v City & County of Honolulu, 65 Hawaii 612, 656 P2d 89, 91 (1982); Leone v City of Utica, 66 AD2d 463, 414 NYS2d 412, 415 (1979), *affd*, 49 NY2d 811, 403 NE2d 964, 426 NYS2d 980 (1980); City of Lampasas v Roberts, 398 SW2d 612, 615 (Tex Civ App 1966); *see generally* Taylor v Kansas City, 353 SW2d 814, 816 (Mo Ct App 1962).

In some states there is still governmental immunity for injuries arising out of conditions in public parks. *See, e.g.*, Wright v City of North Charleston, 271 SC 515, 248 SE2d 480, 482 (1978). This case is criticized in Note, *Torts*, 31 SCL Rev 131, 138-40 (1979).

325 *See* Mooney v Etheridge, 65 Ill App 3d 847, 382 NE2d 826, 830 (1978).

326 Leone v City of Utica, 66 AD2d 463, 414 NYS2d 412, 415 (1979), *affd*, 49 NY2d 811, 403 NE2d 964, 426 NYS2d 980 (1980).

327 Jenkins v City of Miami Beach, 389 So 2d 1195, 1196 (Fla Dist Ct App 1980).

The court held that the negligent maintenance of the fountain had not led to this type of injury in the past and it was not reasonably expected that this type of injury would ever occur.[328] Similarly, a city was not liable where a woman tripped on a water meter box while crossing at night, a parkway which was not intended to be used by pedestrians.[329]

Obvious Defects

The government generally has no duty to eliminate or warn the public of open and obvious defects in a park which the users are aware of or should be aware of in the exercise of reasonable care on their part.[330] For example, a city was entitled to summary judgment where a woman fell in a city park after stepping on a twig or a sweet gum ball near the sweet gum trees, because the city did not violate any duty of care in failing to clean up all twigs or gum balls.[331]

Similarly, in *Rich v City of Lubbock*, the court affirmed a summary judgment for the city where an athlete playing softball in a city park fell and hit a concrete ring, a part of the sprinkler system, in the outfield.[332] The court noted that these rings protruded about one inch above the ground and the athlete knew the rings were in the outfield, although not their exact location.[333] Accordingly, the court concluded that the city had no duty to eliminate this *obvious* danger because the athlete "could have seen it if he had been watching for it, instead [of] watching the ball."[334]

The court's reasoning in *Rich* is mistaken. Outfielders should be expected to watch the ball, not the ground. Therefore, the dangerous condition was not obvious to one playing baseball.

It has been held that a governmental entity which maintains a park or recreational area near a body of water has no duty to warn adults of the dangers of swimming because those dangers involve well-known risks.[335]

---

328 *Id.*

329 Dramstadt v City of West Palm Beach, 81 So 2d 484, 485 (Fla 1955); *see also* Musetto v City of Miami Beach, 82 So 2d 595, 595 (Fla 1955).

330 Shaw v City of Lipscomb, 380 So 2d 812, 814 (Ala 1980); Rich v City of Lubbock, 544 SW2d 958, 959 (Tex Civ App 1976). *See* James, *Tort Liability of Occupiers of Land: Duties Owed to Licensees and Invitees*, 63 Yale LJ 605, 626-27 (1954); *see generally* §6.09.

331 Shaw v City of Lipscomb, 380 So 2d 812, 815 (Ala 1980).

332 544 SW2d 958, 959 (Tex Civ App 1976).

333 *Id.*

334 *Id.*

335 Hall v Lemieux, 378 So 2d 130, 132 (La Ct App 1979). *See generally* §6.07 (in some jurisdictions the dangers of water are deemed *obvious* to all individuals).

Supervision

A city has a duty to provide a reasonable degree of supervision over recreation at public parks[336] and playgrounds.[337] In *Nichter v City of Buffalo*, a city was found negligent where a supervisor of a playground temporarily abandoned her post during lunchtime and one child was injured by another child who was using a swing.[338]

However, there is no requirement that each item of recreational equipment be directly supervised by a governmental employee.[339] In addition, there is no duty to provide supervisory personnel or warning devices to assist individuals in crossing a public street to get to a park.[340]

A landowner may be liable for a plaintiff's injuries that were caused by third parties if there was an unreasonable risk of a foreseeable injury from the third parties. For example, a child who was injured at a park by the illegal fireworks of third parties on July 4th could recover against the village because the village knew or should have known that illegal fireworks had been exploded at the park for some time preceding the accident and still failed to provide adequate supervision there.[341]

One court noted that a park district's lack of funds was *unquestionably irrelevant* in deciding whether the district negligently failed to provide supervision in an area used for sledding.[342] However, the plaintiff's failure to object to this evidence at trial waived this error.[343]

Injury on Private Land

The government can be liable for its failure to take reasonable steps to prevent injury even where the injury occurred on private property, if there was no clear line of demarcation between the public and private properties.[344]

---

336 Peterson v City of New York, 267 NY 204, 196 NE 27, 28 (1935).

337 Nichter v City of Buffalo, 74 AD2d 996, 427 NYS2d 101, 102 (1980); Lopez v City of New York, 4 AD2d 48, 163 NYS2d 562, 565-66 (1957), *affd*, 4 NY2d 738, 171 NYS2d 860 (1958).

338 74 AD2d 996, 427 NYS2d 101, 102 (1980).

339 Nichter v City of Buffalo, 74 AD2d 996, 427 NYS2d 101, 102 (1980); Peterson v City of New York, 267 NY 204, 196 NE 27, 28 (1935).

340 *See* Mooney v Etheridge, 65 Ill App 3d 847, 382 NE2d 826, 830-31 (1978).

341 Caldwell v Village of Island Park, 304 NY 268, 107 NE2d 441, 444-45 (1952). *See generally* Baker v Lane County, 37 Or App 87, 586 P2d 114, 119 (1978) (fairground can be liable for injuries caused by third parties).

342 Compton v Dundee Township Park Dist, 129 Ill App 2d 36, 263 NE2d 146, 148 (1970).

343 *Id.*

344 Leone v City of Utica, 66 AD2d 463, 414 NYS2d 412, 415 (1979), *affd*, 49 NY2d 811, 403 NE2d 964, 426 NYS2d 980 (1980).

In *Leone v City of Utica*,[345] a child playing in a park heard a train whistle and followed the siren sound, left the park, and crossed onto private property which led to the tracks where he fell and had his leg run over by the train. The court held that the city was liable for failing to erect barriers or take other reasonable precautions to prevent a child from leaving the park to go on nearby dangerous property.[346]

Miscellaneous

Where there was no evidence of actual or constructive knowledge that a palm frond was about to fall down over a park bench in a public park, the city was not liable when the frond fell.[347]

A state park district was negligent in failing to replace protective barriers, which had previously been removed, next to a road in a park which resulted in a car falling into an arroyo.[348]

Causation

The government is not liable unless its acts or omissions were a substantial factor in causing the injury.[349] Where there is no causal connection between a city's putative breach of a duty and the plaintiff's injury, the city is entitled to judgment.[350] For example, where a plaintiff failed to prove that had the city provided a supervisor at a park, the supervisor would have prevented a child from falling as she attempted to stand up on a swing, a jury verdict for the child was reversed.[351]

Similarly, the government, the owner of a recreational area, was not liable for failing to warn drivers of the dangers of traveling down a certain road in a recreational area or in maintaining a picnic area near an access road where the injury was caused by a bus with defective tires hitting a pickup truck parked in the area.[352]

Even if the acts or omissions of a governmental entity created an unreasonable degree of danger, it may not be liable if there was a superseding cause

---

345 *Id.*

346 *Id.*

347 Lisk v City of West Palm Beach, 160 Fla 632, 36 So 2d 197, 199 (1948). *But see generally* Middaugh v United States, 293 F Supp 977, 980 (D Wyo 1968) (government liable where it failed to take steps to remove the danger of a tree which had substantially rotted away).

348 Chappell v Dwyer, 611 SW2d 158, 161 (Tex Civ App 1981). *See also* Tex Rev Civ Stat Ann art 6252-19 (18b) (Vernon 1970).

349 *See* Restatement (Second) of Torts §§430, 431 (1965).

350 Nichter v City of Buffalo, 74 AD2d 996, 427 NYS2d 101, 102 (1980).

351 *Id.*

352 Quinn v United States, 439 F2d 335, 340 (8th Cir 1971).

of injury.[353] A subsequent act or omission of another party is a superseding cause of liability which extinguishes the liability of the government if the subsequent act or omission was not a reasonably foreseeable consequence of the government's breach of duty.[354] The test is reasonable foreseeability, and, therefore, it is not dispositive that the subsequent act or omission which caused the injury was done negligently,[355] intentionally,[356] or even criminally.[357]

In *Parness v City of Tempe*, a city was held liable for its failure to remove broken glass at a recreational center.[358] The city argued that the plaintiff's injuries resulted from the superseding act of other children who pushed him, resulting in his falling to the ground on the broken glass. The court rejected this argument because it was reasonably foreseeable that children would push each other and that they would fall on the broken glass left on the ground.[359]

§3.15   National Parks

General Duty of Care

The federal government is not an insurer of the safety of visitors at national parks.[360] It has a duty to exercise reasonable care to lawful visitors,[361] such as invitees or licensees, to keep the premises reasonably safe[362] and to warn of hidden dangers.[363]

For example, the government is generally liable for dangerous conditions

---

353 *See* Restatement (Second) of Torts §440 (1965).

354 Parness v City of Tempe, 123 Ariz 460, 600 P2d 764, 768 (1979).

355 Restatement (Second) of Torts §447 (1965).

356 *Id* at §448.

357 *Id.*

358 123 Ariz 460, 600 P2d 764, 768 (1979).

359 *Id.*

360 Hulet v United States, 328 F Supp 335, 337 (D Idaho 1971).

361 *See generally* Hulet v United States, 328 F Supp 335, 338 (D Idaho 1971). Visitors at national parks are generally considered invitees. *See* Ashley v United States, 215 F Supp 39, 44 (D Neb 1963), *aff'd on other grounds*, 326 F2d 499 (8th Cir 1964); Adams v United States, 239 F Supp 503, 506 (ED Okla 1965). *See generally* §6.02. This is true whether or not they pay an entrance fee, *see* Claypool v United States, 98 F Supp 702, 705 (SD Cal 1951), or an automobile fee, *see* Ashley v United States, 215 F Supp 39, 44 (D Neb 1963), *aff'd on other grounds*, 326 F2d 499 (8th Cir 1964).

362 Piggott v United States, 480 F2d 138, 141 (4th Cir 1973); Adams v United States, 239 F Supp 503, 506 (ED Okla 1965).

363 Ashley v United States, 215 F Supp 39, 45 (D Neb 1963), *aff'd on other grounds*, 326 F2d 499 (8th Cir 1964); *see also* Hulet v United States, 328 F Supp 335, 338 (D Idaho 1971).

at a national park if it created those conditions, had actual knowledge of them or should have discovered them, and failed to warn of those conditions or eliminate the danger.[364] One court stated that this duty is not affected by aesthetic considerations.[365] However, a more accurate statement would be that aesthetic considerations are one factor to be considered in determining whether there was a breach of this duty.

Some potentially dangerous conditions cannot be eliminated without simultaneously destroying the natural beauty of our national parks. In those cases, the government usually will be considered to have exercised reasonable care if it reasonably warned of the dangers. In fact, the courts have been so concerned about destroying the natural conditions of the parks that there have been few decisions which require the government to do more than post warning signs.

An excellent illustration of the courts' reticence to require more than the posting of warnings, and the reasons behind that policy, is the court's opinion in *Henretig v United States*:

> To make the incline less steep in this area would require extensive grading or leveling of the surface. To remove all the rocks germane to the pathway would ... require moving the whole mountain. To place boardwalks and hand rails on every segment of the path would be prohibitively expensive; and all of these measures would detract from that which draws visitors to our parks—the opportunity to observe scenic wonders and the beauty of nature, unspoiled insofar as possible by the touch of man.[366]

Rocks

The government's warning of the danger of falling rocks is reasonable only if the warning is commensurate with the degree of danger.[367] One court held that where the danger of falling rocks was more than incidental and there was a risk of a fatal accident, the government was negligent because it did not post the warning signs near the area with the greatest likelihood of danger.[368] The court held that additional signs with more specific warnings should have been placed at the areas near

---

364 Adams v United States, 239 F Supp 503, 506 (ED Okla 1965).

365 *See* Piggott v United States, 480 F2d 138, 141 (4th Cir 1973).

366 490 F Supp 398, 405 (SD Fla 1980).

367 Hulet v United States, 328 F Supp 335, 337 (D Idaho 1971).

368 *Id.*

the greatest danger.[369] In addition, the court noted that the government should have considered giving oral warnings since these may have a greater impact.[370]

Nevertheless, the government breached no duty of care by failing to construct protective fences or barriers above the trail even though rocks were known to fall at all points on the trail, because that would destroy the natural beauty of the area.[371] In addition, there was no duty to construct protective devices in the areas with the greatest risk of falling rocks because there was not sufficient evidence that the protective devices would significantly reduce the risk of injury.[372]

The National Park Service has no duty to remove small rocks on a trail at a national park when this condition is not unusual and is plainly visible.[373] Indeed, one court buttressed its conclusion that rocks on a trail did not pose an unreasonably dangerous condition by noting that no other injuries were previously reported in this area.[374]

Slope of the Trail

One court held that the natural slope of a trail in a national park was not unreasonably dangerous[375] and, therefore, there was no duty to alter it. Indeed, the fact that the angle of the slope exceeded standards for landscape architects was irrelevant because those standards apply to man-made slopes, not natural ones.[376]

Dangerous Trees

The government has a duty to inspect trees in a national park and to remove trees which may collapse or to warn of the dangers.[377] For example, where a routine inspection would have indicated that a 300-year-old tree had substantially rotted away, the government was liable when the tree fell and killed a camper.[378]

---

369 *Id* at 338.

370 *Id.* Conservative lawyers will rarely advise giving only oral warnings since proof that they were, in fact, given is so easy to controvert.

371 *Id* 337.

372 *Id.*

373 *See* Henretig v United States, 490 F Supp 398, 404 (SD Fla 1980).

374 *Id.*

375 *Id.*

376 *Id* 401.

377 Middaugh v United States, 293 F Supp 977, 980 (D Wyo 1968).

378 *Id* 979.

Boardwalks and Handrails

The Park Service was not negligent in failing to erect boardwalks and handrails along a natural trail in a national park because patrons could see that the trail was unimproved. [379]

Bears

The general rule is that individuals who own or harbor inherently dangerous animals are absolutely liable for the damage those animals cause.[380] Such animals, by their very nature, pose a high degree of danger, and since their owners are under no obligation to keep them, the courts have made the owners insurers of the damage caused by the animals.

However, individuals injured by bears at national parks have not been able to apply this general rule of absolute liability against the government.[381] The federal government is exempt from the usual rule of liability because Congress has required land, in its natural condition, to be set aside in parks to be used and enjoyed by the public for general recreational purposes.[382] This factor is sufficient to relieve the government from being an insurer.[383]

Nonetheless, the federal government generally has a duty to warn of the dangers of bears. Indeed, more detailed warnings regarding bears may be required to be given to hikers and campers than to people driving through national parks because those traveling on foot are exposed to greater danger.[384]

In *Claypool v United States*, the court held that the government was negligent where campers at a national park were told by park rangers that it was safe to sleep outside, even though the rangers knew that a few days earlier a bear had attacked campers while they slept.[385] The rangers' belief that the danger had passed was unjustified under the circumstances.[386]

Even where the government has given warnings, some injured plaintiffs have argued that the warnings did not sufficiently apprise them of the danger or of the proper method of avoiding danger. For example, in *Ashley v United*

---

[379] Henretig v United States, 490 F Supp 398, 404 (SD Fla 1980).

[380] *See* Restatement (Second) of Torts §507 (1977).

[381] Ashley v United States, 215 F Supp 39, 43 (D Neb 1963), *affd on other grounds*, 326 F2d 499 (8th Cir 1964); *see generally* Restatement (Second) of Torts §508 comment a (1977).

[382] 16 USC §1.

[383] Ashley v United States, 215 F Supp 39, 43 (D Neb 1963), *affd on other grounds*, 326 F2d 499 (8th Cir 1964).

[384] *See* Williams v United States (ED Mich Oct 6, 1961), an unpublished opinion, analyzed in Ashley v United States, 215 F Supp 39, 44, 47 (D Neb 1963), *affd on other grounds*, 326 F2d 499 (8th Cir 1964).

[385] 98 F Supp 702, 704 (SD Cal 1951).

[386] *Id.*

States,[387] the government warned a visitor that bears were present in the park, that they were dangerous, and that any attempt to feed them or molest them was also dangerous. The visitor, while napping in his car with the window open and his arm outside the window, was bitten by a bear. The plaintiff argued that an adequate warning would have included the admonition to roll up the car windows if a bear approached. The court rejected this argument because such a detailed warning was not necessary for an adult in light of the other warnings given.[388] In another case, where the government distributed brochures stating that the park was inhabited by dangerous animals, and the plaintiff had read those brochures, a camper bitten by a grizzly bear could not recover because the government had acted reasonably.[389]

No warning is required when the possibility of injury is insignificant. One court held that there is no duty to warn park visitors to roll up the windows in their cars at all times because unprovoked attacks by bears are rare.[390]

In any event, a plaintiff cannot recover unless there is a causal relationship between the failure to warn and the injury.[391] The plaintiff's contention in the *Ashley* case that the government was negligent because it failed to warn visitors to roll up their windows when a bear approached was not accepted because no one saw the bear until after the attack. The government was not negligent because even if the warning had been given, it could not have been heeded because the plaintiff did not see the bear until it was too late to roll up the window.[392]

§3.16 Sidewalks

A municipality owes a duty to all reasonably foreseeable users of its public sidewalks to exercise care in maintaining the sidewalks in a reasonably safe condition for the activities for which they are normally used.[393] For example, the sidewalks must be maintained in a condition reasonably safe for use by bicyclists,[394] roller skaters,[395] and individuals pursuing activities such as

---

387 215 F Supp 39, 47 (D Neb 1963), *aff'd on other grounds*, 326 F2d 499 (8th Cir 1964).

388 *Id.*

389 Rubenstein v United States, 488 F2d 1071, 1072-73 (9th Cir 1973).

390 Ashley v United States, 215 F Supp 39, 47 (D Neb 1963), *aff'd on other grounds*, 326 F2d 499 (8th Cir 1964).

391 *See generally* **§6.08**.

392 Ashley v United States, 215 F Supp 39, 47 (D Neb 1963), *aff'd on other grounds*, 326 F2d 499 (8th Cir 1964).

393 *See* Cygielman v City of New York, 93 Misc 2d 232, 402 NYS2d 539, 542 (Sup Ct 1978).

394 Muallem v City of New York, 82 AD2d 420, 441 NYS2d 834, 837 (1981). *But see* Olsen v City of New York, 49 AD2d 884, 373 NYS2d 214, 215 (1975).

walking, skipping, jumping, or hopping.[396] However, one court held that a city does not have a duty to make the sidewalks safe for users of inherently dangerous instrumentalities such as skateboards.[397]

New York City has a law that provides that the city is not liable for injuries resulting from a defect in its sidewalks unless it had prior actual notice of the defect.[398]

§3.17 Swimming

General Duty of Care

The government is not an insurer of the safety of those who use its recreational facilities to swim or participate in other aquatic activities.[399] However, the government has a duty to use reasonable care to prevent injury to individuals using the government's pools[400] and other bodies of water.[401]

One court held that this duty is not affected by aesthetic considerations.[402] However, those factors may affect whether there was a breach of the duty of reasonable care under the circumstances.

In many cases, the government is not liable for injuries which result from obvious dangers.[403] For example, a woman who slipped on a wet springboard could not recover from the city because the risk of injury was open and obvious.[404]

The government was not negligent when it failed to guard or fence an entire pond, when the portion of the pond not meant for swimming was clearly marked and there was also a natural boundary line composed of trees, underbrush, and shrubs which divided the area meant for swimming from

---

395 Errante v City of New York, 74 AD2d 122, 427 NYS2d 18, 20 (1980).

396 See Cygielman v City of New York, 93 Misc 2d 232, 402 NYS2d 539, 542 (Sup Ct 1978).

397 Id.

398 See Administrative Code of City of New York §394a-1.0. See generally Lipsig, Tort Trends, NYLJ, July 27, 1984, at 1.

399 Bucher v Dade County, 354 So 2d 89, 91 (Fla Dist Ct App 1977); Kaczmarczyk v City & County of Honolulu, 65 Hawaii 612, 656 P2d 89, 91 (1982).

400 Brown v United States, 99 F Supp 685, 687 (SD W Va 1951).

401 Piggott v United States, 480 F2d 138, 141 (4th Cir 1973); Bucher v Dade County, 354 So 2d 89, 91 (Fla Dist Ct App 1977); Ide v City of St Cloud, 150 Fla 806, 8 So 2d 924, 925 (1942) (a city may be negligent in allowing a deep hole in a lake to remain hidden and unguarded).

402 Brown v United States, 99 F Supp 685, 687 (SD W Va 1951). See generally Piggott v United States, 480 F2d 138, 141 (4th Cir 1973).

403 See generally §6.09.

404 Payne v City of Clearwater, 155 Fla 9, 19 So 2d 406, 407 (1944).

the other area.[405] There may also be no duty to patrol a pond in a park to keep out swimmers.[406] One court noted that the cost of guarding against the dangers of swimming in some bodies of water in a park were unreasonably expensive and that if instituted would transform "meccas of restfulness into sanitariums of boredom."[407]

Where the government does not act unreasonably, it is not negligent. For example, the government was not liable where an eight-year-old boy ignored both oral and written warnings not to swim in a canal and drowned.[408]

Ownership and Possession of the Land

The government may have a duty of reasonable care to remove dangers if it owns the land, even if it is not the exclusive possessor of the property.[409] For example, in *Ward v United States*, the government, a lessor, was liable for an individual's drowning because it retained substantial control over the leased premises and the lessee took no substantial action regarding the physical condition of the premises without first consulting the government and obtaining its approval.[410] Indeed, the plaintiff was able to show that the lessee appeared to exercise no control over the swimming facilities, the location of the accident, except to operate a concession stand.[411]

However, in *Ogden v United States*, the court held that the government was not responsible for the drowning of a serviceman's child where the government had no possessory rights to the land, but only bare legal title.[412]

The courts have repeatedly held governments liable for their negligence at beaches and oceans, even though those bodies of water were not owned by the government.[413] For example, the Hawaii Supreme Court, in *Kaczmarczyk v City & County of Honolulu*, held that a city has a duty to warn of dangerous conditions in the ocean, water it did not own, where the ocean is adjacent to city property and the dangerous conditions were reasonably known to the city

---

405 Tuerck v State, 196 Misc 310, 91 NYS2d 842 (Ct Cl 1947).

406 Pope v State, 198 Misc 31, 96 NYS2d 708, 715 (Ct Cl), *affd without opinion*, 277 AD 1157, 101 NYS2d 1020 (1950).

407 *Id.*

408 Avina v United States, 115 F Supp 579, 582 (WD Tex 1953).

409 Ward v United States, 208 F Supp 118, 123 (D Colo 1962).

410 *Id.*

411 *Id.*

412 217 F Supp 94, 96-97 (ND Tex 1963). The court stated that even if the government had possessory rights there was no showing the government had knowledge of the danger and, absent that fact, there was no showing that the government was negligent. *Id* 97.

413 Ide v City of St Cloud, 150 Fla 806, 8 So 2d 924, 925 (1942); Kaczmarczyk v City & County of Honolulu, 65 Hawaii 612, 656 P2d 89, 92 (1982).

and not reasonably observable to the public.[414]

Natural Conditions

The courts have consistently held that the government has no duty to warn of dangerous natural conditions, especially if those conditions change significantly over time.[415] In *Herman v State*, the court held that the government did not have a duty to warn of sandbars at a state beach because the transitory nature of sandbars, which can change location within hours and are impossible to monitor, would render the warnings meaningless.[416] Similarly, there is no duty to warn of or guard against geological formations on the bottom of outdoor bodies of water.[417]

Diving

In *Miller v United States*,[418] the plaintiff dove into shallow water at a boat dock at a national wildlife refuse, struck his head on the bottom of the lake, and was rendered a quadriplegic. The court affirmed a $1 million verdict, holding that the government was negligent because it failed to post warning signs prohibiting diving. This area was unsafe to use for diving because the water was murky and shallow. The government was negligent because, even though it was aware that individuals had previously used this area for swimming and its own safety plan recommended warnings signs, it took no steps to warn of the danger.[419]

Similarly, in *Davis v United States*, a verdict of over $1 million was affirmed where the government improperly failed to warn the public of the danger of subsurface rocks in Devil's Kitchen Lake which, despite its name, appeared to be unthreatening.[420] Although the government was aware of unauthorized swimming and the dangers posed by the underwater rocks in that area, its only warnings were the posting of *no swimming* and *no diving* signs. The *no swimming* sign was an insufficient warning because it could just as easily have been intended to protect the lake from pollution by swimmers rather than protect swimmers from the dangers of the lake.[421] The *no diving* sign was

---

414 656 P2d at 92.

415 Bucher v Dade County, 354 So 2d 89, 90 (Fla Dist Ct App 1977); Herman v State, 94 AD2d 161, 463 NYS2d 501, 502 (1983).

416 94 AD2d 161, 463 NYS2d 501, 502 (1983).

417 Lower Neches Valley Auth v Murphy, 536 SW2d 561, 563 (Tex 1976) (canal); Rowland v City of Corpus Christi, 620 SW2d 930, 934 (Tex Civ App 1981) (marina).

418 597 F2d 614 (7th Cir 1979).

419 *Id* 617.

420 716 F2d 418, 423-24 (7th Cir 1983).

421 *Id.*

also insufficient because it was not explicit about the danger; it should have specifically warned of the dangers of the hidden rocks. [422]

Lifeguards

The government generally has an obligation to have sufficient attendants on duty at its swimming facilities to supervise people and rescue them if necessary.[423] In several cases the government was found negligent because it failed to keep any lifeguards on duty.[424] For example, in *Brown v United States*, the government was negligent in failing to keep an attendant at the pool who was familiar with the operation of a suction pump at the bottom of the pool and knew how to stop the pump if a swimmer's arm became caught in it.[425]

It is not necessary, and probably impossible in any event, for a plaintiff to prove that had even a single lifeguard been present a drowning would not have occurred. The plaintiff's burden is only to show, with reasonable probability, that the drowning resulted from the government's failure to provide a lifeguard.[426] Accordingly, where it was reasonably probable that other children would not have repeatedly pushed a girl under water, ultimately drowning her, had a lifeguard been present, the government was negligent in not providing a lifeguard.[427]

However, the courts have not been particularly receptive to the argument that the government failed to provide sufficient lifeguards where no one else in a public pool saw a swimming accident. In those cases it has been too difficult for the plaintiff to show that one or more lifeguards would, more likely than not, have been able to prevent the accident or lessen the damages.[428]

A lifeguard, or an employee held out to the public as such, is required in the performance of his or her duties to exercise the same degree of care that an ordinarily prudent lifeguard, possessing the requisite training and skills, would exercise under the same or similar circumstances.[429] However, even if the government hired inadequately trained lifeguards, if they performed their duties in essentially the same manner and with the same degree of care as

---

422 *Id.*

423 *See* Pickett v City of Jacksonville, 155 Fla 439, 20 So 2d 484, 487 (1945); Carreira v Territory, 40 Hawaii 513, 521 (1954).

424 Ward v United States, 208 F Supp 118, 121 (D Colo 1962); Brown v United States, 99 F Supp 685, 687 (SD W Va 1951).

425 99 F Supp 685, 687 (SD W Va 1951).

426 Ward v United States, 208 F Supp 118, 122 (D Colo 1962).

427 *Id.*

428 *See, e.g.*, Kaczmarczyk v City & County of Hawaii, 65 Hawaii 612, 656 P2d 89, 94 (1982); Carreira v Territory, 40 Hawaii 513 (1954).

429 Kaczmarczyk v City & County of Honolulu, 65 Hawaii 612, 656 P2d 89, 93 (Hawaii 1982).

adequately trained and skilled lifeguards would have performed under similar circumstances, there is no liability. [430]

§3.18 —Additional Issues

Governments must reasonably maintain their swimming facilities, and their failure to do so is negligence.[431] A government's failure to keep a screen over the open end of a suction pipe used to drain water out of a pool or to warn swimmers of this dangerous condition was negligence.[432] Similarly, a failure to secure properly an umbrella to the back of a lifeguard chair at a government pool, a condition which ultimately resulted in a fatality when the wind picked the umbrella up and hurled it at a boy, was negligence.[433]

The placement of a warning sign does not necessarily relieve the government of taking additional steps to reduce the risk of injury. For example, in *Hodges v United States*, the government was held liable for failing to place a sufficient barrier on an abutment to certain locks to protect children from falling in the locks and drowning.[434] The court reasoned that the placement of a warning notice on a fence, stating that individuals should remain on the inside of the fence, did not discharge the government's duty of reasonable care because young children could not read the warning.[435]

The government also has a duty to remove dangerous conditions created by others.[436] In *Adams v United States*,[437] third parties placed a rope swing over a pool of water used for swimming. While a boy was swinging on the rope, he hit a girl in the water and killed her. The court held that the government was negligent because it failed to take reasonable steps to remove the dangerous condition, viz., allowing individuals to swing on a rope over an area used for swimming. The rope had hung over the swimming area for almost a week and that was a sufficient time for the government, in the exercise of reasonable care, to have learned of the rope's existence and removed it.

Rescue

There is generally no duty for anyone, including the government, to

---

430 656 P2d at 93-94 n 3.

431 *See* Brewer v United States, 108 F Supp 889, 891 (MD Ga 1952); Brown v United States, 99 F Supp 685, 687 (SD W Va 1951).

432 Brown v United States, 99 F Supp 685, 687 (SD W Va 1951).

433 Brewer v United States, 108 F Supp 889, 891 (MD Ga 1952).

434 Hodges v United States, 98 F Supp 281, 287 (SD Iowa 1948).

435 *Id* 286.

436 Adams v United States, 239 F Supp 503, 507 (ED Okla 1965).

437 *Id.*

rescue an individual in danger.[438] Nonetheless, there are several exceptions to this general rule.[439] One of the most important exceptions is where the defendant's actions or omissions placed the plaintiff in danger.[440] Accordingly, the government probably has a duty to rescue an individual in danger at a public pool if the victim was placed in a dangerous condition because of the government's negligence.[441]

The government is also liable for the injuries suffered by one who attempted to rescue an individual placed in danger by the negligence of that governmental entity.[442] For example, where the federal government turned off several turbines at a power station and created a dangerous current downstream for some fishermen, the government was liable for the injuries suffered by those individuals who attempted to rescue the fishermen.[443]

Investigation

A town was not negligent for failing to determine whether a certificate of occupancy for a pool had been issued after the issuance of a residential swimming pool construction permit.[444]

Causation

A plaintiff cannot recover damages from the government unless he or she can establish a causal relationship between the alleged act of negligence and the injury.[445] When there was no such relationship, e.g., where a child's drowning was not substantially caused by the government's putative negligence in leaving a valve in a lock partially opened, the government should be exonerated.[446]

Causation cannot be proven by speculation.[447] In *Marlow v City of Columbia Heights*,[448] a city was granted a directed verdict where the plaintiff, a water skier who cut his foot on an object while walking to shore, was

---

438 W. Prosser, The Law of Torts §56, at 340 (4th ed 1971).

439 Restatement (Second) of Torts §§322, 324 (1965).

440 *Id* §322.

441 *See generally* **§1.23**.

442 Richardson v United States, 248 F Supp 99, 104 (ED Okla 1965). *See generally* Wagner v International RR, 232 NY 176, 133 NE 437, 437-38 (1921) (Cardozo, J) ("danger invites rescue").

443 Richardson v United States, 248 F Supp 99, 104 (ED Okla 1965).

444 Naughton v Sheehan, 56 AD2d 839, 392 NYS2d 75, 76 (1977).

445 Marcum v United States, 452 F2d 36, 38-39 (5th Cir 1971); *see generally* **§6.08**.

446 Marcum v United States, 452 F2d 36, 38-39 (5th Cir 1971).

447 *See* **§6.08**; *see also* **§1.25**.

448 284 NW2d 389, 393 (Minn 1979).

unable to introduce any evidence of what the object was or how or when the object landed in the lake. Absent such evidence, it was impossible to prove, except by speculation, how the government was negligent.

§3.19 Miscellaneous Recreational Activities

Baseball

The government must exercise reasonable care in removing unreasonable dangers near a baseball field.[449] In one case, the government was negligent in failing to remove an abandoned, partially torn down flagpole near a playing field where a boy, while chasing a baseball, ran into it and injured an eye.[450]

Boating

A state was not liable for the deaths of two men who disappeared after they went boating on a reservoir where there was no evidence that the state's acts or omissions bore any relationship to their deaths.[451]

Dancing

Where the government neither knew nor should have known that an acrobatic tap dancer would perform a dance which required an unwaxed floor, there was no liability when the dancer was injured on a waxed floor.[452]

Drag Racing

Where the government did not create an unreasonably dangerous condition and took reasonable, although unsuccessful, steps to stop drag racing in a public area it was not liable.[453]

Fishing

In *Huley v State*[454] a girl was struck in the eye with a fish hook by a young fisherman who was attempting to cast his line. She alleged that the government was negligent for permitting fishing near other recreational

---

449 Smith v United States, 337 F2d 237, 238 (9th Cir 1964).

450 *Id* (however there was no recovery because the plaintiff was contributorily negligent).

451 Trimblett v State, 156 NJ Super 291, 383 A2d 1146, 1147 (1977).

452 Eisenhower v United States, 327 F2d 663, 664 (2d Cir), *cert denied*, 377 US 991 (1964).

453 Harding v Chicago Park Dist, 34 Ill App 3d 425, 339 NE2d 779, 782 (1975).

454 37 Misc 2d 680, 235 NYS2d 679 (Ct Cl 1962).

activities at a state park and for permitting fishing without supervision. The court held that there was no negligence because the situation did not create an unreasonable risk of injury.[455] Indeed, there was no history of prior accidents at the park.[456]

In *Heagy v City & County of Denver*,[457] a fisherman who remained on his boat for two hours after weather conditions turned ominous was thrown into the water and died. The court held that the government defendants, lessors of property to a state recreational department, had no duty to provide rescue facilities.[458] However, even if there were such a duty, there was no negligence in this case because there was no showing of causation, i.e., the plaintiff did not prove that had rescue facilities been available they would more likely than not have saved the fisherman's life.[459]

When causation is difficult to show, some injured fishermen have attempted to rely on the doctrine of res ipsa loquitur. However, these attempts have usually been unsuccessful because the government did not have exclusive control of the situation.[460] One court did not apply this doctrine where several fishermen drowned after they were swept up in a dangerous current, because the plaintiffs pled and proved a specific act of negligence, viz., that when the government turned off several turbines at a power station it created the dangerous current.[461]

Golf

In *United States v Marshall*,[462] a golfer caught in a sudden rain storm got into a covered golf cart, drove over to pick up another member of her party, and headed for shelter under a nearby tree, even though there was a rain shelter a little further away. She drove through an area of *rough* and then realized that she was careening down the side of a hill. The government was not liable because it was not negligent. There was no duty in this case to protect someone from driving through a rough so formidable that it obscured the steep incline of a hill.[463]

---

455 235 NYS2d at 681.

456 *Id.*

457 472 P2d 757 (Colo Ct App 1970).

458 *Id* 759.

459 *Id.*

460 *See* Richardson v United States, 248 F Supp 99, 104 (ED Okla 1965).

461 *Id.*

462 391 F2d 880, 885 (1st Cir 1968).

463 *Id.*

Hunting

The government must exercise reasonable care in its placement of *coyote getters*.[464] In one case it was liable where the coyote getters violated applicable state law.[465] In addition, the government has a duty to warn hunters of coyote getters which, when tripped, eject poison. The government's failure to do so, when it knew or should have known that the area was used for hunting, was negligence.[466]

Motorcycling

The government generally has no duty to warn motorcyclists of open and obvious conditions such as a cable stretched across a road.[467] In *Epling v United States*,[468] the court held that the government owed a duty of reasonable care to motorcyclists using private roads who mistakenly believed they were on public roads. However, a sign placed at the beginning of the private access road which stated that the area was restricted and that it was unlawful to enter the premises without the permission of the government was sufficient to show that the plaintiff was not misled about the private character of the road.[469]

Rafting

Generally there is no duty to warn or guard against obvious dangers.[470] In *Harmon v United States*,[471] one experienced boater and one inexperienced boater drowned on a white-water rafting trip down a river which flowed through several national forests. The *Harmon* court affirmed factual findings that the experienced boater was aware of the dangerous condition of the river and that the inexperienced boater was aware or should have been aware of the danger because both of them wore life jackets and had participated in *lining* the boats[472] down the river. Accordingly, the court held that since the dangers were obvious, the government had no duty to warn of them and also

---

464 Fritz v United States, 216 F Supp 156 (DND), *appeal dismissed*, 324 F2d 959 (8th Cir 1963).

465 *Id.*

466 *Id* (child lost an eye); Worley v United States, 119 F Supp 719, 721 (D Or 1952).

467 Epling v United States, 453 F2d 327, 330 (9th Cir 1971). *See generally* §§6.09, 6.14.

468 453 F2d 327, 329 (9th Cir 1971).

469 *Id.*

470 *See, e.g.,* §6.09.

471 532 F2d 669, 671 (9th Cir 1975).

472 This is a process in which boats are floated through dangerous rapids by ropes attached to the boats and controlled from the shore.

that there was no duty to close the river to boating until the water level had receded.[473]

Skating Rinks

In *Diker v City of St Louis Park*,[474] the court held that a municipality that made an ice-skating rink available to the general public without charge had no duty to provide either supervision of the participants or equipment for the activities. However, if the city assumed such responsibilities, then it had a duty to perform those activities with reasonable care.[475]

A different court ruled that a municipality has a duty to provide general supervision to protect people from foreseeable danger while using city-owned skating rinks.[476]

Unsupervised Play Areas

The government must exercise reasonable care to clean up an area where its employees used ammunition.[477] In one case, the government was held liable for failing to remove a .30 caliber cartridge left by members of the armed forces in an area frequented by children.[478]

Zoos

In *Blanchard v City of Bridgeport*,[479] a two-year-old child crawled underneath a barrier wall at a leopard's cage in a city zoo. The leopard clawed the child's face and scalp, causing serious permanent injuries. The court affirmed a $125,000 verdict against the zoo director, a zoo employee, and the city for their negligence in failing to place a protective bar under the barrier wall that would have prevented a child from crawling into the animal's cage.[480]

---

473 532 F2d 669, 671 (9th Cir 1975).

474 268 Minn 461, 130 NW2d 113, 117 (1964). The *Diker* case is analyzed in Note, *The Minnesota Supreme Court 1963-1964*, 49 Minn L Rev 93, 142 (1964).

475 130 NW2d 113, 117 (Minn 1964).

476 Santangelo v City of New York, 66 AD2d 880, 411 NYS2d 666, 667 (1978).

477 Meara v United States, 119 F Supp 662, 665 (WD Ky 1954).

478 United States v Stoppelmann, 266 F2d 13, 17-18 (8th Cir 1959) (child injured when a cartridge exploded after being hit by a BB pellet causing the BB to lodge in his eye).

479 190 Conn 798, 463 A2d 553 (1983).

480 463 A2d at 555. It was appropriate for plaintiffs to show that the cost of installing a protective bar was less than $100. *Id* at 557.

Liability of Schools

4

§4.01   Introduction

It is estimated that each year over 11.7 million individuals participate in high school and college physical education classes, over 5.4 million participate in varsity sports activities, 5.1 million participate in school intramural activities.[1] In one recent year over 1 million individuals were injured while participating in those activities.[2]

This chapter discusses the liability of athletic associations,[3] athletic directors,[4] boards of education,[5] coaches,[6] principals,[7] superintendents,[8] and teachers[9] for those school-related athletic injuries.[10] In addition, it discusses the schools' liability for negligence[11] in assigning athletic activities,[12] furnishing athletic equipment,[13] supplying facilities,[14] giving instruction,[15] rendering medical assistance,[16] physically contacting the students,[17] and supervising the athletes.[18]

Although most lawsuits have involved students against schools and school personnel, injured spectators[19] and referees[20] have also sued schools.

---

1 Athletic Injuries and Deaths in Secondary Schools and Colleges, Natl Center for Educ Statistics, US Dept Health, Education and Welfare ix (Nov 1979).

2 *Id* 17. Over 110,000 injuries resulted in the student missing over three weeks of athletic or academic activities. *Id.*

Almost 750,000 injuries occurred in varsity sports activities and over 325,000 of those occurred in football. *Id.*

3 *See* §4.02.

4 *See* §4.03.

5 *See* §4.04.

6 *See* §4.05.

7 *See* §4.06.

8 *See* §4.07.

9 *See* §4.08.

10 There has been some commentary in this area. *See, e.g.,* Proehl, *Tort Liability of Teachers,* 12 Vand L Rev 723, 728-29 (1959); Seitz, *Legal Responsibility Under Tort Law Of School Personnel And School Districts As Regards Negligent Conduct Toward Pupils,* 15 Hastings LJ 495, 519 (1964); Vacca, *Teacher Malpractice,* 8 U Rich L Rev 447 (1974); Note, *School Liability For Athletic Injuries,* 21 Washburn LJ 315 (1982).

11 There may also be liability for wilful or wanton acts. *See* §4.17.

12 *See* §4.09.

13 *See* §4.10.

14 *See* §4.11.

15 *See* §4.12.

16 *See* §4.13.

17 *See* §4.14.

18 *See* §4.15.

19 Jackson v Cartwright School Dist, 125 Ariz 98, 607 P2d 975 (1980); Turner v Caddo Parish School Bd, 252 La 810, 214 So 2d 153 (1968). Spectator injuries are discussed in **ch 8.**

Immunity

Public schools and school employees are, by definition, governmental entities and government employees. Accordingly, their acts may be immune from tort liability under the doctrines of sovereign immunity[21] or governmental immunity.[22] Even if those doctrines are not applicable, the liability of schools may be limited under tort claims statutes[23] or other legislative enactments.[24]

In Illinois, an injured student generally cannot recover against a school or school personnel unless the defendant's acts were wilful or wanton.[25] However, in *Gerrity v Beatty*, the Illinois Supreme Court carved out one exception to this general rule and held that a school[26] could be liable for negligently failing to provide adequate football equipment.[27] The *Gerrity* court held that the policy reason for not imposing liability short of wilful or wanton behavior, viz., the fear of jeopardizing the personal relationship between teacher and student, was not present in this area.[28] Therefore, it is not unreasonably burdensome to require schools to use reasonable care in furnishing adequate equipment. Another recent Illinois decision articulated a second exception, holding that a school could be liable for negligently allowing an untrained student to give medical treatment to an injured student.[29]

General Duty of Care

Schools and school personnel are not insurers of the safety of students.[30]

---

20 Studley v School Dist No 38, 210 Neb 669, 316 NW2d 603 (1982).

21 *See* §§3.01, 3.02.

22 *See* §§3.01, 3.02.

23 *See* §3.04.

24 *See* §3.09.

25 *See* Kobylanski v Chicago Bd of Educ, 63 Ill 2d 165, 347 NE2d 705 (1976); *see also* Thomas v Chicago Bd of Educ, 77 Ill 2d 165, 395 NE2d 538, 540-41 (1979); Montag v Board of Educ School Dist No 40, 112 Ill App 3d 1039, 446 NE2d 299, 302 (1983); Morrison v Community Unit School Dist No 1, 44 Ill App 3d 315, 358 NE2d 389, 391 (1976) (action for negligently allowing a student to swim in a place without adequate supervision dismissed).

26 71 Ill 2d 47, 373 NE2d 1323, 1326 (1979). No teachers or coaches were parties to that case. In Thomas v Chicago Bd of Educ, 77 Ill 2d 165, 395 NE2d 538, 540 (1979), the court held that teachers and coaches are immune, absent wilful or wanton conduct, for failing to inspect or supervise the use of equipment.

27 71 Ill 2d 47, 373 NE2d 1323, 1326 (1978); *see also* Lynch v Board of Educ, 72 Ill App 3d 317, 390 NE2d 526, 532 (1979), *aff'd*, 82 Ill 2d 415, 412 NE2d 447 (1980).

28 71 Ill 2d 47, 373 NE2d 1323, 1326 (1978).

29 *See, e.g.*, O'Brien v Township High School Dist 214, 83 Ill 2d 462, 415 NE2d 1015, 1017 (1980).

30 Bradshaw v Rawlings, 612 F2d 135, 138 (3d Cir 1979) (college is not insurer); Stehn v Bernarr MacFadden Foundations, Inc, 434 F2d 811, 813 (6th Cir 1970); Sharp v

However, they have a duty to exercise the reasonable care of a qualified individual[31] under the circumstances.[32] This duty of care extends to students from other schools using their facilities.[33]

Some courts have stated that school personnel have the same duty of care as a reasonably prudent parent under the circumstances.[34] Such language may engender confusion because it is unclear how a prudent parent would act in a classroom since it is teachers, not parents, who run the schools. In addition, a thoughtless application of such language would create a teacher-student immunity doctrine, like the parent-child immunity doctrine,[35] although there is no a priori reason why the rationale for granting immunity in a parent-child situation would apply in a teacher-student context.

One court held that "especial care" must be taken of students because of their youth and because of state compulsory attendance laws.[36] This language is of no particular aid to other courts because it is impossible to discern how especial care differs from *reasonable care under the circumstances*. If there is no distinction, there is no reason for the different wording of the standard of care.

Fairbanks North Star Borough, 569 P2d 178, 182 (Alaska 1977) (implied); Bartell v Palos Verdes Peninsula School Dist, 83 Cal App 3d 492, 147 Cal Rptr 898, 901 (1978); District of Columbia v Cassidy, 465 A2d 395, 398 (DC 1983); Dibortolo v Metropolitan School Dist, 440 NE2d 506, 509 (Ind Ct App 1982); Perkins v State Bd of Educ, 364 So 2d 183, 184 (La Ct App 1978); Reynolds v State, 207 Misc 963, 141 NYS2d 615, 617 (Ct Cl 1955); Tiemann v Independent School Dist No 740, 331 NW2d 250, 251 (Minn 1983); Brackman v Adrian, 63 Tenn App 346, 472 SW2d 735, 739 (Tenn Ct App 1971) (private school is not insurer); Read v School Dist No 211, 7 Wash 2d 502, 110 P2d 179, 181 (1941); Seitz, *Legal Responsibility Under Tort Law Of School Personnel And School Districts As Regards Negligent Conduct Toward Pupils*, 15 Hastings LJ 495, 519 (1964); *see generally* Vacca, *Teacher Malpractice*, 8 U Rich L Rev 447 (1974); Note, *School Liability for Athletic Injuries*, 21 Washburn LJ 315 (1982).

31 *See, e.g.*, Dibortolo v Metropolitan School Dist, 440 NE2d 506, 509 (Ind Ct App 1982).

32 Bellman v San Francisco High School Dist, 11 Cal 2d 576, 81 P2d 894, 897 (1938); Dibortolo v Metropolitan School Dist, 440 NE2d 506, 509 (Ind Ct App 1982); Capers v Orleans Parish School Bd, 365 So 2d 23, 24 (La Ct App 1978); Brooks v Board of Educ, 29 Misc 2d 19, 205 NYS2d 777, 779 (Sup Ct 1960), *affd*, 15 AD2d 495, 222 NYS2d 184 (1961), *affd*, 12 NY2d 971, 189 NE2d 497, 238 NYS2d (1963) (duty to act toward students in a sane and sensible fashion).

Some courts have stated that claims of negligence against schools must be stated with some specificity. *See* Kersey v Harbin, 531 SW2d 76, 80 (Mo Ct App 1975).

33 *See* Eddy v Syracuse Univ, 78 AD2d 989, 433 NYS2d 923, 925 (1980).

34 *See, e.g.*, District of Columbia v Cassidy, 465 A2d 395, 398 (DC 1983); Ehlinger v Board of Educ, 96 AD2d 708, 465 NYS2d 378, 379 (1983).

35 *See* §2.01.

36 *See* Spanel v Mounds View School Dist, 264 Minn 279, 118 NW2d 795, 802 (1962).

One court held that a school was not liable for breach of an implied contract to furnish a safe atmosphere for students.[37] Several courts have held that there is no strict liability, at least if no product is involved.[38]

Schools have generally been unsuccessful in arguing that they cannot be sued for negligence because they stand in loco parentis to the students.[39] That doctrine applies only to the enforcement of authority.[40] However, one Illinois court was receptive to this defense.[41]

It is unclear whether a school is responsible for injuries at events which appear to be school sponsored but, in fact, are not.[42] In *Lynch v Board of Education*, the Illinois Supreme Court held that a school was liable for its teachers' negligence in failing to instruct and equip properly female football players in a powderpuff game, even though the game was not sponsored by the school.[43] The court held that the teachers had the apparent authority of the school board because the practice sessions and game occurred on school property, the girls were allowed to use school locker rooms to change clothes, and the teachers were school coaches.[44] There was a strong dissent which argued that apparent agency principles do not apply to a respondeat superior analysis.[45]

In any event, there is always some chance of injury while participating in physical exercise; however, that does not compel the conclusion that it is unreasonably dangerous to require students to engage in athletic activities.[46]

---

[37] Brown v Calhoun County Bd of Educ, 432 So 2d 1230, 1231 (Ala 1983).

[38] *Id*; District of Columbia v Cassidy, 465 A2d 395, 398 (DC 1983); Dibartolo v Metropolitan School Dist, 440 NE2d 506, 509 (Ind Ct App 1980).

[39] Kersey v Harbin, 531 SW2d 76, 82 (Mo Ct App 1975); Baird v Hosmer, 46 Ohio St 2d 273, 347 NE2d 533, 537 (1976); *see also* Proehl, *Tort Liability of Teachers*, 12 Vand L Rev 723, 728-29 (1959).

[40] Baird v Hosmer, 46 Ohio St 2d 273, 347 NE2d 533, 537 (1976); *see also* Proehl, *Tort Liability of Teachers*, 12 Vand L Rev 723, 728-29 (1959); *but see* Ill Rev Stat ch 122, §§24-24, 34-84(a) (Smith-Hurd 1978).

[41] *See, e.g.*, Kobylanski v Chicago Bd of Educ, 63 Ill 2d 165, 347 NE2d 705 (1976); *but see* Gerrity v Beatty, 71 Ill 2d 47, 373 NE2d 1323, 1326 (1978).

[42] In some cases there is no liability for school-sponsored activities. *See* Bradshaw v Rawlings, 612 F2d 135, 143 (3rd Cir 1979) (Pennsylvania law) (school owed no duty of care to a student injured by another student who became intoxicated at a school-sponsored picnic).

[43] 82 Ill 2d 415, 412 NE2d 447 (1980).

[44] 412 NE2d at 456.

[45] *Id* at 462 (Ryan, J., dissenting).

[46] Cambareri v Board of Educ, 246 AD 127, 284 NYS 892, 894 (1936), *affd*, 283 NY 741, 28 NE2d 968 (1940); *see also* Sims v Etowah County Bd of Educ, 337 So 2d 1310, 1313 (Ala 1976) (physical education is an important aspect of the public school curriculum).

Vicarious Liability

School personnel, such as athletic directors,[47] principals,[48] superintendents,[49] and even individual directors of school boards[50] are not the employers of other school personnel, and, therefore, they are not vicariously liable under the doctrine of respondeat superior for the negligence of others. However, boards of education[51] and school districts[52] can be vicariously liable for the negligence of others. For example, in *Carabba v Anacortes School Dist No 103*, the court held that a school district was liable for a referee's negligence at a wrestling match. The referee failed to stop in a timely manner a contestant from employing a full nelson.[53]

In *Stephenson v College Misericordia*, a college was held not liable where a student was injured while taking horseback riding lessons at a private facility in order to fulfill physical education requirements.[54] The court held that there was no master-servant relationship between the school and the private facility because the school had no right to control the details of the facility's work, the facility was not a school employee, and payment was made by the student directly to the facility.[55] In a different case, the court held that it was a question of fact whether a student temporarily in charge of a golf class was a representative of the school, as asserted by the plaintiff, or merely a fellow student, as claimed by the school.[56]

Insurance

Schools have no duty to provide adequate insurance for injured students.[57] However, a significant number of school districts have insurance policies for athletic injuries which provide unlimited funds for an injured student's

---

47 Fosselman v Waterloo Community School Dist, 229 NW2d 280, 285 (Iowa 1975).

48 *Id*; Cox v Barnes, 469 SW2d 61, 63 (Ky Ct App 1961); Hall v Columbus Bd of Educ, 32 Ohio App 2d 297, 290 NE2d 580, 584 (1972).

49 Fosselman v Waterloo Community School Dist, 229 NW2d 280, 285 (Iowa 1975); Vargo v Svitchan, 100 Mich App 809, 301 NW2d 1, 5 (1980); Smith v Consol School Dist No 2, 408 SW2d 50, 53-54 (Mo 1966); Hall v Columbus Bd of Educ, 32 Ohio App 2d 297, 290 NE2d 580, 584 (1972); De Gooyer v Harkness, 70 SD 26, 13 NW2d 815, 817 (1944).

50 Fosselman v Waterloo Community School Dist, 229 NW2d 280, 285 (Iowa 1975).

51 Domino v Mercurio, 17 AD2d 342, 234 NYS2d 1011, 1019 (1962), *affd*, 13 NY2d 922, 193 NE2d 893, 244 NYS2d 69 (1963).

52 *See, e.g.*, Cal Govt Code §815.2 (West 1980).

53 72 Wash 2d 939, 435 P2d 936, 948 (1967); *see generally* Restatement (Second) of Agency §214 comment a (1957).

54 376 F Supp 1324 (MD Pa 1974).

55 *Id* 1328-29.

56 DeMauro v Tusculum College, Inc, 603 SW2d 115, 117, 120 (Tenn 1980).

57 Friederich v Board of Educ, 59 Ill App 3d 79, 375 NE2d 141, 144-45 (1978).

medical expenses and a fixed weekly payment as long as the student is unable to work.[58] These policies are generally applicable only if the student elects to accept the benefits within three months of the injury and forgoes filing suit.[59]

It is clear that a school's insurance policy which excludes "any and all persons practicing, instructing, or participating in any physical training, sport, athletic activity or contest" is not applicable where a student was injured while running a 50-yard dash as part of a physical education class.[60]

Indemnification

Members of school boards, teachers, and other school personnel may be entitled to legal representation and indemnification from the school under certain conditions.[61] However, one principal's claim for indemnity was rejected because of the school district's governmental immunity.[62]

Defendants

§4.02   Athletic Associations

Virtually all schools belong to athletic associations which regulate the playing of interscholastic sports. These organizations have rarely been sued for the personal injuries of students.[63]

However, in *Peterson v Multnomah County School District*,[64] an injured football player recovered just under $1 million from an athletic association for its negligence in failing to promulgate reasonable safety regulations. The court held that, even if the association had no initial duty to make reasonable safety regulations, once it voluntarily undertook to make them, or to disseminate the safety recommendations of others, it had a duty to act reasonably.[65] The association's failure to disseminate the safety recommendations of the National

---

58 *See* Jackson, *School Districts Fear Suits Over Athletic Injuries*, LA Daily J, May 30, 1984, at 1, col 6; *The Plaintiff Elects to Receive*, 5 Cal Law 11 (July 1985).

59 *See* Jackson, *School Districts Fear Suits Over Athletic Injuries*, LA Daily J, May 30, 1984, at 1, col 6; *The Plaintiff Elects to Receive*, 5 Cal Law 11 (July 1985).

60 Morrison Assurance Co v School Bd, 414 So 2d 581, 582 (Fla Dist Ct App 1982).

61 *See, e.g.*, NY Educ Law §2560 (McKinney Supp 1983); NC Gen Stat §143-300.14 (1983).

62 Larson v Independent School Dist No 314, 289 NW2d 112, 123 (Minn 1979).

63 They have been sued over their policies. *See, e.g.*, Cooper v Oregon State Athletic Assn, 52 Or App 425, 629 P2d 386, *review denied*, 291 Or 504, 634 P2d 1347 (1981).

64 64 Or App 81, 668 P2d 385 (1983), *petition denied*, 295 Or 773, 670 P2d 1036 (1983).

65 668 P2d at 393; *see also* Restatement (Second) of Torts §323 (1965).

Federation of State High School Associations and the American Medical Association that practice games or game condition scrimmages should be prohibited until at least two weeks of practice had been held was negligence where a football player was seriously injured in a contact play on the second day of practice.[66]

§4.03   Athletic Directors

Athletic directors are not insurers of the safety of students.[67] Generally,[68] they have a duty to exercise reasonable care under the circumstances.[69]

In *Vargo v Svitchan*,[70] the court held that athletic directors who are in a position to oversee athletic practice sessions have a duty to stop any unsafe activities. Directors are presumed to know the nature of the class and the physical requirements and limitations of the participants.[71] Therefore, such individuals are liable when they fail to promulgate reasonable safety precautions to minimize injuries to the students.[72]

§4.04   Boards of Education

School boards of education are not insurers of the safety of the students.[73] Generally,[74] a school board has a duty to use due care under the circumstances.[75]

Boards of education, unlike individual directors of the board,[76] can be vicariously liable for the negligence of school employees under the doctrine of respondeat superior.[77] However, absent liability based on respondeat superior,

---

66 669 P2d at 387, 393.

67 *See generally* §4.01.

68 There is no liability if their acts are given immunity. *See* §§3.02, 3.03, 3.04, 4.01.

69 Vargo v Svitchan, 100 Mich App 809, 301 NW2d 1, 5 (1980).

70 *Id.*

71 *Id.*

72 *Id.*

73 Passafaro v Board of Educ, 43 AD2d 918, 353 NYS2d 178, 180 (1974).

74 There is no liability if the boards' acts are granted immunity. *See* §§3.03, 3.04, 4.01. *See, e.g.,* Willis v Dade County School Bd, 411 So 2d 245, 246 (Fla Dist Ct App 1982) (immunity even where physical education teacher acted maliciously).

75 Berman v Philadelphia Bd of Educ, 310 Pa Super 153, 456 A2d 545, 549 (Pa Super Ct 1983).

76 Fosselman v Waterloo Community School Dist, 229 NW2d 280, 285 (Iowa 1975).

77 Domino v Mercurio, 17 AD2d 342, 234 NYS2d 1011, 1019 (1962), *affd*, 13 NY2d 922, 193 NE2d 893, 244 NYS2d 69 (1963) (supervisors negligently allowed speculators to congregate too closely to softball diamond and player ran into a spectator while attempting to field a foul ball). *See also* Cal Govt Code §815.2 (West 1980).

boards of education will usually not be held liable because their duties are usually too general to have been breached vis-a-vis the injured plaintiff.[78] For example, a school board had no duty to build a separate gymnasium for mentally handicapped children, and, therefore, it was not liable when one such child was killed on the way to another gymnasium.[79]

§4.05   Coaches

Generally,[80] coaches have a duty to exercise reasonable care for the safety of their players.[81] Coaches are not insurers of their students' safety.[82]

Coaches have a duty to instruct their players regarding reasonably safe methods to avoid or minimize injury.[83] Their failure to do so can subject their players to crippling injuries and subject themselves to massive liability. In 1982 a jury returned a $6 million verdict against a football coach who taught a player an unsafe method for avoiding a tackle. The resultant injury left the student a quadriplegic.[84]

Sometimes there is no duty to warn of obvious risks.[85] In *Vendrell v School District No 26C*, the court held that a coach had no duty to warn a football player that the use of his head as a battering ram might cause an injury, because that result was obvious.[86] The court buttressed its conclusion by noting that less than two weeks earlier the plaintiff split his helmet when he ran head-on into another football player.[87] The court declared that "no coach could have spoken to him more effectively."[88] Nevertheless, this decision seems particularly harsh. After all, if the player had not been injured when he earlier used his head as a battering ram, it seems reasonable that the lesson he learned was that the helmet would protect his head.

---

[78] *See* Jackson v Board of Educ, 109 Ill App 3d 716, 441 NE2d 120, 121 (1979).

[79] Foster v Houston Gen Ins Co, 407 So 2d 759, 765 (La Ct App 1981), *cert denied*, 409 So 2d 660 (La 1982).

[80] There is no liability if a coach's acts are given immunity. *See* §§3.03, 3.04, 4.01.

[81] *See generally* §4.01. Some courts have held that conclusory allegations of negligence may subject the complaint to dismissal. *See, e.g.*, Smith v Consolidated School Dist No 2, 408 SW2d 50, 55-56 (Mo 1966).

[82] *See generally* §4.01.

[83] *See* §4.12.

[84] *See* Jackson, *School Districts Fear Suits Over Athletic Injuries*, LA Daily J, May 30, 1984, at 1, col 6; *Tough to Tackle*, 70 ABAJ 32 (May 1984). While the case was on appeal, it was settled for slightly under $4 million. *Tough to Tackle*, 70 ABAJ 32 (May 1984).

[85] *See generally* §6.09.

[86] 233 Or 1, 376 P2d 406, 413 (1962).

[87] *Id.*

[88] *Id.*

Coaches are not liable for negligent instruction where the injury did not result from those instructions. In *Passantino v Board of Education*,[89] a base runner in a baseball game was seriously injured when he used his head as a battering ram to bowl over a catcher who was blocking the plate. The jury awarded the plaintiff a $1 million verdict. The *Passantino* court reversed the judgment and held that the coach was not negligent. The coach had congratulated the plaintiff after he put his shoulder into a catcher while attempting to score two weeks earlier. However, the court held that this was not an unreasonably dangerous act which led the plaintiff to use his head to knock down the catcher in the subsequent game because the two plays were dissimilar.

Coaches also have a duty to exercise reasonable care in providing protective equipment.[90] In *Rutter v Northeastern Beaver County School Board*, it was held to be a question of fact whether the coaches were negligent in failing to provide any equipment in a touch football game in which tackling and body blocking occurred.[91]

Coaches can participate in athletic activities with their students if doing so does not create an unreasonable risk of harm.[92] In *Kluka v Livingston Parish School Board*, the court held that a coach did not act unreasonably in wrestling with a strong, well-conditioned athlete who played on two high school athletic teams.[93] The court noted that the coach had a duty to exercise restraint to avoid inflicting injury on the student because of the coach's superior instruction and knowledge, but when there was no breach of that duty, there was no liability.[94]

A coach who knows or should know that a player is injured but nevertheless persuades or permits the athlete to play football and the athlete becomes more seriously injured, is negligent.[95]

Coaches must take reasonable steps to obtain medical assistance.[96] In *Mogabgab v Orleans Parish School Board*,[97] two coaches were found negligent

---

[89] 41 NY2d 1022, 363 NE2d 1373, 395 NYS2d 628 (1977), *revg* 52 AD2d 935, 383 NYS2d 639 (1976).

[90] *See* Rutter v Northeastern Beaver County School Dist, 437 A2d 1198, 1202 (Pa 1981).

[91] 496 Pa 590, 437 A2d 1198, 1202 (Pa 1981).

[92] *See generally* Stafford v Catholic Youth Org, 202 So 2d 333, 336 (La Ct App), *writ ref*, 251 La 231, 203 So 2d 559 (1967).

[93] 433 So 2d 302, 303 (La Ct App 1983).

[94] *Id.*

[95] Morris v Union High School Dist A, 160 Wash 121, 294 P 998, 999 (1931). *See also* LA Daily J, Apr 27, 1983, at 1, col 5 (an injured student who was forced to play football and by doing so significantly aggravated the injury was awarded $1,500,000 by a District of Columbia jury).

[96] Mogabgab v Orleans Parish School Bd, 239 So 2d 456, 460 (La Ct App 1970).

[97] *Id.*

for failing to call a doctor as soon as possible for a player who appeared to be suffering from heat damage and later died. Heat damage causes progressive adverse internal changes in the body that at some point become irreversible.[98] Accordingly, players who appear to suffer from this condition must be given medical attention quickly.[99]

Few doctors will testify that an athlete would not have died if they had been called at a specified time. However, the law does not demand such exactitude.[100] As long as it appears more likely than not that the athlete would have lived, had a doctor been called earlier, the requisite causal relationship is established.[101]

The coaches in *Mogabgab* were also negligent in giving the student aid that was counter-productive.[102] It is important that heat accumulation stop,[103] and, therefore, placing a blanket over the athlete was improper treatment.[104]

There can also be liability for injuries resulting from nonathletic events. For example, a coach who participated in an initiation rite for athletes where a student died after being given an electric shock was held liable.[105] However, a coach was granted a directed verdict where a high school student was pushed and then fell from a six-foot retaining wall at a letterman's outing at the coach's cabin.[106] The court held that there was no failure to supervise because the primary responsibility of the coach was to host the outing.[107]

§4.06 Principals

Principals are not insurers of the students' safety.[108] However, principals generally[109] have a duty to exercise reasonable care under the circumstances.[110]

---

98 Mogabgab v Orleans Parish School Bd, 239 So 2d 456, 460 (La Ct App 1970); Morris v Union High School Dist A, 160 Wash 121, 294 P 998, 999 (1931).

99 Mogabgab v Orleans Parish School Bd, 239 So 2d 456, 460 (La Ct App 1970).

100 *Id.*

101 *Id.*

102 *Id.*

103 Heat can have a pernicious effect on the body. One study concluded that in a recent 23-year period, there were 70 reported school football players who died from heat stroke. *See* Mueller & Schindler, Annual Survey of Football Injury Research 1931-1983.

104 Mogabgab v Orleans Parish School Bd, 239 So 2d 456, 460 (La Ct App 1970).

105 De Gooyer v Harkness, 70 SD 26, 13 NW2d 815, 817 (1944).

106 Arnold v Hafling, 474 P2d 638, 639 (Colo Ct App 1970).

107 *Id.* The court also noted that high school children do not require as much supervision as younger children. *See id.*

108 Kersey v Harbin, 591 SW2d 745, 749 (Mo Ct App 1979).

109 The acts of a principal may be given immunity. *See* §§3.03, 4.01.

110 Pirkle v Oakdale Union Grammar School Dist, 40 Cal 2d 207, 253 P2d 1, 2 (1953).

Principals must take reasonable steps to see that the students are properly supervised by others.[111] In *Larson v Independent School District No 314*,[112] a principal's failure to supervise the actions of an inexperienced physical education teacher resulted in a student becoming a quadriplegic after performing a gymnastic exercise incorrectly. The court upheld a $1 million verdict against the principal.[113] The court held that if the principal believed he lacked the expertise to supervise teachers in this area he should have delegated that responsibility to someone with the appropriate knowledge; it was improper to fail to take any steps to supervise inexperienced teachers.[114] However, in a different case, where a principal did not have the power or authority to direct the detailed conduct of a physical education teacher, the principal was not negligent as a matter of law.[115]

Principals must exercise reasonable care in supervising the maintenance of athletic facilities.[116] Therefore, where a student was injured as a result of a weightlifting room being improperly equipped and designed, the principal was liable.[117]

Where there is no evidence that the principal has acted unreasonably or, even if he or she has, that the acts bore any substantial relationship to a student's injury, the principal is entitled to a judgment in his or her favor.[118] For example, where a student's injuries were not aggravated because the principal failed to provide prompt medical assistance, the principal was exonerated.[119]

One court held that a principal has a ministerial duty to minimize injury to the students and therefore was not immune under a state tort claims act for negligent failure to stop a dangerous game played during recess. *See* Cook v Bennett, 94 Mich App 93, 288 NW2d 609, 611-12 (1979); *see also* Vargo v Svitchan, 100 Mich App 809, 301 NW2d 1, 5 (1980).

In Larson v Independent School Dist No 314, 289 NW2d 112, 116 (Minn 1979) the principal's duties were spelled out in school district manuals.

111 Larson v Independent School Dist No 314, 289 NW2d 112, 116 (Minn 1979); Kersey v Harbin, 591 SW2d 745, 749 (Mo Ct App 1979). *See also* Cal Admin Code tit 5, §5552 (1977) ("Where playground supervision is not otherwise provided, the principal of each school shall provide for the supervision by certificated employees of the conduct and safety, and for the direction of the play, of the pupils of the school who are on the school grounds during recess and other intermissions and before and after school.").

112 289 NW2d 112 (Minn 1979).

113 *Id.* There was expert testimony that indicated a need to supervise closely the teaching of gymnastics when an inexperienced teacher was involved. *Id* 117.

114 *Id.* 117 n 11.

115 *See* Luce v Board of Educ, 2 AD2d 502, 157 NYS2d 123, 127 (1956), *aff'd*, 3 NY2d 792, 143 NE2d 977, 164 NYS2d 43 (1957).

116 Vargo v Svitchan, 100 Mich App 809, 301 NW2d 1, 5 (1980).

117 *Id.*

118 Berg v Merricks, 20 Md App 666, 318 A2d 220, 227-28 (1974); *see also* Arnold v Hafling, 474 P2d 638, 639 (Colo Ct App 1970).

119 Pirkle v Oakdale Union Grammer School Dist, 40 Cal 2d 207, 253 P2d 1, 4 (1953).

§4.07 Superintendents

School superintendents generally[120] have a duty to exercise reasonable care under the circumstances.[121] For example, superintendents have a duty to exercise reasonable care to see that the students are properly supervised.[122] However, school superintendents are not insurers of the safety of students.[123]

School superintendents are not liable for the athletic injuries of students unless they were personally negligent.[124] For example, a county superintendent of schools was entitled to judgment as a matter of law when he did not have the power to take the administrative actions which the plaintiffs alleged were negligent, i.e., the decision to purchase certain equipment, to make curriculum changes, and to require minimum qualifications for physical education teachers.[125]

Superintendents have no duty to instruct students in specific sports, to ascertain a student's knowledge of the sport, or to supervise personally physical education.[126] Therefore, they cannot be held liable for failure to perform those tasks.[127] A school superintendent was entitled to judgment as a matter of law where there was no evidence that he was responsible for a student attempting an advanced gymnastic activity without proper training.[128]

Superintendents are generally not required to develop a physical education curriculum. Where was no showing that the superintendent knew or should have known that the principal had allowed an unsafe physical education curriculum to be developed, there was no liability.[129]

§4.08 Teachers

In no event are teachers[130] insurers of the safety of students.[131] Rather, if

---

120 Their acts may have been given immunity. *See* §§3.03, 3.04, 4.01.

121 *See generally* Kersey v Harbin, 591 SW2d 745, 749 (Mo Ct App 1979); *see also* §4.01.

122 Kersey v Harbin, 591 SW2d 745, 749 (Mo Ct App 1979).

123 *See id.*

124 Smith v Consolidated School Dist No 2, 408 SW2d 50, 55 (Mo 1966); *see also* De Gooyer v Harkness, 70 SD 26, 13 NW2d 815, 817 (1944).

125 Berg v Merricks, 20 Md App 666, 318 A2d 220, 229-30 (1974).

126 Smith v Consolidated School Dist No 2, 408 SW2d 50, 55 (Mo 1966).

127 *Id.*

128 Larson v Independent School Dist No 314, 289 NW2d 112, 119 (Minn 1979).

129 *Id.*

130 There has been some legal commentary on the legal liability of teachers. *See, e.g.,* Proehl, *Tort Liability of Teachers*, 12 Vand L Rev 723, 739 (1959); Seitz, *Legal Responsibility Under Tort Law of School Personnel and School Districts as Regards Negligent Conduct Toward Pupils*, 15 Hastings LJ 495, 519 (1964); Vacca, *Teacher Malpractice*, 8 U Rich L Rev 447 (1974).

their acts are not given immunity,[132] they have the same duty that a reasonable person would have under the same or similar circumstances,[133] i.e., not to expose the students to an unreasonable risk of harm.[134]

Teachers have generally been unsuccessful in claiming that their acts did not subject them to liability because of the doctrine of in loco parentis; that doctrine only applies with respect to the enforcement of authority.[135]

There is inherent physical danger in participating in physical education activities.[136] Therefore, teachers must exercise reasonable care in assigning activities,[137] providing equipment,[138] maintaining the facilities,[139] instructing the students,[140] providing medical assistance,[141] avoiding physical contact,[142] and supervising the activities.[143] Where teachers have not acted unreasonably,

---

131 Kersey v Harbin, 591 SW2d 745, 749 (Mo Ct App 1979); Cirillo v City of Milwaukee, 34 Wis 2d 705, 150 NW2d 460, 466 (1967).

132 See §§3.03, 4.01. In one state, teachers are subjected to liability only when they acted wilfully and wantonly; *mere* negligence is not enough. *See* Thomas v Chicago Bd of Educ, 77 Ill 2d 165, 395 NE2d 538, 541 (1979); Landers v School Dist No 203, 66 Ill App 3d 78, 383 NE2d 645, 647 (1978); *but see* Gerrity v Beatty, 71 Ill 2d 47, 373 NE2d 1323, 1326 (1978).

133 Dibortolo v Metropolitan School Dist, 440 NE2d 506, 509 (Ind Ct App 1982).

Some courts have held that a teacher's duty is similar to a parent's. *See, e.g.*, District of Columbia v Cassidy, 465 A2d 395, 398 (DC 1983); Ehlinger v Board of Educ, 96 AD2d 708, 465 NYS2d 378, 379 (1983). This *rule* has been properly criticized. *See* Proehl, *Tort Liability of Teachers*, 12 Vand L Rev 723, 739-40 n 96 (1959). Among other things, teachers do not have the immunity which is sometimes given to parents. *See* Baird v Hosmer, 46 Ohio St 2d 273, 347 NE2d 533, 536-37 (1976); *but see* Kobylanski v Chicago Bd of Educ, 63 Ill 2d 165, 347 NE2d 705 (1976).

134 Pirkle v Oakdale Union Grammer School Dist, 40 Cal 2d 207, 253 P2d 1, 2 (1953); Perkins v State Bd of Educ, 364 So 2d 183, 184 (La Ct App 1978); Cook v Bennett, 94 Mich App 93, 288 NW2d 609, 611 (1979); Reynolds v State, 207 Misc 963, 141 NYS2d 615, 618 (Ct Cl 1955); La Valley v Stanford, 272 AD 183, 70 NYS2d 460, 462 (1947); Summers v Milwaukie Union High School Dist, 4 Or App 596, 481 P2d 369, 370 (1971); *see also* Proehl, *Tort Liability of Teachers*, 12 Vand L Rev 723, 739 (1959).

Some courts have appeared to impose rigorous pleading requirements in stating a claim against a teacher. *See, e.g.*, Smith v Consolidated School Dist No 2, 408 SW2d 50, 56-57 (Mo 1966).

135 Baird v Hosmer, 46 Ohio St 2d 273, 347 NE2d 533, 537 (1976); *see also* Proehl, *Tort Liability of Teachers*, 12 Vand L Rev 723, 728-29 (1959). *See also* §4.01.

136 Green v Orleans Parish School Bd, 365 So 2d 834, 836 (La Ct App 1978), *writ refused*, 367 So 2d 393 (La 1979); Berg v Merricks, 20 Md App 666, 318 A2d 220, 227 (1974).

137 *See* §4.09.

138 *See* §4.10.

139 *See* §4.11.

140 *See* §4.12.

141 *See* §4.13.

142 *See* §4.14.

143 *See* §4.15; *see also* Kersey v Harbin, 591 SW2d 745, 749 (Mo Ct App 1979); *see also* Cal Educ Code §44807 (West 1978).

but injury still results, they are not liable because all accidents cannot be eliminated.[144]

Some school boards have promulgated standards for safe practices for certain sports. Although the court may not be bound by these standards, the failure of a teacher to comply with them may be considered in determining whether the teacher was negligent.[145]

In any event, a teacher is not liable as a matter of law for injuries which occur at school on a day in which he or she is not at work.[146]

General Principles of Liability

§4.09   Assigning Activities

Schools must exercise reasonable care in assigning pupils to athletic exercises and other physical education activities.[147] Indeed, common sense requires that athletic activities be suited to the age, sex, and physical development,[148] as well as the athletic ability,[149] of the children involved.

Accordingly, a school can be negligent where a teacher directs students to play a game that is too dangerous for the age of the students.[150] However, when the jury concludes that the game was not so dangerous, the school was exonerated.[151] One court held that it was negligence to require improperly matched seventh graders to engage in a hazardous indoor soccer-type game which required them to run toward each other at full speed over a distance of 37 feet.[152]

---

144 Berg v Merricks, 20 Md App 666, 318 A2d 220, 227 (1974).

145 Keesee v Board of Educ, 37 Misc 2d 414, 235 NYS2d 300, 305 (Sup Ct 1962).

146 Cook v Bennett, 94 Mich App 93, 288 NW2d 609, 611 (1979).

147 Luce v Board of Educ, 2 AD2d 502, 157 NYS2d 123, 128 (1956), affd, 3 NY2d 792, 143 NE2d 797, 164 NYS2d 43 (1957); Govel v Board of Educ, 267 AD 621, 48 NYS2d 299, affd without opinion, 293 NY 928, 60 NE2d 133 (1944); see also Proehl, Tort Liability of Teachers, 12 Vand L Rev 723, 746 (1959); see generally §4.20 (gymnastics); §4.22 (soccer).

148 Proehl, Tort Liability of Teachers, 12 Vand L Rev 723, 745 (1959).

149 Luce v Board of Educ, 2 AD2d 502, 157 NYS2d 123, 128 (1956), affd, 3 NY2d 792, 143 NE2d 797, 164 NYS2d 43 (1957); Govel v Board of Educ, 267 AD 621, 48 NYS2d 299, affd without opinion, 293 NY 928, 60 NE2d 133 (1944).

150 Yerdon v Baldwinsville Academy & Cent School Dist, 50 AD2d 714, 374 NYS2d 877, 878-79 (1975) (dicta).

151 Id.

152 Brooks v Board of Educ, 29 Misc 2d 19, 205 NYS2d 777, 779-80 (Sup Ct 1960), affd, 15 AD2d 495, 222 NYS2d 184 (1961), affd, 12 NY2d 971, 189 NE2d 497, 238 NYS2d 963 (1963). ("Perhaps our notions on the subject of education are outmoded but the view that exercises such as these form a necessary part of education impresses us as being absurd," citing Gardner v State, 256 AD 385, 10 NYS2d 274, 276, affd, 281 NY 212, 22 NE2d 344

In *Luce v Board of Education*, the court held that a teacher may be negligent in allowing a child to participate in a rough sport if the teacher had knowledge of the child's previous injuries and should have realized that participation posed an unreasonable risk in aggravating those injuries.[153] However, where a teacher had no knowledge of a student's chronic aneurism of a cerebral artery and the concomitant danger of permitting him to participate in dangerous sports, he was not negligent in allowing the student to participate.[154]

§4.10 Equipment

Schools have a duty to furnish protective equipment to prevent serious injuries to students engaged in athletic activities.[155] Accordingly, a school district was held liable for failing to furnish helmets and face-guards to students engaged in a football game, an activity in which head injuries are common.[156]

In addition, schools must reasonably inspect and maintain athletic equipment and supplies.[157] In *Stanley v Board of Education*,[158] a school board was held liable for injuries suffered by a boy who was hit in the head by a bat that slipped out of the hands of a baseball player. The court affirmed the jury's determination that the school board was negligent in allowing participants in a summer recreational baseball program to use a bat which had no tape and which had a frayed knob.[159] One court held that it was a question of fact whether a school was negligent in allowing students to use gymnastic vaulting horses with exposed holes where the pommels had been removed.[160]

(1939)). *But see generally* Pirkle v Oakdale Union Grammer School Dist, 40 Cal 2d 207, 253 P2d 1, 3 (1953) (if students must be perfectly matched, it may be impossible to field two teams).

153 2 AD2d 502, 157 NYS2d 123, 128 (1956), *affd*, 3 NY2d 792, 143 NE2d 797, 164 NYS2d 43 (1957). *See also* Proehl, *Tort Liability of Teachers*, 12 Vand L Rev 723, 746 (1959).

154 Kerby v Elk Grove Union High School Dist, 1 Cal App 2d 246, 36 P2d 431, 434 (1934).

155 Lynch v Board of Educ, 72 Ill App 3d 317, 390 NE2d 526 (1979), *affd*, 82 Ill 2d 415, 412 NE2d 447 (1980); *see also* §4.18 on baseball; §4.22 on hockey.

156 Lynch v Board of Educ, 72 Ill App 3d 317, 390 NE2d 526 (1979), *affd*, 82 Ill 2d 415, 412 NE2d 447 (1980) (plaintiff's $60,000 verdict affirmed).

157 Tiemann v Independent School Dist No 740, 331 NW2d 250, 251 (Minn 1983); *see also* Vacca, *Teacher Malpractice*, 8 U Rich L Rev 447, 452 (1974); *see generally* §4.20 (gymnastics); §4.22 (hockey).

158 9 Ill App 3d 963, 293 NE2d 417 (1973).

159 293 NE2d at 420.

160 Tiemann v Independent School Dist No 740, 331 NW2d 250, 251 (Minn 1983). The court also held that expert testimony was not required to show negligence in this area. *See id.*

§4.11 Facilities

Schools must take reasonable steps to inspect and maintain their athletic and recreational facilities.[161] A school is liable to an injured student if it knew or should have known of an unreasonably dangerous condition at the school, failed to take reasonable steps to eliminate the danger, and a student was injured by that condition.[162]

There have been several cases where schools have been held liable for allowing glass doors and panels, which can break easily and cause or exacerbate an injury, to remain in areas near athletic activity.[163] For example, in *Eddy v Syracuse University*,[164] a school was held liable for placing glass doors in a gymnasium. The court held that the school was negligent because the glass could have been relatively easily removed and replaced with nonbreakable material, or protection could have been placed over the doors to reduce the risk of injury.[165]

In *Ehlinger v Board of Education*, the court held that a school must allow sufficient unobstructed space for an athlete to slow down after the finish line of a running exercise.[166] In addition, there may also be a duty to warn of the dangers of having inadequate unobstructed space.[167] However, the school was not negligent merely because it did not provide the amount of unobstructed space that was required by a state physical fitness test manual where the school gymnasium which was used was smaller than a standard gymnasium.[168]

Where a school's maintenance of its facilities is not unreasonably dangerous, there is no liability.[169] For example, a school has no duty to pave all areas near a recreation yard in an attempt to remove all rocks and other miscellaneous

---

161 *See* Wilkinson v Hartford Accident & Indem Co, 411 So 2d 22, 24 (La 1982); Tiemann v Independent School Dist No 740, 331 NW2d 250, 251 (Minn 1983); *see generally* Proehl, *Tort Liability of Teachers*, 12 Vand L Rev 723, 746 (1959); *see also* §4.18 (baseball), §4.19 (basketball), §4.20 (gymnastics), §4.21 (playground), §4.22 (track and field).

162 Wilkinson v Hartford Accident & Indem Co, 411 So 2d 22, 24 (La 1982).

163 *Id* (one plate-glass panel had been broken a few years earlier and replaced with safety glass, but the other panel was not replaced); *see also* Thomas v St Mary's Roman Catholic Church, 283 NW2d 254, 257 (SD 1979).

Expert testimony is not necessary to show a school's negligence in placing glass near athletic facilities. *See* 283 NW2d at 257.

164 78 AD2d 989, 433 NYS2d 923, 925 (1980).

165 *Id*.

166 96 AD2d 708, 465 NYS2d 378, 380 (1983).

167 *Id*.

168 *Id*.

169 Hampton v Orleans Parish School Bd, 422 So 2d 202, 204 (La Ct App 1982); Studley v School Dist No 38, 210 Neb 669, 316 NW2d 603, 604-05 (1982).

objects.[170] This is because a child could pick up a rock from virtually anywhere, even if all the areas near the school were paved, and hurl it another student and cause injury.[171] In a similar case, the court held that a child's throwing of a rock was an unforeseeable superseding cause of injury.[172]

Safe Building Statutes

Michigan has a *safe building* statute which imposes liability upon governmental bodies for injuries resulting from dangerous or defective conditions in a public building.[173]

In *Pichette v Manistique Public Schools*, a school was held liable under a safe building statute for injuries resulting from a defective playground slide.[174] The court brushed aside the argument that the statute did not apply because the slide was not a public building or inside a public building.[175] It noted that the statute was broad enough to cover injuries from facilities on the premises of a public building because the legislature intended to protect the public from injury from unsafe public places.[176]

Although these statutes are not limited to physical defects, one court did not find a statutory violation where the injury resulted from an alleged failure to supervise an activity, rather than from a defect in the structure of the building.[177]

§4.12   Instruction

Schools must provide reasonable instructions to students participating in athletic activities.[178]

---

[170] Hampton v Orleans Parish School Bd, 422 So 2d 202, 204 (La Ct App 1982).

[171] *Id.*

[172] Fagan v Summers, 498 P2d 1227, 1229 (Wyo 1972). *See also* §4.16.

[173] Mich Comp Laws §691.1406 (1977); Mich Stat Ann §3.996(106) (Callaghan 1977).

[174] 403 Mich 268, 269 NW2d 143, 149 (1978).

[175] *Id.*

[176] *Id.*

[177] *See* Vargo v Svitchan, 100 Mich App 809, 301 NW2d 1, 7 (1980). The court ignored plaintiff's contention that there was inadequate ventilation in the building, a condition which could have been caused by a defect in the building itself.

[178] *See generally* Darrow v West Genesee Cent School Dist, 41 AD2d 897, 342 NYS2d 611, 612 (1973); Vendrell v School Dist No 26C, 233 Or 1, 376 P2d 406 (1962); *see also* Proehl, *Tort Liability of Teachers*, 12 Vand L Rev 723, 746 (1959); Vacca, *Teacher Malpractice*, 8 U Rich L Rev 447, 452 (1974); *see also* §4.20 (gymnastics).

Where there is no evidence of negligent instruction, the defendant is entitled to a directed verdict. *See* Peck v Board of Educ, 35 AD2d 978, 317 NYS2d 919, 921 (1970).

Generally, this means that students should receive instructions in three areas. First, students should be given information, and possibly a demonstration, on how to perform an athletic activity before the students attempt that activity.[179] The teacher should explain the basic procedures involved in the activity and give some suggestions as to the proper method to perform the assignment.[180] Second, the teacher should identify and clarify the risks that are involved in performing that activity.[181] Finally, the teacher should explain reasonable safety precautions to be observed while engaging in athletic activities.[182] In determining whether the teacher acted reasonably, the courts should consider the age and physical condition of the students and the difficulty and danger of the required activity.[183]

A teacher's failure to give proper instructions to students attempting dangerous athletic activities can have disastrous consequences. In *Stehn v Bernarr MacFadden Foundations, Inc*,[184] a student broke his neck and had his spinal cord severed in a wrestling match. The court held that the instructor was negligent in teaching the students a wrestling maneuver which was not generally recognized or approved by experts, and it upheld a $375,000 verdict for the student.[185] Similarly, in 1982, a superior court jury in Seattle found the local school district liable for over $6 million for its coaches' negligence in teaching a football player an unsafe method of avoiding a tackle. The resultant injury rendered the student a quadriplegic.[186]

A school's duty is only to offer adequate instruction; there is no requirement that each student receive the instruction.[187] It would be a serious blow to schools in general, and particularly universities, which lack serious sanctions to compel attendance, to impose liability where adequate instruction was

---

179 Vacca, *Teacher Malpractice*, 8 U Rich L Rev 447, 452 (1974); *see also* Dibortolo v Metropolitan School Dist, 440 NE2d 506, 510 (Ind Ct App 1982); Green v Orleans Parish School Bd, 365 So 2d 834, 836 (La Ct App 1978), *writ refused*, 367 So 2d 393 (La 1979).

180 Vacca, *Teacher Malpractice*, 8 U Rich L Rev 447, 452 (1974).

181 Green v Orleans Parish School Bd, 365 So 2d 834, 836 (La Ct App 1978), *writ refused*, 367 So 2d 393 (La 1979); Vacca, *Teacher Malpractice*, 8 U Rich L Rev 447, 452 (1974).

182 Darrow v West Genesee Cent School Dist, 41 AD2d 897, 342 NYS2d 611, 612 (1973).

183 Green v Orleans Parish School Bd, 365 So 2d 834, 836 (La Ct App 1978), *writ refused*, 367 So 2d 393 (La 1979). *See also* Proehl, *Tort Liability of Teachers*, 12 Vand L Rev 723, 747 (1959) (activities involving violent body contact or a high degree of skill require more instruction than other activities).

184 434 F2d 811 (6th Cir 1970).

185 *Id. See also* Dibortolo v Metropolitan School Dist, 440 NE2d 506, 510 (Ind Ct App 1982) (teacher can be liable for teaching a dangerous method of performing a vertical jump).

186 *See* Jackson, *School Districts Fear Suits Over Athletic Injuries*, LA Daily J, May 30, 1984, at 1, col 6; *Tough to Tackle*, 70 ABAJ 32 (May 1984). While the case was on appeal, it was settled for slightly less than $4 million. *Id.*

187 Perkins v State Board of Educ, 364 So 2d 183, 184-85 (La Ct App 1978).

offered but not received due to some neglect by the student.[188] Accordingly, a school fulfilled its duty to offer adequate instruction when it made available to a 34-year-old student, who had received prior swimming training, four opportunities to learn the elements of a surface dive, a relatively elementary skill.[189]

§4.13 Medical

Schools must take reasonable precautions to avoid aggravating the condition of an injured student.[190] Where a student had a physical disability from a prior injury and the school had notice of this condition because it had received notes from the student's doctor, the school may have been negligent in insisting, despite the student's protests, that she perform broad jumps as part of gymnastic exercises.[191] Of course, if there were no causal connection between compelling the student to perform the broad jumps and the subsequent injury, the school would not be liable.[192]

Schools must also take reasonable steps to obtain medical assistance for injured students.[193] For example, a school's failure to have a doctor quickly observe a student apparently suffering from heat damage was negligence.[194] However, where there was no proof that a school unreasonably delayed the administration of medical treatment, or that the delay was causally related to the student's death, the school was entitled to a directed verdict.[195]

A coach who renders improper medical treatment can subject him or herself, and the school, to liability.[196]

§4.14 Physical Contact

Teachers can be liable for injuries caused by their unreasonable physical

---

188 *Id.*

189 *Id.*

190 *See* Lowe v Board of Educ, 36 AD2d 952, 321 NYS2d 508, 509-10 (1971). *See also* LA Daily J, Apr 27, 1983, at 1, col 5 (an injured student who was forced to play football and by doing so significantly aggravated an injury was awarded $1.5 million by a District of Columbia jury).

191 Lowe v Board of Educ, 36 AD2d 952, 321 NYS2d 508, 509-10 (1971).

192 *Id. See also* §4.16.

193 Mogabgab v Orleans Parish School Bd, 239 So 2d 456, 460 (La Ct App 1970).

194 *Id.*

195 Peck v Board of Educ, 35 AD2d 978, 317 NYS2d 919, 921 (1970). *See also* §4.16.

196 *Id. See also* Welch v Dunsmuir Joint Union High School Dist, 326 P2d 633, 639 (Cal Ct App 1958) (plaintiff received a verdict of $325,000 because the coach allowed an injured player to be moved off the field before receiving medical aid).

contact with students.[197] For example, a physical education teacher whose physical contact with a student went beyond what was necessary, viz., lifting a student from the floor, shaking him, and then dropping him, was liable for the student's injuries.[198] However, a coach was found not negligent in wrestling with a student where the student's injury was not caused by the coach's excessive violence or superior knowledge of wrestling.[199]

§4.15   Supervision

General Duty of Care

Schools have a duty to exercise reasonable care in supervising athletic activities.[200] This is true whether or not the activities are required, as long as they are sponsored or encouraged by the school.[201] Indeed, one court held that even if the activity were not school sponsored, as long as it reasonably appears to be, the school must provide reasonable supervision.[202] Accordingly, a school's claim that it had no duty to supervise properly a school floor hockey game was dismissed as being without merit.[203] However, a teacher was not liable for lack of supervision where students engaged in tumbling

---

197 Frank v Orleans Parish School Bd, 195 So 2d 451, 453 (La Ct App 1967); *see generally* Cal Educ Code §49001 (West 1978) (there is to be no corporal punishment without the prior written approval of the student's parent or guardian).

198 Frank v Orleans Parish School Bd, 195 So 2d 451, 453 (La Ct App 1967).

199 Kluka v Livingston Parish School Bd, 433 So 2d 302, 304 (La Ct App 1983).

200 Dibortolo v Metropolitan School Dist, 440 NE2d 506, 509 (Ind Ct App 1982); Kersey v Harbin, 591 SW2d 745, 749 (Mo Ct App 1979); Luce v Board of Educ, 2 AD2d 502, 157 NYS2d 123, 128 (1956), *affd*, 3 NY2d 792, 143 NE2d 797, 164 NYS2d 43 (1957). *See also* Green v Orleans Parish School Bd, 365 So 2d 834, 836 (La Ct App 1978), *writ refused*, 367 So 2d 393 (La 1979). *See also* Cal Educ Code §44807 (West 1978); Cal Admin Code tit 5 §5531 (1977) ("All athletic ... activities of pupils, whenever held, if conducted under the name or auspices of a public school or of any class or organization thereof, shall be under the direct supervision of certificated employees of a [school] district....."); NY Educ Law §1709(16) (McKinney 1969); *see also* Proehl, *Tort Liability of Teachers*, 12 Vand L Rev 723, 746 (1959); Vacca, *Teacher Malpractice*, 8 U Rich L Rev 447, 452 (1974); *see generally* Rupp v Bryant, 417 So 2d 658, 666 (Fla 1982) (unclear whether this duty applies to colleges).

This issue is also discussed in §4.18 (baseball); §4.19 (basketball); §4.20 (gymnastics); §4.21 (playground); §4.22 (golf, hockey, track and field, swimming, weight lifting, wrestling).

When there is no evidence of negligent supervision, the defendant is entitled to a directed verdict. *See* Peck v Board of Educ, 35 AD2d 978, 317 NYS2d 919, 921 (1970).

201 Albers v Independent School Dist No 302, 94 Idaho 342, 487 P2d 936, 938 (1971); Bartell v Palos Verdes Peninsula School Dist, 83 Cal App 3d 492, 147 Cal Rptr 898, 901 (1978). *See generally* Rupp v Bryant, 417 So 2d 658, 668 (Fla 1982); Chappel v Franklin Pierce School Dist, 71 Wash 2d 17, 426 P2d 471 (1967).

202 *See* Lynch v Board of Educ, 72 Ill App 3d 317, 390 NE2d 526 (1979), *affd*, 82 Ill 2d 415, 412 NE2d 447 (1980).

203 Sutphen v Benthian, 165 NJ Super 79, 397 A2d 709, 710 (1979).

activities without the knowledge of the teacher before a physical education class commenced.[204]

Several courts have held that there is no duty to supervise children who, of their own volition, use school grounds to engage in athletic activities after school.[205] For example, there is no duty to supervise a high school student's use of high jump equipment when the student borrowed the equipment from the school and used it on school premises, but after regular school hours.[206]

It is, of course, physically impossible for a teacher to watch every student all of the time. The law does not demand the impossible, and, therefore, there is no requirement that every child must be under constant scrutiny.[207] All that is required is that schools exercise reasonable care in supervising their students.[208] This concept has sometimes been referred to as a duty to exercise general supervision.[209]

In determining whether there was reasonable supervision, the courts should consider factors such as the age, experience, judgment, and physical condition of the students, as well as the difficulty of the athletic activity.[210]

Number of Supervisors

Schools must take reasonable care to employ a sufficient number of supervisors.[211] Where no supervision is provided and a student is injured,

---

[204] Banks v Terrebonne Parish School Bd, 339 So 2d 1295, 1297 (La Ct App 1976).

[205] Bartell v Palos Verdes Peninsula School Dist, 83 Cal App 3d 492, 147 Cal Rptr 898, 901 (1978) (a dangerous skateboard game); Bennett v Board of Educ, 16 AD2d 651, 226 NYS2d 593, 594 (1962), affd, 13 NY2d 1104, 196 NE2d 268, 246 NYS2d 634 (1963). *But see* Perkins v State Bd of Educ, 364 So 2d 183, 185 (La Ct App 1978).

[206] Bush v Smith, 154 Ind App 382, 289 NE2d 800, 802 (1973) (plaintiff was hit by a part of this equipment which was thrown in anger by a student who was taunted after unsuccessfully using the equipment).

[207] Hampton v Orleans Parish School Bd, 422 So 2d 202, 203-04 (La Ct App 1982) (three teachers were supervising 170 students); Passafaro v Board of Educ, 43 AD2d 918, 353 NYS2d 178, 180 (1974); Fagan v Summers, 498 P2d 1227, 1228 (Wyo 1972); *see also* Seitz, *Legal Responsibility Under Tort Law of School Personnel and School Districts as Regards Negligent Conduct Toward Pupils*, 15 Hastings LJ 495, 501 (1964) (this is "a frank recognition of the practicalities of the situation").

[208] *See, e.g.*, Dibortolo v Metropolitan School Dist, 400 NE2d 506, 509 (Ind Ct App 1982); Kersey v Harbin, 591 SW2d 745, 749 (Mo Ct App 1979).

[209] *See* Fagan v Summers, 498 P2d 1227, 1228 (Wyo 1972).

[210] *See* Perkins v State Bd of Educ, 364 So 2d 183, 185 (La Ct App 1978); *see also* Vacca, *Teacher Malpractice*, 8 U Rich L Rev 447, 453 (1974).

[211] Capers v Orleans Parish School Bd, 365 So 2d 23, 24-25 (La Ct App 1978). *See generally* Hampton v Orleans Parish School Bd, 422 So 2d 202 (La Ct App 1982) (no negligence where three teachers supervised 170 students).

the school may be liable for failing to provide reasonable supervision.[212]

There is no requirement that the school have notice that a dangerous activity has occurred or is about to occur before a failure to provide supervision is considered negligence.[213] It is usually only necessary that a general danger was foreseeable and that supervision would have probably prevented the accident.[214]

Indeed, one commentator remarked that "[u]nattended school children cannot be expected to await their mentor's long-delayed return timidly, quietly and peaceably. Absence tempts boisterousness."[215]

Accordingly, a school was found liable for negligent supervision when a teacher left eighth graders unattended at a baseball game and some of the students threw pebbles at other students for several minutes, ultimately blinding one of them.[216] In another case, a physical education teacher may have acted unreasonably in leaving a class of about 50 boys unsupervised for almost 30 minutes.[217] The court noted that "boys will be boys."[218] The fact that one of the students was injured by another student's violent acts was not, as a matter of law, a superseding cause of the injury because the teacher's failure to supervise the class was a substantial factor in allowing that dangerous activity to occur.[219]

However, a school was found not liable as a matter of law for a serious eye injury resulting from one student throwing a snowball at another student on the way back from school.[220] Snowball throwing is not inherently dangerous,

---

212 *See* Sheehan v St Peter's Catholic School, 291 Minn 1, 188 NW2d 868, 870 (1971).

213 *Id.*

214 188 NW2d at 871.

215 Comment, *Liability of Texas Public Officials For Their Tortious Acts*, 16 Hous L Rev 100, 122 (1978). *See also* Ohman v Board of Educ, 300 NY 306, 90 NE2d 474, 478 (1949) (Conway, J dissenting):

> Children have a known proclivity to act impulsively without thought of the possibilities of danger. It is precisely this lack of mature judgment which makes supervision so vital. The mere presence of the hand of authority and discipline normally is effective to curb this youthful exuberance and to protect the children against their own folly.

See also Seitz, *Legal Responsibility Under Tort Law of School Personnel and School Districts as Regards Negligent Conduct Toward Pupils*, 15 Hastings LJ 495, 499 (1964) (when a teacher leaves a classroom, the psychology of group behavior increases the risk that horseplay will result).

216 *See* Sheehan v St Peter's Catholic School, 29 Minn 1, 188 NW2d 868, 870 (1971).

217 Cirillo v City of Milwaukee, 34 Wis 2d 705, 150 NW2d 460, 464 (1967).

218 *Id.*

219 *Id.* In fact, some of the students testified that they would have stopped if the teacher had returned. 150 NW2d at 465. *See also* §4.16.

220 Lawes v Board of Educ, 16 NY2d 302, 213 NE2d 667, 266 NYS2d 364 (1965).

and when there was no evidence of danger, the school did not act unreasonably in failing to prevent the snowball from being thrown.[221]

Even when some supervision is given, schools may still be liable if they fail to provide a sufficient number of supervisors in light of the reasonably foreseeable danger.[222]

In *District of Columbia v Cassidy*, the court held, as a matter of law, that one supervisor for about 50 children on a school playground was reasonable.[223] Another court held that supervision of over 250 children by six to eight adults during a lunch recess on fenced school grounds was reasonable.[224] In addition, there was no need for more than one instructor to be present during a physical education class.[225]

In *Foster v Houston General Insurance Co*, the court held that teachers have a duty to maintain closer supervision over children with special problems, viz., mentally handicapped children on a Special Olympics team, while off campus and on route to use a gymnasium.[226] The court held that having only one teacher accompany this team was inadequate supervision because additional personnel would have been able to halt traffic to allow these children to arrive safely at their destination.[227]

There are numerous cases where teachers were found not negligent in the supervision of students because the time between the act creating the danger and the injury was so short that it was impossible to have stopped it.[228] For example, in *Hampton v Orleans Parish School Board*, the teachers were not negligent where a child threw a rock at another child on a

---

221 266 NYS2d at 366.

222 Santee v Orleans Parish School Bd, 430 So 2d 254, 255 (La Ct App 1983) (two teachers for 100 students was insufficient); Gibbons v Orleans Parish School Bd, 391 So 2d 976, 977-78 (La Ct App 1980). *But see* Brown v Calhoun County Bd of Educ, 432 So 2d 1230, 1231 (Ala 1983).

223 465 A2d 395, 398 (DC 1983).

224 Capers v Orleans Parish School Bd, 365 So 2d 23, 24-25 (La Ct App 1978). *See generally* Hampton v Orleans Parish School Bd, 422 So 2d 202 (La Ct App 1982) (no negligence where three teachers supervised 170 students).

225 Fosselman v Waterloo Community School Dist, 229 NW2d 280, 284 (Iowa 1975). *See generally* Lueck v City of Janesville, 57 Wis 2d 254, 204 NW2d 6, 12 (1973) (teacher not liable for failing to have each student under constant scrutiny).

226 407 So 2d 759, 763 (La Ct App 1982).

227 *Id* 764. The court also held they breached a duty to take the safest route to the gymnasium. *Id* at 764-65.

228 *See, e.g.*, Wright v City of San Bernardino High School Dist, 121 Cal App 2d 342, 263 P2d 25, 28 (1953) (a student ran into a ball thrown by another student as the bell rang); District of Columbia v Cassidy, 465 A2d 395, 399 (DC 1983); Norman v Turkey Run Community School Corp, 274 Ind 310, 411 NE2d 614, 618 (1980); Fagan v Summers, 498 P2d 1227, 1228-29 (Wyo 1972). *See also* §4.16.

playground because this incident happened so quickly that it could not have been prevented.[229]

Quality of Supervision

Schools must use reasonable care in employing competent instructors,[230] and the instructors must exercise reasonable care in supervising the students.[231] Indeed, activities involving violent body contact or a high degree of skill, e.g., gymnastics, require more supervision than other activities.[232] However, there is no liability where the teachers did not act unreasonably.[233] For example, a physical education teacher was not negligent in allowing students to go out to the lobby to drink water because the danger arising from their decision to run an informal race in the lobby was not reasonably foreseeable.[234] Similarly, there was no negligence where a physical education teacher directed a student to walk to a first-aid room, a short distance away, after falling off a gymnasium horse. This act posed no unreasonable risk of aggravating the injury.[235] In addition, where a student's actions in performing gymnastic exercises violated the teacher's instructions and the actions were also unforeseeable, the teacher was not liable.[236]

There is usually a duty to warn of reasonably foreseeable dangers. For example, a school may be negligent in failing to warn students of the dangers of running across a courtyard to a playground during physical education class when the school knows that the students do this and also knows that trucks travel in the area.[237] However, a teacher was not negligent in failing to alert softball players that older children were playing softball nearby because the

---

229 422 So 2d 202, 203-04 (La Ct App 1982). Three teachers were supervising 170 students.

230 Reynolds v State, 207 Misc 963, 141 NYS2d 615, 618 (Ct Cl 1955).

231 *See generally* Dibortolo v Metropolitan School Dist, 440 NE2d 506, 509 (Ind Ct App 1982). The teacher must use the judgment of a qualified prudent person under similar circumstances. *See also* Green v Orleans Parish School Bd, 365 So 2d 834, 835 (La Ct App 1978), *writ ref*, 367 So 2d 393 (La 1979); Reynolds v State, 207 Misc 963, 141 NYS2d 615, 618 (Ct Cl 1955).

232 Proehl, *Tort Liability of Teachers*, 12 Vand L Rev 723, 747 (1959).

233 *See generally* Vacca, *Teacher Malpractice*, 8 U Rich L Rev 447, 453 (1974).

234 Wilkinson v Hartford Accident & Indem Co, 411 So 2d 22, 24 (La 1982) (one child ran into a plate glass panel). For additional cases involving injuries from glass panels, see §4.19.

235 Sayers v Ranger, 16 NJ Super 22, 83 A2d 775, 776 (1951), *cert dismissed*, 8 NJ 413, 85 A2d 840 (1952).

236 Berg v Merricks, 20 Md App 666, 318 A2d 220, 225 (1974).

237 Taylor v Oakland Scavenger Co, 17 Cal 2d 594, 110 P2d 1044, 1047-48 (1941). *But see generally* Driscol v Delphi Community School Corp, 155 Ind App 56, 290 NE2d 769, 774 (1972) (no liability where students ran across gymnasium to locker room).

presence of older children on the field would not necessarily alert the teacher to danger.[238]

A school may be liable for negligently supervising athletic activities by allowing the activities to be performed in inadequate facilities. However, the playing of several games simultaneously on a gymnasium floor is generally not considered a source of unreasonable danger, and, therefore, the school is not negligent for allowing such conduct.[239] Similarly, where a baseball game was not played in too small an area, the school was not negligent.[240]

Teachers must take reasonable steps to see that the students wear proper clothing. For example, a teacher was found negligent in permitting a child to participate in a physical education class in bare feet.[241] However, where a student attributed an accident to a teacher's affirmative direction to participate in gymnastic activities while wearing only socks, the student could not also argue that there was a failure to provide supervision in other areas because that was incompatible with the evidence.[242]

There is a duty to anticipate the danger which is reasonably foreseeable because the students are unfamiliar with an athletic activity.[243] Accordingly, a school was liable when a student teacher's ineffective observation and attention allowed one student to hit another with a golf club.[244]

In addition, in *Kessee v Board of Education*, there was liability where a teacher directed a game in which six to eight novices converged on a ball, at a run, and, on meeting, kicked the ball. During the action, a student was kicked by another player and injured.[245] The court held that the risk that an injury would result to someone from such activities was, if not inevitable, at least reasonably foreseeable.[246] Accordingly, the teacher was liable for permitting such a large aggregation of novices to engage in such a dangerous sport, even though the motive, viz., to allow more girls to participate, could be appreciated.[247]

---

238 Germond v Board of Educ, 10 AD2d 139, 197 NYS2d 548, 551 (1960) (student was hit in the face by a baseball bat swung by an older student).

239 Wright v City of San Bernardino High School Dist, 121 Cal App 2d 342, 263 P2d 25, 28 (1953). *See generally* Borushek v Kincaid, 78 Ill App 3d 295, 397 NE2d 172, 174 (1979) (plaintiff's failure to allege the size of the gymnasium or the number of people present subjected the complaint to dismissal for failure to allege an overcrowded condition).

240 *See generally* Underhill v Alameda Elementary School Dist, 133 Cal App 733, 24 P2d 849, 851 (1933).

241 Brod v Central School Dist No 1, 53 AD2d 1002, 386 NYS2d 125, 126 (1976).

242 Passafaro v Board of Educ, 43 AD2d 918, 353 NYS2d 178, 180 (1974).

243 Brahatchek v Millard School Dist, 202 Neb 86, 273 NW2d 680, 687 (1979).

244 *Id.*

245 37 Misc 2d 414, 235 NYS2d 300, 306 (Sup Ct 1962).

246 *Id.*

247 *Id.*

An instructor was not negligent for failing to keep records of weights, ages, heights, and other statistics because he was able to judge the physical, as well as the mental, characteristics of thirty individuals in a wrestling class in determining who to *pair off*, without reference to such records.[248]

§4.16 Causation

Anyone who has ever worked with children knows that whenever children are placed together in the confines of a gymnasium or playground someone frequently gets injured regardless of the precautions taken.[249]

However, schools are not liable for a student's injury unless there is a causal connection between the alleged acts of the school's negligence and the injury.[250] Some courts have held that this causation is shown where the alleged act of negligence sets in motion a chain of circumstances which leads to a foreseeable injury.[251] Accordingly, where a high school student who was rendered a paraplegic because of a gymnastic mishap failed to prove that this accident was caused, at least in part, by the teacher's negligence, the school was not liable as a matter of law.[252] Similarly, although a school may have defective floor boards or hard, rough walls, where there is no showing that a student's injury was caused or aggravated by those conditions, causation is not shown.[253]

Numerous injured students have argued that their accidents were caused by the school's failure to keep appropriate records. They have met with little success because the safe performance of athletic activities is not so scientific. For example, a teacher's failure to keep records of weight, height, and other statistics of the students to enable the matching of wrestling partners was not considered to be the proximate cause of injury.[254] Similarly, the incorrect preparation of an eligibility list which allowed a high school student who was above the prescribed age to play football was not the

---

248 Reynolds v State, 207 Misc 963, 141 NYS2d 615, 618 (Ct Cl 1955).

249 Vacca, *Teacher Malpractice*, 8 U Rich L Rev 447, 448 (1974).

250 *See* Kluka v Livingston Parish School Bd, 433 So 2d 302, 304 (La Ct App 1983); Berg v Merricks, 20 Md App 666, 318 A2d 220, 226 (1974); *see also* §6.08. *See generally* Restatement (Second) of Torts §430 (1965); W. Prosser, The Law of Torts §41, at 239 (4th ed 1971).

251 *See, e.g.*, Dibortolo v Metropolitan School Dist, 440 NE2d 506, 511 (Ind Ct App 1982). Such language is really too broad because in one sense everything is affected by what has occurred previously. See W. Prosser, The Law of Torts §41, at 236 (4th ed 1971).

252 Berg v Merricks, 20 Md App 666, 318 A2d 220, 225-26 (1974).

253 Read v School Dist No 211, 7 Wash 2d 502, 110 P2d 179, 181 (1941).

254 Reynolds v State, 207 Misc 963, 141 NYS2d 615, 618 (Ct Cl 1955).

proximate cause of the injury suffered by a player who was run into by this ineligible player.[255]

Supervision

Many times there are difficult causation questions where a plaintiff alleges that injuries resulted from the school's failure to supervise the students.[256] There was no negligent supervision merely because a gymnastics student slipped on a mat,[257] two students collided while playing a form of tag in a physical education class,[258] or other students suffered athletic injuries.[259]

A school's failure to supervise properly its students is not sufficient to impose liability on the school unless it was also shown that such failure was the proximate cause of the plaintiff's injuries.[260] One court has characterized this as proof that supervision, to a reasonable degree of certainty, would have prevented the injury.[261] For example, when a school's officiating of a hockey game was not the proximate cause of injury, but rather the injury was caused when the plaintiff grabbed another hockey player, the school was not liable.[262] Similarly, there was no liability where a teacher told the students to hurry to finish their athletic activities because there was no evidence that the injury occurred as a result of the plaintiff being rushed.[263]

In *DeMauro v Tusculum College, Inc*, the court held that a college may have negligently breached its duty of reasonable supervision by placing an inexperienced person in charge of a course in golf. The plaintiff was injured when the golfer *shanked* the ball at a 90-degree angle.[264] This decision is questionable because it is unclear whether there was any causal relationship between the plaintiff's injury and the alleged breach of duty. Hitting

---

255 Barrett v Phillips, 29 NC App 220, 223 SE2d 918, 919 (1976).

256 Rivera v Board of Educ, 11 AD2d 7, 201 NYS2d 372, 375 (1960). The doctrine of res ipsa loquitur was not applied where a student was struck in the face by another student's knee in a physical education class because such accidents are not normally due only to a school's negligence. *See* Fosselman v Waterloo Community School Dist, 229 NW2d 280, 283 (Iowa 1975).

257 Cambareri v Board of Educ, 246 AD 127, 284 NYS 892, 894 (1936), *aff'd*, 283 NY 741, 28 NE2d 968 (1940).

258 Ellis v Burns Valley School Dist, 128 Cal App 550, 18 P2d 79, 81 (1933).

259 *See* District of Columbia v Cassidy, 465 A2d 395, 399 (DC 1983); Fosselman v Waterloo Community School Dist, 229 NW2d 280, 284 (Iowa 1975).

260 Brackman v Adrian, 63 Tenn App 346, 472 SW2d 735, 739 (1971); *see also* Pape v State, 90 AD2d 904, 456 NYS2d 863, 864 (1982).

261 *See* Lueck v City of Janesville, 57 Wis 2d 254, 204 NW2d 6, 12 (1973).

262 Pape v State, 90 AD2d 904, 456 NYS2d 863, 864 (1982).

263 Berg v Merricks, 20 Md App 666, 318 A2d 220, 225 (1974).

264 603 SW2d 115, 119, 120 (Tenn 1980).

a golf ball at a 90-degree angle is an unexpected and probably a nonnegligent act.[265]

Where a student is injured by the wrongful act of another student, the school may argue that the second student's wrongful act was a superseding cause of injury. The school is liable when the injury was reasonably foreseeable from the lack of supervision.[266] For example, a second child's act of hitting the plaintiff with a golf club was reasonably foreseeable as a result of improper supervision, and, therefore, this does not break the chain of causation.[267] When the accident is not reasonably foreseeable, the school is not liable.[268]

In *Segerman v Jones*, the court held that a teacher who left, for a few minutes, a class of students who were doing exercises was not liable as a matter of law where one student moved and then, by the improper performance of an exercise, hit and injured another student.[269] The court held that it was not foreseeable that this student, a good athlete, would have moved from his assigned position and also performed the exercise improperly.[270] Accordingly, his acts were a superseding cause of injury breaking the chain of causation.[271] In another case the court held that a child's violent acts were an unforeseeable intervening act which cut off the school's liability.[272]

In any event, a school is not liable for negligent supervision where the accident would have occurred no matter how adequate the supervision might have been. For example, in *Kaufman v City of New York*, a school was not liable as a matter of law when one college basketball player, while jumping for a basketball, hit his head against another player's head and subsequently died, because this collision could not have been stopped.[273]

Res Ipsa Loquitur

The doctrine of res ipsa loquitur permits an inference of negligence to be drawn from the happening of an event if the injury is caused by an agency or instrumentality under the exclusive control and management of the defendant

---

265 *See* §2.11.

266 Brahatchek v Millard School Dist, 202 Neb 86, 273 NW2d 680, 687 (1979).

267 *Id. See also* DeMauro v Tusculum College, Inc, 603 SW2d 115, 120 (Tenn 1980).

268 District of Columbia v Cassidy, 465 A2d 395, 399 (DC 1983) (student's throwing of a stick was an unforeseeable, intervening act). *See also* Sharp v Fairbanks N Star Borough, 569 P2d 178, 183 (Alaska 1977).

269 256 Md 109, 259 A2d 794, 806 (1969).

270 *Id.*

271 *Id.*

272 *See* District of Columbia v Cassidy, 465 A2d 395, 399 (DC 1983) (student struck in eye by stick thrown by another student).

273 30 Misc 2d 285, 214 NYS2d 767, 769 (Sup Ct 1961).

and the occurrence is such as in the ordinary course of things would not happen if reasonable care had been used.[274] This doctrine was not applied in a case involving a school's negligence where a student was struck in the face by another student's knee in a physical education class, because neither element was present.[275]

§4.17 Wilful or Wanton Acts

Wilful and wanton conduct is an act or omission by the defendant which occurred in reckless disregard of probable injury.[276] It is critical to show that the defendant knew or should have known that the conduct posed a high probability of serious harm to others.[277] This behavior is so socially unacceptable that the defendant can be punished by being assessed punitive damages.[278] Furthermore, in one state such conduct subjects schools to liability even though they are generally immune for their negligence.[279]

In most situations this high standard of misconduct is not met. For example, teachers did not wilfully and wantonly disregard their students safety by failing to provide helmets and face-guards for use in a football game because the teachers had stated that the game could be rough and had advised the students to wear mouth-guards.[280] Similarly, a school did not act wilfully in not using spotters in a gymnastic activity where numerous successful vaults had previously been performed.[281] In addition, a school district did not act wilfully or wantonly where the principal intentionally prevented a coach from being present before a practice session.[282]

However, such unacceptable behavior has been shown in a few instances. In *Landers v School District No 203*, the court held that a teacher acted wilfully and wantonly in instructing an obese student, untrained in doing backward somersaults and fearful of attempting the maneuver, to practice

---

274 Fosselman v Waterloo Community School Dist, 229 NW2d 280, 283 (Iowa 1975).

275 *Id.*

276 Pomrehn v Crete-Monee High School Dist, 101 Ill App 3d 331, 427 NE2d 1387, 1390 (1981); *see generally* §6.06.

277 Pomrehn v Crete-Monee High School Dist, 101 Ill App 3d 331, 427 NE2d 1387, 1390 (1981); *see also* O'Brien v Township High School Dist 214, 83 Ill 2d 462, 415 NE2d 1015, 1018 (1980); Montague v School Bd, 57 Ill App 3d 828, 373 NE2d 719, 721 (1978).

278 *See* Rupp v Bryant, 417 So 2d 658, 670 (Fla 1982).

279 *See* O'Brien v Township High School Dist 214, 83 Ill 2d 462, 415 NE2d 1015, 1018 (1980).

280 Lynch v Board of Educ, 72 Ill App 3d 317, 390 NE2d 526 (1979), *affd*, 82 Ill 2d 415, 412 NE2d 447 (1980).

281 Montague v School Bd, 57 Ill App 3d 828, 373 NE2d 719, 721 (1978).

282 Pomrehn v Crete-Monee High School Dist, 101 Ill App 3d 331, 427 NE2d 1387 (1981) (softball player was riding on trunk of car and was injured when the car turned).

this activity on her own, without personal instruction or a preliminary testing of her strength.[283] In addition, a school may have acted wilfully or wantonly where a student was medically treated by an untrained student.[284]

Specific Activities

§4.18   Baseball

Schools are not insurers of the safety of their baseball[285] players.[286] Generally, they have a duty to exercise reasonable care under the circumstances.[287]

Equipment

Schools must take care to provide baseball players with reasonably safe equipment.[288] For example, in *Stanley v Board of Education*, the court held that a school board was negligent in allowing baseball players to use defective equipment where a bat which had a frayed knob and no tape slipped out of the hands of a player injuring an eight-year-old boy.[289]

It is unclear whether a school must provide safety masks for catchers. One recent decision held that safety masks should be provided.[290] However, there

---

283 66 Ill App 3d 78, 383 NE2d 645, 648 (1978). There was expert testimony that an athlete who is overweight has a greater likelihood of injury, and that a fearful athlete is also more likely to be injured. *See* 383 NE2d at 648.

284 O'Brien v Township High School Dist 214, 83 Ill 2d 462, 415 NE2d 1015, 1018 (1980).

285 One study concluded that in the 1982-83 school year, there were no reported fatalities and only two individuals suffered severe functional disabilities while participating in school-sponsored baseball activities. See Mueller & Blyth, Natl Center for Catastrophic Sports Injury Research 1982-83 School Year (1983).

286 *See also* Hanna v State, 46 Misc 2d 9, 258 NYS2d 694, 698 (Ct Cl 1965); Scaduto v State, 86 AD2d 682, 446 NYS2d 529, 530, *affd without opinion*, 56 NY2d 762, 437 NE2d 281, 452 NYS2d 21 (1982).

287 *See* Scaduto v State, 86 AD2d 682, 446 NYS2d 529, 530, *affd without opinion*, 56 NY2d 762, 437 NE2d 281, 452 NYS2d 21 (1982); *see generally* §4.01.

288 *See generally* Hanna v State, 46 Misc 2d 9, 258 NYS2d 694, 698 (Ct Cl 1965) (student umpire injured by foul ball). *See also* §4.10.

289 9 Ill App 3d 963, 293 NE2d 417, 420 (1973).

290 *See* Moschella v Archdiocese of New York Monsignor Farrell High School, 52 AD2d 873, 383 NYS2d 49, 50 (1976). A prior opinion in this case is at 48 AD2d 856, 369 NYS2d 10 (1975).

are several older decisions which came to the opposite conclusion.[291] One such court mistakenly reasoned that playing without a mask was reasonable because it was not customary to provide masks to players.[292] Another court held that there was no negligence because the catcher was a skilled softball player and was aware of the risk of being hit by a bat if a mask were not worn.[293] In short, it used the plaintiff's assumption of the risk as the definitive factor in eliminating a school's duty of care.

Facilities

Schools must provide reasonably safe baseball facilities.[294] Therefore, where a school has actual or constructive knowledge of a dangerous condition on the baseball field and fails to remove it, it may be negligent.[295] In *Ardoin v Evangeline Parish School Board*,[296] the school was liable where a student was injured when he hit a piece of concrete eight inches thick, protruding over one-half inch above the ground between second and third base. The court stated that the softball field had been used for physical education classes for one year and a reasonable examination of the area would have revealed the danger.[297]

A school may not have a duty to screen the bench to protect the players sitting there from being hit by foul balls.[298] In *Dudley v William Penn College*, the court ruled that the school was not negligent because plaintiff's evidence did not show a custom of fencing this area.[299] This reasoning seems incorrect. Compliance with an industry custom should not be an absolute defense; the fact-finder should have been entitled to decide whether the school's failure to screen this area created an unreasonably dangerous condition.

Where the school does not act unreasonably, there is no liability. In *Scaduto v State*,[300] a baseball player was injured when he stepped into a drainage ditch

---

291 *See* Richmond v Employers' Fire Ins Co, 298 So 2d 118, 121 (La Ct App 1974); Brackman v Adrian, 63 Tenn App 346, 472 SW2d 735, 739 (Tenn Ct App 1971).

292 *See* Richmond v Employers' Fire Ins Co, 298 So 2d 118, 121 (La Ct App 1974). The fact that the defendant was in conformity with industry practice should not be an absolute defense. *See generally* §1.01.

293 Brackman v Adrian, 63 Tenn App 346, 472 SW2d 735, 739 (1971).

294 Ardoin v Evangeline Parish School Bd, 376 So 2d 372, 374 (La Ct App 1979); *see generally* §4.11.

295 Ardoin v Evangeline Parish School Bd, 376 So 2d 372, 374 (La Ct App 1979).

296 *Id.*

297 *Id.*

298 Dudley v William Penn College, 219 NW2d 484 (Iowa 1974).

299 *Id* 486-87.

300 86 AD2d 682, 446 NYS2d 529, 530, *affd without opinion*, 56 NY2d 762, 437 NE2d 281, 452 NYS2d 21 (1982).

while attempting to catch a foul ball. The court held that the school was entitled to a judgment in its favor as a matter of law because the ditch was visible, the plaintiff was aware of its location, the slope was gradual, and the ditch fulfilled an important function, viz., draining the playing field.[301] It concluded that there was no duty to provide a perfectly level playing field.[302]

One court held that a school was negligent in using a base in an indoor gymnasium which could slip when it was stepped on.[303] However, the use of a portable backstop in a noncompetitive practice game of baseball was held not to be negligent.[304]

Supervision

Schools must take reasonable care in supervising baseball games.[305] Where they failed to take reasonable care, e.g., allowing spectators to congregate so close to a base line that a catcher chasing a foul ball tripped over them, the school was negligent.[306]

A school is not liable for failure to supervise a baseball game unless the plaintiff can show by a preponderance of the evidence that the injury would not have occurred if the school had provided reasonable supervision.[307] Therefore, where there was no reliable evidence of where a catcher was standing when she was hit by a bat, there was no showing that a school was negligent in failing to have her move farther away from the batter to protect herself.[308]

In addition, there is no liability for failure to supervise in a case where the accident, viz., a plaintiff running head-first into a catcher blocking the plate, could not have been prevented even if a "multitude of supervisory personnel" were present.[309]

In some cases there is no liability for the failure to warn of obvious risks.[310]

---

301 *Id.*

302 *Id.*

303 Bard v Board of Educ, 140 NYS2d 850, 852 (1955).

304 *See generally* Hanna v State, 46 Misc 2d 9, 258 NYS2d 694, 698 (1965).

305 Domino v Mercurio, 17 AD2d 342, 234 NYS2d 1011, 1013 (1962), *affd,* 13 NY2d 922, 193 NE2d 893, 244 NYS2d 69 (1963); *see generally* §4.15.

306 Domino v Mercurio, 17 AD2d 342, 234 NYS2d 1011, 1013 (1962), *affd,* 13 NY2d 922, 193 NE2d 893, 244 NYS2d 69 (1963).

307 *See* Brackman v Adrian, 63 Tenn App 346, 472 SW2d 735, 738 (1971).

308 *Id.*

309 Passantino v Board of Educ, 41 NY2d 1022, 363 NE2d 1373, 395 NYS2d 628 (1977), *revg* 52 AD2d 935, 383 NYS2d 639 (1976) (court reversed a $1 million judgment for plaintiff); *see generally* §4.16.

310 *See generally* §6.09.

In *Stanley v Board of Education*,[311] an eight-year-old softball player was injured at a nearby school when a bat flew out of a player's hands. The school argued that it did not negligently supervise the child because the danger was known and obvious, i.e., the players in the second softball game had previously told the plaintiff to move. This contention was rejected because a warning coming from someone in authority would have a greater effect than a warning from other children, even older ones.[312]

Where the school does not act unreasonably, it is not negligent. In *Richmond v Employers' Fire Insurance Co*,[313] a baseball player was hit in the face by a bat which slipped out of a batter's hands during practice. The batter, a student assistant coach, was standing near the third-base line hitting balls to players who were not getting enough practice fielding the balls hit by another batter standing at home plate. The plaintiff stood near this student coach. The plaintiff alleged that the student coach negligently supervised him by ordering him to move to the left. The court held that this instruction was not an unreasonable act under the circumstances because, by positioning the plaintiff to his left, the student coach afforded the plaintiff the protection of his body against the danger of being hit by a foul ball from the left-handed batter at home plate.[314]

§4.19 Basketball

Schools must exercise reasonable care in maintaining basketball[315] facilities.[316] In *Thomas v St Mary's Roman Catholic Church*,[317] the court affirmed a $125,000 verdict for a basketball player who was injured because his momentum from a play carried him through a glass panel six feet from the edge of the basketball court. The court held that the school was negligent in placing breakable glass panels near a basketball court.[318] The school's argument that it should not be liable because the defect, viz., a breakable

---

[311] 9 Ill App 3d 963, 293 NE2d 417, 421 (1973).

[312] 293 NE2d at 421.

[313] 298 So 2d 118 (La Ct App 1974).

[314] *Id* 121.

[315] One study concluded that in the 1982-83 school year, there were five reported fatalities from school-related basketball activities. See Mueller & Blyth, Natl Center for Catastrophic Sports Injury Research 1982-83 Year.

[316] Thomas v St. Mary's Roman Catholic Church, 283 NW2d 254 (SD 1979); *see generally* §4.11.

[317] 283 NW2d 254 (SD 1979).

[318] *Id.*

glass panel, was open and obvious was rejected because reasonable care in this situation required the school to eliminate the danger.[319]

Where a school had acted reasonably in maintaining a basketball court, a basketball player's claim that he slipped due to the wet condition of the court was rejected.[320] In addition, a school was not liable for allowing a basketball floor to remain dirty where the plaintiff testified he cleaned the floor before the game began and there were no dangerous obstacles on the floor.[321]

Schools must use reasonable care in supervising basketball games.[322] However, generally it is not unreasonable to supervise several sports activities at one time, and, therefore, there was no negligence when a student was injured in a *free play* basketball game.[323]

A school was entitled to judgment as a matter of law when there was no evidence that its failure to supervise a basketball game had a causal connection to an accident, viz., when one player collided with another player while attempting to recover a loose ball.[324] In addition, where there was no basis for concluding that supervisory personnel were needed or could have prevented a basketball accident, a parent's claim that the school negligently supervised a father-son basketball game was dismissed.[325]

§4.20 Gymnastics

Schools must exercise reasonable care to prevent gymnastic[326] injuries.[327] However, they are not insurers, and, therefore, they are not liable merely because a student falls while performing a gymnastic activity.[328]

---

319 *Id* 259 (court properly refused to give an assumption of risk instruction); *see generally* §6.09.

320 Nunez v Isidore Newman High School, 306 So 2d 457, 460 (La Ct App 1975).

321 Albers v Independent School Dist No 302, 94 Idaho 342, 487 P2d 936, 939 (1971).

322 Kerby v Elk Grove Union High School Dist, 1 Cal App 2d 246, 36 P2d 431, 434 (1934); *see generally* §4.15.

323 Kerby v Elk Grove Union High School Dist, 1 Cal App 2d 246, 36 P2d 431, 434 (1934).

324 Albers v Independent School Dist No 302, 94 Idaho 342, 487 P2d 936, 939 (1971).

325 Borushek v Kincaid, 78 Ill App 3d 295, 397 NE2d 172, 174 (1979).

326 One study concluded that in the 1982-83 school year, there were no reported deaths and only one individual suffered a permanent, severe functional disability in a school gymnastic activity. See Mueller & Blyth, Natl Center for Catastrophic Sports Injury Research 1982-83 School Year.

327 Govel v Board of Educ, 267 AD 621, 48 NYS2d 299, 301, *affd without opinion*, 293 NY 928, 60 NE2d 133 (1944).

328 *See* Sayers v Ranger, 16 NJ Super 22, 83 A2d 775, 776 (1951), *cert dismissed*, 8 NJ 413, 85 A2d 840 (1952).

Assigning Activities

Teachers have a duty to take reasonable care to ensure that their students are capable of safely performing gymnastic activities before assigning those activities.[329] Accordingly, schools have been held liable when their teachers knew or should have known that because of a student's mental or physical condition the student was not a proper candidate for certain gymnastic exercises and the student was nevertheless required to perform those exercises.[330] A school was liable for an accident when a student was assigned to perform a gymnastic exercise beyond her ability even though the teacher knew of several recent accidents involving this exercise.[331]

Instruction

Teachers should exercise reasonable care in instructing their students regarding the proper performance of gymnastic exercises.[332] One court held that a school may be negligent in failing to instruct a student in the use of a gymnastic horse.[333]

Equipment

Schools must provide reasonable safety equipment for their students.[334] However, in *Montag v Board of Education*,[335] the court rejected the plaintiff's argument that a school was negligent in failing to provide safety belts to gymnasts during practice sessions. The plaintiff argued that the use of

---

[329] Bellman v San Francisco High School Dist, 11 Cal 2d 576, 81 P2d 894, 898 (1938); Lowe v Board of Educ, 36 AD2d 952, 321 NYS2d 508, 509 (1971); Govel v Board of Educ, 267 AD 621, 48 NYS2d 299, 301, *affd without opinion*, 293 NY 928, 60 NE2d 133 (1944); Summers v Milwaukie Union High School Dist, 4 Or App 596, 481 P2d 369, 370 (1971); Rodriguez v Seattle School Dist No 1, 66 Wash 2d 51, 401 P2d 326, 327 (1965); *see generally* §4.09.

[330] Bellman v San Francisco High School Dist, 11 Cal 2d 576, 81 P2d 894, 898 (1938); Summers v Milwaukie Union High School Dist, 4 Or App 596, 481 P2d 369, 370 (1971). The student's mother had repeatedly requested the school to furnish her with a list of the gymnastic activities so she could ask her doctor whether the activities were dangerous, but the school never complied. *See id.*

[331] Govel v Board of Educ, 267 AD 621, 48 NYS2d 299, 301, *affd without opinion*, 293 NY 928, 60 NE2d 133 (1944).

[332] Rodriguez v Seattle School Dist No 1, 66 Wash 2d 51, 401 P2d 326, 327 (1965) (tumbling); *see also* Dibortolo v Metropolitan School Dist, 440 NE2d 506, 510 (Ind Ct App 1982) (vertical jump).

[333] Lorenzo v Monroe Community College, 72 AD2d 945, 422 NYS2d 230, 231-32 (1979).

[334] *See* Montag v Board of Educ School Dist No 40, 112 Ill App 3d 1039, 446 NE2d 299, 303-04 (1983); *see generally* §4.10.

[335] *See* Montag v Board of Educ School Dist No 40, 112 Ill App 3d 1039, 446 NE2d 299, 303-04 (1983).

the belt in practice would have allowed him to learn more effectively the dismount and this would have prevented the injury when he attempted this exercise later; he did not claim that the use of the belt while performing the gymnastic event in which he was injured would have prevented the injury. The court held that the causal connection between the injury when the exercise was performed and the alleged negligence, viz., not providing safety equipment at an earlier time, was too tenuous to impose liability on the school.[336]

Schools must reasonably inspect and maintain gymnastic equipment.[337] For example, a school may be negligent in allowing students to use a vaulting horse with exposed holes where the pommels were removed.[338]

A school must take reasonable steps to place gymnastic equipment in a position where inexperienced individuals will be unlikely to use it.[339] In addition, a school may be liable if it failed to warn of the dangers of using a springboard in an area with a low ceiling.[340]

Facilities

Schools must take care to provide reasonably safe gymnastic facilities.[341] For example, the failure to have mats in place on the far side of parallel bars may be negligence.[342] In addition, reasonable care must be taken to ensure that the mats used provide sufficient protection.[343] However, a plaintiff's claim that improper matting was used was rejected where the thickness of the matting which would have been required to prevent the injury did not exist.[344] Of course, it is clear that a school is not negligent merely because a student slips on a mat in physical education class while engaging in a gymnastic activity; there must be some act of negligence.[345]

---

336 *Id*; *see generally* §4.16.

337 *See generally* §4.10.

338 Tiemann v Independent School Dist No 740, 331 NW2d 250, 251 (Minn 1983). The fact that it was customary to use vaulting horses with exposed holes does not show that the school was not negligent.

339 Grant v Lake Oswego School Dist No 7, 15 Or App 325, 515 P2d 947, 951-52 (1973).

340 *Id*.

341 Tiemann v Independent School Dist No 740, 331 NW2d 250, 251 (Minn 1983); Govel v Board of Education, 267 AD 621, 48 NYS2d 299, 301, *affd without opinion*, 293 NY 928, 60 NE2d 133 (1944). *See generally* Montag v Board of Educ School Dist No 40, 112 Ill App 3d 1039, 446 NE2d 299, 303-04 (1983); *see also* §4.11.

342 Govel v Board of Education, 267 AD 621, 48 NYS2d 299, 301, *affd without opinion*, 293 NY 928, 60 NE2d 133 (1944).

343 *See* Montag v Board of Educ School Dist No 40, 112 Ill App 3d 1039, 446 NE2d 299, 304 (1983).

344 *Id*.

345 Cambareri v Board of Educ, 284 NYS 892, 894 (1936).

Supervision

Schools have a duty to supervise gymnastic activities in a reasonable manner.[346] However, a school has no duty to place each piece of gymnastic equipment under the direct management or supervision of an instructor or attendant because it would be unreasonable to require this.[347]

In *Banks v Terrebonne Parish School Board*,[348] a school was found not liable as a matter of law where a student in a physical education class performed unauthorized gymnastic activities and injured himself. The plaintiff alleged that an additional supervisor would have seen this activity and stopped it before an accident happened. The court held that there was no liability because the school had acted reasonably, i.e., it would be prohibitively expensive to have sufficient supervisors to monitor all the children constantly.[349] In addition, a school and physical education teacher were not negligent in failing to require a spotter for each gymnastic activity since participants were told they could have one if they wished.[350]

Where the gymnastics teacher has acted reasonably, there is no negligence and no liability. An example of this principle is *Sayers v Ranger*,[351] where a high school student was injured after losing his balance while attempting to leap frog over a gymnastic horse. The appellate court reversed a judgment that the teacher negligently supervised this exercise, holding that the jump was adequately supervised by the teacher as well by as a volunteer student.[352] The court noted that the plaintiff had successfully performed this exercise before and the teacher had told the class that this activity was dangerous and should not be attempted if the students felt they could not perform it without incident.

Finally, schools are not liable for negligently supervising gymnastic activities where even if additional supervisors had been present the injury still would have occurred.[353]

---

346 Lorenzo v Monroe Community College, 72 AD2d 945, 422 NYS2d 230, 231-32 (1979); Govel v Board of Educ, 267 AD 621, 48 NYS2d 299, 301, *affd without opinion*, 293 NY 928, 60 NE2d 133 (1944).

347 Fein v Board of Educ, 104 NYS2d 996, 999 (1951).

348 339 So 2d 1295 (La Ct App 1976).

349 *Id* at 1297.

350 Lueck v City of Janesville, 57 Wis 2d 254, 204 NW2d 6, 12 (1973). *But see generally* Armlin v Board of Educ, 36 AD2d 877, 320 NYS2d 402 (1971).

351 16 NJ Super 22, 83 A2d 775 (1951), *cert dismissed*, 8 NJ 413, 85 A2d 840 (1952).

352 *Id* at 776.

353 Fein v Board of Educ, 104 NYS2d 996, 999 (1951); Lueck v City of Janesville, 57 Wis 2d 254, 204 NW2d 6, 12 (1973); *see generally* **§4.16**.

§4.21 Playground

Schools must exercise reasonable care to prevent playground[354] injuries.[355]

Equipment

A school's placement of playground equipment may subject it to liability.[356] For example, in *Atlantic Christian Schools, Inc v Salinas*, the court upheld a verdict that a school was negligent in maintaining a playground ladder when there were rocks in that area.[357] Another court held that a school was negligent in placing a tether ball pole near monkey bars.[358]

Schools should not allow students to use equipment which poses an unreasonable danger.[359] However, one court held that proof that a six-foot-high horizontal ladder was unsuitable for first grade students to play on because of their age could not be inferred solely from the size of the apparatus.[360]

Some playground conditions are not unreasonably dangerous because the social value of recreation outweighs the risk of harm. One court held that a school was not negligent when it allowed children to use a playground on its premises because the value of recreation was greater than the foreseeable risk of harm from the negligent assembly of a swing set.[361]

Facilities

A school is negligent if it has knowledge, actual or constructive, of an unreasonably dangerous playground condition and fails to remedy it.[362] For

---

[354] There are over 190,000 playground accidents annually which require emergency room treatment, although not all of them occur on school grounds. See US Consumer Prod Safety Commn, Natl Injury Information Clearinghouse, Prod Summary Report (Mar 28, 1984).

[355] *See generally* Proehl, *Tort Liability of Teachers*, 12 Vand L Rev 723, 744 (1959); *see also* §4.01.

[356] Hunt v Board of Educ, 43 AD2d 397, 352 NYS2d 237, 240 (1974) (question of fact whether school was negligent in placing jungle bars extending seven feet above a hardened surface).

[357] 422 So 2d 362, 362 (Fla Dist Ct App 1982).

[358] Gibbons v Orleans Parish School Bd, 391 So 2d 976, 977-78 (La Ct App 1980).

[359] *See generally* Grant v Lake Oswego School Dist No 7, 15 Or App 325, 515 P2d 947, 951-52 (1973).

[360] Cordaro v Union Free School Dist No 22, 14 AD2d 804, 220 NYS2d 656, 657 (1961), *affd*, 11 NY2d 1038, 183 NE2d 912, 230 NYS2d 30 (1962).

[361] Watts v Town of Homer, 301 So 2d 729, 737 (La Ct App 1974). However, the town was liable for its negligent assembly and inspection of the swing sets. *See id* at 734-35.

[362] Gibbons v Orleans Parish School Bd, 391 So 2d 976, 977 (La Ct App 1980) (protruding screw on tether ball pole); Ardoin v Evangeline Parish School Bd, 376 So 2d 372, 374 (La Ct App 1979).

example, where a reasonable inspection would have revealed a piece of concrete embedded in the ground, a school was liable for injuries resulting from a student tripping on that obstacle.[363]

Schools must take care in providing reasonably safe playground facilities. A school was negligent when it encouraged its students to play touch football at a playground located near an unguarded ditch.[364] In that case the plaintiff attempted to touch another player and his momentum led him into the ditch where he fell and injured himself.

Supervision

The kind of supervision required to prevent ordinary playground injuries is, in fact, impossible to obtain.[365] Accordingly, all that is required is that the schools provide reasonable supervision of their school playgrounds during school hours.[366] A school generally has no duty to provide supervision over children using a school playground after school hours.[367]

Several courts have stated that schools have only a duty of general supervision, not a duty to supervise specifically and constantly the use of each individual piece of equipment.[368] A more accurate statement is that schools have a duty to supervise their students while they use playground equipment, but they do not breach that duty unless they act unreasonably and it is generally unreasonable to require a school to supervise the use of each piece of equipment. Indeed, the cost of supervising each piece of playground equipment could be so staggering that schools would cease to provide them.[369]

---

363 Ardoin v Evangeline Parish School Bd, 376 So 2d 372, 374 (La Ct App 1979).

364 Sears v City of Springhill, 303 So 2d 602, 605 (La Ct App 1974). *But see generally* Chimerofsky v School Dist No 63, 121 Ill App 2d 371, 257 NE2d 480, 483 (1970) (not unreasonable to fail to guard or warn of playground dangers).

365 Proehl, *Tort Liability of Teachers*, 12 Vand L Rev 723, 745 (1959).

366 Tashjian v North Colonie Cent School Dist No 5, 50 AD2d 691, 375 NYS2d 467, 468 (1975); Nestor v City of New York, 28 Misc 2d 70, 211 NYS2d 975, 977 (Sup Ct 1961); Ferrill v Board of Educ, 6 AD2d 690, 174 NYS2d 91, 93 (1958); *see also* Cal Educ Code §44807 (West 1978) ("Every teacher in the public schools shall hold pupils to a strict account for their conduct ... on the playground ... ."); Cal Admin Code tit 5, §5552 (1977); NY Educ Law §1709(16) (McKinney 1969) (It shall be the duty of the school district "to employ such persons as may be necessary to supervise, organize, conduct and maintain athletic, playground and social center activities.").

367 *See* Bennett v Board of Educ, 16 AD2d 651, 226 NYS2d 593, 594 (1962), *affd*, 13 NY2d 1104, 196 NE2d 268, 246 NYS2d 634 (1963).

368 *See, e.g.*, Hunt v Board of Educ, 43 AD2d 397, 352 NYS2d 237, 240 (1974); Nestor v City of New York, 28 Misc 2d 70, 211 NYS2d 975, 977 (Sup Ct 1961); Miller v Board of Educ, 291 NYS 633, 634 (1936).

369 *See* Chimerofsky v School Dist No 63, 121 Ill App 2d 371, 257 NE2d 480, 483 (Ill Ct App 1970).

One court held that the risk that young children will fall from nondefective playground equipment is slight when contrasted with the cost of supervising all playgrounds, and, therefore, it not unreasonable for a school to fail to supervise playground activities.[370] Accordingly, a school was entitled to judgment as a matter of law in a case brought by minor who fell from a playground slide.[371]

However, most courts have held that a school is negligent if it does not have a sufficient number of supervisors.[372] In *Decker v Dundee Central School District*,[373] the school negligently supervised a playground where a girl jumped off a bleacher which was taller than she was and was injured. The teacher in that case was 1,000 feet away watching another potential hazard. The *Decker* court held that the school was liable because had there been sufficient supervision in the past the danger of girls jumping from the bleachers would have come to the school's attention and steps would have been taken to prevent its repetition.[374] In a different case, it was a question of fact whether two instructors provided reasonable supervision for 125 to 150 children, ranging in ages from 6 to 12, at a school playground during the lunch recess.[375]

Schools do not have a duty to provide additional slides at a school playground to reduce the likelihood that one child would hit another child while using the slide.[376] Their duty is only to supervise properly the use of the slides which were provided.[377]

A school may be negligent in failing to warn students of the dangers of running across a courtyard to a playground during physical education class when the school knew of the custom of students to do this and also knew that trucks traveled in the area.[378]

A school may also be negligent where it fails to follow its own regulations. In *Tashjian v North Colonie Central School District No 5*,[379] a school was liable for a third grader's baseball injury where school regulations did not allow third-grade students to participate in softball games during recess. It is unclear

---

[370] *See* 257 NE2d at 484.

[371] *Id.*

[372] *See, e.g.*, Santee v Orleans Parish School Bd, 430 So 2d 254, 255 (La Ct App 1983) (two teachers for 100 students insufficient); *see generally* Hunt v Board of Educ, 43 AD2d 397, 352 NYS2d 237, 240 (1974).

[373] 4 NY2d 462, 151 NE2d 866, 176 NYS2d 307, 309 (1958).

[374] *Id.* The dissent argued that even vigilant supervision could not anticipate the unorthodox impulsive self-instigated act of the plaintiff, and, therefore, the defendant was entitled to judgment as a matter of law. *Id* 310 (Burke, J dissenting).

[375] Ferrill v Board of Educ, 6 AD2d 690, 174 NYS2d 91, 93 (1958).

[376] *Id.*

[377] *Id.*

[378] Taylor v Oakland Scavenger Co, 17 Cal 2d 594, 110 P2d 1044, 1047-48 (1941).

[379] 50 AD2d 691, 375 NYS2d 467, 468 (1975).

whether the duty breached was allowing the third grader to play softball in violation of the rules or, irrespective of that, the school failed to supervise the baseball activity. Without analyzing the reasons for the rule prohibiting third graders from playing, it is difficult to know how to apply this decision to other situations.

In any event, if closer supervision would not have averted the injury, the school is not liable.[380] In *Nestor v City of New York*,[381] a teacher was not watching a baseball game when a student was hit by a bat swung by another child. The court held that the teacher was not liable. It rejected the plaintiff's argument that had the teacher been observing the game he could have blown his whistle and thus prevented the accident. The court called the argument pure speculation.[382]

§4.22   Miscellaneous Activities

Boxing

Schools have a duty to warn students of the dangers of participating in dangerous activities, such as boxing,[383] before the students are allowed to engage in such activities.[384] In addition, teachers have a duty to instruct the students as to the proper procedures for defending themselves.[385]

Football

It is obvious that football is a highly dangerous activity. In one recent eight-year period, over 100 high school and 11 college football players died.[386]

---

[380] District of Columbia v Cassidy, 465 A2d 395, 398-99 (DC 1983); Fagan v Summers, 498 P2d 1227, 1228-29 (Wyo 1972); *see generally* §4.16.

[381] 28 Misc 2d 70, 211 NYS2d 975, 977 (1961).

[382] *Id.*

[383] One study concluded that in the 1982-83 school year, there were no reported deaths and only one individual who suffered a permanent, severe functional disability in a school boxing program. See Mueller & Blyth, Natl Center for Catastrophic Sports Injury Research 1982-83 School Year.
Recent medical studies have shown a correlation between boxing and brain damage. *See* Ross, *Boxers-Computed Tomography, EEG, And Neurological Evaluation*, 249 J AMA 211 (Jan 14, 1983) (there is a correlation between brain damage and the number of bouts); *see also* Kaste, *Is Chronic Brain Damage In Boxing A Hazard of the Past?*, Lancet 1186, 1186 (Nov 27, 1982) ("The only way to prevent brain injuries is to disqualify blows to the head."); *see generally* Brayne, *Blood Creative Kinase Isoanzyme BB in Boxers*, Lancet 1308 (Dec 11, 1982).

[384] La Valley v Stanford, 272 AD 183, 70 NYS2d 460, 462 (1947); *see generally* §4.12.

[385] La Valley v Stanford, 272 AD 183, 70 NYS2d 460, 462 (1947); *see generally* §4.12.

[386] See Metropolitan Life Ins Co, 60 Statistical Bull 5 (Jul-Sept 1979). From 1931 to 1975 there were at least 819 deaths directly related to football participation. *See* Maroon, *"Burning Hands" In Football Spinal Cord Injuries*, 238 J AMA 2049, 2049 (1977).

Furthermore, in recent years, an average of over 12 students a year have sustained paralyzing injuries while playing football.[387]

Coaches have a duty to instruct football players about proper safety techniques.[388] In one recent case, a student rendered a quadriplegic because of negligent instruction received a jury verdict of over $6 million.[389]

Schools must also provide reasonable medical assistance to injured football players.[390] In addition, they have a duty to provide reasonable safety equipment.[391]

There is no liability unless the putative act of negligence bears a substantial relationship to the injury.[392] For example, a school's negligence in allowing

---

Interestingly, in light of the large number of football participants, the fatality rate is low. It is estimated that the number of direct fatalities per player exposure is 0.25 participants per 100,000 players. See Mueller & Schindler, Annual Survey of Football Injury Research 1931-1983 (prepared for The National Collegiate Athletic Association, The National Federation of State High School Associations and The American Football Coaches Association).

About 70% of the individuals who suffered catastrophic injuries were playing defense at the time of the injury. Indeed, over half were defensive backs in the process of making a tackle. See Mueller & Blyth, Annual Survey of Catastrophic Football Injuries 1977-82.

[387] Jackson, *School Districts Fear Suits Over Athletic Injuries*, LA Daily J, May 30, 1984, at 1, col 6.

In one survey of high school and college football teams conducted during 1973 to 1975, there was one permanent injury for every 28,000 participants. See Clark, *Survey Reveals 476 Spinal Cord Injuries*, 5 Physician & Sportsmedicine 17 (1977).

[388] *See generally* §4.12. Coaches should explain the dangers of using a head or helmet as a battering ram in blocking, tackling, and butting in football. *See generally* Torg, *The National Football Head and Neck Injury Registry*, 241 J AMA 1477-78 (1979). Indeed, both the NCAA and the National Alliance Football Rules Committee now have rules prohibiting butt-blocking or spearing. *See id* at 1477-78 (1979).

One medical commentator believes that strengthening and development of the head and neck muscles, particularly in long, slender-necked athletes should be required. *See* Maroon, *"Burning Hands" in Football Spinal Cord Injuries*, 238 J AMA 2049, 2051 (1977).

[389] Jackson, *School Districts Fear Suits Over Athletic Injuries*, LA Daily J, May 30, 1984 at 1, col 6; *Tough to Tackle*, 70 ABAJ 32 (May 1984) (case later settled for a little under $4 million).

[390] *See* §4.13. An athlete with spinal trauma or complaints of *burning hands* should be treated as if a fracture or dislocation were present. On the athletic field, after a neurological assessment, the football helmet should not be removed but rather used for cervical support. A stretcher should be used to transport the athlete. *See* Maroon, *"Burning Hands" in Football Spinal Cord Injuries*, 238 J AMA 2049, 2051 (1977).

Painful dysesthesias, or *burning hands*, may be the only complaint of football players with injured spinal cords. Accordingly, if complaints of burning hands are disregarded, complete recovery may be precluded, and the athlete may become a quadriplegic. *Id.*

Coaches may also be liable when they force injured students to play football. *See* §§4.05, 4.13. *See also* LA Daily J, Apr 27, 1983, at 1, col 5 (an injured student who was forced to play football and by doing so significantly aggravated the injury was awarded $1.5 million by a District of Columbia jury).

[391] *See* §4.10. For example, the helmet face mask lowered the incidence of fatal injuries in football. *See* Torg, *The Natl Football Head and Neck Injury Registry*, 241 J AMA 1477 (1979).

[392] *See* §4.16.

an ineligible high school football player to participate was not the proximate cause of the injury when this player collided with another player and killed him.[393] Therefore, the school was entitled to judgment as a matter of law.[394] Similarly, where there was no showing that a teacher's supervision of a football game or his playing in the game contributed to an injury, there was no showing of causation.[395]

Touch football is not usually a dangerous game.[396] Therefore, it is not negligent to allow a team of seventh graders to play a team of eighth graders even though there were differences in weight, height, and age between the two classes.[397] Similarly, it was not negligent to fail to use exponent charts which classify competitors according to weight, height, and age.[398]

Golf

Teachers must exercise reasonable care in supervising golf instruction.[399] Where the instructors of almost 60 high school students failed to watch a student help another student practice a golf swing and a student was fatally hit in the head with the golf club, the school was held liable since the lack of proper supervision was the cause of injury.[400]

One court held that a school was not negligent in having golf students stand in an oval formation to practice hitting golf balls.[401]

Hockey

Schools have a duty to take reasonable care in supervising hockey[402]

---

393 Barrett v Phillips, 29 NC App 220, 223 SE2d 918, 919-20 (1976).

394 *Id.*

395 Read v School Dist No 211, 7 Wash 2d 502, 110 P2d 179, 181 (1941). *See generally* Kluka v Livingston Parish School Bd, 433 So 2d 302, 304 (La Ct App 1983) (not negligent for a coach to wrestle with a student).

396 Pirkle v Oakdale Union Grammer School Dist, 40 Cal 2d 207, 253 P2d 1, 3 (1953).

397 *Id; see generally* §4.09.

398 Pirkle v Oakdale Union Grammer School Dist, 40 Cal 2d 207, 253 P2d 1, 3 (1953).

399 Brahatchek v Millard School Dist, 202 Neb 86, 273 NW2d 680, 687 (1979); *see generally* §§4.12, 4.15.

400 Brahatchek v Millard School Dist, 202 Neb 86, 273 NW2d 680, 687 (1979).

401 Catania v University of Neb, 329 NW2d 354, 355-56 (Neb 1983).

402 One study concluded that in the 1982-83 school year, there were no reported deaths and only one individual suffered a severe functional disability in a school's ice hockey program. *See* Mueller & Blyth, Natl Center for Catastrophic Sports Injury Research 1982-83 School Year.

A different commentator estimates that there are about 50,000 hockey injuries a year from both school and nonschool games and practices. *See Ophthalmologist Wins Hockey Safety Campaign*, 238 J AMA 2591 (1977).

games.[403] However, where this duty is not breached, the school is not liable for plaintiff's injuries.[404]

A school has a duty to provide reasonably safe equipment to its hockey players.[405] In *Everett v Bucky Warren, Inc,*[406] the school failed to exercise reasonable care in providing hockey helmets which it knew or should have known[407] were dangerous because the helmets had gaps which could be penetrated by a hockey puck, and the coach knew other available helmets were safer.[408]

In *Berman v Philadelphia Board of Education,* the court held a school's failure to provide mouth-guards to students playing floor hockey was negligent.[409] The school was aware of the occurrence of mouth injuries in hockey and that there was protective equipment designed to reduce those injuries.[410] Indeed, the physical education teacher had previously requested the school to provide this type of safety equipment.[411] The school's argument that no duty of care was violated because there was no amateur hockey regulation which required mouth-guards was properly rejected because a duty of care can exist independently of any organization's rules.[412]

A school is not liable unless its acts or omissions bear a substantial relationship to the injury.[413] Where a plaintiff was injured as a result of grabbing another hockey player, and not because of any negligent officiating, the school was not liable.[414]

The accident rate in hockey varies from about 25 to 29 accidents per 1,000 players. *See* Hussey, *Ice Hockey Injuries,* 236 J AMA 187 (1976).

403 *See generally* Pape v State, 90 AD2d 904, 456 NYS2d 863, 864 (1982).

404 *Id.*

405 Everett v Bucky Warren, Inc, 380 NE2d 653, 659 (Mass 1978). Almost all serious ocular, orbital, and facial injuries could be prevented by the use of adequate protective devices. See Hussey, *Ice Hockey Injuries,* 236 J AMA 187 (1976).

The Amateur Hockey Association of the United States has mandated full-face protectors for its 400,000 players. *See Ophthalmologist Wins Hockey Safety Campaign,* 238 J AMA 2591, 2591 (1977).

406 376 Mass 280, 380 NE2d 653 (1978).

407 The coach may be held to a higher standard of care than an average person because he or she has substantial knowledge and experience in this area. *See* Restatement (Second) of Torts §289(b) comment m (1965).

408 Everett v Bucky Warren, Inc, 376 Mass 280, 380 NE2d 653, 659 (1978); *see also* Restatement (Second) of Torts §388 (1965).

409 310 Pa Super 153, 456 A2d 545, 549 (1983).

410 *Id.*

411 *Id.*

412 *Id.*

413 *See generally* §4.16.

414 *See generally* Pape v State, 90 AD2d 904, 456 NYS2d 863, 864 (1982).

Soccer

Teachers should explain and demonstrate the proper performance of soccer before the students participate in that activity.[415] In addition, teachers should instruct the students that there should be a minimum of body contact and explain what procedures should be followed when two players arrive at the ball simultaneously.[416]

Teachers must also take reasonable care to ascertain that the students are capable of playing soccer.[417] A school was held liable where an inexperienced physical education class was permitted to play this game, which was dangerous for their level of experience, and a student was injured when several players simultaneously converged on the ball.[418] Furthermore, teachers should not allow unequally matched children to play against each other in a soccer game where there is an unreasonable risk of harm.[419]

Track and Field

Schools have a duty to take reasonable care to supervise track and field[420] events.[421] In *Marques v Riverside Military Academy*,[422] a student hit by a discus after leaving a baseball field successfully sued the school for its negligent supervision of the discus throwers. The school's argument that the errant throw of the discus was an independent, intervening cause which broke the causal connection between the defendant's negligence and the plaintiff's injury was rejected because the school's duty was to exercise reasonable care so that such errant throws will not occur.[423]

Schools must also exercise reasonable care in the placement of track and

---

415 Darrow v West Genesee Cent School Dist, 41 AD2d 897, 342 NYS2d 611, 612 (1973); *see generally* §4.12.

416 *Id.* Darrow v West Genesee Central School Dist, 41 AD2d 897, 342 NYS2d 611, 612 (1973); *see generally* Section 4.12.

417 Keesee v Board of Educ, 37 Misc 2d 414, 235 NYS2d 300, 306 (Sup Ct 1962); *see generally* §4.09.

418 Keesee v Board of Educ, 37 Misc 2d 414, 235 NYS2d 300, 306 (Sup Ct 1962).

419 Brooks v Board of Educ, 29 Misc 2d 19, 205 NYS2d 777 (Sup Ct 1960), *affd*, 15 AD2d 495, 222 NYS2d 184 (1961), *affd*, 12 NYS2d 971, 189 NE2d 497, 238 NYS2d 963 (1963).

420 One study concluded that in the 1982-83 school year, there were three reported fatalities from high school pole vaulting. See Mueller & Blyth, Natl Center for Catastrophic Sports Injury Research 1982-83 School Year. There were six reported fatalities in high school running activities. *See id.*

421 Marques v Riverside Military Academy, 87 Ga App 370, 73 SE2d 574, 577 (1952).

422 87 Ga App 370, 73 SE2d 574, 577 (1952).

423 *Id*; *see generally* §4.16.

field facilities.[424] A school may be liable for placing pole vault uprights on an unstable base and for failure to take reasonable care to prevent the uprights from falling.[425] However, where the jury concluded this did not occur, judgment for the school was affirmed.[426]

In *Johnson v Municipal University of Omaha*,[427] a pole vaulter was injured when he fell on a partially covered wooden box near the uprights. This box, as well as others, was placed in that position to ease the officials' work in expediting the event and to enable the crossbar to be set at a higher position. The court held that the risk of injury did not outweigh the utility of placing the wooden boxes near the uprights, and, therefore, the school was not negligent.[428]

Swimming

Schools should take reasonable care in supervising swimming[429] activities.[430] Accordingly, a school may be negligent in providing swimming instructors who lack training and experience in observing and safeguarding the safety of the students.[431]

The courts have consistently failed to apply the res ipsa loquitur doctrine where a student drowns in a swimming class, because such accidents do not usually occur if only the school was negligent;[432] the victim may have been negligent or other swimmers may have caused the accident.[433]

Weight Lifting

There is a duty to provide the proper training and supervision for weight

---

[424] *See* Johnson v Municipal Univ of Omaha, 187 Neb 24, 187 NW2d 102 (1971); *see generally* §4.11.

[425] *See* Bouillon v Harry Gill Co, 15 Ill App 3d 45, 301 NE2d 627, 631 (1973).

[426] *Id.*

[427] 187 Neb 24, 187 NW2d 102 (1971).

[428] 187 NW2d at 103.

[429] One study concluded that in the 1982-83 school year, four individuals suffered severe functional disabilities in school swimming activities. Three of those accidents occurred while performing a racing dive. See Mueller & Blyth, Natl Center for Catastrophic Sports Injury Research 1982-83 School Year.

[430] Morehouse College v Russell, 109 Ga App 301, 136 SE2d 179, 191 (1964); *see generally* §4.15.

[431] Morehouse College v Russell, 109 Ga App 301, 136 SE2d 179, 191 (1964).

[432] *See, e.g.,* Wong v Waterloo Community School Dist, 232 NW2d 865, 871 (Iowa 1975).

[433] *Id.*

lifting.[434] This is because overexertion and other injuries are foreseeable, indeed frequent, in the absence of proper care.[435]

Wrestling

Schools must take reasonable steps to protect its wrestlers'[436] safety.[437] Wrestlers must obtain a certain degree of skill before it is reasonably safe for them to participate in this sport.[438] However, in one case a physical education teacher was held to have acted reasonably in allowing a physical education class to wrestle *hard* in a 30-second drill after less than a week of training because the class was made up largely of good athletes.[439]

One court held that a teacher's failure to keep records of weights, ages, heights, or other statistics of student wrestlers for determining wrestling partners was not negligence.[440] The teacher in that case was well-acquainted with the students and, therefore, was able to judge the strength and abilities of the members of his 30-person class without reference to those records.[441]

In *Kluka v Livingston Parish School Board*, the court held that a coach did not act unreasonably in wrestling with a student.[442] Although the coach had a

---

434 Vargo v Svitchan, 100 Mich App 809, 301 NW2d 1, 5 (1980).

435 *Id.*

436 One study concluded that in the 1982-83 school year, there were three reports of individuals who suffered permanent, severe functional disabilities from high school wrestling activities. See Mueller & Blyth, Natl Center for Catastrophic Sports Injury Research 1982-83 School Year.

437 Green v Orleans Parish School Bd, 365 So 2d 834, 836 (La Ct App 1978), *writ refused*, 367 So 2d 393 (La 1979). There are no national or, in most areas, local guidelines for teaching wrestling in physical education classes. *See id.*

The use of diuretics for rapid weight loss for making weight in a sport is dangerous because of the side effects of hypotension, weakness, and lethargy. *See* Thornton, *Use of Diuretics For "Making Weight" in Sports is Harmful Practice*, 236 J AMA 200 (1976). Indeed, it may be unethical for a doctor to prescribe diuretics for such purposes. *See id.* The medical dangers of making weight are also analyzed in Hursch, *Food and Water Restriction in the Wrestler*, 241 J AMA 915 (1979).

One medical commentator believes that wrestlers should have one hour's rest between matches at high school or college meets. *See* Cooper, *Are Double Dual High School Wrestling Matches Advisable*, 236 J AMA 200 (1976).

The National Federation of State High School Association's wrestling rules provide that contestants not wrestle in more than four full-length matches during any one day. *Id.*

438 *See* Green v Orleans Parish School Bd, 365 So 2d 834, 836 (La Ct App 1978), *writ refused*, 367 So 2d 393 (La 1979).

439 *Id.*

440 Reynolds v State, 207 Misc 963, 141 NYS2d 615, 618 (Ct Cl 1955).

441 *Id.*

442 433 So 2d 302, 304 (La Ct App 1983).

duty not to injure the student as a result of superior knowledge of wrestling, when the injury occurred because the student caught his leg between two mats, and not as a result of the coach's superior knowledge, there was no liability.[443]

The inclusion of wrestling in a physical education course is proper unless it is specifically prohibited by state law.[444]

---

[443] *Id.*

[444] *See* Smith v Consolidated School Dist No 2, 408 SW2d 50, 53 (Mo 1966).

Landowner Liability to Gratuitous Recreational Users of Property

5

Gratuitous Recreational User Statutes

§5.01 Introduction

Most states have now enacted legislation which limits a landowner's duty of care to individuals who use property, without paying for it, to pursue recreational activities.[1] Most of these laws were patterned, directly or indirectly, on the Model Recreational Users Act, promulgated by the Council of State Governments in 1965.[2]

The Model Act states:

Section 1. The purpose of this act is to encourage owners of land to make land and water areas available to the public for recreational purposes by limiting their liability toward persons entering thereon for such purposes.

Section 2. As used in this act:

(a) 'Land' means land, roads, water, watercourses, private ways and buildings, structures, and machinery or equipment when attached to the realty.

---

[1] Ala Code §§35-15-1 to -5, -20 to -28 (Supp 1981); Ark Stat Ann §§50-1101 to -1107 (1971); Cal Civ Code §846 (West 1982); Conn Gen Stat Ann §§52-557f to -557j (West Supp 1982); Del Code Ann tit 7, §§5901-5907 (1975); Fla Stat Ann §375.251 (West Supp 1983); Ga Code Ann §§51-3-20 to -26 (1982); Hawaii Rev Stat §§520-1 to -8 (1976); Idaho Code §36-1604 (Supp 1981); Ill Ann Stat ch 70, §§31-37 (Smith-Hurd Supp 1981); Ind Code Ann §14-2-6-3 (West 1982); Iowa Code Ann §§111C.1-.7 (West Supp 1981); Kan Stat Ann §§58-3201 to -3207 (1976); Ky Rev Stat Ann §150.645 (Bobbs-Merrill 1980); La Rev Stat Ann §9:2791 (West Supp 1981); Me Rev Stat Ann tit 14, §159-A (Supp 1982); Md Nat Res Code Ann §§5-1101 to -1108 (Supp 1982); Mass Ann Laws ch 21, §17C (Michie/Law Coop 1980); Mich Comp Laws Ann §300.201 (West Supp 1982); Minn Stat Ann §§87.021-.026 (West 1977); Miss Code Ann §89-2-1 (Supp 1982); Mont Code Ann §§70-16-301 to 302 (1981); Neb Rev Stat §§37-1001 to -1008 (1979); Nev Rev Stat §41.510(1) (1979); NH Rev Stat Ann §212:34 (1978); NJ Stat Ann §§2A:42A-2 to -5 (West Supp 1981); NY Gen Oblig Law §9-103 (Consol Supp 1982); ND Cent Code §§53-08-01 to -06 (1982); Ohio Rev Code Ann §§1533.18, .181 (Page 1978); Okla Stat Ann tit 76, §10-15 (West 1976); Or Rev Stat §§105.655-.680 (1979); Pa Stat Ann tit 68, §477-1 to -8 (Purdon Supp 1982); SC Code Ann §§27-3-10 to -70 (Law Co-op 1977); SD Comp Laws Ann §20-9-5 (Supp 1979); Tenn Code Ann §§11-10-101 to -104 (Supp 1982); Tex Rev Civ Stat Ann art 1b (Vernon 1969); Utah Code Ann §57-14-1 (Supp 1981); Vt Stat Ann tit 10, §5212 (1973); Va Code §§15.1-291, 29-130.2 (Supp 1981); Wash Rev Code §§4.24.200, 4.24.210 (Supp 1982); W Va Code §§19-25-1 to -6 (1977); Wis Stat Ann §29.68 (West Supp 1982); Wyo Stat §§34-19-101 to -106 (1977); The discussion of the common law duties of landowners is in ch 6.

There has been some law journal commentary regarding recreational user statutes. *See* Barrett, *Good Sports and Bad Lands: The Application of Washington's Recreational Use Statute Limiting Landowner Liability*, 53 Wash L Rev 1 (1977); Knowles, *Landowners' Liability Towards Recreational Users*, 18 Idaho L Rev 59 (1982); Wilkins, *The Wrongful Death of Willie McCord*, 47 U Cin L Rev 591 (1978); Comment, *Wisconsin's Recreational Use Statute: A Critical Analysis*, 66 Marq L Rev 312 (1983); Note, *Tort Liability and Recreational Use of Land*, 28 Buffalo L Rev 767 (1979); Note, *The Minnesota Recreational Use Statute: A Preliminary Analysis*, 3 Wm Mitchell L Rev 117 (1977); *Note, Torts-Statutes-Liability of Landowner To Persons Entering For Recreational Purposes*, 1964 Wis L Rev 705.

[2] *See* Council of State Governments, XXIV Suggested State Legislation 150-52 (1965). A handful of states had earlier passed similar legislation. Michigan had such a law in 1953, New York in 1956, and New Jersey in 1962.

(b) 'Owner' means the possessor of a fee interest, a tenant, lessee, occupant or person in control of the premises.

(c) 'Recreational purpose' includes, but is not limited to, any of the following, or any combination thereof: hunting, fishing, swimming, boating, camping, picnicking, hiking, pleasure driving, nature study, water skiing, winter sports, and viewing or enjoying historical, archaeological, scenic, or scientific sites.

(d) 'Charge' means the admission price or fee asked in return for invitation or permission to enter or go upon the land.

Section 3. Except as specifically recognized by or provided in Section 6 of this act, an owner of land owes no duty of care to keep the premises safe for entry or use by others for recreational purposes, or to give any warning of a dangerous condition, use, structure, or activity on such premises to persons entering for such purposes.

Section 4. Except as specifically recognized by or provided in Section 6 of this act, an owner of land who either directly or indirectly invites or permits without charge any person to use such property for recreational purposes does not thereby:

(a) Extend any assurance that the premises are safe for any purpose.

(b) Confer upon such person the legal status of an invitee or licensee to whom a duty of care is owed.

(c) Assume responsibility for or incur liability for any person or property caused by an act of omission of such persons.

Section 5. Unless otherwise agreed in writing, the provisions of Sections 3 and 4 of this act shall be deemed applicable to the duties and liability of an owner of land leased to the state or any subdivision thereof for recreational purposes.

Section 6. Nothing in this act limits in any way any liability which otherwise exists:

(a) For willful or malicious failure to guard or warn against a dangerous condition, use, structure, or activity.

(b) For injury suffered in any case where the owner of land charges the person or persons who enter or go on the land for the recreational use thereof, except that in the case of land leased to the state or a subdivision thereof, any consideration received by the owner for such lease shall not be deemed a charge within the meaning of this section.

Section 7. Nothing in this act shall be construed to:

(a) Create a duty of care or ground of liability for injury to persons or property.

(b) Relieve any person using the land of another for recreational purposes from any obligation which he may have in the absence of this act to exercise care in his use of such land and in his activities thereon, or from the legal consequences of failure to employ such care.[3]

Generally, these state statutes provide that a landowner owes no duty of care to individuals who enter[4] onto his or her property without paying consideration. Many statutes also provide that a landowner has no duty of care to third parties injured by the activities of gratuitous recreational users.[5]

Nevertheless, virtually none of the statutes limit a landowner's liability for a wilful or malicious failure to guard or warn against dangerous conditions, uses, structures, or activities on the property. Some statutes also do not limit liability where the injured party was expressly invited, rather than merely being permitted, ot come upon the land.[6] However, one court held that an invitation to the general public was to be considered an invitation to the injured party.[7] This is obviously a matter of some importance to parks and other public recreational areas.

The limited liability provisions cover injuries resulting from the use of real property or personal property, e.g., guns or boats, while pursuing recreational activities on another's land.[8] However, the statutes do not shield a landowner when the injured party never went on his or her property.[9]

The major legislative purpose of these statutes was to reduce the growing tendency of landowners to withdraw their land from recreational access. The thought was that this trend would be slowed if the tort liability that a landowner might otherwise incur from gratuitous users of his or her land could be lowered.[10] Some courts have also discerned a legislative concern

---

3 *See* Council of State Governments, XXIV Suggested State Legislation 150-52 (1965).

4 Some statutes require that permission be given. *See, e.g.,* Ky Rev Stat Ann §150.645 (Bobbs-Merrill 1980).

5 *See, e.g.,* Fla Stat Ann §375.251 (West Supp 1983); Ky Rev Stat Ann §150.645 (Bobbs-Merrill 1980); Neb Rev Stat §37-1003 (1979); SC Code Ann §27-3-40(c) (Law Co-op 1977). *See also* Ind Code Ann §14-2-6-3 (West 1982) (landowner owes no duty of care arising out of the acts or omissions of other persons using the premises). *But see* Potlach Corp v United States Dept of the Army, No 77-2016 (D Idaho May 30, 1980), described in Knowles, *Landowners' Liability Towards Recreational Users,* 18 Idaho L Rev 59, 62 n16 (1982)

6 *See, e.g.,* Cal Civ Code §846 (West 1982).

7 Simpson v United States, 652 F2d 831, 834 (9th Cir 1981). This decision severely limits, if not overrules, Phillips v United States, 590 F2d 297 (9th Cir 1979), which held that the term *express invitation* meant individuals personally selected by the landowner.

8 State *ex rel* Tucker v District Court, 155 Mont 202, 468 P2d 773, 776 (1970).

9 Christians v Homestake Enter, Ltd, 97 Wis 2d 638, 294 NW2d 534, 539 (1980) (plaintiff was injured by exploding blasting caps removed by others from defendant's property), *revd on other grounds,* 101 Wis 2d 25, 303 NW2d 608 (1981).

10 Paige v North Oak Partners, 134 Cal App 3d 860, 863, 134 Cal Rptr 867 (1982). One commentator has written that this purpose will not be significantly encouraged by the limited liability provisions because landowner decisions to allow public access are based on factors such

that it was unfair to allow individuals who entered gratis onto another's land to pursue recreational activities to recover for the landowner's negligence.[11]

Some court decisions have stated that these recreational user laws codified the common law duty of landowners—at least as to licensees.[12] Although that may have been the intent of some legislatures, the statutory language chosen was different from the lexicon of the common law of landowner or premises liability. Therefore, it is inevitable that different results will be reached in some close cases. In any event, a more accurate statement would be that these statutes generally offer more protection to landowners than did the common law. As such, the statutes are a significant aberration in contemporary tort law which has shown a marked trend in increasing the potential liability of defendants.

Several courts have held that these statutes should be strictly construed because they are in derogation of the common law[13] or because immunity from liability for negligence is not favored.[14] Of course, to the extent the statutes codify the common law, they cannot, by definition, be in derogation of those portions of it. Most importantly, these statutes, like all others, should be interpreted in light of their legislative purpose.

---

as privacy and the moral responsibility of compensating injured individuals rather than their tort liability. *See* Barrett, *Good Sports and Bad Lands: The Application of Washington's Recreational Use Statute Limiting Landowner Liability*, 53 Wash L Rev 1, 26-27 (1977). Furthermore, it is not clear that these laws will lower landowners' insurance rates since insurance usually covers other risks unrelated to recreational use. *See id.*

[11] Lostritto v Southern Pac Transp Co, 73 Cal App 3d 737, 749, 140 Cal Rptr 905 (1977).

[12] Crawford v Consumers Power Co, 108 Mich App 232, 310 NW2d 343, 346 (1981); Sega v State, 89 AD2d 412, 456 NYS2d 856, 859 (1982); Rock v Concrete Materials, Inc, 46 AD2d 300, 362 NYS2d 258, 260-61 (1974), *appeal dismissed*, 36 NY2d 772, 329 NE2d 672, 368 NYS2d 841 (1975) ("the purpose of the statute is to codify the common law and prevent the extension of liability to injured licensees in accordance with more liberal approaches taken in other jurisdictions or under the Restatement of Torts"); Hahn v Commonwealth, 18 Pa D&C3d 260, 275 (1980). *See generally* Ky Rev Stat Ann §150.645 (Bobbs-Merrill 1980) (nothing in this section limits in any way any liability which otherwise exists).

[13] Ducey v United States, 713 F2d 504, 510 (9th Cir 1983); Boileau v De Cecco, 125 NJ Super 263, 310 A2d 497, 500 (1973), *affd*, 65 NJ 234, 323 A2d 449 (1974); Tijerina v Cornelius Christian Church, 273 Or 58, 539 P2d 634 (1975); Copeland v Larson, 46 Wis 2d 377, 174 NW2d 745, 749 (1970). Similarly, exceptions to the application of statutes in derogation of the common law should be given a broad reading. *See* Ducey v United States, 713 F2d 504, 510 (9th Cir 1983). Some state statutes have eliminated the common law rule that statutes in derogation thereof should be strictly construed. *See, e.g.*, Cal Civ Code §4 (West 1982) (statutes are to be liberally construed to effect their objects); Tex Rev Civ Stat Ann art 10(8) (Vernon 1969); Utah Code Ann §68-3-2 (1978).

[14] Harrison v Middlesex Water Co, 80 NJ Super 391, 403 A2d 910, 914 (1979).

§5.02   Constitutionality

Recreational user statutes have consistently been held constitutional.[15] There are legitimate state objectives in making available areas of vacant, but private, land to the public.[16] It is reasonable to assume that landowners will restrict access to less land if they are not required to fulfill a duty of care to possible entrants on that land.

Similarly, the statutes' discrimination against licensees[17] or recreational users[18] in favor of owners is not arbitrary or capricious.

When plaintiffs first raised the issue of constitutionality at the appellate level, courts have held that these contentions had been waived.[19]

§5.03   Recreational Activities

Most recreational user statutes specifically list examples of recreational activities covered, such as fishing, hunting, trapping, camping, or hiking.[20] Most also include language to the effect that the list is only representative, not exhaustive, of covered recreational uses.

---

15 Simpson v United States, 652 F2d 831, 833-34 (9th Cir 1981); Parish v Lloyd, 82 Cal App 3d 785, 788, 147 Cal Rptr 431 (1978); Lostritto v Southern Pac Transp Co, 73 Cal App 3d 737, 747-49, 140 Cal Rptr 905 (1977); Abdin v Fischer, 374 So 2d 1379, 1381 (Fla 1979); Crawford v Consumers Power Co, 108 Mich App 232, 310 NW2d 343, 345 (1981); Estate of Thomas v Consumers Power Co, 58 Mich App 486, 228 NW2d 786, 791, *affd on this issue, revd on other grounds*, 394 Mich 459, 231 NW2d 653 (1975); Goodson v City of Racine, 61 Wis 2d 554, 213 NW2d 16, 20 (1973) (not an illegal law or violative of equal protection).

16 Estate of Thomas v Consumers Power Co, 58 Mich App 486, 228 NW2d 786, 791, *affd on this issue, revd on other grounds*, 394 Mich 459, 231 NW2d 653 (1975).

17 *Id.*

18 Moss v Department of Natural Resources, 62 Ohio St 2d 138, 404 NE2d 742, 745 (1980).

19 Gard v United States, 594 F2d 1230, 1235 (9th Cir), *cert denied*, 444 US 866 (1979); Crawford v Consumers Power Co, 108 Mich App 232, 310 NW2d 343, 345 (1981).

20 Numerous other activities, some of them nonrecreational, are also included. *See, e.g.*, Ark Stat Ann §50-1102(c) (1971) (pleasure driving); Conn Gen Stat Ann §52-557j (West Supp 1982) (snowmobile, motorcycle, pleasure driving, viewing or enjoying scenic sites); Idaho Code §36-1604(b)(3) (Supp 1981) (animal riding); Ind Code Ann §14-2-6-3 (West 1982) ("any other purpose"); Iowa Code Ann §11C.2 (West Supp 1981) (going to or from a recreational use); Me Rev Stat Ann tit 14 §159-A (Supp 1982) (gathering forest products); Md Nat Res Code Ann §5-1101(c) (Supp 1982) (includes activities of 4-H and FFA clubs); Mont Code Ann §70-16-301 (1981) (pleasure expeditions); NH Rev Stat Ann §212:34 (1978) (removal of furlwood); NJ Stat Ann §2A:42A-2 (West Supp 1981) (training of dogs); NY Gen Oblig Law §9-103 (McKinney Supp 1984) (training of dogs, speleological activities, hang gliding); ND Cent Code §53-08-01 (1982) (using land for purposes of the user); Tenn Code Ann §11-10-101(6) (Supp 1982) (using land for purposes of the user); Va Code §29-103.2 (Supp 1982) (skydiving); Wash Rev Code §4.24.210 (Supp 1982) (clam digging, riding animals); Wis Stat Ann §29.68 (West 1968) (berry picking, climbing of observation towers).

Courts have, accordingly, found these statutes applicable to other nonspecified recreational activities such as snowmobiling,[21] swimming and diving,[22] horseback riding,[23] motorbiking,[24] riding a jeep up and down hills for fun,[25] use of the property as access to a beach[26] and the normal activities afforded by public parks.[27]

However, not all jurisdictions have applied these statutes to activities which were not specifically listed. A recent New York decision, *Rochette v Town of Newburgh*, stated that the statute's applicability is strictly limited to the activities specified.[28] Therefore, it held that iceboat racing is not covered even though the New York statute specifically covers boating. Similarly, a golfer[29] and a musician[30] were not considered to be engaged in recreational activities.

Some recreational activities which are included in the statute are so similar to others which are not that fine distinctions may need to be drawn. For example, statutes which include hiking do not necessarily also include walking. In *Gerkin v Santa Clara Valley Water District*, the court held that hiking meant taking a long walk for pleasure or exercise. Therefore, when a child slipped and injured herself while walking her bicycle across a bridge, the statute would not apply if the child's purpose in crossing the bridge was to use a telephone and buy candy at a store located on the other side of the creek.[31]

The *Gerkin* decision can be read to mean that an individual who walks and bicycles is not engaged in a covered recreational activity if there is any reason for the trip other than merely enjoying the outdoors. If that is the proper interpretation, the decision is questionable because the use of a telephone for a social call and the purchase of candy hardly seem like activities which are so inconsistent with walking or bicycling for pleasure or exercise that they preclude application of the statute.

The *Gerkin* court also held that a plaintiff's subjective intent regarding whether he or she was pursuing a recreational activity was not dispositive of whether the statute should apply. That determination must be based on a reasonable person's belief of whether the activity was recreational.

---

21 Estate of Thomas v Consumers Power Co, 58 Mich App 486, 228 NW2d 786, 790, *affd in part, revd in part on other grounds*, 394 Mich 459, 231 NW2d 653 (1975).

22 Anderson v Brown Bros, 65 Mich App 409, 237 NW2d 528 (1975).

23 Crabtree v Shultz, 57 Ohio App 2d 33, 384 NE2d 1294, 1296 (1977).

24 Krevics v Ayars, 141 NJ Super 511, 358 A2d 844, 846 (1976).

25 Lauber v Narbut, 178 NJ Super 591, 429 A2d 1074, 1077 (1981).

26 Power v Union Pac RR, 655 F2d 1380, 1387 (9th Cir 1981).

27 Watson v City of Omaha, 209 Neb 835, 312 NW2d 256, 259 (1981) (slippery slide).

28 88 AD2d 614, 449 NYS2d 1013, 1016 (1982).

29 Quesenberry v Milwaukee County, 106 Wis 2d 685, 317 NW2d 468, 473 (1982).

30 Villanova v American Fedn of Musicians, 123 NJ Super 57, 301 A2d 467, 469 (1973).

31 95 Cal App 3d 1022, 157 Cal Rptr 612 (1979).

Accordingly, when there was a dispute whether the plaintiff was hiking rather than walking, it was critical to consider the path taken, the length and purpose of the journey, and the topography and prior use of the land, as well as the plaintiff's subjective intent.[32]

In *Fisher v United States*, the court seemingly held that a plaintiff's subjective intent was irrelevant and that an objective, reasonable person standard should be followed in determining whether the injured party was engaged in a recreational activity.[33] Accordingly, the recreational user statute was applied in *Fisher* when a girl was killed while playing on a snowplow blade at a national wildlife refuge which she visited on a school field trip.

In contrast, in *Orawsky v Jersey Central Power & Light Co*, the court gave great weight to a plaintiff's subjective intent regarding whether he was pursuing a recreational activity.[34] When a state statute listed fishing as one of the covered recreational activities, an individual who was fishing for pleasure, even though intending to sell the fish, was bound by the limited liability provisions since he was not in the business of fishing or even fishing primarily to make money.

Gerkin, Fisher, and *Orawsky* can be reconciled as follows: When the plaintiff's subjective intent was to pursue a covered recreational activity, that fact should be given great, if not conclusive, weight regarding whether the limited liability provisions should apply. However, when the plaintiff's subjective intent was not to pursue a covered recreational activity, an objective, reasonable person standard should be used to ascertain whether a recreational activity was being pursued.

If a person is allowed entry for both recreational and nonrecreational purposes, such as a business-related sports activity, it is unclear whether the statute should apply. One commentator has argued that the statute should be inapplicable if the nonrecreational purpose alone would have allowed entry.[35]

When an injury occurs in an activity incidental to a recreational use, the statute is usually applied. For example, in *Curtiss v County of Chemung*, the court held that the statute should be considered when several boys who were hunting and hiking were injured after they entered a shed which subsequently collapsed.[36] The statute was also applied when a woman who was hiking took a break and sat down on a guardrail which then broke.[37]

---

32 *Id.*

33 534 F Supp 514, 516 (D Mont 1982).

34 472 F Supp 881, 885 (ED Pa 1977).

35 Note, *The Minnesota Recreational Use Statute: A Preliminary Analysis*, 3 Wm Mitchell L Rev 117, 153 (1977).

36 78 AD2d 908, 433 NYS2d 514, 515 (1980).

37 Sega v State, 89 AD2d 412, 456 NYS2d 856, 858 (1982).

A plaintiff can also be injured while attempting to discourage others from using the property in a recreational manner. In *Smith v Scrap Disposal Corp*,[38] the plaintiff was driving some friends home after a day of fishing. One friend jumped out of the car and attempted to drive a bulldozer located in the area. The plaintiff stated that he was injured while he was trying to stop his friend from using the bulldozer. The court reversed a summary judgment for the defendant and held that if the plaintiff went on the defendant's land solely to dissuade his friends from using the bulldozer, the statute would not apply.[39]

A similar analysis was applied to a rescuer who drowned while trying to save two boys who, while ice skating, had fallen through the ice. The statute was not applied since the rescue attempt was not a recreational activity.[40] This decision presents an analytical problem because it was unclear whether the rescuer was already on the land and engaged in a recreational activity when he attempted the rescue. Indeed, when it was undisputed that a rescuer was engaged in a recreational activity before beginning the rescue attempt, the court held that the individual was a "trespasser... before he became a hero" and applied the statute.[41]

§5.04 Types of Landowners and Land Occupiers

Most recreational user statutes define the term landowner broadly and include the possessor of a fee interest or life estate, and tenants, lessees, occupants, or persons in control of the premises.[42]

Operators of recreational facilities are in control of the premises and therefore can avail themselves of these statutes.[43]

Some of these statutes have been construed to cover state employees when there is statutory support for that construction.[44]

§5.05 — Commercial Enterprises

It is quite clear that the legislative intent behind these recreational user

---

38 96 Cal App 3d 525, 158 Cal Rptr 134 (1979).

39 *Id.*

40 Harrison v Middlesex Water Co, 80 NJ Super 391, 403 A2d 910, 915 (1979).

41 Lovell v Chesapeake & Ohio RR, 457 F2d 1009, 1011 (6th Cir 1972).

42 *See, e.g.,* Ga Code Ann §51-3-21(3) (1982); Ill Ann ch 70 §32 (Smith-Hurd Supp 1981); NY Gen Oblig Law §9-103 (Consol Supp 1982); Ohio Rev Code Ann §1533.181 (Page 1978); Pa Stat Ann tit 68, §477-2(2) (Purdon Supp 1984); Tex Rev Civ Stat Ann art 1b (Vernon 1969).

43 Pratt v State, 408 So 2d 336, 342-43 (La Ct App 1981), *cert denied,* 412 So 2d 1098 (La 1982).

44 Wirth v Ehly, 93 Wis 2d 433, 287 NW2d 140, 145 (1980).

statutes was to limit the liability of landowners from gratuitous users of their property. The most common method of determining whether a landowner is covered by the statute is to discover whether he or she charged the plaintiff for the use of the land—not whether the landowner was engaged in business. Indeed, only a few states specifically prohibit commercial enterprises from benefiting from recreational user statutes.[45]

However, even when the statute does not specifically preclude businesses from its definition of landowner, some courts have construed the statute to mean that the limited liability provisions did not apply to landowners engaged in a commercial activity, including those who did not charge the plaintiff a fee.[46] For example, in *Donaher v Patridge Creek Country Club*, the court held that a golf course could not avail itself of the statute when a prospective golfer was injured by an errant golf ball, since it was a commercial enterprise.[47]

Not all courts have agreed with the *Donaher* analysis. A retail business operation which supplied a free boat ramp was protected under a recreational user statute when a plaintiff slipped on algae on the ramp.[48] The court held that since there was no charge for the ramp, the statute applied.

In states which exclude commercial enterprises from their definition of landowner, it is important to be able to distinguish enterprises which are commercial from those which are not. One court defined a commercial enterprise as having a primary objective of making a profit.[49] The charging of fees, standing alone, is not dispositive evidence of a commercial enterprises.[50]

It may be difficult to know when an entity's primary objective is to make a profit. It is, for example, unclear whether this is a subjective or objective test. If it is subjective, it probably gives too much weight to the opinion of an interested party. If it is objective, a very poorly managed company which lost money or operated close to break-even might be considered noncommercial.

It may be helpful to note whether the enterprise qualifies as a not-for-profit entity under the federal tax law[51] (i.e., organized and operated exclusively for

---

[45] *See, e.g.*, Ala Code §33-15-3 (1977); La Rev Stat Ann §9:2791 (West Supp 1981); Minn Stat Ann §87.021(5) (West 1977)

[46] *See, e.g.*, Baroco v Araserv, Inc, 621 F2d 189, 193 (5th Cir 1980); Cedeno v Lockwood, Inc, 250 Ga 799, 301 SE2d 265, 267 (1983). This case is noted in Gershon, *Torts*, 35 Mercer L Rev 291, 309 (1983).

[47] 116 Mich App 305, 323 NW2d 376, 378, *appeal dismissed*, 325 NW2d 2 (Mich 1982). *See also* Kesner v Trenton, 216 SE2d 880, 855 (W Va 1975).

[48] *See* Sea Fresh Frozen Prods, Inc v Abdin, 411 So 2d 218, 220 (Fla Dist Ct App), *petition denied*, 419 So 2d 1195 (Fla 1982); Abdin v Fischer, 374 So 2d 1379, 1379-80 (Fla 1979). *See also* §5.18.

[49] Pratt v State, 408 So 2d 336, 342 (La Ct App 1981), *cert denied*, 412 So 2d 1098 (La 1982).

[50] *See id.*

[51] 26 USC §501(c)(7).

pleasure or recreation, where no part of the net earnings inures to the benefit of any private shareholder). It should be noted, however, that under this test most country clubs would be considered noncommercial enterprises; a result which is contrary to that reached in *Donaher*.[52]

§5.06 —Governments

Federal Government

Under the Federal Tort Claims Act, the United States is entitled to the benefit of laws which are applicable to private individuals under like circumstances.[53] Accordingly, the United States can obtain the benefit of state recreational user statutes when they would be applicable to a private individual,[54] but not otherwise.[55]

The major purpose of these statutes is to encourage landowners to open their land by limiting their potential liability. Theoretically, this can be achieved by including the federal government as a landowner since the government could close off its land if it felt its potential liability were too great.[56] However, even if the legislative purpose were to encourage only private landowners to open their land, the federal government is still entitled to the protection of these statutes. The Tort Claims Act mandates that a state may not protect private citizens from liability without also protecting the federal government.[57]

---

[52] *See, e.g.*, Augusta Golf Assn v United States, 338 F Supp 272 (SD Ga 1971); Columbia Country Club v Livingston, 252 SC 490, 167 SE2d 300 (1969).

[53] 28 USC §2674. *See* Rayonier Inc v United States, 352 US 315, 319 (1957); Otteson v United States, 622 F2d 516, 517 (10th Cir 1980); §3.11.

[54] Van Tagen v United States, 557 F Supp 256, 259 (ND Cal 1983); Mandel v United States, 545 F Supp 907, 912 (WD Ark 1982); Fisher v United States, 534 F Supp 514, 516 (D Mont 1982); Hahn v United States, 493 F Supp 57, 59 (MD Pa), *aff'd without opinion*, 639 F2d 733 (3d Cir 1980); Blair v United States, 433 F Supp 217, 218 (D Nev 1977); Smith v United States, 383 F Supp 1076, 1081 (D Wyo 1974), *aff'd on other grounds*, 546 F2d 872 (10th Cir 1976); Garfield v United States, 297 F Supp 891, 899 (WD Wis 1969). *But cf* Delta Farms Reclamation Dept v Superior Court, 33 Cal 3d 699, 660 P2d 1168, 190 Cal Rptr 494, *cert denied*, 104 S Ct 277 (1983) (state cannot use recreational user statute even though it is entitled to all defenses that would be available to a private person).

[55] Miller v United States, 597 F2d 614, 616 (7th Cir 1979). This decision may have misapplied Illinois law. *See* Johnson v Stryker Corp, 70 Ill App 3d 717, 388 NE2d 932, 934 (1979).

[56] Jones v United States, 693 F2d 1299, 1303 (9th Cir 1982): Otteson v United States, 622 F2d 516, 519 (10th Cir 1980); Gard v United States, 594 F2d 1230, 1233 (9th Cir), *cert denied*, 444 US 866 (1979).

[57] McClain v United States, 445 F Supp 770, 771 (D Or 1978).

State and Municipal Governments

A few states have explicitly included state government land in their definition of covered property,[58] while others have explicitly excluded it.[59] Most state statutes, however, do not specifically address this issue.

In the absence of an explicit provision in the statute to the contrary, most courts have ruled that state and municipal governments are entitled to the limited liability benefits of these statutes. They have reasoned that the definition of a landowner is broad enough to cover public entities.[60] Other courts have reached this result without an analysis of the issue.[61]

However, some courts have held that local governmental units cannot obtain the benefit of these statutes.[62] They have reasoned that since the statutes were passed to encourage *private* landowners to open their land to public use, no purpose can be served by limiting the liability of public landowners.[63] Moreover, it has been suggested that governmental units do not need this type of limited liability since they can be adequately protected by the applicable state tort claims act.[64]

Michigan has adopted a third alternative. In *Anderson v Brown Brothers*,

---

[58] *See, e.g.*, Idaho Code §36-1604(b)(1) (Supp 1981); Ohio Rev Code Ann §1533.18 (Page 1978); Tenn Code Ann §11-10-103 (Supp 1982); Va Code §15.1-291 (Supp 1981); Wash Rev Code §4.24.210 (Supp 1982); Wis Stat Ann §29.68 (West Supp 1982).

[59] *See, e.g.*, Hawaii Rev Stat §520-2 (1976).

[60] *See* Stone Mountain Memorial Assn v Herrington, 225 Ga 746, 171 SE2d 521, 523 (1969); Watson v City of Omaha, 209 Neb 835, 312 NW2d 256, 259 (1981); Trimblett v State, 156 NJ Super 291, 383 A2d 1146, 1149 (1977); Magro v City of Vineland, 148 NJ Super 34, 371 A2d 815 (1977); Sega v State, 89 AD2d 412, 456 NYS2d 856, 859 (1983); McCord v Ohio Divn Parks & Recreation, 54 Ohio St 2d 72, 375 NE2d 50, 52 (1978) (strongly criticized in Wilkins, *The Wrongful Death of Willie McCord*, 47 U Cin L Rev 591 (1978)); McCarver v Manson Park & Recreation Dept, 92 Wash 2d 370, 597 P2d 1362, 1365 (1979). *But see* Primo v City of Bridgeton, 162 NJ Super 394, 392 A2d 1252, 1257 (1978).

In some of these jurisdictions, the statutes were later amended to include government land. *See, e.g.*, Ohio Rev Code Ann §533.181 (Page 1978).

[61] *See* Glover v City of Mobile, 417 So 2d 175 (Ala 1982); Rushing v State, 381 So 2d 1250, 1251 (La Ct App 1980); Wight v State, 93 Misc 2d 560, 403 NYS2d 450 Ct Cl 1978); Hogg v Clatsop County, 46 Or App 129, 610 P2d 1248, 1250 n 2 (1980); *see also* Mattison v Hudson Falls Cent School Dist, 91 AD2d 1133, 458 NYS2d 726, 728 (1983) (school district can avail itself of statute).

[62] *See* Delta Farms Reclamation Dept v Superior Court, 33 Cal 3d 699, 660 P2d 1168, 190 Cal Rptr 494, *cert denied*, 104 S Ct 277 (1983); Metropolitan Dade County v Yelvington, 392 So 2d 911, 912 & n 2 (Fla Dist Ct App), *review denied*, 389 So 2d 1113 (Fla 1980); Rushing v State, 381 So 2d 1250, 1251 (La Ct App 1980); Champ v Butler County, 18 Pa D&C3d 282 (1981); Watterson v Commonwealth, 18 Pa D&C3d 276 (1980); Hahn v Commonwealth, 18 D&C3d 260 (1980).

[63] Goodson v City of Racine, 61 Wis 2d 554, 213 NW2d 16, 19 (1973).

[64] *see* Wilkins, *The Wrongful Death of Willie McCord*, 47 U Cin L Rev 581, 602 (1978).

the court held that municipal governments engaged in governmental, as distinguished from propietary, functions can use the statute as a defense.[65]

One court held that even if the government did not raise the defense of the recreational user statute in the trial court, it could raise the issue on appeal.[66]

One unpublished decision held that a statutory amendment which included government property within its coverage should not be applied retroactively.[67]

§5.07 — Easement Holders

The Michigan courts have consistently construed the recreational user statute to include easement holders, such as electric companies having only an utility easement, under the definition of landowners.[68] The result was that individuals tragically injured when they came into contact with live power lines were unable to recover damages from the power company.[69] Those decisions may be criticized because the easement holders in those cases, the power companies, did not have the right to prevent the injured person from using the land. The limited liability provided in the statute did not encourage the easement holder to allow recreational use of the property, and therefore, the easement holder should not have been given the statute's benefits.[70]

The California statute is atypically worded. It only applies to an "owner of any estate" in real property.[71] In *Darr v Lone Star Industries*, the court held that *estate* should be given its usual real property meaning, viz., an interest in land which is or may become possessory.[72] Accordingly, since an easement holder has only a nonpossessory interest in the property, the holder does not have an estate in land and cannot claim the benefit of the statute.[73]

However, a different California appellate court reached the opposite conclusion.[74] It held that this issue should be decided by analyzing the purpose of the statute, not by *technicalities* of common law rules of real property. When

---

65 65 Mich App 409, 237 NW2d 528, 532 (1976).

66 *See* Sega v State, 89 AD2d 412, 456 NYS2d 856, 858 (1982).

67 Matre v State of Idaho, No 74080 (Idaho Aug 11, 1981), discussed in Knowles, *Landowners' Liability Toward Recreational Users*, 18 Idaho L Rev 59, 67 n 31 (1982).

68 *See* Crawford v Consumers Power Co, 108 Mich App 232, 310 NW2d 343, 345 (1981); Estate of Thomas v Consumers Power Co, 58 Mich App 486, 228 NW2d 786, 789, *affd on this issue, revd on other grounds*, 394 Mich 459, 231 NW2d 653 (1975).

69 *See* Crawford v Consumers Power Co, 108 Mich App 232, 310 NW2d 343, 345 (1981); Estate of Thomas v Consumers Power Co, 58 Mich App 486, 228 NW2d 786, 789, *affd on this issue, revd on other grounds*, 394 Mich 459, 231 NW2d 653 (1975).

70 *See* Atkinson, *Torts*, 22 Wayne L Rev 629, 661 (1976).

71 Cal Civ Code §846 (West 1982).

72 Restatement Property §9 (1936); 3 Powell on Real Property ¶405, at 34-10 (1981).

73 94 Cal App 3d 895, 900-01, 157 Cal Rptr 90 (1979).

74 Smith v Scrap Disposal Corp, 96 Cal App 3d 525, 528-29, 158 Cal Rptr 134 (1979).

a defendant has the right to bar access to its portion of the land, it should be allowed the statute's protection so it will not exercise its power to close off the land.

§5.08 —Former Owners

Recreational user statutes can only be used by present landowners, not former ones.[75] This interpretation is consistent with the major legislative purpose of these laws. Former owners, by definition, do not have the power to restrict access to the property and, therefore, should not be given limited tort liability when they do not limit access.

It should be noted, however, that the general common law rule places liability for injury from defective premises upon the person who has control and possession of the premises, not the prior owner.[76] Therefore, former owners may not require the benefits of the statute to limit their liability.

§5.09 —Tenants, Lessees, and Licensees

Many state recreational user statutes include tenants in their definition of parties entitled to limited liability.[77]

Whether a lessee's rights under a lease are sufficient to consider the lessee a tenant is a question of fact to be determined by analyzing the lease terms. Obviously, conclusory words or labels are not dispositive. When the parties are in a true landlord-tenant relationship (i.e., the tenant is entitled to exclusive possession of a defined space for a specified time) the lessee is entitled to the benefit of these statutes.[78]

In *Anderson v Brown Brothers*, the court held that when property is leased from a municipal government which has no governmental immunity, the lessees are precluded from claiming the benefits of these statutes.[79] This decision is troublesome since it ignored the plain wording of the applicable statute, viz., that tenants or lessees are parties entitled to limited liability. Moreover, the decision undercuts the legislative purpose. Since tenants can restrict access to their property, the failure to give them limited liability

---

[75] Thone v Nicholson, 84 Mich App 538, 269 NW2d 665, 667 (1978).

[76] *See id*; Rock v Concrete Materials, Inc, 46 AD2d 300, 362 NYS2d 258, 261 (1974), *appeal dismissed*, 36 NY2d 772, 329 NE2d 672, 368 NYS2d 841 (1975). *See also* W. Prosser, Torts §64, at 412 (4th ed 1971).

[77] *See, e.g.*, Mich Comp Laws Ann §§300.201, 317.176 (West Supp 1982) (also covers owner's agent).

[78] State *ex rel* Tucker v District Court, 155 Mont 202, 468 P2d 773, 777 (1970).

[79] 65 Mich App 409, 237 NW2d 528, 532 (1975).

may lead them to prohibit the public from using their land for recreational activities.

A party with exclusive, albeit temporary, rights to possession of the property can avail itself of these statutes. For example, when a railroad has the exclusive right to use railroad tracks for a period of time, it is entitled to limited liability when there is a recreational injury there.[80]

In *O'Shea v Claude C. Wood Co*, the courts held that a defendant whose license to use property did not include the right to exclusive occupation against the injured plaintiff could not obtain the benefits of these statutes.[81] This decision appears sound. The legislative intent was to encourage landowners and occupiers to leave their property open for recreational purposes. If a defendant did not have the power to restrict access to the property, it should not be given limited liability for not exercising that nonexistant power.

Some statutes provide that the owner of land leased to the state may agree in writing that the statutory limitations on liability are inapplicable.[82] These waivers of statutory protection should not be implied. Accordingly, a *hold harmless* provision in a lease, standing alone, is not a waiver of the limited liability provided by the statute.[83]

§5.10 Location and Quality of the Land

Most of the statutes explicitly include recreational activities on all property.[84] Nevertheless, the courts have not usually construed the statutes so broadly. They have repeatedly limited their application to situations where it was believed that limited liability would entice landowners to allow their land to be used for recreational purposes. Accordingly, the courts have required

---

80 *See* Power v Union Pac RR, 655 F2d 1380, 1387 (9th Cir 1981); *see also* State *ex rel* Tucker v District Court, 155 Mont 202, 468 P2d 773, 776 (1970).

81 97 Cal App 3d 903, 911, 159 Cal Rptr 125 (1979).

82 *See, e.g.*, Ill Stat Ann ch 70, §35 (Smith-Hurd Supp 1981).

83 Stephens v United States, 472 F Supp 998, 1010 (CD Ill 1979).

84 *See* Wash Rev Code §4.24.210 (Supp 1982) (includes urban land). Some statutes specifically include abandoned caves or mines. *See* Iowa Code Ann §111C.2 (West Supp 1981). *But see* Ill Ann Stat ch 70 §32(e) (Smith-Hurd Supp 1981) (land must be outside city limits and not subdivided into blocks and lots); Miss Code Ann §89-2-1 (Supp 1982) (must publish notice of availability of land); Okla Stat Ann tit 76, §11 (West 1976) (appears to include only land for farming or ranching); SD Comp Laws Ann §20-9-5 (Supp 1979) (only rural real estate used exclusively for agricultural purposes); Vt Stat Ann tit 10 §5212(a)(1) (Supp 1981) (land must be unposted, outside city limits, and more than 500 feet from any residential or commercial building); Va code §29-130.2 (Supp 1982) (statute does not apply to land used primarily for residential or commercial purposes and not routinely used by others).

that the injuries occur on large tracts of land or water[85] or on relatively undeveloped property[86] for the statutes to apply.

One statute was construed to apply only to property open to the general public or to particular classes of the public such as the Boy Scouts or Little League Baseball players.[87]

However, two federal courts construing the Illinois recreational user statute held that areas which are primarily maintained for recreational use as parks were not covered by the statute.[88] These decisions appear to have been limited, at least in part, by a state appellate court decision.[89] It is now difficult to state Illinois law in this area with much precision.

In any event, most courts have implied or directly held that parks and other areas primarily meant for recreation are covered by these statutes.[90] This seems to be the preferred approach.

The decision to open new parks or playgrounds and to continue to keep present ones open, is based on a cost-benefit analysis. The analysis may, of course, be made sub rosa, and noneconomic factors are obviously considered. Nevertheless, to the extent decision makers perceive that the future cost of paying for injuries or insurance (or both) is high, the future availability of these areas will be jeopardized.

§5.11 — Artificial Conditions

Several New Jersey decisions have held that the statute should not be applied when the injury was a result of an artificial condition on the land. For example, in *Primo v City of Bridgeton*, the statute was not applied when an

---

[85] Erickson v Century Management Co, 154 Ga App 508, 268 SE2d 779 (1980). This decision was disapproved in Cedeno v Lockwood, Inc, 250 Ga 799, 301 SE2d 265, 267 (1983).

[86] Michalovic v Genesee-Monroe Racing Assn, 79 AD2d 82, 436 NYS2d 468, 470 (1981); *see also* Comment, *Wisconsin's Recreational Use Statute: A Critical Analysis*, 66 Marq L Rev 312, 334 (1983).

[87] Stone Mountain Memorial Assn v Herrington, 225 Ga 746, 171 SE2d 521, 523 (1969).

[88] Miller v United States, 597 F2d 614, 616 (7th Cir 1979); Stephens v United States 472 F Supp 998, 1012 (CD Ill 1979).

[89] Johnson v Stryker Corp, 70 Ill App 3d 717, 388 NE2d 932, 934 (1979).

[90] Glover v City of Mobile, 417 So 2d 175 (Ala 1982); Stone Mountain Memorial Assn v Herrington, 225 Ga 746, 171 SE2d 521 (1969); Van Gordon v Portland Gen Elec Co, 59 Or 740, 652 P2d 817, 819 (1982); Thomas v Jeane, 411 So 2d 744 (La Ct App 1982); McCarver v Manson Park & Recreation Dist, 92 Wash 2d 370, 597 P2d 1362, 1366 (1979). *But see* Primo v City of Bridgeton, 162 NJ Super 394, 392 A2d 1252, 1257 (1978); Note, *The Minnesota Recreational Use Statute: A Preliminary Analysis*, 3 Wm Mitchell L Rev 117, 138 (1977).

individual was injured on a slide in a park.[91] Similarly, in *Diodato v Camden County Park Commission*, the statute was not applied when a plaintiff injured himself when he dove into a pond and hit a submerged trash barrel.[92]

There is no a priori reason why artificial conditions are not covered. Indeed, such an interpretation is contrary to the relevant state statute which provides that there is no duty to warn of *"any* hazardous *condition* of the land or in connection with the use of *any structure."*[93] Not surprisingly, other courts have rejected any putative distinction between natural or artificial conditions.[94]

§5.12 — Construction Projects

In *Paige v North Oak Partners*, the court held that the recreational user statute was inapplicable when minors were injured while riding their bicycles on a temporary construction project. The court noted that the plaintiff's purpose was undoubtedly recreational but held that it was inconceivable that the legislature intended to encourage owners and building contractors to allow children to play on their temporary contruction projects.[95]

The *Paige* decision can be criticized because the court failed to articulate a reasoned distinction between property covered by the statute and property not covered. Ad hoc determinations of what property is covered by recreational user statutes offer no guidance for future situations and promote uncertainty in this area. Consequently, cautious land occupiers may bar access to their land.

Other courts have allowed contractors to obtain the benefit of these statutes.[96]

§5.13 — Keep-Out Signs

A few statutes limit coverage to property which is *not* posted with signs prohibiting tresspassing.[97] Several other statutes state that it is irrelevant

---

91 162 NJ Super 394, 392 A2d 1252, 1257 (1978).

92 162 NJ Super 275, 392 A2d 665, 671 (1978).

93 *See* NJ Stat Ann §2A:42A-3 (West Supp 1982) (emphasis added).

94 Wirth v Ehly, 93 Wis 2d 433, 287 NW2d 140, 147 (1980); *see also* Mattison v Hudson Falls Cent School Dist, 91 AD2d 1133, 458 NYS2d 726, 728 (1983) (bench on baseball field).

95 134 Cal App 3d 860, 863, 864, 184 Cal Rptr 867 (1982).

96 Fanny v Pike Indus, 119 NH 108, 398 A2d 841 (1979); Denton v L. W. Vail Co, 23 Or App 28, 541 P2d 511 (1975).

97 Vt Stat Ann tit 10, §5212(a)(1) (1973).

whether or not the property is posted.[98] The overwhelming majority of statutes, however, are silent on this issue.

In *Georgia Power Co v McGruder*, the Georgia Supreme Court ruled that the state recreational user statute did not apply when the defendant had posted keep-out signs. In that case a 10-year-old boy drowned when he disregarded two large signs which stated: *Danger. For your own safety please keep out. Rough waters. Gates at dam operate automatically.*[99]

The *McGruder* decision is highly questionable on two grounds. First, it is unclear what the defendant did wrong. Had the sign stated *please be careful* or *please keep out* the court may have held the statute applicable. If this interpretation is correct, the decision is a triumph of form over substance.

Second, and more critically, the decision represents poor public policy. The logical result of this interpretation will be that landowners will not post warnings. This will allow them to claim the benefits of the limited liability provisions of the statute. Unfortunately, this will give the recreational enthusiast less knowledge of the dangers lurking in the area and also reduce the opportunity to recover damages when injured.

Not surprisingly, other courts have reached the opposite conclusion in similar cases.[100]

§5.14 —Residential Land

Most courts have ruled that recreational user statutes were not intended to apply to injuries in residential areas. Accordingly, these statutes were not applied when an injury occurred on a vacant lot in a residential area[101] or on an asphalt parking lot.[102]

Similarly, in *Harrison v Middlesex Water Co*, the New Jersey Supreme Court held that the recreational user statute did not apply when an individual drowned in a lake on an improved tract of land situated in a highly populated

---

98 NJ Stat Ann §2A:42A-3(a) (West Supp 1982); NY Gen Oblig Law §9-1031(a) (Consol Supp 1982).

99 229 Ga 811, 194 SE2d 440 (1972). *See also* Christians v Homestake Enters, Ltd, 47 Wis 2d 638, 294 NE2d 534, 539 (1980) (alternative holding), *revd on other grounds*, 101 Wis 2d 25, 303 NW2d 608 (1981).

100 Johnson v Stryker, 70 Ill App 3d 717, 388 NE2d 932, 933 (1979).

101 Shepard v Wilson, 123 Ga App 74, 179 SE2d 550, 551 (1970). Property is not considered residential when the injured party turned off a paved road, travelled down a sand road bordered by swamps, and crossed a dilapidated bridge to reach it. *See* Orawsky v Jersey Cent Power & Light Co, 472 F Supp 881, 884 (ED Pa 1977).

102 Michalovic v Genessee-Monroe Racing Assn, 79 AD2d 82, 436 NYS2d 468, 470 (1981).

suburban community.[103] The *Harrison* court also criticized an earlier New Jersey appellate decision[104] which applied the statute when the injury occurred on a large, undeveloped tract of land, since the land was in close proximity to developed, residential property.

However, the statute was applied when a girl was injured while walking a horse in a pasture field close to where at least two families lived.[105]

Where the statute only covered agricultural land, it was not applied to an injury occurring on property within a city district.[106]

§5.15   —Swimming Pools

The courts have uniformly failed to apply recreational user statutes to injuries occurring in residential[107] or motel[108] swimming pools. These decisions appear to be correct. It is unlikely that the state legislatures intended to limit the liability of these pool owners. Regardless of the statutory limited liability provisions, these landowners generally would not allow their pools to be used without their permission.

In *Boileau v DeCecco*,[109] the court held the recreational user statute inapplicable to injuries occurring in a residential swimming pool but did so on a tortured reading of the statutory text. The relevant state statute provided that, with certain exceptions, a landowner owed no duty of care to gratuitous recreational users irrespective of whether special no-trespassing notices were posted.[110] The court reasoned that these no-trespassing signs were used only in rural areas and, therefore, that the recreational user statute should not be applied to suburban lands. However, there is no textual support for the court's view that the recreational user statute should be limited to land where these special no-trespassing signs could be posted.

---

103 80 NJ 391, 403 A2d 910, 913, 915 (1979). *See generally* Wirth v Ehly, 93 Wis 2d 433, 287 NW2d 140, 146 (1980) (statute clearly applies when injury is in rural or semirural environment).

104 Tallaksen v Ross, 167 NJ Super 1, 400 A2d 485, 486 (1979); *but see* Harrison v Middlesex Water Co, 80 NJ 391, 403 A2d 910, 913 (1979) ("the Act does not grant immunity from liability to the owners or occupiers of land situate... in residential and populated neighborhoods").

105 Crabtree v Shultz, 57 Ohio App 2d 33, 384 NE2d 1294, 1295-96 (1977).

106 Kucher v Pierce County, 24 Wash App 281, 600 P2d 683, 688 (1979). The Washington statute now covers all land. *See* Wash Rev Code §4.24.210 (Supp 1982).

107 *See* Herring v Hauck, 118 Ga App 623, 165 SE2d 198, 199 (1968); *but see* McWilliams v Guzinski, 71 Wis 2d 57, 237 NW2d 437, 446 (1976) (Hansen, J, dissenting) (would apply statute when young child drowned in a neighbor's swimming pool).

108 Erickson v Century Management Co, 154 Ga App 508, 268 SE2d 779 (1980).

109 125 NJ Super 263, 310 A2d 497, 499 (1973), *aff'd*, 65 NJ 234, 323 A2d 449 (1974).

110 *See* NJ Stat Ann §2A:42A-3 (West Supp 1982).

§5.16   Tortious Conduct

Recreational user statutes generally exempt landowners from all claims of negligence, whether active or passive.[111] It is usually irrelevant whether or not the owner's negligence arose out of the natural condition of the land.[112]

In some cases the statutes have been construed to allow plaintiff's nuisance claims. Accordingly, a person injured by a dangling high-voltage wire can claim that he or she was injured by a nuisance and that the recreational user statute is inapplicable.[113] However, other courts have reached the opposite conclusion.[114]

One state statute was construed to bar strict liability claims against a landowner.[115]

§5.17   —Wilful, Wanton, or Malicious Acts

Virtually all state statutes provide that certain conduct by the landowners is not deserving of limited liability.[116] Generally, the state law provides that the limited liability provisions shall not apply when the landowner's conduct was a *wilful or wanton* failure to guard or to warn against a dangerous condition, use, structure, or activity.[117] Some states use a slightly different wording. For example, in some jurisdictions a landowner's "wilful or malicious"[118] or "reckless"[119] failure to guard or warn of danger or a landowner's gross negligence is not given limited liability.[120]

Some statutes use the words wilful and wanton in the conjunctive. However,

---

111 *See* Crawford v Consumers Power Co, 108 Mich App 232, 310 NW2d 343, 345-46 (1981).

112 *Id*; *see also* §5.11.

113 Crawford v Consumers Power Co, 108 Mich App 232, 310 NW2d 343, 347 (1981). However, this decision may be an inaccurate statement of Michigan law. *See* Burnett v City of Adrian, 414 Mich 448, 326 NW2d 810, 824 n 24 (Moody, J, concurring).

114 North v Toco Hills, Inc, 160 Ga App 116, 286 SE2d 346, 348 (1981).

115 Thomas v Jeane, 411 So 2d 744, 747 n 4 (La Ct App 1982).

116 *But see* Idaho Code §36-1604 (Supp 1981); Ohio Rev Code Ann §§1533.18, .181 (Page 1978), neither of which, at least on their face, allow any claims against landowners by gratuitous recreational users. The Washington statute, Wash Rev Code §4.24.210 (Supp 1982), provides that the only claims which are still allowed are for "known dangerous artificial latent conditions for which warning signs are not conspicuously posted."

117 Cal Civ Code §846 (West 1982); *but see* Minn Stat Ann §87.021 (West 1977) (only includes wilful action).

118 *See, e.g.*, Fla Stat Ann §375.251 (West Supp 1983).

119 *See, e.g.*, Or Rev Stat §105.675 (1979).

120 Mich Comp Laws Ann §300.201 (West Supp 1982); SC Code Ann §27-3-60(a) (Law Co-op 1977). In Michigan, gross negligence is another name for the last clear chance doctrine; it does not refer to conduct analogous to wilful or wanton acts. *See* Bennett v City of Adrian, 414 Mich 448, 326 NW2d 810, 811, 814 (1982).

at least one court hinted that the disjunctive was proper.[121]

The courts have experienced difficulty in articulating what a wilful, wanton, or malicious act represents. Indeed, the Michigan Supreme Court has stated that "to reconcile the confused and disparate pronouncements of Michigan's appellate judiciary concerning the concepts of gross negligence and willful and wanton misconduct ... [would] disown much of what has been written in this Court and in the Court of Appeals in earlier cases. ..."[122]

Some courts have stated that the plaintiff must show: that the defendant's conduct would naturally or probably result in injury; that the defendant knew or reasonably should have known that its conduct would so result in injury; and that the defendant continued that course of conduct in reckless disregard of the foreseeable consequences.[123] Other courts have held that wilful or wanton acts are an extreme departure from ordinary care in a situation where a high degree of danger is apparent.[124]

Obviously, there must be more than mere negligence.[125] Therefore, the failure to comply with a local ordinance is not, standing alone, wilful or malicious.[126]

In *Odar v Chase Manhattan Bank*, the court held that even when a landowner knew that the property was frequently used for recreational purposes by others, the failure to fence, post, patrol, or prevent individuals from entering the property was not wilful or malicious.[127] Of course, this standard is appropriate only when there is no probable risk of serious injury.

Landowner's Knowledge of Prior Accidents or Dangers

A landowner's knowledge of serious prior accidents and a subsequent failure

---

121 Lovell v Chesapeake & Ohio RR, 547 F2d 1009, 1011 (6th Cir 1972).

122 *See* Burnett v City of Adrian, 414 Mich 448, 326 NW2d 810, 811 (1982); *see also* Thone v Nicholson, 84 Mich App 538, 269 NW2d 665, 672 (1978) ("It is well-recognized that many cases have misused and misapplied the terms gross negligence and wilful and wanton misconduct, and that this area of the law is fraught with confusion and wrong statements of the law.").

123 Mandel v United States, 545 F Supp 907, 913 (WD Ark 1982). *See also* Van Tagen v United States, 557 F Supp 256, 259 (ND Cal 1983); O'Shea v Claude C Wood Co, 97 Cal App 3d 903, 912, 159 Cal Rptr 125 (1979). Defendant's conduct must probably result in injury or the requisite indifference to harm will not have been shown. *See* Burnett v City of Adrian, 414 Mich 448, 326 NW2d 810, 812 (1982).

124 Stephens v United States, 472 F Supp 998, 1016-17 (CD Ill 1979); *see also* Hogg v Clatsop County, 46 Or App 129, 610 P2d 1248, 1249 (1980) (failure to exercise ordinary care when it is apparent that disastrous consequences could occur).

125 Rushing v State, 381 So 2d 1250, 1252 (La Ct App 1980).

126 Herring v R. L. Mathis Certified Dairy Co, 121 Ga App 373, 173 SE2d 716, 722, *appeal dismissed*, 400 US 922 (1970); *see also* Gard v United States, 594 F2d 1230, 1235 (9th Cir), *cert denied*, 444 US 866 (1979).

127 138 NJ Super 474, 351 A2d 389 (1976).

to guard against or warn of them may indicate a wanton failure to act.[128] In *Simpson v United States*, a landowner knew that an individual had previously fallen into a scalding hot-water pool in a park, knew of the dangerous condition of the creek bank, and still failed to post a warning that the bank might collapse. The court held that it was a question of fact whether the owner wilfully and maliciously failed to warn.[129] However, in a questionable decision, a landowner was held not to have acted recklessly as a matter of law for failure to warn of the dangers of hot springs even when it had actual knowledge of prior serious injuries caused by the springs.[130]

The absence of prior accidents is some indication that there is no serious risk of danger.[131] Accordingly, maintaining an electrical line about 12 feet above a lake when there were no previous accidents was not wilful or malicous.[132]

However, the absence of prior injuries may only mean that it took some time for the inevitable to occur.[133] When a landowner failed to warn of or guard against the risks posed by submerged tree stumps which it knew were located in an area used for swimming, the landowner acted wilfully and wantonly.[134]

In contrast, absent any indication of danger, a landowner is under no obligation to examine the depths of a river. A landowner did not act wantonly when it did not warn or guard against the dangers of an unknown submerged rock which a plaintiff hit while diving into a river.[135]

In *Hamilton v United States*, a landowner erected a chain link fence to prohibit passage beyond that point. A plaintiff went through a break in the fence and ultimately was injured. The court held that the landowner did not commit a wilful or malicious act because it did not know of the break.[136]

A landowner did not wilfully fail to guard or warn against danger when it posted a cable which served as a fence to prevent property damage.[137]

---

128 Van Tagen v United States, 557 F Supp 256, 260 (ND Cal 1983) (government failed to erect guardrail or warning sign at a sharp curve on a road in a federal recreational area).

129 652 F2d 831, 834 (9th Cir 1981).

130 Van Gordon v Portland Gen Elec Co, 59 Or App 740, 652 P2d 817, 819 (1982).

131 Jones v United States, 693 F2d 1299, 1304-05 (9th Cir 1982).

132 Rushing v State, 381 So 2d 1250, 1252 (La Ct App 1980).

133 Stephens v United States, 472 F Supp 998, 1017 (CD Ill 1979); *see also* Lostritto v Southern Pac Transp Co, 73 Cal App 3d 737, 745, 140 Cal Rptr 905 (1977). *Cf* Lucchesi v Kent County Road Commn, 109 Mich App 524, 312 NW2d 86, 93 (1981) ("Having baited a trap for even the most prudent . . . , defendant could not stand by idly and await a victim.").

134 Stephens v United States, 472 F Supp 988, 1017 (CD Ill 1979).

135 Mandel v United States, 545 F Supp 907, 913 (WD Ark 1982).

136 371 F Supp 230, 235 (ED Va 1974) (there also was no showing of negligence under these facts).

137 Lauber v Narbut, 178 NJ Super 591, 429 A2d 1074, 1077 (1981); *see also* Wirth v Ehly, 93 Wis 2d 433, 287 NW2d 140, 147 (1980) (the act of placing a wire cable across a road, standing alone, is not a wilful or malicious act).

However, the placing of a cable across a motorbike trail when the cable was indistinguishable from the surroundings at dusk, with no warning posted, may be a wilful act unprotected by the recreational user statute.[138]

The leaving of a road-grading machine where it was being used was not gross or wanton negligence as a matter of law. The grader was not inherently dangerous to children, and there was no showing that the landowner knew that children had played on the grader.[139]

Obvious Dangers

The failure to guard or warn of obvious dangers is not a wilful or wanton act. Indeed, usually it is not even negligence. Accordingly, the failure to warn of the dangers of shallow water is not a wilful act.[140]

In several cases landowners were held not responsible to snowmobilers who failed to observe objects visible except for the darkness of night, and consequently hit them.[141] The landowners were exonerated even though the injuries occurred at night and it appeared that the objects, a gate[142] and a partially snow-covered bench on a baseball field,[143] were not seen because it was dark.

Similarly, the failure to warn of a concrete dock which was plainly visible except under the most adverse weather conditions was not negligence—much less a wilful failure to warn.[144]

A landowner's failure to warn of a stream or to construct a bridge over it is not wilful or wanton. Therefore, a motorcyclist who was injured when he struck the bank of a creek while riding along a railroad track could not recover.[145]

---

138 Krevics v Ayars, 141 NJ Super 511, 358 A2d 844, 845-46 (1976); *see also* Cutway v State, 89 AD2d 406, 456 NYS2d 539, 541 (1982) (landowner liable for placing a relatively inconspicuous cable across a dirt roadway used by motorized recreational vehicles).

139 Town of Big Stone Gap v Johnson, 184 Va 375, 35 SE2d 71, 74 (1945) (statute dealt with government's liability for some recreational accidents).

140 Orawsky v Jersey Cent Power & Light Co, 472 F Supp 811, 884 (ED Pa 1977).

141 *See, e.g.*, Rock v Concrete Materials, Inc, 46 AD2d 300, 362 NYS2d 258, 261 (1974), *appeal dismissed*, 36 NY2d 772, 329 NE2d 672, 368 NYS2d 841 (1975); *see also* La Carte v New York Explosives Corp, 72 AD2d 873, 421 NYS2d 949 (1979).

142 *See, e.g.*, Rock v Concrete Materials, Inc, 46 AD2d 300, 362 NYS2d 258, 261 (1974), *appeal dismissed*, 36 NY2d 772, 329 NE2d 672, 368 NYS2d 841 (1975). Other courts have also held that otherwise visible conditions which were concealed only by darkness are not hidden perils which must be guarded or have warnings posted. *See* Mazzeffi v Schwanke, 52 Ill App 3d 1032, 368 NE2d 441, 442-43 (1977), *cert denied*, 439 US 869 (1978) (case did not construe a recreational user statute).

143 Mattison v Hudson Falls Cent School Dist, 91 AD2d 1133, 458 NYS2d 726, 727 (1983).

144 Wight v State, 93 Misc 2d 560, 403 NYS2d 450, 453 (Ct Cl 1978).

145 Thone v Nicholson, 84 Mich App 538, 269 NW2d 665, 672 (1978).

Gross Negligence

A landowner's gross negligence is generally not shielded by recreational user statutes. In a Michigan case, the plaintiff alleged that a landowner knew of unmarked guy wires which violated an industry safety code, was aware of the risk of these wires to snowmobilers, and could have eliminated the risk, but failed to do so. The allegations stated a claim for relief irrespective of a recreational user statute.[146] Similarly, where landowners knew that children were using a gravel pit as a swimming pool, and knew that this was dangerous, but failed to take successful action to deter the conduct of the children, there was a question of fact concerning the landowners gross negligence and liability.[147]

One court held that a landowner's knowledge that children used its dock to fish and its failure to exercise ordinary care to prevent them from doing so presented a jury question regarding its gross negligence when a child fell off the dock and drowned.[148] However, the failure to post warnings or to construct a bridge so a motorcyclist riding along an abandoned railroad right-of-way would not strike the bank of a stream is not gross negligence.[149]

Decisions Using Common Law Principles

There are several decisions in this area which should be used with care because they rely on common law principles, rather than the language of the recreational user statute. In *Wright v Alabama Power Co*,[150] the court held that the defendant was entitled to a directed verdict. The only evidence of wilful or malicious conduct was that an adult, while riding backward on an inner tube attached by a ski rope to a power boat, was injured when he collided with a partially submerged fence. Although the *Wright* decision appears to have reached the correct result, its analysis is confusing. It appears to have been decided under an analysis of the common law duty owed to licensees. The court should have determined whether the failure to guard or warn of the fence was a wilful or malicious act under the recreational user statute.[151]

---

146 Estate of Thomas v Consumers Power Co, 394 Mich 459, 231 NW2d 653 (1975).

147 Taylor v Matthews, 40 Mich App 74, 198 NW2d 843, 852 (1972).

148 Magerowski v Standard Oil Co, 274 F Supp 246, 248 (WD Mich 1967).

149 Thone v Nicholson, 84 Mich App 538, 269 NW2d 665, 672 (1978).

150 355 So 2d 322 (Ala 1978).

151 *See also* Driskill v Alabama Power Co, 374 So 2d 265, 267 (Ala 1979) (landowner not liable for injuries resulting when operator of a motorboat ran into a submerged tree trunk). In Bilbao v Pacific Power & Light Co, 257 Or 360, 479 P2d 226, 228 (1971), the court criticized jury instructions which dealt with both the recreational user statute and the common law duty owed invitees.

Several New York and Pennsylvania courts have held that since their respective state recreational user statutes codified the common law, landowners still must warn of traps or unreasonably hazardous defects which they know of and which the injured party could not discover upon reasonable inspection.[152]

Therefore, New York and Pennsylvania formulations of the appropriate standard of conduct under the recreational user statutes focus on traps and unreasonably hazardous defects; words which are not in the relevant statutes. They should instead focus on the words of the statute which declare that a landowner owes no duty "to warn of any hazardous condition or use of [the premises] ... however a landowner's willful or malicious failure to guard, or to warn against, a dangerous condition ... [or] use of the premises" is not given partial immunity.[153]

A landowner almost certainly commits a wilful or malicious act when it knows of a hazardous defect, realizes that individuals using the land would not reasonably discover the defect, and fails to warn or guard against the dangers of the defect. If that premise is accepted, then there is no difference in result whether common law principles or the recreational user statute language is applied. Indeed, the decisions in New York and Pennsylvania to date would probably have been the same under either test. Nevertheless, the risk in applying a slightly differently worded standard is that a different, and possibly erroneous, result might be reached in a close case.

Summary Judgment

There is language in many decisions cautioning courts to be wary of granting summary judgment when issues which may involve questions of intent or motive, such as wilfulness, are present. Such statements are correct. However, when there is no genuine dispute of material fact, even in cases involving wilfulness, summary judgment is appropriate.[154]

§5.18 Charge or Consideration

State legislatures have given landowners limited tort liability in exchange for the landowners allowing gratuitous recreational activities on their property.

---

152 *See* Mattison v Hudson Falls Cent School Dist, 91 AD2d 1133, 458 NYS2d 726, 727 (1983); Sega v State, 89 AD2d 412, 456 NYS2d 856, 859 (1982); Curtis v County of Chemung, 78 AD2d 908, 433 NYS2d 514, 516 (1980); Rock v Concrete Materials, Inc, 46 AD2d 300, 362 NYS2d 258 (1974), *appeal dismissed*, 36 NY2d 772, 329 NE2d 672, 368 NYS2d 841 (1975); Hahn v Commonwealth 18 Pa D&C2d 260, 275 (1980).

153 NY Gen Oblig Law §9-103 (McKinney Supp 1982); Pa Stat Ann tit 68, §§477-3, -6 (Purdon Supp 1982).

154 Gard v United States, 594 F2d 1230, 1234 n2 (9th Cir), *cert denied*, 444 US 866 (1979).

The statutes have differentiated the entrepreneur landowner, whose land is open for commercial activities, from the landowner who opens its land on a gratuitous basis by whether the landowner received a charge or consideration from the user of the land.[155]

The legislatures properly felt that landowners who charge for access to their property do not need, or deserve, limited liability. Indeed, a probable assumption is that owners who charge for access can or should buy insurance to cover the risks of accidents.[156]

The states have differed in their expressed intent to cover only gratuitous recreational use. Many states refuse to give limited liability when there is a *charge*. This is usually defined as the price or fee asked of those who wish to enter on the land.[157] Other states exclude commercial activities[158] or landowners who receive consideration[159] or compensation[160] for allowing access to their land.

A significant number of states specifically provide that money received for leasing land to the government is not a charge or consideration which precludes application of these statutes.[161] One state even excludes rent paid by groups, organizations, or corporations from its definition of charge.[162]

Incidental Fees

Incidental fees have usually not been construed to be a charge or consideration. For example, a true parking fee, meaning one not charged to individuals entering on foot and not based on the number of people in the vehicle, will not preclude a landowner from claiming the statute's protection.[163] Similarly,

---

155 Ducey v United States, 713 F2d 504, 514 (9th Cir 1983).

156 *See generally* Ducey v United States, 713 F2d 504, 511 (9th Cir 1983).

157 *See, e.g.*, Ga Code Ann §51-3-21(1) (1982); Ill Ann Stat ch 70 §32(d) (Smith-Hurd Supp 1981); Kan Stat Ann §58-3202(d) (1976); Neb Rev Stat §37-1008 (1978); Pa Stat Ann tit 68, §477-2(4) (Purdon Supp 1982).

158 *See, e.g.*, Ala Code §35-15-3 (1977); La Rev Stat Ann §9:2791 (West Supp 1981); Minn Stat Ann §87.021(5) (West 1977). *See also* §5.05.

159 *See, e.g.*, Cal Civ Code §846 (West 1982); NY Gen Oblig Law §9-103 (Law Co-op Supp 1981); Ohio Rev Code Ann §1533.18 (Page 1978); Wis Stat Ann §29.68 (West Supp 1982).

160 *See, e.g.*, Idaho Code §36-1604(3) (Supp 1981).

161 *See, e.g.*, Conn Gen Stat Ann §52-557h (West Supp 1982); Del Code Ann tit 7, §5906 (1975); Hawaii Rev Stat §520-5(2) (1976).

162 Neb Rev Stat §37-1005 (1978).

163 Stone Mountain Memorial Assn v Herrington, 225 Ga 746, 171 SE2d 521, 523 (1969); *see also* Smith v United States, 383 F Supp 1076, 1078 (D Wyo 1974), *affd*, 546 F2d 872 (10th Cir 1976). However, one commentator believes that if the only realistic access to a recreational area is by automobile and if the parking fees would be available for the park's upkeep, the payment of parking fees should be considered a charge. Barrett, *Good Sports and*

payments for gas, food, and canoe or inner tube rental[164] are not consideration for using the facilities since these items could have been provided by the
plaintiffs.[165] However, 50 cent hunting permits for small game were held to
be consideration, even when there was no charge to use the park facilities.[166]
Furthermore, payment for permission to camp was consideration for the use
of a cabana and access to a river.[167]

A fee to enter[168] and use a trailer site is an entrance fee and would preclude
application of the statute.[169] However, where there was a charge for using
a ballfield, but a diving injury occurred after the plaintiff left the field, no
consideration was received.[170]

In any event, if a landowner attempted to avoid liability by charging fees for
the use of all facilities rather than for the use of the land, it would, in essence,
be charging an entrance fee and the court should consider it as such.[171]

Payment of Consideration

There is, obviously, no mechanical need to have each plaintiff pay the
defendant. When each person is charged, regardless of who makes actual
payment, the landowner has an equal duty of care to all.[172] Indeed, the
California statute, which is atypical, is broad enough to be construed to
include individuals for whom no fee was received by the landowner, as long
as the landowner received some consideration from other individuals using
the premises for the same purpose.[173]

A citizen's payment of taxes is not consideration for the use of government
land.[174]

Bad Lands: The Application of Washington's Recreational Use Statute Limiting Landowner Liability,
53 Wash L Rev 1, 12 (1977).

164 Jones v United States, 693 F2d 1299, 1303-04 (9th Cir 1982); *but see* Ducey v United
States, 713 F2d 504, 513-14 ((9th Cir 1983).

165 Moss v Department of Natural Resources, 62 Ohio St 2d 138, 404 NE2d 742, 745
(1980).

166 Garfield v United States, 297 F Supp 891, 899 (WD Wis 1969).

167 Graves v United States, 692 F2d 71, 73 (9th Cir 1982).

168 *But see* Wis Stat §29.68 (West Supp 1982) (entrance fee paid to the government is not
consideration).

169 Huth v State, 64 Ohio St 2d 143, 413 NE2d 1201, 1203 (1980).

170 Diodato v Camden County Park Commn, 162 NJ Super 275, 392 A2d 665, 670
(1978).

171 Moss v Department of Natural Resources, 62 Ohio St 2d 138, 404 NE2d 742, 745
(1980).

172 Graves v United States, 692 F2d 71, 73 (9th Cir 1982).

173 *See* Cal Civ Code §846 (West 1982).

174 Hahn v United States, 493 F Supp 57, 59 (MD Pa), *affd without opinion*, 639 F2d 773
(3d Cir 1980); Hamilton v United States, 371 F Supp 230, 234-35 (ED Va 1974); Hahn v
Commonwealth, 18 Pa D&C3d 260, 265 nl (1980); Moore v City of Torrance, 101 Cal App

The commercial value of advertising or goodwill has not usually been construed to be consideration. Accordingly, when a proprietor allows access to land for advertising purposes, there is no charge.[175] Similarly, the goodwill to be derived from signs on the property is not a charge.[176]

The courts have reached inconsistent results in determining whether the limited liability provisions should apply when the injured party did not pay money to the landowner. In *Kesner v Trenton*,[177] the court held there was a charge even when there was no payment. Two girls fell and drowned while wading in a lake. Although the landowner imposed no charge for the use of the lake, the court held that the statute was inapplicable because the landowner: operated a money-making marina (and the girls' father was attempting to rent a boat there); and expected to attract prospective customers by allowing people to swim at no cost.[178]

The decision severely strained the relevant statute, which defined *charge* as the amount of money asked in return for an invitation to enter the land. It was clear that there was no charge to anyone to go swimming.

Furthermore, there was no showing that the girls were going to use the rented boat. In light of that fact, the case suggests that if anyone in a family takes some affirmative steps to pay the landowner for some prospective service, the entire family has paid a charge, and the landowner has no limited liability under the statute. This holding is directly contrary to the result reached in several other decisions.

In *Garfield v United States*, the court held that the statute limited one spouse's recovery for her injuries because she paid no consideration; however, the statute did not apply to her husband since he paid consideration.[179] The *Garfield* court further held that the wife's claim for her mental distress injuries, which resulted from her husband's physical injuries, were limited by the statute because she paid no consideration. Finally, the

---

3d 66, 72, 166 Cal Rptr 192 (1979) (payment of taxes by the parents of an injured child is not consideration).

175 Bourn v Herring, 225 Ga 67, 166 SE2d 89, 92 (1969).

176 Epps v Chattahoochee Brick Co, 140 Ga App 426, 231 SE2d 443, 444 (1976).

177 216 SE2d 880, 885 (W Va 1975).

178 *See also* Copeland v Larson, 46 Wis 2d 337, 174 NW2d 745, 751 (1970) (*valuable consideration* means what constitutes an invitee at common law). The Wisconsin statute was subsequently amended and valuable consideration was defined. It remains unclear whether a different result would occur under the new language since, on its face, the statute does not directly address prospective income.

The statutory definition of consideration in Wisconsin now excludes "payments to landowners either in money or in kind if the total payments do not have an aggregate value in excess of $150 annually." This applies to payments from all users, not just the injured person. Quesenberry v Milwaukee, 106 Wis 2d 685, 317 NW2d 468, 472 (1982).

179 297 F Supp 891, 899-902 (WD Wis 1969); *see also* Stephens v United States, 472 F Supp 998, 1011 (CD Ill 1979).

court held that the husband's damages for loss of his wife's consortium and for her medical expenses were also limited by statute since she had not paid an entrance fee.

The courts have also reached different conclusions regarding the applicability of the statute to a landowner when the landowner's lessee received consideration from the injured party. In *Thomas v Jeane*, the court held that the landowner must receive the consideration before it will be precluded from using the statute's limited liability provisions; payment to the landowner's lessee is insufficient.[180]

However, in *Graves v United States Coast Guard*, the court reached the opposite conclusion.[181] It held that the statute did not require the payment of consideration to the landowner. Payment to the landowner's lessee was sufficient to render the statute inapplicable to the landowner.[182] In a different case, the court held that the landowner received consideration when it charged a racing association $10 to use the land and the association subsequently charged the plaintiff $6 as an entrance fee to participate in a motorcycle race on that land.[183]

The consideration exception to the recreational user statute was also applicable when payment was made to a concessionaire to purchase goods and to rent a boat slip. The landowner was entitled to a percentage, albeit an insignificant one, of the concessionaire's gross receipts,[184] and there was an implicit commitment by the owner to allow individuals to enter the recreational area to use the concession facilities.[185]

§5.19 Children

A few statutes explicitly consider children to be in the category of individuals who have only limited rights against landowners under recreational user statutes.[186] Several other statutes specifically state that they do not reduce a

180 411 So 2d 744, 747 (La Ct App 1982).

181 692 F2d 71 (9th Cir 1982).

182 *But see* Jones v United States, 693 F2d 1299, 1303-04 (9th Cir 1982) (payment to a concessionaire is not consideration to a landowner).

183 Thompson v United States, 592 F2d 1104, 1108 (9th Cir 1979).

184 Ducey v United States, 713 F2d 504, 513-14 (9th Cir 1983) (it was held irrelevant that the landowner was never paid by the concessionaire); *but see* Jones v United States, 693 F2d 1299, 1303-04 (9th Cir 1982) (fee paid to concessionaire was not consideration paid to landowner).

185 Ducey v United States, 713 F2d 504, 513-14 (9th Cir 1983).

186 Ala Code §35-15-21 (Supp 1981); Ill Ann Stat ch 70, §32(e) (Smith-Hurd Supp 1981); SC Code Ann §27-3-20(e) (Law Co-op 1977); *see also* Hawaii Rev Stat §520-2(5) (1976) (house guest). Since a prior Oregon recreational user statute retained the attractive nuisance doctrine, it can be argued the repeal of that statute and its subsequent reenactment without

landowner's liability to children.[187] Most statutes, however, are silent on this point, and the courts have to decide whether recreational user statutes reduce a landowner's liability to children under §339 of the Restatement (Second) of Torts, the attractive nuisance doctrine, or any similar theory.

Several courts have assumed, without clearly analyzing the issue, that children are in the class of individuals owed limited duties by landowners under these recreational user statutes.[188] Other courts have reached the same conclusion by reasoning that the legislature wanted to limit landowners' liability to anyone who gratuitously uses the land.[189]

However, in *Smith v Crown-Zellerbach, Inc*, the court reached the opposite result. It held that repeals by implication are disfavored. Since the state legislature did not affirmatively abolish the attractive nuisance doctrine[190] when it passed the recreational user statute, it would not find an implied repeal of that doctrine.[191]

The court's analysis is weak. The presumption against implied repeal only applies when there are two apparently inconsistent statutes.[192] The theory is that the legislature could have repealed the prior statute, if that were the intended result, rather than pass a new law. This theory has no application when, like here, a legislature is writing on a clean legislative slate. The legislature clearly could have wished to change the existing case law of the attractive nuisance doctrine, and new legislation would have been the route to accomplish that result.

---

that provision evidences a legislative intent that the new statute applies to children. *See* 1963 Or Laws ch 524, §§1-2 (repealed 1971) (formerly codified at Or Rev Stat §30.790).

187 Ind Code Ann §14-2-6-3 (West 1982) (does not affect law of attractive nuisance or invited guests); Minn Stat Ann §87.025 (West 1977) (statute does not apply where trespasser could otherwise maintain an action); SD Comp Laws Ann §20-9-5 (Supp 1979) (does not affect law of attractive nuisance); Tex Rev Civ Stat Ann art 1b (Vernon 1969) (does not modify, extend, or change doctrine of attractive nuisance); Wash Rev Code §4.24.210 (Supp 1982) (does not limit or expand doctrine of attractive nuisance). *See also* Ky Rev Stat Ann §150.645 (Bobbs-Merrill 1980) (nothing in this section limits, in any way, any liability which otherwise exists).

188 *See* Heider v Michigan Sugar Co, 375 Mich 490, 134 NW2d 637 (1965), *cert dismissed*, 385 US 362 (1966); Taylor v Mathews, 40 Mich App 74, 198 NW2d 843, 846 (1972); Magerowski v Standard Oil Co, 274 F Supp 246, 247 (WD Mich 1967).

189 Blair v United States, 433 F Supp 217, 218 (D Nev 1977); Johnson v Stryker Corp, 70 Ill App 3d 717, 388 NE2d 932, 935 (1979); Tallaksen v Ross, 167 NJ Super 1, 400 A2d 485 (1979); Magro v City of Vineland, 148 NJ Super 34, 371 A2d 815, 818 (1977) (explicitly rejecting two prior cases to the contrary); Wirth v Ehly, 93 Wis 2d 433, 287 NW2d 140, 147 (1980). *But cf* Space v National RR Passenger Corp, 555 F Supp 163, 167 (D Del 1983) (state guest statute does not apply to child trespassers).

190 In many jurisdictions the name is a misnomer since there is no requirement that a nuisance must be attractive. *See* Restatement (Second) of Torts §339 (1965).

191 638 F2d 883, 885 (5th Cir 1981).

192 *See* 2A C. Sands, Statutes and Statutory Construction §51.01, at 289 (4th ed 1973).

Some state legislatures explicitly did not want to modify a landowner's present duty of care to children.[193] When a state recreational user statue disclaimed any intent to alter the law of attractive nuisance, it was interpreted to mean that there should be no change in the exceptions to that doctrine either.[194]

Most of the commentators have felt that these statutes were not intended to change a landowner's duty of care to children.[195] It is not self-evident why this interpretation is correct. Because children compose a significant percentage of the population of gratuitous recreational users, the legislatures could easily have reasoned that if landowners' duty to children were not reduced, many landowners would not make their land available for recreational use and the statutes would be ineffective.

In any event, it is evident that many court decisions which limit the scope of recreational user statutes have children as plaintiffs. This may be an indication that courts are not anxious to reduce a landowner's duty of care to children.

---

193 *See, e.g.,* Wash Rev Code §4.24.210 (Supp 1982).

194 Ochampaugh v City of Seattle, 91 Wash 2d 514, 588 P2d 1351, 1356 (1979) (bodies of water are not dangers covered by the attractive nuisance doctrine).

195 *See* Malone, *Torts,* 25 La L Rev 47, 48 (1964) (no one can seriously believe the legislature intended to abolish the attractive nuisance doctrine); J. Page, The Law of Premises Liability §5.20, at 117 (1976).

Common Law Liability of Landowners and Occupiers

6

General Principles of Liability

Specific Recreational Activities

§6.01 Introduction

Traditionally under the common law, a land occupier's[1] duty of care varied

---

[1] Land occupiers, not necessarily landowners, are the beneficiaries of these common law rules. *See* 2 F. Harper & F. James, The Law of Torts §27.2, at 1433 (1956).

along a continuum, depending on the status of the entrant.[2] An invitee,[3] usually someone on the land because of a business relationship with the land occupier, was owed the highest standard of care and could usually recover when injured by the land occupier's negligence. A licensee,[4] usually someone on the land with the permission of the land occupier, was generally owed a lower standard of care. Trespassers,[5] individuals on the land of another without permission, were owed the least care; usually a land occupier's only responsibility to them was to refrain from wilful or wanton acts.[6] Under no circumstances was a land occupier an insurer of the safety of entrants on the land.[7]

Great Britain, the country which originally held that a land occupier's duty of care was dependent on the status of the entrant, abolished the distinctions between invitees and licensees in 1957.[8] Two years later, the United States Supreme Court noted that the traditional method of determining a land occupier's liability was a "semantic morass" and refused to apply the distinctions between invitees and licensees in an admiralty case.[9]

In 1968, the California Supreme Court held in *Rowland v Christian*, a case which did not involve a recreational accident, that a land occupier owed all entrants on the land a duty of due care, thereby abolishing the classification system.[10] Numerous other jurisdictions followed *Rowland* and abolished all distinctions between the entrant's status.[11] Accordingly, in these jurisdictions, absent a statute to the contrary, a land occupier is liable for recreational

---

2 The origins of common law entrant classification system are somewhat uncertain. *See* Comment, *Duty of Owners and Occupiers of Land to Persons Entering the Premises: Should Pennsylvania Abandon the Common Law Approach*, 17 Duq L Rev 153, 154 (1979).

The first case in this country to adopt the classification system was Sweeny v Old Colony & Newport RR, 92 Mass (10 Allen) 368 (1865).

3 *See* §6.02.

4 *See* §6.03.

5 *See* §6.04.

6 *See* §6.06.

7 Barnaby v Rice, 75 AD2d 179, 428 NYS2d 973, 974-75 (1980), *affd without opinion*, 53 NY2d 720, 421 NE2d 846, 439 NYS2d 354 (1981).

8 *See* Occupiers' Liability Act, 1957, 5 & 6 Eliz 2, ch 31.

9 Kermarec v Compagnie Generale Transatlantique, 358 US 625, 631 (1959).

10 69 Cal 2d 108, 443 P2d 561, 70 Cal Rptr 97 (1968).

11 *See, e.g.*, Smith v Arbaugh's Restaurant, Inc, 469 F2d 97 (DC Cir 1972), *cert denied*, 412 US 939 (1973); Mile High Fence Co v Radovich, 175 Colo 537, 489 P2d 308 (1971); Bourg v Redden, 351 So 2d 1300, 1302 (La Ct App 1977); Ovellete v Blanchard, 116 NH 552, 364 A2d 631 (1976); Basso v Miller, 40 NY2d 233, 352 NE2d 868, 386 NYS2d 564 (1976); Mariorenzi v Joseph DiPonte, Inc, 114 RI 294, 333 A2d 127 (1975). *See also* Annot, 22 ALR4th 294 (1983).

accidents caused by its negligence.[12] In addition, several state courts partially followed *Rowland*, abolishing distinctions between invitees and licensees or licensees and trespassers.[13]

At one time it was believed that *Rowland* presaged the modern rule in this area. However, it is now clear that the overwhelming majority of states still determine a land occupier's liability based on the entrant's status.[14]

Even in jurisdictions which abolished the common law classifications for determining the standard of care, the plaintiff's status is relevant in determining the foreseeability of his or her presence on the land and the probability of injury.[15] For example, a school should reasonably have foreseen the presence in its gymnasium of a student from another university who was there without express permission.[16]

Exceptions to the Application of the Classification System

Even in several jurisdictions which retain the classification system, the courts have held that a land occupier has an obligation to exercise reasonable care in the conduct of its activities. The continuum of duties based on the entrant's status only applies to injuries arising out of a *condition* of the property.[17] These courts reason that it is largely irrelevant that a plaintiff was

---

12 *See, e.g.*, Drake v State, 97 Misc 2d 1015, 416 NYS2d 734 (Ct Cl 1979), *aff'd*, 75 AD2d 1016, 432 NYS2d 676 (1980).

13 *See, e.g.*, Geremia v State, 58 Hawaii 502, 573 P2d 107, 111 (1977); Schofield v Merrill, 386 Mass 244, 435 NE2d 339, 341-42 (1982); (no distinction between duties owed to invitees and licensees); Flom v Flom, 291 NW2d 914, 917 (Minn 1980); Antoniewicz v Reszcynski, 70 Wis 2d 836, 236 NW2d 1 (1975). *See also* Conn Gen Stat Ann §52-557a (Supp 1977).
Some commentators have argued that distinctions between licensees and invitees should be abolished. *See* Comment, *The Outmoded Distinction Between Licensees and Invitees*, 22 Mo L Rev 186, 186 (1957).

14 *See, e.g.*, Madison v Deseret Livestock Co, 419 F Supp 914, 918 (D Utah 1976) (Utah law), *aff'd in part, vacated in part*, 574 F2d 1027 (10th Cir 1978); Holcombe v Harris, 143 Ga App 173, 237 SE2d 677 (1977); Huyck v Heckla Mining Co, 101 Idaho 299, 612 P2d 142, 144 (1980); Gerchberg v Loney, 223 Kan 446, 576 P2d 593, 598 (1978); Caroff v Liberty Lumber Co, 146 NJ Super 353, 369 A2d 983, 985 (1977). *See generally* Annot, 22 ALR4th 294 (1983).

15 Johnson v Krueger, 36 Colo App 242, 539 P2d 1296, 1298 (1975); Eddy v Syracuse Univ, 78 AD2d 989, 433 NYS2d 923, 925 (1980).

16 Eddy v Syracuse Univ, 78 AD2d 989, 433 NYS2d 923, 925 (1980). The duty of care of schools is discussed in **ch 4**.

17 Martin v Shea, 432 NE2d 46, 47 (Ind Ct App 1982); Ragnone v Portland School Dist No 1J, 291 Or 617, 633 P2d 1287, 1291 (1981); Bradshaw v Minter, 206 Va 450, 143 SE2d 827, 830 (1965). *See also* Mangione v Dimino, 39 AD2d 128, 332 NYS2d 683, 687 (1972). New York subsequently held that the appropriate standard is always reasonable care under the circumstance. *See* Scurti v City of New York, 40 NY2d 433, 354 NE2d 794, 795, 387 NYS2d 55 (1976); Basso v Miller, 40 NY2d 233, 352 NE2d 868, 386 NYS2d 564, 568 (1976). *See generally* Note, *Landowners' Liability in New Jersey: The Limitation of Traditional Immunities*, 12 Rut LJ 599, 608 (1958).

standing on a defendant's land, when an injury arose from an *activity* of the landowner. For example, a school may be liable for its negligence when a possible licensee, a school employee on medical leave who nevertheless came back to school one day, was injured by a student in an unsupervised gym class.[18]

In addition, a land occupier has a duty to exercise reasonable care to stop or curtail dangerous acts of individuals on the land when they could injure others not on the premises. However, a landowner who could not have reasonably anticipated those dangers was not held liable.[19]

Another exception to the rigid classification system holds that a possessor of land owes a duty of reasonable care to a public officer or employee, e.g., a park ranger, who enters on the land in the performance of a public duty. Though clearly not an invitee, the public officer who suffers harm because of a condition on a part of the land open to the public can hold the land possessor liable for negligence.[20]

Dangerous Condition Created by Others

When a dangerous artificial condition is created by third parties, the land occupier must have failed to act after obtaining actual knowledge of the condition before liability will be imposed.[21] This follows the general rule that a land occupier has no duty to inspect the premises periodically in order to ascertain whether third parties have created dangerous conditions.

Generally, a landowner is not subject to liability for harm caused by a dangerous condition on the land when the condition came into existence after the landowner gave up possession of the land to others.[22] Accordingly, a landowner was not liable when a participant in a motorcycle race was injured because of the allegedly negligent marking of the race course; an event which

---

Some courts have referred to a land occupier's liability for its activities as *active* negligence and its liability for the condition of the property as *passive* negligence. *See* Heald v Cox, 480 SW2d 107, 109 (Mo Ct App 1972).

[18] Ragnone v Portland School Dist No 1J, 291 Or 617, 633 P2d 1287, 1291 (1981).

[19] Sanderson v Beaugh, 367 So 2d 14, 17 (La Ct App 1978).

[20] Caroff v Liberty Lumber Co, 146 NJ Super 353, 369 A2d 983, 987 (1977); Restatement (Second) of Torts §345(2) (1965). *See generally* Comment, *Torts—Abolition of the Distinction Between Licensees and Invitees Entitles All Lawful Visitors To a Standard of Reasonable Care*, 8 Suffolk UL Rev 795, 798-99 (1974).

[21] Caliguire v City of Union, 104 NJ Super 210, 249 A2d 603, 606 (1967), *aff'd*, 53 NJ 182, 249 A2d 577 (1969).

[22] Thompson v United States, 592 F2d 1104, 1109 (9th Cir 1979); Grant v Hipsher, 257 Cal App 2d 375, 64 Cal Rptr 892, 896 (1967); Restatement (Second) of Torts §355 (1965). The exceptions to this general rule are listed in Restatement (Second) of Torts §§357-362 (1965).

occurred after a motorcycle racing association took possession of the land from the landowner.[23]

However, where a landowner leases property knowing that a structural change in the property is necessary to comply with local safety laws, e.g., swimming pools must be surrounded by a fence in some jurisdictions, the owner must comply with those laws.[24] Furthermore, where a tenant makes the structural change, but the change does not comply with the local ordinance and the owner has knowledge of this, the owner has a duty to terminate the tenancy or compel the tenant to comply with the law.[25] Where an owner failed to fulfill this responsibility and a child consequently drowned, the owner was held liable.[26]

Injury Did Not Occur as a Result of a Condition on Defendant's Property

Landowners are not liable when neither the injury nor the events leading up to the injury occurred on their land. In *Barnaby v Rice*,[27] a two-year-old child drowned in a body of water 400 feet behind the defendant's home. The court held that the landowner was not negligent as a matter of law. There was no evidence that the child entered the water by crossing over defendant's land rather than from a neighbor's property. Moreover, the defendant did not create a dangerous condition through mere failure to erect a fence around the land.[28]

Right to Control the Use of the Land

Where a defendant has no right to control the use of property, failure to exercise control will not create liability. Accordingly, a hotel was not liable when a man dove off a seawall into shallow ocean water and seriously injured himself because there was a public easement to use the seawall.[29]

Liability of Commercial and Public Recreational Facilities

The liability of commercial[30] and public[31] recreational facilities is analyzed

---

23 Thompson v United States, 592 F2d 1104, 1109 (9th Cir 1979).

24 Grant v Hipsher, 257 Cal App 2d 375, 64 Cal Rptr 892, 897 (1967).

25 *Id.*

26 *Id.*

27 75 AD2d 179, 428 NYS2d 973 (1980), *affd without opinion*, 53 NY2d 720, 421 NE2d 846, 439 NYS2d 354 (1981).

28 428 NYS2d at 975.

29 Jones v Halekulani Hotel, Inc, 557 F2d 1308, 1310-11 (9th Cir 1977).

30 *See* ch 1.

31 *See* chs 3, 4.

in more detail in other chapters of this book. Although this chapter includes such cases, the primary focus is on the common law liability of homeowners or owners of vacant land, since that topic is not generally discussed elsewhere in the book.[32]

§6.02 Invitees

Definition of Invitee

There are primarily two disparate definitions of an invitee. One definition, usually called the economic benefit test, considers an individual an invitee when a land occupier receives an actual or potential benefit from the individual's entry onto the land.[33] The economic benefit test regards entrance as a quid pro quo. Because the occupier receives an actual or potential pecuniary benefit, there is an obligation to keep the premises reasonably safe.[34]

The second definition, usually called the invitation test, is more widely followed[35] and is applied where the land occupier holds out the premises as suitable for the purpose for which the visitor entered.[36] This test is based on an implied representation by the occupier that the premises will be reasonably safe for those who are encouraged to enter.

Both tests often reach the same result.[37] However, the invitation test, unlike the economic benefit test, would cover an individual's use of governmental or other not-for-profit organizations' recreational facilities.[38]

It is clear from the foregoing definitions that actual receipt of an invitation is largely irrelevant in determining whether an individual is an invitee.[39] In

---

[32] *But see* ch 5.

[33] Restatement (Second) of Torts §§332, 343 (1965); W. Prosser, The Law of Torts §61, at 394 (4th ed 1971). *See generally* Epps v Chattahoochee Brick Co, 140 Ga App 426, 231 SE2d 443, 444 (1976).

[34] *See* Comment, *The Common Law Tort Liability of Owners and Occupiers of Land*, 36 Md L Rev 816, 824 (1977).

[35] *See* W. Prosser, The Law of Torts §61, at 389 (4th ed 1971).

[36] *See* Copeland v Larson, 46 Wis 2d 337, 174 NW2d 745, 748 (1970); *see generally* Raponotti v Burnt-Mill Arms, Inc, 113 NJ Super 173, 273 A2d 372, 376 (1971) (a guest of a tenant at an apartment complex is an invitee).

[37] *See, e.g.,* Mitchell v Gay, 111 Ga App 867, 143 SE2d 568, 572 (1965) (patron at horseback riding facility was an invitee); Lexington Country Club v Stevenson, 390 SW2d 137, 140 (Ky Ct App 1965) (woman hit by golf ball while passenger in car going to country club was an invitee).

[38] *See, e.g.,* Rowland v City of Corpus Christi, 620 SW2d 930, 933-34 (Tex Civ App 1981).

[39] *See generally* Thomas v St Mary's Roman Catholic Church, 283 NW2d 254 (SD 1979) (a basketball player on a visiting team is a business invitee of the school although not personally invited to use the facilities).

fact, social guests, usually recipients of an invitation, are generally considered licensees.[40]

It is also obvious from the definitions that most patrons at commercial recreational facilities are invitees. A more detailed analysis of liability in that situation is given in other chapters of the book.[41] This section focuses primarily on the dividing line between invitees on one hand and licensees, and trespassers on the other and the general duty of care owed invitees.

Members of the public who are invited to enter land for a purpose for which the land is held open are clearly invitees.[42] For example, people who enter an exposition park in response to a general public invitation are invitees.[43]

A spectator at a baseball game who was admitted without an entrance fee was held an invitee, and not a licensee. This was because, pursuant to an advertising plan of the club, he was allowed free admittance because he had purchased a T-shirt with the baseball team's name on it and wore it to the stadium.[44] The court held that the T-shirt was a "semblance of a ticket."[45] However, it was a jury question whether a mother who entered a speedway because of a free pass given to her son, a driver in the race, was an invitee or a licensee.[46]

If a landowner's general invitation is sought to be limited to the particular portion of the premises owned, it must expressly make the limitation apparent to the invitee or obstruct or otherwise segregate the limited portion.[47] A landowner could be liable for injuries to an invitee which occurred on someone else's property if the landowner appeared to control the premises where the injury occurred and failed to exclude this additional property from the invitation.[48]

However, the true owner of the additional property could also be liable for injuries occurring on that land if it knew of the general invitation to enter the land, knew or should have known of the invitation's overbreadth, and failed either to give notice that the general invitation did not cover this property or to guard or warn of the unreasonably dangerous condition on the property.[49]

---

40 *See* Restatement (Second) of Torts §332 comment a (1965); *see also* **§6.04**.

41 *See* **chs 1, 8**.

42 Restatement (Second) of Torts §332(2) (1965).

43 Mesa v Spokane World Exposition, 18 Wash App 609, 570 P2d 157, 159 (1977).

44 Stroud v Bridges, 275 SW2d 503, 505 (Tex Civ App 1955).

45 *Id* 505.

46 Bickford v International Speedway Corp, 654 F2d 1028, 1032 (5th Cir 1981).

47 Mesa v Spokane World Exposition, 18 Wash App 609, 570 P2d 157, 159 (1977).

48 *Id.*

49 *Id.*

A landowner's invitation may be limited to only a portion of the land owned.[50] If the injured party unreasonably strays beyond the area of invitation, his or her status will change from invitee to licensee or trespasser. A plaintiff who climbed over a guardrail and used a bridge as a diving platform, when the bridge was not designed to be used as such and there were signs prohibiting diving, was transformed from an invitee to a licensee or trespasser.[51] However, where there are disputed facts regarding whether the landowner gave adequate notice that a portion of the property was closed to the public, the fact-finder should determine the status of the injured party.[52]

Many courts have held that where a governmental body maintains recreational property which is open to the public, everyone who uses the land for that purpose is an invitee.[53] However, when an individual enters onto government-owned recreational property without at least implied permission, he or she is not an invitee.[54] In *Oliver v City of Atlanta*, the court held that a landowner's chain link fence surrounding the property was dispositive of the landowner's lack of invitation to the public to come on the premises.[55] However, this broad holding should not be followed blindly, because in *Oliver* it was also undisputed that the park was closed to the public and there were several keep-out signs posted.

General Duty of Care

A land occupier owes an invitee a duty to use reasonable care to keep the premises reasonably safe for his or her visit and to warn of any hidden

---

50 *See* City of Lampasas v Roberts, 398 SW2d 612, 615 (Tex Civ App 1966) (to create a zone in a park where children or others are not allowed, the land occupier must fence the property or at least post warning signs).

51 Dougherty v Hernando County, 419 So 2d 679, 681 (Fla Dist Ct App 1982).

52 Egede-Nissen v Crystal Mountain, Inc, 93 Wash 2d 127, 606 P2d 1214, 1218 (1980) (jury question regarding whether ski operator gave adequate notice that the ski lift was closed to the public).

53 *See* Watts v Town of Homer, 301 So 2d 729, 734 (La Ct App) (playground), *cert denied*, 305 So 2d 130 (La 1974); Caldwell v Village of Island Park, 304 NY 268, 107 NE2d 441, 443 (1952) (park); Baker v Lane County, 28 Or App 53, 558 P2d 1247, 1250 (1977), *appeal after remand*, 37 Or App 87, 586 P2d 114, 117 (1978) (fairgrounds); Treps v City of Racine, 73 Wis 2d 611, 243 NW2d 520, 523 (1976) (parking lot in city park). *See generally* Teaney v City of St Joseph, 520 SW2d 705 (Mo Ct App 1975) (park); City of Anadarko v Swain, 42 Okla 741, 142 P 1104 (1914) (park); Paraska v Scranton, 313 Pa 227, 169 A 434, 435 (1933) (park); Ramirez v City of Cheyenne, 34 Wyo 67, 241 P 710 (1925) (playground); W. Prosser, The Law of Torts §61, at 388-90 (4th ed 1971).

54 Smith v United States, 383 F Supp 1076, 1081 (D Wyo 1974) (artificial lake appeared to be abandoned); *but see* Crabtree v Schultz, 57 Ohio App 2d 33, 384 NE2d 1294, 1295-96 (1977) (a girl invited on another's land to exercise their horses and to clear their stable may be an invitee).

55 147 Ga App 790, 250 SE2d 519, 521 (1978).

danger.[56] There is generally no duty to warn of known dangers, obvious dangers, or dangers which should have been observed in the exercise of ordinary care.[57] The possessor of land is not an insurer of the invitee's safety.[58]

A land occupier who knew or should have known of hidden dangerous conditions and failed to warn or guard against those perils is usually liable.[59] A defendant who had actual knowledge of submerged tree stumps and also knew that the water would be used by the public for recreation was liable to an injured plaintiff. The defendant's failure to post warnings of the stumps where divers would see them or prohibit diving in the area of danger was negligence.[60]

In contrast, landowners did not breach their duty of care to a young girl who was injured when her horse was startled by a motorbike when they made it generally known that motorbikes were not to be taken near horses, a neighborhood boy was specifically told not to ride his motorbike in an area where people might be near horses, and the landowners had no knowledge that the neighborhood boy failed to heed this instruction.[61]

Warning of an unreasonably dangerous condition may be insufficient to insulate a land occupier from liability in some situations, e.g., where it is known that a warning would not be effective. In those situations, reasonable care dictates that the occupier should guard against the dangerous condition.[62] For example, a municipality which maintains a swimming pool probably has an obligation, in addition to posting swimming-may-be-dangerous signs, to provide safety and rescue equipment as well as lifeguards.[63]

The possessor of land must also exercise reasonable care to eliminate the danger of invitees being injured by the conduct of third parties.[64] However, when there was no actual knowledge, or even a reason to believe that there

---

56 Smith v United States, 383 F Supp 1076, 1081 (D Wyo 1974); Cornutt v Bolin, 404 So 2d 38, 40 (Ala 1981); Rowland v City of Corpus Christi, 620 SW2d 930, 933 (Tex Civ App 1981); Ga Code Ann §51-3-1 (1982); *see generally* James, *Tort Liability of Occupiers of Land: Duties Owed to Licensees and Invitees*, 63 Yale LJ 605 (1954); Comment, *Duty of Owners and Occupiers of Land to Persons Entering the Premises: Should Pennsylvania Abandon the Common Law Approach*, 17 Duq L Rev 153, 156 (1979).

57 Rice v Florida Power & Light Co, 363 So 2d 834, 839 (Fla Dist Ct App 1978) (university was entitled to summary judgment where a pilot in a model airplane was electrocuted as he hit uninsulated power lines over university property); *see also* **§6.09**.

58 Ambrose v Kent Island Yacht Club, Inc, 22 Md App 133, 321 A2d 805, 807 (1974).

59 Hulet v United States, 328 F Supp 335, 338 (D Idaho 1971); Rice v Florida Power & Light Co, 363 So 2d 834, 839 (Fla Dist Ct App 1978).

60 Stephens v United States, 472 F Supp 998, 1013 (CD Ill 1979).

61 Crabtree v Shultz, 57 Ohio App 2d 33, 384 NE2d 1294, 1296 (1977).

62 *See* James, *Tort Liability of Occupiers of Land: Duties Owed to Licensees and Invitees*, 63 Yale LJ 605, 626-27 (1954).

63 *See* §§3.17, 3.18.

64 Ambrose v Kent Island Yacht Club, Inc, 22 Md App 133, 321 A2d 805, 807 (1974).

was danger, this duty was not breached.[65] Accordingly, when a yacht club was unaware of the danger of children throwing a baseball back and forth at a high speed, the club was entitled to summary judgment when another child was injured as a result of an errant throw.[66]

§6.03 Licensees

Definition of Licensee

A licensee is a person who enters on or uses another's premises with the express or implied permission of the owner or person in control.[67] Permission may be implied where the owner acquiesces in the known customary use of property by the public.[68] Many times, licensees are referred to with the pejorative adjective of *bare*, *naked*, or *mere*. Use of these nonsubstantive adjectives may indicate that the court is not going to weigh the licensee's interest highly.

Duty of Care

The duties a land occupier owes to licensees differ depending on which state law applies. The Restatement (Second) of Torts provides that a possessor of land is subject to liability for bodily harm to gratuitous licensees by a natural or artificial condition thereon if: (1) it knows of the condition and realizes that it involves an unreasonable risk to them and has reason to believe that they will not discover the condition or realize the risk; and (2) it invites or permits them to enter or remain upon the land, without exercising reasonable care (a) to make the conditions reasonably safe or (b) to warn of the condition and the risk involved.[69]

Generally, a prerequisite for liability under the Restatement (Second) of Torts is that the landowner *knew* of the unsafe condition.[70] The landowner's

---

65 *Id.*

66 331 A2d at 808.

67 Cox v Hayes, 34 Mich App 527, 532, 192 NW2d 68, 70-71 (1971); Rowland v City of Corpus Christi, 620 SW2d 930, 933 (Tex Civ App 1981); Ga Code Ann §51-3-2 (1982); *see generally* James, *Tort Liability of Occupiers of Land: Duties Owed to Licensees and Invitees*, 63 Yale LJ 605 (1954).

68 Thone v Nicholson, 84 Mich App 538, 269 NW2d 665, 669 (1978).

69 Restatement (Second) of Torts §342 (1965). A few states continue to follow the First Restatement of Torts. *See, e.g.,* Brown v Lesh, 604 SW2d 636, 638 (Mo Ct App 1980) (injury from swing set).

70 However, a few courts have held that actual realization is unnecessary; liability attachs when the risk of harm is reasonably forseeable. *See, e.g.,* Madison v Deseret Livestock Co, 419 F Supp 914, 918 (D Utah 1976) (Utah law), *affd in part, vacated in part,* 574 F2d 1027 (10th Cir 1978).

permission to allow entry does not necessitate inspection of the premises to discover unknown dangers.[71] Since a licensee receives the use of the premises as a gift, he or she has no right to demand that the land be made safe.

The land occupier usually has a duty not to injure a licensee wilfully or wantonly.[72] Likewise, there is a duty not to injure negligently a licensee after discovering the licensee is in peril.[73]

Some courts have held that a land occupier owes no duty to warn a licensee of a potentially dangerous condition unless the occupier does some positive act that creates a new hidden danger, pitfall, or trap which the licensee could not avoid by the use of reasonable care and skill.[74] A defendant who knew that children played in a pond and had been warned of the potential dangers to the children was held not liable when a child drowned because the defendant had not taken any affirmative steps amounting to wilfulness.[75] In some cases it is a question of fact whether a landowner created a hidden danger, e.g., whether placing enamel paint on a patio around a pool may have increased the risk of slipping.[76]

Most courts have held that a land occupier's duty of care to licensees extends to situations where the occupier has actual knowledge of dangers which would not reasonably be observed by others.[77] By extending permission to enter the land, the land occupier represents that it is as safe as it appears to be, and

---

[71] W. Prosser, The Law of Torts §60, at 376 (4th ed 1971).

[72] Some states have codified this low standard of care. *See, e.g.,* Ga Code Ann §51-3-2 (1982); *see also* Del Code Ann tit 25, §1501 (Supp 1982) (no cause of action unless wilful or wanton act). The Delaware statute applies only when no consideration was given. When a father visited his daughter's house and his payments to her were gifts, not money given in consideration of being able to visit her, the statute was applicable. *See* Whitney v Brann, 394 F Supp 1, 8 (D Del 1975), *aff'd without opinion,* 530 F2d 966 (3d Cir), *cert denied,* 426 US 922 (1976).

For an analysis of what constitutes wilful or wanton conduct, see §6.06.

[73] Bryant v Morley, 406 So 2d 394, 395 (Ala 1981); McMullan v Butler, 346 So 2d 950, 951 (Ala 1977); Barbre v Indianapolis Water Co, 400 NE2d 1142, 1146 (Ind Ct App 1980) (diving into shallow water); McCurry v YMCA, 210 Neb 278, 313 NW2d 689, 691 (1981) (hole in basketball court).

[74] *See, e.g.,* Wright v Alabama Power Co, 355 So 2d 322, 325 (Ala 1978).

[75] Montega Corp v Grooms, 128 Ga App 333, 196 SE2d 459 (1973).

[76] Bisnett v Mowder, 114 Ariz 213, 560 P2d 68, 70 (Ct App 1977).

[77] *See* Epling v United States, 453 F2d 327, 330 (9th Cir 1971) (Ariz law); Hulet v United States, 328 F Supp 335, 338 (D Idaho 1971); Carlson v Tucson Racquet & Swim Club, 127 Ariz 247, 619 P2d 756, 757 n1 (Ct App 1980) (must warn of known hidden perils or traps); Washington v Trend Mills, Inc, 121 Ga App 659, 175 SE2d 111, 113 (1970); West v Faubro, 66 Ill App 3d 815, 384 NE2d 457, 459 (1978); Rowland v City of Corpus Christi, 620 SW2d 930, 933, 935 (Tex Civ App 1981), *writ ref nre* (defendant had no knowledge of dangerous conditions on bottom of bay so was not liable); City of Houston v Riggins, 586 SW2d 188, 192 (Tex Civ App 1978), *writ ref nre*; Comment, *Duty of Owners and Occupiers of Land to Persons Entering the Premises: Should Pennsylvania Abandon the Common Law Approach,* 17 Duq L Rev 153, 155-56 (1979).

when he or she knows that it is not, failure to give a warning appears to be "something like fraud."[78] Nevertheless, a landowner who allowed cement blocks to edge past a parking lot did not act unreasonably because this posed a slight risk of anything more serious than a minor injury.[79]

A few courts have imposed a higher duty of care. For example, it has been held that a land occupier has a duty to anticipate reasonably a licensee's presence and must use reasonable care to prevent the licensee from being injured.[80] At the other end of the continuum, one court held that a possessor of land owes no duty to a licensee with respect to "a mere dangerous statical condition of the premises"[81]—a phrase which defies understanding. In that case, the court upheld a demurrer to a complaint alleging that a young child drowned in a residential pool because the doors leading to a pool were left open.

In any event, a jury instruction which gave the wrong standard of care was reversible error.[82]

§6.04   —Social Guests

Courts have reached inconsistent results regarding the status of social guests. Although some decisions have labelled social guests as invitees,[83] most have considered them licensees.[84]

---

78 W. Prosser, The Law of Torts §60, at 381 (4th ed 1971).

79 West v Faubro, 66 Ill App 3d 815, 384 NE2d 457, 459 (1978).

80 *See, e.g.*, Wren v Harrison, 165 Ga App 847, 303 SE2d 67, 70 (1983) ("It is usually wilful or wanton not to exercise ordinary care to prevent injuring a licensee who is actually known to be, or reasonably is expected to be, within range of a dangerous act being done"); Herring v Hauck, 118 Ga App 623, 165 SE2d 198, 199 (1968).

81 *See, e.g.*, Handiboe v McCarthy, 114 Ga App 541, 151 SE2d 905, 907 (1966); *see also* Barbre v Indianapolis Water Co, 400 NE2d 1142, 1146 (Ind Ct App 1980) (not liable for any defects in the condition of the land).

The *Handiboe* court's ruling has now been modified regarding child licensees. *See* Gregory v Johnson, 249 Ga 151, 289 SE2d 232 (1982).

82 Holland Builders, Inc v Leck, 395 So 2d 579, 581 (Fla Dist Ct App), *petition dismissed*, 402 So 2d 610 (Fla 1981).

83 *See, e.g.*, Chauvin v Atlas Ins Co, 166 So 2d 581, 583 (La Ct App 1964) (swimming guest). *But see* Lear v United States Fire Ins Co, 392 So 2d 786, 788 (La Ct App 1980) (status is not dispositive of duty owed). *See also* Christensen v Potratz, 100 Idaho 352, 597 P2d 595, 598 (1979) (social guest, a hunter, was owed duty of reasonable care by host, owner of camper); Wood v Camp, 284 So 2d 691, 695 (Fla 1973) (social guests are entitled reasonable care under the circumstances); Conn Gen Stat Ann §52-557a (West Supp 1982) (the standard of care owed to a social invitee shall be the same as that owed a business invitee).

Several commentators have argued that social guests should be treated as invitees. *See, e.g.*, Note, *Torts—Duty of Occupier to Social Guests*, 19 La L Rev 906, 910 (1959); Comment, *Status of the Social Guest: A New Look*, 7 Wm & Mary L Rev 313, 318-20 (1966) (ease of obtaining homeowner liability insurance supports a higher duty of care).

84 *See, e.g.*, United States v Marshall, 391 F2d 880, 883 (1st Cir 1968) (PR law); Madison v Deseret Livestock Co, 419 F Supp 914, 917 (D Utah 1976) (invitation to pheasant hunt),

Social guests of a tenant in an apartment building are usually classified as invitees while using the common walkways and common facilities.[85] However, when a tenant's social guest was injured while taking an unconventional path to the pool, viz., behind a dumpster, over a ladder, and over uneven terrain, rather than using a walkway, the apartment owner was not negligent since the guests conduct was not reasonably forseeable.[86]

Furthermore, when a guest goes beyond the area of invitation the guest becomes a trespasser or licensee, depending on whether he or she goes there with the consent of the apartment owner.[87] Accordingly, when a guest climbed onto a retaining wall and dove into an apartment pool, knowing that it was not open for tenant use, the guest was a trespasser.[88] Even without actual knowledge that the pool was closed, the decrepit condition of a pool filled with algae, scum, beer cans, and dead birds was notice that the pool was not presently open for use.[89]

§6.05 Trespassers

Definition of Trespasser

A trespasser is a person who enters or remains upon land in the possession of another without the possessor's consent or a privilege to do so.[90] Although

---

affd in part, vacated in part, 574 F2d 1027 (10th Cir 1978); Bryant v Morley, 406 So 2d 394, 395 (Ala 1981); McMullan v Butler, 346 So 2d 950, 951 (Ala 1977) (swimming pool guest); Bisnett v Mowder, 114 Ariz 213, 560 P2d 68, 69 (Ct App 1977) (swimming pool guest); Barry v Cantrell, 150 Ga App 439, 258 SE2d 61 (1979) (injured while sitting on hammock); Ramsey v Mercer, 142 Ga App 827, 237 SE2d 450 (1977) (injured by a gun at a private residence); Telak v Maszczenski, 248 Md 476, 237 A2d 434, 438 (1968) (classified guest at swimming pool as licensee by invitation); Brown v Lesh, 604 SW2d 636, 638 (Mo Ct App 1980) (used residential swing set).

One commentator has argued that this is the preferable approach. *See* James, *Tort Liability of Occupiers of Land: Duties Owed to Licensees and Invitees*, 63 Yale LJ 605, 611-12 (1954) (noting, however, that the prevalence of insurance may militate in favor of a higher standard of care).

85 *See generally* Raponotti v Burnt-Mill Arms, Inc, 113 NJ Super 173, 273 A2d 372, 376 (1971); Restatement (Second) of Torts §360 (1965). *But see* Pedone v Fontainebleau Corp, 322 So 2d 79, 80 (Fla Dist Ct App 1975) (a trespasser does not become an invitee because he talked with a hotel guest).

86 Hancock v Alabama Home Mortgage Co, Inc, 393 So 2d 969, 970-71 (Ala 1981).

87 *See* Toole v Levitt, 492 SW2d 230, 234 (Tenn Ct App 1972).

88 *Id.*

89 *Id.*

90 West v Faubro, 66 Ill App 3d 815, 384 NE2d 457, 458 (1978); Rowland v City of Corpus Christi, 620 SW2d 930, 933 (Tex Civ App 1981) ("without any right, lawful authority, or express or implied invitation, permission or license"); Restatement (Second) of Torts §329 (1965).

a trespasser's status can change, a conversation a trespasser has with a hotel guest near a hotel pool is insufficient to transform his or her status from a trespasser into an invitee.[91]

The placement of chain link fences and keep-out signs around property shows an owner's lack of consent to the public to use the property. Individuals who nevertheless enter upon the property are trespassers.[92] One court stated that a fence which surrounds a pool "informs those who come thereon that what lies beyond is private."[93]

It is sometimes difficult to know whether an individual had a landowner's consent to use some, but not all, of the property. Where there were no warning signs or barriers indicating a boundary line dividing a park from contiguous property being developed for a softball field, and many children used the area under development as a park, there was a question of fact whether the injured party was a trespasser on the property being developed.[94]

One privilege which allows entry onto the land of another is that of private necessity, i.e., where the entry is for the purpose of advancing or protecting one's interest.[95] When this privilege applies, the entrant is a licensee.[96] Accordingly, a bicyclist who swerved onto another's property to avoid an automobile, and hit a concrete block covered by grass, was a licensee, and not a trespasser.[97]

General Duty of Care

Generally, a defendant owes no duty to a trespasser except to refrain from wilfully or wantonly injuring him or her.[98] This low standard

---

91 Pedone v Fontainebleau Corp, 322 So 2d 79, 80 (Fla Dist Ct App 1975).

92 Oliver v City of Atlanta, 147 Ga App 790, 250 SE2d 519, 521 (1978).

93 Earnest v Regent Pool, Inc, 288 Ala 63, 257 So 2d 313, 315 (1972).

94 Caine v New Castle County, 379 A2d 1112, 1115 (Del 1977).

95 West v Faubro, 66 Ill App 3d 815, 384 NE2d 457, 458 (1978); Restatement (Second) of Torts §329 comment a (1965).

96 West v Faubro, 66 Ill App 3d 815, 384 NE2d 457, 458 (1978); Restatement (Second) of Torts §345 (1965).

97 West v Faubro, 66 Ill App 3d 815, 384 NE2d 457, 459 (1978).

98 Locke v Liquid Air Corp, 725 F2d 1331, 1334 (11th Cir 1984) (Ala law); Carlson v Tucson Racquet & Swim Club, 127 Ariz 247, 619 P2d 756, 758 (Ct App 1980); Earnest v Regent Pool, Inc, 288 Ala 63, 257 So 2d 313, 315 (1972); Oliver v City of Atlanta, 147 Ga App 790, 250 SE2d 519, 521 (1978); Huyck v Heckla Mining Co, 101 Idaho 299, 612 P2d 142, 144 (1980); Osterman v Peters, 260 Md 313, 272 A2d 21, 22 (1971); Schofield v Merrill, 386 Mass 244, 435 NE2d 339, 340-41 (1982) (landowner granted summary judgment against adult trespasser severely injured while jumping into water at a quarry); Ausmer v Sliman, 336 So 2d 730, 731 (Miss 1976); Latimer v City of Clovis, 83 NM 610, 495 P2d 788, 794 (Ct App 1972); Starr v Clapp, 40 NC App 142, 252 SE2d 220, 221, *affd*, 298 NC 275, 258 SE2d 348 (1979); Toole v Levitt, 492 SW2d 230, 233 (Tenn Ct App 1972); Rowland v City of Corpus Christi, 620 SW2d 930, 933 (Tex Civ App 1981); Ochampaugh v City of

of care is not easily breached.[99]

Dean Prosser believes that the explanation why land occupiers owe trespassers a limited duty of care is because, in a country based on private ownership, it is considered desirable policy to allow the land possessor to use the land in its own discretion, without the burden of watching for and protecting those who come there without permission or right.[100] However, this explanation is not totally satisfactory. All land occupiers, even adverse possessors,[101] are entitled to these special rules of limited liability. There is no a priori reason why adverse possessors, basically long-term trespassers, should be favored over short-term trespassers in a system based on private ownership of property.

Commentators have severely criticized the reasons cited for the limited duty owed trespassers.[102] Furthermore, because of an increasing feeling that human safety is of more importance than a land occupier's unrestricted freedom to use its land as is deemed fit, which usually has meant a desire to be free from the burdens of taking precautions, numerous exceptions to the limited duty owed trespassers have emerged.[103]

One of the most important exceptions applies where the trespasser is discovered or should reasonably have been anticipated. In this situation, the landowner's duty is usually to warn of known dangers not open to ordinary observation.[104] Indeed, one court has stated that a duty of reasonable care is owed under these circumstances.[105]

A court may hold that a land occupier acted reasonably by warning of the danger. In *Grant v City of Duluth*, the court reversed a $224,000 verdict for a trespasser who was killed when he hit a chain while riding down a slide

---

Seattle, 91 Wash 2d 514, 588 P2d 1351, 1353 (1979). *See generally* James, *Tort Liability of Occupiers of Land: Duties Owed to Trespassers*, 63 Yale LJ 144 (1953); Comment, *Duty of Owners and Occupiers of Land to Persons Entering the Premises: Should Pennsylvania Abandon the Common Law Approach*, 17 Duq L Rev 153, 155 (1979).

Some state statutes impose the same low standard of care. *See, e.g.,* Del Code Ann tit 25, §2501 (Supp 1982) (no cause of action unless wilful or wanton act).

99 *See, e.g.,* Pedone v Fontainebleau Corp, 322 So 2d 79, 80 (Fla Dist Ct App 1975) (hotel did not act wilfully or wantonly when it failed to provide lifeguards or adequate safety equipment at a pool and a trespasser drowned). For a more detailed discussion of what constitutes wilful or wanton conduct, see **§6.06**.

100 W. Prosser, The Law of Torts §58, at 359 (4th ed 1971).

101 *See* Restatement (Second) of Torts §328E & comment a (1965).

102 2 F. Harper & F. James, The Law of Torts §27.3, at 1436-40 (1956); W. Prosser, The Law of Torts §58, at 358-59 (4th ed 1971).

103 W. Prosser, The Law of Torts §58, at 360 (4th ed 1971). The major exceptions are listed in Restatement (Second) of Torts §§334-339 (1965).

104 Pedone v Fontainebleau Corp, 322 So 2d 79, 80 (Fla Dist Ct App 1975); Latimer v City of Clovis, 83 NM 610, 495 P2d 788, 794 (Ct App 1972).

105 Latimer v City of Clovis, 83 NM 610, 495 P2d 788, 794 (1972).

at a closed amusement park.[106] The court held that even if the amusement park knew or should have known that trespassers used the equipment when the park closed at night, there was no duty to maintain the premises in a reasonably safe condition. In this case, reasonable care was used to warn of the dangerous conditions, viz., the amusement park surrounded the slide with a six-foot fence and posted no-trespassing and danger signs.[107]

A second important exception to the land occupier's otherwise low standard of care is applied when the trespasser is a child.[108]

Not all states have adopted these two exceptions that increase the standard of care owed trespassers. A few jurisdictions have held that a land occupier owes no higher duty than to refrain from wilful or wanton injury to known trespassers[109] or to child trespassers.[110]

It is clear that a defendant must be the possessor of property before he or she can limit the duty owed to trespassers. A defendant who placed a cable across a dirt path on someone else's property was a trespasser, as was the motorcyclist who struck the cable. Therefore the defendant could not rely on the motorcyclist's status as a trespasser to limit responsibility for the injury.[111]

A jury instruction which gave the wrong standard of care was reversible error.[112]

§6.06 — Wilful or Wanton Acts

Wilful or wanton acts occur when the land occupier knows of the probable consequences of its acts but acts recklessly or with indifference to the results.[113] Obviously, a wilful or wanton act requires more than negligence.

There is no wilful or wanton act unless the land occupier knew that the probable consequences of the act would result in injury.[114] This test must be applied using foresight, not hindsight. Accordingly, a landowner was not

---

106 672 F2d 677, 680 (8th Cir 1982).

107 *Id.*

108 *See* §6.07.

109 Oliver v City of Atlanta, 147 Ga App 790, 250 SE2d 519, 521 (1978).

110 *See* Osterman v Peters, 260 Md 313, 272 A2d 21, 22 (1971); *see also* §6.07.

111 McLamb v Jones, 23 NC App 670, 209 SE2d 854, 856 (1974).

112 Holland Builders, Inc v Leck, 395 So 2d 579, 581 (Fla Dist Ct App), *petition dismissed*, 402 So 2d 610 (Fla 1981).

113 McDonnell v Flaherty, 636 F2d 184, 187 (7th Cir 1980) (Ind law); Boyce v Pi Kappa Alpha Holding Corp, 476 F2d 447, 452 (5th Cir 1973) (Fla law); Starr v Clapp, 40 NC App 142, 252 SE2d 220, 221, *affd*, 298 NC 275, 258 SE2d 348 (1979). The appellate decision in *Starr* is entitled to no precedential weight in North Carolina since it was affirmed by an equally divided supreme court. *See* 258 SE2d at 350.

114 Mims v Brown, 49 Ala App 643, 275 So 2d 159, 161 (1973).

liable when a 13-year-old boy climbed onto a barbeque pit cover and was injured diving into a pool. The landowner was not present when the injury occurred, had no knowledge that anyone had previously dived into the pool from the barbeque cover, and had not placed the barbeque cover near the pool so that it could be used as diving board.[115]

Actions that would not be considered a breach of duty toward an adult may be considered wilful and wanton when applied to a child.[116] For example, a landowner may be liable for leaving young children unsupervised in the backyard when one gate leading to the swimming pool was open.[117]

The failure to warn or guard against obvious dangers is usually not negligence; a fortiori it is not a wilful or wanton act. Courts have usually found the dangers of swimming and diving to have been understood by the plaintiff.[118] For example, in *Carlson v Tucson Racquet & Swim Club*,[119] a 16-year-old boy who was not a member or guest of a member of a private club used the club's swimming pool and sustained a major permanent injury in a diving accident. The court affirmed a summary judgment for the club since the plaintiff, a trespasser or licensee, was owed a limited duty, and the club did not wilfully or intentionally injure him or fail to warn of a hidden peril in the pool.[120]

Baseball

There was no liability when a 13-year-old was injured when he put his hand in a conveyor to retrieve a baseball. Even if the defendant should have anticipated the presence of children, there was no wilful or wanton conduct in operating an unguarded conveyor belt near a vacant lot.[121]

Bicycling

The mere failure to warn bicyclists of hidden, sharp debris lying alongside a bicycle path was not wilful or wanton misconduct as a matter of law.[122] To be successful, a plaintiff would have to show, at a minimum, that there was a probability of falling from his or her bicycle at that point in the path.

---

115 Herring v Hauck, 118 Ga App 623, 165 SE2d 198, 199 (1968).

116 Adler v Copeland, 105 So 2d 594, 596 (Fla Dist Ct App 1958).

117 *Id.*

118 *See, e.g.,* Carlson v Tucson Racquet & Swim Club, 127 Ariz 247, 619 P2d 756 (Ct App 1980).

119 *Id.*

120 *Id.*

121 Washington v Trend Mills, Inc, 121 Ga App 659, 175 SE2d 111, 113 (1970) (also held no liability under the recreational user statute).

122 Smith v Goldman, 53 Ill App 3d 362, 368 NE2d 1052, 1055 (1977).

Boating

There was no wilful or wanton conduct when a plaintiff's boat hit a partially submerged barge because the defendant had earlier told the plaintiff that he was on private property and instructed him to leave.[123]

Motorcycling

An adult motorcyclist who was injured by riding into a barbed wire fence on a construction project could not recover since the defendant's actions in placing a fence there and in failing to warn of it were not wilful or wanton.[124] There was no evidence that the defendants were aware or should have been aware of persistent trespassers where the fence was located. Furthermore, the road was clearly not prepared for public use; it was impassable in part and blocked by piles of boulders.

Swimming and Diving

In numerous instances of swimming and diving accidents, the landowner has been exonerated because it did not act with a sufficient degree of misconduct.[125] An apartment owner committed no wilful or wanton injury by leaving a cleaning net near a pool where a trespassing child tripped on it, fell, rolled into the pool, and drowned.[126] There also was no wilful or wanton conduct when a residential swimming pool was left filled with water while the owners traveled for an extended period of time.[127] In a different case, allegations that the defendant failed to provide adequate lighting, to fence and lock the pool, or to warn that the pool was not filled with water were insufficient to show wilful conduct.[128]

Many local governmental bodies have enacted ordinances requiring swimming pools to be properly fenced. Some courts have held that the failure to comply with the law to erect a fence and gate around a residential swimming pool is not only evidence of negligence, but also possibly tantamount to the

---

123 Votava v Material Serv Corp, 74 Ill App 3d 208, 392 NE2d 768, 772 (1979).

124 Denton v L. W. Vail Co, Inc, 23 Or App 28, 541 P2d 511, 515 (1975); *see also* §6.14.

125 *See, e.g.,* Epps v Chattahoochee Brick Co, 140 Ga App 426, 231 SE2d 443, 445 (1976).

126 Ausmer v Sliman, 336 So 2d 730, 731 (Miss 1976).

127 Osterman v Peters, 260 Md 313, 272 A2d 21, 23 (1971). *See also* Poston v Vanderlee, 144 Ga App 833, 242 SE2d 727 (1978) (landowner was entitled to summary judgment in a child drowning case even though the pool was unfenced, the ladder providing access to pool was in place, and the owner was aware children played in the area). The *Poston* decision may have been incorrectly decided since it appears from the undisputed facts that a jury could infer a wilful or wanton act.

128 Boyce v Pi Kappa Alpha Holding Corp, 476 F2d 447, 452 (5th Cir 1973) (Florida law).

infliction of intentional, wilful, and wanton injury subjecting the owner to liability to a trespasser.[129] However, other courts have concluded that fences and gates which are not in compliance with local codes are not dispositive of whether the landowner committed a wilful or wanton act.[130] The failure to construct a swimming pool to the minimum specifications recommended by a private association is not negligence per se, much less a wilful or wanton act.[131]

The dangers of varying depths, sharp drop-offs, and shallow shorelines are inherent in outdoor bodies of water.[132] Accordingly, the owners of a reservoir were entitled to summary judgment because they did not act wantonly in failing to warn of or to eliminate such dangers in a case where a plaintiff dove into shallow water and was seriously injured.[133] Courts have also held that owners of land containing outdoor bodies of water did not act wantonly when they failed to take any steps to reduce the risk of injury even though they knew of the presence of trespassing children and knew of the danger posed by the body of water.[134]

§6.07   Children

Background

There has long been a strong judicial sentiment that the harsh results reached in cases of injured trespassers should be ameliorated when the plaintiffs were children.[135] Even when it was obvious that land occupiers had no duty to individuals coming on their land, except to refrain from wilful or wanton acts, social policy required that children be treated differently because of the value of their lives and their lessened ability to protect themselves.

---

129 Healy v City of New Rochelle, 25 AD2d 446, 266 NYS2d 861, 863 (1966). The *Healy* court may have stretched to find a wilful act because the land occupier breached no duty of care at that time, absent a finding of wilfullness. New York subsequently abolished the distinctions between the status of entrants, thereby allowing a licensee to recovery for the land occupier's negligence. *See* Basso v Miller, 40 NY2d 233, 352 NE2d 868, 386 NYS2d 564 (1976).

130 *See* Boyce v Pi Kappa Alpha Holding Corp, 476 F2d 447, 453 (5th Cir 1973) (Florida law); Osterman v Peters, 260 Md 313, 272 A2d 21, 23 (1971).

131 Chauvin v Atlas Ins Co, 166 So 2d 581, 583-84 (La Ct App 1964).

132 Barbre v Indianapolis Water Co, 400 NE2d 1142 (Ind Ct App 1980).

133 *See id* 1146.

134 *See, e.g.,* Locke v Liquid Air Corp, 725 F2d 1331, 1337 (11th Cir 1984) (Alabama law); Cox v Alabama Water Co, 216 Ala 35, 112 So 352 (1927).

135 *See generally* Prosser, *Trespassing Children*, 47 Cal L Rev 427 (1959).

Indeed, in 1873, the United States Supreme Court in *Sioux City & Pacific Railroad v Stout*, a decision far ahead of its time, recognized that land occupiers owed a duty of reasonable care to child trespassers.[136] In *Stout*, the Court affirmed a verdict for the plaintiff, a child who had trespassed on another's land and injured himself while playing with a railroad turntable as a result of the defendant's negligence.

Stout was not quickly followed in the state courts. In fact, even courts which increased a landowner's duty to trespassing children did not directly adopt the straightforward analysis in *Stout*. Rather, they fashioned an *attractive nuisance* doctrine which generally required that the child must have been *attracted* to an unreasonably dangerous instrumentality or condition before a land occupier's duty of care increased beyond merely refraining from committing wilful or wanton acts.[137]

The First Restatement of Torts, published by the American Law Institute in 1934, radically altered the law in this area. It did not restate the extant law in this area but rather adopted a new position. It held that land occupiers were liable to young child trespassers for artificial conditions maintained on the land if:

1. The land occupier knew or should have known that such children were likely to trespass

2. The landowner realized or should have realized that the condition created an unreasonable risk of serious harm

3. The young children did not realize the risk

4. The utility of maintaining the condition is slight as compared to the risk of injury[138]

This section of the Restatement received widespread acceptance and was adopted by numerous state courts.

In 1965, the Restatement (Second) of Torts was published. Section 339 of that Restatement provides:

---

136 84 US (17 Wall) 657 (1874). The decision is only of historical interest now since *Erie RR v Tompkins*, 304 US 64 (1938) holds that state law, not federal law, should be applied in such instances.

137 *See generally* J. Page, The Law of Premises Liability §2.9, at 15 (1976). In fact, Justice Holmes in *United Zinc & Chem Co v Britt*, 258 US 268 (1922) adopted the allurement requirement of the attractive nuisance doctrine. The *Britt* court held that a land occupier was not liable when a child died from swimming in a poisoned pool because the child did not see the pool until after he trespassed. This case is not representative of one of Justice Holmes's better opinions, and it was effectively overruled a few years later. *See Best v District of Columbia*, 291 US 411 (1934).

138 *See* Restatement of the Law of Torts §339 (1934).

A possessor of land is subject to liability for physical harm to children trespassing thereon caused by an artificial condition upon the land if:

(1) The place where the condition exists is one upon which the possessor knows or has reason to know that the children are likely to trespass; and

(2) The condition is one of which the possessor knows or has reason to know and which he realizes or should realize will involve an unreasonable risk of death or serious bodily harm to such children; and

(3) The children because of their youth do not discover the condition or realize the risk involved in intermeddling with it or in coming within the area made dangerous by it; and

(4) The utility to the possessor of maintaining the condition and the burden of eliminating the danger are slight as compared with the risk to children involved; and

(5) The possessor fails to exercise reasonable care to eliminate the danger or otherwise to protect the children.

Whether the conditions of §339 are met is usually a question of fact for the jury.[139]

Numerous states have adopted §339 as a correct statement of their law.[140] However, some courts still cling to the attractive nuisance doctrine,[141] and a few courts hold that landowners owe no duty of due care to trespassers of any age.[142]

---

139 Mascarena v Booth, 174 Mont 11, 568 P2d 182, 185 (1977).

140 Gregory v Johnson, 249 Ga 151, 289 SE2d 232, 235 (1982); Crawford v Pacific W Mobile Estates, Inc, 548 SW2d 216, 219 (Mo Ct App 1977); Baker v Lane County, 28 Or App 53, 558 P2d 1247, 1249 (1977), *appeal after remand*, 37 Or App 87, 586 P2d 114 (1978);
Metropolitan Govt v Counts, 541 SW2d 133, 136 (Tenn 1976); McWilliams v Guzinski, 71 Wis 2d 57, 237 NW2d 437, 438-39 (1976); Mass Gen Laws ch 231, §85Q (Supp 1984) (duty to child trespassers); Note, *A New Beginning For the Attractive Nuisance Doctrine in Georgia*, 34 Mercer L Rev 433, 433 (1982) (citing cases which show that a majority of the states have adopted the approach of the Restatement). *But see* Earnest v Regent Pool, Inc, 288 Ala 63, 257 So 2d 313, 317 (1972) (§339 not followed).

141 *See, e.g.*, Miller v Perry, 308 F Supp 863, 865 (DSC 1970) (South Carolina law) (however the court also found no liability under §339 of the Restatement); Ochampaugh v City of Seattle, 91 Wash 2d 514, 588 P2d 1351, 1354 (1979).

142 *See, e.g.*, Murphy v Baltimore Gas & Elec Co, 290 Md 186, 428 A2d 459, 465 (1981); Osterman v Peters, 260 Md 313, 272 A2d 21, 22 (1971) (drowning in residential swimming pool). It is also generally believed that New Hampshire, Ohio, and Vermont do not recognize a special duty of landowners to children. *See* Soule v Massachusetts Elec Co, 378 Mass 177, 390 NE2d 716, 720 n 10 (1979); Note, *A New Beginning For the Attractive Nuisance Doctrine in Georgia*, 34 Mercer L Rev 433, 439 n 52 (1982). This appears to be an open question in Nevada. *See* Kimberlin v Lear, 88 Nev 492, 500 P2d 1022 (1972).

Condition Attractive to Child

The Restatement does not require that the child be *attracted* to the potentially dangerous condition. Rather, the landowner can be liable if it knew or should have known that children were likely to trespass.[143] Of course, if a condition is attractive to children, it is more likely that the landowner should foresee a trespass.[144]

Nonetheless, there are still a few jurisdictions which do not impose a higher duty of care on the landowner unless the child was enticed upon the land by the condition which caused the harm.[145] For example, in *Johnson v Bathey*, the Florida Supreme Court affirmed a defendant's summary judgment because the plaintiff, a nine-year-old boy who was injured while swimming, came on the land to collect surplus vegetables. He was not *allured* onto the premises to swim.[146]

Natural Conditions

The Restatement basically provides that a land possessor owes a duty of reasonable care to children with regard to artificial conditions on the land. It is unclear whether this duty should also extend to natural conditions. The Restatement expresses no opinion on this matter.

Although the commentators have felt that there is no principled distinction between artifical and natural conditions,[147] the courts have generally held that a landowner owes no duty of reasonable care for dangerous natural conditions.[148] Indeed, there are repeated statements in the decisions that land in its natural state and with normal topographical features, e.g., rolling hills, is not inherently dangerous and that land occupiers have no duty to warn or to guard against natural conditions.[149] Accordingly, claims that landowners

---

143 See Restatement (Second) of Torts §339 (1965).

144 Skaggs v Junis, 27 Ill App 2d 251, 169 NE2d 684, 689 (1960).

145 *See, e.g.*, Ausmer v Sliman, 336 So 2d 730, 731 (Miss 1976); *see generally* Metropolitan Govt v Counts, 541 SW2d 133, 136 (Tenn 1976); Note, *A New Beginning For the Attractive Nuisance Doctrine in Georgia*, 34 Mercer L Rev 433, 440 (1982).

146 376 So 2d 848, 849 (Fla 1979).

147 *See* 2 F. Harper & F. James, The Law of Torts §27.5, at 1452-53 (1956); Prosser, *Trespassing Children*, 47 Cal L Rev 427, 446-47 (1959).

148 *See, e.g.*, Caliguire v City of Union, 104 NJ Super 210, 249 A2d 603, 607 (1967), *aff'd*, 53 NJ 182, 249 A2d 577 (1969).

Some artificial conditions resemble nature, e.g., a canal or a ditch, and when an individual is injured there, the general rule applying to natural conditions may apply. *See* Meyer v General Elec Co, 46 Wash 2d 251, 280 P2d 257, 258 (1955); *see also* Plotzki v Standard Oil, 228 Ind 518, 92 NE2d 632, 634 (1950).

149 Beechy v Village of Oak Forest, 16 Ill App 3d 240, 305 NE2d 257, 260 (1973); McIntyre v McIntyre, 558 SW2d 836, 837 (Tenn 1977); *see also* McDermott v Kaczmarek, 2 Wash App 643, 469 P2d 191, 197 (1970).

were liable for injuries from riding a sled down an embankment[150] and for the drowning of a child in an ocean cove[151] have been rejected. However, it is a jury question whether a horse on private land is an artificial condition.[152]

The broad statements in the cases above are obviously incorrect as a matter of fact since land in its natural state can be unreasonably dangerous. The proper analysis is not whether, as a general proposition, the risks posed by the natural conditions are unreasonably dangerous, but whether the specific condition which caused harm was unreasonably dangerous. However, one of the hidden assumptions in those decisions may have been that clear lines of demarcation of nonliability are necessary because land cannot be made child-proof and plaintiffs' counsel, after injury has occurred, can usually be inventive enough to articulate some extra precaution which should have been taken.

Trespassers and Licensees

A few courts have stated that a landowner's duty of reasonable care to children only applies when they entered upon the land uninvited.[153] These statements clearly indicate poor reasoning. There is no legitimate reason to entitle trespassing children to a standard of reasonable care when child licensees are afforded a lower standard of care. Indeed, such reasoning appears perverse, and numerous courts have held that a landowner's duty of reasonable care applies to all children, irrespective of their status as trespassers or as licensees.[154]

Plaintiff's Awareness of the Risk

Where the injured child understands or appreciates the peril and is able to avoid the danger, it is generally held that the §339 of Restatement is inapplicable. There can be no recovery since the rule is intended for the protection of children who, because of their immaturity and inexperience, are unable to appreciate and avoid the danger to which they are exposed.[155] The

---

150 Beechy v Village of Oak Forest, 16 Ill App 3d 240, 305 NE2d 257, 260 (1973).

151 Loney v McPhillips, 268 Or 378, 521 P2d 340, 344 (1974).

152 Hoffer v Meyer, 295 NW2d 333, 337 (SD 1980).

153 See, e.g., Wren v Harrison, 165 Ga App 847, 303 SE2d 67, 70 (1983); McIntyre v McIntyre, 558 SW2d 836, 837 (Tenn 1977); see also Jackson v Board of Educ, 109 Ill App 3d 716, 441 NE2d 120, 122 (1982) (children at school playground were invited).

154 See, e.g., Dougherty v Graham, 161 Conn 248, 287 A2d 382, 385 (1971). Grimes v Hettinger, 566 SW2d 769, 772 (Ky Ct App 1978); Crawford v Pacific W Mobile Estates, Inc, 548 SW2d 216, 218 n 1 (Mo Ct App 1977). See also Restatement (Second) of Torts §343B (1965); W. Prosser, The Law of Torts §60, at 382 (4th ed 1971); Note, A New Beginning For the Attractive Nuisance Doctrine in Georgia, 34 Mercer L Rev 433, 446 (1982).

155 Carlson v Tucson Racquet & Swim Club, 127 Ariz 247, 619 P2d 756, 758 (Ct App 1980); Lister v Campbell, 371 So 2d 133, 136 (Fla Dist Ct App 1979); Richards v Marlow, 347 So 2d 281, 283 (La Ct App), writ denied, 350 So 2d 676 (La 1977); Ostroski v

fact that warnings were given is not dispositive of whether the injured child realized the risk.[156]

Often, the most probative evidence of whether a child understood the risks of participating in a recreational activity is the child's own testimony, at least when an awareness of the risk is admitted.[157] Accordingly, when a 13-year-old boy, who injured himself by placing his hand in a conveyor to retrieve a baseball, admitted that he was aware of the dangers of the machine, he could not recover.[158] Similarly, a boy of normal intelligence who testified that he knew it was *wrong* to dive into shallow water could not recover for diving injuries.[159]

It cannot be denied that some risks are so obvious to some individuals that a land occupier is not liable when the plaintiff ignores the risk and is consequently injured, even in the face of plaintiffs' protestations to the contrary. Accordingly, landowners are not usually liable to older children injured while swimming or diving since the risks of those activities are usually obvious to the participants.[160]

A significant number of courts have held that the perils of ponds, pools, lakes, streams, and other bodies of water are *obvious* as a matter of law.[161] Such

---

Mount Prospect Shop-Rite, Inc, 94 NJ Super 374, 228 A2d 545, 549 (dangers of sliding down snow-covered hill), *cert dismissed*, 49 NJ 369, 230 A2d 400 (1967); Prosser, *Trespassing Children*, 47 Cal L Rev 427, 461 (1959).

[156] *See* Latimer v City of Clovis, 83 NM 610, 495 P2d 788, 793 (1972) (deceased's brother testified he had forgotten his mother's warnings to stay away from the pool).

[157] Lister v Campbell, 371 So 2d 133, 136 (Fla Dist Ct App 1979); *see generally* §9.03.

[158] Washington v Trend Mills, Inc, 121 Ga App 659, 175 SE2d 111, 112 (1970).

[159] Lister v Campbell, 371 So 2d 133, 136 (Fla Dist Ct App 1979).

[160] Carlson v Tucson Racquet & Swim Club, 127 Ariz 247, 619 P2d 756, 758 (Ct App 1980) (16-year-old diver); O'Keefe v South End Rowing Club, 64 Cal 2d 729, 414 P2d 830, 51 Cal Rptr 534 (1966) (15-year-old diver); Prince v Wolf, 92 Ill App 3d 505, 417 NE2d 679, 682 (1981) (15-year-old swimmer); Barbre v Indianapolis Water Co, 400 NE2d 1142, 1146 (Ind Ct App 1980) (17-year-old diver); *see also* Lister v Campbell, 371 So 2d 133, 136 (Fla Dist Ct App 1979).

[161] Glover v City of Mobile, 417 So 2d 175, 179 (Ala 1982); Jones v Comer, 237 Ark 500, 374 NW2d 465, 467 (1964); Stanley v Security Athletic Assn, 152 Colo 19, 380 P2d 53, 56 (1963); Montega Corp v Grooms, 128 Ga App 333, 196 SE2d 459, 462 (1973); Pasierb v Hanover Park Dist, 103 Ill App 3d 806, 431 NE2d 1218, 1221 (1981); Barbre v Indianapolis Water Co, 400 NE2d 1142, 1146 (Ind Ct App 1980) (even young children are presumed to understand and appreciate the dangers common to bodies of water); Hecht v Des Moines Playground & Recreation Assn, 227 Iowa 81, 287 NW 259 (1939); McCormick v Williams, 194 Kan 81, 397 P2d 392, 394 (1965); Ausmer v Sliman, 336 So 2d 730, 731 (Miss 1976); Metropolitan Govt v Counts, 541 SW2d 133, 136 (Tenn 1976); Ochampaugh v City of Seattle, 91 Wash 2d 514, 588 P2d 1351, 1355 (1979); *see also* Mims v Brown, 49 Ala App 643, 275 So 2d 159, 161 (1973) (not applicable to residential synthetic swimming pool with only a small amount of water in it).

In Wren v Harrison, 165 Ga App 847, 303 SE2d 67, 69 (1983), the court held that the attractive nuisance doctrine did not apply to natural bodies of water but could apply to artificial bodies of water such as residential swimming pools. There is no logical basis for such a distinction.

statements must ring particularly hollow to over 125,000 individuals who are sufficiently injured annually in recreational accidents involving swimming or other water activities to require emergency room treatment.[162] In any event, under this analysis children are deemed to realize the risks and therefore do not qualify for recovery under §339 or the attractive nuisance doctrine.[163] Sometimes this rule is not applied where unusual elements of danger exist, such as a trap or hidden hazard, that a child would be unlikely to appreciate,[164] or where there is a special attraction present, e.g., a diving board[165] or a bank of white sand.[166]

Other courts have correctly rejected the pigeon-hole analysis that implies that the risks of water hazards are always obvious.[167] The proper test is whether the specific child who was injured was aware of the danger. Indeed, it is clear that the age of some children, e.g., those one or two years old, effectively precludes their understanding of virtually all risks, including the danger posed by bodies of water.[168]

Plaintiff's Age

The courts have reached different conclusions regarding when a plaintiff is too old to impose a higher duty of care on a land occupier.[169] It

---

162 *See* US Consumer Product Safety Commn, Natl Injury Information Clearinghouse, Product Summary Report (Mar 28, 1984).

163 Glover v City of Mobile, 417 So 2d 175, 179 (Ala 1982); Montega Corp v Grooms, 128 Ga App 333, 196 SE2d 459, 462 (1973); Pasierb v Hanover Park Dist, 103 Ill App 3d 806, 431 NE2d 1218, 1221 (1981); Barbre v Indianapolis Water Co, 400 NE2d 1142, 1146 (Ind Ct App 1980); Ausmer v Sliman, 336 So 2d 730, 731 (Miss 1976); Metropolitan Govt v Counts, 541 SW2d 133, 136 (Tenn 1976); Ochampaugh v City of Seattle, 91 Wash 2d 514, 588 P2d 1351, 1355 (1979).

164 Townes v Hawaii Properties, Inc, 708 F2d 333, 335 (8th Cir 1983) (Arkansas law). *But see* Locke v Liquid Air Corp, 725 F2d 1331, 1334 (11th Cir 1984) (Alabama law) ("water, including water concealing a submerged hazardous condition, is an obvious and patent danger reasonably anticipated by any child of sufficient maturity to be allowed abroad without supervision").

165 Smith v Evans, 178 Kan 259, 284 P2d 1065, 1066-67 (1955).

166 Allen v William P McDonald Corp, 42 So 2d 706, 707 (Fla Dist Ct App 1949).

167 King v Lennen, 53 Cal 2d 340, 348 P2d 98, 100, 1 Cal Rptr 665 (1959); Giacona v Tapley, 5 Ariz App 494, 428 P2d 439, 442 (1967); Samson v O'Hara, 239 So 2d 151, 152 (Fla Dist Ct App 1970); Bartlett v Heersche, 204 Kan 392, 462 P2d 763 (1969); Saxton v Plum Orchards, Inc, 215 La 378, 40 So 2d 791 (1949); Crawford v Pacific W Mobile Estates, Inc, 548 SW2d 216, 221-22 (Mo Ct App 1977); Latimer v City of Clovis, 83 NM 610, 495 P2d 788, 793 (Ct App 1972); Lynch v Motel Enters, Inc, 248 SC 490, 151 SE2d 435, 437 (1966); McWilliams v Guzinski, 71 Wis 2d 57, 237 NW2d 437, 438 (1976) (insufficiently guarded residential swimming pool).

168 *See generally* §9.04.

169 *See generally* Restatement (Second) of Torts §339 comment c (1965); Note, *A New Beginning For the Attractive Nuisance Doctrine in Georgia*, 34 Mercer L Rev 433, 446 (1982).

should be noted that the First Restatement's provision that §339 was limited to *young* children was eliminated in the Second Restatement. Indeed, children as old as 16 years have been allowed to take their case to a jury regarding whether they were without the necessary discretion and judgment essential to their own security.[170] Nonetheless, an analysis of actual decisions shows that there are few recoveries by children more than 14 years old.[171] It is important to note that there is some support for the proposition that the child's mental development as well as age should be taken into account.[172]

Activities Not Unreasonably Dangerous

Land occupiers are not liable unless they knew or should have known that a condition on their land was unreasonably dangerous.[173] Courts have held that certain activities are not unreasonably dangerous and that landowners are not liable to plaintiffs injured pursuing those activities. For example, plaintiffs were not entitled to use the attractive nuisance doctrine when

---

Some courts have stated that the infant trespasser rule does not apply to children who can travel unsupervised. *See, e.g.,* McWilliams v Guzinski, 71 Wis 2d 57, 237 NW2d 437, 440 (1976). However, *McWilliams* held that the true test is whether the child appreciated the specific danger which later befell the child, not whether the child, as a general proposition, could travel unsupervised. *See* 237 NW2d at 440-41. *See generally* Annot, 26 ALR3d 25 (1967).

170 Skaggs v Junis, 27 Ill App 251, 169 NE2d 684, 689 (1960); Scheck v Houdaille Constr Materials, Inc, 121 NJ Super 335, 297 A2d 17, 20 (1972) (14-year-old can use this doctrine).

171 Carlson v Tucson Racquet & Swim Club, 127 Ariz 247, 619 P2d 756, 758 (Ct App 1980) (16-year-old cannot take advantage of this rule); Barbre v Indianapolis Water Co, 400 NE2d 1142, 1146 (Ind Ct App 1980) (17-year-old not entitled to special consideration); Jones v Maryland Casualty Co, 256 So 2d 358, 360 (La Ct App 1971) (14-year-old is too old to take advantage of this special rule for children); Richards v Marlow, 347 So 2d 281, 283 (La Ct App), *writ denied*, 350 So 2d 676 (La 1977) (this special rule was not applied to a 13-year-old); Gordon v CHC Corp, 236 So 2d 733, 736 (Miss 1970) (an intelligent boy who completed the fourth grade was not too young to appreciate the danger of water); James, *Tort Liability of Occupiers of Land: Duties Owed to Trespassers,* 63 Yale LJ 144, 167 (1953) (rarely applied to children over 14 years old); Prosser, *Trespassing Children,* 47 Cal L Rev 427, 439 (1959) (the great majority of the recoveries have been by children 12 years old or under).

172 W. Prosser, The Law of Torts §59, at 374-75 (4th ed 1971).

173 Weatherby v Meredith, 341 So 2d 139, 140 (Ala 1976). *See also* Venable v Langford, 116 Ga App 257, 157 SE2d 34, 37 (1967) (land occupier not liable when minor went onto the land to see a companion's horse but, instead, took a leaky boat onto a lake and drowned; there was no peril until the boat was moved).

In Johnson v Kreuger, 36 Colo App 242, 539 P2d 1296 (1975), the court held the landowners were not negligent as a matter of law in leaving a clearly visible tree stump on their land. It was not reasonably foreseeable that a child would run onto their land while playing football and fail to see this stump because he was looking back to see where the football pass was being thrown and not looking where he was going. *See* 539 P2d at 1298.

they injured themselves falling from a treehouse,[174] "walking the barrel,"[175] being hit by a volleyball net pole,[176] or riding a bicycle.[177] Nevertheless, the better view is to limit the broad wording in some of these cases to the specific facts.[178] In a different context, the same activity could be unreasonably dangerous.

Negligence Standard

The Restatement essentially provides that a land occupier will be liable for negligence. The land occupier is not an insurer of the safety of trespassing children.[179] A failure to provide doors leading to a swimming pool which would close even if they were unlocked, was negligence since open doors to unguarded pools present a serious risk of injury.[180]

However, a landowner who erected a six-foot high chain link fence, topped with barbed wire, around a swimming pool was not liable when it was impossible to ascertain how the decedents got through the fence and into the pool where they ultimately drowned. The defendant made a reasonable effort to keep people out and was not obligated to erect and maintain an impenetrable wall around the pool.[181]

Former Owners

The attractive nuisance doctrine and §339 of the Restatement only apply to present landowners and occupiers, not former ones.[182] The general rule is that former possessors of land are not liable for injuries caused to others by any dangerous condition, natural or artificial, which existed when the possession of

---

174 Hickey v Charlton, 335 So 2d 389, 391 (Ala 1976).

175 Patterson v Recreation & Park Commn, 226 So 2d 211, 216 (La Ct App), *cert denied*, 254 La 925, 228 So 2d 483 (1969).

176 Downey Memorial Church Interdenominational, Inc, v Knowlton, 290 So 2d 549, 550 (Fla Dist Ct App), *cert denied*, 300 So 2d 896 (Fla 1974).

177 Appling v Stuck, 164 NW2d 810, 813, 815 (Iowa 1969).

178 *See generally* James, *Tort Liability of Occupiers of Land: Duties Owed to Trespassers*, 63 Yale LJ 144, 170 (1953).

179 Samson v O'Hara, 239 So 2d 151, 152 (Fla Dist Ct App 1970).

180 Clifford v Recreation & Park Commn, 289 So 2d 373, 376 (La Ct App 1973), *writ denied*, 293 So 2d 168 (1974). *See also* Mitchell v Akers, 401 SW2d 907, 912 (Tex Civ App 1966).

181 Staley v Security Athletic Assn, 152 Colo 19, 380 P2d 53, 56 (1963); *see also* Butler v Continental Ins Co, 374 So 2d 170, 171 (La Ct App 1979); Crawford v Pacific W Mobile Estates, Inc, 548 SW2d 216, 221 (Mo Ct App 1977) (landowner is not required to child-proof premises against an obvious danger); McWilliams v Guzinski, 71 Wis 2d 57, 237 NW2d 437, 439 (1976) (pool owner not required to make it impossible for children to get into the pool).

182 Brock v Rogers & Babler, Inc, 536 P2d 778, 781 (Alaska 1975).

the land was transferred.[183] One who lacks possession and control of property normally should not be held liable for injuries which it is no longer able to prevent.[184] However, if the prior occupier concealed or failed to disclose the dangerous condition, it is liable if the present owner did not know or did not have reason to know of the condition.[185]

§6.08   Causation

It is, of course, black-letter law that a defendant's act or omission must have caused the plaintiff's injury before the defendant can be held liable. Traditionally, this test was articulated as whether the injury would not have occurred *but for* the defendant's behavior.[186] However, many recent decisions have found liability when the defendant's act or omission was only a substantial factor in bringing about the injury.[187]

There are, unfortunately, numerous cases where an injury occurred and no one witnessed it or can recall how it happened. In those situations, although it may be difficult to prove what caused the accident, defendants are not, ipso facto, entitled to a judgment.

In *Johnson v Harris*,[188] it was not known how a young child got into a pool and drowned. The defendants argued that since the child's entry was just as likely to have occurred absent any negligent act on their part as through negligence, viz., their failure to have a pool fence in compliance with city regulations, they were not liable. The court rejected this argument and upheld a jury verdict against the defendants, reasoning that the more reasonable inference was that the child got to the pool because the fence was not in compliance with the city code.

Most other decisions have also upheld the plaintiff's theory of causation when that theory can be proved by reasonable inference,[189] even when it is contrary to the opinion of an expert witness.[190] However, causation cannot

---

183 Brock v Rogers & Babler, Inc, 536 P2d 778, 781 (Alaska 1975); *see generally* Restatement (Second) of Torts §352 (1965).

184 Brock v Rogers & Babker, Inc, 536 P2d 778, 782 (Alaska 1975).

185 Brock v Rogers & Babler, Inc, 536 P2d 778, 781-82 (Alaska 1975); *see generally* Restatement (Second) of Torts §352 (1965).

186 W. Prosser, The Law of Torts §41, at 239 (4th ed 1971).

187 *Id* 240.

188 23 Ariz App 103, 530 P2d 1136, 1138 (1975).

189 *See, e.g.*, Crawford v Pacific W Mobile Estates, Inc, 548 SW2d 216, 223 (Mo Ct App 1977) (drowning); B.M.&R. Interests v Snyder, 453 SW2d 360, 363 (Tex Civ App 1970), *writ ref nre* (fall from a pool slide); Mitchell v Akers, 401 SW2d 907, 912 (Tex Civ App 1966), *writ ref nre* (drowning in residential pool; gate around pool not in compliance with city ordinance); *see generally* §1.25.

190 Flom v Flom, 291 NW2d 914, 917 (Minn 1980).

properly be proved by speculation or conjecture. Therefore, when causation is an insoluble mystery,[191] or when there is no relationship between the defendant's acts and the injury,[192] the plaintiff will lose.

§6.09   Duty to Warn or Guard against Obvious Dangers

A land occupier is generally not required to eliminate known or obvious hazards that a person would reasonably be expected to avoid, unless the owner should anticipate that the person could be harmed despite such knowledge or obviousness.[193] The reason being that the person's knowledge[194] of the condition eliminates the unreasonable nature of the hazard.[195]

Accordingly, a pool owner generally has no duty to warn of the usual dangers of swimming or diving,[196] including the risks posed by shallow water.[197] Indeed, one court rejected a plaintiff's claim that he was deceived regarding an above-ground pool's depth because of an optical illusion when it was obvious that the plaintiff was aware of the pool's total depth.[198] Similarly, there was no landowner negligence when an adult slipped on a puddle of water at the edge of a pier and was severely injured.[199]

---

191 Butler v Continental Ins Co, 374 So 2d 170, 171 (La Ct App 1979) (drowning); Bougon v Traders & General Ins Co, 146 So 2d 535, 539 (La Ct App 1962) (swimming accident).

192 Burchinal v Gregory, 41 Colo App 490, 586 P2d 1012, 1014 (1978) (no failure to supervise where plaintiff admitted that spotters could not have helped him successfully complete a flip on a trampoline); McClur v Suter, 63 Ill App 3d 378, 379 NE2d 1376, 1379 (1978) (boy may have drowned regardless of whether lifesaving personnel and equipment available); Brown v Lesh, 604 SW2d 636, 639 (Mo Ct App 1980) (insufficient showing of relationship between a swing set's rusty chains and injury); Andrews v Taylor, 34 NC App 706, 239 SE2d 630, 632 (1977) (no showing that availability of lifeguards or rescue equipment would have prevented swimming death).

193 See Dougherty v Graham, 161 Conn 248, 287 A2d 382, 385 (1971) (gully located at the bottom of hill that plaintiff used to toboggan); Burnett v City of Adrian, 414 Mich 448, 326 NW2d 810, 818 n 16 (1982) (Moody, J, concurring); see also Restatement (Second) of Torts §343A (1965); James, Tort Liability of Occupiers of Land: Duties Owed to Licensees and Invitees, 63 Yale LJ 605, 626-27 (1954) (where knowledge of danger is not sufficient to avoid it, e.g., icy stairs, the landowner should take steps to reduce the danger).

194 The obvious nature of the hazard supplies knowledge.

195 2 F. Harper & F. James, The Law of Torts §27.13, at 1491 (1956).

196 See Christman v Senyk, 34 Ohio Misc 47, 293 NE2d 126, 127 (1972). See also §6.16.

197 See generally Chauvin v Atlas Ins Co, 166 So 2d 581, 584 (La Ct App 1964) (diving is fraught with danger, and diver is required to make investigation); Telak v Maszczenski, 248 Md 476, 237 A2d 434, 438 (1968); Christman v Senyk, 34 Ohio Misc 47, 293 NE2d 126, 127 (1972).

198 Shuman v Mashburn, 137 Ga App 231, 223 SE2d 268, 270-71 (1976).

199 Friedrich v Department of Transp, 60 Hawaii 32, 586 P2d 1037, 1041 (1978).

A landowner was not responsible for injuries caused by a depression in an outdoor basketball court, a condition that was open and obvious.[200] However, a 10-inch-by-12-inch hole in an area where persons were known to play catch was not an open and obvious danger, and the failure to fix the hole or warn of its dangers was held to be negligence.[201]

This same general rule applies to children as long as they are old enough to realize the risks of the danger.[202] When an experienced 12-year-old swimmer drowned, the landowner was held to be not negligent in permitting her to swim since the child was aware of the risks of swimming in cloudy water.[203] Similarly, a defendant had no duty to warn a 15-year-old boy of the dangers of using trampolines when the boy already understood and appreciated the dangers.[204]

Specific Recreational Activities

§6.10 Baseball

A land occupier generally has no duty to warn or guard against obvious dangers.[205] Therefore, when a social guest was hit in the eye by a batted baseball, she could not recover against her host, the landowner. The danger presented by the host's children playing baseball[206] should have been observed by the guest because she was directly facing the part of the yard where the baseball game was being played. Since the danger was obvious, the host breached no duty of care and was not negligent as a matter of law.[207]

§6.11 Bicycling

Possessors of land may, under some circumstances, have a duty to warn bicyclists[208] of hidden defects in or upon a bicycle path.[209] However, there is

---

200 McCurry v YMCA, 210 Neb 278, 313 NW2d 689, 691 (1981).

201 Treps v City of Racine, 73 Wis 2d 611, 243 NW2d 520, 523 (1976).

202 *See* §6.07.

203 Grimes v Hettinger, 566 SW2d 769, 773 (Ky Ct App 1978).

204 Burchinal v Gregory, 41 Colo App 490, 586 P2d 1012, 1013 (1978).

205 *See* §6.09.

206 It is estimated that there are over 300,000 accidents annually which require emergency room treatment from nonorganized baseball. *See* US Consumer Product Safety Commn, Natl Injury Information Clearinghouse, Product Summary Report (Mar 28, 1984).

207 Lear v United States Fire Ins Co, 392 So 2d 786, 789 (La Ct App 1980).

208 It is estimated that there are about 570,000 bicycle accidents a year which require emergency room treatment. *See* US Consumer Product Safety Commn, Natl Injury Information

no duty to warn bicyclists of all concealed objects that lie near a bicycle path which might serve to aggravate a bicyclist's injuries in a fall.[210]

It is not unreasonable for a land occupier to fail to warn of all concealed objects near a bike path because the economic and aesthetic cost of doing so outweighs the benefit to bicyclists.[211] Furthermore, it is common knowledge that a fall from a bicycle may result in injury and that hidden debris may well be present along bike paths.[212] Of course, if a landowner knew of concealed objects that could cause serious injury near a bike path and also knew that there was a significant liklihood of a fall occurring in that area, the landowner would probably be liable for failure to warn or guard against the danger.[213]

Landowners may also be liable to bicyclists for negligently maintaining their property, thereby creating conditions which cause[214] or aggravate a bicyclist's injuries.[215]

§6.12   Firearms

In *Cornutt v Bolin*,[216] a woman invited a relative to her house to clean a gun. The woman failed to mention that the gun was loaded and the relative was killed when the gun discharged. The court held that the woman owed the relative a duty of reasonable care, the standard of care owed invitees, because she received a benefit from the visit and upheld a $100,000 verdict against her.[217]

A landowner generally has no duty to warn guests in the house of obvious dangers.[218] Accordingly, when a guest's possession of a gun was apparent to everyone, another guest who was injured when the gun discharged could not recover against the host.[219] Indeed, the court held that it was irrelevant

---

Clearinghouse, Product Summary Report (Mar 28, 1984).

209 Smith v Goldman, 53 Ill App 3d 362, 368 NE2d 1052, 1054 (1977).

210 *Id.*

211 *Id.*

212 *Id.*

213 *See* §6.06.

214 *See* McKeever v New York Tel Co, 254 AD 872, 5 NYS2d 6, 8, *affd without opinion*, 279 NY 651, 18 NE2d 44 (1938). The dissent argued that the danger of injury was not reasonably foreseeable and noted that there were no prior accidents in the last 20 years due to the condition of the property. *Id* (Lazansky, J, dissenting).

215 *See* Muallem v City of New York, 104 Misc 2d 207, 428 NYS2d 173, 176 (Sup Ct 1980), *modified on other grounds*, 82 AD2d 420, 441 NYS2d 834 (1981).

216 404 So 2d 38, 40 (Ala 1981).

217 *Id.*

218 Joyner v Jones, 97 Idaho 647, 551 P2d 602, 604 (1976); *see generally* §6.09.

219 Joyner v Jones, 97 Idaho 647, 551 P2d 602, 604 (1976).

that the host failed to inform the injured guest of the other guest's earlier brandishing of a gun because this could not have added to the obviousness of the danger.[220]

A landowner is generally not responsible for protecting guests from uninvited persons who attend a party.[221] However, even if there were such a duty, a guest's attempt to take a gun from an uninvited person was an unforeseeable event which eliminated the landowner's proximate causation of the injury.[222]

One court held that when landowners have not undertaken to supervise children in their backyard, they have no duty to supervise the children.[223] Accordingly, when one neighbor's child injured another child while playing with a toy rifle on defendant's land, the landowners were not negligent as a matter of law since they did not owe plaintiff a duty to supervise the children.[224]

§6.13 Horseback Riding

Most courts have held that landowners owe a duty of reasonable care to all individuals allowed on the land for horseback riding, regardless of the status of the plaintiffs.[225]

The owner of a horse is not liable for injuries the horse caused a rider unless the owner knew or should have known that the horse was dangerous.[226] For example, a host who knew of the dangerous proclivities of a horse to buck, and that it required special handling to control that tendency, should have warned a guest of the danger.[227] Even if the horse is not vicious, the owner may be liable if he or she knew or should have known that the horse was unsafe for the rider, an inexperienced equestrian.[228] A horse is not presumed dangerous merely because an accident occurred.[229]

---

220 *Id.*

221 *Id.*

222 551 P2d at 605.

223 Gordon v Harris, 86 AD2d 948, 448 NYS2d 598, 599 (1982).

224 448 NYS2d at 599.

225 Heald v Cox, 480 SW2d 107, 110 (Mo Ct App 1972); Bradshaw v Minter, 206 Va 450, 143 SE2d 827, 830 (1965). *See generally* §6.01.
For other cases involving liability for horseback riding accidents, *see* §2.17.

226 *See generally* McKinney v Cochran, 197 Kan 524, 419 P2d 931, 935 (1966).

227 Heald v Cox, 480 SW2d 107, 111 (Mo Ct App 1972).

228 Brooks v Mack, 222 Or 139, 352 P2d 474, 477 (1960); Bradshaw v Minter, 206 Va 450, 143 SE2d 827, 830 (1965).

229 Whitney v Brann, 394 F Supp 1, 6 (D Del), *aff'd without opinion*, 530 F2d 966 (3d Cir 1975), *cert denied*, 426 US 922 (1976).

When an owner neither knew nor should have known of the propensity of a horse to disobey the commands of its rider and run wild, the owner was entitled to a summary judgment.[230] Similarly, an owner who had no knowledge of a horse's violent propensities was not liable for failing to warn a rider of these characteristics, especially when the rider was an experienced equestrian.[231]

There is generally no duty to warn a guest riding a horse of obvious dangers.[232] It is common knowledge that open ground in most parts of the country is frozen during the winter.[233] Accordingly, there is no duty to warn a guest riding a horse of the dangers of riding on such land.[234]

Several states impose liability on the owner of an animal, including a horse, for injuries caused by the animal.[235] In Illinois, when a person peaceably conducting him or herself in a place where he or she may lawfully be is injured by an animal, the owner of the animal is held strictly liable.[236] Accordingly, a female horse rider recovered from the horse's owner when, without provocation, the horse carried her in a direction she did not want to go and she was consequently struck by a truck.[237]

§6.14 Motorcycling

Generally, the simple existence of unauthorized motorbike activity on landowners' property imposes no affirmative duty upon the landowners to inquire into the situation or to bear responsibility for the risks inherent in that activity.[238] Landowners were entitled to summary judgment when a motorcyclist resting in a shack was injured by a firecracker thrown into the shack by other youths because the landowners committed no unreasonable act.[239]

Public or Private Roads

Many recreational motorcycling injuries occur on what are, in fact, private roads. However, it is often unclear whether the road was private or public and

---

230 Pearce v Shanks, 153 Ga App 693, 266 SE2d 353, 354 (1980).

231 McKinney v Cochran, 197 Kan 524, 419 P2d 931, 935 (1966).

232 419 P2d 931. *See generally* §6.09.

233 McKinney v Cochran, 197 Kan 524, 419 P2d 931, 934 (1966).

234 *Id.*

235 *See, e.g.,* Ill Rev Stat ch 8, §366 (Smith-Hurd 1975); La Civ Code Ann art 2321 (West 1979).

236 *See* Ill Rev Stat ch 8, §366 (Smith-Hurd 1975).

237 Chittum v Evanston Fuel & Material Co, 92 Ill App 3d 188, 416 NE2d 5, 7 (1980).

238 Bellflower v Penrise, 548 F2d 776, 779 (8th Cir 1977).

239 *Id.*

even if it were private, whether the landowner impliedly invited the public to use it.

The mere acquiescence by a land occupier in the public use of its private land does not amount to an implied invitation of use that gives rise to the correlative duty to exercise reasonable care. Indeed, the acquiescence may only mean that the land occupier does not want to incur the costs involved in keeping others off the land. But when the landowner induces public use of the property, it will be liable for negligence. Clearly, the line between acquiescence and inducement is very fine.

When a private road was commonly used by the public as a shortcut between a state highway and a county road, and the private land around the private road was regularly used for recreational activities by the public, a jury verdict finding inducement was upheld.[240]

Similarly, when a private access road was regularly used, and the landowner failed to post signs stating that the road was private, the injured party may have been led to believe that the road was public.[241] In fact, land occupiers who know or should know that others will reasonably believe their private road to be a public highway are liable for failure to exercise reasonable care to maintain the road in a reasonably safe condition for travel.[242]

In contrast, when a landowner had no actual knowledge of the public's use of old dirt roads on the property for motorcycling, there was no implied invitation, and the landowner was not liable in negligence when a trespassing motorcyclist fell into a mine shaft at the trail's end.[243]

There was no implied invitation when it was unquestioned that a road was private property,[244] nor when a cable barricade with a *No Admittance* sign was posted.[245] Similarly, when there was a sign at the beginning of the road

---

[240] Vickers v Gifford-Hill & Co, Inc, 534 F2d 1311, 1317-18 (8th Cir 1976) (Arkansas law).

[241] Rogers v Bray, 16 Wash App 494, 557 P2d 28, 29-30 (1977). *See generally* Restatement (Second) of Torts §367 (1965).

[242] *See* Lucier v Meriden-Wallingford Sand & Stone Co, 153 Conn 422, 216 A2d 818, 822 (1966); Restatement (Second) of Torts §367 (1965).

[243] Holcombe v Harris, 143 Ga App 173, 237 SE2d 677, 680 (1977). The court did not discuss whether it was wilful or wanton to fail to guard or warn of a mine shaft at the trail's end.

[244] Huyck v Heckla Mining Co, 101 Idaho 299, 612 P2d 142, 143 (1980).

[245] Bosiljevac v Ready Mixed Concrete Co, 182 Neb 199, 153 NW2d 864, 867 (1967). The court's reasoning may be in error. The plaintiff failed to see the barrier and, therefore, had no actual knowledge, at least from the barrier, of being on private property. The proper question is whether the plaintiff had an implied invitation to use the road which led up to the barrier. Of course, even with an invitation, the barrier may have been so obvious that there was no unreasonable act of the landowner. If so, defendant may still have been properly entitled to judgment.

indicating that the road was private, as well as a cable barricade with a sign stating, *Do Not Enter*, there was no implied invitation.[246]

When the motorcyclists are trespassers and there was no implied invitation to use the property, in most jurisdictions the land occupier only owes them the duty to refrain from wilful or wanton acts.[247] However, when the land occupier knows of the trespassers and also knows that they will not discover an artifical condition on the land, the land occupier must exercise reasonable care to warn of the risks of the condition.[248]

Obvious Dangers

There is generally no duty to warn or guard against the dangers of conditions which are open to ordinary observation.[249] Accordingly, a motorcyclist who was injured when his bike hit the bank of a ditch could not recover against the landowner because the ditch was readily observable.[250] Similarly, a motorcyclist who parked his bike and was hit by another motorcyclist could not recover from the landowner because it was undisputed that the injured cyclist was aware of the dangers inherent in an area used as a motorcycle racing track.[251]

Children

A child motorcyclist will rarely be able to use the attractive nuisance doctrine or §339 of the Restatement (Second) of Torts because he or she will usually be considered old enough to have discovered and appreciated the risks involved.[252]

Lessor

Motorcyclists injured on leased land may attempt to recover from the lessor. However, the general rule is that a lessor is not liable to individuals who were injured by dangerous conditions on the land which came into existence

---

[246] Epling v United States, 453 F2d 327, 328-29 (9th Cir 1971) (Arizona law).

[247] An uninvited licensee is basically entitled to the same duty of care in some jurisdictions. *See* Morris v Florentes, Inc, 421 So 2d 582, 583 (Fla Dist Ct App 1982).

[248] *See* Lucier v Meriden-Wallingford Sand & Stone Co, 153 Conn 422, 216 A2d 818, 822 (1966).

[249] *See* §6.09.

[250] *See* Morris v Florentes, Inc, 421 So 2d 582, 583 (Fla Dist Ct App 1982). The court suspected that the dirt bikers specifically sought rough terrain because that is where their vehicles are designed to be used and their skills best demonstrated. *Id* 583 n 2.

[251] *See* Bovino v Metropolitan Dade County, 378 So 2d 50, 51 (Fla Dist Ct App 1979).

[252] McIntyre v McIntyre, 558 SW2d 836, 838 (Tenn 1977); *see generally* §6.07.

after the lessee took possession.[253] Accordingly, a plaintiff who was injured in a motorcycle race because of the negligent marking of the race course or the failure to control the spectators properly could not recover against the lessor of that land.[254]

Wilful or Wanton Acts

The courts have usually held that a landowner's placing of cable across a private road is not a wanton act, or even negligence, when the cable is easily observable.[255]

One court held that a one-inch yellow steel cable hanging between two yellow posts which had a 30-inch aluminum reflector was *readily observable*.[256] Hence, when a trespassing motorcyclist ran into it, the landowner was not liable for committing a wilful or wanton act. However, the posting of a rust-colored cable gate, not readily visible and with no warning signs other than a faded pink-colored rag, may have been wilful or wanton conduct.[257]

When landowners were unaware of trespassing motorcyclists but erected a cable-gate on a private road to protect their property from known trespassing motorists, they did not act wilfully or wantonly.[258]

§6.15   Playground Equipment and Activities

Playground   injuries   are   common   occurrences,[259]   especially   when

---

253 Restatement (Second) of Torts §355 (1965); W. Prosser, The Law of Torts §63, at 400 (4th ed 1971). The primary exceptions to this general rule are stated in §§357-362 of the Restatement.

254 Thompson v United States, 592 F2d 1104, 1109 (9th Cir 1979).

255 *See generally* Epling v United States, 453 F2d 327, 330 (9th Cir 1971) (Arizona law) (could have seen cable if traveling at close to posted speed limit); Gaboury v Ireland Road Grace Brethren, 441 NE2d 227, 231 (Ind Ct App 1982) (jury question whether cable was obvious danger); *see generally* **§6.06**.

256 Huyck v Hecla Mining Co, 101 Idaho 299, 612 P2d 142, 144 (1980). The court bolstered its conclusion by noting that the motorcyclist's daughter was able to stop without striking the barrier. However, it is possible that the daughter stopped because she saw her father's accident, not the barrier.

257 Vickers v Gifford-Hill & Co, 534 F2d 1311, 1317 n 11 (8th Cir 1976).

258 Starr v Clapp, 40 NC App 142, 252 SE2d 220, 223, *affd*, 298 NC 275, 258 SE2d 348 (1979). However, the appellate decision is without precedential value because the North Carolina Supreme Court affirmance was by an equally divided vote. *See* 258 SE2d at 350.

259 It is estimated that there are over 190,000 playground accidents which require emergency room treatment annually, although not all of them occur on private land. *See* US Consumer Product Safety Commn, Natl Injury Information Clearinghouse, Product Summary Report (Mar 28, 1984). The commission estimates the annual injury rate as follows:

1.   Slides and sliding boards, 40,000
2.   Monkey bars and playground climbing equipment, 45,500

unsupervised children are playing. However, unless the landowner's conduct was, at a minimum, unreasonable, it will not be liable since landowners are not insurers.[260]

In *Lester v Dunn*, the court held that hosts are responsible for injuries to their guests when: (1) the host knows or should have known that there was an unreasonable risk of harm and should have known that the guests would not realize the danger; (2) the host fails to exercise reasonable care to make the condition safe or to warn of the risk involved; and (3) the guests neither know nor should have known of the risk involved.[261] In that case, it was a question of fact whether the defendant was liable when a neighbor's child was injured on the property while using a swing set because it was not clear that those elements were satisfied.[262]

Nonetheless, in *Weatherby v Meredith*,[263] the Alabama Supreme Court held that a three-year-old social guest could not recover for injuries from a swing set. The court held that the prerequisite for liability under §339 of the Restatement (Second) of Torts, an unreasonable risk of harm, was not present. The swing set, which consisted of a platform swing, two ordinary swings, a glider, and a slide, was not a dangerous instrumentality.[264]

It has also been held that monkey bars are not an inherently dangerous condition or trap, and that a plaintiff injured by such playground equipment cannot recover against a landowner.[265] Similarly, the placement of a bench and table near a tree did not create a dangerous condition because the injured child was capable of appreciating the risk.[266]

There is no duty of landowners to supervise constantly the playtime activities of children.[267] The fact that the defendants permitted children to play on picnic tables near a low-hanging tree branch does not establish a duty to supervise.[268]

---

3.   Swings and swing sets, 77,000
4.   Seesaws or teter boards, 9,000
5.   Playground equipment, 5,200
6.   Miscellaneous playground equipment 18,000

260 Rice v Argento, 59 AD2d 1051, 399 NYS2d 809, 810 (1977).

261 436 F2d 300, 302 (DC Cir 1970) (Maryland law); *see also* Restatement (Second) of Torts §342 (1965).

262 436 F2d at 302.

263 341 So 2d 139, 140 (Ala 1976).

264 *Id.*

265 Alegre v Shurkey, 396 So 2d 247, 248 (Fla Dist Ct App 1981).

266 Bazos v Chouinard, 96 Ill App 3d 526, 421 NE2d 566, 570-71 (1981).

267 *Id.*

268 *Id.*

Contribution

Landowners may have an action for contribution against a minor's parents. In *Cole v Sears Roebuck & Co*,[269] a child was injured while playing with a swing set on a neighbor's property, and the child sued the neighbors. The neighbors filed a third-party action for contribution against the plaintiff's parents for negligent supervision. The court held that there was no parent-child tort immunity in this situation and, therefore, the third-party complaint stated a claim for relief.[270]

§6.16   Residential Swimming Pools

General Duty of Care

The owner of a residential swimming pool is not an insurer of the safety[271] of the individuals who use the pool.[272] One court stated that the duty of care of an owner of a residential swimming pool is less than the duty of care of a commercial or public swimming facility,[273] a statement which does not provide much practical aid since an owner of a residential pool owes the applicable duty of care under the circumstances, and the circumstances of a residential pool are different from a commercial or public one.

In states that have abolished the distinctions among trespassers, licensees, and invitees, pool owners owe a duty of reasonable care to pool users.[274]

In other states, the pool owner's duty of care usually varies with the status of the entrant.[275] However, since users of residential swimming pools will rarely

---

269 47 Wis 2d 629, 177 NW2d 866 (1970).

270 177 NW2d at 869.

271 It is presently estimated that there are almost 100,000 swimming pool accidents which require emergency room treatment each year, although this figure is not limited to residential swimming pool injuries. *See* US Consumer Product Safety Commn, Natl Injury Information Clearinghouse, Product Summary Report (Mar 28, 1984). That figure is broken down as follows:

1.   Built-in swimming pools, 29,200
2.   Above-ground swimming pools, 2,000
3.   Miscellaneous swimming pools, 43,500
4.   Diving and diving boards, 17,000
5.   Swimming pool equipment, 3,000
6.   Swimming pool slides, 1,800

272 Samson v O'Hara, 239 So 2d 151, 152 (Fla Dist Ct App 1970); Gregory v Johnson, 249 Ga 151, 289 SE2d 232, 235 (1982).

273 Jones v Maryland Casualty Co, 256 So 2d 358, 361 (La Ct App 1971).

274 *See* Naughton v Sheehan, 56 AD2d 839, 392 NYS2d 75, 76 (1977); *see also* §6.01.

275 *See* §6.01.

be considered invitees, an owner's duty of care will usually be something less than reasonable care under the circumstances.[276] It is, therefore, not surprising that pool owners have usually been held not liable in such states. [277]

The pool owner's duty of care is not dependent on the entrant's status when the alleged negligence was a result of the owner's *activity*, e.g., a failure to control the horseplay of third parties near the pool, rather than a *condition* of the property.[278]

It has generally been held that there is no duty to warn of obvious dangers.[279] Indeed, some courts have held that landowners have no duty to warn of or eliminate dangerous conditions at swimming pools because the hazards of water are generally appreciated by everyone, even children of tender years.[280] However, there are decisions to the contrary.[281]

Unfortunately, it is not always easy to know whether the danger was *obvious*,—a statement which must be tinged with irony for the layperson. One court held that it was a jury question whether an owner who recently painted the patio around the pool, making the patio more slippery than before to wet, bare feet, had a duty to warn of the danger of slipping near a pool.[282]

There is no duty for the owner of a residential swimming pool to provide lifeguards.[283]

Vicarious Liability for Negligence by Others

A pool owner was held not vicariously responsible for the negligent acts of his mother in attempting to rescue a child in the pool, even when she provided

---

276 *See* §§6.03-6.05.

277 *See, e.g.,* McMullan v Butler, 346 So 2d 950, 951 (Ala 1977); Mims v Brown, 49 Ala App 643, 275 So 2d 159, 161 (1973); Holland v Krawski, 25 Conn Supp 406, 206 A2d 648 (1964); Odom v Lee, 145 Ga App 304, 243 SE2d 699, 699 (1978); Poston v Vanderlee, 144 Ga App 833, 242 SE2d 727, 727 (1978); Osterman v Peters, 260 Md 313, 272 A2d 21 (1971); Telak v Maszczenski, 248 Md 476, 237 A2d 434 (1968).

278 Martin v Shea, 432 NE2d 46, 47 (Ind Ct App 1982). *See generally* §6.01.

279 Schuman v Mashburn, 137 Ga App 231, 223 SE2d 268, 270 (1976); Grimes v Hettinger, 566 SW2d 769, 776 (Ky Ct App 1978).

280 *See, e.g.,* Grimes v Hettinger, 566 SW2d 769, 772 (Ky Ct App 1978) (child was 12-years-old); *see also* Mims v Brown, 49 Ala App 643, 275 So 2d 159, 161 (1973) (attractive nuisance doctrine not applied to a residential, synthetic swimming pool with only a small amount of water in it); Jones v Maryland Casualty Co, 256 So 2d 358, 360 (La Ct App 1971) (attractive nuisance doctrine was not applied to 14-year-old).

281 *See, e.g.,* Samson v O'Hara, 239 So 2d 151, 152 (Fla Dist Ct App 1970); McWilliams v Guzinski, 71 Wis 2d 57, 237 NW2d 437, 440 (1976) (child was four-years-old).

282 Bisnett v Mowder, 114 Ariz 213, 560 P2d 68, 70 (1977).

283 Grimes v Hettinger, 566 SW2d 769, 774 (Ky Ct App 1978).

him with various other services, such as maintaining his home.[284] The court reasoned that she was a nonservant agent because the owner had no control over her physical acts, and therefore, there was no vicarious liability.[285]

However, in a different case, a court noted that a landowner who instructed his children to look after the other swimmers in the pool would be liable for the negligence of the children in performing that task.[286]

Fences

Many local governments have passed ordinances requiring residential swimming pool owners to fence their pools.[287] Violation of such ordinances may be negligence per se.[288] Indeed, under some circumstances, the failure to comply with the fencing requirement is a wilful and wanton act.[289] However, one court held that even if an owner of a residential swimming pool violated a local fencing ordinance, an injured trespasser could not recover because there was no breach of the applicable duty of care. The *mere* violation of a statute is not wilful conduct.[290]

Even without an ordinance requiring a fence, an owner's failure to enclose adequately a residential swimming pool may be negligence, at least where the cost to do so was minimal and the owner knew or should have known of the risk to children.[291] Indeed, an insufficiently fenced swimming pool in a residential neighborhood may be an attractive nuisance,[292] although there are also decisions to the contrary.[293]

---

284 Jones v Maryland Casualty Co, 256 So 2d 358, 362 (La Ct App 1971).

285 *Id; see also* Restatement (Second) of Agency §250 (1958).

286 *See* Grimes v Hettinger, 566 SW2d 769, 775 (Ky Ct App 1978).

287 *See, e.g.,* Johnson v Harris, 23 Ariz App 103, 530 P2d 1136, 1137 (1975); Giancona v Tapley, 5 Ariz App 494, 428 P2d 439, 440 (1967); Grant v Hipsher, 257 Cal App 2d 375, 64 Cal Rptr 892, 896 (1967); Osterman v Peters, 260 Md 313, 272 A2d 21, 23 (1971).

Some city ordinances regulating residential swimming pools have been struck down as illegal zoning regulations. *See, e.g.,* Garnett v Incorporated Village of Atlantic Beach, 84 Misc 2d 460, 376 NYS2d 802, 804 (1975).

288 Restatement (Second) of Torts §286 (1965); *see generally* §1.24.

289 *See generally* Healy v City of New Rochelle, 25 AD2d 446, 266 NYS2d 861, 863 (1966).

290 *See* Osterman v Peters, 260 Md 313, 272 A2d 21, 23 (1971).

291 Giacona v Tapley, 5 Ariz App 494, 428 P2d 439, 442 (1967) (applied §339 of the Restatement (Second) of Torts); King v Lennen, 53 Cal 2d 340, 348 P2d 98, 100-01, 1 Cal Rptr 665 (1959); Reynolds v Wilson, 51 Cal 2d 94, 331 P2d 48, 52 (1958); Gregory v Johnson, 249 Ga 151, 289 SE2d 232, 235 (1982).

292 Banks v Mason, 132 So 2d 219, 222 (Fla Dist Ct App), *cert denied,* 136 So 2d 348 (Fla 1961).

293 Naughton v Sheehan, 56 AD2d 839, 392 NYS2d 75, 75-76 (1977).

Diving

It has sometimes been held that a pool owner has no duty to warn of obvious danger, e.g., the shallowness of the water in the pool.[294] Similarly, a land owner is under no duty to warn a 12-year-old, proficient swimmer and diver of the danger of a sliding board in a residential swimming pool.[295]

The owner of a residential swimming pool is not liable when there was no hidden dangerous condition in the pool.[296] For example, a landowner was exonerated when a 19-year-old man voluntarily, and despite protests by others, dived from the roof of the landowner's house into a swimming pool containing only shallow water.[297] In *Christman v Senyk*, a child was injured by diving into a swimming pool. The pool owners were entitled to a directed verdict because they had cautioned the child, an experienced diver, to be careful.[298]

Pool owners who had no knowledge that a minor might dive into shallow areas in the pool breached no duty of care by failing to instruct or warn the minor not to dive in those areas.[299] The court noted that there might have been a higher duty of care if the pool owners had undertaken the supervision of the minor; however, that higher standard was not applied because supervision had not been undertaken.[300]

Pool owners are not negligent for failure to take steps to reduce the risk of injury from unforeseeable accidents, e.g., a child who climbs onto the cover of a barbeque pit and dives into a pool, and is consequently injured.[301]

Acts of Third Parties

A property owner, or one in control or possession of real property, has the duty to exercise reasonable control over the conduct of those permitted to enter upon the land.[302] This duty arises when the owner is aware of the necessity for such control and has a reasonable opportunity to exercise control over the third parties' conduct.[303]

---

[294] Shuman v Mashburn, 137 Ga App 231, 223 SE2d 268, 270 (1976); *see generally* §6.09.

[295] Grimes v Hettinger, 566 SW2d 769, 773 (Ky Ct App 1978).

[296] Christman v Senyk, 34 Ohio Misc 47, 293 NE2d 126, 127 (1972).

[297] Bradshaw v Paduano, 55 AD2d 828, 390 NYS2d 308, 309-10 (1976).

[298] 34 Ohio Misc 47, 293 NE2d 126, 127 (1972).

[299] Bryant v Morley, 406 So 2d 394, 396 (Ala 1981).

[300] *Id.*

[301] Herring v Hauck, 118 Ga App 623, 165 SE2d 198, 199 (1968).

[302] Mangione v Dimino, 39 AD2d 128, 332 NYS2d 683, 685 (1972).

[303] *Id.*

Hosts who breach this duty by failing to stop or limit the horseplay of third parties near a pool can be liable for a plaintiff's injury.[304] For example, a pool guest who was rendered a quadriplegic when hit from behind by another guest who was fooling around stated a claim for negligence against the pool owner.[305] In that case the court held that a property owner who observed social guests repeatedly attempting to throw another guest into a swimming pool but took no action to stop the activity may be liable when the guest was injured when finally thrown into the pool.[306] However, when there was no evidence that swimmers were engaged in horseplay, boisterous conduct, or any other dangerous activity, a landowner was not negligent when a guest was injured.[307]

Rescue

A person is generally under no duty to attempt to rescue another person known to be in danger of drowning.[308] However, a duty to aid one in peril has been imposed when a special relationship exists between the parties.[309] For example, a duty to aid a social guest has been imposed upon a host.[310]

However, a host is not liable for failure to render aid unless he or she knows or has reason to know of the guest's peril.[311] There is no continuing duty to discover the peril of persons in danger of drowning.[312] Furthermore, if there was not sufficient time to rescue a swimmer in peril, there is no liability.[313]

In *Handiboe v McCarthy*,[314] a four-year-old child visited another child in the

---

304 Martin v Shea, 432 NE2d 46, 49 (Ind Ct App 1982); Grimes v Hettinger, 566 SW2d 769, 774 (Ky Ct App 1978); *see also* Restatement (Second) of Torts §318 (1965).

305 Martin v Shea, 432 NE2d 46, 49 (Ind Ct App 1982).

306 *Id.*

307 Grimes v Hettinger, 566 SW2d 769, 774 (Ky Ct App 1978).

308 *Id* 775; *see also* Restatement (Second) of Torts §314 comment e, illustration 4 (1965). There has been some interesting law journal commentary in this area. *See, e.g.,* D'Amato, *The Bad Samaritan Paradigm,* 70 NWUL Rev 798 (1975); Weinrib, *The Case For A Duty To Rescue,* 90 Yale LJ 247 (1980); Note, *Beyond Good Samaritans and Moral Monsters: An Individualistic Justification of the General Legal Duty To Rescue,* 31 UCLA 252 (1983).

309 Grimes v Hettinger, 566 SW2d 769, 775 (Ky Ct App 1978). A handful of states require a person to rescue someone in danger. *See, e.g.,* Minn Stat Ann §604.05 (West Supp 1984); Vt Stat Ann tit 12 §519 (1973). It is unclear whether the Vermont statute provides for a private cause of action. *See* Franklin, *Vermont Requires Rescue,* 25 Stan L Rev 51, 57 (1972).

310 Grimes v Hettinger, 566 SW2d 769, 775 (Ky Ct App 1978).

311 *Id.*

312 *Id.*

313 *Id* 776.

314 114 Ga App 541, 151 SE2d 905 (1966).

neighborhood and drowned in the friend's swimming pool. The children were apparently being cared for by a servant employed by the friend's parents. The court held that there was no legal duty to rescue unless the injury was due to the fault of the defendant. In this case, the court held that the servant was not at fault and dismissed the complaint.[315]

The *Handiboe* decision is flawed in three major ways, although the result may have been correct under Georgia law at that time. First, the court only analyzed the case in terms of a duty to rescue. However, there was at least one other major issue: the defendant's potential liability for negligent supervision, i.e., allowing the child to get into the pool in the first place. In addition, the defendant may also have been negligent under a second theory, i.e., in hiring or retaining this servant if she had a history of acting irresponsibly. However, the facts were insufficiently developed to know whether this second theory was applicable.

Second, although it is not obvious that the servant had a duty to supervise the child,[316] this issue should have been discussed, not ignored. Furthermore, if this duty to supervise were breached, then there is the additional issue of whether the owner is vicariously liable for the servant's negligence.[317]

Third, even if the owner had, at that time,[318] only the limited duty to refrain from wilful or wanton conduct, the court never analyzed, at least explicitly, whether that duty was breached.

Quality of Water

Where the lack of clarity of the water at a residential pool was considered a dangerous, but obvious, condition, the owner had no duty to warn a 12-year-old experienced swimmer.[319]

Causation

When there is no evidence of what caused a child's drowning, the landowner is not liable.[320] However, there is always a potential problem of causation when an unnoticed drowning occurs. In one close case, the court held that there was sufficient evidence of causation to go to the jury.

---

315 151 SE2d at 907.

316 *See, e.g.*, Gordon v Harris, 86 AD2d 948, 448 NYS2d 598, 599 (1982).

317 *Contrast* Jones v Maryland Casualty Co, 256 So 2d 358, 362 (La Ct App 1971) *with* Grimes v Hettinger, 566 SW2d 769, 775 (Ky Ct App 1978).

318 Restatement (Second) of Torts §339 has now been adopted. *See* Gregory v Johnson, 249 Ga 151, 289 SE2d 232, 235 (1982).

319 Grimes v Hettinger, 566 SW2d 769, 773 (Ky Ct App 1978).

320 Butler v Continental Ins Co, 374 So 2d 170, 172 (La Ct App 1979); *see generally* §§1.25, 6.08.

The court found four possible ways in which the deceased child could have entered a residential swimming pool, and only two of them would have been possible had the pool owner acted reasonably under the circumstances.[321]

§6.17 Skydiving

A land occupier generally has no duty to warn of or guard against obvious dangers.[322] In *Hammerlind v Clear Lake Star Factory Skydiver's Club*, a skydiver was fatally injured when he landed in a lake.[323] The plaintiff's estate argued that the airport owner was liable, even though the injury did not occur on airport property, for failure to close the airport to skydiving.

The *Hammerlind* court rejected this argument and affirmed a directed verdict for the landowner because the lake posed an obvious danger to parachutists, given its proximity to the drop zone and the general danger of water to jumpers.[324] Furthermore, the landowner could not have reasonably anticipated harm despite the obvious danger because no similar accident had previously occurred, and the landowner could rely on the skydiving club to check the jumper's equipment.

§6.18 Sledding and Tobogganing

A land occupier generally has no duty to warn of or guard against obvious dangers.[325] Therefore, when a plaintiff knew of a gully at the bottom of a hill but still proceeded to toboggan the landowner was not liable when the plaintiff was injured after hitting the gully.[326]

Similarly, a 15-year-old boy was held to have realized the risks when he had been sledding for over three hours and had ridden down an incline at least 15 times before he lost control of the sled and hit a tree.[327] Therefore, the landowner was exonerated.

---

[321] Johnson v Harris, 23 Ariz App 103, 530 P2d 1136, 1138 (1975).

[322] *See* **§6.09**.

[323] 258 NW2d 590, 594 (Minn 1977).

[324] *See id* 594; *see also* Restatement (Second) of Torts §343A(1) (1965).

[325] *See* **§6.09**.

[326] Dougherty v Graham, 161 Conn 248, 287 A2d 382, 385 (1971).

[327] Scheffer v Braverman, 89 NJ Super 452, 215 A2d 378, 381 (1965).

Products Liability

7

General Principles of Liability

Specific Activities and Products

General Principles of Liability

§7.01 Introduction

In the last 20 years there has been a marked transformation in the liability of manufacturers, distributors, and retailers of products, including recreational products.[1] This is due, in substantial part, to the publication in 1965 of the Restatement (Second) of Torts which imposed strict liability on companies for marketing unreasonably dangerous products.[2] Today, over 40 states have adopted §402A of the Restatement (Second) of Torts or a substantially similar principle of liability.[3] In addition, strict liability principles have been applied under federal law.[4]

A person injured by a defective product may sue under strict liability as well as several other related theories of recovery, e.g., negligence,[5]

---

[1] *See generally* Frakt, *Recreational And Leisure Product Liability*, 1 J Prod L 5 (1982); Wilkinson, *Sports Products Liability*, 17 Trial 58 (Nov 1981).

[2] *See* Restatement (Second) of Torts §402A (1965). This book ignores, almost completely, cases decided prior to 1965 because it is highly questionable in light of the major changes in product liability law whether the reasoning in those cases would be followed today.

The California Supreme Court adopted the principle of strict liability in 1962 in Greenman v Yuba Power Prod, Inc, 59 Cal 2d 57, 377 P2d 897, 27 Cal Rptr 697 (1962). Although *Greenman* was decided before §402A had been officially adopted by the American Law Institute, it was not unaffected by it. The author of *Greenman*, Justice Traynor, was a member of the Reporter's Advisory Committee to the Restatement and a draft of §402A had been disseminated prior to the publication of *Greenman. See* Wade, *On Product "Design Defects" And Their Actionability*, 33 Vand L Rev 551, 554 (1980).

Strict products liability was originally introduced as a new concept of warranty, sounding in tort, to which certain warranty defenses, such as lack of privity, were inapplicable. Corbin v Coleco Indus, 748 F2d 411, 416 (7th Cir 1984); *see generally* Prosser, *The Fall Of The Citadel (Strict Liability To The Consumer)*, 50 Minn L Rev 791 (1966); Prosser, *The Assault Upon The Citadel (Strict Liability To The Consumer)*, 69 Yale LJ 1099 (1960). One court stated that the advantage of strict liability was that it was a "release from the shackles of warranty language." Blevins v Cushman Motors, 551 SW2d 602, 609 (Mo 1977).

[3] *See* Comment, *Products Liability—Tort Reform: An Overview Of Washington's New Act*, 17 Gonz L Rev 357, 365 (1982); *see, e.g.*, Anderson v Heron Engg Co, 198 Colo 391, 604 P2d 674, 676 (1979); Nicolodi v Harley Davidson Motor Co, 370 NE2d 68, 72 (Fla Dist Ct App 1979); Lukowski v Vecta Educ Corp, 401 NE2d 781, 786 (Ind Ct App 1980); Blevins v Cushman Motors, 551 SW2d 602, 606 (Mo 1977); Pegg v General Motors Corp, 258 Pa Super 59, 391 A2d 1074 (1978); Ark Stat Ann §85-2-318.2 (1983); Ga Code §51-1-11 (1982); Ind Code Ann §34-4-20A-1 to -8 (Burns 1984); SC Code Ann §15-73-10 (Law Co-op 1977).

[4] Pavlides v Galveston Yacht Basin, Inc, 727 F2d 330, 338 (5th Cir 1984) (Death on the High Seas Act); Arthur v Avon Inflatables, Ltd, 156 Cal App 3d 401, 405, 203 Cal Rptr 1 (1984).

[5] *See generally* **ch** 1.

misrepresentation,[6] breach of warranty,[7] or violation of a Consumer Product Safety Commission rule.[8] As a practical matter, in many cases the distinctions between these theories of recovery blur.[9] This has caused significant confusion for the litigants and for the courts. There is authority that if the plaintiff cannot articulate a meaningful distinction between the different theories of recovery, he or she can proceed under only one theory.[10] However, several courts have held that even if the defendant receives a favorable verdict on the strict products liability claim, it is not entitled to judgment as a matter of law on related theories.[11]

In any event, it is generally considered that strict liability provides the most expansive liability for defendants[12] and, therefore, this theory is discussed extensively throughout this chapter. Generally, the courts have imposed strict liability where a person was injured by a defective[13] condition of a product which rendered the product unreasonably dangerous[14] and this defect existed when the product left[15] the company's control.[16] Accordingly, *strict* liability

---

6 *See* §7.06.

7 *See* §§7.04, 7.05.

8 *See* 15 USC §2072(a); Aimone v Walgreen's Co, 601 F Supp 507, 510 (ND Ill 1985). It has been held that punitive damages are not recoverable for violations of the Consumer Product Safety Act. *See* Payne v A. O. Smith, 578 F Supp 733, 738 (SD Ohio 1983); *but see* Young v Robertshaw Controls Co, 560 F Supp 288, 294 (NDNY 1983) (question of state law).

9 Flaminio v Honda Motor Co, 733 F2d 463, 467 (7th Cir 1984); Dietz v Waller, 141 Ariz 107, 685 P2d 744, 749 (1984); Cronin v JBE Olson Corp, 8 Cal 3d 121, 501 P2d 1153, 1162, 104 Cal Rptr 433 (1972); Evangeline v Billings Cycle Center, 626 P2d 841, 843 (Mont 1981); *see also* Nicolodi v Harley Davidson Motor Co, 370 So 2d 68, 72 (Fla Dist Ct App 1979); Lewis v Big Powderhorn Mt Ski Corp, 69 Mich App 437, 245 NW2d 81, 83 (1976); J. White & R. Summers, Uniform Commercial Code 325 (1980); Birnbaum, *Unmasking The Test For Design Defect: From Negligence [To Warranty] To Strict Liability To Negligence*, 33 Vand L Rev 593, 601 (1980); *but see* Gorman v Saf-T-Mate, Inc, 513 F Supp 1028, 1038 (ND Ind 1981) (express warranty is different from misrepresentation).

10 Corbin v Coleco Indus, 748 F2d 411, 416 (7th Cir 1984).

11 Randall v Warnaco, Inc, 677 F2d 1226, 1231-32 (8th Cir 1982); Schenck v Pelkey, 176 Conn 245, 405 A2d 665, 671-72 (1978); Brown v Yamaha Motor Corp, 38 Wash App 914, 691 P2d 577, 579-80 (1984).

12 There is one primary exception, although it is not applicable in most recreational accident cases. Strict liability generally only provides a recovery for personal injuries. Colonial Park Country Club v Joan of Arc, 746 F2d 1425, 1428-29 (10th Cir 1984). In contrast, under warranty law, there is recovery for purely economic losses.

13 *See* §7.03.

14 The giving of the jury instruction regarding "unreasonable danger" in 3 E. Devitt & C. Blackmar, Federal Jury Practice And Instructions §82.03 (3d ed 1977) is not error. *See* Schwartz v American Honda Motor Co, Inc, 710 F2d 378, 382 (7th Cir 1982).

15 Plaintiff must prove in her case-in-chief that the defect existed when the product left defendant's possession. This burden does not arise only when defendant argues the product was subsequently altered. Hiller v Kawasaki Motors Corp, USA, 671 P2d 369, 371 (Alaska 1983).

does not mean absolute liability.[17] Product manufacturers or sellers are not transformed into insurers under this doctrine and products need not be made accident-proof.[18]

Strict liability is imposed by operation of law as a matter of public policy for the protection of the public.[19] It has been justified on the basis that the manufacturer or seller is in a better position than the consumer to guard against defects in the product.[20] It is imposed independent of contractual considerations and since one cannot contract away this responsibility, exculpatory agreements limiting or eliminating this liability are unenforceable.[21]

Strict products liability primarily focuses on the defect in the product, rather than on the defendant's behavior.[22] Therefore, it is commonly said that there is no requirement that the plaintiff prove that the defendant was negligent.[23] However, such statements oversimplify the analysis. In both negligence and strict liability cases, the probability and magnitude of the risk is to be balanced against the utility of the product.[24] The distinction between the two theories of recovery lies in the fact that the inability of the defendant to know and

---

An unforeseen modification of the product after it leaves the manufacturer's hands is not the manufacturer's responsibility. Landrine v Mego Corp, 95 AD2d 759, 464 NYS2d 516, 518 (1983).

16 Deitz v Waller, 141 Ariz 107, 685 P2d 744, 747 (1984); Ogg v City of Springfield, 121 Ill App 3d 25, 458 NE2d 1331, 1339 (1984); O'Brien v Muskin Corp, 94 NJ 169, 463 A2d 298, 303 (1983); Fitzgerald Marine Sales v LeUnes, 659 SW2d 917, 918 (Tex Civ App 1983); *see also* Barris v Bob's Drag Chutes & Equip, 685 F2d 94, 99 (3d Cir 1982) (Pennsylvania law); Pawlak v Brown, 430 So 2d 1346, 1348 (La Ct App 1983); Novak v Piggly Wiggly Puget Sound Co, 22 Wash App 407, 591 P2d 791, 794 (1979).
The disastrous consequences to a manufacturer of mistakenly admitting in a pleading that it manufactured a defective water slide are analyzed in Beeck v Aquaslide 'N' Dive Corp, 350 NW2d 149 (Iowa 1984).

17 Sabich v Outboard Marine Corp, 60 Cal App 3d 591, 131 Cal Rptr 703, 706 (1976); Dippel v Sciano, 37 Wis 2d 443, 155 NW2d 55, 63 (1967).

18 Hunt v Harley Davidson Motor Co, Inc, 147 Ga App 44, 248 SE2d 15, 16-17 (1978); Genteman v Saunders Archery Co, 42 Ill App 3d 294, 355 NE2d 647, 652 (1976); Bolm v Triumph Corp, 33 NY2d 151, 305 NE2d 769, 350 NYS2d 644, 649 (1973); *see also* American Safety Equip Co v Winkler, 640 P2d 216 (Colo 1982); *see generally* Dickerson, *Products Liability: How Good Does A Product Have To Be?*, 42 Ind LJ 301 (1967).

19 Sipari v Villa Olivia Country Club, 63 Ill App 3d 985, 380 NE2d 819, 823 (1978).

20 Dixon v Four Seasons Bowling Alley, Inc, 176 NJ Super 540, 424 A2d 428, 430 (1980).

21 Sipari v Villa Olivia Country Club, 63 Ill App 3d 985, 380 NE2d 819, 823 (1978). Exculpatory agreements are discussed in **ch 10**.

22 O'Brien v Muskin Corp, 94 NJ 169, 463 A2d 298, 304 (1983).

23 *See* O'Brien v Muskin Corp, 94 NJ 169, 463 A2d 298, 303 (1983); Keeton, *Product Liability And The Meaning of Defect*, 5 St Mary's LJ 30, 34-35 (1973).

24 *See generally* Pavlides v Galveston Yacht Basin, Inc, 727 F2d 330, 337 (5th Cir 1984). A reasonable firm would not sell the product if it knew the risk involved. *Id.*

prevent the risk is a defense to a negligence claim, but not to a strict liability action.[25]

Strict liability is generally applied only where the product is dangerous to an extent beyond that which would be contemplated by an ordinary person with the ordinary knowledge common to the community as to its characteristics,[26] an objective test.[27] This has sometimes been held to mean that there is no recovery if the injury is caused by the obvious propensities of a product.[28] Accordingly, a motorcycle helmet without a face guard is not unreasonably dangerous because the helmet could not reasonably be expected to guard against blows to the face.[29] In one case, the court stated, in dicta, that a motorcycle was not unreasonably dangerous where it presented no unforseen hazard for the intended user, an experienced motorcyclist.[30]

The majority rule is that there is recovery under strict products liability only for physical harm.[31] Accordingly, a country club's strict liability claim against a food supplier for damages for lost membership resulting from a serious case of botulism poisoning was rejected.[32]

Plaintiffs

Section 402A, by its terms, can only be invoked by injured users or consumers.[33] Indeed, comment o to that section states that no position is taken on whether other injured parties can recover under this theory.[34] In *Kately v Wilkinson*, the court held that the operator (and owner) of a boat could sue

---

[25] Barras v Touzet's, Inc, 423 So 2d 1239, 1242 (La Ct App 1982).

[26] Restatement (Second) of Torts §402A comment i (1965).

[27] Vincer v Esther Williams All-Aluminum Swimming Pool Co, 69 Wis 2d 326, 230 NW2d 794, 798 (1975). Plaintiff's awareness of the danger is a factor to consider in assessing whether there was contributory or comparative negligence or assumption of the risk. *See id.* These defenses are discussed in **ch 9**.

[28] Walker v Maxwell City, Inc, 117 Ill App 3d 571, 453 NE2d 917, 922 (1983); Magnuson v Rupp Mfg, Inc, 171 NW2d 201, 208 (Minn 1969); O'Brien v Muskin Corp, 94 NJ 169, 463 A2d 298, 304 (1983); *see generally* Marshall, *An Obvious Wrong Does Not Make A Right: Manufacturers' Liability For Patently Dangerous Products*, 48 NYUL Rev 1066 (1973); Comment, *Obviousness Of Product Dangers As A Bar to Recovery: Minnesota Apparently Adopts The Latent-Patent Doctrine*, 3 Wm Mitchell L Rev 241 (1977).

[29] O'Brien v Muskin Corp, 94 NJ 169, 463 A2d 298, 304 (1983); *see generally* **§7.17**.

[30] Rainbow v Albert Elia Bldg Co, 79 AD2d 287, 436 NYS2d 480, 483 (1981), *affd without opinion*, 56 NY2d 550, 434 NE2d 1345, 449 NYS2d 967 (1982).

[31] Colonial Park Country Club v Joan of Arc, 746 F2d 1425, 1428 (10th Cir 1984); *see generally* Note, *Economic Loss in Products Liability*, 66 Colum L Rev 917 (1966).

[32] Colonial Park Country Club v Joan of Arc, 746 F2d 1425, 1428 (10th Cir 1984).

[33] Restatement (Second) of Torts §402A (1965). A friend of the purchaser who was injured using the product was allowed to sue under strict liability. *See* Wentworth v Kawasaki, Inc, 508 F Supp 1114, 1117 (DNH 1981) (snowmobile).

[34] *See* Restatement (Second) of Torts §402A comment o (1965).

the boat's manufacturer and retailer under strict liability for the emotional trauma she suffered from watching the boat collide, because of a defect in the boat's steering column, with a close friend who was water skiing.[35]

A manufacturer has no duty of care to nonusers of its product in cases of an omission[36] to act.[37] In *Carrier v Riddell, Inc*, the plaintiff was not using the defendant-manufacturer's football helmet at the time of his injury. The plaintiff argued that had this manufacturer properly warned the other players on his high school team who used its helmets, he would have learned of the warnings and acted accordingly. The court rejected this argument because where there is no duty to act, there can be no liability.[38]

In *Pegg v General Motors Corp*, an equally divided court affirmed a lower court decision that a lawbreaker, an individual who had stolen a small quantity of swimming pool sanitizer and was injured when it later ignited, could not recover under strict liability.[39]

Defendants

Strict products liability applies to the entire distribution chain,[40] including manufacturers, wholesalers, and retailers, and also to those who hold themselves out as manufacturers or suppliers.[41] However, by its terms §402A only applies to those who *sell* products.[42] Accordingly, a university athletic director, football coach, and athletic trainer were not liable, as a matter of law, under strict products liability for providing a defective football helmet to a college football player because they did not *sell* the helmet.[43] Similarly, a pool manufacturer was not strictly liable for a pool ladder it did not manufacture,[44] a carpenter was not liable for wood it did not sell which was used

---

35 148 Cal App 3d 576, 588, 195 Cal Rptr 902 (1983). The case is discussed in Diamond, *Dillon v. Legg Revisited: Toward A Unified Theory Of Compensating Bystanders And Relatives For Intangible Injuries*, 35 Hastings LJ 477, 495 (1984).

36 E.g., a failure to act. This is in contrast to a commission of an act. *See* Carrier v Riddell, Inc, 721 F2d 867, 868 (1st Cir 1983).

37 *Id.*

38 *Id* 870.

39 258 Pa Super 59, 391 A2d 1074 (1978); *but cf* §6.05 (many jurisdictions hold that landowners owe a duty of care to trespassers).

40 Garcia v Joseph Vince Co, 84 Cal App 3d 876, 148 Cal Rptr 843, 848 (1978); Cobb v Insured Lloyds, 387 So 2d 13, 20 (La Ct App 1980); Sipari v Villa Country Club, 63 Ill App 3d 985, 380 NE2d 819, 824 (1978).

41 *See* Sipari v Villa Country Club, 63 Ill App 3d 985, 380 NE2d 819, 825 (1978); Dudley Sports Co v Schmitt, 151 Ind App 217, 279 NE2d 266, 273 (1972); Restatement (Second) of Torts §400 (1965).

42 Restatement (Second) of Torts §402A (1965).

43 Hemphill v Sayers, 552 F Supp 685, 689 (SD Ill 1982).

44 Kaloz v Risco, 120 Misc 2d 586, 466 NYS2d 218, 220 (Sup Ct 1983).

in bleachers[45] and a homeowner engaged in erecting a swimming pool in his backyard was not liable to a visitor who fell because of a defective ladder.[46]

It has been held that strict liability does not apply to lessors,[47] such as country clubs which rent golf carts.[48] In addition, liability is imposed only on sellers engaged in the business of selling that product.[49] Accordingly, an amusement ride operator who sold a ride to a second operator was not liable when a person was injured while using this ride at the second operator's establishment.[50]

§7.02 Frequently Occurring Issues

Products

An assumption of strict products liability is that injuries from products constitute a discrete problem meriting special treatment.[51] Otherwise, it would be inappropriate to distinguish product injuries from other personal injuries, liability for which is governed by negligence.[52] However, courts have not always clearly articulated the features of a product case and the policies which distinguish product injuries from other personal injuries.[53]

Accordingly, it is sometimes not easy to determine whether a *product* was involved.[54] Navigational charts have been considered products.[55] However, a

---

[45] Parker v Warren, 503 SW2d 938, 945 (Tenn Ct App 1973).

[46] Yearke v Zarcone, 57 AD2d 457, 395 NYS2d 322, 327 (1977).

[47] Bona v Graefe, 264 Md 69, 285 A2d 607, 611 (1972) (golf cart); Katz v Slade, 460 SW2d 608, 613 (Mo 1970); *see generally* Fraser, *Application of Strict Tort Liability To The Leasing Industry: A Closer Look*, 34 Bus Law 605 (1979); Comment, *Finance Lessor Liability Under Section 402A Restatement (Second) of Torts*, 7 Am J Trial Advoc 155 (1983); *but see* Opera v Hyva, Inc, 86 AD2d 373, 450 NYS2d 615, 618 (1982) (strict liability applies to firms in the business of renting ski equipment).

[48] *See* §7.14.

[49] Restatement (Second) of Torts §402A (1965). However, actions can be brought against dissolved corporations where they accrued prior to dissolution and the statute of limitations has not run. Gassert v Commercial Mechanisms, Inc, 277 NW2d 392, 394 (Minn 1979).

[50] Allen v Nicole, Inc, 172 NJ Super 442, 412 A2d 824, 826 (1980).

[51] Powers, *Distinguishing Between Products And Services In Strict Liability*, 62 NCL Rev 415, 418 (1984).

[52] *Id.*

[53] *Id* 423-30.

[54] *See generally* Wunsch, *The Definition Of A Product For Purposes Of Section 402A*, 50 Ins Couns J 344 (1983); Comment, *Products Liability - Tort Reform: An Overview Of Washington's New Act*, 17 Gonz L Rev 357, 360 n 13 (1982).

[55] *See* Brocklesby v United States, 753 F2d 794, 800 (9th Cir 1985) (California law); Saloomey v Jeppesen & Co, 707 F2d 671, 676-77 (2d Cir 1983) (Colorado law).

hockey ticket has been held not to be a product.[56] One court rejected an injured motorcyclist's claim that a narrow street with a sharp curve was a defective product which should subject the developer to strict liability.[57]

Some plaintiffs injured by products which were used in the providing of a service have been unsuccessful in urging that strict liability should be applied.[58] For example, in *Dixon v Four Seasons Bowling Alley, Inc*,[59] the plaintiff was injured when she fell and a chipped portion of a bowling ball cut her finger. The court held that the bowling alley was not strictly liable, reasoning that if the plaintiff alleged that the premises were unsafe, she would have to prove that the bowling establishment was negligent and her burden should not be lessened because the injury resulted from the condition of a ball rather than a condition of a different part of the premises.[60]

Subsequent Remedial Measures

There are two reasons why evidence of a defendant's subsequent[61] remedial measures is generally inadmissible in negligence actions as proof that the defendant previously acted unreasonably.[62] First, it is reasoned that the changes are not relevant to the manufacturer's objective conduct and perceptions prior to the accident.[63] Second, there is the policy consideration of not wanting to discourage the repair of potentially unsafe conditions.[64] However, the changes are admissable for other purposes, e.g., to challenge a defendant's expert's opinion that a certain design would be uneconomical.[65]

Some courts have allowed subsequent remedial repairs and corrections to be introduced as evidence of prior wrongful conduct in cases involving strict product liability,[66] although there is authority to the contrary.[67] However, this

---

56 *See* Kennedy v Providence Hockey Club, Inc, 119 RI 70, 376 A2d 329, 333 (1977).

57 Milam v Midland Corp, 282 Ark 15, 665 SW2d 284, 285 (1984).

58 *See generally* J. White & R. Summers, Uniform Commercial Code 348-49 (1980); Powers, *Distinguishing Between Products And Services In Strict Liability*, 62 NCL Rev 415 (1984); §7.04.

59 176 NJ Super 540, 424 A2d 428 (1980).

60 424 A2d at 431; *see generally* §7.10.

61 Changes made after the purchase, but before the accident are admissible. Lavin v Fauci, 170 NJ Super 408, 406 A2d 978, 981 (1979).

62 Bolm v Triumph Corp, 71 AD2d 429, 422 NYS2d 969, 974 (1979); *see, e.g.*, Fed R Evid 407.

63 Bolm v Triumph Corp, 71 AD2d 429, 422 NYS2d 969, 974 (1979); Haysom v Coleman Lantern Co, 89 Wash 2d 474, 573 P2d 785, 790 (1978).

64 Bolm v Triumph Corp, 71 AD2d 429, 422 NYS2d 969, 974 (1979); Haysom v Coleman Lantern Co, 89 Wash 2d 474, 573 P2d 785, 790 (1978).

65 Lavin v Fauci, 170 NJ Super 408, 406 A2d 978, 980-81 (1979).

66 Herndon v Seven Bar Flying Serv Inc, 716 F2d 1322, 1331 (10th Cir 1983); Robbins v Farmers Union Grain Terminal Assn, 552 F2d 788 (8th Cir 1977); Ault v International

evidence is inadmissible if there is no showing that the change was made because the prior condition was defective.[68]

In jurisdictions where evidence of subsequent repairs is admissible regarding strict liability claims, care must be taken that the defendant is not unduly prejudiced where the plaintiff is pursuing both strict liability and negligence claims. One court held that in cases involving both strict liability and negligence, it was better practice to word the jury instructions regarding subsequent remedial measures affirmatively, i.e., to state that the evidence only applies to the strict liability claim.[69] However, it was not reversible error to word the instructions negatively, i.e., to state that the evidence of subsequent remedial measures does not apply to the negligence claim.[70]

Presence or Absence of Similar Accidents

Evidence of similar[71] accidents is generally admissible because it is relevant to the defendant's notice of a problem, the magnitude of the danger involved, the defendant's ability to correct a known defect, and causation.[72] However, to be admissible these other accidents must have occurred under substantially similar conditions to those existing during the plaintiff's accident and they must not have occurred at a time too remote in relation to the plaintiff's accident.[73] In addition, evidence of similar accidents may be excluded if the

---

Harvester Co, 13 Cal 3d 113, 528 P2d 1148, 117 Cal Rptr 812 (1974); Millette v Radosta, 84 Ill App 3d 5, 404 NE2d 823 (1980); Caprara v Chrysler Corp, 52 NY2d 114, 417 NE2d 545, 436 NYS2d 251 (1981); Caldwell v Yamaha Motor Co, 648 P2d 519, 525 (Wyo 1982).

[67] Flaminio v Honda Motor Co, 733 F2d 463, 469 (7th Cir 1984) (citing numerous other cases); Werner v Unjohn Co, 628 F2d 848, 857 (4th Cir 1980); Lavin v Fauci, 170 NJ Super 403, 406 A2d 978, 980 (1979); *see also* Opera v Hyva, Inc, 86 AD2d 373, 450 NYS2d 615, 617 (1982) (not admissible in design defect cases because strict liability is not different from negligence).

In *Flaminio* the court held that Rule 407 was to be applied even though state law was to the contrary. *See* 733 F2d at 470-72.

[68] Caldwell v Yamaha Motor Co, 648 P2d 519, 525 (Wyo 1982).

[69] Hiller v Kawasaki Motors Corp, USA, 671 P2d 369, 374 (Alaska 1983).

[70] *Id.*

[71] Evidence of subsequent accidents may also be admissible because it relates to causation. Weeks v Remington Arms Co, 733 F2d 1485, 1491 n 10 (11th Cir 1984); Bolm v Triumph Corp, 71 AD2d 429, 422 NYS2d 969, 975 (1979).

[72] Weeks v Remington Arms Co, 733 F2d 1485, 1491 (11th Cir 1984); *see also* Cole v New York Racing Assn, 24 AD2d 993, 266 NYS2d 267, 270 (1965), *affd,* 17 NY2d 761, 217 NE2d 144, 270 NYS2d 421 (1966).

[73] Weeks v Remington Arms Co, 733 F2d 1485, 1491 (11th Cir 1984). Where the prior accidents are only offered to show the defendant's notice of a problem, the requirement that the prior accidents be substantially similar is weakened. *See* Warshaw v Rockresorts, Inc, 57 Hawaii 645, 562 P2d 428, 434 (1977).

value of such evidence is disproportionate to the danger of unfair surprise, prejudice, confusion of the issues, or undue consumption of time.[74]

In some cases, evidence of similar accidents will be contained in written reports. The reports may be inadmissible hearsay if they contain information by individuals who did not have a business duty to observe and report how the accidents occurred.[75]

The defendant is generally allowed to show that the product had a history of use without any accidents occurring.[76] In *Belfry v Anthony Pools, Inc*, the court allowed the defendant to introduce evidence that there had been no previous accidents because this showed the defendant's lack of knowledge of the defect and also showed whether the defendant exercised a reasonable duty of care.[77]

To lay a proper foundation for testimony concerning the absence of similar prior accidents, the defendant must show that the absence occurred while the product was being used similarly to the way the plaintiff used the product.[78] The defendant must also show that the absence occurred under conditions which were substantially similar to those surrounding the accident which gave rise to the suit.[79]

Defenses

A plaintiff who was comparatively negligent,[80] who voluntarily and unreasonably proceeded to encounter a known risk arising out of the defective product[81] or misused the product,[82] may have his or her recovery limited.[83]

---

[74] Warshaw v Rockresorts, Inc, 57 Hawaii 645, 562 P2d 428, 434 (1977).

[75] Warshaw v Rockresorts, Inc, 57 Hawaii 645, 562 P2d 428, 433 (1977).

[76] *See* Belfry v Anthony Pools, Inc, 80 Mich App 118, 262 NW2d 909, 912 (1977).

[77] *Id.*

[78] Leischner v Deere & Co, 127 Ill App 3d 175, 468 NE2d 182, 183 (1984).

[79] *Id.* In *Leischner* the defendant's witness stated that there were no other reports of the alleged defect. The court assumed that a substantial amount of the other snowmobiles were used similarly to the way plaintiff used his snowmobile. *See id.*

[80] *See* Pavlides v Galveston Yacht Basin, Inc, 727 F2d 330, 341 (5th Cir 1984) (action was brought under the Death on the High Seas Act); *see generally* Feinberg, *The Applicability Of A Comparative Negligence Defense In A Strict Products Liability Suit*, 42 Ins Couns J 39 (1975); Hasten, *Comparative Liability Principles: Should They Now Apply To Strict Products Liability Actions In Ohio*, 14 U Toledo L Rev 1151 (1983); Voelker, *The Application of Comparative Negligence To Strict Products Liability*, 59 Chi-Kent L Rev 1043 (1983); Woods, *Product Liability: Is Comparative Fault Winning The Day*, 36 Ark L Rev 360 (1983); §§9.01, 9.04.

[81] Dias v Daisy-Heddon, 180 Ind App 657, 390 NE2d 222, 225 (1979); *see generally* §§9.01-9.03.

[82] Sipari v Villa Olivia Country Club, 63 Ill App 3d 985, 380 NE2d 819, 824 (1978); Dias v Daisy-Heddon, 390 NE2d 222, 225 (Ind Ct App 1979); *see generally* Woodward v First of Ga Ins Co, 333 So 2d 709, 711 (La Ct App), *writ denied*, 338 So 2d 295 (La 1976). In Illinois, misuse is not an affirmative defense. Plaintiff must show in the case-in-chief that

The statute of limitations may also bar a plaintiff's claim.[84]

Indemnity and Contribution

In many cases, the retailer can receive complete indemnification from the manufacturer when the manufacturer is the primary wrongdoer.[85] However, in *Four Winns, Inc v Cincinnati Insurance Co*,[86] the court held that a retailer of a boat was not entitled to indemnity as a matter of law against the boat's manufacturer. The court held that indemnity was proper only where the party seeking that relief was without fault.[87] Therefore, if the retailer failed to inspect the boat and an inspection would have revealed the defect, the retailer could not recover from the manufacturer.[88]

A manufacturer who settles a product liability action with the plaintiff may bring a subsequent action against other joint tortfeasors for contribution.[89] However, a defendant sued solely under strict products liability may not collect from a negligent third party in a contribution action because there is no right to contribution between parties whose liability is imposed on different grounds.[90]

A manufacturer who paid damages to a plaintiff may be subrogated to the plaintiff's claim against a doctor whose negligence aggravated the plaintiff's injuries.[91]

---

he or she did not misuse the product. Schwartz v American Honda Motor Co, 710 F2d 378, 380 (7th Cir 1983) (Illinois law).

[83] *See generally* ch 9.

[84] Weeks v Remington Arms Co, 733 F2d 1485 (11th Cir 1984); Ferguson v Sturm, Ruger & Co, 524 F Supp 1042, 1044 (D Conn 1981); Neikirk v Central Ill Light Co, 128 Ill App 3d 1069, 471 NE2d 1027 (1984); Bernick v Jurden, 293 SE2d 405, 411-13 (NC 1982); *see generally* McGovern, *The Variety, Policy And Constitutionality Of Product Liability Statutes Of Repose*, 30 Am UL Rev 579 (1981); Comment, *Limiting Liability: Products Liability And A Statute Of Repose*, 32 Baylor L Rev 137 (1980).

[85] Heiman v Boatel Co, 1975-77 Prod Liab Rep (CCH) ¶7570, at 14,433 (8th Cir 1976) (yacht); Rosehoro v Yamaha Intl Corp, 1978-79 Prod Liab Rep (CCH) ¶8425, at 18,082 (DDC 1979) (motorcycle).

[86] 471 NE2d 1187 (Ind Ct App 1984).

[87] *Id* 1189.

[88] *Id.*

[89] Home Ins Co v Advance Mach Co, 443 So 2d 165, 168 (Fla Dist Ct App 1983). The bringing of this contribution action does not waive matters protected by the attorney-client privilege in the first lawsuit. *Id.*

A defendant who loses at trial is entitled to reduce the damage award by the present value of the settlement paid by other joint tortfeasors. *See* Franck v Polaris E-Z Go Div of Textron, 157 Cal App 3d 1107, 204 Cal Rptr 321, 328 (1984); *see generally* Leisure Group, Inc v Williams, 351 So 2d 374, 375 (Fla Dist Ct App 1977).

[90] Bike v American Motors Corp, 101 FRD 77, 83 (ED Pa 1984); Fenton v McCrory Corp, 47 FRD 260, 262 (WD Pa 1969); *see generally* Aalco Mfg Co v City of Espanola, 95 NM 66, 618 P2d 1230, 1231-32 (1980).

[91] *See* Reese v AMF-Whitely, 420 F Supp 985, 989 (D Neb 1976).

Punitive Damages

Punitive damages may be granted in a products liability case where there is evidence of wilfulness, wantonness, maliciousness, recklessness, oppression, or outrageous conduct.[92] Indeed, in one case, an award of punitive damages was upheld even though the compensatory damage issues had been settled.[93] However, where such reprehensible behavior was absent, no punitive damages were allowed.[94]

When a party's knowledge of the defective condition is an element of liability, e.g., for punitive damages, both parties should be allowed to present evidence either establishing or refuting the existence of such knowledge.[95] For example, a football helmet manufacturer is entitled to show that it could not have been aware of any defect in its helmet because the vast majority of other helmet manufacturers constructed their helmets using the same method used by the defendant.[96]

Insurance

In *Smith v Maryland Casualty Co*,[97] an insurance policy for a church excluded coverage for injuries which occurred after possession of a product was transferred from the insured. Accordingly, the church was not afforded coverage where a boy was injured by a slingshot he received at a church bazaar because at the bazaar the product was transferred from the church to others.[98]

§7.03 Defective Products

To recover on a claim of strict products liability, the plaintiff must prove that the product was defective.[99] This generally means that the product was not

---

92 Detroit Marine Engg, Inc v Maloy, 419 So 2d 687, 693 (Fla Dist Ct App 1982); Wussow v Commercial Mechanisms, Inc, 97 Wis 2d 136, 293 NW2d 897, 905 (1980); *see also* Owen, *Punitive Damages In Products Liability Litigation*, 74 Mich L Rev 1256 (1976); Note, *Allowance Of Punitive Damage Awards In Product Liability Claims*, 6 Ga L Rev 613 (1972).

93 Wussow v Commercial Mechanisms, Inc, 97 Wis 2d 136, 293 NW2d 897, 905 (1980).

94 Detroit Marine Engg, Inc v Maloy, 419 So 2d 687, 693 (Fla Dist Ct App 1982); Ogg v City of Springfield, 121 Ill App 3d 25, 458 NE2d 1331, 1342 (1984).

95 Galindo v Riddell, Inc, 107 Ill App 3d 139, 437 NE2d 376, 384 (1982).

96 *Id.*

97 246 Md 485, 229 A2d 120, 122 (1967).

98 *Id.*

99 Collins v Caldor of Kingston, Inc, 73 AD2d 708, 422 NYS2d 524, 527 (1979). The term *defect* is really no more than a conclusion that the product failed to meet an appropriate standard. *See* O'Brien v Muskin Corp, 94 NJ 169, 463 A2d 298, 304 (1983).

There has been extensive law journal commentary in this area. *See, e.g.*, Prosser, *The Fall*

reasonably fit for the ordinary purposes for which such products are intended or reasonably expected to be used.[100] In addition, in most, but not all,[101] jurisdictions a product is not defective unless it is unreasonably dangerous.[102]

The plaintiff must plead some facts showing a defect or the complaint will be dismissed.[103] However, defects can be established through circumstantial evidence.[104] There is even authority that the plaintiff need not establish a specific defect.[105] The fact that the product malfunctioned is some proof of a defect.[106]

There are three types of product defects: manufacturing defects, design defects, and lack of proper instructions or warnings.[107] Each will be discussed in this section.

Manufacturing Defects

A manufacturing defect results when a product does not perform as intended by the manufacturer.[108] The classic example is a mass-produced product which leaves the assembly lacking a part.[109] Where this occurs, the

---

of the Citadel (Strict Liability To The Consumer), 50 Minn L Rev 791 (1966); Keeton, Product Liability And The Meaning of Defect, 5 St Mary's LJ 30 (1973); Birnbaum, Unmasking The Test For Design Defect: From Negligence [To Warranty] To Strict Liability To Negligence, 33 Vand L Rev 593 (1980); Wade, On Product Design Defects and Their Actionability, 33 Vand L Rev 551 (1980).

100 Anderson v Heron Engg Co, 40 Colo App 191, 575 P2d 16, 18 (Colo Ct App 1978) (ski lift), revd on other grounds, 198 Colo 391, 604 P2d 674 (1979); Parker v Warren, 503 SW2d 938, 945 (Tenn Ct App 1973) (poor grade lumber used for bleachers but no showing that lumber company knew what lumber was to be used for); Prosser, The Fall Of The Citadel (Strict Liability To The Consumer), 50 Minn L Rev 791, 826 (1966); see also Restatement (Second) of Torts §402A comment g (1965) (in a condition not contemplated by the ultimate consumer).

101 See, e.g., McPhail v Municipality of Culebra, 598 F2d 603, 606 (1st Cir 1979) (Puerto Rico law); Butand v Suburban Marine & Sporting Goods, Inc, 543 P2d 209, 214 (Alaska 1975); Cronin v JBE Olson Corp, 8 Cal 3d 12, 501 P2d 1153, 104 Cal Rptr 443 (1972).

102 Collins v Caldor of Kingston, Inc, 73 AD2d 708, 422 NYS2d 524, 527 (1979); see generally Wade, On The Nature Of Strict Tort Liability For Products, 44 Miss LJ 825 (1973); §7.01.

103 Rice v Walker, 359 So 2d 891, 892 (Fla Dist Ct App 1978).

104 Wolff v Whittaker Marine & Mfg Co, 484 F Supp 1021, 1027 (ED Mo 1979).

105 Id.

106 Id.

107 Hemphill v Sayers, 552 F Supp 685, 693 (SD Ill 1982); Franck v Polaris E-Z Go Div of Textron, Inc, 157 Cal App 3d 1107, 204 Cal Rptr 321, 324 (1984); Beeck v Aquaslide 'N' Dive Corp, 350 NW2d 149, 159 (Iowa 1984); Sheehan v Anthony Pools, 50 Md App 614, 440 A2d 1085, 1089 (1982); O'Brien v Muskin Corp, 94 NJ 169, 463 A2d 298, 303 (1983); Opera v Hyva, Inc, 86 AD2d 373, 450 NYS2d 615, 617 (1982).

108 O'Brien v Muskin Corp, 94 NJ 169, 463 A2d 298, 304 (1983).

109 Id.

manufacturer is strictly liable for any injuries, even where it was not at fault.[110]

Design Defects

A product which is defectively designed is one in which there is an unreasonable risk of harm, even though the product was made according to the manufacturer's plans and specifications.[111] In such cases, the plaintiff claims that the entire product line is defective.[112]

A manufacturer has a duty to design products so that they are reasonably fit for the purposes for which they are intended[113] and also reasonably safe for other reasonably foreseeable uses of the product.[114] In determining what risks are foreseeable, the manufacturer is held to the status of an expert.[115]

It is reasonably foreseeable that some recreational products, e.g., motorcycles and snowmobiles, will be involved in collisions.[116] Therefore, manufacturers have a duty to design those products so that users are not subjected to unreasonable risks of injury when the inevitable collision happens.[117]

In many cases, whether the plaintiff's use of the product was reasonably foreseeable is a question of fact. The plaintiff may wish to depose the manufacturer's advertising personnel,[118] review product advertisements,[119] and review patent applications for the product[120] to learn the manufacturer's objective beliefs concerning the reasonably foreseeable uses of its product. If the plaintiff's use of the product was not reasonably foreseeable, the manufacturer is not liable, either because the product was not defective or because the design defect did not cause the accident.[121]

---

[110] Opera v Hyva, Inc, 86 AD2d 373, 450 NYS2d 615, 617 (1982).

[111] 450 NYS2d at 618.

[112] Smith v Ariens Co, 375 Mass 620, 377 NE2d 954, 958 (1978).

[113] *See* Restatement (Second) of Torts §398 (1965).

[114] *See* Szyplinski v Midwest Mobile Home Supply Co, 308 Minn 152, 241 NW2d 306, 310 (1976) (it is not foreseeable that a shop lift, a device used to raise snowmobiles when they are being repaired, would be climbed by child).

[115] Pavlides v Galveston Yacht Basin, Inc, 727 F2d 330, 338 (5th Cir 1984).

[116] Smith v Ariens Co, 375 Mass 620, 377 NE2d 954, 957 (1978).

[117] *See* Cota v Harley Davidson, 141 Ariz 7, 684 P2d 888, 895 (App 1984) (motorcycle); Smith v Ariens Co, 375 Mass 620, 377 NE2d 954, 957 (1978) (snowmobile); Bolm v Triumph Corp, 33 NY2d 151, 305 NE2d 769, 773-74 (1973) (motorcycle); *see also* **§§7.17, 7.19.**

[118] Swartz, *Leisure Time Product-Related Torts*, in 1983 SMU Products Liability Institute 5-11 (1983).

[119] Woods v International Harvester Co, 697 F2d 635, 638 (5th Cir 1983); Blevins v Cushman Motors, 551 SW2d 602, 613 (Mo 1977) (golf cart).

[120] *See* Weeks v Remington Arms Co, 733 F2d 1485, 1490 (11th Cir 1984).

[121] Gellenbeck v Sears, Roebuck & Co, 59 Mich App 339, 229 NW2d 443, 446 (1975).

A manufacturer who designs a defective product is strictly liable for injuries it causes.[122] Therefore, it is sometimes said that there is liability even where the manufacturer acted with reasonable care.[123] However, such statements are overly simplistic.

The determination of whether there is a design defect is usually made by performing a risk–utility analysis.[124] This compares the product's utility with the risk and severity of injury[125] and what alternative designs were available and feasible.[126] Some factors used in this test are:

1. The usefulness and desirability of the product to users and the public
2. The safety of the product
3. The availability of a substitute product
4. The ability to eliminate the risk of injury without impairing the utility of the product[127]

If no alternatives were available, recourse to a unique design is more defensible.[128]

The plaintiff's strongest evidence of the feasibility of an alternative design is the actual use of the alternative design by the defendant or others at the time the product was manufactured.[129] Even if a safer alternative was not being used, evidence that it was available, known, or capable of being developed is relevant in determining whether the alternative was feasible.[130] In contrast, the defendant's strongest rebuttal evidence is that a particular design alternative was impossible due to the state of

---

[122] Blevins v Cushman Motors, 551 SW2d 602, 606 (Mo 1977).

[123] Id.

[124] O'Brien v Muskin Corp, 94 NJ 169, 463 A2d 298, 306 (1983); Landrine v Mego Corp, 95 AD2d 759, 464 NYS2d 516, 518 (1983).

[125] See O'Brien v Muskin Corp, 94 NJ 169, 463 A2d 298, 306 (1983); Boatland, Inc v Bailey, 609 SW2d 743, 746 (Tex 1980).

[126] Murphy v Chestnut Mt Lodge, Inc, 124 Ill App 3d 508, 464 NE2d 818, 823 (1984); Opera v Hyva, Inc, 86 AD2d 373, 450 NYS2d 615, 618 (1982); Boatland, Inc v Bailey, 609 SW2d 743, 746 (Tex 1980).

[127] See O'Brien v Muskin Corp, 94 NJ 169, 463 A2d 298, 306 (1983); Boatland, Inc v Bailey, 609 SW2d 743, 746 (Tex 1980).

[128] O'Brien v Muskin Corp, 94 NJ 169, 463 A2d 298, 305 (1983). The existence of a safer and equally efficacious design diminishes the justification for using the challenged design. Id.

[129] Boatland, Inc v Bailey, 609 SW2d 743, 748-49 (Tex 1980).

Of course, a manufacturer may have a duty to make products pursuant to a safer design even if the custom of the industry is not to use that alternative. O'Brien v Muskin Corp, 94 NJ 169, 463 A2d 298, 305 (1983).

[130] Boatland, Inc v Bailey, 609 SW2d 743, 748-49 (Tex 1980).

the art.[131] However, is is not universally agreed that state-of-the-art evidence is dispositive of the risk–utility analysis.[132] That is, a product may embody the state of the art and still fail to satisfy the risk–utility equation.[133]

It should be remembered that the defendant's ability to rebut the plaintiff's evidence is not limited to showing that a particular alternative was impossible. The defendant is entitled to rebut the plaintiff's evidence of feasibility, i.e., a suggested alternative may not be feasible because of the time necessary for its application and implementation or because it is significantly more expensive or impairs the usefulness of the product.[134]

The risk–utility analysis considers the reasonableness of the manufacturer's actions and, therefore, is really a negligence analysis.[135] However, a few courts have held that strict liability for design defects and for negligence are not coextensive.[136] Accordingly, a jury verdict which found both that a product was not reasonably dangerous and that the defendant was negligent was upheld.[137]

In any event, a review of the published cases shows that products which exceed all known standards have generally been found not to be defectively designed.[138] Accordingly, the value of such evidence to the defendant at trial seems self-evident.

---

131 *Id.*

132 Murphy v Chestnut Mt Lodge, Inc, 124 Ill App 3d 508, 464 NE2d 818, 823 (1984); *see generally* Robb, *A Practical Approach To Use Of State Of The Art Evidence In Strict Products Liability Cases*, 77 Nw UL Rev 1 (1977); Note, *Product Liability Reform Proposals: The State Of The Art Defense*, 43 Alb L Rev 944 (1979).

133 O'Brien v Muskin Corp, 94 NJ 169, 463 A2d 298, 305 (1983); *but see* Gross, *State Of The Art: Still Alive And Well in New Jersey*, Legal Times, Sept 17, 1984, at 12.

A plaintiff's requested jury instruction that the state-of-the-art defense is inapplicable was refused where the defense did not rely on this argument. Walker v Maxwell City, Inc, 117 Ill App 3d 571, 453 NE2d 917, 925 (1983).

134 Boatland, Inc v Bailey, 609 SW2d 743, 748-49 (Tex 1980).

135 *See* Flaminio v Honda Motor Co, 733 F2d 463, 467 (7th Cir 1984); O'Brien v Muskin Corp, 94 NJ 169, 463 A2d 298, 304 (1983); Opera v Hyva, Inc, 86 AD2d 373, 450 NYS2d 615, 618 (1982); Birnbaum, *Unmasking The Test For Design Defect: From Negligence [To Warranty] To Strict Liability To Negligence*, 33 Vand L Rev 593, 649 (1980); *see also* Cronin v JBE Olson Corp, 8 Cal 3d 121, 501 P2d 1153, 1162, 104 Cal Rptr 433 (1972).

136 Brown v Yamaha Motor Corp, 38 Wash App 914, 691 P2d 577, 579 (1984).

It has been noted that strict products liability focuses on whether a defect is unreasonably dangerous as contemplated by a reasonable consumer, while negligence focuses on whether the manufacturer's conduct is reasonable. 691 P2d at 579-80; *see also* Blevins v Cushman Motors, 551 SW2d 602, 607-08 (Mo 1977).

137 691 P2d at 580.

138 *See, e.g.*, Garcia v Joseph Vince Co, 84 Cal App 3d 879, 148 Cal Rptr 843, 847 (1978) (fencing mask); Palvides v Galveston Yacht Basin, Inc, 727 F2d 330, 338 (5th Cir 1984) (motorboat).

Instructions and Warnings

A manufacturer has a duty to instruct users as to the safe use of the product and also to warn of the dangers of using its product,[139] even if the product has no manufacturing or design defects.[140] This rule is based on the principles of social utility and self-determination.[141] There is a duty to instruct and warn because the costs of providing such information are small in relation to the benefits gained by users.[142] In addition, users of the product need this information to determine whether to expose themselves to the risks involved.[143]

The standard for determining whether such information should be given is generally based on what is reasonable under the circumstances, the usual formulation of the duty of care in negligence cases.[144] The factors to be considered are the normal expectations of the consumer as to how the product will perform, the degree of simplicity or complication in the operation or use of the product, the nature and magnitude of the danger to which the user is exposed, the likelihood of injury, and the feasibility and beneficial effect of including the information.[145]

An adequate warning must be reasonably designed to alert a consumer to the specific risks involved.[146] It should be targeted to the *average user* of the product.[147] Therefore, where the product is marketed to the general public,

---

[139] Pavlides v Galveston Yacht Basin, Inc, 727 F2d 330, 338 (5th Cir 1984); Anderson v Heron Engg Co, Inc, 198 Colo 391, 604 P2d 674, 676 (1979); Pegg v General Motors Corp, 258 Pa Super 59, 391 A2d 1074, 1083 (1978).

The warning does not have to be on the product. Temple v Velcro USA, Inc, 148 Cal App 3d 1090, 196 Cal Rptr 531, 533 (1983).

[140] Pavlides v Galveston Yacht Basin, Inc, 727 F2d 330, 338 (5th Cir 1984); Anderson v Heron Engg Co, Inc, 198 Colo 391, 604 P2d 674, 676 (1979).

[141] Pavlides v Galveston Yacht Basin, Inc, 727 F2d 330, 338 (5th Cir 1984) (motorboat).

[142] *Id.*

[143] *Id.*

[144] Flaminio v Honda Motor Co, Ltd, 733 F2d 463, 467-68 (7th Cir 1984) (Wisconsin law) (no error to instruct using the language only of negligence and not of strict liability); Cavers v Cushman Motor Sales, Inc, 95 Cal App 3d 350, 157 Cal Rptr 142, 148 (1979); Opera v Hyva, Inc, 86 AD2d 373, 450 NYS2d 615, 618 (1982); *see generally* Cavers v Cushman Motor Sales, Inc, 95 Cal App 3d 338, 157 Cal Rptr 142, 149 (1979).

Indeed, this standard of reasonableness is even used in jurisdictions which do not require proof that the defect was *unreasonably dangerous* in manufacturing defect cases. *See* Cavers v Cushman Motor Sales, Inc, 95 Cal App 3d 350, 157 Cal Rptr 142, 148 (1979).

[145] Cavers v Cushman Motor Sales, Inc, 95 Cal App 3d 350, 157 Cal Rptr 142, 148 (1979) (golf cart).

[146] Pavlides v Galveston Yacht Basin, Inc, 727 F2d 330, 338 (5th Cir 1984).

One court held that unless there is relevant extrinsic evidence, the determination of the adequacy of a written warning is for the court. Temple v Velcro USA, Inc, 148 Cal App 3d 1090, 196 Cal Rptr 531, 533 (1983).

[147] Pavlides v Galveston Yacht Basin, Inc, 727 F2d 330, 338 (5th Cir 1984).

the warning must be useful to members of the public.[148] A manufacturer cannot assume that persons using a complex product, e.g., a boat, know how it should be used.[149] However, the warnings are not insufficient merely because they were not heeded.[150]

There is generally no duty to warn of dangers that could be readily recognized by the ordinary user.[151] Further, even if there were such a duty, if the plaintiff was cognizant of the danger, the manufacturer is not liable for failing to warn because the lack of the warning was not the proximate cause of the injury.[152] For example, in *Sherk v Daisy-Heddon*, the estate of a boy who was killed by a BB from an air rifle could not recover from the rifle's manufacturer for defective warnings because the individual who shot the rifle disobeyed his parent's directions not to use the rifle and he realized the rifle's lethal properties.[153] In addition, where the plaintiff had actual knowledge of the specific risk but proceeded to use the product, the plaintiff may have his or her recovery limited because of contributory negligence or assumption of the risk.[154]

There is also no duty to warn of all possible idiosyncratic reactions to a product.[155] This is true, in part, because the warnings would be so voluminous that they would never be read.

Once the plaintiff has shown that the manufacturer failed to provide an adequate warning, the burden shifts to the manufacturer to show that the representations made by third parties, such as a retailer, gave the plaintiff adequate and specific knowledge of the hazards associated with the product.[156] However, if the manufacturer's warnings were inadequate and the manufacturer cannot show that the plaintiff had actual knowledge of the risks involved, it is generally presumed that a plaintiff would have read the warnings and acted to minimize the risk to him or herself.[157]

---

148 *Id* 339.

149 *Id.*

150 Temple v Velcro, USA, Inc, 148 Cal App 3d 1090, 196 Cal Rptr 531, 533 (1983); *see generally* Sherk v Daisy-Heddon, 498 Pa 594, 450 A2d 615, 619-20 (1982).

151 Prince v Parachutes, Inc, 685 P2d 83, 88 (Alaska 1984); Temple v Velcro, USA, Inc, 148 Cal App 3d 1090, 196 Cal Rptr 531, 533 (1983); *see generally* Sherk v Daisy-Heddon, 498 Pa 594, 450 A2d 615, 619-20 (1982).

152 Durkee v Cooper of Canada, Ltd, 99 Mich App 693, 298 NW2d 620, 622 (1980).

153 498 Pa 594, 450 A2d 615, 619-20 (1982).

154 Pavlides v Galveston Yacht Basin, Inc, 727 F2d 330, 340 (5th Cir 1984); Prince v Parachutes, Inc, 685 P2d 83, 88 (Alaska 1984); *see generally* §§9.01-9.04.
The burden of proof on this issue is on the defendant. Prince v Parachutes, Inc, 685 P2d 83, 88 (Alaska 1984). These defenses are discussed in **ch 9**.

155 Pell v Victor J. Andrew High School, 123 Ill App 3d 423, 462 NE2d 858, 864 (1984).

156 Pavlides v Galveston Yacht Basin, Inc, 727 F2d 330, 340 (5th Cir 1984) (motorboat).

157 Pavlides v Galveston Yacht Basin, Inc, 727 F2d 330, 340 (5th Cir 1984); Dias v Daisy-Heddon, 390 NE2d 222, 225 (Ind Ct App 1979); Menard v Newhall, 135 Vt 53, 373 A2d 505, 506 (1977).

This presumption is necessary because otherwise it would be necessary to have the plaintiff testify that he or she would have heeded the warning, and such testimony would be speculative.[158] Of course, the manufacturer is entitled to rebut this presumption by showing that the plaintiff was blind, illiterate, intoxicated, or otherwise would not have been affected by the warning.[159]

The duty of a manufacturer to warn of potential hazards in its products is sometimes greater than the duty of a mere vendor to warn.[160] This is because those two parties may have different information as to the product's hazards.[161] For example, a boat manufacturer who had received accident reports which called into question the safety of its design had a greater duty to warn than a boat rental company which was without knowledge of the prior accidents.[162]

The fact that a product met or exceeded all applicable government regulations and private standards is not dispositive of whether there was a failure to warn.[163]

§7.04   Warranties

The warranty provisions of the Uniform Commercial Code (UCC), applicable in all states except Louisiana, and the federal Magnuson-Moss Warranty Act[164] contain the exclusive provisions for actions for breach of warranty involving the sale of goods;[165] no common law actions remain.[166] It is, therefore, important to be familiar with the most important provisions of the UCC and federal law.[167]

---

[158] Nissen Trampoline Co v Terre Haute First Natl Bank, 332 NE2d 820, 826 (Ind Ct App 1975), *revd on other grounds*, 358 NE2d 974 (Ind 1976); Note, *Products Liability*, 50 Tex L Rev 577, 581 (1972).

[159] Technical Chem Co v Jacobs, 480 SW2d 602, 606 (Tex 1972) (nonrecreational accident case).

[160] Martell v Boardwalk Enters, Inc, 748 F2d 740, 749 (2d Cir 1984).

[161] *Id.*

[162] *Id.*

[163] Pavlides v Galveston Yacht Basin, Inc, 727 F2d 330, 337 (5th Cir 1984).

[164] *See* 15 USC §§2301-2312.

[165] Most recreational products are *goods* as that term is defined in the UCC *See, e.g.,* Corbin v Coleco Indus, 748 F2d 411, 414 (7th Cir 1984); Sheehan v Anthony Pools, 50 Md App 614, 440 A2d 1085, 1089 (1982); *but see* Kennedy v Providence Hockey Club, Inc, 376 A2d 329, 333 (RI 1977) (tickets to a hockey game are not goods and injured spectator cannot sue under warranty law).

[166] *See generally* Corbin v Coleco Indus, 748 F2d 411, 414 (7th Cir 1984).

[167] The primary source of warranty law is the UCC. The federal warranty law is, in essence, a supplement to the UCC.

Sale of Goods

By their terms, the warranty provisions of the UCC only apply to *sellers* of goods.[168] Therefore, nonsellers, such as football coaches who supply helmets to their players, are not liable under these provisions.[169] Similarly, a pool manufacturer was not liable for a defect in a pool ladder which it did not manufacture.[170]

In addition, if the defendant did not sell a *good*, it is generally not liable under the UCC for breach of warranty. Accordingly, it is usually held that a plaintiff who was injured by a defendant who was providing a service, e.g., leasing a golf cart,[171] operating an amusement ride,[172] or operating a health club,[173] has no action for breach of express or implied warranty because there was no sale of a good.[174] However, in *Anthony Pools v Sheehan*, the court held that a pool construction company was liable for breach of the implied warranty of merchantability for defects in a diving board for an in-ground swimming pool.[175] The court reasoned that warranty law applied because the diving board, although provided as part of a service, retained its character as a good after the service was performed.[176]

Further, even though the warranty obligations of nonseller defendants are not found directly in the UCC, the provisions may be applied by analogy.[177] Indeed, one court held that the lessor of a golf cart warrants that the cart is in reasonably good condition.[178]

Implied Warranties

Under the UCC, there are two major implied warranties: the warranty

---

168 *See* UCC §§2-313, 2-314, 2-315; *but see* J. White & R. Summers, Uniform Commercial Code 348-49 (1980) (sellers of services may also be liable).

169 Hemphill v Sayers, 552 F Supp 685, 689 (SD Ill 1982).

170 Kaloz v Risco, 120 Misc 2d 586, 466 NYS2d 218, 220 (1983).

171 *See* Bona v Graefe, 264 Md 69, 285 A2d 607, 609 (1972); *but see* Baker v City of Seattle, 79 Wash 2d 198, 484 P2d 405, 407 (1971).

172 *See* Shaw v Fairyland at Harvey's Inc, 26 AD2d 576, 271 NYS2d 70, 71 (1966).

173 *See* Marie v European Health Spas, Inc, 79 AD2d 749, 434 NYS2d 802, 804 (1980).

174 *But see* Smith v Alexandria Arena, Inc, 294 F Supp 695, 697 (ED Va 1969) (warranty applied where defendant rented ice skates).
There has been a significant amount of law journal commentary in this area. *See* Farnsworth, *Implied Warranties Of Quality In Non-Sale Cases*, 57 Colum L Rev 653 (1957); Comment, *Sale of Goods In Service-Predominated Transactions*, 37 Fordham L Rev 115 (1968); Note, *Contracts For Goods And Services And Article 2 of The Uniform Commercial Code*, 9 Rut-Cam LJ 303 (1978); Comment, *Sales-Service Hybrid Transactions: A Policy Approach*, 28 Sw LJ 575 (1974).

175 295 Md 285, 455 A2d 434, 441 (1983).

176 *Id.*

177 J. White & R. Summers, Uniform Commercial Code 327, 346 (1980).

178 *See* Baker v City of Seattle, 79 Wash 2d 198, 484 P2d 405, 407 (1971).

of merchantability and the warranty of fitness for a particular purpose.[179] These two implied warranties arise by operation of law[180] and may not be disclaimed by a seller of consumer goods.[181]

The implied warranty of merchantability, applicable only to sellers who are merchants with respect to goods of that type,[182] means that, at a minimum, the goods must be fit for the ordinary purposes for which such goods are used.[183] Goods which do not meet this standard are also defective under strict liability.[184] However, where a plaintiff could not articulate any distinction between strict liability and the implied warranty of merchantability, he was only allowed to prosecute under one theory.[185]

A person injured by a product which was not fit for the ordinary purposes for which such goods are used may sue for breach of this implied warranty.[186] In *Hauter v Zogarts*, the court held that a golf training device was not merchantable because it was marketed to novice golfers who would not hit the ball solidly, thereby incurring a substantial risk that they would be hit by the ball.[187]

The implied warranty that the goods are fit for a particular purpose of

---

179 UCC §§2-314, 2-315.

180 Hauter v Zogarts, 14 Cal 3d 104, 534 P2d 377, 385, 120 Cal Rptr 681 (1975).

181 Sheehan v Anthony Pools, 50 Md App 614, 440 A2d 1085, 1089 (1982); *but see* UCC §2-316; Corbin v Coleco Indus, 748 F2d 411, 414 (7th Cir 1984).

182 UCC §2-314; Corbin v Coleco Indus, 748 F2d 411, 414 (7th Cir 1984). Individuals such as a university athletic director or football coach who did not sell a football helmet to the plaintiff are not liable as a matter of law under this provision. Hemphill v Sayers, 552 F Supp 685, 689 (SD Ill 1982). Similarly, in Allen v Nicole, Inc, 172 NJ Super 442, 412 A2d 824, 825-26 (1980), the court held that a seller of an amusement ride who was not in the business of selling those rides was not liable for breach of the implied warranty of merchantability.

183 UCC §2-314(2)(c); Corbin v Coleco Indus, Inc, 748 F2d 411, 414 (7th Cir 1984); Kelly v Koppers Co, 293 So 2d 763, 764 (Fla Dist Ct App), *cert denied*, 302 So 2d 415 (Fla 1974); (manufacturer of swimming pool paint not liable where plaintiff alleged the paint camouflaged an injured swimmer and hindered the rescue); Poppell v Waters, 126 Ga App 385, 190 SE2d 815, 817 (1972) (bicycle manufacturer not liable for manufacturing a bicycle without a headlight or a front reflector); Sabloff v Yamaha Motor Co, 113 NJ Super 279, 273 A2d 606, 611 (1971) (manufacturer liable for improper assembly by its dealers). The fact that a rifle exploded while it was being loaded was some evidence that the rifle was unfit for the ordinary purposes for which it was intended. Jones v Cranman's Sporting Goods, 142 Ga App 838, 237 SE2d 402, 404 (1977).

184 Corbin v Coleco Indus, 748 F2d 411, 416 (7th Cir 1984); *see also* J. White & R. Summers, Uniform Commercial Code 325, 355-56 (1980). Of course, economic damages are recoverable under warranty law, while usually only personal injury damages are compensable under strict liability.

185 *See* Corbin v Coleco Indus, 748 F2d 411, 416 (7th Cir 1984).

186 Hauter v Zogarts, 14 Cal 3d 104, 534 P2d 377, 385, 120 Cal Rptr 681 (1975).

187 *Id.*

the buyer, which usually does not arise in consumer cases,[188] applies where the seller[189] has reason to know of that purpose at the time of the purchase and the buyer is relying on the seller's skill and judgment to select or furnish suitable goods.[190] A case tried on the implied warranty of fitness for a particular purpose may also, in effect, try the issue of implied warranty of merchantability and, if so, it is not error to give a jury instruction on this second issue even if it was not pleaded.[191]

Express Warranty

Section 2-313 of the UCC provides that a description of the goods or affirmation of fact regarding the goods which becomes a basis of the bargain of sale is an express warranty that the goods will conform to those statements.[192]

At one time, sellers were allowed some room to *puff* their products without incurring liability if the product did not live up to the representation.[193] However, the zone of allowable puffing has become increasingly restricted.[194] Further, the more specific the information given by the seller, the more likely the information will be considered not puffing, but an express warranty.[195] For example, in *Hauter v Zogarts*[196] the California Supreme Court held that where the shipping carton of a golf training device stated that the golf ball would not hit a player using the device, the manufacturer expressly warranted that aspect of safety. In that case, the manufacturer was liable, as a matter of law, for breach of express warranty because the ball hit the player.[197] The manufacturer's argument that the warranty only applied where the ball was hit properly was rejected because there was no such written statement or disclaimer; the manufacturer's unarticulated, subjective intent was irrelevant.[198]

Not all courts have imposed liability for untrue statements. In *Salk v Alpine Ski Shop, Inc*, decided the same year as *Hauter*, the Rhode Island Supreme Court held that a skier whose bindings did not release could not recover for breach of express warranty even though the ski bindings manufacturer's

---

188 J. White & R. Summers, Uniform Commercial Code 359 (1980).

189 Individuals who did not sell the product are not liable. Hemphill v Sayers, 552 F Supp 685, 689 (SD Ill 1982).

190 UCC §2-315; Corbin v Coleco Indus, 748 F2d 411, 414 (7th Cir 1984).

191 Gellenbeck v Sears, Roebuck & Co, 59 Mich App 339, 229 NW2d 443, 445 (1975).

192 UCC §2-313.

193 Hauter v Zogarts, 14 Cal 3d 104, 534 P2d 377, 384-85, 120 Cal Rptr 681 (1975).

194 *Id; see generally* Opera v Hyva, Inc, 86 AD2d 373, 450 NYS2d 615, 619 (1982); Prosser, *Products Liability (Strict Liability To The Consumer)*, 50 Minn L Rev 791, 837 (1966).

195 J. White & R. Summers, Uniform Commercial Code 329 (1980).

196 14 Cal 3d 104, 534 P2d 377, 384-85, 120 Cal Rptr 681 (1975).

197 *Id.*

198 534 P2d at 385-87.

advertisement stated "Cubco is the precise binding ... that releases when it's supposed to .... Both heel and toe release at the exact tension you set. And release whichever way you fall."[199] The court held that no binding can be set at a tension sufficiently low to release during a slow fall and still keep the skier on skies during normal skiing.[200] Accordingly, it reasoned that the advertisement was not a blanket guarantee that the bindings would release in every dangerous situation.[201] The court's analysis is questionable. If bindings cannot always be set to *release when they are supposed to*, the manufacturer should not make such representations.

§7.05 —Privity and Other Issues

Privity

At one time, decades ago, a plaintiff had to have purchased the good from the seller before he or she could sue for breach of warranty. This rule, prohibiting a purchaser from recovering from other companies up the distribution chain, such as the manufacturer, and also not allowing a nonpurchaser, e.g., a family member of the purchaser, to recover for injuries from the product, was considered harsh and has been weakened. However, there is presently no uniform rule defining the necessary relationship, usually called *privity*, between the plaintiff and the defendant which is required before the plaintiff can sue to enforce the defendant's warranty. Accordingly, this is a fertile field for litigation.

There are two types of privity, vertical and horizontal. Vertical privity focuses on the proper defendant in the marketing and distribution chain, i.e., whether someone other that the retailer can be liable.[202] The UCC takes no position on this issue.

Horizontal privity focuses on the proper plaintiff, i.e., whether someone other than the person who purchased the product can sue for injuries. The UCC does not take a position on this issue,[203] although it offers three

---

199 115 RI 309, 342 A2d 622, 626 (1975).

200 *Id.*

201 *Id.*

202 *See* Drake v Wham-O Mfg Co, 373 F Supp 608, 609 (ED Wis 1974) (consumer cannot recover from manufacturer under implied warranty where he purchased the good from a retailer).

203 Bernick v Jurden, 293 SE2d 405, 414 (NC 1982); UCC §2-318 comment 3. The Texas and California legislatures took no position on this when they adopted the rest of the UCC. *See* Cal Code Comment to Cal Coml Code §2318 (West 1964); Tex Bus & Com Code Ann §2.318 (Vernon 1968).

alternatives. Alternative A, adopted in over one-half of the states,[204] provides that a warranty, whether express or implied, extends to all natural persons who are in the family or household of the buyer as well as guests if it is reasonable to expect that such persons may use, consume, or be affected by the goods and that those persons may suffer personal injuries from the product.[205]

This provision was applied in *Corbin v Coleco Industries*.[206] In that case, the plaintiff did not purchase an above-ground pool from the manufacturer, but rather from an individual who had in turn purchased it from someone else. The court held that the plaintiff was not in the family or household of the original purchaser and, therefore, he could not assert, as a matter of law, a claim for breach of implied warranty.[207] Similarly, in *Hemphill v Sayers*, the court held that a college football player who was supplied a football helmet by the school could not sue the manufacturer for breach of warranty. The student was neither the purchaser of the helmet nor in the family or household of the purchaser.[208]

Alternative B, adopted by only five states,[209] applies to any natural person who may reasonably be expected to use, consume, or be affected by the goods and who suffers personal injuries.[210] Alternative C, adopted by 16 states,[211]

---

204 *See* Alaska Stat §45.02.318 (1984); Ariz Rev Stat Ann §47-2318 (1984); Conn Gen Stat Ann §42-2-318 (West 1984); DC Code Ann §28:2-318 (1981); Fla Stat Ann §672.318 (West Supp 1984); Ga Code Ann §11-2-318 (1982); Idaho Code §28-2-318 (1980); Ill Ann Stat ch 26, §2-318 (Smith-Hurd 1963); Ind Code Ann §26-1-2-318 (Burns 1974); Ky Rev Stat §355.2-318 (1972); Mich Comp Laws Ann §440.2318 (West 1967); Miss Code §75-2-318 (1981); Mo Stat Ann §400.2-318 (1965); Mont Code Ann §30-2-318 (1983); Neb Rev Stat §2-318 (1980); Nev Rev Stat §104.2318 (1984): NJ Stat Ann §12A:2-318 (West 1962); NM Stat Ann §55-2-318 (1978); NC Gen Stat §99B-2(b) (1979); Ohio Rev Code Ann §1302.31 (Page 1979); Okla Stat Ann tit 12A, §2-318 (West 1963); Or Rev Stat §72.3180 (1983); Pa Cons Stat Ann tit 13, §2318 (Purdon 1984); Tenn Code Ann §47-2-318 (1979); Wash Rev Code Ann §62A.2-318 (1966); W Va Code §46-2-318 (1966); Wis Stat Ann §402.318 (West 1964).

205 UCC §2-318 alternative A.

206 748 F2d 411, 414 (7th Cir 1984). The *Corbin* court overruled Filler v Rayex Corp, 435 F2d 336 (7th Cir 1970), a prior decision on this issue.

207 748 F2d 411, 414 (7th Cir 1984); *see also* Bolm v Triumph Corp, 71 AD2d 429, 422 NYS2d 969, 976 (1979) (plaintiff could not recover from a motorcycle manufacturer because plaintiff purchased the motorcycle secondhand from a prior owner); *see generally* Hulsebosch v Ramsey, 435 SW2d 161, 164 (Tex Civ App 1968).

208 552 F Supp 685, 692-93 (SD Ill 1982).

209 *See* Ala Code §7-2-318 (1984); Kan Stat Ann §84-2-318 (1983); Md Code Ann §2-318 (1975); NY Consol Laws Serv, Uniform Commercial Code §2-318 (1981); Vt Stat Ann tit 9A, §2-318 (1966).

210 UCC §2-318 alternative B.

211 *See* Ark Stat Ann §85-2-318.1 (Supp 1983); Colo Rev Stat §4-2-318 (1974); Hawaii Rev Stat §490:2-318 (1976); Iowa Code Ann §554.2318 (West Supp 1984); Minn Stat §336.2-318 (1984); ND Cent Code §41-02-35 (1981); RI Gen Laws §6A-2-318 (Supp

is even more expansive than Alternative B because it allows an action for economic injuries as well as personal injuries.[212]

Failure to plead facts showing that the plaintiff is in the class of persons who can sue for breach of warranty subjects the complaint to dismissal.[213]

Damages

Generally, the damages for breach of warranty are the difference between the value of goods purchased and the value they would have had if they had been as warranted.[214] However, consequential damages may be recovered for personal injuries.[215]

Notice

The UCC provides that where a tender has been accepted, the buyer must, within a reasonable time[216] after it discovers or should have discovered the breach, notify the seller or be barred from recovery.[217] This provision applies in personal injury cases,[218] although there is authority to the contrary.[219] The determination of whether a reasonable time passed before notice was given is usually a question for the fact-finder.[220]

The UCC does not specifically require that nonpurchasers give notice

---

1984); SC Code Ann 36-2-318 (Law Co-op 1977); SD Codified Laws Ann §57A-2-318 (1980); Utah Code Ann §70A-2-318 (1980); Wyo Stat §34-21-235 (1977); *see generally* Del Code Ann §2-318 (1975); Me Rev Stat Ann tit 11, §2-318 (Supp 1984); Mass Gen Laws Ann ch 106, §2-318 (West 1984); NH Rev Stat Ann §382-A:2-318 (Supp 1983); Va Code §8.2-318 (1965).

212 UCC §2-318 alternative C.

213 Taylor v American Honda Motor Co, Inc, 555 F Supp 59, 63 (MD Fla 1982).

214 UCC §2-714(2); Corbin v Coleco Indus, 748 F2d 411, 414 (7th Cir 1984); Noreli Indus v Kleinert's, Inc, 57 AD2d 792, 394 NYS2d 687, 688 (1977).

215 UCC §§2-714(3), 2-715(2)(b); Corbin v Coleco Indus, 748 F2d 411, 414 (7th Cir 1984).

216 A reasonable time for notification from a retail consumer is to be judged by different standards so that in his or her case it will be extended, for the rule of requiring notification is designed to defeat commercial bad faith, not to deprive a good faith consumer of his remedy. Official Comment to UCC §2-607.

217 UCC §2-607(3)(a).

218 Taylor v American Honda Motor Co, 555 F Supp 59, 63 (MD Fla 1982) (citing other cases); Page v Camper City & Mobile Home Sales, 297 So 2d 810, 812 (Ala 1974).

The notice does not have to be in writing. Page v Camper City & Mobile Home Sales, 297 So 2d 810, 811 (Ala 1974).

219 Fischer v Mead Johnson Labs, 41 AD2d 737, 341 NYS2d 257 (1973); Hill v Joseph T. Ryerson & Son v United States Steel Corp, 268 SE2d 296 (W Va 1980).

220 *See* Jones v Cranman's Sporting Goods, 142 Ga App 838, 237 SE2d 402, 404 (1977).

to the defendant prior to filing suit.[221] Nevertheless, comment 5 to §2-607 of the UCC states that nonbuyers are required to give notice.[222] In this confusion, some courts have held that notice is not required by nonbuyers who suffer personal injuries from the product.[223] In addition, at least one court concluded that notice to the *seller* only means that notice is required to be given to the entity which directly sold the product to the plaintiff, not a company further up the distribution chain such as a manufacturer.[224]

Reliance

The UCC does not specifically require that the plaintiff rely on the warranty before he or she can recover.[225] Its only provision dealing with this issue is that affirmations of fact must be part of *the basis of the bargain* before a warranty is created,[226] a phrase which is patently ambiguous.[227]

In any event, the element of reliance can often be inferred in express warranty cases from the purchase or use of the product if the natural tendency of the representations made by the seller is to induce such purchase or use.[228] For example, in *Bernick v Jurden* reliance was inferred where a manufacturer of a hockey mouthguard promoted its product through hockey catalogs and parent guides with the representation that the mouthguard supplied "maximum protection to the lips and teeth."[229] The court held that the natural tendency of that statement by the manufacturer would be to induce a mother to purchase the product for her hockey player son.[230]

Two leading commentators believe that the better view is that there should be no reliance requirement for a nonpurchasing user.[231] Reliance by the purchaser should be enough because if the purchaser was not induced to buy the product, no harm would have come to the plaintiff.[232]

---

221 Tomczuk v Town of Cheshire, 26 Conn Supp 219, 217 A2d 71, 74 (1965).

222 UCC §2-607 comment 5.

223 *See* Taylor v American Honda Motor Co, Inc, 555 F Supp 59, 64 (MD Fla 1982); Tomczuk v Town of Cheshire, 26 Conn Supp 219, 217 A2d 71 (1965); J. White & R. Summers, Uniform Commercial Code 423 (1980).

224 Tomczuk v Town of Cheshire, 26 Conn Supp 219, 217 A2d 71 (1965).

225 *See* UCC §§2-313, 2-314, 2-315; J. White & R. Summers, Uniform Commercial Code 345-46 (1980).

226 *See* UCC §2-313.

227 J. White & R. Summers, Uniform Commercial Code 338 (1980).

228 Bernick v Jurden, 293 SE2d 405, 413 (NC 1982).

229 *Id* 414.

230 *Id.*

231 2 L. Frumer & M. Friedman, Products Liability at §16.04(4)[b], at 4A-268 (1984).

232 *Id.*

Magnuson-Moss Warranty Act

The federal Magnuson-Moss Warranty Act, only applicable where a written warranty is given,[233] requires the warrantor to use simple, readily understood, and to some extent, standard language in describing the warranty.[234] However, the act does not require that written warranties be given.[235] Further, it basically does not regulate substantive warranty terms, although it does prohibit a company from disclaiming any implied warranties.[236] Congress provided that the successful plaintiff is entitled to recover attorneys' fees.[237]

This federal law is probably not a significant factor in most recreational accident litigation for two reasons. First, several courts have held that the act does not create a federal cause of action for personal injury claims.[238] Second, the act generally requires that the plaintiff afford the defendant a reasonable opportunity to cure, i.e., to replace or repair the product or refund the purchase price.[239] An injured bicyclist who admitted in his deposition that he failed to give the manufacturer an opportunity to cure was barred from recovery.[240] More importantly, most plaintiffs who suffer personal injuries are interested in damages beyond those provided by a cure.

Defenses

Most courts do not consider plaintiff's assumption of the risk as a defense to a claim for breach of warranty.[241] However, the courts have reached inconsistent results regarding whether a plaintiff's contributory negligence is a defense to a warranty action.[242] The distinctions between contributory negligence and assumption of risk are fuzzy in many jurisdictions, and,

---

233 *See* 15 USC §2302.

234 *Id; see* Eddy, *Effects Of The Magnuson-Moss Act Upon Consumer Product Warranties*, 55 NCL Rev 835 (1977).

235 Gorman v Saf-T-Mate, Inc, 513 F Supp 1028, 1031 (ND Ind 1981).

236 *See* 15 USC §2308; J. White & R. Summers, Uniform Commercial Code 326 n 6 (1980).

237 *See* 15 USC §2310(d)(2).

238 *See* Washington v Otasco, Inc, 603 F Supp 1295, 1296 (ND Miss 1985); Gorman v Saf-T-Mate, Inc, 513 F Supp 1028, 1036 (ND Ind 1981).

239 15 USC §2310(e).

240 Washington v Otasco, Inc, 603 F Supp 1295, 1297 (ND Miss 1985).

241 J. White & R. Summers, Uniform Commercial Code 412 (1980); *see also* **§9.02**.

242 *Id* 411-12; *see also* Brenner v President & Fellows Of Harvard College, No 79-1308-T (D Mass July 21, 1983) (available on Lexis) (contributory or comparative negligence is not a defense to breach of implied warranty); *see also* **§9.04**.

therefore, care should be taken to see whether such a defense is applicable in each particular instance.[243]

The statute of limitations commences to run when there is a breach of the warranty, which is usually when there is a tender of delivery of the defective good.[244]

§7.06 Misrepresentations

The Restatement (Second) of Torts §402B allows recovery for physical harm to a consumer resulting from a seller's misrepresentation of material facts to the public of the character or quality of the chattel sold, even if the misrepresentation is innocent and not made fraudulently or negligently.[245] This principle, adopted by several jurisdictions,[246] does not require either a defective product or one that is unreasonably dangerous.[247] Rather, it imposes strict liability on sellers for their misrepresentations of material facts. However, a manufacturer's failure to state material facts, e.g., its failure to warn of latent hazards, is not covered by this provision.[248]

Section 402B does not contain a privity requirement.[249] Therefore, an injured plaintiff need not have purchased the product to recover.[250] Further, §402B provides a basis for recovery in addition to those provided under general warranty law.[251] Accordingly, one defendant's argument that there was no need to adopt this section as state law because warranty law covered this area was rejected.[252]

---

243 *See* §9.01.

244 *See, e.g.*, 15 USC §2308; J. White & R. Summers, Uniform Commercial Code 326 n 6 (1980).

245 American Safety Equip Corp v Winkler, 640 P2d 216, 219 (Colo 1982); Restatement (Second) of Torts §402B (1965); Sales, *The Innocent Misrepresentation Doctrine: Strict Tort Liability Under Section 402B*, 16 Hous L Rev 239 (1979).

246 *See, e.g.*, Hauter v Zogarts, 14 Cal 3d 104, 534 P2d 377, 120 Cal Rptr 681 (1975); American Safety Equip Corp v Winkler, 640 P2d 216 (Colo 1982); Klages v General Ordinance Equip Corp, 240 Pa Super 356, 367 A2d 304 (1976); Ford Motor Co v Lonon, 217 Tenn 400, 398 SW2d 240 (1966); Crocker v Winthrop Labs, 514 SW2d 429 (Tex 1974).

247 American Safety Equip Corp v Winkler, 640 P2d 216, 219 (Colo 1982); *see also* Sales, *The Innocent Misrepresentation Doctrine: Strict Tort Liability Under Section 402B*, 16 Hous L Rev 239 (1979).

248 Sherk v Daisy-Heddon, 285 Pa Super 320, 427 A2d 657, 664-65 (1981), *revd on other grounds*, 498 Pa 594, 450 A2d 615 (1982).

249 *See* Hauter v Zogarts, 14 Cal 3d 104, 534 P2d 377, 381 n 4, 120 Cal Rptr 681 (1975); Restatement (Second) of Torts §402B (1965).

250 Hauter v Zogarts, 14 Cal 3d 104, 534 P2d 377, 381 n4, 120 Cal Rptr 681 (1975).

251 American Safety Equip Corp v Winkler, 640 P2d 216, 221 (Colo 1982).

252 *Id* (citing cases).

The Colorado Supreme Court, in *American Safety Equipment Corp v Winkler*, provided the rationale for §402B:

> [I]t is sound policy to permit a consumer, who purchases a product on the strength of the manufacturer's representations, to obtain direct recovery from the manufacturer on a theory of strict liability ... [I]t is the manufacturer who, through the design and testing of its products, knows of their particular qualities and capabilities. A consumer, on the other hand, knows only the information he has been able to glean from the manufacturer's marketing materials. Because of its superior knowledge, the manufacturer should not be permitted to avoid responsibility for its misrepresentations to the consumer, even though the misrepresentations were neither fraudulently nor negligently made.
>
> Further, imposing strict liability on manufacturers who misrepresent their products does not impose an undue burden. A manufacturer intends to reap economic benefit from the public representations it makes regarding the character and quality of its products, and must assume the economic consequences for physical harm resulting from misrepresentations it has made about its products. Manufacturers should not benefit economically from representations they make to the public and, at the same time, be insulated from liability for misrepresentations which result in physical harm.[253]

Traditionally, manufacturers were not liable for misrepresentation for *puffing*, their self-laudatory opinions of the high quality of their products.[254] There is, however, a trend toward imposing liability for inaccurate puffing.[255] Further, an unqualified statement of safety is actionable if untrue.[256] For example, in *Hauter v Zogarts*, the court held, as a matter of law, that the manufacturer of a "Golfing Gizmo," a training device for golfers, misrepresented its product where the shipping carton label stated that the product was "completely safe" and that the "ball will not hit player," but a novice golfer using the product was injured by the ball.[257]

In *Hauter*, the manufacturer argued that it should not be liable because there are certain inherent risks in golfing and, therefore, the plaintiff's reliance on the misrepresentation of safety was not reasonable. The court rejected this argument because the specific cause of the injury, the golf ball striking the

---

253 640 P2d 216, 220-21 (Colo 1982).
254 Hauter v Zogarts, 14 Cal 3d 104, 534 P2d 377, 381, 120 Cal Rptr 681 (1975).
255 *Id.*
256 *Id.*
257 *Id.*

golfer on his follow-through, was not an inherent risk of golfing, but a risk of using this product.[258]

Specific Activities and Products

§7.07 Amusement Parks and Rides

In several cases, the courts have held that individuals injured on amusement rides[259] cannot recover under products liability law. For example, in *Siciliano v Capital City Shows, Inc*,[260] the New Hampshire Supreme Court held that the owner of an amusement park cannot be strictly liable for injuries caused by an amusement machine because it does not supply a *product*, but rather provides a service. The passenger acquires no property rights in the ride[261] and, therefore, the owner can only be liable for negligence.[262]

Products liability law was also not applied in *Allen v Nicole, Inc*,[263] where a child injured on a *pony cart* amusement ride sued, among others, the company which had sold that ride to the amusement park. Strict products liability law only applies to firms in the business of selling that product.[264] In this case, the seller was another amusement park operator who had sold the ride, as it had done with other amusement facilities, when it wished to change the rides it offered to the public. Therefore, this seller was really a consumer of amusement park rides because it used the rides in its business.[265] The court concluded that this firm's incidental sale of rides was not a meaningful part of its business and, therefore, UCC §402A was inapplicable.[266]

---

[258] *Id* at 382.

[259] Over 8,000 individuals are seriously injured each year on amusement rides. *See* US Consumer Prod Safety Commn, Natl Injury Information Clearinghouse, Prod Summary Rep (Mar 28, 1984).

One study concluded that the Comission's report overstated the actual number of injuries. *See* E. Maasoumi, An Analysis of the Sampling Validity, the Estimation Procedure and the Estimates of Injuries Related to Amusement Park Rides Produced by the Consumer Prod Safety Commn (1980) (unpublished).

Some studies have shown that the vast majority of amusement park ride accidents are not caused by equipment defects, but by human error. *See* Scanlon, *Revving Up A Regulatory Merry-Go-Round*, Wall St J, July 14, 1984, at 24, col 4.

[260] 124 NH 719, 475 A2d 19, 25 (1984).

[261] *Id.*

[262] *See* §7.02; *see generally* §1.02.

[263] 172 NJ Super 442, 412 A2d 824 (1980).

[264] 412 A2d at 826.

[265] *Id.*

[266] *Id.*

Recovery under warranty law has also been circumscribed. In *Shaw v Fairyland at Harvey's Inc*, the court held that an owner of an amusement park was not liable to an injured patron for breach of warranty because there was no *sale* of a good.[267] Indeed, in *Allen*, warranty law was not applied to the seller of the ride to the amusement park because that defendant was not a *merchant* in the business of selling amusement rides.[268] This was true even though the supplier had previously sold other rides.[269]

Amusement parks are, of course, generally liable for their negligence.[270] For example, the parks,[271] as well as the manufacturers of the amusement devices,[272] may be liable for failing to warn of the dangers of using the devices.

A manufacturer of an amusement park ride was entitled to indemnity from the operator of the park for an injury from a defective ride because the manufacturer shipped an improved part to the park, without charge, but it was never installed and the original part caused the plaintiff's injuries.[273]

§7.08 Boating

Boating is a very dangerous activity. In recent years, about 1,200 individuals have died annually in recreational boating accidents.[274]

Sellers of boats may be liable for manufacturing defects, design defects, failing to issue proper instructions or warnings, and negligence. However, care must be taken in choosing the most appropriate theory. In *McPhail v Muncipality of Culebra*,[275] the aluminum mast of a Hobie Cat came in contact with a high-tension wire, killing the sailor. Although the boat manufacturer might have been liable for using a defective design[276] this theory was not presented at trial and the appellate court ruled that it was too late to advance this argument on appeal.

---

267 26 AD2d 576, 271 NYS2d 70, 71 (1966); *see generally* **§7.04**.

268 412 A2d at 824-25.

269 *Id.*

270 *See generally* **§1.02**. The American Society for Testing and Materials has promulgated 4 safety standards for amusement rides and devices. *See* ASTM F846-83, F853-83, F698-83, F770-82.

271 Buck v Tweetsie RR, 44 NC App 588, 261 SE2d 517, 519 (1980).

272 *Id.*

273 Rekab, Inc v Frank Hrubetz & Co, 261 Md 141, 274 A2d 107, 112 (1971).

274 United States Dept of Transp, Boating Statistics 1983 at 11 (June 1984). However, the fatality rate, which is based on the number of fatalities per number of boats, has shown a significant downward trend in the last 20 years. *See id.*

275 598 F2d 603 (1st Cir 1979).

276 A grounding device might have been attached to the boat at a minimal cost. *See id* 605. However, defendant's expert came to a different conclusion. *See id.*

Manufacturing Defects

Boating manufacturers are liable for manufacturing defects.[277] In *Harris v Bardwell*, the driver of a boat moved suddenly after he was struck by an insect, causing the boat to make an abrupt turn. At that point, the screws securing the pedestal of his seat to the boat's floor became loose and the driver was thrown into the water where he was cut by the boat's propeller.[278] The manufacturer was liable because a high performance boat should have the driver's seat satisfactorily attached to the floor.[279] It was no defense that the installation method used by the manufacturer was the accepted and customary method in the industry.[280] In a different case, a boat manufacturer was held liable for allowing air pockets to remain in the steering wheel.[281]

A boat manufacturer is only liable for defects which are unreasonably dangerous beyond the extent which could be reasonably contemplated by the ordinary user.[282] Therefore, a defective steering wheel on a boat which did not affect the steering was not a *defect*.[283] In *Fitzgerald Marine Sales v LeUnes*,[284] the steering wheel, through a manufacturing flaw, was not as strong as it should have been and, as a result, it broke when it was used as a restraint by the driver. However, the court held that one does not expect the steering wheel to be used to brace a boater and, therefore, when it fails in that task, the manufacturer is not liable.[285]

Boat retailers may also be liable for manufacturing flaws.[286] In *Harris v Bardwell*,[287] the court held that a retailer who knew or should have known of a defect by making a reasonable inspection of the boat is just as liable as the manufacturer. However, the retailer does not have to disassemble the boat to look for latent defects.[288] Accordingly, a retailer who could not reasonably

---

[277] Detroit Marine Engg, Inc v Maloy, 419 So 2d 687, 690 (Fla Dist Ct App 1982); Harris v Bardwell, 373 So 2d 777, 780 (La Ct App 1979).

[278] 373 So 2d 777, 780 (La Ct App 1979).

[279] *Id* ($175,000 judgment affirmed).

[280] *Id.*

[281] Detroit Marine Engg, Inc v Maloy, 419 So 2d 687, 690 (Fla Dist Ct App 1982).

[282] Fitzgerald Marine Sales v LeUnes, 659 SW2d 917, 919 (Tex Ct App 1983); Restatement (Second) of Torts §402(A) (1965).

[283] Fitzgerald Marine Sales v LeUnes, 659 SW2d 917, 919 (Tex Ct App 1983).

[284] *Id.*

[285] *Id.* (a $109,000 judgment for the plaintiff was reversed).

[286] *See* Dietz v Waller, 141 Ariz 107, 685 P2d 744, 747 (1984); Marrillia v Lyn Craft Boat Co, 271 So 2d 204, 206 (Fla Dist Ct App 1973); Harris v Bardwell, 373 So 2d 777, 780 (La Ct App 1979).

[287] 373 So 2d 777, 780 (La Ct App 1979); *see also* Marrillia v Lyn Craft Boat Co, 271 So 2d 204, 206 (Fla Dist Ct App 1973).

[288] *Id*; *see also* Hebert v Vice, 413 So 2d 342, 345 (La Ct App 1982).

have learned that the screws in the pedestal base of the boat's seat were not properly installed was not liable for this defect.[289]

In *Dietz v Waller*, the court held that a motorboat retailer may be strictly liable for a defect which arose while the boat was in its control.[290] Although there was no direct evidence that the boat was defective when it was sold to the plaintiff, there was circumstantial evidence of a defect, viz., the boat leaked from the start and it sunk on a clear, calm day while it was being used by an experienced boater.[291]

Design Defects

Boat manufacturers must design boats that are not unreasonably dangerous.[292] In *Detroit Marine Engineering, Inc v Maloy*, the court, in affirming a $1 million judgment, held that the plastic steering wheel was defectively designed because there was no attempt to round off its corners and, in addition, the spokes which were attached to the hub of the wheel were too thin.[293] Similarly, in *Ogg v City of Springfield*, the manufacturer of a Hobie Cat was held liable for a defective design because the boat was unreasonably dangerous when it contacted electricity, a reasonably foreseeable occurrence.[294]

Of course, a boat is not defectively designed merely because an accident occurred.[295] A Robalo motorboat which had a large void space in the bilge and a through-hull bilge drain in the rear of the bilge below the waterline was not defectively designed because the boat was not unreasonably dangerous.[296]

The courts have not required boat manufacturers to install a kill switch, a safety device which cuts electrical power to the boat's motor.[297] In *Young v Tide Craft, Inc*, the court held that the lack of a kill switch was not a defect because the danger posed by the absence of the switch, viz., being thrown

---

289 Harris v Bardwell, 373 So 2d 777, 780 (La Ct App 1979).

290 141 Ariz 107, 685 P2d 744, 747 (1984).

291 685 P2d at 748.

292 *See* Pavlides v Galveston Yacht Basin, Inc, 727 F2d 330, 337-38 (5th Cir 1984); Detroit Marine Engg, Inc v Maloy, 419 So 2d 687, 690 (Fla Dist Ct App 1982); Ogg v City of Springfield, 121 Ill App 3d 25, 458 NE2d 1331, 1339 (1984); *see generally* Trojan Boat Co v Lutz, 358 F2d 299, 299 (5th Cir 1966); Standard v Meadors, 347 F Supp 908, 909, 911 (ND Ga 1972).

Demonstrative evidence of a better designed product is admissible. Ogg v City of Springfield, 121 Ill App 3d 25, 458 NE2d 1331, 1339-40 (1984).

293 419 So 2d 687, 690 (Fla Dist Ct App 1982).

294 121 Ill App 3d 25, 458 NE2d 1331, 1342 (1984) (approximately $300,000 judgment).

295 *See generally* Pavlides v Galveston Yacht Basin, Inc, 727 F2d 330, 337-38 (5th Cir 1984).

296 *Id.*

297 *See* Boatland, Inc v Bailey, 609 SW2d 743 (Tex 1980); Young v Tide Craft, Inc, 270 SC 453, 242 SE2d 671, 679-80 (1978).

overboard, was not beyond the boater's contemplation.[298] Therefore, the boat was not dangerous to an extent beyond that comtemplated by an ordinary consumer.[299] The *Young* court also concluded that the failure to install a kill switch did not breach an implied warranty or show a failure to exercise due care.[300]

In *Arthur v Avon Inflatables, Ltd*,[301] the court held that a life raft manufacturer may be liable not just for a physical defect of the raft, but also for failing to have reasonable life-saving equipment on board. In that case, a yacht sank in the Pacific Ocean and the crew attempted to save themselves by using defendant's life rafts. Unfortunately, the rafts, which were promoted in yachting magazines as the *finest emergency lifecraft*, did not contain either an emergency position indicating radio beacon (EPIRB) which continuously transmits a distress signal over a range of 200 miles or solar stills which desalinize sea water. The crew, in the life rafts, drifted for weeks. During that time several crew members died. The *Arthur* court held that the life rafts may have been unreasonably dangerous because they failed to contain life-saving equipment.[302]

§7.09 —Particular Issues

Warnings and Instructions

A boat manufacturer has a duty to give proper instructions for using the boat and also to warn of potential hazards.[303]

The warnings must advise the boat user of the specific nature and magnitude of the danger.[304] The manufacturer is held to the standard of an expert in determining whether an injury could occur if warnings were not given.[305] Therefore, a manufacturer who knew or should have known of a risk of injury in using the boat should, at a minimum, warn of that danger.[306]

---

298 242 SE2d at 680. The *Young* decision is criticized in Birnbaum, *Unmasking The Test For Design Defect: From Negligence [To Warranty] To Strict Liability To Negligence*, 33 Vand L Rev 593, 611-12 (1980).

299 *See* Restatement (Second) of Torts §402A comment i (1965). The test is objective, i.e., of a reasonable person. *See* 242 SE2d at 679-80.

300 242 SE2d at 680.

301 156 Cal App 3d 401, 203 Cal Rptr 1 (1984).

302 156 Cal App 3d at 408.

303 *See* Martell v Boardwalk Enters, Inc, 748 F2d 740, 748 (2d Cir 1984); Pavlides v Galveston Yacht Basin, Inc, 727 F2d 330, 339 (5th Cir 1984); Sharton v J. H. Westerbeke Corp, 11 Mass App 925, 415 NE2d 880, 881-82 (1981).

304 Pavlides v Galveston Yacht Basin, Inc, 727 F2d 330, 339 (5th Cir 1984).

305 *Id.*

306 *Id.*

In *Pavlides v Galveston Yacht Basin, Inc,*[307] four men drowned in the cold waters of the Gulf of Mexico after their motorboat submerged. The court held that the motorboat was defective because there was no warning that an accidental slipping out of a plug in the bilge drain could begin a series of events which could easily lead to the boat's submerging, a situation which was not obvious to an ordinary consumer.[308] Other courts have held that watercraft manufactures should have warned of a craft's lack of visibility,[309] lack of stability,[310] and unusual handling characteristics,[311] and that the diaphragm of a fuel pump should be checked regularly.[312]

However, there is usually no duty to warn of obvious dangers.[313] Therefore, one court held that a boat manufacturer was not liable for failing to warn of the danger of sailing a boat into a power line.[314]

A boat manufacturer may have a greater duty than a retailer to warn of potential hazards in the boat.[315] This is because those two parties may have different information regarding the product's hazards.[316] For example, a boat manufacturer that had received accident reports calling into question the safety of the boat's design had a greater duty to warn of the danger than a boat rental company that was without knowledge of the prior accidents.[317]

Where inadequate warnings are given, it is generally presumed that the boat user would have read the appropriate warnings, had they been provided, and acted to minimize the risks.[318] For example, in *Pavlides* the court held that had the purchaser of a motorboat been apprised of the potentially fatal effects of allowing a bilge drain to become accidently unplugged, he would have taken appropriate action such as installing a warning device or not purchasing the boat.[319]

---

307 727 F2d 330 (5th Cir 1984).

308 *Id.*

309 *See* Martell v Boardwalk Enters, Inc, 748 F2d 740, 747 (2d Cir 1984) (over $800,000 damages).

310 *Id.*

311 *Id.*

312 *See* Schedlbauer v Chris-Chraft Corp, 381 Mich 217, 160 NW2d 889, 891-92 (1968).

313 McPhail v Municipality of Culebra, 598 F2d 603, 606-07 (1st Cir 1979).

314 *Id.*

315 Martell v Boardwalk Enters, Inc, 748 F2d 740, 749 (2d Cir 1984).

316 *Id.*

317 *Id.*

318 Pavlides v Galveston Yacht Basin, Inc, 727 F2d 330, 340 (5th Cir 1984); *see also* §7.03.

319 Pavlides v Galveston Yacht Basin, Inc, 727 F2d 330, 341 n 20 (5th Cir 1984).

The fact that a motorboat met or exceeded all applicable governmental regulations and private standards is not dispositive evidence that the manufacturer provided sufficient warnings.[320]

A boat manufacturer must also provide correct instructions and directions for the repair and maintenance of the boat.[321] In *Sharton v J. H. Westerbeke Corp*, a sailboat manufacturer was held liable for the damages caused when a boater followed the incorrect instruction manual for the upkeep of the engine.[322]

Causation

A plaintiff, suing for negligence, breach of warranty, or strict liability, can recover from a defendant only where the defendant's acts or omissions were a substantial factor in causing the injury.[323] The causal relationship between a plaintiff's injury and a defendant's acts or omissions may be proven by direct evidence or reasonable inferences from the facts; however, it may not be proven by conjecture.[324] In many cases, the line between reasonable inference and conjecture is difficult to discern.[325]

In several recent cases the courts have held that the plaintiff did not sustain his or her burden of proof regarding causation.[326] In *Wolff v Whittaker Marine & Manufacturing Co*, the court held that the boat manufacturer was not liable because the plaintiff did not show, by a preponderance of the evidence, that the boat's explosion was caused by a design or manufacturing defect.[327] In that case, the plaintiff failed sufficiently to negate other possible causes of the explosion, e.g., negligent fuel procedures or tampering with the fuel lines, which were not defects attributable to the manufacturer.[328]

A defendant is generally liable for the damages which flow from its wrongful acts or omissions, including damages from reasonably foreseeable intervening

---

320 Pavlides v Galveston Yacht Basin, Inc, 727 F2d 330, 337 (5th Cir 1984).

321 Sharton v J. H. Westerbeke Corp, 11 Mass App 925, 415 NE2d 880, 881-82 (1981).

322 *Id.*

323 Gasquet v Commercial Union Ins Co, 391 So 2d 466, 472-73 (La Ct App 1980) (airboat manufacturer not liable because the accident was solely a result of operator error); Young v Tide Craft, Inc, 270 SC 453, 242 SE2d 671, 675 (1978).

324 Schedlbauer v Chris-Chraft Corp, 381 Mich 217, 160 NW2d 889, 896-97 (1968).

325 *See id.*

326 *See* Wolff v Whittaker Marine & Mfg Co, 484 F Supp 1021, 1029 (ED Mo 1979); Young v Tide Craft, Inc, 270 SC 453, 242 SE2d 671, 679 (1978).

327 484 F Supp 1021, 1029 (ED Mo 1979).

328 Wolff v Whittaker Marine & Mfg Co, 484 F Supp 1021, 1029 (ED Mo 1979).

acts.[329] However, in *Young v Tide Craft, Inc*,[330] a verdict of approximately $200,000 against the boat manufacturer was reversed because the subsequent wrongful actions of a repair shop were not reasonably foreseeable. In *Young*, the operator of a boat took the watercraft to a repair company. The repair firm spliced the steering cable, a highly unsafe method of repair, rather than repairing it and, as a result, the cable snapped. This set in motion a series of events which ultimately killed the boater. The court held that the boat manufacturer was not liable because it was unforeseeable that such an unsafe repair method would be utilized.[331]

Punitive Damages

Punitive damages are available only to punish egregious misconduct.[332] In *Ogg v City of Springfield*,[333] the court affirmed the awarding of no punitive damages even though the manufacturer of a Hobie Cat knew, and had known for years, of the dangers of electrocution if the boat struck a power line. In that case, there was evidence that it was neither safe nor feasible to use all nonmetallic parts in the boat and, therefore, the risk of danger could not be eliminated.[334]

Indemnity and Contribution

Some defendants held liable for injuries have attempted to seek indemnity or contribution from others in the distribution chain. However, in *Four Winns, Inc v Cincinnati Insurance Co*,[335] the court held that a retailer of a boat was not entitled to indemnity, as a matter of law, against the boat's manufacturer. The court held that indemnity was proper only where the party seeking that relief was without fault.[336] Therefore, if the retailer failed to inspect the boat and an inspection would have revealed the defect, the retailer could not recover from the manufacturer.[337]

A manufacturer of a defective inboard-outboard engine which caused the plaintiff's pleasure boating accident was not allowed to be indemnified by the manufacturer of the boat for a design defect because the alleged defect, viz.,

---

329 *Id.*

330 270 SC 453, 242 SE 671, 676 (1978).

331 *Id.* The fact that the competence of repair companies varied did not change the result. *See id.*

332 *See* §7.02.

333 121 Ill App 3d 25, 458 NE2d 1331, 1342 (1984).

334 *Id.*

335 471 NE2d 1187 (Ind Ct App 1984).

336 *Id* 1189.

337 *Id.*

that the boat should have had a longer and more efficient forward rail, had no relationship to the cause of the plaintiff's injury.[338]

§7.10 Bowling

There have been few product liability actions for bowling injuries. This may be due, in part, to the fact that bowling balls and pins do not cause many injuries. However, another reason may be decisions such as *Dixon v Four Seasons Bowling Alley, Inc*,[339] which held that strict liability principles are inapplicable when a patron sues a bowling facility because the injury resulted more from a defective service than a defective product.

In *Dixon* a bowler was injured when she fell and cut her finger on a chipped bowling ball. The court held the bowling facility primarily provided a service and the supplying of a product, viz., the ball, was "incidental" to the use of the premises. It based its conclusion on nine factors:

1. The plaintiff selected the ball
2. The defendant did not assist her in selecting the ball
3. The plaintiff did not rely on the defendant's expertise in making the selection
4. The defect was a chip in the ball and this was obvious
5. There was no separate charge for the ball
6. The plaintiff could have brought her own ball
7. The ball was part of a broader service supplied
8. The plaintiff's actual possession of the ball was intended to be very short
9. The ball was not to be removed from the premises[340]

Accordingly, products liability law was not applicable.[341]

The *Dixon* court also noted that application of strict products liability was inappropriate because the bowling ball was not placed in the stream of commerce.[342] Although this may have been true for the bowling facility, this reasoning would not appear to apply to the bowling ball manufacturer. However, the manufacturer was not sued in *Dixon*.

---

338 Outboard Marine Corp v Apeco Corp, 348 So 2d 5, 5-6 (Fla Dist Ct App 1977).

339 176 NJ Super 540, 424 A2d 428, 431 (1980).

340 *Id*.

341 *Id; see generally* Powers, *Distinguishing between Products and Services in Strict Liability*, 62 NCL Rev 415 (1984). The liability of commercial bowling facilities is discussed in §1.04.

342 176 NJ Super 540, 424 A2d 428, 431 (1980).

§7.11 Fencing

Manufacturers of fencing[343] equipment must design their products so they are not defective when used in an intended or reasonably foreseeable manner.[344] In *Garcia v Joseph Vince Co*,[345] the plaintiff was injured when an opponent's sabre, narrower than the regulations permitted, broke through his fencing mask. The court held that the mask manufacturer was not strictly liable because sabres with sharp corners can penetrate all standard fencing masks[346] and the mask was not intended to be used against a sharp sabre.[347]

Further, even if the use of the mask while fencing with unduly narrow sabres had been reasonably foreseeable, the court held that the manufacturer was entitled to judgment as a matter of law because there is no strict liability where the product is reasonably safe for use but has inherent dangers that are impossible to eliminate.[348] In this case, the court concluded that a fencing mask cannot be designed which will prevent penetration by a sharp-edged sabre.[349] Therefore, it is inappropriate to impose strict liability on the mask manufacturer for failing to produce a mask which can do the impossible.[350]

A blade which was so thin and sharp that it could pierce the protective mask could be considered defective because this is not the type of weapon intended to be used during a fencing contest.[351] However, in *Garcia* the court held that where the plaintiff could not prove which of two blade manufacturers produced this defective blade, both manufacturers were properly entitled to a directed verdict.[352] The court distinguished this situation from the famous hunting accident case of *Summers v Tice*[353] where the plaintiff was allowed to go to the jury even though he did not know which of two hunters shot him because both defendants had acted improperly in shooting. In *Garcia* one defendant was clearly innocent.[354]

---

[343] It is estimated that over 1,500 individuals are seriously injured each year in fencing activities. *See* United States Prod Safety Commn, Natl Injury Information Clearinghouse, Prod Summary Report (Mar 28, 1984).

[344] Garcia v Joseph Vince Co, 84 Cal App 3d 879, 148 Cal Rptr 843, 848 (1978).

[345] *Id.*

[346] *Id.*

[347] *Id.*

[348] *Id*; Prosser, *The Fall of the Citadel (Strict Liability to the Consumer)*, 50 Minn L Rev 791, 812 (1966); Restatement (Second) of Torts §402A comment k (1965).

[349] Garcia v Joseph Vince Co, 84 Cal App 3d 879, 148 Cal Rptr 843, 848 (1978). Other cases have been reported where a jagged sword pierced a fencing mask. *See* LA Times, July 29, 1982, pt III, at 4.

[350] Garcia v Joseph Vince Co, 84 Cal App 3d 879, 148 Cal Rptr 843, 848 (1978).

[351] 148 Cal Rptr at 846 (1978).

[352] *Id.*

[353] 33 Cal 2d 80, 199 P2d 1 (1948). This case is discussed in **§2.08**.

[354] Garcia v Joseph Vince Co, 84 Cal App 3d 879, 148 Cal Rptr 843, 847 (1978).

§7.12   Firearms

Manufacturers of firearms do not have to design an accident-proof product.[355] However, they are liable for unreasonably dangerous defects in their products.[356] In addition, sellers of handguns may be absolutely liable because the use of a handgun is an ultrahazardous activity,[357] although there is contrary authority.[358]

The definition of *defect* in firearm cases is critical because it can be argued that if the gun discharged, it did what it was designed and intended to do.[359] Indeed, a manufacturer should be able to assume that the average consumer understands that a loaded firearm can result in death or serious injury.[360] However, one commentator has concluded that if firearm buyers were aware of the true risks of harm which are inherent in most firearms manufactured today, many popular models would find no market.[361]

Manufacturing Defects

Manufacturers are strictly liable for manufacturing flaws.[362] In *Philippe v*

Further, the subsequent landmark decision in *Sindell v Abbott Laboratories*, a non-recreational accident case imposing liability on pharmaceutical companies based on their market share where plaintiff could not ascertain which company marketed the specific drug which caused the injury, specifically distinguished *Garcia* and did not overrule it. *See* 26 Cal 3d 588, 607 P2d 924, 163 Cal Rptr 132, 139 n 18 (1980).

355 Cobb v Insured Lloyds, 387 So 2d 13, 19 (La Ct App 1980). The liability of firearms retailers is discussed in §1.07.

356 *See generally* Goff, *Defective Firearms*, 20 Trial 36 (Nov 1984); Halbrook, *Tort Liability for the Manufacture, Sale and Ownership of Handguns?*, 6 Hamline L Rev 351 (1983); Siegel, *Liability of Manufacturers for the Negligent Design and Distribution of Handguns*, 6 Hamline L Rev 321 (1983); Teret & Wintemute, *Handgun Injuries: The Epidemiologic Evidence for Assessing Legal Responsibility*, 6 Hamline L Rev 341 (1983); Turley, *Manufacturers' and Suppliers' Liability to Handgun Victims*, 10 N Ky L Rev 41 (1982); Turley & Harrison, *Strict Liability of Handgun Suppliers*, 6 Hamline L Rev 285 (1983); Note, *A Shot at Stricter Controls: Strict Liability for Gun Manufacturers*, 15 Pac LJ 171 (1983).

357 *See* Richman v Charter Arms, 571 F Supp 192 (ED La 1983); *see generally* Restatement (Second) of Torts §§519, 520 (1977).

358 *See* Martin v Harrington & Richardson, Inc, 743 F2d 1200 (7th Cir 1984).

359 Goff, *Defective Firearms*, 20 Trial 36, 37 (Nov 1984); *see generally* Note, *Handguns and Products Liability*, 97 Harv L Rev 1912 (1984) (products liability law should not be applied to handguns which performed exactly as they were intended).

Cal Civ Code §1714.4 (West 1985) provides that no firearm shall be deemed defective in design on the basis that the benefits of the product do not outweigh the risk of injury posed by its potential to cause serious injury or death when discharged.

360 Goff, *Defective Firearms*, 20 Trial 36, 37 (Nov 1984).

361 *Id.*

362 Philippe v Browning Arms Co, 375 So 2d 151, 155 (La Ct App 1979), *aff'd*, 395 So 2d 310 (La 1981).

Browning Arms Co, the manufacturer was held liable because the safety of its shotgun malfunctioned.[363] The manufacturer's reliance on the *feel* of assemblers, employees who were not skilled gunsmiths, in manufacturing the safety of the shotgun without testing it created an unreasonable risk of harm.[364]

In *Bender v Colt Industries*, the court held the manufacturer of a colt single-action army revolver liable when the firearm was known to have a defective sear.[365] The manufacturer offered the interesting defense that this gun was an exact replica of an 1873 gun and since the plaintiff purchased the gun as a replica, nothing in its design and construction could be considered a defect. The court rejected this argument because the firearm was not a "museum piece sold to be mounted on velvet and encased in a frame,"[366] but was intended to be used.

Retailers which inspect a rifle may be liable for any patent defect which the inspection might reveal.[367] In addition, retailers may be negligent in not discovering any defects which a reasonable inspection would have uncovered.[368]

Design Defects

Firearms must be designed without unreasonable defects.[369] In *Cobb v Insured Lloyds*, the court held that the defendant was liable for a design defect because the gun could fire from what was believed to be a safe position.[370] Such a gun is unreasonably dangerous because consumers do not reasonably expect a gun to discharge with the safety on or without the trigger being pulled.[371]

Generally, firearms manufacturers have no duty to install a design improvement in firearms which are already on the market.[372] For example, in *Stephan v Marlin Firearms Co*, the court held that the manufacturer had

---

363 *Id.*

364 *Id.*

365 517 SW2d 705, 708 (Mo Ct App 1974).

366 *Id* 707.

367 Jones v Cranman's Sporting Goods, 142 Ga App 838, 237 SE2d 402, 404-05 (1977).

368 *Id.*

369 Cobb v Insured Lloyds, 387 So 2d 13, 20 (La Ct App 1980) (distributor held liable); *see also* Moore v Remington Arms Co, 100 Ill App 3d 1102, 427 NE2d 608 (1981).

370 387 So 2d 13, 19 (La Ct App 1980).

371 *See* Goff, *Defective Firearms*, 20 Trial 36, 37 (Nov 1984).

However, one commentator believes that a shotgun may discharge if it is dropped from any height over four feet, whether or not the safety is on. *See id.*

The major trade organization has not come up with an acceptable drop standard. *See id.* One such standard is found at 18 USC §§921-928.

372 Stephan v Marlin Firearms Co, 353 F2d 819, 823 (2d Cir 1965), *cert denied*, 384 US 959 (1966).

no duty to install a design improvement in a gun which was submitted back to the manufacturer for specific repairs unrelated to the improvement.[373]

Warnings

Firearms manufacturers and distributors have a duty to warn of unreasonable dangers involved in the foreseeable use of their products.[374] Accordingly, firearms manufacturers may be liable for failing to warn that the weapon could fire with the hammer in the full forward position[375] or with the safety on.[376] One defendant argued that it had no duty to warn of obvious dangers, but this argument was not accepted because the danger of a revolver firing with the hammer in the full forward position was not obvious.[377]

Warranties

Sellers of defective firearms may also be liable under the Uniform Commercial Code's implied warranty provisions.[378] In *Jones v Cranman's Sporting Goods*, the court held that the fact that the rifle exploded during loading was some evidence that it was unfit for the ordinary purpose for which it was intended.[379]

One court stated that it was *doubtful* whether the Code's implied warranties apply to a firearm which had been purchased secondhand.[380]

BB Guns and Air Rifles

Sellers of BB guns and air rifles[381] may be strictly liable for design defects in the guns.[382] However, they are not liable, and may even be entitled to summary judgement, where the gun functioned correctly even though a person was injured.[383]

A BB gun is not defectively designed merely because BBs can ricochet

---

373 *Id.*

374 Cobb v Insured Lloyds, 387 So 2d 13, 19 (La Ct App 1980).

375 *Id* 18.

376 Weeks v Remington Arms Co, 733 F2d 1485, 1490 (11th Cir 1984).

377 Cobb v Insured Lloyds, 387 So 2d 13, 18 (La Ct App 1980).

378 *See* §7.04.

379 142 Ga App 838, 237 SE2d 402, 404 (1977).

380 *See* Hulsebosch v Ramsey, 435 SW2d 161, 164 (Tex Civ App 1968).

381 Each year, over 30,000 individuals injured from air guns and BBs require emergency room treatment. *See* US Consumer Prod Safety Commn, Natl Injury Information Clearinghouse, Prod Summary Report (Mar 28, 1984).

382 *See* Collins v Caldor of Kingston, Inc, 73 AD2d 708, 422 NYS2d 524, 526 (1979); Novak v Piggly Wiggly Puget Sound Co, 22 Wash App 407, 591 P2d 791, 794 (1979).

383 *See* Collins v Caldor of Kingston, Inc, 73 AD2d 708, 422 NYS2d 524, 526 (1979).

and cause harm when shot at a hard surface.[384] Indeed, in *Novak v Piggly Wiggly Puget Sound Co*, the court held that A BB gun was not unreasonably dangerous, even when judged by the standard of an ordinary child consumer, because there was nothing the manufacturer could have done to stop the BBs shot from a gun from ricocheting after they hit a hard surface.[385]

Sellers of BB guns are generally not liable for failing to warn of dangers which are known or should have been known to the user.[386] For example, it has been held that shooting a BB gun at a person[387] and using carbon dioxide cartridges to power pellet guns[388] were obvious dangers and the manufacturer was not liable for failing to warn of these dangers. Indeed, one court held that a directed verdict for the manufacturer would have been appropriate in such a case.[389]

The courts have reached the conclusion that there is usually no liability for failing to warn of obvious dangers for three reasons. First, if the danger is known, the BB gun is not dangerous beyond that which would be contemplated by the ordinary consumer with the ordinary knowledge common to the community.[390] Therefore, strict liability does not apply. Second, where the danger was obvious, a warning would serve no useful purpose.[391] After all, the law does not require an idle act. Third, if the user of the BB gun knew of the danger, the failure to warn was not the proximate cause of the injury.[392] The accident was caused by the user's actions, not the manufacturer's omission.[393]

In addition, the manufacturer is not liable for failing to warn where the user was warned by others.[394] In *Menard v Newhall*,[395] a father instructed his son on the use of a BB gun, but the son ignored those instructions. The court

---

[384] Novak v Piggly Wiggly Puget Sound Co, 22 Wash App 407, 591 P2d 791, 794 (1979).

[385] *Id.*

[386] Holmes v JC Penney Co, 133 Cal App 3d 216, 220, 183 Cap Rptr 777 (1982); Bookout v Victor Comptometer Corp, 40 Colo App 417, 576 P2d 197, 198 (1978); Sherk v Daisy-Heddon, 498 Pa 594, 450 A2d 615, 618 (1982); Menard v Newhall, 135 Vt 53, 373 A2d 505, 507 (1977).

[387] Bookout v Victor Comptometer Corp, 40 Colo App 417, 576 P2d 197, 198 (1978); Sherk v Daisy-Heddon, 498 Pa 594, 450 A2d 615, 618 (1982); Menard v Newhall, 135 Vt 53, 373 A2d 505, 507 (1977).

[388] Holmes v JC Penney Co, 133 Cal App 3d 216, 220, 183 Cal Rptr 777 (1982).

[389] Bookout v Victor Comptometer Corp, 40 Colo App 417, 576 P2d 197, 198 (1978).

[390] Menard v Newhall, 135 Vt 53, 373 A2d 505, 507 (1977).

[391] Holmes v JC Penney Co, 133 Cal App 3d 216, 220, 183 Cal Rptr 777 (1982).

[392] *See generally* Sherk v Daisy-Heddon, 498 Pa 594, 450 A2d 615, 620 (1982) (BB gun user failed to check whether safety was on).

[393] *Id.*

[394] Menard v Newhall, 135 Vt 53, 373 A2d 505, 507 (1977).

[395] *Id.*

held that the manufacturer was entitled to summary judgment because in that case no warning by it would have been effective to stop the accident.[396]

Obviously, a manufacturer is not liable for failing to warn where it gave an adequate warning.[397] For example, in *Novak v Piggly Wiggly Puget Sound Co*, the court held that the manufacturer was not liable because it warned that a BB shot at a hard surface could ricochet.[398]

Retailers and manufacturers are not per se liable for the sale of BB guns to minors.[399] In addition, manufacturers have no duty to sell only to retailers which agree to refrain from selling the BB guns to minors.[400]

Misuse

Manufacturers of BB guns are generally not liable where the user misused the product.[401] In *Sherk v Daisy-Heddon*, the court held that the manufacturer was not liable where the user knew that BBs fired from a gun could cause serious injury and death, and nevertheless shot the BB gun at another individual at close range.[402]

Evidence

Proof of prior similar accidents is generally admissible to establish a firearms manufacturer's prior knowledge of the defect.[403] However, this evidence is generally not admissible unless the accidents were caused by a similar factor.[404]

Causation

Sellers of firearms are only liable if their wrongful acts or omissions played a substantial role in causing a plaintiff's injuries.[405] Therefore, a manufacturer

---

396 *Id.*

397 Collins v Caldor of Kingston, Inc, 73 AD2d 708, 422 NYS2d 524, 526 (1979); Novak v Piggly Wiggly Puget Sound Co, 22 Wash App 407, 591 P2d 791, 795 (1979).

398 22 Wash App 407, 591 P2d 791, 795 (1979).

399 *See* Jimenez v Zayre Corp, 374 So 2d 28, 29 (Fla Dist Ct App 1979).

400 *See* Novak v Piggly Wiggly Puget Sound Co, 22 Wash App 407, 591 P2d 791, 796 (1979).

401 *See* Sherk v Daisy-Heddon, 498 Pa 594, 450 A2d 615, 618 (1982); *see also* §§7.02, 9.02, 9.04.

402 498 Pa 594, 450 A2d 615, 618 (1982).

403 *See* Moore v Remington Arms Co, 100 Ill App 3d 1102, 427 NE2d 608, 614 (1981); *see also* §7.02. This knowledge can also form the basis for a punitive damage award because it can show the manufacturer's indifference to safety. Moore v Remington Arms Co, 100 Ill App 3d 1102, 427 NE2d 608, 614 (1981).

404 Moore v Remington Arms Co, 100 Ill App 3d 1102, 427 NE2d 608, 614 (1981).

405 *See* Hulsebosch v Ramsey, 435 SW2d 161, 164 (Tex Civ App 1968).

was not responsible where the cartridge clip was not in good condition, but the clip did not cause the accident.[406]

Punitive Damages

In *International Armament Corp v King*,[407] the Texas Supreme Court affirmed an award of $1.5 million in punitive damages against an importer of a Spanish shotgun. The court held punitive damages were appropriate where the defendant was consciously indifferent to the safety of the plaintiff, i.e., the defendant knew about the peril, but its acts or omissions demonstrated that it did not care.[408] In this case, punitive damages were allowed because there was evidence that the importer knew of the poor workmanship of the shotguns, knew that the gun could misfire if the internal mechanism did not fit properly and yet failed to inspect each gun or issue a warning about the safety system.[409]

In contrast, in *Moore v Remington Arms Co*, the court reversed an $85,000 punitive damages award against a gun manufacturer because there was no showing that the manufacturer was aware of the existence of a defect, much less than it was flagrantly indifferent to the public safety.[410]

§7.13 Football

Each year, about 420,000 individuals are seriously injured while playing football.[411] Although not all of those accidents are caused by defective equipment, in some cases, where defective equipment did cause the accident, individuals have suffered catastrophic injuries. Accordingly, there have been several multimillion-dollar jury verdicts in football equipment cases.[412] One

---

406 *Id.*

407 686 SW2d 595 (Tex 1985).

408 *Id* 597.

409 *Id* 597-98.

410 100 Ill App 3d 1102, 427 NE2d 608, 618 (1981).

411 *See* US Consumer Prod Safety Commn, Natl Injury Information Clearinghouse, Prod Summary Rep (Mar 28, 1984).

There have been several studies of the causes of football injuries. *See, e.g.*, Mueller & Schindler, Annual Survey of Football Injury Research 1931-1983 (1984); Mueller & Blyth, Annual Survey of Catastrophic Football Injuries 1977-1982 (1983).

412 *See, e.g.*, Underwood, *An Unfolding Tragedy*, Sports Illustrated, Aug 14, 1972, at 72; Note, *Injuries Resulting From Nonintentional Acts In Organized Contact Sports: The Theories Of Recovery Available To The Injured Athlete*, 12 Ind L Rev 687, 689 (1979); *see* LA Times, May 13, 1982, pt II, at 1 ($3.5 million awarded by jury for defective football helmet).

The costs of adverse jury verdicts and liability insurance have reduced the number of helmet manufacturers operating in this country in recent years. *See* Beumler, *Liability In Professional Sports: An Alternative To Violence*, 22 Ariz L Rev 919, 921 n 19 (1980).

verdict was for over $11 million.[413] Some of these seven-figure awards have been affirmed on appeal.[414] Of course, there also have been verdicts in favor of the manufacturer.[415]

Strict products liability principles only apply to parties who are in the production and marketing chain.[416] Accordingly, a student injured by a defective football helmet purchased and supplied by the school has limited remedies against the school and its officials. For example, in *Hemphill v Sayers*, a college student injured by a defective football helmet was not entitled, as a matter of law, to recover from a university athletic director, football coach, and athletic trainer under strict products liability law because they were not in the chain of commerce for the helmet.[417]

In addition, the Uniform Commercial Code's implied warranty of fitness for a particular purpose applies only to warranties made by a *seller* to a buyer.[418] Therefore, nonsellers such as university athletic department officials are not liable as a matter of law under this theory.[419] Similarly, university athletic department officials are not liable for breach of the implied warranty of merchantability because that warranty applies only to sellers who are *merchants*.[420]

In some cases, a college football player who was supplied a defective football helmet by the school may not be able to recover from the helmet's manufacturer for breach of warranty.[421] In *Sayers*, the court held that Illinois adopted the privity version of Uniform Commercial Code §2-318 which extends warranty protection only to the purchaser or members or guests of the purchaser's family.[422] Accordingly, in that case the student was not protected under warranty law because the school purchased the helmet.[423]

It is clear, however, that the helmet manufacturer is strictly liable for injuries caused by its defective helmet.[424] A helmet may be defective because it

---

413 *See, e.g.*, NY Times, Feb 27, 1985, at 20, col 1 (jury awarded $11,000,000 to injured high school player who broke his neck in ramming another player with his helmet).

414 *See, e.g.*, Rawlings Sporting Goods Co v Daniels, 619 SW2d 435 (Tex Civ App 1981) ($1,500,000 verdict); Fiske v MacGregor, 464 A2d 719 (RI 1983) ($2,100,000 verdict).

415 *See, e.g.*, Struder v Riddell Co, ____ SW2d ____ (Tenn Ct App 1984) (available on Lexis).

416 Hemphill v Sayers, 552 F Supp 685, 689 (SD Ill 1982).

417 *Id.*

418 *Id.*

419 *Id.*

420 *Id*

421 *Id* 692-93.

422 *See generally* §7.05.

423 552 F Supp 685, 692-93 (SD Ill 1982).

424 *See generally* Philo & Stine, *The Liability Path To Safer Helmets*, 13 Trial 38 (Jan 1977).

was defectively manufactured[425] or designed,[426] or because the manufacturer failed to issue appropriate warnings.[427]

In *Rawlings Sporting Goods Co v Daniels*,[428] the court held that a football helmet which indented inward over one and a half inches after a *head-to-head* collision between two football players was defectively manufactured. The helmet failed to perform its intended purpose, i.e, to protect the wearer from head injuries.[429] A different court held that a helmet's failure to meet the Z90.1 safety standard promulgated by the American National Standards Institute may be a defect and, therefore, the manufacturer was not entitled to a directed verdict.[430]

Every manufacturer has a duty to warn of dangers in the use of its products of which it knows or should know.[431] Indeed, where there is no warning, the presumption is that the user would have read and acted upon an adequate warning.[432] In *Daniels*, the court held that a football helmet manufacturer must warn of known limitations in the protective abilities of the helmet with which the user is not equally familiar.[433] In that case, the manufacturer knew that football players run a significant risk of head injury even where they wear helmets because the helmets are not able to protect against all brain injuries. The manufacturer also knew that most purchasers of football helmets do not realize that helmets do not protect against all head injuries. Accordingly, the manufacturer, who has superior knowledge of the product's limitations, must warn of the limitations.[434]

A helmet manufacturer has no duty of care to nonusers of the product for its omission[435] to act.[436] In *Carrier v Riddell, Inc*,[437] the manufacturer of a football helmet was granted summary judgment where the plaintiff was not using the defendant-manufacturer's helmet at the time of the injury but the helmet of another manufacturer. The court rejected the plaintiff's theory that

---

425 Hemphill v Sayers, 552 F Supp 685, 693 (SD Ill 1982).

426 *Id*; Fiske v MacGregor, 464 A2d 719, 723 (RI 1983).

427 Hemphill v Sayers, 552 F Supp 685, 693 (SD Ill 1982).

428 619 SW2d 435 (Tex Civ App 1981).

429 *Id* 438.

430 Byrns v Riddell, Inc, 113 Ariz 264, 550 P2d 1065, 1069 (1976); *but see* Galindo v Riddell, Inc, 107 Ill App 3d 139, 437 NE2d 376, 382-83 (1982).

431 Rawlings Sporting Goods, Inc v Daniels, 619 SW2d 435, 439 (Tex Civ App 1981).

432 *Id*.

433 *Id*.

434 *Id* 437-39.

435 E.g., a failure to act. This is in contrast to a commission of an act. *See* Carrier v Riddell, Inc, 721 F2d 867, 868 (1st Cir 1983).

436 *Id*.

437 721 F2d 867 (1st Cir 1983).

had the defendant-manufacturer properly warned the other players on his high school team of the dangers of using its helmets, he would have learned of the warnings and acted appropriately. Where there is no duty to act, there can be no liability.[438]

Evidence

A manufacturer's knowledge of the dangerous condition of its helmet can be shown in many ways. It has been held that a manufacturer's report on the dangers of its helmets[439] and a medical journal article on football injuries which the defendant's personnel had read were admissible evidence.[440]

One court held that evidence that a football helmet failed one organization's safety standard was inadmissible.[441] The committee responsible for developing that standard was concerned with protective headgear for vehicular uses and there was no showing that the standards were applicable to nonvehicular uses.[442]

Care must be taken to show whether there was a causal relationship between the football helmet and the injury. A former professional football player who had no proven expertise in analyzing the cause of a football injury should not have been qualified as an expert or allowed to testify on this issue.[443] Similarly, a doctor's survey showing that football helmet designs were not a contributing cause of neck injuries was inadmissible because there was no showing that a scientifically accurate method was used in the survey.[444]

In appropriate circumstances, experiments can be used to prove causation. Generally, experiments are incompetent as evidence unless the essential conditions of the experiment are shown to be the same as those existing at the time of the accident.[445] However, when an experiment is not represented to be an enactment of the accident, but deals only with whether one theory of causation was possible, the exact conditions need not be duplicated.[446] Accordingly, experiments showing whether a football helmet could have come into contact with a plaintiff's cervical spine when his head and neck were in

---

438 *Id* 870.

439 Galindo v Riddell, Inc, 107 Ill App 3d 139, 437 NE2d 376, 382-83 (1982).

440 *Id.*

441 *Id; but see* Byrns v Riddell, Inc, 113 Ariz 264, 550 P2d 1065, 1069 (1976).
There is one academic study regarding safety standards for athletic helmets. *See* Mahajan, *Standards For Athletic Helmets—State Of The Art And Recommendations* prepared for the Consumer Prod Safety Commn (Apr 1, 1974).

442 Galindo v Riddell, Inc, 107 Ill App 3d 139, 437 NE2d 376, 382-83 (1982).

443 *Id.*

444 *Id.*

445 437 NE2d at 381.

446 *Id.*

a hyperextended position tested the probability of one theory of causation and were admissible.[447]

Punitive Damages

Where a party's knowledge of the product's defective condition is an element of liability, e.g., for punitive damages, both parties should be allowed to present evidence either establishing or refuting the existence of such knowledge.[448] For example, the defendant is entitled to show that it could not have been aware of a design defect in its helmet because the vast majority of other helmet manufacturers constructed their helmets in the same method.[449]

In *Rawlings Sporting Goods Co v Daniels*, an award of $750,000 punitive damages was affirmed because the manufacturer was knowingly indifferent to the safety of users of its helmets.[450] The manufacturer knew that its helmets would not protect against all head injuries, and knew that most purchasers of the helmets did not realize this, but the manufacturer still failed to warn of the danger.[451]

§7.14   Golf

Sellers of golf equipment[452] are liable for defects in the design or manufacture of equipment of which a plaintiff was not aware and which made the equipment unsafe for its intended purpose.[453] For example, in *Hauter v Zogarts*, the court held, as a matter of law, that a golf training device was defectively designed because a person using the device under normal conditions was likely to injure him or herself by entangling the club in the cord attached

---

447 *Id.* Plaintiff tried to show such contact was possible through x-rays. Defendant attempted to show such contact was impossible through expert testimony performed on dummies, cadavers and x-rayed individuals. *See id* 380.

448 Galindo v Riddell, Inc, 107 Ill App 3d 139, 437 NE2d 376, 384 (1982).

449 *Id.*

450 619 SW2d 435, 440-41 (Tex Civ App 1981).

451 *Id.*

452 About 4,500 individuals each year are seriously injured while using a golf cart. *See* US Consumer Prod Safety Commn, Natl Injury Information Clearinghouse, Prod Summary Report (Mar 28, 1984).

453 Blevins v Cushman Motors, 551 SW2d 602, 608 (Mo 1977) (golf cart); *see also* Sipari v Villa Olivia Country Club, 63 Ill App 3d 985, 380 NE2d 819, 825 (1978); *see generally* Dixon v Outboard Marine Corp, 481 P2d 151, 157 (Okla 1970).

The cause of a defect in a golf cart can be shown by expert testimony given with a reasonable degree of engineering certainty. *See* Gifford v Bogey Hills Golf & Country Club, Inc, 426 SW2d 98, 101-02 (Mo 1968).

to the ball.[454] A different court held that an unstable three-wheel golf cart may have been defectively designed.[455]

Most golf equipment, e.g., a golf cart, is capable of being made safe for its intended and ordinary purpose.[456] Accordingly, the equipment should not be treated as an unavoidably unsafe product.[457]

Sellers of golf equipment must provide instructions regarding the proper operation of their product.[458] In addition, they must warn, at a minimum, of the nonapparent dangers of using their products.[459] However, where a plaintiff was cognizant of the danger, e.g., a plaintiff knew that if he stood up in a golf cart, the cart might tip over,[460] then the failure to warn is not actionable.[461]

In any event, there is no liability merely because a golfer was injured.[462] A patron who fell on a miniature golf course could not recover from the operator of the course because the only conceivable defect was that the green and steps near it were wet, but it had been raining and the plaintiff failed to show that the steps were unreasonably slick.[463]

Rented Golf Carts

A country club which rents golf carts must take reasonable care to see that the carts are in good condition.[464] While the country club is not an insurer, it is liable to lessees or third persons for injuries caused by a defect in the cart of which the club was aware or which it should have discovered by reasonable

---

454 14 Cal 3d 104, 534 P2d 377, 120 Cal Rptr 681 (1975).

455 Blevins v Cushman Motors, 551 SW2d 602, 608 (Mo 1977).

456 *Id.*

457 *Id; see generally* Restatement (Second) of Torts §402A comment k (1965).

458 Dixon v Outboard Marine Corp, 481 P2d 151, 155 (Okla 1970).

459 *Id; see also* Cavers v Cushman Motor Sales, Inc, 95 Cal App 3d 338, 157 Cal Rptr 142 (1979).

460 Dixon v Outboard Marine Corp, 481 P2d 151, 155 (Okla 1970).

461 *Id* 157.

462 Lash v Noland, 321 So 2d 104, 105 (Fla Dist Ct App 1975); Sanders v Stutes, 400 So 2d 1159, 1161 (La Ct App 1981).

463 Sanders v Stutes, 400 So 2d 1159, 1161 (La Ct App 1981).

464 Lash v Noland, 321 So 2d 104, 105 (Fla Dist Ct App 1975); Fort Lauderdale Country Club v Winnemore, 189 So 2d 222, 223-24 (Fla Dist Ct App 1966); Terry v Midvale Golf & Country Club, 73 AD2d 1049, 425 NYS2d 900, 901 (1980) (court held that plaintiff must accept $150,000 damages or a new trial); Roberts v William N. & Kate B. Reynolds Memorial Park, 281 NC 48, 187 SE2d 721, 724 (1972); *see also* §1.09.

The doctrine of res ipsa loquitur does not apply because the country club does not have exclusive control of the cart. *See* Hutchins v Southview Golf Club, Inc, 343 SW2d 223, 224 (Mo Ct App 1960).

care.[465] For example, it may be negligence to rent a golf cart after removing a rubber-covered brake pedal safety device because without the cover the brake pedal may be difficult to use with conventional spiked golf shoes.[466]

However, lessors of golf carts may not be liable for defective carts under other theories of recovery. Several courts have held that strict liability principles do not apply to country clubs which rent golf carts.[467] In *Katz v Slade* the court reasoned that strict liability was inappropriate because the cart was provided only as an "incidental and collateral"[468] convenience to the golfer. It was rented for a short period of time, for use in a specified area and for a small fee.[469] Indeed, the court concluded that the transaction more closely resembled a license and, therefore, there should be liability only for negligence.[470]

In *Bona v Graefe*, the court also held that warranty principles do not apply to lessors of golf carts.[471] However, there is contrary authority.[472]

In Florida, country clubs have additional exposure for liability. In that state the owner of an instrumentality which has the capability of causing death or destruction is vicariously liable for the negligence of anyone using that instrumentality with the owner's knowledge and consent.[473] This expands liability well beyond respondeat superior and agency principles.[474] Accordingly, a golfer injured by another golfer's negligent operation of a golf cart can recover from the country club which rented the cart to the negligent golfer.[475]

§7.15 Gymnastics

Manufacturers of gymnastic[476] equipment must provide equipment which

---

[465] Lash v Noland, 321 So 2d 104, 105 (Fla Dist Ct App 1975); Gifford v Bogey Hills Golf & Country Club, Inc, 426 SW2d 98, 102 (Mo 1968); Roberts v Williams N. & Kate B. Reynolds Memorial Park, 281 NC 48, 187 SE2d 721, 724 (1972).

[466] Fort Lauderdale Country Club v Winnemore, 189 So 2d 222, 223-24 (Fla Dist Ct App 1966) (cart driver's actions were not intervening cause of accident).

[467] *See* Bona v Graefe, 264 Md 69, 285 A2d 607, 609, 611 (1972); Katz v Slade, 460 SW2d 608, 613 (Mo 1970); *see generally* §7.02.

[468] 460 SW2d 608, 613 (Mo 1970).

[469] *Id.*

[470] *Id.*

[471] 264 Md 69, 285 A2d 607, 609, 611 (1972).

[472] *See Baker v City of Seattle*, 79 Wash 2d 198, 484 P2d 405, 407 (1971); *see generally* Farnsworth, *Implied Warranties of Quality in Non-Sale Cases*, 57 Colum L Rev 653 (1957).

[473] *See* Meister v Fisher, 462 So 2d 1071, 1072 (Fla 1984).

[474] *Id.*

[475] *Id* 1073.

[476] It is estimated that over 50,000 individuals are seriously injured in gymnastic accidents each year, although not all of those injuries are from defective gymnastic equipment. *See* US Consumer Prod Safety Commn, Prod Summary Report (Mar 28, 1984).

is not defective.[477] This means, among other things, that they must adequately warn of the dangers of using their equipment.[478] Warnings are inadequate if they:

1. Do not specify the risk presented by the product
2. Are inconsistent with how a product would be used
3. Do not provide the reason for the warnings
4. Do not reach foreseeable users[479]

In *Pell v Victor J. Andrew High School*, a mini-trampoline manufacturer was held liable for over $3 million for a gymnast's injury.[480] The court held that the warnings on the trampoline were inadequate for two reasons. First, they did not specify the risk of severe spinal cord injury if the trampoline was used without a spotter or safety harness.[481] Second, the warnings were placed in areas where they would not be seen, viz., underneath the trampoline where they faced the floor and on the sides of the metal frames where they were covered by the frame pads.[482] Although the actual placement of the warnings was done by the person who assembled the trampoline, and not the manufacturer, the manufacturer was liable because its instructions for assembling the trampoline failed to specify that the warnings should be visible to a gymnast.[483]

In *Nissen Trampoline Co v Terre Haute First National Bank*,[484] a case with an unusual procedural history, the Indiana Supreme Court effectively held that an *aqua diver*, a trampoline used to enter the water, was not unreasonably dangerous even where there were no instructions for use. The defendant won the jury trial. The trial judge, however, granted a new trial. This decision

---

477 Pell v Victor J. Andrew High School, 123 Ill App 3d 423, 462 NE2d 858, 862-63 (1984); Curtiss v YMCA, 82 Wash 2d 455, 511 P2d 991, 996 (1973) (the manufacturer was liable because of an improperly fastened gymnastic bar); *see generally* Goodman v Metallic Ladder Mfg Co, 181 Conn 62, 434 A2d 324 (1980) (nylon loops on the diving pad portion of the trampoline were defective); Tiemann v Independent School Dist No 740, 331 NW2d 250, 251 (Minn 1983); *see generally* §1.10.

478 Pell v Victor J. Andrew High School, 123 Ill App 3d 423, 462 NE2d 858, 862-63 (1984); *see generally* Tiemann v Independent School Dist No 740, 331 NW2d 250, 251 (Minn 1983) (manufacturer not liable).

479 Pell v Victor J. Andrew High School, 123 Ill App 3d 423, 462 NE2d 858, 862-63 (1984).

480 *Id.* The manufacturer's contribution claim against a joint tortfeasor was dismissed as untimely when it was filed after the original lawsuit was over. *See* 462 NE2d at 867.

481 462 NE2d at 863.

482 *Id.*

483 *Id.*

484 358 NE2d 974 (Ind 1976).

was affirmed by the appellate court. The state supreme court held that the trial court's actions were procedurally incorrect because the court failed to set forth the appropriate evidence of wrongdoing and since the supreme court failed to remand this case back to the lower court to see whether such evidence existed, it held, sub silentio, that no such evidence was possible.

A trampoline manufacturer usually has no duty, under negligence or strict liability, to warn of dangers actually known to the users of the trampoline.[485] Accordingly, a manufacturer was entitled to summary judgment where the plaintiff claimed the manufacturer failed to warn of the dangers of landing on one's head because the plaintiff realized this danger.[486]

Causation

Generally, a defendant is liable if its conduct contributed in whole or in part to the plaintiff's injury.[487] This is true even where there are intervening acts or omissions of others, as long as those intervening acts or omissions were reasonably foreseeable.[488]

A mini-trampoline manufacturer who failed to provide adequate warnings was not entitled to judgment as a matter of law when it argued that the school's failure to provide proper gymnastic supervision was a superseding cause of the injury.[489] It was objectively foreseeable that users of a mini-trampoline would not always be under the direct supervision of a coach and that a coach would not have sufficient knowledge of the dangers unless the warnings were adequate.[490] Therefore, the manufacturer's failure to warn adequately of the dangers of using a mini-trampoline was a contributing cause of the injury.[491]

Evidence

One court allowed evidence pertaining to safety standards for full-size trampolines in a case involving a mini-trampoline because there was some showing that the same standards were applicable, at least in part, to both sizes of trampolines.[492]

---

485 Garrett v Nissen Corp, 84 NM 16, 498 P2d 1359, 1363 (1972).

486 *Id.*

487 Pell v Victor J. Andrew High School, 123 Ill App 3d 423, 462 NE2d 858, 863 (1984).

488 *Id.* This is usually a question of fact for the jury. *Id.*

489 462 NE2d at 864.

490 *Id* 863-64 (over $3 million verdict affirmed).

491 *Id.*

492 *See* Pell v Victor J. Andrew High School, 123 Ill App 3d 423, 462 NE2d 858, 865-66 (1984).

§7.16 Hockey

A hockey[493] helmet manufacturer must design the helmet to be reasonably safe for its intended use.[494] In *Everett v Bucky Warren, Inc*, a hockey helmet was consciously designed, by a person with no engineering background, to have gaps between its three sections to facilitate adjustment. Unfortunately, a puck landed in one of the gaps in the helmet, causing serious injury.[495] The court held that the manufacturer was liable for failing to design a product which would properly protect the head.[496] The court also noted that the manufacturer failed to make any safety tests for this design, although it knew that other manufacturers were producing helmets of a one-piece design.[497]

Sellers of hockey equipment must warn of the latent risks of injury from using their products.[498] However, they generally have no duty to warn of dangers which are apparent.[499] Accordingly, in *Durkee v Cooper of Canada, Ltd*, the court held that a hockey helmet manufacturer was under no duty to warn an adult hockey player of the dangers of using a helmet which did not completely cover his head because the adult was aware of the dangers.[500]

The purchase of a ticket to a hockey game is not a *product* so the owner of the facilities is not liable to a spectator for injuries under either strict liability or warranty principles.[501]

§7.17 Motorcycling

Manufacturing and Assembling Defects

Motorcycle manufacturers are strictly liable for manufacturing defects in

---

493 About 25,000 individuals are seriously injured each year playing ice hockey, although not all of them are injured by defective equipment. *See* US Consumer Prod Safety Commn, Prod Summary Report (Mar 28, 1984).

494 Everett v Bucky Warren, Inc, 376 Mass 280, 380 NE2d 653, 658 (1978); Durkee v Cooper of Canada, Ltd, 99 Mich App 693, 298 NW2d 620, 623 (1980) (question of fact whether hockey helmet manufacturer acted reasonably in manufacturing a helmet which allowed a player to be injured by a blow to the head).

There is one academic study regarding safety standards for athletic helmets. *See* Mahajan, *Standards For Athletic Helmets—State Of The Art And Recommendations* prepared for the Consumer Prod Safety Commn (Apr 1, 1974).

One jury recently awarded $3.5 million to a child severely injured because of a defective hockey helmet. LA Times, Oct 9, 1983, §III, at 9, col 1.

495 376 Mass 280, 380 NE2d 653, 658 (1978).

496 *Id.*

497 *Id.*

498 Durkee v Cooper of Canada, Ltd, 99 Mich App 693, 298 NW2d 620, 621 (1980).

499 *Id.*

500 298 NW2d at 622.

501 Kennedy v Providence Hockey Club, Inc, 119 RI 70, 376 A2d 329, 333 (1977).

their motorcycles.[502] Therefore, their compliance with industry standards is not dispositive of whether there was a defect.[503]

A motorcycle dealer may be negligent in failing to assemble the drive chain and sprocket assembly correctly.[504] The distributor can also be liable for the dealer's negligence where it had the contractual right to control the manner in which the dealer performed warranty service.[505] In addition, it has been held that a manufacturer is liable for the improper assembly of a motorcycle by a dealer where the manufacturer relied on the dealer to assemble the motorcycle.[506]

Design Defects

Motorcycle manufacturers are also strictly liable for design defects where the injury occurred while the motorcycle was used in a reasonably foreseeable manner.[507] Juries have awarded seven-figure verdicts in such cases.[508]

The determination of whether the design is defective usually involves an analysis of the utility of the current design versus the likelihood and severity of injury.[509] One court noted that motorcycles have limited utility and, therefore, if there are serious risks of operation, the product should not be manufactured.[510] However, in a different case the court stated in dicta that a motorcycle was not defectively designed because it was not unreasonably dangerous where it presented no unforeseen hazard for the intended user.[511]

A motorcycle manufacturer's compliance with the applicable federal standards[512] or industry standards[513] is not dispositive of whether there was a

---

502 *See* Harley Davidson Motor Co v Wisniewski, 50 Md App 339, 437 A2d 700, 705 (1982) ($500,000 verdict); Abbott v American Honda Motor Co, 682 SW2d 206, 211 (Tenn Ct App 1984).

503 Abbott v American Honda Motor Co, 682 SW2d 206, 211 (Tenn Ct App 1984).

504 *See* Peeples v Kawasaki Heavy Indus, 288 Or 143, 603 P2d 765, 769 (1979).

505 *Id.*

506 Sabloff v Yamaha Motor Co, 113 NJ Super 279, 273 A2d 606, 612 (1971); *but see* Peeples v Kawasaki Heavy Indus, 288 Or 143, 603 P2d 765, 769 (1979) (manufacturer not liable for dealer's failure to check and adjust the chain and sprocket assembly).

507 Rainbow v Albert Elia Bldg Co, 79 AD2d 287, 436 NYS2d 480, 483 (1981), *aff'd without opinion*, 56 NY2d 550, 434 NE2d 1345, 449 NYS2d 967 (1982).

508 Cota v Harley Davidson, 141 Ariz 7, 684 P2d 888 (Ct App 1984) ($3,500,000 verdict affirmed); *see also* LA Daily J, July 15, 1983, at 1, col 4 (a young woman received a jury verdict of $6.5 million for her injuries from a defective design of a 1972 Yamaha motorcycle).

509 *See* §7.03.

510 Pawlak v Brown, 430 So 2d 1346, 1349-50 (La Ct App 1983).

511 Rainbow v Albert Elia Bldg Co, 79 AD2d 287, 436 NYS2d 480, 483 (1981), *aff'd without opinion*, 56 NY2d 550, 434 NE2d 1345, 449 NYS2d 967 (1982).

512 *See* 49 CFR §§571.122, 571.123; *see also* Schwartz v American Honda Motor Co, 710 F2d 378, 383 (7th Cir 1983).

513 Abbott v American Honda Motor Co, 682 SW2d 206, 211 (Tenn Ct App 1984).

design defect.[514] However, failure to comply with the federal regulations may be a defect.[515]

Motorcycles must be designed to be reasonably safe when used in a foreseeable manner.[516] This is broader than use exactly in accordance with the manufacturer's instructions.[517] In *Pawlak v Brown*, the court held that it was foreseeable that a three-wheel motorcycle would be driven on the shoulder of a driveway with a passenger even though the manufacturer's instructions stated that the product was to be used for off-the-road purposes and was not designed to carry two people.[518]

The courts have consistently held that motorcycle manufacturers may be liable under the *crashworthiness doctrine*, i.e., motorcycles must be designed to minimize the likelihood or severity of injuries when the motorcycle is involved in an accident.[519] This is true whether the cyclist is injured coming in contact with external forces in the first collision or involved in a second collision.[520] In fact, this doctrine is cognizable in negligence, strict product liability, and breach of implied warranty.[521]

Several courts have held that motorcycle manufacturers have no duty to install *crash bars*, i.e., tubular steel bars which bolt to the motorcycle frame in front of the rider's knees.[522] One court reasoned that the absence of such a device was not an unreasonably dangerous defect because the plaintiff was an experienced cyclist who was aware of the dangers of riding a cycle without those bars.[523] In another case the manufacturer was not liable because there

---

[514] Evidence of compliance with federal and industry standards is admissible if the standards relate to the alleged defect. *See* Schwartz v American Honda Motor Co, 710 F2d 378, 383 (7th Cir 1983); Abbott v American Honda Motor Co, 682 SW2d 206, 211 (Tenn Ct App 1984).

[515] Bernotas v Harley Davidson, Inc, 543 F Supp 519, 521 (WD Pa 1982) (kickstand failed to move to the rear and upward upon contacting the road).

[516] Pawlak v Brown, 430 So 2d 1346, 1350 (LA Ct App 1983).

[517] *Id*.

[518] *Id* 1350.

[519] *See, e.g.*, Taylor V American Honda Motor Co, 555 F Supp 59, 61 (MD Fla 1982); Stueve v American Honda Motors Co, 457 F Supp 740, 759 (D Kan 1978); Cota v Harley Davidson, 141 Ariz 7, 684 P2d 888, 895 (Ct App 1984); Nicolodi v Harley Davidson Motor Co, 370 So 2d 68, 71 (Fla Dist Ct App 1979); Bolm v Triumph Corp, 33 NY2d 151, 305 NE2d 769, 773-74 (1973); *see generally* Note, *Second Collision Liability: A Critique Of Two Approaches To Plaintiff's Burden Of Proof*, 68 Iowa L Rev 811 (1983).

[520] *See* Nicolodi v Harley Davidson Motor Co, 370 So 2d 68, 71 (Fla Dist Ct App 1979).

[521] *Id* 72.

[522] *See* Hunt v Harley Davidson Motor Co, 147 Ga App 44, 248 SE2d 15 (1978); Rainbow v Albert Elia Bldg Co, 79 AD2d 287, 436 NYS2d 480, 482 (1981), *aff'd without opinion*, 56 NY2d 550, 434 NE2d 1345, 449 NYS2d 967 (1982).

[523] *See* Hunt v Harley Davidson Motor Co, 147 Ga App 44, 248 SE2d 15, 17 (1978).

was no showing that the crash bars worked.[524]

Instructions and Warnings

Motorcycle manufacturers must give proper instructions for using their products and also must adequately warn of the risks of using their products.[525] An adequate warning is one calculated to bring home to a reasonably prudent user the nature and extent of the danger in using the product.[526] Manufacturers must consider who the users of their product will be, e.g., children.[527] In *Evridge v American Honda Motor Co*, the court held that it was a question of fact whether a motorbike manufacturer's written warnings in two different places on the bike and also in the owner's manual were adequate.[528]

A manufacturer or distributor of a motorcycle usually has no duty to warn of a danger which is within the common knowledge and understanding of ordinary users.[529] Therefore, there is no duty to warn that the fuel tank might explode in a high-speed crash.[530] In contrast, a motorcycle manufacturer was found liable where it failed to warn prospective purchasers of its motorcycles that with the fuel switch in the *on* position, gasoline could spill from the gas tank when the motorcycle was tilted.[531]

§7.18 — Particular Issues

Misrepresentation

The Restatement (Second) of Torts §402B imposes strict liability on sellers of products for physical harm caused by their misrepresentations.[532] A plaintiff must prove three elements to recover:

1. There must have been a misrepresentation of a material fact concerning the character or quality of a chattel

---

524 *See* Rainbow v Albert Elia Bldg Co, 79 AD2d 287, 436 NYS2d 480, 482 (1981), *affd without opinion*, 56 NY2d 550, 434 NE2d 1345, 449 NYS2d 967 (1982).

525 Pawlak v Brown, 430 So 2d 1346, 1349 (La Ct App 1983).

526 Evridge v American Honda Motor Co, 685 SW2d 632 (Tenn 1985).

527 *Id* 637.

528 *Id.*

529 Height v Kawasaki Heavy Indus, 190 NJ Super 7, 461 A2d 757, 758 (1983).

530 *Id.*

531 Stapleton v Kawasaki Heavy Indus, 608 F2d 571, 572 (5th Cir 1979), *modified on other grounds*, 612 F2d 905 (5th Cir 1980).

532 *See* Restatement (Second) of Torts §402B (1965); *see also* **§7.06**.

2. The misrepresentation must have been made to the public

3. Physical harm must have resulted to a consumer from justifiable reliance on the misrepresentation[533]

In *American Safety Equipment Corp v Winkler*, the court held that *justifiable reliance* requires the user of a motorcycle helmet to exercise his or her knowledge and intelligence reasonably in relying on the represented facts; an unsupportable subjective reliance on a seller's representation is not actionable.[534] In *Winkler*, a policeman was injured on a motorcycle while using a general purpose helmet rather than a motorcycle helmet. The court concluded that there was no showing that the policeman justifiably relied on the seller's illustration of a motorcyclist on the helmet box containing a general purpose helmet because that box was specifically color-coded to highlight its inappropriateness for motorcycling.[535] Accordingly, the plaintiff's claim under this theory failed as a matter of law.[536]

Motorcycle Helmets

It is beyond doubt that motorcycle riders who do not wear helmets have a much greater likelihood of incurring fatal injuries than riders who do use helmets.[537] Accordingly, all cyclists should wear helmets. In some states, they are required to do so by law.[538]

Generally, motorcycle helmet manufacturers are liable only for defects which make their helmets unreasonably dangerous.[539] This requirement has sometimes been construed to mean that a helmet must be more dangerous than it appears to be to the ordinary consumer.[540] One court held that a motorcycle helmet which did not have a face guard was not unreasonably dangerous because it was obvious that the helmet offered no protection in that area.[541] Therefore, the helmet was not more dangerous than it appeared to be.[542]

---

533 American Safety Equip Corp v Winkler, 640 P2d 216, 222 (Colo 1982).

534 *Id* 223.

535 *Id.* 222.

536 *Id.*

537 *See* Coben, *Motorcycle Helmets*, 19 Trial 62, 62 (Nov 1983).

538 *See, e.g.*, Penney v City of N Little Rock, 248 Ark 1158, 455 SW2d 132 (1970); Ariz Rev Stat §28-964(A) (1976); Hawaii Rev Stat §286-81 (1976).

539 Walker v Maxwell City, Inc, 117 Ill App 3d 571, 453 NE2d 917, 922 (1983); *see also* Restatement (Second) of Torts §402A (1965); **§7.03.**

540 Walker v Maxwell City, Inc, 117 Ill App 3d 571, 453 NE2d 917, 922 (1983); *see also* Restatement (Second) of Torts §402A comment i (1965).

541 Walker v Maxwell City, Inc, 117 Ill App 3d 571, 453 NE2d 917, 922 (1983).

542 *Id.*

Three organizations have promulgated safety standards for motorcycle helmets: The Canadian Standards Association Standard For Safety Helmets For Motorcycle Riders (CSA - 0230), the American National Standards Institute Specification For Protective Headgear For Vehicular Users (ANSI - Z90.1) and the Snell Memorial Foundation Standard.[543] In addition, the Department of Transportation has issued a safety standard in MVSS 218.[544] Each of the standards measures three different qualities of the helmet:

1. Shock-absorption
2. Resistance to penetration
3. Ability to remain on the cyclist's head[545]

The standards do not require impact protection for the face.[546]

Motorcycle helmets sold in this country must satisfy certain federal safety standards.[547] The failure to comply with those standards is a defect,[548] although a plaintiff must still prove causation to prevail.

Damages

In *Pawlak v Brown*, the court held that a defendant is only liable for injuries which were reasonably foreseeable.[549] Therefore, a motorcycle manufacturer was not liable for the psychic injuries of the father of an injured motorcyclist.[550]

Punitive damages are only proper where the defendant was guilty of an egregious act or omission.[551] In *Harley Davidson Motor Co v Wisniewski*, the court reversed a $1.9 million punitive damage verdict because there was no evidence establishing that the motorcycle manufacturer had substantial knowledge of the existence of the danger from an improper assembly process.[552]

---

543 Coben,*Motorcycle Helmets*, 19 Trial 62, 65 (Nov 1983).

544 *Id.*

545 *Id.* It may still be negligent to manufacture a helmet which complies with these standards. *See* Cornier v Spagna, 101 AD2d 141, 475 NYS2d 7, 12-13 (1984).

546 Walker v Maxwell City, Inc, 117 Ill App 3d 571, 453 NE2d 917, 922 (1983).

547 *See* 15 USC §1381 *et seq*; FMVSS No 218; *see also* Coben, *Motorcycle Helmets*, 19 Trial 62, 64 (Nov 1983).

548 Cornier v Spagna, 101 AD2d 141, 475 NYS2d 7, 11 (1984).

549 430 So 2d 1346, 1353 (La Ct App 1983).

550 *Id.*

551 *See generally* Owen, *Punitive Damages in Products Liability Litigation*, 74 Mich L Rev 1256 (1976); §7.02.

552 50 Md App 339, 437 A2d 700, 704-05 (1982).

Evidence

Evidence of other motorcycle accidents involving the same product is admissible to show the product's dangerous nature if the accidents occurred under the same or substantially similar conditions.[553] Such evidence is probative of whether a defect existed and if so, whether it caused the accident.[554] However, the defendant can introduce evidence of no prior reports of problems regarding the alleged defect because this evidence is also relevant to those two issues.[555]

One court held that a recall letter alone was insufficient to create a question of fact regarding the presence of a defect in the product,[556] although there is authority to the contrary.[557] However, a recall letter is admissible evidence as long as there is first some independent proof that the particular product in question suffered from the same defect.[558] Of course, where the letter acknowledges a defect under certain conditions, and the plaintiff fails to show that those conditions existed on the day of the accident, the letter is not admissible.[559]

In *Carr v Suzuki Motor Co*,[560] the court held that it was reversible error to show a videotape of a professional motorcycle rider when the plaintiff was an amateur rider who was severely injured when he was thrown off the motorcycle. The court reasoned that the tape was of questionable relevancy because the skills of the professional rider who knew of the defect, viz., only one shock absorber was working, could have masked the effects that the defect would have had on an amateur rider who did not know what had gone awry.[561] Further, even if the tape were relevant, it was unreasonably prejudicial because the professional was not thrown off the motorcycle as the plaintiff was.[562]

Causation

A defendant must have played a substantial role in producing a plaintiff's

---

553 McInnes v Yamaha Motor Corp, 659 SW2d 704, 710 (Tex Ct App 1983).

554 *Id*.

555 Schwartz v American Honda Motor Co, 710 F2d 378, 383 (7th Cir 1983); Caldwell v Yamaha Motor Co, 648 P2d 519, 526-27 (Wyo 1982).

556 Harley Davidson Motor Co v Daniel, 244 Ga 284, 260 SE2d 20, 22 (1979).

557 *See* Harley Davidson Motor Co v Carpenter, 350 So 2d 360, 361 (Fla Dist Ct App 1977).

558 Calhoun v Honda Motor Co, 738 F2d 126, 133-34 (6th Cir 1984); Harley Davidson Motor Co v Daniel, 244 Ga 284, 260 SE2d 20, 22 (1979); *but see* Matsko v Harley Davidson Motor Co, 325 Pa Super 452, 473 A2d 155, 159 (1984).

559 Calhoun v Honda Motor Co, 738 F2d 126, 133-34 (6th Cir 1984).

560 280 Ark 1, 655 SW2d 364, 365 (1983).

561 *Id*.

562 *Id*.

injuries before it can be held liable.[563] Proof of this causal relationship can, and usually is, shown by circumstantial evidence.[564] However, the plaintiff must show more than the fact that the defendant may have caused the accident.[565]

In *Calhoun v Honda Motor Co,*[566] the jury awarded the plaintiff over $1.2 million for a motorcycle accident. However, the trial court granted judgment n.o.v. for the manufacturer because the plaintiff failed to produce any credible evidence of causation and the sixth circuit affirmed this judgment. In *Calhoun,* the plaintiff, while on a Honda 750 CB motorcycle, rear-ended a stopped truck and, as a result, lost his memory of the accident. He alleged that the motorcycle was defective because the effectiveness of the rear brake pad was reduced in heavy rain. However, it was not raining on the day of the accident.[567] Further, although the pad had gotten slightly wet at a car wash, the plaintiff failed to show the brake's drying time or the amount of time which elapsed between the car wash and the accident.[568] Therefore, the plaintiff's expert's testimony about causation amounted to guesswork.[569]

A motorcycle manufacturer is not liable where subsequent to its act or omission, there is a superseding cause of the accident, i.e., a new, independent, and unexpected occurrence, which appears to be the real cause of the plaintiff's injuries.[570] However, the chain of causation flowing from the manufacturer's act or omission is not broken by the occurrence of an intervening event which was reasonably foreseeable.[571]

The determination of whether a superseding factor occurred is usually a question of fact.[572] In *Evridge v American Honda Motor Co,* the Tennessee Supreme Court held that it was a question of fact whether it was reasonably foreseeable that a parent and a child would fail to heed a motorbike

---

[563] *See* Evangeline v Billings Cycle Center, 626 P2d 841, 843 (Mont 1981).

[564] *See* Calhoun v Honda Motor Co, 738 F2d 126, 130 (6th Cir 1984); McGuire v Nelson, 167 Mont 188, 536 P2d 768, 773 (1975); Sabloff v Yamaha Motor Co, 113 NJ Super 279, 273 A2d 606, 610 (1971) (shown by expert opinion).

[565] *See* Evangeline v Billings Cycle Center, 626 P2d 841, 843 (Mont 1981); Cornier v Spagna, 101 AD2d 141, 475 NYS2d 7, 11 (1984).

[566] *See* Calhoun v Honda Motor Co, 738 F2d 126, 130 (6th Cir 1984).

[567] *Id* at 132-33.

[568] *Id.*

[569] *Id.* However, there is authority that the plaintiff need not produce much evidence of causation to defeat the defendant's motion for summary judgment. *See* Hughes v American Jawa, Ltd, 529 F2d 21, 25 (8th Cir 1976).

[570] Evridge v American Honda Motor Co, 685 SW2d 632 (Tenn 1985); Abbott v American Honda Motor Co, 682 SW2d 206, 212 (Tenn Ct App 1984).

[571] Abbott v American Honda Motor Co, 682 SW2d 206, 212 (Tenn Ct App 1984).

[572] Evridge v American Honda Motor Co, 685 SW2d 632, 636 (Tenn 1985).

manufacturer's warning that the vehicle was to be used only by one person.[573] Another court held that a parent's failure to instruct and supervise a child properly in the use of the motorcycle may be a superseding cause of the child's injury.[574]

§7.19 Snowmobiles

A snowmobile[575] manufacturer has a duty to design products that are reasonably fit for their foreseeable uses.[576] In *Franck v Polaris E-Z Go Division of Textron*, the court held that a snowmobile which had the sharp corners of the metal cleats attached to the moving track was defectively designed because the cleats could snag a rear passenger's foot and sweep it into the machine.[577] This danger could have been reduced by rounding off the corners and this would not have adversely affected the performance of the machine.[578] However, in *Magnuson v Rupp Manufacturing, Inc*, the court held that a snowmobile with an obvious design flaw, viz., the spark plug faced the driver and was located about six inches above the driver's seat, was not defective because the plaintiff was fully aware of the danger.[579]

Foreseeable use focuses on what is reasonably foreseeable to the manufacturer; the subjective knowledge of the consumer is irrelevant.[580] Accordingly, a snowmobile manufacturer's advertisement which illustrated various uses of the product, e.g., jumping an embankment, is highly probative that such uses were reasonably foreseeable.[581] However, one court held that it was not reversible error to refuse to admit such an advertisement into evidence where there was other evidence relating to foreseeable uses of the snowmobile.[582]

---

573 *Id.*

574 Abbott v American Honda Motor Co, 682 SW2d 206, 212 (Tenn Ct App 1984).

575 It is estimated that about 11,000 individuals are seriously injured each year while using snowmobiles. *See* US Consumer Prod Safety Commn, Natl Injury Information Clearinghouse, Prod Summary Report (Mar 28, 1984).

In Wisconsin, over 100 individuals have died in snowmobile accidents since 1976. *See* Wis Div of Health, Dept of Health & Soc Servs, Snowmobile Deaths By Age And Sex (1984).

576 Wolfgram v Bombardier, Ltd, No 81-1117 (6th Cir Sept 7, 1982) (available on Lexis); Smith v Ariens Co, 375 Mass 620, 377 NE2d 954, 957 (1978).

577 Franck v Polaris E-Z Go Div of Textron, 157 Cal App 3d 1107, 204 Cal Rptr 321, 325 (1984) (affirmed a $300,000 jury verdict for plaintiff).

578 *Id.*

579 285 Minn 32, 171 NW2d 201, 208 (1969).

580 Hiller v Kawasaki Motors Corp, USA, 671 P2d 369, 373 (Alaska 1983). Indeed, it is also irrelevant that plaintiff did not see the advertisement and that the advertisement was shown after the accident occurred. *Id.*

581 *Id.*

582 *Id.*

Accidents are reasonably foreseeable. Therefore, snowmobile manufacturers must design their products in a fashion which will not subject snowmobilers to an unreasonable risk of injury if the snowmobile is involved in a collision.[583] For example, in *Smith v Ariens Co*,[584] a person using a snowmobile hit her head on protusions from a brake bracket after the snowmobile collided with a rock. The court held that this type of injury was foreseeable and, therefore, the manufacturer should have designed the snowmobile to eliminate or minimize this danger.[585]

In a defective design case, the plaintiff must show that the defect existed at the time the product left the manufacturer.[586] One court held that where snowmobiles from a specific manufacturer arrived at a distributor with the defective brake brackets protruding above the handlebar, and other snowmobiles from this manufacturer also had this defect, it could be inferred that the defect was present when the snowmobile left the manufacturer.[587]

A snowmobile manufacturer is not under a duty to provide replacement of worn parts or to guard against injury resulting from the wear and deterioration of parts.[588]

In *Szyplinski v Midwest Mobile Home Supply Co*,[589] the court held that a retail store may be liable for the negligent display of a shop lift, a device which raises snowmobiles when they are being repaired, because it acted unreasonably in allowing a child access to this lift.

Evidence

The presence of a manufacturer's name on the snowmobile is sufficient evidence to allow the fact-finder to conclude that the snowmobile was, in fact, manufactured by that company.[590] This is true for two interrelated reasons. First, it is more likely than not that the name on the product correctly identifies the manufacturer because trade names are protected by law.[591] Second, because of that first reason, it is efficient for the judicial system to allow such evidence to be heard by the fact-finder, although the defendant can introduce contrary evidence.[592]

---

583 *Id.*

584 Smith v Ariens Co, 375 Mass 620, 377 NE2d 954, 957 (1978).

585 *Id.*

586 *Id.*

587 *Id* 958-59.

588 Wolfgram v Bombardier, Ltd, No 81-1117 (6th Cir Sept 7, 1982) (available on Lexis).

589 308 Minn 152, 241 NW2d 306, 310 (1976).

590 Smith v Ariens Co, 375 Mass 620, 377 NE2d 954, 956 (1978).

591 *Id.*

592 *Id.*

A snowmobile manufacturer's witness's testimony that it had not received any reports, other than plaintiff's, of handlebar fatigue failure for four years was admissible.[593] This testimony was relevant to whether there was a defect and whether the alleged defect caused the accident.[594]

There is no inherent need to have expert testimony on the issue of defective design.[595] One court held that it is within the common knowledge of a jury whether unshielded metal protrusions on a snowmobile handlebar created an unreasonable risk of harm.[596] However, where an expert did testify on the defective design and manufacture of a snowmobile, the trial court could reject his opinion and grant a directed verdict for the other side. The expert had not studied the snowmobile industry, had no factual information regarding other similar snowmobile accidents, and had not performed any tests to determine how this accident occurred.[597]

Causation

The defendant is not liable unless its acts or omissions were a substantial factor in producing the plaintiff's injury.[598] This is usually a question of fact.[599] However, a plaintiff's proof that a snowmobile accident occurred is not enough, standing alone, to show a defective product.[600] A manufacturer is entitled to judgment as a matter of law where the plaintiff fails to provide any proof that his or her injuries were caused by a design or manufacturing flaw in the snowmobile.[601]

If a defendant's acts or omissions played a role in causing the injury, the defendant is liable; its actions or omissions need not be the sole factor or even the primary factor in causing the accident.[602] Therefore, a jury instruction which requires that the snowmobile manufacturer's acts be *the* cause of the accident before there is liability is improper.[603]

---

[593] Payson v Bombardier, Ltd, 435 A2d 411, 413 (Me 1981).

[594] *Id.*

[595] Smith v Ariens Co, 375 Mass 620, 377 NE2d 954, 957-58 (1978).

[596] *Id.*

[597] Haffner v Cody, 102 Wis 2d 721, 308 NW2d 420 (1981) (available on Lexis).

[598] Clark v Leisure Vehicles, Inc, 96 Wis 2d 607, 292 NW2d 630, 635-36 (1980).

[599] Bjorklund v Hantz, 296 Minn 298, 208 NW2d 722, 724 (1973).

[600] Olson v Arctic Enters, Inc, 349 F Supp 761, 764 (D ND 1972); Burke v Bombardier, Ltd, 111 Mich App 183, 314 NW2d 473, 475 (1981).

[601] Olson v Arctic Enters, Inc, 349 F Supp 761, 764 (D ND 1972); Burke v Bombardier, Ltd, 111 Mich App 183, 314 NW2d 473, 475 (1981).

[602] Clark v Leisure Vehicles, Inc, 96 Wis 2d 607, 292 NW2d 630, 635-36 (1980). However, there is no liability if the accident was caused by a superseding factor.

[603] *Id.*

Indemnity

A retailer found negligent in failing to discover and correct a snowmobile's defects may be entitled to be indemnified by the manufacturer.[604]

§7.20   Snow Skiing

Sellers of ski[605] equipment may be held strictly liable for manufacturing defects or design defects in their products or for failing to instruct on the proper use, or warn of the dangers, of their products.[606]

In *Anderson v Heron Engineering Co*, the Colorado Supreme Court held that a ski lift may be defective because the manufacturer failed to instruct how to test whether the torque was properly applied.[607] This is true even where the ski facility's employees, the people who would adjust the torque, were experts in the area, unless the employees were specifically aware of the potential problem and how to solve it.[608] It is no defense in a strict liability action that the ski lift manufacturer had no previous knowledge of the problem.[609] Although that may be important exculpatory evidence in an action for negligence, a manufacturer's knowledge of the defect is assumed in strict liability claims.[610]

A seller of ski equipment may defend an allegation that it gave inadequate instructions by showing that the suggested alternative was not within the state of the art at the time the equipment was produced.[611] However, the custom in the industry does not establish the state of the art and, therefore, one court held that evidence of the industry custom was inadmissible.[612]

Ski equipment manufacturers must warn of the dangers that may arise

---

[604] *See* Bjorklund v Hantz, 296 Minn 298, 208 NW2d 722, 724 (1973). Whether a collision occurred because of an improperly placed tail light wire or for other causes unrelated to the snowmobile was for the jury.

[605] Over 40,000 individuals are seriously injured each year while snow skiing, although all of those accidents are not due to defective equipment. *See* US Consumer Prod Safety Commn, Natl Injury Information Clearinghouse, Prod Summary Rep (Mar 28, 1984).

Improved technology in ski equipment has led to fewer injuries; however, the injuries which do occur tend to be more serious. Barrell & Shuster, *USA Today*, Mar 8, 1985, §C, at 1, col 3.

[606] Anderson v Heron Engg Co, 198 Colo 391, 604 P2d 674, 678-79 (1979); Opera v Hyva, Inc, 86 AD2d 373, 450 NYS2d 615, 617 (1982).

[607] Anderson v Heron Engg Co, 198 Colo 391, 604 P2d 674, 678-79 (1979).

[608] *Id.*

[609] *Id.*

[610] *Id.*

[611] Opera v Hyva, Inc, 86 AD2d 373, 450 NYS2d 615, 618 (1982).

[612] *Id.*

from the improper use and handling of their product.[613] It is not sufficient merely to give instructions for proper use; warnings must be given of the consequences of failing to follow the instructions.[614] For example, in *Anderson* the court held that the lift manufacturer should have instructed as to the specific torque for a clamp, and also should have warned of the dangers of tightening it too much, viz., the chair could slip back and knock a rider in the next chair to the ground.[615]

Ski facilities are generally not liable to injured patrons under strict product liability or breach of implied warranty principles.[616] In *Bolduc v Herbert Schneider Corp*, the New Hampshire Supreme Court held that a passenger who fell from a ski tramway could not recover from the ski facility under strict product liability or implied warranty because the facility provided a service, not a product.[617] A similar result was reached where the plaintiff was injured while riding a rope-tow at a ski facility.[618]

Warranties

At one time, sellers of ski equipment were allowed some room to *puff* their products without liability attaching for misstatements.[619] This zone of no liability has diminished in recent years.[620] It is now usually a question of fact whether advertisements for ski equipment are warranties and a part of the bargain of sale or allowable puffing.[621]

Where specific representations relating to the safety of the facilities are given, an express warranty may be created.[622] For example, if a ski lift manufacturer stated in a sales brochure that the lift was *safe* and that brochure was seen or relied on by the ski facility when it purchased the lift, the plaintiff is entitled to a jury instruction that the ski lift was expressly warranted to be safe.[623]

However, not all courts have imposed liability so quickly. In *Salk v Alpine Ski Shop, Inc*, the Rhode Island Supreme Court held that a manufacturer of

---

613 Anderson v Heron Engg Co, 198 Colo 391, 604 P2d 674, 678 (Colo 1979).

614 604 P2d at 677.

615 *Id.*

616 *See* Hunt v Sun Valley Co, 561 F2d 744, 747 (9th Cir 1977); Lewis v Big Powderhorn Mt Ski Corp, 69 Mich App 437, 245 NW2d 81 (1976); Bolduc v Herbert Schneider Corp, 117 NH 566, 374 A2d 1187, 1189 (1977).

617 117 NH 566, 374 A2d 1187, 1189 (1977).

618 Lewis v Big Powderhorn Mt Ski Corp, 69 Mich App 437, 245 NW2d 81, 82 (1976).

619 *See generally* §§7.04, 7.06.

620 *See generally* §§7.04, 7.06.

621 *See* Opera v Hyva, Inc, 86 AD2d 373, 450 NYS2d 615, 619 (1982).

622 *See* Anderson v Heron Engg Co, 198 Colo 391, 604 P2d 674, 676 (1979).

623 *Id.*

ski bindings was not liable for breach of express warranty for advertisements which said "Cubco is the precise binding ... that releases when it's supposed to ... Both heel and toe release at the exact tension you set. And release whichever way you fall".[624] The court stated than no binding can be set at a tension sufficiently low to release during a slow fall and still keep the skier on the skis during normal skiing and, therefore, the advertisement was not a blanket guarantee that the bindings would release in every dangerous situation.[625] This decision appears poorly reasoned. If the manufacturer's goods cannot meet the representation made in the advertisement, the manufacturer should be held liable for the misstatement.

Subsequent Remedial Measures

Subsequent remedial measures are usually not admissible to prove that the defendant was previously negligent.[626] However, such evidence is admissible for other purposes.[627] For example, in *Opera v Hyva, Inc*, the court held that evidence of post-accident changes in a ski binding manufacturer's user manual was admissible to prove the feasibility of using a different system of adjusting the bindings.[628]

Causation

The mere occurrence of a skiing accident, standing alone,[629] usually does not support an inference that the defendant was negligent.[630] This is because liability cannot be predicated on surmise or conjecture.[631] In *Murphy v Chestnut Mountain Lodge, Inc*, a ski resort was granted a directed verdict where the plaintiff alleged that the resort failed to provide him with skis with a safety device allowing the bindings to release when excessive force was exerted because the plaintiff did not prove that the skis given to him lacked

---

624 115 RI 309, 342 A2d 622, 626 (1975).

625 *Id.*

626 Opera v Hyva, Inc, 86 AD2d 373, 450 NYS2d 615, 616 (1982); *see generally* Fed R Evid 407.

627 Opera v Hyva, Inc, 86 AD2d 373, 450 NYS2d 615, 616 (1982); *see generally* Fed R Evid 407.

628 86 AD2d 373, 450 NYS2d 615, 616 (1982).

629 In Tarlowe v Metropolitan Ski Slopes, Inc, 28 NY2d 410, 271 NE2d 515, 322 NYS2d 665, 667 (1971), the court held that plaintiff made out a prima facie case where his expert gave his opinion on the cause of a ski accident even though the expert did not explain the reasons for the opinion.

630 *See* Murphy v Chestnut Mt Lodge, Inc, 124 Ill App 3d 508, 464 NE2d 818, 821 (1984); Salk v Alpine Ski Shop, Inc, 115 RI 309, 342 A2d 622, 625 (1975). An exception to this general rule is the res ipsa loquitur doctrine.

631 Murphy v Chestnut Mt Lodge, Inc, 124 Ill App 3d 508, 464 NE2d 818, 821 (1984).

such devices.[632] Similarly, a retailer and a manufacturer of ski bindings were granted a directed verdict where the plaintiff's only evidence of liability was that the bindings failed to release because unless the plaintiff was traveling at a certain minimum velocity, the bindings would not release even if they were properly adjusted.[633]

In addition, a seller of ski bindings was not strictly liable for failing to warn of the dangers involved in using its product where the plaintiff failed to produce evidence that had he been warned of the dangers of skiing, he would have acted differently, i.e., he would not have skied or he would have purchased other bindings.[634]

Insurance

An insurance company which issued a general comprehensive liability policy has a duty to defend, and possibly a duty to pay, an action brought by a company which bought defective ski straps from its insured, a manufacturer of ski straps, and used them in its ski bindings.[635]

§7.21 Swimming Pools and Related Products

Each year over 125,000 individuals injured while swimming or diving require emergency room treatment.[636] Tragically, recreational diving[637] results in more cases of quadriplegia than all other recreational activities combined.[638]

---

[632] 464 NE2d at 823.

[633] Salk v Alpine Ski Shop, Inc, 115 RI 309, 342 A2d 622, 625 (1975).

[634] 342 A2d at 626.

[635] *See* Sturges Mfg Co v Utica Mut Ins Co, 37 NY2d 69, 371 NYS2d 444, 447 (1975).

[636] *See* US Consumer Prod Safety Commn, Natl Injury Information Clearinghouse, Prod Summary Report (Mar 28, 1984).

[637] If the water is four feet or less in depth and the diver's entry angle is 45 degrees or greater, there will be only a fraction of a second between breaking the surface and striking the bottom. Unless the elbows are firmly locked, injury is inevitable. *See* Gabrielsen & Olenn, *Swimming Pool Litigation: Educating For Safety*, 18 Trial 39, 40 (Feb 1982).

[638] *See* Gabrielsen & Olenn, *Swimming Pool Litigation: Educating For Safety*, 18 Trial 39, 39 (Feb 1982); Swartz, *Leisure Time Product-Related Torts*, 1983 SMU Prod Liab Inst 5-7. Each year about 500-700 individuals, predominantly adult males or teenagers of adult size, will break their necks while diving or sliding into swimming pools or other water areas. Indeed, more adults or individuals of adult size will break their necks in pools than will drown. Gabrielsen & Olenn, *Swimming Pool Litigation: Educating For Safety*, 18 Trial 39, 39 (Feb 1982); Swartz, *Leisure Time Product-Related Torts*, 1983 SMU Prod Liab Inst 5-8.

In one study, alcohol consumption by the diver was not a material factor in diving accidents. Gabrielsen & Olenn, *Swimming Pool Litigation: Educating For Safety*, 18 Trial 39, 39 (Feb 1982).

It is estimated that about 140 million individuals swim at least once a year. There are about 5 million swimming pools in this country and the number is increasing. *See* Gabrielsen & Olenn, *Swimming Pool Litigation: Educating For Safety*, 18 Trial 39, 40 (Feb 1982); Swartz,

Accordingly, in some cases, injured plaintiffs have recovered seven-figure verdicts.[639]

Traditionally, sellers of swimming pools were not found liable for swimming and diving injuries because the pools were not considered unreasonably dangerous.[640] For example, in *Colosimo v May Department Store Co*, the court held that an above-ground pool was not unreasonably dangerous because a reasonable consumer would know that a dive into a small, above-ground backyard pool containing less than three feet of water carried with it a substantial risk of injury.[641]

Similarly, in *Vincer v Esther Williams All-Aluminum Swimming Pool Co*, the Wisconsin Supreme Court held that a swimming pool which lacked a self-closing gate to prevent entry to the pool was not defective as a matter of law.[642] In *Vincer* the pool contained a rectractable ladder which was left down and a small child was severely injured. The court held that the pool manufacturer was not liable because the risk of harm to small children when the retractable ladder is left down and children are left unsupervised is obvious.[643] Therefore, the pool was not defective because it was not more dangerous than a reasonable consumer would expect.[644] However, two recent decisions have abruptly reversed that trend.

In *Corbin v Coleco Industries*,[645] the plaintiff, a 27-year-old man of average height, dove from the lip of a four-foot-deep, above-ground swimming pool. He intended to do a belly flop, but for some unknown reason his body twisted in mid-air and his head hit the pool bottom, rendering him a quadriplegic. The Seventh Circuit held that the above-ground pool may have been unreasonably

---

Leisure Time Product-Related Torts, 1983 SMU Prod Liab Inst 5-7.

639 *See* Swartz, *Leisure Time Product-Related Torts*, 1983 SMU Prod Liab Inst 5-16 (a $6 million jury verdict was received when the plaintiff was rendered a quadriplegic after he dove into a four-foot, above-ground pool).

640 *See* Colosimo v May Dept Store Co, 466 F2d 1234, 1235 (3d Cir 1972); Vincer v Esther Williams All-Aluminum Swimming Pool Co, 69 Wis 2d 326, 230 NW2d 794, 798 (1975); Hensley v Muskin Corp, 65 Mich App 662, 238 NW2d 362, 362 (1975); *see also* Telak v Maszczenski, 248 Md 476, 237 A2d 434, 441 (1968).

Pool manufacturers are not liable for defects in products, e.g., a pool ladder, they did not sell. *See* Kaloz v Risco, 120 Misc 2d 586, 466 NYS2d 218, 220-21 (Sup Ct 1983).

Safety guidelines have been published. *See* US Dept of Health and Human Servs, Center for Disease Control, Suggested Health and Safety Guidelines for Public Spas and Hot Tubs (rev Jan 1985).

The liability of commercial swimming facilities is discussed in §§1.22, 1.23, 1.24, 1.25.

641 466 F2d 1234, 1235 (3d Cir 1972). In addition, the court held that the cause of the injury was plaintiff's error in judgment in diving into a shallow pool. *See id* 1235-36.

642 69 Wis 2d 326, 230 NW2d 794, 798 (1975).

643 *Id*.

644 230 NW2d at 799.

645 748 F2d 411 (7th Cir 1984).

dangerous because the lip and sides of the pool were insufficently rigid, so a diver attempting a belly flop from a standing position on the lip would be thrown off balance and would enter the water at a steeper angle than intended.[646] In addition, the court held that it was not obvious that the lip of the pool wobbled or that a wobbly lip increased the danger of a dive.[647] Therefore, the pool manufacturer was not entitled to summary judgment.

In *O'Brien v Muskin Corp*,[648] the court held that it was a jury question whether an above-ground swimming pool with vinyl liners was defectively designed. The court held that a product may be defectively designed if the risk and severity of injury outweigh the utility of the product.[649] Therefore, it is possible that a jury could conclude that a swimming pool, a luxury product which is dangerous, should not be put on the market even if the product has been made as safely as possible.[650] There can be liability under this theory even where the plaintiff cannot prove the existence of a safer, alternative design.[651] Indeed, the *O'Brien* court held that the plaintiff may establish a prima facie case that an above-ground swimming pool was defectively designed by establishing that such pools are marketed primarily for recreational, rather than therapeutic, purposes and that because of their design, injury is likely.[652]

Pool manufacturers may also be liable for their negligence. The *Corbin* court held that a pool manufacturer may have to warn of the dangers of diving into a shallow pool, a danger which appears, at first, to be self-evident. In that case, the plaintiff's expert witness testified that although people generally understand the dangers of diving into shallow water, they believe there is a safe way to do it, viz., by executing a flat, shallow dive.[653] The court held, therefore, that since people understand that there is a safe way to dive into the pool, the danger of diving is not obvious and the manufacturer must warn of this danger.[654]

In fact, the manufacturer's failure to warn may have been the proximate cause of the accident in *Corbin*.[655] The plaintiff intended to perform a flat and shallow dive and if he understood that this was safe to do, a warning to

---

646 *Id* 420; *see generally* Gabrielson & Olenn, *Swimming Pool Litigation: Educating for Safety*, 18 Trial 39, 41 (Feb 1982); Swartz, *Leisure Time Product-Related Torts*, 1983 SMU Prod Liab Inst at 5-8.

647 748 F2d at 420.

648 94 NJ 169, 463 A2d 298, 306 (1983).

649 *Id.*

650 *Id.*

651 *Id.*

652 463 A2d at 306.

653 748 F2d 411 (7th Cir 1984).

654 *Id.*

655 *Id.*

the contrary by the manufacturer might well have stopped him from making the dive.

Pool Slides

Pool slide manufacturers and operators may be liable for defects in the slides under strict liability,[656] negligence,[657] or breach of implied warranties.[658] Indeed, there is a case where a plaintiff severely injured by a defective pool slide received a seven-figure verdict.[659]

The United States Product Safety Commission has promulgated safety standards for swimming pool slides.[660] A manufacturer's violation of these standards may be proof that the slide was defective.[661] However, one court properly excluded as irrelevant pool slide standards promulgated by the Consumer Product Safety Commission nine years after a slide was sold.[662]

In *Barras v Touzet's Inc*, the court held that a water slide was not unreasonably dangerous where the drop from the end of the flume to the water was about one foot.[663]

One academic study concluded that the position of the slider on entering the water is far more important than the configuration of the slide in determining whether there is a substantial risk of injury.[664]

Chemicals

A swimming pool sanitizer may have been defective because it was sold with inadequate warnings.[665] Although the sanitizer was taken out of its original container when it was given to the plaintiff by another person, an adequate warning might have spurred that third party to warn the plaintiff

---

656 *See* Barras v Touzet's Inc, 423 So 2d 1239 (La 1982).

657 Schenck v Pelky, 176 Conn 245, 405 A2d 665, 670 (1978).

658 *Id; see generally* §7.04.

659 *See* Gaston v Aquaslide 'N' Dive Corp, 487 F Supp 16 (ED Tenn 1980) ($1,000,000 damages allowed).

660 *See* 16 CFR §1207; *see also* US Dept of Health & Human Servs, Centers for Disease Control, Suggested Health and Safety Guidelines for Recreational Water Slide Flumes (1981). The commission's regulations were once successfully challenged. *See* Aqua Slide 'N' Dive v Consumer Prod Safety Commn, 569 F2d 831 (5th Cir 1978).

661 15 USC §2072(a).

662 Schenck v Pelkey, 176 Conn 245, 405 A2d 665, 669 (1978).

663 423 So 2d 1239 (La Ct App 1982).

664 *See* Nova University, Human Habitability Studies, The Effect of Various Water Slide Configurations on the Velocity and Depth of Penetration of Human Bodies of Different Physical Characterisitics 22 (Nov 1973).

665 Pegg v General Motors Corp, 258 Pa Super 59, 391 A2d 1074, 1083 (1978).

of the risks.[666] Of course, the manufacturer can argue at trial that this constituted an abnormal use and, therefore, it was a superseding cause of injury.[667] In addition, the manufacturer is not liable where the plaintiff was a lawbreaker.[668]

In *Moreno v Leslie's Pool Mart*, the court held that an employee who was injured by fumes from pool chemicals could sue his employer, a company which manufactured pool chemicals and also sold the chemicals in retail stores, for strict liability.[669] He was not barred by workers' compensation because of the dual capacity doctrine, i.e., he was injured by a product for sale to the public.[670]

Evidence

In *Belfry v Anthony Pools, Inc*, the court admitted evidence that similarly designed pools had a history of use without any accident claims being asserted.[671] This evidence was probative, although not conclusive, on the issues of foreseeability of injury, notice of the defective condition, and whether the product was designed safely.[672]

In *Spotto v Hayward Manufacturing Co*,[673] the court allowed an expert to testify about conditions that existed in a pool on the day of an accident by examining the pool 10 years later because there was a reasonable likelihood that the conditions had not changed in the interim.

Causation

A plaintiff cannot show by conjecture that the defendant's acts or omissions caused his or her injury.[674] For example, in *Shield v California Pool Service, Inc*,[675] the plaintiff alleged a diving board was defective because the guardrails did not extend out far enough. The court directed a verdict against the plaintiff because there was no evidence she fell from the unguarded portion of the board.[676]

---

666 *Id.*

667 *Id.*

668 *Id.*

669 Moreno v Leslie's Pool Mart, 110 Cal App 3d 179, 167 Cal Rptr 747 (1980).

670 *Id.* The California legislature substantially eliminated the dual capacity doctrine. *See* Cal Lab Code §3602(a) (West Supp 1984).

671 80 Mich App 118, 262 NW2d 909, 912 (1977).

672 262 NW2d at 912.

673 2 Conn App 663, 482 A2d 91 (1984).

674 Shield v California Pool Serv, Inc, 515 SW2d 342, 244 (Tex Civ App 1974); *see generally* §1.25.

675 515 SW2d 342 (Tex Civ App 1974).

676 *Id* 344.

§7.22 Toys and Games

Manufacturers of toys and games[677] are under no duty to design and construct products that are accident-proof.[678] Their duty is usually just to make the toys and games free from unreasonable dangers.[679] This means, at a minimum, that toy and game manufacturers must comply with the United States Consumer Product Safety Commission standards in this area.[680]

Toys that fall apart, causing injury, may be defective. In *Bailey v Montgomery Ward & Co*,[681] a child testified that he was well acquainted with the use of a pogo stick, but that when he used one on a Christmas morning, it broke and injured him. The court held that a pogo stick was expected to be subjected to harsh contact with the pavement and may also be knocked to the ground, and that failure to take such rugged use may be a defect.[682]

Unfortunately, there are very few toys or playthings that are so inherently harmless that they cannot be used to injure a child.[683] In many cases, toys which are reasonably safe when properly used can become dangerous when used by an imaginative child[684] or when mishandled by others.[685] However, in those situations, the sellers of the toys may not be liable.[686] For example, in *Rader v Milton Bradley Co*, a child was struck in the mouth by a toy called a Time Bomb which was thrown by a different child to the floor, and then struck the plaintiff. The court held that the toy manufacturer

---

[677] It is estimated that there are about 750,000 injuries as a result of toy-related incidents each year. Swartz, *Toys-R-Dangerous*, 18 Trial 28, 29 (Feb 1982).

During 1976, over 7,000 children under 10 years old were treated in hospital emergency rooms for injuries related to small parts. *See id* 30. About one-half of the victims in the Consumer Product Safety Commission death certificate file on small parts were under three years old. *Id*.

[678] *See* §7.01.

[679] *See* Landrine v Mego Corp, 95 AD2d 759, 464 NYS2d 516, 518 (1983); §7.01.

Children are usually more vulnerable to quality defects. Therefore, one commentator concluded that a higher level of quality control should be required of manufacturers who make products for children. *See* Swartz, *Toys That Harm*, 12 Trial 40, 42 (Dec 1976).

[680] *See* 16 CFR §§1501, 1502; *see also* 15 USC §2072(a). The American Natl Standards Inst has published a voluntary toy standard. *see* ANSI/UPS PS72-76 (1977).

[681] 6 Ariz App 213, 431 P2d 108 (1967).

[682] 431 P2d at 113-14.

[683] Atkins v Arlans Dept Store, 522 P2d 1020, 1022 (Okla 1974).

[684] Maramba v Newman, 82 Ill App 2d 95, 227 NE2d 80, 81 (1967); Atkins v Arlans Dept Store, 522 P2d 1020, 1022 (Okla 1974).

[685] Radar v Milton Bradley Co, 62 Misc 2d 610, 309 NYS2d 393, 396 (Civ Ct 1970).

[686] *See generally* Maramba v Newman, 82 Ill App 2d 95, 227 NE2d 80, 84 (1967) (retailer not liable for injuries from boomerang).

was not liable because one of the players was unable to make a complete toss.[687]

Several courts have held that the sellers of a lawn dart game were not liable, as a matter of law, where a child was injured by a dart thrown by another child.[688] The courts have held that the dangers with lawn darts are inherently obvious and, therefore, the game is not dangerous to an extent beyond that which would be contemplated by the ordinary consumer with the ordinary knowledge common to the community.[689] Further, a warning that a dart should not be thrown in the direction of anyone was unnecessary because such a warning would hardly have done more than apprise even a minor of what he or she already knew.[690]

The United States Consumer Product Safety Commission has promulgated a rule precluding the sale of lawn darts in toy stores or store departments dealing predominantly in toys or other children's articles.[691] In *Aimone v Walgreen's Co*, the court held that a manufacturer was not liable, as a matter of law, for violating this rule where it took numerous precautions so that the darts were not sold as toys, e.g., it did not sell its lawn darts to toy stores and its catalog, invoices, and cartoons all stated that the darts were not a toy.[692] However, in that case the court held that it was a question of fact whether a retailer violated the commission's rule.[693]

The manufacturer, wholesaler, and retailer of a slingshot owe a duty of care to those affected by its use.[694] In *Moning v Alfono*, the Michigan Supreme Court held that it was a question of fact whether those parties breached that duty by marketing slingshots directly to children.[695] The court reasoned that it may be unreasonably dangerous to market a toy which could cause serious injuries directly to minors.[696] However, in *Bojorquez v House of Toys, Inc*, a California court, traditionally known for being sympathetic to plaintiffs, held that a wholesaler and a retailer were not negligent, as a matter of law, for selling slingshots to children, the class of persons for whom they were

---

687 62 Misc 2d 610, 309 NYS2d 393, 396 (Civ Ct 1970).

688 *See* Aimone v Walgreen's Co, 601 F Supp 507, 514-15 (ND Ill 1985); Atkins v Arlans Dept Store, 522 P2d 1020, 1022 (Okla 1974).

689 Aimone v Walgreen's Co, 601 F Supp 507, 514-15 (ND Ill 1985).

690 *Id.*

691 16 CFR §1500.86(a); *see also* 16 CFR §1500.18(a)(4).

692 601 F Supp 507, 513-14 (ND Ill 1985).

693 *Id* 511-12.

694 Moning v Alfono, 400 Mich 425, 254 NW2d 759, 762 (1977).

695 254 NW2d at 775. The *Moning* decision is discussed in Note, *Handguns and Products Liability*, 97 Harv L Rev 1912, 1920 (1984).

696 254 NW2d at 765.

intended.[697] The *Bojorquez* court held that a ban of such products should come from the legislature, and not from the courts.[698] In addition, the court held that the sellers were not liable for failing to warn of the dangers because the dangers had been well known ever since David slew Goliath.[699]

In *Landrine v Mego Corp*, the court also held that there is no duty to warn where the customer is already aware of the hazards because they are common knowledge.[700] In that case, a child died after she swallowed a balloon used to inflate a doll which could simulate the blowing of bubble gum. There was no duty to warn because it is self-evident that swallowing a balloon is dangerous.[701] The court also held that even if the danger were not self-evident to the child, this would not change the result because if a warning were required, it would be directed to the child's guardian and it is self-evident to an adult that balloons should not be ingested.[702]

An unforeseen modification of the product after it leaves the manufacturer's hands is not its responsibility.[703] Therefore, where there is no evidence that a balloon manufacturer knew or should have known that its balloons would be inserted into a doll, any injury resulting from the use of the doll cannot be charged to the balloon manufacturer.[704]

Statutes

The federal government[705] and about one-half of the states[706] have statutes

---

697 62 Cal App 3d 930, 133 Cal Rptr 483, 484 (1976).

698 *Id.*

699 *Id.*

700 95 AD2d 759, 464 NYS2d 516 (1983) (balloons are not inherently dangerous).

701 *Id.*

702 *Id.*

703 Landrine v Mego Corp, 95 AD2d 759, 464 NYS2d 516, 518 (1983).

704 *Id.*

705 *See* 15 USC §§1261-1274. There may be no implied private cause of action under this statute. *See* Riegal Textile Corp v Celanese Corp, 649 F2d 894, 903, 906 (2d Cir 1981); Doane v Metal Bluing Prod, Inc, 568 F Supp 744, 746 (NDNY 1983); *but see* Cross v Board of Supervisors, 326 F Supp 634, 638 (ND Cal 1968).

706 *See, e.g.,* Conn Gen Stat Ann §§21a-72, 21-335 (West Supp 1984); Cal Health & Safety Code §§12500-12725, 28759-28772 (West Supp 1984); Fla Stat Ann §501.065 (West 1972); Ill Ann Stat ch 111½, ¶252-15 (Smith-Hurd 1977); Kan Stat Ann §65-2701 (1980); La Rev Stat Ann §319 (West 1974); Me Rev Stat Ann tit 6, §277 (1979), tit 8, §211 (1980), tit 26, §121 *et seq* (Supp 1984); Md Health-Environment Code Ann §7-201(K) (1982); Mass Gen Laws Ann ch 94, §270 (West 1984), ch 148, §39 (West Supp 1984), ch 270, §10 (West 1970); Mich Comp Laws Ann §259.781 (West 1977), §286.451 (West 1979), §750.243a (West Supp 1984); Minn Stat Ann §325F.08 (West Supp 1984); Miss Code Ann §97-37-33 (1973); Mo Ann Stat §578.100 (Vernon 1979); Mont Code Ann §50-30-202 (1983); Neb Rev Stat §§28-1243 to -1250, 28-1430 (1979); NH Rev Stat Ann §339-A:3 (1984); NJ Stat Ann §21:2-1 *et seq* (West 1969); NY Gen Bus Law §396-K (McKinney 1984), Penal §270.00 (McKinney 1980), Pub Health §1371 (McKinney Supp 1984); Ohio Rev Code Ann

regulating the sale or manufacture of dangerous toys. Much of the state legislation is similar to federal law.[707]

Many states, as well as the United States Consumer Product Safety Commission,[708] regulate fireworks.[709] A few states also regulate stuffed toys[710] and toy missiles or rockets.[711]

§7.23 Miscellaneous Products

Air Balloons

A velcro manufacturer is not liable, as a matter of law, for a hot air balloonist's injuries where it had clearly warned the plaintiff, as well as other balloonists, that its material was not meant to secure deflation panels in hot air balloons and that it was unsafe to ride in a balloon which used velcro material for a closure device.[712]

Archery

In *Genteman v Saunders Archery Co*,[713] the manufacturer of a *string silencer*

---

§§3713.01-37.13.99 (Page Supp 1984); Or Rev Stat §§453.001-.992, 480.110-.170 (1983); Pa Stat Ann §§1271-1277, 16581-16583 (Purdon Supp 1984); SC Code Ann §§23-35-10 to -170, 23-39-10 to -120 (Law Co-op Supp 1984); Tenn Code Ann §§68-27-101 to -203 (Supp 1984); Tex Civ Stat Ann art 4476-13 (Vernon Supp 1985); Wis Stat Ann §§100.37, 167.10 (West Supp 1984).

707 *See, e.g.*, Conn Gen Stat Ann §21a-335 (West Supp 1984); Fla Stat Ann §501.065 (West 1972); Ill Rev Stat ch 111½, ¶252-15 (Smith-Hurd 1977); Kan Stat Ann §65-2701 (1980); Md Health-Environment Code Ann §7-201(K) (1982); Mich Comp Laws Ann §286.451 (West 1979); Mont Code Ann §50-30-202 (1983); NH Rev Stat Ann §§339-A:3 (1984); Or Rev Stat §§453.001-.992 (1983); SC Code Ann §§23-39-10 to -120 (Law Co-op Supp 1984); Tenn Code Ann §§68-27-101 to -203 (Supp 1984); Tex Civ Stat Ann art 4476-13 (Vernon Supp 1985); Wis Stat Ann §100.37 (West Supp 1984).

708 *See* 16 CFR §1507.

709 *See, e.g.*, Cal Health & Safety Code §§12500-12725 (West Supp 1985); Me Rev Stat Ann tit 8, §211 (1980); Mass Gen Laws Ann ch 148, §39 (West Supp 1984); Mich Comp Laws Ann §750.243a (West Supp 1984); Neb Rev Stat §§28-1244 to -1250 (1979); NJ Stat Ann §21:2-1 *et seq* (West 1969); NY Penal Law §270.00 (McKinney 1980); Or Rev Stat §§480-110-.170 (1983), Pa Stat Ann §1271-1277, 16581-16583 (Purdon Supp 1984); SC Code Ann §§23-35-10 to -170 (Supp 1984); Wis Stat Ann §167.10 (West Supp 1984).

Each year, about 8,000 individuals are seriously injured by fireworks. *See* US Consumer Prod Safety Commn, Natl Injury Information Clearinghouse, Prod Summary Rep (Mar 28, 1984).

710 *See, e.g.*, Conn Gen Stat Ann §21a-72 (West Supp 1984); Me Rev Stat Ann tit 26, §121 *et seq* (Supp 1984); Mass Gen Laws Ann ch 94, §270 (West 1984).

711 *See, e.g.*, Me Rev Stat Ann tit 6, §277 (1979); Mich Comp Laws Ann §259.781 (West 1977).

712 *See* Temple v Velcro USA, Inc, 148 Cal App 3d 1090, 196 Cal Rptr 531, 533 (1983).

713 42 Ill App 3d 294, 355 NE2d 647 (1976).

was found not liable when an archery bow broke, and the silencer hit the bottom of the bow, bounced up, and hit the archer's eye. The plaintiff's argument that the manufacturer's change, to using plastic, in the manufacturing of the silencer showed that its previous use of another material was defective was unsuccessful.[714] The court noted that the manufacturer changed to plastic for a reason unrelated to safety, viz, that the silencer could be manufactured more quickly using plastic.[715] Therefore, it was improper to conclude that the change showed that the prior condition was defective.[716]

In addition, the plaintiff may have misused the product. Generally, the longer the product has been out of the control of the manufacturer and in active use by the consumer, the greater the likelihood that some intervening instrumentality such as product misuse may have caused the failure.[717] In this case, there was evidence that the silencer was improperly used in two ways: first, it was attached to the bow contrary to written instructions and second, it was used for an improper purpose, viz., for target practice rather than for actual hunting.[718] The second improper use of the product was important because the silencer would be fired significantly more in practice than in actual hunting and the product failed, in part, because it was used too often.[719]

Baseball

In *Filler v Rayex Corp*,[720] the plaintiff was wearing athletic sunglasses while playing baseball, but he still lost the ball in the sun. The ball hit the sunglasses, shattering them and forcing glass splinters into the plaintiff's eye. The manufacturer was held liable under all three of the plaintiff's theories of recovery.[721] First, the sunglass lenses were so thin that they were unreasonably dangerous and, therefore, the manufacturer was strictly liable for the injury.[722] Second, the manufacturer was liable for breach of the implied warranty of fitness because the sunglasses were advertised to give *eye protection* but they did not have the safety features of plastic or shatterproof glass.[723] Third, the manufacturer was negligent in failing to warn of the dangers

---

[714] 355 NE2d at 651.

[715] *Id.*

[716] *Id.*

[717] *Id* 652.

[718] *Id.*

[719] *Id.*

[720] 435 F2d 336 (7th Cir 1970).

[721] A $100,000 judgment was affirmed.

[722] 435 F2d 336, 338 (7th Cir 1970) (Indiana law).

[723] *See id.* The court's ruling that privity is not required for breach of implied warranty was later overruled. *See Corbin v Coleco*, 748 F2d 411, 415 (7th Cir 1984).

of the lenses which could shatter on impact.[724] The manufacturer of the sunglasses was not allowed to benefit from the principle that liability should not be imposed for unavoidably unsafe products because, even assuming that it were impossible to manufacture shatterproof sunglasses for athletes, this exception is not applicable where the manufacturer failed to warn of the dangers.[725]

In *Dudley Sports Co v Schmitt*, the court held that a baseball pitching machine was negligently designed.[726] The distributor of this machine was held liable because the machine was unreasonably dangerous in a manner not reasonably expected by users of the machine, viz., the arm of the machine could deliver a swift, crippling blow even though it was unplugged.[727] The distributor was also liable for failing to warn of this latent risk.[728] The distributor's compliance with industry standards was considered irrelevant.[729]

A manufacturer of a catcher's mask was granted a new trial where the catcher, Johnny Roseboro of the Los Angeles Dodgers, failed to produce sufficient evidence that the mask was defective when it left the manufacturer's plant.[730]

Bicycles

Bicycle manufacturers are generally not liable for defects in the bicycles which are apparent.[731] Accordingly, in *Poppell v Waters*, the court held that there is no liability for designing a bicycle which did not have a headlight or front reflector because the dangers of riding a bicycle at night without a headlight or a front reflector are obvious.[732]

A bicycle retailer that received the bicycles in parts from the manufacturer and assembled them itself may be liable for improper assembly.[733] In one case the manufacturer was liable for the retailer's improper assembly because it knowingly relied on the retailer, its authorized dealer, to put the bicycles in a completed state.[734]

---

724 *See* 435 F2d at 338.

725 *See id.*

726 151 Ind App 217, 279 NE2d 266, 274 (1972).

727 *Id.*

728 279 NE2d at 275.

729 *Id* 276.

730 Roseboro v Rawlings Mfg Co, 275 Cal App 2d 43, 79 Cal Rptr 567, 569 (1969).

731 Poppell v Waters, 126 Ga App 385, 190 SE2d 815, 817 (1972).

732 *Id.*

733 *See* Caporale v Raleigh Indus, 382 So 2d 849, 850 (Fla Dist Ct App 1980); Means v Sears, Roebuck & Co, 550 SW2d 780 (Mo 1977) ($40,000 damages).

734 *See* Caporale v Raleigh Indus, 382 So 2d 849, 851 (Fla Dist Ct App 1980).

A bicycle retailer is not liable for a bicycle accident under the res ipsa loquitur doctrine because the bicycle was not in its control at the time of the accident.[735]

The United States Consumer Product Safety Commission has promulgated safety standards for bicycles.[736] The violation of these standards is actionable.[737]

Bleachers

In *Lukowski v Vecta Educational Corp*,[738] the court held that a company which had contracted to manufacture and install bleachers for a high school gymnasium was not liable, as a matter of law, under strict products liability where it had not finished its work, but the school nevertheless allowed the public in and a spectator fell off the back of the bleachers. The court held the manufacturer had not yet *sold or delivered* the product since its work was not finished and, therefore, strict products liability law was inapplicable.[739]

In a different case, the bleacher manufacturer was not liable because the defect, viz., a metal railing which protruded from the end of the bleachers, was obvious.[740]

Horseback Riding

In *Llewellyn v Lookout Saddle Co*,[741] the plaintiff fell from a horse. The court held that the manufacturer of the girth buckle was not liable because the plaintiff could not carry his burden of proof on causation.[742] The plaintiff was unable to testify as to the cause of the accident and his expert failed to test the broken girth buckle. Therefore, the buckle manufacturer was held not liable because the buckle may have broken later as a result of, rather than as the cause of, the fall.[743]

The court also held that the plaintiff could not rely on the doctrine of res ipsa loquitur.[744] The girth had been in the possession of the plaintiff or his family for 10 months and when it was not in use, it was kept in a

---

735 *See* Hacker v Shofer, 251 Md 672, 248 A2d 351, 353 (1968).

736 *See* 16 CFR §1512.

737 *See* 15 USC §2072(a).

738 401 NE2d 781 (Ind Ct App 1980).

739 *Id* 787.

740 *See* DiPerna v Roman Catholic Diocese, 30 AD2d 249, 292 NYS2d 177, 179 (1968).

741 315 So 2d 69, 71 (La Ct App 1975).

742 *Id* 73; *see generally* §1.13.

743 315 So 2d 69, 74 (La Ct App 1975).

744 *Id; see generally* §1.13.

common area to which over 15 other families had access.[745] Therefore, the girth was not under the defendant's control and the res ipsa loquitur doctrine was inapplicable.[746]

Horse Racing

In *Cole v New York Racing Association*,[747] a professional jockey fell off his horse, hit a railing, and died when he struck his head on a raised concrete base that was part of the railing. The court held that the owner and operator of the Aqueduct race track was negligent in erecting and maintaining those above-ground concrete footings.[748] The architect who designed this track testified that his original plans had the footings level with the ground as a safety precaution, but the plans were changed to save money.[749]

Lawn Chairs

In *Kontz v K-Mart Corp*, the Eighth Circuit held that a retailer has no duty to warn of the potential dangers of lawn chairs because such chairs are neither latently dangerous when used as anticipated nor unavoidably unsafe.[750] The court also ruled that it was not error to exclude a United States Consumer Products Safety Commission study showing that there were about 8,000 injuries a year from folding or beach chairs because there was no showing that those injuries were similar to plaintiff's.[751]

Off-Road Vehicles

Off-road vehicles can be dangerous. Over 25,000 individuals are seriously injured each year while using them.[752]

In *Woods v International Harvester Co*, a vehicle designed for off-road terrain, which was advertised as being able to travel through water and came with an instruction booklet that contemplated the use of the vehicle in "deep water," was held to be defective because it could cause fatal injuries if

---

[745] 315 So 2d 69, 74 (La Ct App 1975).

[746] *Id*.

[747] 24 AD2d 933, 266 NYS2d 267 (1965), *affd*, 17 NY2d 761, 217 NE2d 144, 270 NYS2d 421 (1966).

[748] 266 NYS2d at 269-70.

[749] *Id*.

[750] 712 F2d 1302, 1304 (8th Cir 1983) (Missouri law).

[751] *Id*.

[752] *See* US Consumer Prod Safety Commn, Natl Injury Information Clearinghouse, Prod Summary Report (Mar 28, 1984).

used in water over 25 inches deep.[753] Therefore, a $900,000 judgement was affirmed.[754]

In *Sabich v Outboard Marine Corp*, the court held, in affirming a $600,000 judgment, that an off-road vehicle was unreasonably dangerous because although the vehicle had a tendency to tip over when going down steep inclines, the manufacturer did not warn of this danger.[755]

Parachuting

In *Prince v Parachutes, Inc*,[756] a parachutist was injured using a parachute designed for more experienced users. The court held that the parachute manufacturer was not entitled to summary judgment regarding its duty to warn because it was a question of fact whether an ordinary parachutist would readily recognize that this parachute, which had been marketed for only a short period of time, should be used by experienced parachutists.[757] The plaintiff's subjective knowledge of the hazards of using this parachute was not relevant to the manufacturer's duty to warn, but only to the plaintiff's comparative negligence.[758]

Playground Equipment

There is a significant amount of danger in using playground equipment. Each year over 190,000 individuals injured while using playground equipment require emergency room treatment.[759]

In *Gellenbeck v Sears, Roebuck & Co*,[760] the court dealt with litigation between two parties in the distribution chain after a child was injured when a swing set chain, suffering from *strain aging*, broke while the child was being twirled on the swing. The manufacturer argued that it was not liable to the wholesaler for breach of the implied warranty of fitness for a particular purpose because it had no reason to know that the purchaser was relying on it to use its skill or judgment in selecting proper chains. However, the court concluded that the wholesaler bought the chain from the manufacturer, who sold other types of swing equipment, because the manufacturer furnished it

---

[753] 697 F2d 635, 637-38 (5th Cir 1983).

[754] *Id*.

[755] 60 Cal App 3d 591, 131 Cal Rptr 703, 708-09 (1976).

[756] 685 P2d 83, 88 (Alaska 1984).

[757] *Id*.

[758] *Id* 88-89.

[759] *See* US Consumer Prod Safety Commn, Natl Injury Information Clearinghouse, Prod Summary Report (Mar 28, 1984).

[760] 59 Mich App 339, 229 NW2d 443 (1975).

an independent laboratory report that the chain was proper.[761] Therefore, it was reasoned that the chain was purchased because of the manufacturer's assurances that it was suitable for use in swings.[762]

Race Cars

In *Barris v Bob's Drag Chutes & Safety Equipment, Inc,*[763] a driver in a sprint car wearing a Y-type shoulder harness was involved in a collision. The car was catapulted into the air and flipped end-over-end, and the harness apparently failed to restrain the driver properly. The court reversed a directed verdict for the harness manufacturer.[764] It held that a jury could have concluded that the shoulder harness was defective under strict liability principles because the harness did not have a sufficient number of stitches and the stitches which were present were not arranged to maximize the harness's strength.[765]

In another case, the jury awarded almost $10 million in damages where defective race car tires contributed to a race car driver's death.[766]

Reducing Equipment

In *Shugar v Pat Walker Figure Perfection Salons International,*[767] the plaintiff, while using defendant's vibrating and reducing machine, felt weak. She later went to a doctor and learned that she had a kidney stone. The court held that defendant was not entitled to summary judgment because there was a question of fact regarding whether the machine was safe.[768] Although the facts in the case are not sufficiently developed, this ruling appears wrong. If the plaintiff did not know of her kidney stone and the machine was otherwise safe, a warning of possible dangers, none of which the plaintiff realized would be applicable, would have been ignored as meaningless. Therefore, the defendant should not be liable for failing to warn of a danger which the plaintiff reasonably believed was nonexistent.

---

761 229 NW2d at 445.

762 *Id.*

763 685 F2d 94 (3d Cir 1982).

764 *Id* 100.

765 *Id.*

766 *See* LA Times, Apr 4, 1984, §III, at 5, col 1.

767 541 SW2d 511 (Tex Civ App 1976).

768 *Id* 513.

Spectators

8

§8.01 Introduction

Stadium owners and operators are not insurers of the safety of their patrons.[1] However, they generally have a duty to exercise reasonable care to keep all of their premises in a reasonably safe condition under the circumstances.[2]

---

[1] Hartzell v United States, 539 F2d 65, 69 (10th Cir 1976); Harrell v Martin, 345 So 2d 868, 869 (Fla Dist Ct App 1977); Ingersoll v Onondaga Hockey Club, 245 AD 137, 281 NYS 505, 506 (1935); Jones v Three Rivers Management Corp, 483 Pa 75, 394 A2d 546, 549 (1978); *see generally* ch 6.

[2] Hartzell v United States, 539 F2d 65, 68 (10th Cir 1976); Harrell v Martin, 345 So 2d 868, 869 (Fla Dist Ct App 1977); Lemoine v Springfield Hockey Assn, 307 Mass 102, 29 NE2d 716, 718 (1940); Merritt v Nickelson, 407 Mich 544, 287 NW2d 178, 180 (1980); Lindgren v Voge, 260 Minn 262, 109 NW2d 754, 757 (1961) (toilet facilities at a speedway must be reasonably safe); Jones v Three Rivers Management Corp, 483 Pa 75, 394 A2d 546, 549 (1978); *see also* Restatement (Second) of Torts §343 (1965); *see generally* ch 6.

A cotenant of real estate who did not occupy it owed no duty of reasonable care to spectators invited onto the property by her cotenant. Merritt v Nickelson, 407 Mich 544, 287 NW2d 178, 181 (1980).

In one case a spectator at a baseball game who was admitted without paying an entrance fee was held an invitee, not a licensee. Pursuant to an advertising plan of the club, children who bought a t-shirt with the baseball team's name on it at a local retail store and wore it to

In several cases, sponsors of recreational activities were held not to have a duty of care toward spectators injured by third parties on property they did not control.[3] In *Kilpatrick v University Mall Shopping Center*,[4] the court held that the sponsors of a horse show at a shopping center owed no duty of care to a spectator who was struck by an automobile. The automobile was driven by another spectator in the parking lot, the place where the horses could be viewed. The sponsors were not liable because they did not own the parking lot and had no authority or power to control it. Similarly, in *Ziginow v Redford Jaycees*, the sponsor of a fireworks display was granted a directed verdict where two individuals were injured, one fatally, by an automobile while they were walking to their own automobile after a fireworks display because the sponsor owed no duty of care to spectators after they left the area.[5]

Generally, a defendant is not liable for injuries which result from an open and obvious condition of which a plaintiff, in the exercise of due care for his or her own safety, is or should be aware.[6] In *Larrea v Ozark Water Ski Thrill Show, Inc*,[7] a spectator at a water ski show fell on a rock in the parking lot. The court held that the recreational facility was not negligent as a matter of law because the plaintiff should have recognized that the obvious, rustic nature of the facility required care.[8]

The custom of other recreational facilities is admissible evidence in proving whether a particular facility breached its duty of care.[9] In fact, one court held that it was reversible error not to allow the defendant to introduce such evidence.[10] Nevertheless, a sports facility's compliance with an industry custom does not end the inquiry into whether the facility breached a duty of care because the court, not the recreational industry, makes the final determination

---

the stadium were admitted without charge. The court held that the t-shirt was a "semblance of a ticket." Stroud v Bridges, 275 SW2d 503, 505 (Tex Civ App 1955).

3 Ziginow v Redford Jaycees, 133 Mich App 259, 349 NW2d 153, 155 (1983); Kilpatrick v University Mall Shopping Center, 68 NC App 629, 315 SE2d 786, 788-89, *review denied*, 311 NC 758, 321 SE2d 136 (1984).

4 68 NC App 629, 315 SE2d 786, 788-89, *review denied*, 311 NC 758, 321 SE2d 136 (1984).

5 133 Mich App 259, 349 NW2d 153, 155 (1983). The court also held that even if there were a duty of care, there was no breach of that duty because the evidence showed that rerouting traffic would have increased the danger to children in the neighborhood. *See* 349 NW2d at 156.

6 Hartzell v United States, 539 F2d 65, 69 (10th Cir 1976); Larrea v Ozark Water Ski Thrill Show, Inc, 562 SW2d 790, 794 (Mo Ct App 1978); *see generally* §§1.01, 6.02.

7 562 SW2d 790, 794 (Mo Ct App 1978).

8 *Id.*

9 James v Rhode Island Auditorium, Inc, 60 RI 405, 199 A 293, 298 (1938).

10 Shurman v Fresno Ice Rink, Inc, 91 Cal App 2d 469, 205 P2d 77, 81 (1949).

of what type of conduct is reasonable under the circumstances.[11] Similarly, a facility's compliance with statutes and safety regulations is also not dispositive of whether it acted with reasonable care in a particular situation.[12]

Recreational facilities must provide reasonable protection to spectators from the dangers of being hit by players or objects used by the players.[13] Most courts have held that baseball clubs must provide sufficient screened seats for as many spectators as may reasonably be expected to want them on an ordinary occasion.[14] As a result, in many baseball cases, the club has been held not liable.[15] However, the courts have usually held that other sports organizations must provide a reasonable amount of screening for their spectators,[16] a standard which is harder to meet.

There are a handful of court decisions which have concluded that the dangers of being hit by an object from the playing arena, e.g., a hockey puck, are well-known to individuals who sit in unprotected areas and, therefore, there is no duty for the proprietor to construct safety barriers to protect those individuals.[17] In addition, several courts have held that schools were not required to provide physical barriers along the field to protect spectators from players who run out of bounds.[18] One court decided that it was reasonable not to construct a barrier because the barrier would preclude the school from using the field for other events.[19] There seems little doubt that the solicitude of the courts for the schools, nonprofit entities which never seem to have enough money, would not apply to commercial sporting organizations.

The Alabama Supreme Court recently held that recreational facilities generally have no duty to remove debris dropped on their premises during a

---

11 Uline Ice, Inc v Sullivan, 187 F2d 82, 84 (DC Cir 1950); *see generally* §1.01.

12 Christou v Arlington Park—Washington Park Race Tracks, Corp, 104 Ill App 3d 257, 432 NE2d 920, 924 (1982). However, the facility should be allowed to introduce evidence that it did not violate any safety statute. *Id.*

13 Brown v San Francisco Ball Club, 99 Cal App 2d 484, 222 P2d 19, 21 (1950); Clark v Monroe County Fair Assn, 203 Iowa 1107, 212 NW 163, 166 (1927); Knebel v Jones, 266 SW2d 470, 476 (Tex Civ App 1954).

14 *See* Brown v San Francisco Ball Club, 99 Cal App 2d 484, 222 P2d 19, 21 (1950); Knebel v Jones, 266 SW2d 470, 476 (Tex Civ App 1954).

15 *See* Brown v San Francisco Ball Club, 99 Cal App 2d 484, 222 P2d 19, 21 (1950); Knebel v Jones, 266 SW2d 470, 476 (Tex Civ App 1954); *see generally* §8.03.

16 *See* Uline Ice, Inc v Sullivan, 187 F2d 82, 84 (DC Cir 1950); Shanney v Boston Madison Square Garden Corp, 296 Mass 168, 5 NE2d 1, 2 (1936).

17 Ingersoll v Onondaga Hockey Club, 245 AD 137, 281 NYS 505, 508 (1935); Hammel v Madison Square Garden Corp, 156 Misc 311, 279 NYS 815, 816 (Sup Ct 1935); *see also* §§9.07, 9.16.

18 *See* Turner v Caddo Parish School Bd, 214 So 2d 153, 157 (La 1968); Perry v Seattle Dist No 1, 66 Wash 2d 800, 405 P2d 589, 593 (1965).

19 Turner v Caddo Parish School Bd, 214 So 2d 153, 157 (La 1968).

sporting event because patrons should realize that this will occur.[20] However, a different court held that sporting facilities must take reasonable care to remove the debris.[21] In any event, where a racetrack had taken reasonable steps to remove the debris, viz., it had a sufficient crew of cleaners on duty, it was not liable.[22]

It is generally held that there is no duty to protect a spectator from being injured by the misconduct of other spectators unless the operator of the facility had notice of the likelihood of the injury before it happened and failed to act prudently.[23]

Clubs may be liable for the wrongful acts of their players.[24] In one case the court held that a club would be liable for a player's violent act which injured a spectator if the player acted, at least in part, in an attempt to win the game or make it interesting. However, if the player acted in anger or oblivious to the playing of the game, the employer is not liable.[25] A different court held that an employer is not liable because striking a spectator is outside the scope of the player's employment.[26]

Players also owe a duty of reasonable care to spectators and bystanders.[27] In *Osborne v Sprowls*, the Illinois Supreme Court held that an older and stronger student breached this duty by attempting to catch a football in the presence of nonparticipants because it would have been safer to play football in a nearby area, farther away from the bystanders.[28]

§8.02 Automobile Racing

An automobile racetrack facility is not an insurer of the safety of the

---

[20] *See* Gray v Mobile Grayhound Park, Ltd, 370 So 2d 1384, 1388 (Ala 1979).

[21] *See* McMillan v Mountain Laurel Racing, Inc, 240 Pa Super 248, 367 A2d 1106, 1110 (1976).

[22] Paranzino v Yonkers Raceway, 9 Misc 2d 378, 170 NYS2d 280, 282 (Sup Ct 1957).

[23] Weldy v Oakland High School Dist, 19 Cal App 2d 429, 65 P2d 851, 852 (1937); Gill v Chicago Park Dist, 85 Ill App 3d 903, 407 NE2d 671, 673 (1980) (criminal assault); Aaser v City of Charlotte, 265 NC 494, 144 SE2d 610, 615 (1965).

[24] M.J. Uline Co v Cashdan, 171 F2d 132, 133-34 (DC Cir 1948). In some cases, there is a question whether the person causing the harm is an employee or independent contractor. *See generally* Ulrich v Minneapolis Boxing & Wrestling Club, Inc, 268 Minn 328, 129 NW2d 288, 293 (1964); §§2.02, 2.17, 8.05, 8.07.

[25] MJ Uline Co v Cashdan, 171 F2d 132, 133-34 (DC Cir 1948).

[26] Wiersma v City of Long Beach, 41 Cal App 2d 8, 106 P2d 45, 49 (1940); *but see* Langess v Ketonen, 42 Wash 2d 394, 255 P2d 551, 555 (1953); *see also* McFatridge v Harlem Globe Trotters, 69 NM 271, 365 P2d 918 (1961).

[27] Osborne v Sprowls, 84 Ill 2d 390, 419 NE2d 913, 916 (1981).

[28] 419 NE2d at 917.

spectators.[29] One court held that the commercial operation of a stock car race is not an ultrahazardous activity imposing strict liability on the enterprise.[30] However, a racetrack facility has a duty to exercise reasonable care for the safety of its patrons.[31]

Racetrack facilities which know or should know of the dangers to spectators in certain areas must erect appropriate safety barriers[32] of sufficient strength[33] to protect the spectators.[34] In fact, a facility's failure to comply with the industry custom regarding the strength of the safety barrier may be evidence of its negligence.[35] In addition, the facility may be liable for failing to provide a safety zone for spectators[36] or warn them of the dangers of remaining in certain areas.[37]

There may be no need for the plaintiff to elicit expert testimony regarding the appropriate standard of care to be exercised in providing protective barriers.[38] However, one court held that a facility was not liable where

---

[29] Harrell v Martin, 345 So 2d 868, 869 (Fla Dist Ct App 1977); Alden v Norwood Arena, 332 Mass 267, 124 NE2d 505, 508 (1955); Taylor v Hardee, 232 SC 338, 102 SE2d 218, 222 (1958); Rogers v Black Hills Speedway, Inc, 217 NW2d 14, 17 (SD 1974).

[30] *See* Blake v Fried, 173 Pa Super 27, 95 A2d 360, 365 (1953); *see generally* Restatement (Second) of Torts §§519, 520 (1977).

[31] Harrell v Martin, 345 So 2d 868, 869 (Fla Dist Ct App 1977); Alden v Norwood Arena, 332 Mass 267, 124 NE2d 505, 507 (1955); Taylor v Hardee, 232 SC 338, 102 SE2d 218, 222 (1958); Rogers v Black Hills Speedway, Inc, 217 NW2d 14, 17 (SD 1974); Kuemmel v Vradenburg, 239 SW2d 869, 871 (Tex Civ App 1951); Atlantic Rural Exposition v Fagan, 195 Va 13, 77 SE2d 368, 373 (1953) (track owner and its lessee); Virginia State Fair Assn v Burton, 182 Va 365, 28 SE2d 716, 718 (1944) (this is true even though the defendant hired an independent contractor to produce the races); *see generally* §§6.02, 8.01.
One court held that the owner of a track is not liable where it did not operate the track, even though it received a percentage of the gate receipts as rent. *See* Sam v Theriot, 49 So 2d 484, 487 (La Ct App 1950).
A spectator who improperly went into a pit area may be considered a trespasser and, therefore, may be owed a lower duty of care. *See* Kelley v Sportsmen's Speedway, 80 So 2d 785, 792-93 (Miss 1955); *see generally* §6.05.
A speedway's conduct may be wilful and wanton. One court held that it was a jury question whether a speedway which allowed a teenager to drive a pickup truck over 30 miles per hour in an infield area filled with pedestrians exhibited such behavior. *See* Bickford v International Speedway Corp, 654 F2d 1028, 1033 (5th Cir 1981).

[32] Cessna v Coffeyville Racing Assn, 179 Kan 766, 298 P2d 265, 267 (1956); Rogers v Black Hills Speedway, Inc, 217 NW2d 14, 19 (SD 1974); Atlantic Rural Exposition v Fagan, 195 Va 13, 77 SE2d 368, 374 (1953); Virginia State Fair Assn v Burton, 182 Va 365, 28 SE2d 716, 719 (1944).

[33] Kuemmel v Vradenburg, 239 SW2d 869, 872 (Tex Civ App 1951).

[34] They must also warn of the dangers. Alden v Norwood Arena, 332 Mass 267, 124 NE2d 505, 508 (1955) (failure to warn that wheels may come off the automobiles).

[35] Kuemmel v Vradenburg, 239 SW2d 869, 873 (Tex Civ App 1951).

[36] Virginia State Fair Assn v Burton, 182 Va 365, 28 SE2d 716, 719 (1944).

[37] Rogers v Black Hills Speedway, Inc, 217 NW2d 14, 19 (SD 1974).

[38] Atlantic Rural Exposition v Fagan, 195 Va 13, 77 SE2d 368, 374 (1953).

the plaintiff failed to introduce any evidence of what the proper height for protective fences would have been.[39]

Racetrack speedways must be designed to be reasonably safe.[40] Therefore, a racing association which fails to bank the curves may be negligent.[41]

Racetrack facilities must reasonably inspect their premises.[42] Accordingly, racetracks have been held negligent in failing to inspect the grandstands to learn whether the wood was safe to sit on[43] and in failing to inspect the track to discover loose nails that had been left there.[44]

However, when the facility did not know, and would not have known in the exercise of reasonable care, of danger, it had no duty to warn or eliminate the danger.[45] For example, in *Harrell v Martin*,[46] a spectator at an automobile racetrack was injured when a car slid on a ramp causing the ramp to *kick back* against the spectator as he was walking by to purchase refreshments. The court held that the facility was not negligent because it did not create the situation, did not know or have reason to know of the danger and, therefore, it had no duty to warn or eliminate the danger.[47]

Racing organizations may be liable for their employees' negligence.[48] In *Zieman v World Amusement Service Association*, a driver negligently attached the steering apparatus to the wheel of his automobile and, as a result, the car went out of control and hit a spectator.[49] The court held that the driver's employer may be liable for the spectator's injuries.[50]

Insurance

In *Underwriters at Lloyd's of London v Hunefeld*, the court held that an insurance policy for the owners of a drag racing strip covered an accident where an automobile went out of control and hit a spectator.[51] The

---

39 *See* Blake v Fried, 173 Pa Super 27, 95 A2d 360, 364 (1953).

40 *See generally* Cessna v Coffeyville Racing Assn, 179 Kan 766, 298 P2d 265, 267 (1956).

41 *Id.*

42 Taylor v Hardee, 232 SC 338, 102 SE2d 218, 221 (1958); Virginia State Fair Assn v Burton, 182 Va 365, 28 SE2d 716, 719 (1944).

43 Taylor v Hardee, 232 SC 338, 102 SE2d 218, 221 (1958).

44 Virginia State Fair Assn v Burton, 182 Va 365, 28 SE2d 716, 719 (1944).

45 Harrell v Martin, 345 So 2d 868, 870 (Fla Dist Ct App 1977).

46 *Id.*

47 *Id.*

48 Zieman v World Amusement Serv Assn, 209 Iowa 1298, 228 NW 48 (1929).

49 *Id.*

50 *Id.*

51 230 Cal App 2d 31, 40 Cal Rptr 659, 664 (1964).

policy excluded coverage for accidents occurring in the pit area. However, the words *pit area* were not defined in the policy, and the court gave them a narrow construction.[52] In addition, the insurance company argued that an exclusion for *mechanics* was applicable because the spectator intended to perform such activities. However, the court rejected this argument because the injured party had not yet engaged in that activity when he was injured.[53]

Several courts have held that injuries from a race car, a vehicle which was designed for use primarily *off public roads*, were not covered by an automobile insurance policy.[54]

§8.03   Baseball

Baseball clubs are not insurers of their patrons' safety.[55] However, they must use reasonable care to protect their patrons from injury.[56] This includes a duty to keep the premises in a reasonably safe condition and to warn of concealed dangers.[57]

Virtually all baseball stadiums have large amounts of spectator seating which provide no protection from batted balls. This is a result, at

---

[52] 40 Cal Rptr at 665.

[53] *Id* 664.

[54] *See* Williams v Cimarron Ins Co, 406 SW2d 173, 175 (Tex Civ App 1966); Beagle v Automobile Club Ins Co, 18 Ohio Ops 2d 280, 176 NE2d 542, 544 (1960); *but see* Carney v American Fire & Indem Co, 371 So 2d 815, 817 (La 1979); *see also* **§2.17.**

[55] Brown v San Francisco Ball Club, 99 Cal App 2d 484, 222 P2d 19, 20 (1950); Ratcliff v San Diego Baseball Club, 27 Cal App 2d 733, 81 P2d 625, 626 (1938); Maytnier v Rush, 80 Ill App 2d 336, 225 NE2d 83, 87 (1967); Akins v Glens Falls City School Dist, 53 NY2d 325, 424 NE2d 531, 441 NYS2d 644, 646 (1981); Jones v Three Rivers Management Corp, 483 Pa 75, 394 A2d 546, 549 (1978); Keys v Alamo City Baseball Co, 150 SW2d 368, 370 (Tex Civ App 1941).

[56] Ratcliff v San Diego Baseball Club, 27 Cal App 2d 733, 81 P2d 625, 626 (1938); Maytnier v Rush, 80 Ill App 2d 336, 225 NE2d 83, 87 (1967); Akins v Glens Falls City School Dist, 53 NY2d 325, 424 NE2d 531, 441 NYS2d 644, 646 (1981); Jones v Three Rivers Management Corp, 483 Pa 75, 394 A2d 546, 549 (1978); Keys v Alamo City Baseball Co, 150 SW2d 368, 370 (Tex Civ App 1941); *see generally* **§§6.02, 8.01**; *but see generally* Employers Casualty Co v Hagendorfer, 393 So 2d 999, 1003 (Ala 1981) (Embry, J, concurring) (ball park owes no duty to protect against the risks inherent in the nature of the activity taking place at that time).
One court held that a little league organization was not liable when a spectator was injured on a ramp because it did not own the premises and the owner was responsible for conditions in the common areas. Jackson v Cartwright School Dist, 125 Ariz 98, 607 P2d 975, 977 (App 1980).

[57] Brown v San Francisco Ball Club, 99 Cal App 2d 484, 222 P2d 19, 20 (1950).
One court held that there is no duty to remove or warn of obvious dangers. *See* Jackson v Cartwright School Dist, 125 Ariz 98, 607 P2d 975, 980 (Ct App 1980) (spectator slipped on dust and gravel on a ramp).

least in part, of the wish of stadium owners to cater to the many spectators who prefer to watch baseball games without looking through protective fencing.[58] In addition, for some spectators an important part of the enjoyment of attending a baseball game is the chance to obtain foul balls as souvenirs.[59] These legitimate desires of the patrons, coupled with the fact that watching a baseball game is not inherently dangerous, means that reasonable care does not require a baseball club to provide the spectators with complete protection from all balls going into the stands.[60] Accordingly, the critical question in most cases is only how much protective fencing is required.[61]

Most courts have held that baseball clubs must provide sufficient screened seats for as many spectators as may be reasonably expected to want them on an ordinary occasion.[62] Indeed, in *Akins v Glens Falls City School District*, the New York Court of Appeals recently held that the owner of a baseball field has a duty to provide adequate protection for the number of spectators who are reasonably expected to prefer such seating in the area behind home plate, where the danger of being struck by a ball is the greatest.[63] The plaintiff in *Akins* introduced no evidence that the backstop was inadequate or that there were an insufficient number of screened seats and, therefore, the court held

---

58 Akins v Glens Falls City School Dist, 53 NY2d 325, 424 NE2d 531, 441 NYS2d 644, 646 (1981); Knebel v Jones, 266 SW2d 470, 476 (Tex Civ App 1954); Keys v Alamo City Baseball Co, 150 SW2d 368, 369 (Tex Civ App 1941).

59 Powless v Milwaukee County, 6 Wis 2d 78, 94 NW2d 187, 190 (1959).

60 Brown v San Francisco Ball Club, 99 Cal App 2d 484, 222 P2d 19, 21 (1950); Maytnier v Rush, 80 Ill App 2d 336, 225 NE2d 83, 87 (1967); Akins v Glens Falls City School Dist, 53 NY2d 325, 424 NE2d 531, 441 NYS2d 644, 646 (1981); Knebel v Jones, 266 SW2d 470, 476 (Tex Civ App 1954); Keys v Alamo City Baseball Co, 150 SW2d 368, 369 (Tex Civ App 1941).

61 Akins v Glens Falls City School Dist, 53 NY2d 325, 424 NE2d 531, 441 NYS2d 644, 646 (1981).

62 Quinn v Recreation Park Assn, 3 Cal 2d 725, 46 P2d 144 (1935); Brown v San Francisco Ball Club, 99 Cal App 2d 484, 222 P2d 19, 21 (1950); Ratcliff v San Diego Baseball Club, 27 Cal App 2d 733, 81 P2d 625, 626 (1938); Anderson v Kansas City Baseball Club, 231 SW2d 170, 173 (Mo 1950); Knebel v Jones, 266 SW2d 470, 476 (Tex Civ App 1954); Keys v Alamo City Baseball Co, 150 SW2d 368, 371 (Tex Civ App 1941); *see also* Davidoff v Metropolitan Baseball Club, 61 NY2d 996, 475 NYS2d 367, 368 (1984).

One court held that it was irrelevant that all of the screened seats had already been taken by others. *See* Knebel v Jones, 266 SW2d 470, 476 (Tex Civ App 1954).

In Rudnick v Golden West Broadcasters, 156 Cal App 3d 793, 202 Cal Rptr 900, 902 (1984) the court held that the club owner was not entitled to summary judgment where it made no showing of the number of requests reasonably expected for screened seats.

Clubs must also provide reasonable precautions against bats which slip out of a batter's hands. Ratcliff v San Diego Baseball Club, 27 Cal App 2d 733, 81 P2d 625, 626 (1938).

63 53 NY2d 325, 424 NE2d 531, 441 NYS2d 644, 646 (1981); *see also* Ratcliff v San Diego Baseball Club, 27 Cal App 2d 733, 81 P2d 625, 626 (1938).

that the defendant was entitled to judgment as a matter of law.[64] There was a strong dissent in *Akins* which argued that the jury should determine whether the stadium owner acted reasonably by weighing the likelihood and severity of injuries caused by baseballs hit into the unprotected spectator areas against the cost of providing additional screening.[65]

The screening which is provided must provide reasonable protection from batted baseballs.[66] In *Edling v Kansas City Baseball & Exhibition Co*, a club was held liable where the ball went through a hole in the protective screen and injured a spectator.[67]

The owner of a baseball stadium must take reasonable precautions to protect spectators from being hit by wildly thrown baseballs which are not in play.[68] In *Maytnier v Rush*,[69] a spectator at Wrigley Field, home of the Chicago Cubs, was hit by an errant ball thrown by a prospective relief pitcher *warming up* along the foul lines while the game was going on. The court held that spectators required additional protection in this situation because they would be expected to watch the game, not the practice routines of relief players and, therefore, would not be able to protect themselves from these errant throws.[70]

Reasonable protection must also be provided to spectators who are likely to be hit by a baseball while walking through the stadium.[71] In *Jones v Three Rivers Management Corp*,[72] the Pennsylvania Supreme Court upheld a $125,000 damage award to a woman who was hit by a baseball while walking on a concourse to buy some refreshments. The court noted that the opening in the concourse which allowed the ball to hit her was not associated with the ordinary manner in which baseball is viewed.[73] Accordingly, the opening was not "part of the spectator sport of baseball"[74] and the stadium owner owed a duty of care to protect spectators when they were not sitting in their seats, but were still subject to being hit by a baseball.

---

64 441 NYS2d at 647.

65 441 NYS2d at 649 (Cooke, J, dissenting).

66 Edling v Kansas City Baseball & Exhibition Co, 168 SW 908, 910 (Mo Ct App 1914).

67 *Id.*

68 Maytnier v Rush, 80 Ill App 2d 336, 225 NE2d 83 (1967).

69 *Id.*

70 225 NE2d at 89.

71 Olds v St Louis Natl Baseball Club, 232 Mo App 897, 104 SW2d 746, 749, 751 (1937); Jones v Three Rivers Management Corp, 483 Pa 75, 394 A2d 546 (1978).

72 483 Pa 75, 394 A2d 546 (1978).

73 394 A2d at 551.

74 *Id* 552.

Most courts have held that baseball clubs have no duty to warn spectators of the danger of baseballs being hit into unscreened areas of the stands.[75] In one case the club was held not liable even where an usher told a spectator that an unscreened seat was safe.[76] However, in *Falkner v John E Fetzer, Inc*,[77] a spectator struck by a batted ball at a Detroit Tigers baseball game received a jury verdict of about $250,000 because of the defendant's failure to warn her of the dangers of being hit by a baseball. Unfortunately for the plaintiff, the appellate court reversed her judgment because she failed to present any evidence that if a proper warning had been given, she would have taken precautions to prevent the injury.[78]

Baseball clubs must reasonably maintain their stadiums.[79] Accordingly, clubs have been held liable for failing to provide sufficient safeguards to prevent patrons from falling through the back of the grandstands[80] and failing to remove a hole in the ground near a concession stand.[81]

Baseball clubs must provide spectators with reasonable protection from the acts of other spectators.[82] In *Noble v Los Angeles Dodgers*, a case which illustrates the adage that one should not start what one cannot finish, the court held that a spectator who initiated a fight in the parking lot following a night game could not recover, as a matter of law, for the injuries he received in the altercation.[83] The court noted that it was a "sad commentary" that today it was foreseeable that a crime could occur at almost any time and

---

75 Anderson v Kansas City Baseball Club, 231 SW2d 170, 173 (Mo 1950); Keys v Alamo City Baseball Co, 150 SW2d 368, 369 (Tex Civ App 1941); *but see* Friedman v Houston Sports Assn, No 79-27215 (Tex Civ Ct July 10, 1985) ($180,000 jury verdict for failing to warn). However, the court in *Friedman* entered judgment for the defendant.

Such a warning, if it were given, would be resented by many patrons. Keys v Alamo City Baseball Co, 150 SW2d 368, 369 (Tex Civ App 1941).

76 *See* Anderson v Kansas City Baseball Club, 231 SW2d 170, 173 (Mo 1950).

77 113 Mich App 500, 317 NW2d 337 (1982).

78 317 NW2d at 339.

79 Martin v Angel City Baseball Assn, 3 Cal App 2d 586, 40 P2d 287, 288 (1935) (liable for unsafe construction of a stairway); Louisville Baseball Club v Butler, 289 Ky 785, 160 SW2d 141, 143-44 (Ct App 1942); Murray v Pittsburgh Athletic Co, 324 Pa 486, 188 A 190, 193 (1936) (gate moved and injured a spectator); Stroud v Bridges, 275 SW2d 503, 504 (Tex Civ App 1955).

80 Stroud v Bridges, 275 SW2d 503, 504 (Tex Civ App 1955).

81 Louisville Baseball Club v Butler, 289 Ky 785, 160 SW2d 141, 143-44 (Ct App 1942).

82 Lee v National League Baseball Club, 4 Wis 2d 168, 89 NW2d 811 (1958) (an older woman was injured when other spectators rushed to retrieve a foul ball which landed close to her). The *Lee* case is criticized in Note, *Torts: Negligence: Duty of A Place of Amusement To Protect Patrons Against Acts of Third Persons*, 6 UCLA L Rev 494 (1959).

It has been reported that spectators have grown more violent in recent years, possibly due to the consumption of alcohol. *See* Wolff, *Drunkenness: Ugly Pastime For Some Baseball Fans*, NY Times, June 16, 1985, at 23, col 5.

83 168 Cal App 3d 912, 214 Cal Rptr 396 (1985).

place.[84] It further noted that the plaintiff's expert concluded, and the jury agreed with him, that the Dodgers' security was not adequate.[85] However, the plaintiff's judgment was reversed because there was no showing that the lack of reasonable security measures caused the fight that the plaintiff initiated.[86]

§8.04 Football

Owners and operators of football stadiums are not insurers of the safety of their patrons.[87] However, they must use reasonable care under the circumstances.[88] One court reasoned that *the circumstances* means that a school may be required to take less care at an intramural contest than at a varsity game because in an intramural game no admission is charged, the school does not make a profit, and attendance is small.[89]

Most courts have held that schools were not negligent in failing to provide a physical barrier along the football field to protect the spectators from players who run out of bounds.[90] In *Turner v Caddo Parish School Board* the court held that it was reasonable not to construct such a barrier because the barrier would preclude the school from using the field for some other activities and even where the field could be used for other events, the barrier would increase the risk of the danger.[91] The *Turner* court also held that a school was not negligent in failing to warn spectators of the dangers of players running out of bounds because it was reasonable to assume that spectators were aware of this danger.[92]

Unfortunately, it is a sad reality that spectators may be assaulted by other spectators. However, in *Gill v Chicago Park District* the court held that an owner and a lessee of a football stadium had no duty to protect a spectator from a criminal assault by other spectators when there was no showing that the defendants had notice of the likelihood of the assault before it happened.[93]

---

84 214 Cal Rptr at 397.

85 *Id* 398-99.

86 *Id* 399.

87 Hartzell v United States, 539 F2d 65, 69 (10th Cir 1976) (Colorado law).

88 *Id*; Perry v Seattle School Dist No 1, 66 Wash 2d 800, 405 P2d 589, 593 (1965); *see generally* §§6.02, 8.01.

89 Perry v Seattle School Dist No 1, 66 Wash 2d 800, 405 P2d 589, 593 (1965).

90 *See* Turner v Caddo Parish School Bd, 214 So 2d 153, 157 (La 1968); Perry v Seattle Dist No 1, 66 Wash 2d 800, 405 P2d 589, 593 (1965); *see generally* §9.13.

Reasonable protection can be provided in other ways, e.g., by stationing teachers near the field to keep the spectators away from the danger. *See* Turner v Caddo Parish School Bd, 214 So 2d 153, 157 (La 1968).

91 *See* 214 So 2d 153, 157 (La 1968).

92 *See id*; *see also* §9.13.

93 *See* 85 Ill App 3d 903, 407 NE2d 671, 673 (1980).

Football is sometimes played under adverse weather conditions. In those situations, the stadium may be filled with ice and snow. However, the stadium owner is not liable for the injuries of a spectator who slipped on an icy stairway unless the owner failed to use reasonable care.[94]

§8.05 Hockey

It is clear that hockey clubs are not insurers of the safety of their patrons.[95] They do, however, generally have a duty to use reasonable care.[96] This usually means that the clubs should eliminate or warn of dangers which they should realize exist and which are not reasonably expected to be realized by their patrons.[97]

Hockey leagues do not owe a duty of care to spectators at league games.[98] Accordingly, in *Riley v Chicago Cougars Hockey Club, Inc*, the court held that the World Hockey Association had no duty to use care to avoid injury to spectators at hockey games between its member teams and a directed verdict in its favor would have been appropriate.[99]

The customs and practices of other hockey clubs are admissible evidence in proving whether a particular club breached its duty of care.[100] In fact, one court held that the trial court committed reversible error when it failed to allow the defendant to introduce such evidence.[101] Of course, a club's compliance with the custom in this industry is not dispositive of whether the

---

94 Hartzell v United States, 539 F2d 65, 69 (10th Cir 1976) (Colorado law).

95 Uline Ice, Inc v Sullivan, 187 F2d 82, 84 (DC Cir 1950); Tite v Omaha Coliseum Corp, 12 NW2d 90, 93 (Neb 1943); Ingersoll v Onondaga Hockey Club, 245 AD 137, 281 NYS 505, 506 (1935); Rich v Madison Square Garden Corp, 149 Misc 123, 266 NYS 288, 289 (1933), *affd without opinion*, 241 AD 722, 270 NYS 915 (1934).

96 Lemoine v Springfield Hockey Assn, 307 Mass 102, 29 NE2d 716, 718 (1940); Tite v Omaha Coliseum Corp, 12 NW2d 90, 93 (Neb 1943); Ingersoll v Onondaga Hockey Club, 245 AD 137, 281 NYS 505, 506 (1935); Rich v Madison Square Garden Corp, 149 Misc 123, 266 NYS 288, 289 (Sup Ct 1933), *affd without opinion*, 241 AD 722, 270 NYS 915 (1934); Aaser v City of Charlotte, 265 NC 494, 144 SE2d 610, 614 (1965); James v Rhode Island Auditorium, Inc, 60 RI 405, 199 A 293, 295 (1938); *see generally* §§6.02, 8.01.

The fact that injuries infrequently occur does not eliminate the club's duty of care. Riley v Chicago Cougars Hockey Club, Inc, 100 Ill App 3d 664, 427 NE2d 290, 293 (1981).

One court held that an owner's duty of care may be delegated to a lessee under provisions in the lease. Riley v Chicago Cougars Hockey Club, Inc, 100 Ill App 3d 664, 427 NE2d 290, 293 (1981).

97 Lemoine v Springfield Hockey Assn, 307 Mass 102, 29 NE2d 716, 718 (1940).

98 Riley v Chicago Cougars Hockey Club, Inc, 100 Ill App 3d 664, 427 NE2d 290, 293-94 (1981).

99 *Id.*

100 Shurman v Fresno Ice Rink, Inc, 91 Cal App 2d 469, 205 P2d 77, 81 (1949); James v Rhode Island Auditorium, Inc, 60 RI 405, 199 A 293, 298 (1938).

101 *See* Shurman v Fresno Ice Rink, Inc, 91 Cal App 2d 469, 205 P2d 77, 81 (1949).

club breached a duty of care in a particular case because the court, not the hockey industry, is the final arbiter of what type of care is reasonable.[102]

Most courts have held that hockey clubs must provide a reasonable amount of screening to protect spectators sitting in their seats from being injured by pucks which are hit into the stands.[103] In addition, there may be a duty to warn of the dangers of being hit by a puck in the unprotected areas of the stands.[104]

A proprietor's warnings of the danger may not be sufficient to satisfy its duty of reasonable care.[105] In *Shurman v Fresno Ice Rink, Inc*, the court held that the facility may have been negligent even though it posted warning signs because the plaintiffs, who were unfamiliar with hockey, asked for the "best seats" and they were directed to seats in an unprotected area.[106]

Nevertheless, several New York courts have held that hockey clubs were not liable where a spectator sitting in an area without a protective net was hit by a puck.[107] They reasoned that the clubs breached no duty of care by failing to take safety precautions because the danger of being hit by a puck was well-known.[108] In fact, one court held that a club had no duty to inquire whether patrons were aware of the dangers of being hit by a puck.[109]

A hockey rink proprietor was not entitled to summary judgment in a case where a spectator on her way back to her seat after purchasing refreshments was hit by a puck because there was no showing that the proprietor took

---

102 Tite v Omaha Coliseum Corp, 12 NW2d 90, 95 (Neb 1943); Shurman v Fresno Ice Rink, Inc, 91 Cal App 2d 469, 205 P2d 77, 81 (1949); James v Rhode Island Auditorium, Inc, 60 RI 405, 199 A 293, 298 (1938).

Industry practice cannot be allowed to set the standard for reasonable conduct because what is common may be unreasonably dangerous. Uline Ice, Inc v Sullivan, 187 F2d 82, 84 (DC Cir 1950); *see also* §§1.01, 8.01.

103 Uline Ice, Inc v Sullivan, 187 F2d 82, 84 (DC Cir 1950); Shanney v Boston Madison Square Garden Corp, 296 Mass 168, 5 NE2d 1, 2 (1936); *but see* §9.16.

In one recent case, a spectator who was sitting in the first row of the balcony, an area with no safety protection, recovered $90,000 after he was hit in the head by a puck. *See* Riley v Chicago Cougars Hockey Club, Inc, 100 Ill App 3d 664, 427 NE2d 290, 293 (1981).

104 Uline Ice, Inc v Sullivan, 187 F2d 82, 84 (DC Cir 1950); Shanney v Boston Madison Square Garden Corp, 296 Mass 168, 5 NE2d 1, 2 (1936). The *Uline* court also held that it was a jury question whether additional screening should be provided even though some spectators do not like this obstruction of their view of the game. *See* 187 F2d at 84.

105 Shurman v Fresno Ice Rink, Inc, 91 Cal App 2d 469, 205 P2d 77, 80-81 (1949).

106 *Id.*

107 Ingersoll v Onondaga Hockey Club, 245 AD 137, 281 NYS 505, 508 (1935); Hammel v Madison Square Garden Corp, 156 Misc 311, 279 NYS 815, 816 (Sup Ct 1935); *see generally* §9.16.

108 Ingersoll v Onondaga Hockey Club, 245 AD 137, 281 NYS 505, 508 (1935); Hammel v Madison Square Garden Corp, 156 Misc 311, 279 NYS 815, 816 (Sup Ct 1935); *see generally* §9.16.

109 *See* Ingersoll v Onondaga Hockey Club, 245 AD 137, 281 NYS 505, 508 (1935).

any precautions to prevent patrons standing in the aisles from being hit by pucks.[110] Reasonable care may require the proprietor to protect patrons who are moving in the aisles because their attention is not directed toward the game and, therefore, they may not see pucks hit in their direction.[111]

Although it is foreseeable that pucks will go into the stands, it is not reasonably foreseeable for other objects to go from the rink into the spectator sections of the stadium.[112] In *Rich v Madison Square Garden Corp*, one player *body checked* another player and as a result, a hockey stick went into the stands and injured a spectator.[113] The court held that the owner of the rink was not responsible because there is no liability for failing to eliminate a danger which was not reasonably foreseeable and this accident was not reasonably foreseeable.[114]

Hockey spectators have also been injured by the conduct of other spectators. However, the operator of the hockey facility is liable for these injuries only if it knew or should have known of the danger, but failed to act prudently.[115] In *Aaser v City of Charlotte*, a spectator was hit by a puck shot by a group of boys in a stadium corridor. The court held that the plaintiff could not recover from the stadium owner because there was no showing that the owner knew or should have known[116] of the danger and, therefore, could not have taken steps to avoid it.[117]

Hockey clubs may be liable for the wrongful acts of their players.[118] In *M.J. Uline Co v Cashdan*,[119] a hockey player raised his stick above his head and attempted to hit an opposing player, but missed, and instead struck a spectator. The spectator sued the player's employer, arguing that the assault was within the scope of the player's employment. The court held that the violent act was within the player's scope of employment if the player was motivated, at least in part, by trying to win the game or make it interesting.[120] However, if the player struck the blow only in anger and if he was completely

---

110 Parsons v National Dairy Cattle Congress, 277 NW2d 620, 624 (Iowa 1979).

111 *Id* 625. A patron's view of the game may also be obscured when walking to a concession stand. *Id*.

112 Rich v Madison Square Garden Corp, 149 Misc 123, 266 NYS 288, 289 (Sup Ct 1933), *aff'd without opinion*, 241 AD 722, 270 NYS 915 (1934).

113 *Id*.

114 *Id*.

115 Aaser v City of Charlotte, 265 NC 494, 144 SE2d 610, 615 (1965).

116 There was evidence that the boys had been playing in that area for less than five minutes. *Id*.

117 *Id*.

118 M.J. Uline Co v Cashdan, 171 F2d 132 (DC Cir 1948); *see also* §8.01.

119 171 F2d 132 (DC Cir 1948).

120 *Id* 133.

indifferent to his work at that time, his employer was not liable for his acts.[121]

§8.06   Horse Racing

Racetrack operators are not insurers of their patrons' safety.[122] However, they must exercise reasonable care under the circumstances.[123] In several cases, injured spectators did not recover because there was no showing that the facility knew or should have known of the danger and failed to act prudently.[124]

A racetrack's compliance with statutes and safety regulations is not dispositive evidence that the track was not negligent.[125] However, such evidence is relevant to the issue of whether the track breached a duty of care.[126] In *Christou v Arlington Park — Washington Park Race Tracks Corp*,[127] a patron was pushed into a plate glass door at the clubhouse and was injured when his body went partially through the glass. The court held that the race-track facility should have been allowed to show that there was no legal requirement to use safety glass in the clubhouse door.[128] Indeed, the facility

---

121 *Id* 133-34.

122 Clark v Monroe County Fair Assn, 203 Iowa 1107, 212 NW 163, 165 (1927); Cale v Johnson, 177 Kan 576, 280 P2d 588, 591 (1955); Morrison v Union Park Assn, 129 Me 88, 149 A 804, 805 (1930); Maryland State Fair v Henderson, 164 Md 507, 165 A 698, 700 (1933); Phillips v Butte Jockey Club & Fair Assn, 46 Mont 338, 127 P 1011, 1012 (1912); Cofone v Narragansett Racing Assn, 103 RI 345, 237 A2d 717, 720 (1968); Kane v Burrillville Racing Assn, 73 RI 264, 54 A2d 401, 403 (1947).

123 Clark v Monroe County Fair Assn, 203 Iowa 1107, 212 NW 163, 165 (1927); Cale v Johnson, 177 Kan 576, 280 P2d 588, 591 (1955); Morrison v Union Park Assn, 129 Me 88, 149 A 804, 805 (1930); Maryland State Fair v Henderson, 164 Md 507, 165 A 698, 700 (1933); Phillips v Butte Jockey Club & Fair Assn, 46 Mont 338, 127 P 1011, 1013 (1912); Redmond v National Horse Show Assn, 78 Misc 383, 138 NYS 364, 365 (1912); Hallyburton v Burke County Fair Assn, 119 NC 526, 26 SE 114, 115 (1896); Cofone v Narragansett Racing Assn, 103 RI 345, 237 A2d 717, 720 (1968); Kane v Burrillville Racing Assn, 73 RI 264, 54 A2d 401, 403 (1947); *see generally* §§6.02, 8.01.

124 Maryland State Fair v Henderson, 164 Md 507, 165 A 698, 700 (1933) (fell on a piece of wire); Phillips v Butte Jockey Club & Fair Assn, 46 Mont 338, 127 P 1011, 1013 (1912) (tripped on a nail in the grandstand).

125 Christou v Arlington Park — Washington Park Race Tracks Corp, 104 Ill App 3d 257, 432 NE2d 920, 924 (1982).

126 *Id.*

127 *Id.*

128 *Id.* The state of the law at the time of the trial, in contrast to at the time of the accident, may be relevant where it can be shown that the purpose of a statute enacted after the accident was to eliminate that hazard. However, the failure to enact a statute can rarely be shown to be due to the absence of danger and, therefore, such evidence has been excluded at trial. *Id.* Accordingly, the court held that it was irrelevant that the Illinois legislature did not require existing buildings to install safety glass. *Id.*

should have been permitted to introduce the applicable statutes to prove this point.[129]

It is well-known that horses may become unmanageable.[130] Accordingly, the racetrack must provide safety barriers of sufficient height to protect spectators from horses attempting to go into the grandstand.[131] In addition, the racetrack must provide sufficiently well-constructed gates around the track to protect spectators when the horses hit those gates.[132]

Horse racing facilities have a duty to use reasonable care in keeping and maintaining the equipment around the track in a reasonably safe condition.[133] Fire extinguishers must be reasonably placed, secured, and maintained so as to be readily accessible to one removing an extinguisher for a proper purpose, but not easily removable by inadvertent contact.[134] A facility may be negligent if the fire extinguisher can be dislodged too easily.[135] Similarly, a racetrack must take reasonable precautions to prevent an overhead door from coming down and hitting a spectator.[136]

It is inevitable that there will be some contact and jostling among the spectators at a racetrack.[137] However, the facility must take reasonable care to keep this contact to an acceptable level.[138] In one case a racetrack was found negligent in failing to station police officers at the head of the stairways because their presence would cause most spectators to exercise more restraint.[139]

The facility must take reasonable care to remove debris dropped on the floor by spectators.[140] However, it is impossible to prevent patrons from throwing debris on the ground and beyond the power of the facility to remove all debris constantly. Therefore, one court held that where the racetrack had a sufficient crew of cleaners on duty and there was no showing by the plaintiff that the

---

129 *Id.*

130 Clark v Monroe County Fair Assn, 203 Iowa 1107, 212 NW 163, 166 (1927); Redmond v National Horse Show Assn, 78 Misc 383, 138 NYS 364, 366 (Sup Ct 1912); *see also* §1.14.

131 Clark v Monroe County Fair Assn, 203 Iowa 1107, 212 NW 163, 166 (1927).

132 Redmond v National Horse Show Assn, 78 Misc 383, 138 NYS 364, 366 (Sup Ct 1912).

133 Phelps v Burrillville Racing Assn, 73 RI 84, 53 A2d 753, 755 (1947).

134 *Id.*

135 Kane v Burrillville Racing Assn, 73 RI 264, 54 A2d 401, 403 (1947).

136 Cofone v Narragansett Racing Assn, 103 RI 345, 237 A2d 717, 723 (1968).

137 Paranzino v Yonkers Raceway, 9 Misc 2d 378, 170 NYS2d 280, 282 (Sup Ct 1957).

138 *Id.*

139 *Id.*

140 McMillan v Mountain Laurel Racing Inc, 240 Pa Super 248, 367 A2d 1106, 1110 (1976).

debris had remained on the ground for an appreciable amount of time, the racetrack was not liable.[141]

Insurance

In *Totten v Underwriters at Lloyd's of London*, the court held that an accident which occurred at a horse show in another city was not within the scope of a horse stable's insurance policy which only covered accidents arising out of the ownership, maintenance, or use of the premises, or necessary or incidental operations.[142]

§8.07 Wrestling

Operators of wrestling exhibitions must exercise reasonable care for their patrons' safety.[143] However, they are not insurers[144] and, therefore, are not liable unless they fail to act reasonably.

A wrestling facility must provide reasonably safe premises.[145] For example, a facility's failure to warn spectators sitting close to the contest of the dangers of being struck by a wrestler thrown from the ring is negligence.[146] Similarly, failure to place the seats at a safe distance from the ring to protect spectators from being hit by a wrestler knocked out of the ring is also negligence.[147]

However, a facility is not required to take action which will unreasonably impair the enjoyment of the match by the other patrons.[148] Therefore, the court in *Pierce v Murnick* held that there was no duty to provide shields or barriers between the ring and the spectators to protect the spectators from being injured by a wrestler who was thrown out of the wrestling arena.[149]

---

141 *See* Paranzino v Yonkers Raceway, 9 Misc 2d 378, 170 NYS2d 280, 282 (Sup Ct 1957); *see also* §8.01.

142 176 Cal App 2d 440, 445, 1 Cal Rptr 520 (1959).

143 Silvia v Woodhouse, 356 Mass 119, 248 NE2d 260, 263 (1969); Pierce v Murnick, 265 NC 707, 145 SE2d 11, 12 (1965); Whitfield v Cox, 189 Va 219, 52 SE2d 72, 73-74 (1949); *see generally* §§6.02, 8.01.

144 Pierce v Murnick, 265 NC 707, 145 SE2d 11, 12 (1965); Whitfield v Cox, 189 Va 219, 52 SE2d 72, 73-74 (1949).

145 Silvia v Woodhouse, 356 Mass 119, 248 NE2d 260, 263 (1969); Whitfield v Cox, 189 Va 219, 52 SE2d 72, 75 (1949).

146 Silvia v Woodhouse, 356 Mass 119, 248 NE2d 260, 263 (1969). This danger is not so obvious that there is no duty to warn of it. *Id.*

147 *Id*; *but see* §9.23.

148 Pierce v Murnick, 265 NC 707, 145 SE2d 11, 12 (1965).

149 *Id.*

It has been noted that wrestling matches are not "quiet and dignified" affairs.[150] However, in *Whitfield v Cox*,[151] a noisy and undignified exhibition quickly became dangerous when some unknown person threw a whiskey bottle into the crowd. The court held that the wrestling facility was not negligent because there was no showing that the facility breached a duty of care.[152] Drinking was prohibited and no one knew who threw the bottle. Accordingly, there was no showing that the facility knew or should have known of the danger and failed to act prudently.[153] Similarly, in *Ulrich v Minneapolis Boxing & Wrestling Club, Inc*, the Minnesota Supreme Court held that a sponsor of a wrestling match was not negligent in failing to provide a reasonably safe exit from the ring for a referee where there was no showing that the sponsor knew or should have known that a spectator would come up to the referee on his way out and touch him, inciting the referee to hit the spectator.[154]

There have been numerous incidents in which a wrestler or a referee struck and injured a spectator. Generally, the courts have held that if the promoter employed the wrestler or referee, the promoter may be liable, either under respondeat superior for the employee's negligence or for its own negligence in hiring an employee with dangerous tendencies.[155] However, if the employee had not previously exhibited dangerous behavior, the promoter may not be liable under respondeat superior because striking a spectator may be outside the scope of the employee's employment.[156]

§8.08 Miscellaneous Activities

Basketball

A spectator injured by a basketball thrown into the stands either negligently or intentionally by a player may recover from the player's employer.[157]

Demolition Derby

In *Khanoyan v All American Sports Enterprises, Inc*,[158] a spectator at a

---

150 Whitfield v Cox, 189 Va 219, 52 SE2d 72, 75 (1949).

151 *Id.*

152 *Id.*

153 *Id.*

154 268 Minn 328, 129 NW2d 288, 292 (1964).

155 129 NW2d at 293; Caldwell v Maupin, 61 Ohio App 161, 22 NE2d 454, 454-55 (1939); Langness v Ketonen, 42 Wash 2d 394, 255 P2d 551, 555 (1953); *see also* §8.01.

156 Wiersma v City of Long Beach, 41 Cal App 2d 8, 106 P2d 45, 49 (1940); *but see* Langness v Ketonen, 42 Wash 2d 394, 255 P2d 551, 555 (1953).

157 McFatridge v Harlem Globe Trotters, 69 NM 271, 365 P2d 918 (1961); *see also* §8.01.

158 229 Cal App 2d 785, 40 Cal Rptr 596 (1964).

demolition derby, an automobile contest where the winner was the driver of the last vehicle still in operating condition, was hit by a portion of a fan blade from one of the colliding vehicles. The court held that the plaintiff was entitled to a res ipsa loquitur jury instruction because a spectator sitting in an area designated for viewing this event is not ordinarily injured by a flying object in the absence of someone's negligence.[159] However, the court also held that the defendant was allowed to introduce evidence of the absence of prior accidents at this facility.[160]

Dog Racing

Operators of dog racing exhibitions are not insurers of their patrons' safety.[161] However, they generally must exercise reasonable care under the circumstances.[162] Accordingly, they may be negligent where they created a slippery condition on the stairs in a spectator area.[163]

Dog racing exhibitors are not liable where they did not act unreasonably.[164] In *Carr v Mile High Kennel Club*,[165] a spectator, while on his way to place a bet, was struck and tripped by another patron. The court held that the exhibitor was not liable because there was no showing that it knew or should have known of this altercation and failed to take reasonable steps to prevent it.[166]

It has also been held that owners and operators of dog racing facilities have no duty to remove known dangers.[167] In *Gray v Mobile Greyhound Park, Ltd*,[168] a woman slipped on a plastic cup near a ticket window. The court noted that patrons generally should know that debris accumulates on the walkways during a sporting event and, therefore, the exhibitor has no duty to remove it.[169] However, the court did concede that at some point it would be unreasonable for the defendant not to clean up the debris.[170]

---

159 40 Cal Rptr at 601.

160 *Id* 602.

161 Wells v Palm Beach Kennel Club, 35 So 2d 720, 721 (Fla 1948).

162 Gray v Mobile Greyhound Park, Ltd, 370 So 2d 1384, 1388 (Ala 1979); *see also* Wells v Palm Beach Kennel Club, 35 So 2d 720, 721 (Fla 1948) (there is a continuous duty to look after the safety of the patrons); *see generally* **§§6.02, 8.01**.

163 Arnold v Miami Beach Kennel Club, 88 So 2d 617, 617 (Fla 1956).

164 Gray v Mobile Greyhound Park, Ltd, 370 So 2d 1384, 1388 (Ala 1979); Carr v Mile High Kennel Club, 125 Colo 251, 242 P2d 238, 239-40 (1952).

165 125 Colo 251, 242 P2d 238 (1952).

166 242 P2d 239-40.

167 Gray v Mobile Greyhound Park, Ltd, 370 So 2d 1384, 1388 (Ala 1979).

168 *Id.*

169 *Id; see also* **§8.01**.

170 370 So 2d 1384, 1389 (Ala 1979).

Golf

A golfing establishment is not an insurer of the safety of spectators at a golf tournament.[171] However, it has a duty to exercise reasonable care.[172] Further, if a company holds itself out to the public as being the operator of the golf course and if the injured spectator believed that the company was the operator, that company may be liable for the operator's negligence even though a different, undisclosed firm actually operated the premises.[173]

In *Duffy v Midlothian Country Club*, the court held that an operator of a golf club may be negligent in placing a concession stand in an area between two fairways because it was foreseeable that a golf ball would strike a spectator who was in that area to purchase some refreshments.[174] Indeed, in that case the spectator received a jury verdict of $450,000.[175]

However, there is no liability where the operator did not act unreasonably.[176] For example, in *Thompson v Sunset Country Club*, the country club was not liable where a spectator, while walking down a grassy slope, kicked a rock which was concealed by the grass and injured herself.[177] The operator had no knowledge of the rock and it was not unreasonable to fail to remove all obstacles on the course.[178]

The president of a golf club is not vicariously liable for the club's negligence.[179] Therefore, unless the corporate officer personally breached a duty of care, he or she is entitled to judgment in his favor.[180]

Snowmobiles

The sponsor of a snowmobile race must exercise reasonable care to protect spectators at the race.[181] In *Boetsch v Rockland Jaycees*,[182] a riderless snowmobile crossed over a snowbank and struck a spectator who was standing near a curve

---

171 Thompson v Sunset Country Club, 227 SW2d 523, 525 (Mo Ct App 1950).

172 Duffy v Midlothian Country Club, 92 Ill App 3d 193, 415 NE2d 1099, 1103 (1980); Thompson v Sunset Country Club, 227 SW2d 523, 525 (Mo Ct App 1950); *see generally* §§6.02, 8.01.

173 Buck v Clauson's Inn at Coonamesett, Inc, 349 Mass 612, 211 NE2d 349, 351 (1965).

174 92 Ill App 3d 193, 415 NE2d 1099, 1104 (1980).

175 *See* Duffy v Midlothian Country Club, No 75 L 12096 (Cook County, Ill, Aug 1983) *reported in* 69 ABAJ 1616 (1983) (spectator lost an eye when she was struck by errant golf ball).

176 Thompson v Sunset Country Club, 227 SW2d 523, 525 (Mo Ct App 1950).

177 *Id* 526.

178 *Id.*

179 Buck v Clauson's Inn at Coonamesett, Inc, 349 Mass 612, 211 NE2d 349, 351 (1965).

180 *Id.*

181 Boetsch v Rockland Jaycees, 288 A2d 102, 105 (Me 1972); *see generally* §§6.02, 8.01.

182 288 A2d 102, 105 (Me 1972).

in the racetrack, in an area marked *off limits* in a race brochure. However, this area was not designated off limits by any visible markings such as a sign or a rope and no one policed this area. In addition, several other spectators were standing in this area, an indication that it was not generally understood that this area was truly off limits.[183] Accordingly, the court held that the sponsor may have been negligent in allowing spectators to remain in this area.[184]

Soap Box Derby

Sponsors and operators of soap box derbies owe a duty of reasonable care to spectators of those events.[185] Accordingly, they may be negligent in allowing a race where the grade was too steep,[186] spectators stood in front of rope barricades rather than behind them,[187] the drivers of the vehicles were not required to demonstrate proper skills,[188] the participants used flimsy vehicles which were improperly inspected,[189] and there was not a sufficient safety zone to allow the cars to stop safely.[190] In addition, one court held that their duty of care was not necessarily discharged merely because they provided for police supervision.[191]

---

183 *Id.*

184 *Id* 106.

185 Macon Telegraph Publishing Co v Graden, 79 Ga App 230, 53 SE2d 371, 374 (1949); *see also* Cummings v General Motors Corp, 146 Conn 443, 151 A2d 884, 888 (1959); *see generally* §§6.02, 8.01.
This duty of reasonable care applies even if the event is held on public property. Watford v Evening Star Newspaper Co, 211 F2d 31, 33 (DC Cir 1954); Murphy v Jarvis Chevrolet Co, 310 Ill App 534, 34 NE2d 872 (1941).

186 Cummings v General Motors Corp, 146 Conn 443, 151 A2d 884, 887 (1959).

187 Watford v Evening Star Newspaper Co, 211 F2d 31, 35 (DC Cir 1954).

188 Macon Telegraph Publishing Co v Graden, 79 Ga App 230, 53 SE2d 371, 374 (1949).

189 *Id.*

190 Cummings v General Motors Corp, 146 Conn 443, 151 A2d 884, 888 (1959).

191 Watford v Evening Star Newspaper Co, 211 F2d 31, 35 (DC Cir 1954).

Traditional Defenses

9

§9.01 Introduction

There have been two traditional defenses in cases involving accidents in sports and recreational activities: assumption of the risk[1] and contributory negligence.[2] The defendant has the burden of proving both of these defenses.[3]

The major distinction drawn between contributory negligence and assumption of risk is that the former is tested by an objective standard, i.e., whether the plaintiff failed to act as a reasonable person,[4] while the latter is tested by a subjective standard, i.e., whether this plaintiff actually understood and voluntarily accepted the risk of danger.[5]

The distinction between the two defenses has not always been kept clear.[6] In fact, one court noted that the distinction between assumption of the risk and contributory negligence "is slight [and] often difficult to pinpoint."[7] It has even been held that these two defenses were so similar that it was not error to give jury instructions on only one of them.[8]

Even in jurisdictions where the distinction between the defenses has been noted, it is understood that in some areas the defenses overlap.[9] For example, where the plaintiff unreasonably[10] encounters a known risk, he or she may be contributorily negligent and assume the risk of injury.[11] However, if the plaintiff reasonably encounters a known risk, he or she is not contributorily

---

[1] *See* §§9.02, 9.03.

[2] *See* §9.04.

[3] Wilkinson v Hartford Accident & Indem Co, 411 So 2d 22, 24 (La 1982); Hooper v Mougin, 263 Md 630, 284 A2d 236, 238 (1971); Adam Dante Corp v Sharpe, 483 SW2d 452, 456 (Tex 1972).

[4] Kennedy v Providence Hockey Club, Inc, 119 RI 70, 376 A2d 329, 333 (1977).

[5] *See* Berman v Philadelphia Bd of Educ, 456 A2d 545, 550 (Pa Super Ct 1983) (notes the objective and subjective standards which are applied); Kennedy v Providence Hockey Club, Inc, 119 RI 70, 376 A2d 329, 332 (1977); *see generally* Dorry v Lafluer, 399 So 2d 559, 563 (La 1981) (plaintiff did not assume the risk of injury from a puddle on the floor of roller skating rink unless he knew of the existence of the puddle in the area where he fell; his knowledge of puddles in another area of the rink is not enough to prove his assumption of the risk).

[6] Woods, *The Trend Toward Comparative Fault*, 20 Trial 16, 16 (Nov 1984) (it is also difficult to distinguish these defenses from product misuse); *see also* Note, *Contributory Negligence And Assumption Of Risk—The Case For Their Merger*, 56 Minn L Rev 47 (1971).

[7] *See* Hooper v Mougin, 263 Md 630, 284 A2d 236, 238 (1971).

[8] *See* Dorobek v Ride-A-While Stables, 262 Cal App 2d 554, 68 Cal Rptr 774, 778 (1968); Eisenhart v Loveland Skiing Corp, 33 Colo App 120, 517 P2d 466 (1973).

[9] Segoviano v Housing Auth, 143 Cal App 3d 162, 167, 191 Cal Rptr 578 (1983).

[10] E.g., the danger of proceeding exceeds the benefits to be derived.

[11] Segoviano v Housing Auth, 143 Cal App 3d 162, 167, 191 Cal Rptr 578 (1983); Provence v Doolin, 91 Ill App 3d 271, 414 NE2d 786, 794 (1980).

negligent, even though he or she may assume the risk.[12] Accordingly, a plaintiff who voluntarily and unreasonably assumes the risk of danger is guilty of contributory negligence and his or her recovery will be eliminated or restricted, even in a state which has abolished the defense of assumption of the risk.[13]

The courts have not yet reached unanimity regarding whether a plaintiff's assumption of the risk is a complete bar to recovery in a comparative negligence state. The Rhode Island Supreme Court recently held that assumption of the risk was a complete defense.[14] However, there is support for the contrary view.[15]

The courts have repeatedly held that the plaintiff's contributory negligence[16] and assumption of the risk[17] are questions of fact to be decided by the fact-finder at a trial, not by a court on motions for a summary judgment or a directed verdict. In addition, the comparison of the plaintiff's and defendant's negligence is rarely decided correctly as a matter of law.[18] This is especially so where the negligence of a minor is being compared with the negligence of an adult.[19]

However, assumption of the risk and contributory negligence may be decided as a matter of law where all reasonable understandings of the facts show that they are applicable.[20] Accordingly, in an appropriate case the defendant is entitled to summary judgment.[21]

The defendant's failure to tender appropriate jury instructions regarding these defenses generally waives its right to argue that such instructions should

---

12 However, if the plaintiff's conduct was not unreasonable, there are strong policy reasons which militate against considering this conduct a defense. *See* Segoviano v Housing Auth, 143 Cal App 3d 162, 167, 191 Cal Rptr 578 (1983); *see generally* §9.02.

13 *See* Hale v O'Neill, 492 P2d 101, 103 (Alaska 1971); Provence v Doolin, 91 Ill App 3d 271, 414 NE2d 786, 794 (1980); *see generally* Stephenson v College Misericordia, 376 F Supp 1324, 1327 (MD Pa 1974) (where the two doctrines overlap, assumption of risk is merged into contributory negligence).

14 *See* Kennedy v Providence Hockey Club, Inc, 119 RI 70, 376 A2d 329, 333 (1977).

15 *See* Manassa v New Hampshire Ins Co, 332 So 2d 34, 36 (Fla Dist Ct App 1976); *see also* Segoviano v Housing Auth, 143 Cal App 3d 162, 167, 191 Cal Rptr 578 (1983).

16 Dibortolo v Metropolitan School Dist, 440 NE2d 506, 511 (Ind Ct App 1982); Jackson v Livingston Country Club, Inc, 55 AD2d 1045, 391 NYS2d 234, 235 (1977); *see also* Haddock v Smithson, 30 NC App 228, 226 SE2d 411, 414, *cert denied*, 290 NC 776, 229 SE2d 32 (1976) (plaintiff was mentally retarded).

17 Dibortolo v Metropolitan School Dist, 440 NE2d 506, 511 (Ind Ct App 1982); Hooper v Mougin, 263 Md 630, 284 A2d 236, 238 (1971); Jackson v Livingston Country Club, Inc, 55 AD2d 1045, 391 NYS2d 234, 235 (1977).

18 Cirillo v City of Milwaukee, 34 Wis 2d 705, 150 NW2d 460, 465 (1967).

19 150 NW2d at 465-66.

20 Simmons v Wexler, 94 Cal App 3d 1007, 1012, 156 Cal Rptr 810 (1979).

21 *See* Benjamin v Deffet Rentals, Inc, 66 Ohio St 2d 86, 419 NE2d 883 (1981).

have been given.[22] In addition, if the defendant was unable to produce evidence of any facts supporting these defenses during the trial, it was not error for the court to refuse to instruct the jury on these issues.[23]

Defenses

§9.02   Assumption of the Risk

Plaintiffs who voluntarily assume a risk of harm arising out of the conduct of the defendant usually cannot recover when injury from that harm actually results.[24] This defense, derived from the maxim *volenti non fit injuria*, i.e., no wrong is done to one who consents,[25] is usually labeled assumption of the risk.

Judge Cardozo described this defense, in a classical fashion, in *Murphy v Steeplechase Amusement Co*, where the plaintiff was injured on an amusement park ride:

> One who takes part in such a sport accepts the dangers that inhere in it so far as they are obvious and necessary ... The antics of the clown are not the paces of the cloistered cleric. The rough and boisterous joke, the horseplay of the crowd, evokes its own guffaws, but they are not

---

[22] Ogg v City of Springfield, 121 Ill App 3d 25, 458 NE2d 1331, 1338 (1984).

[23] Willis v YMCA, 28 NY2d 375, 270 NE2d 717, 321 NYS2d 895, 897 (1971).

[24] *See* Restatement (Second) of Torts §496A (1965); Gary v Party Time Co, 434 So 2d 338 (Fla Dist Ct App 1983); *see generally* Parsons v National Dairy Cattle Congress, 277 NW2d 620, 622 (Iowa 1979); Meistrich v Casino Arena Attractions, 31 NJ 44, 155 A2d 90 (1959); Olson v Hansen, 216 NW2d 124, 127 (Minn 1974); Note, *Utah's Inherent Risks of Skiing Act*, 1980 Utah L Rev 355, 358.
This defense has been discussed extensively by the commentators. *See, e.g.*, Bohlen, *Voluntary Assumption Of Risk*, 20 Harv L Rev 14 (1906); James, *Assumption Of Risk: Unhappy Reincarnation*, 78 Yale LJ 185 (1968); James, *Assumption Of Risk*, 61 Yale LJ 141 (1952); Wade, *The Place Of Assumption Of Risk In The Law Of Negligence*, 22 La L Rev 5 (1961).

[25] At least in the overwhelming number of jurisdictions which do not restrict the assumption of risk defense to master-servant cases. *See* Kennedy v Providence Hockey Club, Inc, 119 RI 70, 376 A2d 329, 332 (1977); *see generally* Hogenson v Service Armament Co, 77 Wash 2d 209, 461 P2d 311, 314 (1969).
The defense of assumption of the risk originally applied only to injuries received in the workplace. Felgner v Anderson, 375 Mich 23, 133 NW2d 136, 141 (1965). In some states, assumption of risk is still limited to cases involving an employment relationship or an express consent. Provence v Doolin, 91 Ill App 3d 271, 414 NE2d 786, 793 (1980); Koclanes v Hertenstein, 130 Ill App 2d 916, 266 NE2d 119, 120 (1971); Felgner v Anderson, 375 Mich 23, 133 NW2d 136, 153-54 (1965); *see also* Note, *Torts*, 41 Notre Dame Law 104 (1965).

the pleasures of tranquility. The plaintiff was not seeking a retreat for meditation. ... The timorous may stay at home.[26]

The assumption of the risk defense, which seems so intuitively just in theory, has proven extremely difficult to apply in practice. Indeed, one court described this concept as an "enigma wrapped in a mystery."[27] Justice Frankfurter once remarked:

> The phrase 'assumption of risk' is an excellent illustration of the extent to which uncritical use of words bedevils the law. A phrase begins life as a literary expression; its felicity leads to its lazy repetition; and repetition soon establishes it as a legal formula, indiscriminately used to express different and sometimes contradictory ideas.[28]

Indeed, the courts have not used this phrase to convey a consistent concept.[29] Some courts have held that assumption of the risk means that the defendant had no duty to protect the plaintiff from certain risks,[30] while other courts have held the plaintiff's own misconduct barred his or her recovery.[31] As a result, great care must be used in applying cases decided by different courts.

Although there are significant differences among the states, the assumption of the risk defense generally applies where the plaintiff voluntarily consents, whether the consent is express or implied, to accept the danger of a known and appreciated risk of the sport or recreational activity.[32]

Express Assumption of the Risk

A plaintiff may expressly assume the risk of danger either orally or in

---

26 250 NY 479, 166 NE 173, 174 (1929).

27 Blackburn v Dorta, 348 So 2d 287, 290 (Fla 1977); *see also* Turpin v Shoemaker, 427 SW2d 485, 488 (Mo 1968) (the doctrine "has been continued, if indeed not conceived, in controversy").

28 Tiller v Atlantic Coast Line RR, 318 US 54, 68 (1943) (concurring opinion).

29 *See* Restatement (Second) of Torts §496A comment c (1965); *see also* W. Keeton, D. Dobbs, R. Keeton & D. Owen, Prosser And Keeton On Torts §68 (1984).

30 O'Connell v Walt Disney World Co, 413 So 2d 444, 448 (Fla Dist Ct App 1982). This concept is sometimes also called primary assumption of risk. *See* Meistrich v Casino Arena Attractions, 31 NJ 44, 155 A2d 90 (1959).

31 *See generally* W. Keeton, D. Dobbs, R. Keeton & D. Owen, Prosser And Keeton On Torts §68 (1984). This concept is sometimes also called secondary assumption of risk. *See* Meistrich v Casino Arena Attractions, 31 NJ 44, 155 A2d 90 (1959).

32 *See* Segoviano v Housing Auth, 143 Cal App 3d 162, 167, 191 Cal Rptr 578 (1983); Turpin v Shoemaker, 427 SW2d 485, 489 (Mo 1968); Diderou v Pinecrest Dunes, Inc, 34 AD2d 672, 310 NYS2d 572, 573 (1970); *see also* Benjamin v Deffet Rentals, Inc, 66 Ohio St 2d 86, 419 NE2d 883, 886 (1981).

writing.[33] Some courts have considered this principle in terms of waiver.[34] When a participant in a recreational activity expressly volunteers to take certain chances, he or she waives the right to be free from those bodily contacts which are inherent in the chances taken.[35] Parties who rely on such an express waiver by the participant and allow a recreational activity to proceed should be protected.[36]

The manifestation of a plaintiff's express assumption of the risk, sometimes called an exculpatory agreement, is discussed extensively in other sections of this book.[37]

Implied Assumption of the Risk

A plaintiff may impliedly assume the risk of injury.[38] This arises where the plaintiff, aware of the risk created by the negligence of the defendant, proceeds voluntarily. The plaintiff's consent is implied from his or her conduct in going forward although aware of the risk.[39]

The plaintiff's actions in assuming the risk may be unreasonable or reasonable. Where the conduct is unreasonable, it is no different from contributory negligence.[40]

Where the plaintiff acted reasonably his or her conduct is not, by definition, contributory negligence.[41] Further, if the plaintiff's conduct was reasonable, there appears no legitimate basis to bar or reduce his or her recovery.[42]

---

[33] Kuehner v Green, 436 So 2d 78, 80 (Fla 1983); *see generally* V. Schwartz, Comparative Negligence §9.2, at 158-59 (1974).

A release is evidence of "actual consent" to assume the risk of injury. *See* Gary v Party Time Co, 434 So 2d 338, 339 n 3 (Fla Dist Ct App 1983).

[34] Kuehner v Green, 436 So 2d 78, 80 (Fla 1983); Hooper v Mougin, 263 Md 630, 284 A2d 236, 238 (1971).

[35] Kuehner v Green, 436 So 2d 78, 80 (Fla 1983).

[36] *Id.*

[37] *See* §§10.01-10.03.

[38] *See* Restatement (Second) of Torts §496C (1965).

[39] In contrast, express assumption of the risk is shown by the plaintiff's communication, either oral or written, that he or she will assume the risk of injury.

[40] Segoviano v Housing Auth, 143 Cal App 3d 162, 167-68, 170-72, 191 Cal Rptr 578 (1983); Isker v Gardner, 360 NW2d 468, 470 (Minn Ct App 1985); *see generally* §9.04.

[41] Segoviano v Housing Auth, 143 Cal App 3d 162, 167-68, 170-72, 191 Cal Rptr 578 (1983).

[42] Segoviano v Housing Auth, 143 Cal App 3d 162, 167-68, 170-72, 191 Cal Rptr 578 (1983) (citing cases from Florida, Maine, Minnesota, Texas and Wisconsin); O'Connell v Walt Disney World Co, 413 So 2d 444, 448 (Fla Dist Ct App 1982) (dealing with non-contact sports); Parsons v National Dairy Cattle Congress, 277 NW2d 620, 621-22 (Iowa 1979). This assumes, of course, that there is no enforceable exculpatory agreement. *See* §§10.01, 10.02.

There are, however, decisions to the contrary.[43]

One court has reasoned that if contact sports are to continue to serve a legitimate recreational function in our society, assumption of the risk must remain a viable defense to negligence actions spawned from these athletic endeavors.[44]

Products Liability

Some courts have held that a plaintiff's assumption of the risk is a defense to strict liability claims,[45] although other courts have held to the contrary.[46] It also has been held that a plaintiff's assumption of the risk is not a defense to a breach of warranty action.[47]

Recent Trend

In recent years, this defense has become disfavored and has been limited by statute[48] and court order.[49] However, this trend has not been universal and several states, spurred at least in part by court decisions limiting the defense, have enacted statutes specifying that the defense is still viable.[50]

§9.03 —Scope of the Risk Assumed

Traditionally, participants in athletic events and spectators at those events have been held to have assumed the risks of injury normally associated with

---

43 *See, e.g.*, Kennedy v Providence Hockey Club, Inc, 119 RI 70, 376 A2d 329 (1977) (contributory negligence and assumption of risk do not merge).

44 *See* Kuehner v Green, 436 So 2d 78, 79 (Fla 1983).

45 Zahrte v Sturm Ruger & Co, 709 F2d 26, 28 (9th Cir 1983) (Montana law); Kinka v Harley-Davidson Motor Co, 1975-77 Prod Liab Rep (CCH) ¶7665, at 14, 821 (Ill App Ct 1976); Benjamin v Deffet Rentals, Inc, 66 Ohio St 2d 86, 419 NE2d 883, 885 n 4 (1981); Richards v Marlow, 347 So 2d 281, 284 (La Ct App), *writ denied*, 350 So 2d 676 (La 1977); *see also* §7.02.

46 Kennedy v Providence Hockey Club, Inc, 119 RI 70, 376 A2d 329, 333 (1977); *see also* §7.02.

47 Kennedy v Providence Hockey Club, Inc, 119 RI 70, 376 A2d 329, 333 (1977); *see also* §7.05.

48 *See, e.g.*, NY Civ Prac Law §1411 (McKinney 1976); Or Rev Stat §18.475 (1983).

49 *See* Blair v Mt Hood Meadows Dev Corp, 291 Or 293, 630 P2d 827, 831, *modified on other grounds*, 291 Or 703, 634 P2d 241 (1981).

50 Pa Cons Stat Ann tit 42, §7102 (Purdon 1982); Utah Code Ann §78-27-53 (Supp 1983); Vt Stat Ann tit 12, §1037 (Supp 1984) (a person who takes part in any sport accepts as a matter of law the dangers that inhere therein insofar as they are obvious and necessary).

the sport.[51] However, they did not assume the risk of injury from fellow participants and spectators who acted in an unexpected or unsportsmanlike manner.[52]

Several courts have held that a plaintiff does not assume the risk of another's negligence.[53] For example, in *De Gooyer v Harkness*, the court held that an athlete who knew he would be given an electrical shock as part of an initiation rite could assume every proper precaution for his safety would be taken; he did not assume the risk of negligence by others in administering this ritual.[54] However, such broad statements as to the applicability of this defense are misleading. As the discussion in the preceding sections reveals, the assumption of the risk defense is grounded upon the plaintiff's actual understanding of the risk of danger and his or her voluntary acceptance of that risk.[55]

Accordingly, it is imperative to define precisely what risk the plaintiff actually assumed. Defendants will argue that the risk assumed should be defined broadly; plaintiffs will argue that the risk assumed should be defined narrowly. Therefore, an uncritical application of this defense is destined to result in injustice.

The case of *Rutter v Northeastern Beaver County School District*[56] illustrates the problem of defining what risk was actually assumed by the plaintiff. In that case the plaintiff, a high school student, was blinded after being struck in the eye by a fellow football player during spring practice. The plaintiff sued, among others, his coaches for their failure to supervise this practice and their failure to provide protective equipment. The trial court held that the plaintiff

---

51 Niemczyk v Burlson, 538 SW2d 737, 742 (Mo Ct App 1976); Cadieux v Board of Educ, 25 AD2d 579, 266 NYS2d 895, 896 (1966); McGee v Board of Educ, 16 AD2d 99, 226 NYS2d 329, 321 (1962); Hooper v Mougin, 263 Md 630, 284 A2d 236, 240 (1971) (does not assume unusual or abnormal risks of sports activity).

There has been extensive commentary in the law journals. *See, e.g.,* Note, *Tort Liability In Professional Sports*, 44 Alb L Rev 696 (1980); Comment, *Assumption Of Risk And Vicarious Liability In Personal Injury Actions Brought By Professional Athletes*, 1980 Duke LJ 742; Note, *Professional Sports And Tort Liability: A Victory For The Intentionally Injured Player*, 1980 Det CL Rev 687; *Torts*, 15 Gonz L Rev 867 (1980); Note, *Compensating Injured Professional Athletes: The Mystique Of Sport Versus Traditional Tort Principles*, 55 NYUL Rev 971 (1980); Scalf & Robinson, *Injuries Arising Out Of Amateur And Professional Sports: Viability Of The Assumption Of Risk Defense*, 27 Def LJ 419 (1978).

52 Kuehner v Green, 436 So 2d 78, 80 (Fla 1983); Bourque v Duplechin, 331 So 2d 40, 42 (La Ct App 1976); *see generally* ch 2.

53 *See, e.g.,* Jackson v Livingston Country Club, 55 AD2d 1045, 391 NYS2d 234, 235 (1977) (golf); Humbyrd v Spurlock, 345 SW2d 499, 502 (Mo Ct App 1961) (roller rink); Carabba v Anacortes School Dist No 103, 72 Wash 2d 939, 435 P2d 936, 948 (1967) (football); *see also* Proehl, *Tort Liability of Teachers*, 12 Vand L Rev 723, 747 (1959).

54 70 SD 26, 13 NW2d 815, 817 (1944).

55 *See* §§9.01, 9.02.

56 496 Pa 590, 437 A2d 1198, 1205 (1981). This case was commented upon in Note, *Tort Law*, 21 Duq L Rev 815 (1983).

assumed the risk of all injuries related to training for and playing football and granted the defendants' motion for a nonsuit. However, a plurality of the Pennsylvania Supreme Court noted that it was possible that the plaintiff only assumed the risk of injuries related to training for and playing football while under the direction of coaches who furnished watchful supervision and protective equipment when needed.[57] Accordingly, the plaintiff was entitled to have a jury determine the scope of the risk assumed.[58]

Actual Knowledge

It is usually held that this defense applies only where the plaintiff had actual knowledge of risk of injury[59] because one cannot meaningfully consent unless one knows the real danger.[60] Therefore, it is irrelevant what the plaintiff "should have"[61] known.

Nevertheless, a purely subjective standard does not ignore the realities of life. Although the appropriate test is what this plaintiff realized, the testimony of the plaintiff is not dispositive.[62] The taking of an oath is not always followed by truthful testimony and, therefore, a jury is not required to believe the plaintiff's version of what risks were assumed. For example, in *Fuller v State*,[63] a boy dove into shallow water injuring himself. Although he testified that he did not think there was any danger, this testimony was properly disbelieved in light of the evidence that he was originally afraid to

---

57 496 Pa 590, 437 A2d 1198, 1205 (1981).

58 *Id; see also* Kuehner v Green, 436 So 2d 78, 80 (Fla 1983).

59 Chase v Shasta Lake Union School Dist, 259 Cal App 2d 612, 66 Cal Rptr 517, 519-20 (1968); Anderson v Heron Engg Co, 198 Colo 391, 604 P2d 674, 678 (1979); Kennedy v Providence Hockey Club, Inc, 119 RI 70, 376 A2d 329, 332 (1977).

The test of whether a user of a product has assumed the risk is also subjective. In determining whether the risk was assumed, the fact-finder should consider all applicable factors such as the user's age, experience, knowledge, and understanding, as well as the obviousness of the defect and the danger it poses. *See* Sipari v Villa Country Club, 63 Ill App 3d 985, 380 NE2d 819, 824 (1978).

60 Turpin v Shoemaker, 427 SW2d 485, 490 (Mo 1968) (doctrine not applied when plaintiff was fatally injured in "quick draw" gun contest because he did not know his opponent's gun was loaded).

The plaintiff's actual knowledge of the risk is rarely susceptible to proof by direct evidence. Curran v Green Hills Country Club, 24 Cal App 3d 507, 101 Cal Rptr 158, 160 (1972).

61 Anderson v Heron Engg Co, 198 Colo 391, 604 P2d 674, 678 (1979). The presumptions regarding whether a child is contributorily negligent do not apply by analogy. Berman v Philadelphia Bd of Educ, 456 A2d 545, 550 (Pa Super Ct 1983).

62 McPherson v Sunset Speedway, Inc, 594 F2d 711, 715 (8th Cir 1979); Curran v Green Hills Country Club, 24 Cal App 3d 507, 101 Cal Rptr 158, 160 (1972); Dorry v Lafluer, 399 So 2d 559, 563 (La 1981) (one need not take plaintiff's disclaimer of knowledge of the risk at face value).

63 51 Cal App 3d 942, 125 Cal Rptr 586 (1975).

dive and a companion had already struck the bottom of the ocean with his feet when he dove into this water.[64] It has also been held, for the same reason, that a plaintiff assumed the risks of injury which were "common knowledge."[65] In any event, proof of this issue can be complicated if the injury caused the plaintiff to suffer retrograde amnesia of the events preceding the accident.[66]

Voluntary Acceptance

The assumption of the risk defense is grounded upon the plaintiff's voluntary acceptance of the risk.[67] Generally, a person's participation in a sporting activity shows a willingness to submit to the physical contact which is permitted by the rules of the activity.[68] However, participation usually does not show consent to physical contact which is prohibited by rules of the game, even if the participant knows that other players have a history of using excessive force.[69]

The plaintiff's acceptance of a risk is not voluntary if the defendant's tortious conduct has left him or her no reasonable alternative course of conduct if he or she wishes to exercise a right or privilege.[70] For example, in *Rutter v Northeastern Beaver County School District*,[71] a plurality of the Pennsylvania Supreme Court held that a high school student trying out for a football team is probably exercising a right or privilege connected with his schooling of which his coaches have no right to deprive him. Therefore, the coaches who required, as a condition of playing on the high school football team, a player to participate in a practice session in which he was not allowed to wear protective equipment may have eliminated the *voluntariness* of the player's actions and, therefore, the player may not have accepted the risk of injury.[72] A student may not voluntarily assume the risk of injury where he or she participated in an athletic activity because of the urgings of the coach and the pressures of pride and team spirit[73] or as part

---

[64] 125 Cal Rptr at 595.

[65] *See* Benjamin v Deffet Rentals, Inc, 66 Ohio St 2d 86, 419 NE2d 883, 887 (1981).

[66] Chase v Shasta Lake Union School Dist, 259 Cal App 2d 612, 66 Cal Rptr 517, 520 (1968).

[67] Restatement (Second) of Torts §496E(1) (1965).

[68] Restatement (Second) of Torts §50 comment b (1965).

[69] *Id.*

[70] Restatement (Second) of Torts §496E(2) (1965).

[71] 496 Pa 590, 437 A2d 1198, 1205 (1981). This case was commented upon in Note, *Tort Law*, 21 Duq L Rev 815 (1983).

[72] 496 Pa 590, 437 A2d 1198, 1205 (1981).

[73] *See* Proehl, *Tort Liability of Teachers*, 12 Vand L Rev 723, 746 (1959).

of a physical education class.[74] A professional jockey may not voluntarily assume the risk where there is a requirement that he or she fulfill all racing engagements.[75]

The defense is not applicable where the plaintiff had no reasonable alternatives available to him or her because in that case it cannot be said that the plaintiff voluntarily assumed the risk.[76] One court held that forgoing participation in a sport was not a reasonable alternative and, therefore, the plaintiff did not assume the risk merely because he engaged in an activity although he had the option not to do so.[77]

The plaintiff's consent is to the defendant's conduct, not to the actual consequences.[78] Obviously, no rational person would consent to serious injury; however, the fact that serious injury occurred does not mean there was no consent.[79] For example, a person who willing engaged in a boxing match, but who unexpectedly died because of a blow, had no claim against the other boxer, although he had not consented to being killed.[80]

§9.04 Contributory and Comparative Negligence

Contributory negligence is conduct which falls below the standard which the plaintiff should meet for his or her own protection and which is a contributing cause of the plaintiff's injuries.[81] It frequently involves the plaintiff's inadvertent failure to notice danger.[82] However, absent notice to the contrary, a patron at a sports or recreational facility can usually assume that the premises are reasonably safe.[83]

Traditionally, a plaintiff's contributory negligence was a complete bar to recovery, even if the plaintiff was only slightly negligent and the defendant

---

74 *See generally* Keesee v Board of Educ, 37 Misc 2d 414, 235 NYS2d 300, 306 (Sup Ct 1962).

75 Martino v Park Jefferson Racing Assn, 315 NW2d 309, 314 (SD 1982).

76 Segoviano v Housing Auth, 143 Cal App 3d 162, 191 Cal Rptr 578 (1983); Restatement (Second) of Torts §496E comment c (1965).

77 *See* Segoviano v Housing Auth, 143 Cal App 3d 162, 191 Cal Rptr 578 (1983).

78 *See* McAdams v Windham, 208 Ala 492, 94 So 742 (1922) (also held defendant committed no negligence).

79 *Id.*

80 *Id.*

81 *See* Stephenson v College Misericordia, 376 F Supp 1324, 1327 (MD Pa 1974); Provence v Doolin, 91 Ill App 3d 271, 414 NE2d 786, 793 (1980); Passantino v Board of Educ, 52 AD2d 935, 383 NYS2d 639 (1976) (reversed a $1,000,000 judgment for plaintiff because of the plaintiff's contributory negligence); *see also* Ga Code §51-11-7 (1981); Restatement (Second) of Torts §463 (1965).

82 Segoviano v Housing Auth, 143 Cal App 3d 162, 167, 191 Cal Rptr 578 (1983).

83 Parker v Warren, 503 SW2d 938, 943 (Tenn Ct App 1973).

was primarily negligent.[84] This harsh rule was properly criticized and the criticism eventually was well received.

Most states now[85] apply comparative negligence principles[86] in allocating responsibility for the plaintiff's injuries. In general, comparative negligence compares the plaintiff's contributory negligence with the defendant's negligence and allows the plaintiff to recover damages only for the percentage of the injury caused by the defendant's conduct.

In the states which have adopted the *pure* form of this doctrine, the plaintiff can recover if the defendant's negligence played any part in causing the injury or aggravating the damages, even if the plaintiff was primarily at fault.[87] However, in a significant number of states, the plaintiff can recover only if his or her negligence was less than the defendant's[88] or his or

---

[84] *See* Fleming, *Forward: Comparative Negligence At Last—By Judicial Choice*, 64 Cal L Rev 239 (1976); Restatement (Second) of Torts §467 (1965).

[85] Comparative negligence was first adopted in Mississippi in 1910. *See* Woods, *The Trend Toward Comparative Fault*, 20 Trial 16, 17 (Nov 1984).

[86] *See, e.g.,* Ark Stat Ann §27-1764 (1979) (compares fault of all parties); Colo Rev Stat §13-21-111 (1974); Conn Gen Stat Ann §52-572h (West 1985); Ga Code Ann §51-11-7 (1982); Hawaii Rev Stat §663-31 (1976); Kan Stat Ann §60-258a (1983); La Civ Code Ann art 2323 (West Supp 1985); Me Rev Stat Ann tit 14, §156 (1980); Mass Gen Laws Ann ch 231, §85 (West 1985); Minn Stat Ann §604.01 (West 1984) (compares fault); Miss Code Ann §11-7-15 (1972); Mont Code Ann §§27-1-701, 27-1-702 (1979); Neb Rev Stat §25-1151 (1979); Nev Rev Stat §41.141 (1983); NH Rev Stat Ann §507:7-A (1983); NY Civ Prac Law §1411 (McKinney 1976); Ohio Rev Code Ann §2315.19 (Page 1981); Or Rev Stat §18.470 (1983); Pa Stat Ann tit 42, §7102 (Purdon 1982); RI Gen Laws §9-20-4 (Supp 1984); SD Comp Laws Ann §20-9-2 (1979); Tex Rev Civ Stat Ann art 2212a (Vernon Supp 1985); Utah Code Ann §78-27-37 (1976); Vt Stat Ann tit 12, §1036 (Supp 1984); Wash Rev Code Ann §4.22.005 (Supp 1985) (compares fault); Wis Stat Ann §895.045 (West 1983); Wyo Stat §1-1-109 (1977).

In some states, this doctrine is purely a creation of case law. *See* Kaatz v State, 572 P2d 775 (Alaska 1977); Li v Yellow Cab Co, 13 Cal 3d 804, 119 Cal Rptr 858, 532 P2d 1226 (1975); Hoffman v Jones, 280 So 2d 431 (Fla 1973); Alvis v Ribar, 85 Ill 2d 1, 421 NE2d 886 (1981); Placeb v City of Sterling Heights, 405 Mich 638, 275 NW2d 571 (1979); Scott v Rizzo, 20 NM St Bar Bull 289, 634 P2d 1234 (Feb 12, 1981); Bradley v Appalachian Power Co, 256 SE2d 879 (W Va 1979).

Only eight states have failed to adopt comparative negligence. *See* Woods, *The Trend Toward Comparative Fault*, 20 Trial 16, 17 (Nov 1984) (Alabama, Delaware, Kentucky, Maryland, North Carolina, South Carolina, Tennessee, and Virginia).

[87] *See* Woods, *The Trend Toward Comparative Fault*, 20 Trial 16, 17 (Nov 1984) (Alaska, Arizona, California, Florida, Illinois, Iowa, Louisiana, Michigan, Mississippi, New Mexico, New York, Rhode Island, Washington).

One commentator has argued that comparing fault is not well suited for most sports cases because of the difficulty of ascertaining the appropriate *fault* of a plaintiff who knowingly engaged in a game with inherent risks of injury. *See* Lambert, *Tort Law and Participant Sports*, 4 J Contemp L 211, 216 (1978). However, all human activities have inherent risks of injury and there is no a priori reason why juries cannot compare fault in sports cases if they can compare fault in all other types of activities.

[88] *See, e.g.,* Colo Rev Stat §13-21-111 (1974); Conn Gen Stat §52-572h (1985); Hawaii Rev Stat §663-31 (1976); Kan Stat Ann §60-258a (1983); Me Rev Stat Ann tit 14, §156

her negligence was slight.[89] In addition, even where the defendant's acts were wilful and wanton, it is usually held that the plaintiff's contributory negligence is compared with the defendant's conduct and some reduction of the award is made to account for the plaintiff's behavior.[90]

A handful of states still completely bar the plaintiff's recovery when he or she was contributorily negligent.[91] Indeed, in *Harrison v Montgomery County Board of Education*, Maryland's highest court recently held that a high school student who was left a quadriplegic as a result of a gymnastics accident was not entitled to any recovery because of the student's contributory negligence.[92]

Products Liability

Most courts have held that the plaintiff's contributory negligence is not a defense to strict products liability claims.[93] This is because the user or

---

(1980); Mass Gen Laws Ann ch 231, §85 (West 1985); Minn Stat Ann ch 604 (West 1984); Mont Code Ann §27-1-702 (1979); Nev Rev Stat §41.141 (1983); NH Rev Stat Ann §507:7-A (1983); Ohio Rev Code Ann §2315.19 (Page 1981); Or Rev Stat §18.470 (1983); Pa Cons Stat Ann tit 42, §7102 (Purdon 1982); Tex Rev Civ Stat Ann art 2212a (Vernon Supp 1985); Utah Code Ann §78-27-37 (1976); Vt Stat Ann tit 12, §1036 (Supp 1984); Wis Stat Ann §895.045 (West 1983); Wyo Stat §1-1-109 (1977).

89 *See, e.g.*, Neb Rev Stat §25-1151 (1979); *see also* Woods, *The Trend Toward Comparative Fault*, 20 Trial 16, 17 (Nov 1984).

90 Davis v United States, 716 F2d 418, 429 (7th Cir 1983) (citing cases indicating that this is the majority rule); *but see* Acosta v Daughtry, 268 So 2d 416, 420 (Fla Dist Ct App 1972).

91 *See* Golden v McCurry, 392 So 2d 815 (Ala 1980); Harrison v Montgomery County Bd of Educ, 295 Md 442, 456 A2d 894 (1983); McGraw v Corrin, 303 A2d 641 (Del Sup Ct 1973). In addition, Kentucky, North Carolina, South Carolina, Tennessee, Virginia, and the District of Columbia. *See* Digges & Klein, *Comparative Fault in Maryland: The Time Has Come*, 41 Md L Rev 276, 277 n 6 (1982).

92 295 Md 442, 456 A2d 894 (1983).

93 Khoder v AMF, Inc, 539 F2d 1078, 1081 (5th Cir 1976) (Louisiana law); Brenner v President and Fellows of Harvard College, No 79-1308-T (D Mass July 21, 1983) (available on Lexis); OS Stapley v Miller, 103 Ariz 556, 447 P2d 248, 253 (1968); Abbott v American Honda Motor Co, 682 SW2d 206, 209 (Tenn Ct App 1984); Belfrey v Anthony Pools, Inc, 80 Mich App 118, 262 NW2d 909, 910 (1977); Pegg v General Motors Corp, 258 Pa Super 59, 391 A2d 1074, 1084 n14 (1978); *see also* Ariz Rev Stat §12-2501 *et seq* (Supp 1984); Conn Gen Stat §52-572L (1985); *see generally* Randall v Warnaco, Inc, 677 F2d 1226, 1230 n 3 (8th Cir 1982) (North Dakota law); *but see* Stueve v American Honda Motors Co, 457 F Supp 740, 758 (D Kan 1978) (Kansas law); Butand v Suburban Marine & Sporting Goods, Inc, 555 P2d 42, 43 (Alaska 1976); Fiske v MacGregor, 464 A2d 719, 727 (RI 1983) (citing cases from other jurisdictions); *see* Davis, *Comparative Negligence, Comparative Contribution, And Equal Protection In The Trial And Settlement Of Multiple Defendant Product Cases*, 10 Ind L Rev 831 (1977); Feinberg, *The Applicability Of A Comparative Negligence Defense In A Strict Products Liability Suit*, 42 Ins Counsel J 39 (1975); Hasten, *Comparative Liability Principles: Should They Now Apply To Strict Products Liability Actions In Ohio*, 14 U Tol L Rev 1151 (1983); Schwartz, *Strict Liability And Comparative Negligence*, 42 Tenn L Rev 171 (1974); Voelker, *The Application Of Comparative Negligence To Strict Products Liability*, 59 Chi-Kent L Rev 1043 (1983); Woods, *Product Liability: Is Comparative Fault Winning The Day*, 36 Ark L Rev 360 (1983).

consumer of a product has no duty to search for or guard against the possibility of defects in the product.[94] However, a more accurate analysis of this issue is that contributory negligence may be a defense, but since the plaintiff has no duty to search for product defects, the failure to do so is not contributory negligence.

It has repeatedly been held that the defendant is entitled to prevail if the plaintiff discovered the defect, was aware of the danger, and then proceeded unreasonably to use the product.[95] In addition, the defendant is entitled to prevail if the plaintiff was injured while using the product in a fashion which was not reasonably foreseeable.[96] This means, as a practical matter, that the plaintiff may recover even if he or she took unreasonable actions so long as those actions were reasonably foreseeable and did not involve a knowing use of a defective product. Accordingly, the courts have held that driving a snowmobile too fast[97] or carelessly using a diving board[98] are not defenses in product liability cases.

It has also been held that contributory negligence is not a defense to implied warranty claims,[99] although there is authority to the contrary.[100] Where the plaintiff alleges that the defendant breached an implied warranty, the potential defense is the plaintiff's abuse or misuse of the product.[101]

The confusion encountered in synthesizing strict liability and comparative negligence was a strong factor in spawning the doctrine of *comparative fault*,[102] a concept which has been adopted by several states.[103] This doctrine, as

---

94 OS Stapley v Miller, 103 Ariz 556, 447 P2d 248, 253 (1968).

95 *See* Butand v Suburban Marine & Sporting Goods, Inc, 543 P2d 209, 211 (Alaska 1975); OS Stapley v Miller, 103 Ariz 556, 447 P2d 248, 253 (1968); Sheehan v Anthony Pools, 50 Md App 614, 440 A2d 1085, 1090, 1092 (1982); Abbott v American Honda Motor Co, 682 SW2d 206, 209 (Tenn Ct App 1984); Means v Sears, Roebuck & Co, 550 SW2d 780, 787 n 6 (Mo 1977); *see generally* Khoder v AMF, Inc, 539 F2d 1078, 1081 (5th Cir 1976); Luque v McLean, 8 Cal 3d 136, 501 P2d 1163, 1169, 104 Cal Rptr 443, 449 (1972); Restatement (Second) of Torts §402A comment n (1965).

96 *See* Butand v Suburban Marine & Sporting Goods, Inc, 555 P2d 42, 46 (Alaska 1976); OS Stapley v Miller, 103 Ariz 556, 447 P2d 248, 253 (1968); Genteman v Saunders Archery Co, 42 Ill App 3d 294, 355 NE2d 647, 651-52 (1976) (archery string silencer improperly mounted and used for wrong activity).

97 *See* Butand v Suburban Marine & Sporting Goods, Inc, 543 P2d 209, 212 (Alaska 1975).

98 *See* Sheehan v Anthony Pools, 50 Md App 614, 440 A2d 1085, 1092 (1982).

99 *See* Schenck v Pelkey, 176 Conn 245, 405 A2d 665, 671 (1978); Dixon v Outboard Marine Corp, 481 P2d 151, 155 (Okla 1970).

100 *See* Fiske v MacGregor, 464 A2d 719, 727 (RI 1983) (citing cases from other jurisdictions).

101 Belfrey v Anthony Pools, Inc, 80 Mich App 118, 262 NW2d 909, 910 (1977).

102 Woods, *The Trend Toward Comparative Fault*, 20 Trial 16, 19 (Nov 1984).

103 *See, e.g.*, Ark Stat Ann §27-1763 (1979); Colo Rev Stat §13-21-406 (1977); Me Rev Stat Ann tit 14, §156 (1980); Minn Stat §604.01 (1978); NY Civ Prac Law §1411 (McKinney

the name implies, compares the fault of the plaintiff, usually a knowing assumption of the risk of danger from a defective product or the misuse of a product,[104] and the fault of the defendant, viz., marketing a defective product, and allocates damages on the applicable percentage of fault.[105] A consumer's negligent failure to discover a defect, usually considered contributory negligence, has been held not to be fault.[106] Accordingly, in *Pell v Victor J. Andrew High School*, the court held that this doctrine did not apply where the plaintiff, unaware of the danger, was injured while somersaulting on a mini-trampoline.[107]

Expert Knowledge

Although a plaintiff with expert knowledge may be held to a standard of reasonable care for people with such knowledge,[108] when the defendant fails to introduce any evidence as to what constitutes reasonable care for such experts, the plaintiff's acts must be measured as if he or she were a person without that special expertise.[109]

Children

Children, at least while engaging in activities appropriate for their age,[110] are usually held to the standard of care expected of a child of their age, intelligence, and experience.[111] Therefore, they are not contributorily

---

1976); Wash Rev Code §4.22.020 (1977); *see also* Gustafson v Benda, 661 SW2d 11, 15 (Mo 1983); *see generally* Woods, *The Trend Toward Comparative Fault*, 20 Trial 16, 20-21 (Nov 1984).

104 Pell v Victor J. Andrew High School, 123 Ill App 3d 423, 462 NE2d 858, 865 (1984).

105 *Id.*

106 *Id.*

107 *Id.* There was no evidence that the plaintiff was misusing the product. *Id.*

108 *See* Restatement (Second) of Torts §289(b) (1965).

109 *See* Hooper v Mougin, 263 Md 630, 284 A2d 236, 238 (1971) (plaintiff, a hunting guide, was injured in a hunting accident).

110 Bixenman v Hall, 251 Ind 527, 242 NE2d 837, 839 (1968).

111 *See* Smith v United States, 546 F2d 872, 878 (10th Cir 1976) (14-year-old boy who fell into thermal pool in national park was contributorily negligent); Smith v United States, 337 F2d 237, 238 (9th Cir 1964); United States v Stoppelmann, 266 F2d 13, 19 (8th Cir 1959); Taylor v Oakland Scavenger Co, 17 Cal 2d 594, 110 P2d 1044, 1049 (1941); Lewis v Northern Ill Gas Co, 97 Ill App 3d 227, 422 NE2d 889, 891 (1981); Dibortolo v Metropolitan School Dist, 440 NE2d 506, 512 (Ind Ct App 1982); Wilkinson v Hartford Accident & Indem Co, 411 So 2d 22, 24 (La 1982); Parker v Roszell, 617 SW2d 597, 599 (Mo Ct App 1981); Brahatcek v Millard School Dist, 202 Neb 86, 273 NW2d 680, 687 (1979); Jordan v Bero, 158 W Va 28, 210 SE2d 618, 626 (1974).

In one state, for a child under 13 years old, due care is such care as the child's mental and physical capacities enable him or her to exercise in the actual circumstances of the occasion and situation under investigation. *See* Ga Code §51-1-5 (1981); *see also* Townsend v Moore, 165 Ga App 606, 302 SE2d 398, 400 (1983).

negligent unless their acts or omissions were unreasonable when judged against the care used by other similar children.

Some courts have used presumptions to aid them in determining whether a child was contributorily negligent. It has sometimes been held that children under seven years of age are irrebuttably presumed to be incapable of negligence; children between seven and fourteen years of age are granted a rebuttable presumption that they are incapable of negligence; and children over fourteen years old face a rebuttable presumption that they are capable of negligence.[112] However, other states do not utilize any presumptions.[113]

Young children are rarely found negligent for following the instructions of their parents.[114] This is quite understandable because, absent unusual circumstances, a parent's judgment will be superior to a child's and the parent is expected to look out for the child's safety. In addition, few juries, bodies which usually include a few parents, would be expected to conclude that a child should be judged unreasonable for obeying a parent's instructions. Indeed, the cases almost uniformly hold that a child is contributorily negligent only where the child acts without or contrary to parental guidance.[115]

Imputed Contributory Negligence

Generally, a parent's negligence is not imputed to the child to reduce the child's recovery.[116] Similarly, a wife's contributory negligence is usually

---

It has been held that individuals over 14 years of age with no known physical or mental defects must conform to the standard of care of adults. *See* Walker v Hamby, 503 SW2d 118, 122 (Tenn 1973).

112 *See* Kopera v Moschella, 400 F Supp 131, 135 (SD Miss 1975) (Mississippi law) (minor under seven years old is conclusively presumed incapable of contributory negligence), *affd*, 526 F2d 1405 (5th Cir 1976); Berman v Philadelphia Bd of Educ, 310 Pa Super 153, 456 A2d 545, 549 (1983); *see generally* Townes v Hawaii Properties, Inc, 708 F2d 333, 335 (8th Cir 1983) (Arkansas law) (eight-year-old child can be contributorily negligent); Goode v Walt Disney World Co, 425 So 2d 1151, 1156 (Fla Dist Ct App 1982) (four-year-old child cannot be contributorily negligent); Lewis v Northern Ill Gas Co, 97 Ill App 3d 227, 422 NE2d 889, 891 (1981); Latimer v City of Clovis, 83 NM 610, 495 P2d 788, 795 (1972) (five-year-old child cannot be contributorily negligent as a matter of law); Bell v Page, 271 NC 396, 156 SE2d 711, 715 (1967) (there is a rebuttable presumption that children between seven and fourteen years of age are incapable of contributory negligence).

Nine-month-old babies assume no risks and are incapable of negligence. *See* Lewis v Buckskin Joe's, Inc, 156 Colo 46, 396 P2d 933, 940 (1964).

113 *See* Shelanie v National Fireworks Assn, 487 SW2d 921, 923 (Ky Ct App 1972); Hamel v Crosietier, 109 NH 505, 256 A2d 143, 145 (1969).

114 Haft v Lone Palm Hotel, 3 Cal 3d 756, 478 P2d 465, 478-79, 91 Cal Rptr 745 (1970).

115 *See id* (citing cases).

116 *See, e.g.*, Haft v Lone Palm Hotel, 3 Cal 3d 756, 478 P2d 465, 478-79 & n 21, 91 Cal Rptr 745 (1970); Restatement (Second) of Torts §488 (1965).

not imputed to her husband to bar his claim.[117] However, state law differs significantly regarding whether a statutory beneficiary of the proceeds in a wrongful death action may share in the proceeds where the beneficiary is contributorily negligent.[118]

Specific Activities

§9.05 Amusement Parks, Rides, and Devices

Assumption of the Risk

Several courts have held that amusement park patrons assumed the risk of injury because they realized the dangers of using the attractions.[119] In *Murphy v Steeplechase Amusement Co,* Judge Cardozo, in an eloquent opinion in which he stated that "the timorous should stay at home,"[120] held that a patron who fell on *The Flopper,* a moving ride which sometimes threw its riders, assumed the risk of injury because the purpose of the ride was to make it difficult to stand straight. Similarly, in *Bonanno v Continental Casualty Co,* the court held that the plaintiff assumed the risk of being frightened, jostled, and pushed about when she entered a haunted house attraction.[121] The court reasoned that the plaintiff had to realize that the very nature of the attraction was to cause patrons to react in bizarre, frightened, and unpredictable ways.[122]

In another case the court directed a verdict for the amusement park because the plaintiff's own testimony confirmed that she knew the dangers of riding an amusement device which bounced violently.[123] However, where the plaintiff was not aware of the dangers of an amusement ride, the park was not entitled to judgment as a matter of law.[124]

---

117 *See* Dashiell v Keauhou-Kona Co, 487 F2d 957, 961 (9th Cir 1973) (wife was driving a golf cart and both husband and wife were injured); Restatement (Second) of Torts §487 (1965).

118 *See* Restatement (Second) of Torts §493 (1965); *see also* Latimer v City of Clovis, 83 NM 610, 495 P2d 788, 795 (1972) (parents cannot recover under such a statute where they were negligent).

119 *See* Murphy v White City Amusement Co, 242 Ill App 56 (1926); Bonanno v Continental Casualty Co, 285 So 2d 591, 592 (La Ct App 1973); Wood v Conneaut Lake Park, Inc, 417 Pa 58, 209 A2d 268, 271 n 3, *cert denied,* 382 US 865 (1965) (roller coaster).

120 250 NY 479, 166 NE 173, 174 (1929).

121 285 So 2d 591, 592 (La Ct App 1973).

122 *Id.*

123 Murphy v White City Amusement Co, 242 Ill App 56 (1926).

124 Russo v Range, Inc, 76 Ill App 3d 236, 395 NE2d 10 (1979).

Contributory Negligence

Patrons who act unreasonably may be contributorily negligent.[125] A plaintiff's failure to keep a proper lookout when she attempted to avoid an unusual crowd reaction to a ride may be contributory negligence.[126] Similarly, a patron who left a tavern, which had amusement devices, to follow a quarrel between other patrons may have been contributorily negligent.[127]

In *Brown v Columbia Amusement Co*, a mother was found not contributorily negligent in allowing her young child to ride an amusement device unattended.[128] The attendant at the park knew that the child was riding alone and, therefore, the park made an implied promise to look after the child.[129] It was reasonable to believe that the park would not allow a child to use an amusement device alone if that act were dangerous.

In some cases, an injured child is simply too young to be contributorily negligent.[130] Indeed, in *Goode v Walt Disney World Co*, the court held that a four-year-old boy could not be contributorily negligent.[131]

§9.06 Automobile Racing

Assumption of the Risk

Automobile race car drivers generally assume the known and appreciated risks in that activity.[132] This includes the risks of colliding with another car or the surrounding fence.[133] It also includes the risk that the car accelerator will *hang* and fail to release.[134]

Drivers do not assume the risk that the racing facility will not have

---

125 Adamson v Hand, 93 Ga App 5, 90 SE2d 669, 672 (1955); Furlow v Campbell, 459 SW2d 284, 287-88 (Mo 1970).

126 Furlow v Campbell, 459 SW2d 284, 287-88 (Mo 1970).

127 Adamson v Hand, 93 Ga App 5, 90 SE2d 669, 672 (1955).

128 91 Mont 174, 6 P2d 874, 879 (1934).

129 *Id.*

130 Goode v Walt Disney World Co, 425 So 2d 1151, 1156 (Fla Dist Ct App 1982); *see generally* §9.04.

131 425 So 2d 1141, 1156 (Fla Dist Ct App 1982).

132 *See generally* Seymour v New Bremen Speedway, Inc, 31 Ohio App 2d 141, 287 NE2d 111, 113 (1971); Luckey v Adams, 397 SW2d 519, 522 (Tex Civ App 1965).

133 *See generally* Seymour v New Bremen Speedway, Inc, 31 Ohio App 2d 141, 287 NE2d 111, 113 (1971); Luckey v Adams, 397 SW2d 519, 522 (Tex Civ App 1965); Huckaby v Confederate Motor Speedway, Inc, 276 SC 629, 281 SE2d 223, 224 (1981).

134 Luckey v Adams, 397 SW2d 519, 522 (Tex Civ App 1965).

firefighting personnel or machinery.[135] Nonetheless, in *Seymour v New Bremen Speedway, Inc*, there was no evidence of what further injury occurred because the facility did not have sufficient firefighting capabilities and, therefore the facility was held not liable.[136]

Members of a pit crew may assume some risks in this sport.[137] In *Provence v Doolin*, the court held that a pit crewman in an automobile race assumed, as a matter of law, the risks of being hit by an automobile.[138] In that case the crewman testified that his participation in the event was voluntary and that he was aware of the risks of cars going out of control.[139]

In several cases, spectators at automobile racing events were held to have assumed the risk of injury.[140] In *Morton v California Sports Car Club*, the court held that the plaintiff, a member of a car racing club who was aware that racing cars travel at a high rate of speed, assumed the risk of injury, as a matter of law, when he watched an automobile race near a turn which was virtually unprotected rather than sitting in a safer area such as the grandstand.[141] Similarly, in *Shela v Warren*, an individual who had previously attended stock car races and had even been employed as an announcer of such races was held to have assumed the risk of injury as a matter of law when he went to the pit, a dangerous area where he knew he was not supposed to be.[142] However, a different court held that spectators did not assume the risk of injury where they had no knowledge of the dangers of sitting in a particular area.[143]

---

135 *See generally* Seymour v New Bremen Speedway, Inc, 31 Ohio App 2d 141, 287 NE2d 111, 114-15 (1971).

136 *Id*.

137 Provence v Doolin, 91 Ill App 3d 271, 414 NE2d 786, 794 (1980).

138 *Id*.

139 414 NE2d at 789, 794.

140 *See* McPherson v Sunset Speedway, Inc, 594 F2d 711, 714-15 (8th Cir 1979); Morton v California Sports Car Club, 163 Cal App 2d 685, 329 P2d 967, 968-69 (1958); Shula v Warren, 395 Pa 428, 150 A2d 341, 345 (1959); *but see* Atlantic Rural Exposition, Inc v Fagan, 195 Va 13, 77 SE2d 368, 375 (1953) (spectator does not assume the risk of a wheel coming off an automobile and going into the spectator section).

A signed exculpatory agreement may be some evidence that plaintiff assumed the risk of injury. Celli v Sports Car Club of Am, Inc, 29 Cal App 3d 511, 105 Cal Rptr 904, 911 (1972).

141 163 Cal App 2d 685, 329 P2d 967, 968-69 (1958). The court also noted, although it was not directly relevant to an assumption of risk analysis, that most of the accidents at sports car races occur on the turns because of the additional gravitational stresses which are exerted there. *Id*.

The *Morton* case is discussed at Note, *Torts: Assumption Of Risk At Sports Car Event*, 10 Hastings LJ 344 (1959).

142 395 Pa 428, 150 A2d 341, 345 (1959).

143 Rogers v Black Hills Speedway, Inc, 217 NW2d 14, 19-20 (SD 1974); *see also* Alden v Norwood Arena, 332 Mass 267, 124 NE2d 505, 507 (1955) (spectator did not assume the

Contributory Negligence

Several courts have held that automobile racing is so dangerous that drivers[144] and members of a pit crew[145] were contributorily negligent as a matter of law for participating in that activity.

It is common knowledge that drinking and driving is a dangerous combination. Indeed, the combination is so fraught with peril that in *Allgeier v Grimes* the court held that a passenger in a car involved in a drag race which was operated by a driver who had too much to drink was contributorily negligent as a matter of law.[146] No prudent person would have ridden with a driver who had been drinking to such an extent that his or her ability to drive was affected.[147]

Spectators at automobile racing contests who do not act unreasonably are not contributorily negligent.[148] For example, a spectator who sat in an area reserved for spectators was not contributorily negligent when he was hit by an automobile, because it was reasonable to sit there.[149] In fact, one court held that a spectator who did not sit in the bleachers was not contributorily negligent because there were not enough seats in the bleachers to accommodate all of the spectators.[150] However, a spectator who was injured when he walked onto the track was contributorily negligent.[151]

§9.07 Baseball

Assumption of the Risk

Baseball players generally assume the obvious, inherent risks of that sport.[152] Accordingly, it is usually held that baseball players assume the risk that a bat may slip out of a batter's hands.[153]

---

risk that a wheel would come off an automobile); *see generally* Goade v Benevolent & Protective Order of Elks, 213 Cal App 2d 189, 28 Cal Rptr 669, 671-72 (1963).

[144] *See* Luckey v Adams, 397 SW2d 519, 522 (Tex Civ App 1965).

[145] *See* Provence v Doolin, 91 Ill App 3d 271, 414 NE2d 786, 794 (1980).

[146] 449 SW2d 911, 913 (Ky Ct App 1970).

[147] *Id.*

[148] Celli v Sports Car Club of Am, Inc, 29 Cal App 3d 511, 105 Cal Rptr 904, 912 (1972); Sam v Theriot, 49 So 2d 484, 486 (La Ct App 1950); Ellingson v World Amusement Serv Assn, 175 Minn 563, 222 NW 335, 338 (1928).

[149] Sam v Theriot, 49 So 2d 484, 486 (La Ct App 1950).

[150] *See* Ellingson v World Amusement Serv Assn, 175 Minn 563, 222 NW 335, 338 (1928).

[151] Endorf v Johnson, 59 SD 549, 241 NW 519, 520 (1932).

[152] *See* Richmond v Employers' Fire Ins Co, 298 So 2d 118, 122 (La Ct App 1974).

[153] *See* Richmond v Employers' Fire Ins Co, 298 So 2d 118, 122 (La Ct App 1974)

Several courts have discussed whether a baseball player assumes the risk of injury on the base paths.[154] In *Passentino v Board of Education*, the court reversed a $1 million judgment and held that a base runner assumed the risk of injury, as a matter of law, when he ran headfirst into a catcher who was holding the ball and blocking the plate.[155] However, in *Bourque v Duplechin*, the court noted that although a second baseman may assume the risk of an injury from being spiked by someone sliding into second base, a relatively common occurrence, he did not assume the risk of a base runner running into him at full speed and hitting him in the chin, when he was standing out of the runner's path and five feet away from the base.[156]

A baseball player may assume the risk of playing on a dangerous field.[157] For example, in one case the court held that a player who was injured when he fell in a hole on a baseball field that had many holes assumed that risk of injury.[158] The plaintiff's argument, that he did not assume this risk because he had his eyes on the ball and, therefore, did not see the hole in the ground, was not accepted.[159]

In *Maddox v City of New York*,[160] Elliot Maddox, an outfielder for the New York Yankees, was injured while chasing a fly ball when one of his feet hit a wet spot, causing him to slip. His other foot then became stuck in a mud puddle and buckled. The defendant argued that Maddox assumed the risk of injury as a matter of law by continuing to play on what he knew was a wet field. The court rejected this argument.[161] It held that since he was carrying out his assigned responsibilities at the time of the injury, it could be inferred that he was acting pursuant to a superior's instructions and in that

---

(during practice); Gaspard v Grain Dealers Mut Ins Co, 131 So 2d 831, 834 (La Ct App 1961); Brackman v Adrian, 472 SW2d 735, 738 (Tenn Ct App 1971) (although the court held that the school did not negligently supervise the game, its language showed that it applied an assumption of the risk analysis); *see also* Bourque v Duplechin, 331 So 2d 40, 42 (La Ct App 1976).

154 Bourque v Duplechin, 331 So 2d 40, 42 (La Ct App 1976) (second baseman was spiked); Ross v Clouser, 637 SW2d 11 (Mo 1982) (question of fact whether third baseman assumed the risk of being hit by a base runner); Passentino v Board of Educ, 41 NY2d 1022, 363 NE2d 1373 (1977), *revg* 52 AD2d 935, 383 NYS2d 639 (1976) (reversed a $1 million judgment for plaintiff).

155 41 NY2d 1022, 363 NE2d 1373 (1977), *revg* 52 AD2d 935, 383 NYS2d 639 (1976).

156 331 So 2d 40, 42 (La Ct App 1976).

157 Maddox v City of New York, 121 Misc 2d 358, 467 NYS2d 772 (Sup Ct 1983); Luftig v Steinhorn, 21 AD2d 760, 250 NYS2d 354, 355 (1964).

158 *See* Luftig v Steinhorn, 21 AD2d 760, 250 NYS2d 354, 355 (1964).

159 *Id; but see* Garafano v Neshobe Beach Club, Inc, 126 Vt 566, 238 A2d 70, 76 (1967).

160 121 Misc 2d 358, 467 NYS2d 772 (Sup Ct 1983).

161 467 NYS2d at 774.

event, his actions might not have been voluntary and, therefore, this defense might be inapplicable.[162]

Several courts have held that spectators at a baseball game assumed the risk of being hit by a baseball.[163] In *Vines v Birmingham Baseball Club, Inc*,[164] the Alabama Supreme Court held that a spectator assumed the risk of injury because on the day of the accident there were several signs placed in open and obvious locations around the field warning spectators of the dangers of being hit by a ball and these signs were also near the entrances which the plaintiff must have passed to enter the stadium. In addition, the baseball club had seats which were protected by a screen, but the plaintiff did not sit in that area.[165] Indeed, it has been held that a spectator sitting in an unscreened seat assumed the risk of injury as a matter of law even where there was evidence that she was unaware of the risk of being hit by a baseball because she had never sat in the stands of a baseball game before and, in fact, did not watch this game, but rather talked with a friend.[166]

In *Dillard v Little League Baseball*, the court held that an umpire at a little league baseball game assumed the risk, as a matter of law, of getting hit in the groin by a ball thrown by a pitcher, even when he had called "time out."[167] The court held that the umpire, who had coached in this league for two years, must have been aware of the wild pitches and errant play of nine-year-old boys.[168] The court noted:

> It cannot be said that it would be a total surprise for a nine year old to throw a pitch after the umpire had called time out and before the umpire had called a resumption of play. This kind of mistake, error, inadvertence or lack of attention is fully to be expected during the heat of a game from so young a player. Plaintiff assumed such a risk. ...[169]

---

162 *Id.*

163 *See* Vines v Birmingham Baseball Club, Inc, 450 So 2d 455, 456 (Ala 1984); Brown v San Francisco Ball Club, 99 Cal App 2d 484, 222 P2d 19, 21 (1950); Anderson v Kansas City Baseball Club, 231 SW2d 170, 173 (Mo 1950); Ingersoll v Onondaga Hockey Club, 245 AD 137, 281 NYS 505, 507 (1935) (dicta); *see also* Schentzel v Philadelphia Natl League Club, 173 Pa Super 179, 96 A2d 181, 186 (1953); *see generally* **§8.03**; *but see* Edling v Kansas City Baseball & Exhibition Co, 168 SW 908, 910 (Mo Ct App 1914).

164 450 So 2d 455, 456 (Ala 1984).

165 *Id.*

166 Brown v San Francisco Ball Club, 99 Cal App 2d 484, 222 P2d 19, 21 (1950).

167 55 AD2d 477, 390 NYS2d 735 (1977).

168 390 NYS2d at 737.

169 *Id.*

Contributory Negligence

In *Passentino v Board of Education*,[170] a case discussed earlier in this section regarding assumption of the risk, the court reversed a $1 million judgment. The court concluded that the base runner was contributorily negligent when he ran into the catcher; he should have ran around the catcher or back to third base.[171]

Several courts have held that it was unreasonable to play on a dangerous baseball field.[172] In one case, a boy was found to be contributorily negligent when he ran into an abandoned, partially removed flagpole located near a baseball field.[173]

Spectators must also exercise reasonable care for their own protection.[174] In *Powless v Milwaukee County*, the court held that a spectator who continued to look down at her scorecard even though she heard the crack of a bat hitting a ball and heard a commotion indicating that the ball was coming in her direction was contributorily negligent.[175]

§9.08 Bicycling

More bicyclists are injured each year than participants in any other sporting or recreational activity.[176] In one recent year, over 570,000 bicyclists required emergency room treatment for their injuries.[177]

Bicyclists who do not act in a reasonably prudent manner may be contributorily negligent and their recovery may be restricted or eliminated.[178]

---

170 41 NY2d 1022, 363 NE2d 1373 (1977), *revg* 52 AD2d 935, 383 NYS2d 639 (1976).

171 *Id.*

172 *See* Maddox v City of New York, 121 Misc 2d 358, 467 NYS2d 772 (Sup Ct 1983); Luftig v Steinhorn, 21 AD2d 760, 250 NYS2d 354, 355 (1964).

173 Smith v United States, 337 F2d 237, 238-39 (9th Cir 1964).

174 Powless v Milwaukee County, 6 Wis 2d 78, 94 NW2d 187, 191 (1959); Edling v Kansas City Baseball & Exhibition Co, 168 SW 908, 910 (Mo Ct App 1914) (spectator was not contributorily negligent in failing to dodge a ball which came through a hole in a protective screen); *see generally* Knebel v Jones, 266 SW2d 470, 475 (Tex Civ App 1954).

175 6 Wis 2d 78, 94 NW2d 187, 191 (1959).

176 US Consumer Prod Safety Commn, Natl Injury Information Clearinghouse, Prod Summary Report (Mar 28, 1984).

177 *Id.* Over 800 bicyclists were fatally injured in 1983. *See* US Dept of Transportation, Fatal Accident Reporting System 1983, at 92. In 1972-1977, it was estimated that there were about 1,000 fatalities each year. *See* Cross & Fisher, A Study of Bicycle/Motor-Vehicle Accidents: Identification of Problem Types and Countermeasure Approaches 1 (prepared for the US Dept of Transportation, Sept 1977).

Head injuries account for 75% of all bicycle deaths. *See* The Washington Area Bicyclist Assn, A Consumer's Guide to Bicycle Helmets (Apr 1984).

178 Valenzuela v Bracamonte, 126 Ariz 472, 616 P2d 932, 933 (App 1980).

The courts have held that bicyclists who fail to keep proper lookout,[179] fail to yield the right-of-way,[180] fail to stop at a stop sign,[181] or ride their bicycles, without lights, at night[182] may be contributorily negligent.[183]

Bicyclists generally must follow the rules of the road.[184] In fact, in one case the court held that a bicyclist's violation of the rules of the road, viz., crossing the road without looking, was contributory negligence.[185] However, if a bicyclist's violation of a statute did not cause the accident, then the violation is not evidence of contributory negligence.[186]

A child bicyclist is usually held to the standard of care that a similar child of the same age and intelligence would be expected to exercise under the circumstances.[187] Accordingly, in some cases, child bicyclists may be found not contributorily negligent in situations, e.g., operating a bicycle at night, without lights, and on the wrong side of the highway,[188] where an adult bicyclist probably would be contributorily negligent.

However, several child bicyclists have been held contributorily negligent as

---

[179] Boudreaux v Allstate Ins Co, 258 So 2d 710, 712 (La Ct App 1972).

[180] *Id.*

[181] Green v Kersey, 189 So 2d 236 (Fla Dist Ct App 1966).

[182] Fusilier v City of Houma, 421 So 2d 418, 420 (La Ct App 1982).

[183] Rosvold v Johnson, 284 Minn 162, 169 NW2d 598, 599 (1969) (rode a tricycle onto a public road).

[184] *See* Maxwell v Gossett, 126 Ariz 98, 612 P2d 1061, 1063 (1980); Owen v Burcham, 100 Idaho 441, 599 P2d 1012, 1018 (1979); Finch v Christensen, 84 SD 420, 172 NW2d 571, 573 (1969); Jordan v Bero, 158 W Va 28, 210 SE2d 618, 627 (1974).

In some cases, the rules for bicyclists only apply where the bicycles are used on roadways. *See* Maxwell v Gossett, 126 Ariz 98, 612 P2d 1061, 1063-64 (1980); Crawford v Miller, 18 Wash App 151, 566 P2d 1264, 1265-66 (1977).

In one study about 75% of the bicyclists were in some form of violation of traffic rules when a bicycle-motor vehicle accident occurred. *See* Roland, Hunter, Stewart & Campbell, Investigation of Motor Vehicle/Bicycle Collision Parameters 9 (prepared for the US Dept of Transportation, Feb 19, 1979) (the principal violation of the bicyclist was use of an improper lane).

[185] *See* Leonard v Bratcher, 258 Md 186, 265 A2d 246, 247-48 (1970).

[186] *See* Maxwell v Gossett, 126 Ariz 98, 612 P2d 1061, 1062-63 (1980); Wilson v Wylie, 86 NM 9, 518 P2d 1213, 1216 (Ct App 1973), *cert denied*, 86 NM 5, 518 P2d 1209 (1974); Poczkalski v Cartwright, 64 AD2d 445, 410 NYS2d 488, 489 (1978).

[187] *See* Conway v Tamborini, 68 Ill App 2d 190, 215 NE2d 303 (1966); Taylor v Armiger, 277 Md 638, 358 A2d 883, 889-90 (1976); Richards v Goff, 26 Md App 344, 338 A2d 80, 87 (1975); Zaepfel v City of Yonkers, 56 Ad2d 867, 392 NYS2d 336, 338 (1977); Moe v Kettwig, 68 NW2d 853, 860 (ND 1955); Finch v Christensen, 84 SD 420, 172 NW2d 571, 574 (1969).

An adult standard of care has been applied where the bicycle was powered by a motor. *See* Fishel v Givens, 47 Ill App 3d 512, 362 NE2d 97, 102 (1977); *see generally* §2.12.

[188] Finch v Christensen, 84 SD 420, 172 NW2d 571, 574 (1969).

a matter of law for their unreasonable acts.[189] For example, child bicyclists have been held contributorily negligent as a matter of law when they failed to yield the right-of-way to an automobile,[190] went around a blind corner on the wrong side of the road,[191] and failed to observe dangerous obstacles in their path.[192]

Virtually all courts have held that the common law doctrine imposing a lesser standard of care on minors than adults applies even where the minor bicyclist has violated a traffic regulation.[193] Therefore, a minor's violation of a statute is not negligence per se.[194] The child's actions are judged by what is reasonable for a child of similar age, experience, and intelligence.[195] If a similar child would have violated the law, the child bicyclist is not contributorily negligent in doing so.[196]

Bicyclists who do not act unreasonably are not guilty of contributory negligence.[197] Even if a bicyclist was contributorily negligent, the bicyclist can still recover if the defendant had the last clear chance to avoid the accident but failed to do so.[198]

The plaintiff's contributory negligence is usually not a defense in a strict products liability action.[199] Therefore, in *Khoder v AMF, Inc* the court held that the plaintiff's alleged negligence in assembling a bike was irrelevant and the giving of a jury instruction on this issue was reversible error.[200]

---

189 Lewis v Northern Ill Gas Co, 97 Ill App 3d 227, 422 NE2d 889, 891 (1981); Richards v Goff, 26 Md App 344, 338 A2d 80, 87 (1975).

190 Richards v Goff, 26 Md App 344, 338 A2d 80, 87 (1975); Oddis v Greene, 11 Md App 153, 273 A2d 232, 235 (1971).

191 Fishel v Givens, 47 Ill App 3d 512, 362 NE2d 97, 103 (1977).

192 Lewis v Northern Ill Gas Co, 97 Ill App 3d 227, 422 NE2d 889, 891 (1981).

193 *See* Herrell v Pimsler, 307 F Supp 1166, 1169 (DDC 1969); Williams v Gilbert, 239 Ark 935, 395 SW2d 333, 336 (1965); Davis v Bushnell, 93 Idaho 528, 465 P2d 652, 654 (1970); Kronenberger v Husky, 38 Ill 2d 376, 231 NE2d 385, 386-87 (1967); Bixenman v Hall, 251 Ind 527, 242 NE2d 837, 839-40 (1968); Goldberg v Board of Regents of the Univ, 81 AD2d 981, 439 NYS2d 769, 769 (1981); Poczkalski v Cartwright, 64 AD2d 445, 410 NYS2d 488, 489 (1978); Rudes v Gottschalk, 159 Tex 552, 324 SW2d 201 (1959).

194 Herrell v Pimsler, 307 F Supp 1166, 1169 (DDC 1969); Rudes v Gottschalk, 159 Tex 552, 324 SW2d 201 (1959).

195 Poczkalski v Cartwright, 64 AD2d 445, 410 NYS2d 488, 489 (1978).

196 *Id.*

197 *See* LaCroix v Middle South Serv, Inc, 345 So 2d 136, 138 (La Ct App), *writ refused*, 346 So 2d 716 (La 1977); Thibodeaux v Fireman's Fund Ins Co, 325 So 2d 318, 322 (La Ct App 1975).

198 *See* Dufrene v Dixie Auto Ins Co, 373 So 2d 162, 165 (La 1979); Boudreaux v Allstate Ins Co, 258 So 2d 710, 713 (La Ct App 1972).

199 Khoder v AMF, Inc, 539 F2d 1078, 1081 (5th Cir 1976) (La law); *see generally* §9.04.

200 539 F2d 1078, 1081 (5th Cir 1976) (Louisiana law).

Some defendants have attempted to argue that a parent's negligent supervision of a child bicyclist was the real cause of the accident.[201] However, the courts have held that if the child bicyclist did not commit a negligent act, then any negligence on the part of the parent in permitting the child to use the bicycle would be, at best, a remote cause of the injury and not sufficient to preclude or reduce the child's recovery.[202]

§9.09 Boating

Assumption of the Risk

Boaters usually assume the ordinary and normal hazards incidental to the sport.[203] However, boaters usually do not assume the risk of injury caused by the negligence of others.[204]

Accordingly, in many cases, passengers on a boat did not assume the risk of danger caused by the boat operator's unreasonable acts.[205] For example, a passenger did not assume the risk of injury caused by the operator's sharp turns,[206] excessive speed,[207] or failure to use headlights on a dark night.[208] However, passengers may assume the risk of riding with a boat operator who is intoxicated or *high*, if the passengers knew of the operator's condition, and this condition was the cause of the accident.[209]

Contributory Negligence

A boater's recovery may be eliminated or restricted where the boater knew or should have known of the dangers, but failed to take reasonable safety precautions.[210] What is reasonable depends on the circumstances.

---

201 *See* Owen v Burcham, 100 Idaho 441, 599 P2d 1012, 1020 (1979); *see generally* Wilson v Wylie, 86 NM 9, 518 P2d 1213, 1220 (Ct App 1973), *cert denied*, 86 NM 5, 518 P2d 1209 (1974).

202 *See* Owen v Burcham, 100 Idaho 441, 599 P2d 1012, 1020 (1979); *see generally* Wilson v Wylie, 86 NM 9, 518 P2d 1213, 1220 (Ct App 1973), *cert denied*, 86 NM 5, 518 P2d 1209 (1974).

203 Carroll v Aetna Casualty & Sur Co, 301 So 2d 406, 408 (La Ct App 1974); *see also* §9.12 (fishing); §9.23 (water skiing).

204 Holman v Reliance Ins Co, 414 So 2d 1298, 1309 (La Ct App 1982).

205 Holman v Reliance Ins Co, 414 So 2d 1298, 1309 (La Ct App 1982); Carroll v Aetna Casualty & Sur Co, 301 So 2d 406, 408-09 (La Ct App 1974).

206 *See* Holman v Reliance Ins Co, 414 So 2d 1298, 1309 (La Ct App 1982).

207 *See* Carroll v Aetna Casualty & Sur Co, 301 So 2d 406, 408-09 (La Ct App 1974).

208 *Id.*

209 *See* Holman v Reliance Ins Co, 414 So 2d 1298, 1309 (La Ct App 1982).

210 *See* Harmon v United States, 532 F2d 669, 672 (9th Cir 1975); *see also* §9.12 (fishing); §9.23 (water skiing).

Boaters should take reasonable steps to learn of conditions on the water.[211] However, in *Lane v United States*, the operator of a cabin cruiser was found not contributorily negligent even though he did not review, or have available, a chart published by the National Oceanic and Atmospheric Administration which indicated water conditions in the area where the operator intended to take the boat.[212] The court held that the operator was an experienced navigator and generally familiar with water conditions where the boat was traveling and, therefore, he was not negligent in failing to review a chart of those conditions.[213]

Boat passengers are not expected to act like navigators.[214] Therefore, they are not obligated to watch for sudden or unexpected dangers in the water and their failure to do so is usually not contributory negligence.[215] Indeed, it is reasonable for passengers to rely upon the operator to be alert for such dangers.[216] Accordingly, a passenger who rode in a boat which did not use headlights on a dark night was found not contributorily negligent because the passenger was not required to watch for potential obstacles in the boat's path.[217] In a different case, the court held that a passenger in a boat was not contributorily negligent in failing to warn the boat's driver of a rapidly approaching boat.[218]

In some cases, boaters may be affected by alcohol or other drugs.[219] In *Holman v Reliance Insurance Co*, a passenger was found not contributorily negligent in a boating accident, even though she smoked one marijuana cigarette some time prior to the accident.[220] There was no showing that she was under the influence of this drug to a degree which substantially affected her ability to use reasonable care for her safety.[221] Similarly, in *Carroll v Aetna Casualty & Surety Co*, the court affirmed a finding that a guest was not contributorily negligent for riding in a boat with a driver whose blood had a .10 per cent alcoholic content, enough alcohol that an expert testified that

---

211 *See generally* Lane v United States, 529 F2d 175, 180 (4th Cir 1975).

212 *Id.*

213 *Id.*

214 *See* Carroll v Aetna Casualty & Sur Co, 301 So 2d 406, 409 (La Ct App 1974).

215 *Id.*

216 *Id.*

217 *Id.*

218 Reed v Reed, 182 Neb 136, 153 NW2d 356, 358 (1967) (boat operator was fully cognizant of the situation).

219 *See generally* National Transp Safety Bd, Recreational Boating Safety & Alcohol 15, 17 (1983); Schmalz, *Increasing Problem Of Drunken Boating Spurring New Laws*, NY Times, Sept 2, 1984, at 23, col 1.

220 414 So 2d 1298, 1307-08 (La Ct App 1982).

221 *Id.* Indeed, another passenger was injured and he had not smoked any marijuana. *Id.*

it would have affected the driver's ability to operate the boat properly.[222] In that case, the fact-finder believed the passenger's testimony that he observed nothing to indicate that the driver was under the influence of alcohol.[223] Other fact-finders may not have found the testimony that the driver was not under the influence, made by a person who himself had been drinking, so credible.

Indeed, not all courts have so discounted drinking alcohol and smoking marijuana.[224] In *Kuntz v Windjammer "Barefoot" Cruises, Ltd*, the court held that the damages for the wrongful death of a woman diver should be reduced 50 per cent because her motor functions were significantly diminished by her drinking alcohol and smoking marijuana the night before the dive.[225]

The plaintiff's actions or omissions are judged by what is reasonable under the circumstances.[226] Therefore, in an emergency, where there is less time to react, the appropriate standard of care is that of a reasonable person acting in an emergency; the plaintiff is not to be judged by what would be reasonable if the plaintiff had more time to react.[227] In *Pavlides v Galveston Yacht Basin, Inc*, a case involving a boat manufacturer's failure to warn of certain dangers in using a boat, the court held that the reasonableness of the plaintiff's actions in leaving[228] his boat, which had submerged in the Gulf of Mexico, and attempting to swim to a nearby rig should be judged by whether that was reasonable conduct in an emergency situation.[229]

A jury instruction on contributory negligence should not be given, even if the plaintiff's conduct was unreasonable, if the plaintiff's conduct did not cause the accident or aggravate the injuries.[230] In *Gasquet v Commercial Union Insurance Co*,[231] an airboat hit a sandbar, and a passenger was injured. There was no evidence that the airboat passenger's failure to hold onto his seat was the proximate cause of the accident, or caused or aggravated his injuries.[232] Therefore, a jury instruction on the plaintiff's alleged contributory negligence should not have been given.[233]

---

222 301 So 2d 406, 408 (La Ct App 1974).

223 *Id*.

224 *See* Kuntz v Windjammer "Barefoot" Cruises, Ltd, 573 F Supp 1277 (WD Pa 1983).

225 *Id* 1282-83.

226 Pavlides v Galveston Yacht Basin, Inc, 727 F2d 330, 341 n 21 (5th Cir 1984).

227 *Id*.

228 It is generally believed that the proper safety procedure to follow when the boat capsizes is to stay with the boat. *See id* 337 n 12.

229 *See id* 341 n 21 (5th Cir 1984).

230 Gasquet v Commercial Union Ins Co, 391 So 2d 466, 475 (La Ct App 1980).

231 *Id*.

232 *Id*.

233 *Id*.

§9.10 Bowling

Assumption of the Risk

Bowlers generally assume the known and appreciated risks of danger which occur while bowling.[234] They do not, however, assume unknown risks.[235] In *Elias v New Laurel Radio Station, Inc*, an experienced bowler apparently stepped into a wet substance while paying for using the lanes and, as a result, later slipped while bowling.[236] The court held that the bowler did not, as a matter of law, assume that risk because he did not know he stepped into the liquid substance until after his injury.[237] The court reasoned that the bowler's knowledge of the risks of bowling with a wet shoe was irrelevant because he was not aware that his shoe was, in fact, wet.[238]

Contributory Negligence

Generally, the plaintiff has the burden of proof regarding the defendant's negligence and the defendant shoulders the burden of proof regarding the plaintiff's contributory negligence.[239] However, the plaintiff may not recover if, while presenting his or her case against the defendant, the plaintiff reveals factors which show that he or she was contributorily negligent.[240] In that event, the plaintiff may lose even though the defendant presents no evidence.[241]

In *Matteo v Sharon Hill Lanes, Inc*, a bowler lost his traction because of a liquid substance on his shoe.[242] In presenting his case, the bowler admitted he did not inspect his shoes before bowling although he knew of the presence of beverages in the area and the danger resulting from moisture on his shoes. The *Matteo* court held that this evidence was sufficient to enable the defense to obtain a jury instruction that the plaintiff may have been contributorily negligent.[243]

Where the plaintiff did not act unreasonably, there was no contributory

---

234 *See generally* §§9.02, 9.03.

235 Elias v New Laurel Radio Station, Inc, 146 So 2d 558, 561-62 (Miss 1962).

236 *Id.*

237 *Id* 561-62.

238 *Id.*

239 *See* Matteo v Sharon Hill Lanes, Inc, 216 Pa Super 188, 263 A2d 910, 912 (1970); Restatement (Second) of Torts §477 (1965).

240 *See* Matteo v Sharon Hill Lanes, Inc, 216 Pa Super 188, 263 A2d 910, 912 (1970).

241 *See id.*

242 *Id.*

243 263 A2d at 913.

negligence.[244] In *McGillivray v Eramian*,[245] the plaintiff was injured when a splinter which was sticking up from the wooden approach to the lanes lodged in his finger. The court held that the bowler was not contributorily negligent because there was no evidence that the bowler's delivery was improper or that he observed, prior to his delivery, that the approach to the lane had splinters.[246]

In *Geraghty v Burr Oak Lanes*, a prospective bowler was injured in an unlighted parking lot when his foot became wedged between a railroad tie and a telephone pole, obstacles which were obscured by the weeds.[247] The court held that this did not show contributory negligence as a matter of law.[248]

§9.11 Firearms

Assumption of the Risk

Users of firearms generally assume the risk of injury where they have actual knowledge of the particular risk, appreciate its magnitude, and yet voluntarily choose to use the weapon.[249]

The courts have reached conflicting conclusions regarding whether one assumes the risk that a firearm is loaded.[250] In *Greaves v Galchutt*, the Minnesota Supreme Court held that two children who took turns shooting a rifle at each other, believing that the rifle was unloaded, assumed the risk of injury when the rifle discharged a bullet.[251] The injured child argued that he did not assume the risk because he did not know the rifle was loaded. The court held, however, that the risk assumed was that the rifle was loaded.[252] However, in *Turpin v Shoemaker*, the Missouri Supreme Court did not apply

---

[244] *See* Geraghty v Burr Oak Lanes, 5 Ill 2d 153, 125 NE2d 47 (1955); McGillivray v Eramian 309 Mass 430, 35 NE2d 209, 210 (1941).

[245] 309 Mass 430, 35 NE2d 209, 210 (1941).

[246] *Id.*

[247] 5 Ill 2d 153, 125 NE2d 47 (1955).

[248] 125 NE2d at 52.

[249] *See* Mack v Barney, 125 Ariz 5, 606 P2d 823, 824 (Ct App 1980); Parker v Roszell, 617 SW2d 597, 600 (Mo Ct App 1981); *see generally* Hooper v Mougin, 263 Md 630, 284 A2d 236, 239-40 (1971).

[250] *Compare* Acosta v Daughtry, 268 So 2d 416, 422-23 (Fla Dist Ct App 1972) (a child did not assume the risk that a friend would fire a pistol at him without first checking to see whether the pistol was loaded); Turpin v Shoemaker, 427 SW2d 485, 490 (Mo 1968) *with* Greaves v Galchutt, 289 Minn 335, 184 NW2d 26, 28 (1971); LaBarge v Stewart, 84 NM 222, 501 P2d 666, 668, *cert denied*, 84 NM 219, 501 P2d 663 (1972) (participant assumed the risk of injury while engaging in a game of Russian roulette).

[251] 289 Minn 335, 184 NW2d 26, 28 (1971).

[252] *Id.*

the assumption of the risk doctrine where the plaintiff was fatally injured in a *quick draw* firearm contest because the plaintiff did not know his opponent's gun was loaded.[253]

A party does assume the risk of danger from the intended discharge of a loaded firearm.[254] In *Gregory v Hester*,[255] two boys, each with a BB gun, stood next to each other and shot at a piece of cardboard on a chain link fence. One boy's BB ricocheted back from the target and struck the plaintiff, blinding him in one eye.[256] The court concluded that the danger that a BB would ricochet is inherent in shooting BBs. Therefore, even though the ricochet was not expected, it was an assumed risk and the plaintiff could not recover.[257]

This defense usually does not apply where the plaintiff is not cognizant of the risk.[258] The fact that firearms are inherently dangerous is not sufficient to impose constructive knowledge of all dangers on the plaintiff.[259] For example, a hunter does not assume the risk that a gun's safety will not protect him or her in the absence of specific knowledge that the safety is not working.[260]

Firearms users usually do not assume the risk of injury from the negligent acts of others.[261] Therefore, hunters usually do not assume the risk of being shot by another hunter.[262] In *Mack v Barney*, the court held that a hunter did not assume the risk of being injured when a companion's rifle went off because he did not know that the safety in the companion's rifle was not engaged.[263]

Contributory Negligence

Hunters who are aware or should be aware of a dangerous situation and yet fail to exercise reasonable care to protect themselves may be contributorily

---

[253] 427 SW2d 485, 490 (Mo 1968).

[254] Gregory v Hester, 123 Ga App 406, 181 SE2d 104, 107 (1971).

[255] *Id.*

[256] *Id.*

[257] *Id.*

[258] *See generally* Greaves v Galchutt, 289 Minn 335, 184 NW2d 26, 28 (1971).

[259] Turpin v Shoemaker, 427 SW2d 485, 490 (Mo 1968); Hogenson v Service Armament Co, 77 Wash 2d 209, 461 P2d 311, 315 (1969); *see also* Mack v Barney, 125 Ariz 5, 606 P2d 823, 824 (Ct App 1980).

[260] Philippe v Browning Arms Co, 375 So 2d 151, 155 (La Ct App 1979), *aff'd on other grounds*, 395 So 2d 310 (La 1981).

[261] *See* Gregory v Hester, 123 Ga App 406, 181 SE2d 104, 107 (1971).

[262] *See* Hooper v Mougin, 263 Md 630, 284 A2d 236, 239-40 (1971); Parker v Roszell, 617 SW2d 597, 600 (Mo Ct App 1981).

[263] 125 Ariz 5, 606 P2d 823, 824 (Ct App 1980).

negligent.[264] For example, a hunter who knew of a defect in his gun's safety for three years but still used the gun for hunting was contributorily negligent as a matter of law.[265] Similarly, a hunter who failed to warn of his presence, when he was located in an area where he was not supposed to be, may have been contributorily negligent.[266] In addition, a person who engaged in a *quick draw* gun contest may have been contributorily negligent in failing to make an adequate inspection of his opponent's gun to ascertain whether all live ammunition had been removed.[267]

A hunting guide may be held to the standard of care used by reasonable hunting guides.[268] However, in *Hooper v Mougin*, the defendant offered no evidence of what this standard was and, therefore, the guide was only held to the standard of care of a person without special hunting expertise.[269]

A hunter's violation of a statute may show that he or she acted unreasonably.[270] However, such an action is not contributory negligence unless it was a proximate cause of the injury.[271] In *Breithaupt v Sellers*, the court held that a hunter who did not wear the required[272] *hunter orange*, a fluorescent orange color, on his head or chest, and was shot by another hunter, was not necessarily contributorily negligent as a matter of law.[273] The plaintiff's failure to follow the statute was not necessarily the cause of his injury; the defendant may have caused this accident by firing his gun at the plaintiff even if the hunter had worn the required clothing.[274]

In many cases, hunters injured by a fellow hunter did not act unreasonably and, therefore, were not contributorily negligent.[275] In *Boose v Digate*, the defendant argued that the plaintiff was contributorily negligent as a matter

---

[264] *See* Hooper v Mougin, 263 Md 630, 284 A2d 236, 239 (1971); Houk v Pennington, 550 SW2d 584, 588 (Mo Ct App 1977); Turpin v Shoemaker, 427 SW2d 485, 490 (Mo 1968).

[265] *See* Baker v Rosemurgy, 4 Mich App 195, 144 NW2d 660, 662-63 (1966).

[266] *See* Houk v Pennington, 550 SW2d 584, 588 (Mo Ct App 1977); Wren v Steiger, 23 Ohio App 2d 135, 261 NE2d 191, 194 (1970); *see generally* Bookout v Victor Comptometer Corp, 40 Colo App 417, 576 P2d 197, 199 (1978) (Pierce, J, concurring) (it was unreasonable for the plaintiff to allow a child to shoot BB gun at him).

[267] *See* Turpin v Shoemaker, 427 SW2d 485, 490 (Mo 1968).

[268] *See generally* Hooper v Mougin, 263 Md 630, 284 A2d 236, 238 (1971).

[269] *Id.*

[270] *See generally* Breithaupt v Sellers, 390 So 2d 870, 873 (La 1980).

[271] *Id.*

[272] *See* La Rev Stat Ann §56:143 (West Supp 1984).

[273] 390 So 2d 870, 873 (La 1980).

[274] *Id.*

[275] *See* Mileur v Briggerman, 110 Ill App 3d 721, 442 NE2d 1356, 1359 (1982); Boose v Digate, 107 Ill App 2d 418, 246 NE2d 50, 54 (1969); Hooper v Mougin, 263 Md 630, 284 A2d 236, 239 (1971).

of law because before the defendant's shot was fired, the plaintiff saw that the defendant, who was tracking a duck, had raised his gun but the plaintiff failed to take sufficient safety measures.[276] The court rejected this argument because by the time the defendant's intention to shoot became apparent to the plaintiff it was too late for the plaintiff to make an audible signal.[277] In addition, the plaintiff's efforts in attempting to avoid injury by falling to the ground were reasonable.[278]

In *Mileur v Briggerman*, a turkey hunter wearing camouflage was shot from behind by another hunter who thought he was, in fact, a turkey.[279] The court held that the plaintiff was not contributorily negligent in failing to keep a proper lookout for other hunters because a hunter is not required to anticipate that another hunter will mistake him or her for a turkey.[280] Further, the plaintiff did not act unreasonably because he had no time to react to a shot which came from behind.[281]

Similarly, a hunting guide who was injured by a pellet when the hunter, after sighting a bird, quickly pivoted and, without hesitation, shot in his direction, was held not contributorily negligent.[282] The guide did not act unreasonably by merely being present in a hunting area.[283]

A hunter is not contributorily negligent when he or she brings a firearm to a fellow hunter's house. In *Woodward v First of Georgia Insurance Co*,[284] a high school student brought a revolver over to a friend's house and was injured as a result of his friend's negligence. The court held that the plaintiff was not contributorily negligent because the students had hunted together for several years and there was no evidence which would have led a reasonable person to believe that his friend would carelessly handle the firearm.[285] Similarly, in *Acosta v Daughtry*, the court held that a child who loaded a gun while his friend was out of the room, but did not tell him, was not contributorily negligent when the friend came back in the room and fired the gun at him.[286]

---

276 107 Ill App 2d 418, 246 NE2d 50, 54 (1969).
277 *Id.*
278 *Id.*
279 110 Ill App 3d 721, 442 NE2d 1356, 1359 (1982).
280 *Id.*
281 *Id.*
282 Hooper v Mougin, 263 Md 630, 284 A2d 236, 239 (1971).
283 *Id.*
284 333 So 2d 709, 711 (La Ct App), *writ denied*, 338 So 2d 295 (La 1976).
285 *Id.*
286 268 So 2d 416, 421 (Fla Dist Ct App 1972).

§9.12 Fishing

Assumption of the Risk

Anglers usually assume all ordinary and normal hazards incident to that sport.[287] However, where there was no evidence that a fisherman knew of the dangers, he did not assume the risk.[288]

In *Seaboard Properties, Inc v Bunchman*, a novice fisherman may not have assumed the risk of breaking his back when his skiff hit a high wave in the coastal waters off the Atlantic Ocean.[289] The court held that it could not conclude as a matter of law that the plaintiff, a college graduate and a successful businessman, should have realized the dangers inherent in riding in a small boat when he had never previously engaged in this sport.[290] Similarly, other fishermen did not assume the risk of being caught in a dangerous current of water when the government, without adequate warning, turned off some turbines because the fishermen were not aware of this danger.[291]

The courts have reached conflicting results regarding whether individuals injured by an angler's casting assumed that risk. In *Hawayek v Simmons* it was held that a fisherman did not assume the risk of being struck in the eye by a fellow fisherman whose lure took a lateral and horizontal tangent when the fisherman made an overhead-forward cast.[292] The court reasoned that fishermen do not assume the risk of negligence by others.[293] However, in *Hurley v State*, a girl who stood on a dock where fishing was permitted assumed the risk of a fisherman's hook going astray while he was casting his line.[294] In that case, the plaintiff had stayed on the dock long enough to have observed the fisherman and was capable of realizing the danger of remaining in that area.[295]

One court held that a fisherman did not assume the risk by failing to wear a life jacket because there was no real danger in engaging in this quiet activity.[296]

---

[287] *See* Lockhart v Martin, 159 Cal App 2d 760, 324 P2d 340 (1958); Hawayek v Simmons, 91 So 2d 49, 54-55 (La Ct App 1956); *see generally* Seaboard Properties, Inc v Bunchman, 278 F2d 679, 682-83 (5th Cir 1960); Johnson v State Farm Fire & Casualty Co, 303 So 2d 779, 785 (La Ct App 1974).

[288] *See* Seaboard Properties, Inc v Bunchman, 278 F2d 679, 682-83 (5th Cir 1960).

[289] *Id.*

[290] *Id.*

[291] *See* Richardson v United States, 248 F Supp 99, 104 (ED Okla 1965).

[292] 91 So 2d 49, 54-55 (La Ct App 1956).

[293] *Id.*

[294] 37 Misc 2d 680, 235 NYS2d 679, 681 (Ct Cl 1962).

[295] 235 NYS2d at 682.

[296] *See* Johnson v State Farm Fire & Casualty Co, 303 So 2d 779, 786 (La Ct App 1974).

Contributory Negligence

Anglers who fail to act reasonably may be contributorily negligent.[297] In *Heagy v City & County of Denver*, the court held that a fisherman who remained on a fishing boat for two hours after weather conditions had turned ominous was contributorily negligent as a matter of law.[298] However, a different court concluded that failure to wear a life jacket while fishing was not contributory negligence because the risk of danger from not wearing the jacket is not great.[299]

§9.13   Football

There is no question that football is a violent sport.[300] Indeed, the court in *Vendrell v School District No 26C* stated:

> The playing of football is a body contact sport. The game demands that the players come into physical contact with each other constantly, frequently with great force. ... Body contacts, bruises, and clashes are inherent in the game. There is no other way to play it. No prospective player need be told that a participant in the game of football may sustain injury. That fact is self-evident. It draws to the game the manly; they accept its risks, blows, clashes and injuries without whimper.[301]

Accordingly, most courts have traditionally held that football players assume the obvious risks in playing that sport.[302] In *Vendrell* the court held that a player assumed the risk of his coach's negligence in selecting defective equipment because he uncovered the defect, but failed to inform anyone of his finding and also did not select substitute equipment.[303]

---

[297] Johnson v State Farm Fire & Casualty Co, 303 So 2d 779, 785 (La Ct App 1974).

[298] 472 P2d 757, 759 (Colo Ct App 1970).

[299] *See* Johnson v State Farm Fire & Casualty Co, 303 So 2d 779, 785 (La Ct App 1974).

[300] One study estimated that over 400,000 football players in one year required emergency room treatment. *See* US Consumer Prod Safety Commn, Natl Injury Information Clearinghouse, Prod Summary Report (Mar 28, 1984).

[301] 233 Or 1, 376 P2d 406, 412-13 (1962); *see also* Colclough v Orleans Parish School Bd, 166 So 2d 647, 649 (La Ct App 1964) ("Football, as it is played in America, is a rough and rugged game requiring much brawn and physical effort and contact on the part of the players").

[302] *See* Hale v Davies, 86 Ga App 126, 70 SE2d 923, 925 (1952); Whipple v Salvation Army, 261 Or 453, 495 P2d 739, 743 (1972); Vendrell v School Dist No 26C, 233 Or 1, 376 P2d 406, 414 (1962).

[303] 233 Or 1, 376 P2d 406, 412 (1962).

However, in the last few years, several courts have reasoned that foot-ball players, even professional ones, do not assume many of the risks of injury.[304] In *Hackbart v Cincinnati Bengals, Inc*,[305] a professional football player, Dale Hackbart, was struck in the back of his head and neck by the forearm of another player, "Booby" Clark, after a play. The trial court ruled that in light of the known level of violence in pro-fessional football, the plaintiff assumed the risk of injury.[306] The Tenth Circuit reversed this decision on multiple grounds, most of which did not deal directly with the assumption of the risk defense. However, the court did state that there were limits on the acceptable conduct by play-ers and strongly implied that the risk of an the intentional striking of a player, conduct which is prohibited by the rules of the game, is not assumed.[307]

The assumption of the risk defense may not be applicable where the player's decision to participate was not entirely voluntary.[308] In *Rutter v Northeastern Beaver County School District*, a plurality of the Pennsylvania Supreme Court held that it was a question of fact whether a football player who was not wearing protective equipment while playing *jungle football*, a rough variant of two-handed touch football, during summer practice assumed the risk of being blinded by another player.[309] The court reasoned that if the player was compelled to accept the risks of jungle football in order to exercise his right or privilege to play high school football, he did not voluntarily assume the risk and this defense was inapplicable.[310] This was especially the case if the player had no reasonable alternative to avoid the danger, i.e., he had to play jungle football without protective equipment or he could not play on the school football team.[311]

In addition, the *Rutter* court's plurality opinion concluded that there was a question of fact whether the player knowingly assumed the risk of injury.[312]

---

[304] *See* Hackbart v Cincinnati Bengals, Inc, 601 F2d 516, 520 (10th Cir 1979); Segoviano v Housing Auth, 143 Cal App 3d 162, 191 Cal Rptr 578 (1983); Rutter v Northeastern Beaver County School Dist, 496 Pa 590, 437 A2d 1198, 1204 (1981).

[305] 601 F2d 516, 520 (10th Cir 1979).

[306] 435 F Supp 352, 356 (D Colo 1977).

[307] 601 F2d at 520-21.

[308] *See* Rutter v Northeastern Beaver County School Dist, 496 Pa 590, 437 A2d 1198, 1204 (1981).

[309] *Id* at 1206. The court's plurality opinion also argued that the assumption of the risk defense should no longer be applied. *Id.*
This case was commented upon in Note, *Tort Law*, 21 Duq L Rev 815 (1983).

[310] 437 A2d at 1205.

[311] *Id.*

[312] 437 A2d at 1204.

The plaintiff testified that he did not realize the risk of blindness and the court did not hold that this testimony was unbelievable.[313]

In general, playing flag football is not so unreasonably dangerous that participants, by making the decision to participate, act so improvidently that they cannot recover for their injuries.[314] In *Segoviano v Housing Authority*,[315] the court held that no jury instruction on either contributory negligence or assumption of risk was proper in a flag football game accident. In *Segoviano*, the plaintiff, a young man, was injured when he fell, seriously injuring his left shoulder, after he was pushed out of bounds by an opposing player attempting to stop him from scoring a touchdown. The court held that the plaintiff's decision to play football was not contributory negligence because there were no facts which indicated that this decision fell below the standard of care which a person of ordinary prudence would exercise to avoid injury to himself under the circumstances. There was no showing that the plaintiff lacked the skill or physical capacity to play the game or suffered some physical or emotional impairment which would have made his decision to play unreasonable.[316]

The fact that the plaintiff had a reasonable alternative available, i.e., not playing, does not render the decision to play unreasonable.[317] Recreational activities such as flag football usually benefit the participants as well as society, and they should be encouraged.[318] These activities must be distinguished from true forms of unreasonable conduct such as riding with an intoxicated driver.[319] Further, the plaintiff's awareness that injury could result from a fellow participant's violation of the rules does not make the plaintiff's decision to participate unreasonable.[320]

Most courts have held that spectators at football games assumed the risk and were contributorily negligent when they were injured by a player running out of bounds.[321] It is common knowledge that players run beyond the playing field, and, therefore, spectators must take appropriate precautions.[322] However, one court held that a person who stayed in an area reasonably

---

[313] *Id.*

[314] Segoviano v Housing Auth, 143 Cal App 3d 162, 191 Cal Rptr 578 (1983).

[315] *Id.*

[316] 143 Cal App 3d at 175.

[317] *Id.*

[318] *Id.*

[319] *Id.*

[320] *Id.*

[321] *See* Colclough v Orleans Parish School Bd, 166 So 2d 647, 649-50 (La Ct App 1964); Cadieux v Board of Educ, 25 AD2d 579, 266 NYS2d 895, 896 (1966); Perry v Seattle School Dist No 1, 66 Wash 2d 800, 405 P2d 589, 594 (1965); *see also* Turner v Caddo Parish School Bd, 214 So 2d 153, 156 (La 1968) (dicta).

[322] Colclough v Orleans Parish School Bd, 166 So 2d 647, 649-50 (La Ct App 1964).

removed from a *tackle-the-football* game and did not participate in that game was not contributorily negligent when a player in that game, while attempting to catch an errant pass, collided with him.[323]

§9.14 Golf

Assumption of the Risk

Golfers who are familiar with the sport generally have been held to have assumed the normal, inherent risks of engaging in that activity.[324] However, golfers usually do not assume unreasonable risks.[325] Accordingly, it is usually held that golfers do not assume the risk of a negligent act of another golfer.[326]

Most courts have held that golfers do not assume the risk of injury caused by another golfer's failure to give a proper warning.[327] In *Allen v Pinewood Country Club Inc*, the court held that a golfer who was standing in front of, and with his back turned toward, another golfer addressing his ball did not assume the risk that the second golfer would hit the ball without warning him of the impending shot.[328] Similarly, in *Jenks v McGranaghan*, a golfer did not assume the risk of injury where a second golfer failed to warn him that there was a reasonable possibility that a golf ball might strike him.[329]

Golfers also usually do not assume the risk of injury caused by another golfer's unreasonable swing of a golf club.[330] They can rely upon the

---

[323] *See* Osborne v Sprowls, 84 Ill 2d 390, 419 NE2d 913, 917 (1981).

[324] *See* Thomas v Shaw, 217 Ga 688, 124 SE2d 396, 397 (1962); Reardon v Country Club, 353 Mass 702, 234 NE2d 881, 883 (1968); *see generally* Note, *Torts-Assumption Of Risks-Golf Courses*, 14 Mercer L Rev 295 (1962).

[325] Reardon v Country Club, 353 Mass 702, 234 NE2d 881, 883 (1968); Hollenbeck v Downey, 113 NW2d 9, 13 (Minn 1962) (person who shags golf balls on a driving range does not assume the risk of being hit by a golf ball as a matter of law).

[326] *See* Thomas v Shaw, 217 Ga 688, 124 SE2d 396, 397 (1962); Brady v Kane, 111 So 2d 472, 474 (Fla Dist Ct App 1959); Duke's GMC, Inc v Erskine, 447 NE2d 1118, 1123 (Ind Ct App 1983); Jackson v Livingston Country Club, Inc, 55 AD2d 1045, 391 NYS2d 234, 235 (1977) (failure to shout "fore"); *see also* Toohey v Webster, 97 NJL 545, 117 A 838, 839 (1922).

[327] *See* Allen v Pinewood Country Club, Inc, 292 So 2d 786, 789 (La Ct App 1974); Jenks v McGranaghan, 32 AD2d 989, 299 NYS2d 228, 230 (1969).

[328] 292 So 2d 786, 789 (La Ct App 1974).

[329] 32 AD2d 989, 299 NYS2d 228, 230 (1969).

[330] *See* Tannehill v Terry, 11 Utah 2d 368, 359 P2d 911, 912 (1961) (jury verdict for defendant was affirmed).

This assumption is not justified where the plaintiff places himself or herself in the arc of the defendant's swing if he or she knew the defendant was going to swing. *Id.*

assumption that fellow golfers will not swing their golf clubs while they are standing so close that the club could strike someone.[331]

Some courts have concluded that golfers do not assume the risk that another golfer will hit a golf ball when it is dangerous to do so.[332] For example, a golfer did not assume the risk of being struck by a fellow golfer's practice shot when the person taking the practice shot should have been stationary because a third golfer was teeing off.[333] Similarly, a plaintiff did not assume the risk that a member of his own party would drive the ball while he was standing in full view of the person addressing the ball and near the intended line of flight of the ball, but had his back turned to the impending play.[334]

In a few cases, the courts have held that golfers assumed, as a matter of law, the risk of being hit by a golf ball.[335] In *Rindley v Goldberg*, a golfer who was standing on a green and watching another golfer in her party hit a ball toward the green, assumed, as a matter of law, the risk of being hit by that golf ball.[336] In another case, the court held that a golfer who was not in the zone of reasonably anticipated danger assumed the risk of injury by a golf ball which went awry.[337] However, a student who was standing at a 90-degree angle from the golfer as he addressed the tee, in an area where she had been instructed to stand, did not assume the risk, as a matter of law, that she would be hit by a *shanked* ball.[338]

A golfer may rely, at least to some extent, on the obligation of the golf club owner to keep its premises in a reasonably safe condition.[339] Accordingly, a golfer who was hit by a ball as soon as she emerged from a tree-lined stretch of path after one hole did not assume that risk as a matter of law.[340]

In several cases, the courts have held that golfers did not assume the risk of golf cart accidents.[341] In *Sipari v Villa Olivia Country Club*, the court held that a golfer did not assume, as a matter of law, the risk of a defectively

---

331 *Id.*

332 Brady v Kane, 111 So 2d 472, 474 (Fla Dist Ct App 1959); Allen v Pinewood Country Club, Inc, 292 So 2d 786, 790 (La Ct App 1974).

333 Brady v Kane, 111 So 2d 472, 474 (Fla Dist Ct App 1959).

334 Allen v Pinewood Country Club, Inc, 292 So 2d 786, 790 (La Ct App 1974).

335 *See, e.g.*, Rindley v Goldberg, 297 So 2d 140, 141 (Fla Dist Ct App 1974); Mazzuchelli v Nissenbaum, 355 Mass 788, 244 NE2d 729, 730 (1969).

336 297 So 2d 140, 141 (Fla Dist Ct App 1974).

337 *See* Mazzuchelli v Nissenbaum, 355 Mass 788, 244 NE2d 729, 730 (1969); DeMauro v Tusculum College, Inc, 603 SW2d 115, 120 (Tenn 1980).

338 *See* DeMauro v Tusculum College, Inc, 603 SW2d 115, 120 (Tenn 1980).

339 Reardon v Country Club, 353 Mass 702, 234 NE2d 881, 884 (1968); *see generally* §1.09.

340 Reardon v Country Club, 353 Mass 702, 234 NE2d 881, 884 (1968).

341 *See* Sipari v Villa Olivia Country Club, 63 Ill App 3d 985, 380 NE2d 819, 824 (1978); Nepstad v Randall, 82 SD 615, 152 NW2d 383, 386 (1967).

designed golf cart tipping over because the golfer had no knowledge of this hidden danger in the cart.[342] Similarly, in *Nepstad v Randall*, the South Dakota Supreme Court held that a golfer who rode on the hood of another golfer's golf cart and, therefore, had nothing to grasp for support did not assume the risk of injury caused by the defendant driver's unexpected negligent driving of the cart.[343]

Individuals living near golf courses may be injured by errant balls.[344] However, In *Curran v Green Hills Country Club*, the court held that a homeowner hit by an errant golf ball did not assume the risk of such an injury.[345] There was no evidence that the homeowner knew that golfers were near his home at the time of the accident and if there were no golfers nearby, there was no knowledge of any present danger.[346] The homeowner's general knowledge that golfers sometimes played in the nearby area was held to be insufficient knowledge of the actual risk of imminent danger.[347] Therefore, this defense was inapplicable.[348]

Contributory Negligence

Golfers who act unreasonably may be contributorily negligent.[349] However, a golfer was not contributorily negligent when he stood in front of, and with his back facing, another golfer since he was unaware that the second golfer was going to strike the ball.[350] Similarly, a golfer was not contributorily negligent as a matter of law when she was hit by a golf ball as she emerged from a tree-lined path after finishing one hole because it was not clear she acted unreasonably.[351]

A golfer may be contributorily negligent when he or she is hit by another golfer's swing of a golf club.[352] However, in *Morrison v Sudduth*, the Fifth Circuit held that a golfer who began to move out of the other golfer's way as soon as he gave the club to him, and who was not observing the

---

[342] 63 Ill App 3d 985, 380 NE2d 819, 824 (1978).

[343] 82 SD 615, 152 NW2d 383, 386 (1967).

[344] *See* Curran v Green Hills Country Club, 24 Cal App 3d 507, 101 Cal Rptr 158, 160 (1972).

[345] *Id.*

[346] *Id.*

[347] *Id.*

[348] *Id.*

[349] *See* Allen v Pinewood Country Club, Inc, 292 So 2d 786, 790 (La Ct App 1974); Reardon v Country Club, 353 Mass 702, 234 NE2d 881, 883 (1968); Wood v Postelthwaite, 6 Wash App 885, 496 P2d 988, 995 (1972).

[350] *See* Allen v Pinewood Country Club, Inc, 292 So 2d 786, 790 (La Ct App 1974).

[351] *See* Reardon v Country Club, 353 Mass 702, 234 NE2d 881, 883 (1968).

[352] *See generally* Morrison v Sudduth, 546 F2d 1231, 1233 (5th Cir 1977).

golfer, but rather watching his feet to avoid tripping over a light, did not act unreasonably.[353]

Most courts have held that golfers were not contributorily negligent as a matter of law where they fell on the grounds.[354] It is usually a question of fact whether the golfer should have realized the danger and acted accordingly.[355] However, one court held that a spectator at a golf tournament could not recover for injuries she sustained when she fell in a parking lot because she knew of the conditions and they were not unreasonably dangerous.[356]

Child golfers are contributorily negligent when they act below a reasonable standard of care for similar children.[357] They are usually not held to an adult standard of reasonable self-care.[358] In *Outlaw v Bituminous Insurance Co*, a child crouched behind his golf bag for protection while an adult golfer was preparing to drive a ball.[359] Unfortunately, the child raised his head above the golf bag and was struck in the eye by the ball.[360] The court held that the child was not contributorily negligent in leaving a place of safety because the danger from this act was the same danger which imposed a duty on the adult golfer not to drive the ball when a child was in the reasonably foreseeable path of the ball, and the risk which defines the duty of care of the adult golfer cannot excuse the breach of that duty.[361] The court also concluded that this child's act did not fall below the standard of conduct for similar children.[362]

A child hit by another golfer's club may not be contributorily negligent.[363] In *Brahatcek v Millard School District*, a ninth grader was fatally injured when he stood too close to another student who was showing him how to swing a golf club and was hit by the club.[364] The court held that the student, who had never played golf before or even received instruction about this sport, was not contributorily negligent as a matter of law.[365]

---

[353] *Id.*

[354] *See, e.g.*, Misenhamer v Pharr, 99 Ga App 163, 107 SE2d 875 (1959); McCarthy v River Forest Golf Club, 62 Ill App 3d 483, 379 NE2d 19, 20-21 (1978).

[355] *See* Misenhamer v Pharr, 99 Ga App 163, 107 SE2d 875, 879 (1959).

[356] *See* Pound v Augusta Natl, Inc, 158 Ga App 166, 279 SE2d 342, 344-45 (1981).

[357] *See* Outlaw v Bituminous Ins Co, 357 So 2d 1350, 1352 (La Ct App), *writ ref*, 359 So 2d 1293 (La 1978).

[358] *Id; see generally* §§2.11, 9.04, 9.15, 9.16, 9.22.

[359] 357 So 2d 1350, 1352 (La Ct App), *writ ref*, 359 So 2d 1293 (La 1978).

[360] *Id.*

[361] *Id* 1353 (affirmed a $150,000 judgment for the child).

[362] *Id.*

[363] *See* Brahatcek v Millard School Dist, 202 Neb 86, 273 NW2d 680, 687-88 (1979).

[364] *Id.*

[365] *Id.*

The plaintiff may still recover, even if he or she was contributorily negligent, where the defendant had the last clear chance to avoid the injury, but failed to do so.[366] The last clear chance doctrine only applies where the defendant has sufficient time to take some preventive action.[367] As a practical matter, there is usually insufficient time after a golf ball is struck for the defendant to warn the plaintiff of the danger, and, therefore, in many cases this doctrine is inapplicable.[368]

Product Misuse

A golfer's misuse of a product may preclude the golfer from recovering in a strict liability action.[369] However, a golfer who may have been driving a golf cart at full speed when it tipped over was not misusing the product as a matter of law.[370] The golfer's use of the cart was for an intended purpose and the jury reasonably could have concluded that it was foreseeable that the cart would be driven at full speed.[371]

One court held that a person who briefly uses a rented golf cart has no duty to inspect the cart's internal mechanism.[372]

§9.15 Gymnastics

Assumption of the Risk

Most courts have held that gymnasts injured by an obvious danger in that sport assumed the risk of that injury.[373] For example, gymnasts who landed on the edge of the trampoline[374] or unsuccessfully attempted to *leap frog* over a gymnasium horse were held to have assumed those risks.[375]

This defense is especially applicable where the gymnast is well educated[376] or was told that this activity was dangerous and should not be attempted if it could not be completed successfully.[377]

---

[366] Wood v Postelthwaite, 6 Wash App 885, 496 P2d 988, 996 (1972).

[367] 496 P2d at 997.

[368] *Id.*

[369] Sipari v Villa Olivia Country Club, 63 Ill App 3d 985, 380 NE2d 819, 825 (1978).

[370] *Id.*

[371] *Id.*

[372] *See* Vander Veer v Tyrrell, 27 AD2d 958, 278 NYS2d 916, 918 (1967).

[373] *See generally* Cohen, *Gymnastics Litigation: Meeting The Defenses*, 16 Trial 34 (Aug 1980); §§9.02, 9.03.

[374] *See* Williams v Lombardini, 38 Misc 2d 146, 238 NYS2d 63, 65 (Sup Ct 1963).

[375] *See* Sayers v Ranger, 16 NJ Super 22, 83 A2d 775, 776 (1951).

[376] *See* Williams v Lombardini, 38 Misc 2d 146, 238 NYS2d 63, 65 (1963).

[377] *See* Sayers v Ranger, 16 NJ Super 22, 83 A2d 775, 776 (1951).

Gymnasts can assume, unless they are aware of evidence to the contrary, that the protective pads around a trampoline are properly installed and afford adequate protection.[378] Accordingly, even though falling on a pad covering the edge of a trampoline may be one of the usual hazards of engaging in a gymnastic activity,[379] an athlete did not, as a matter of law, assume that risk where the gymnastics facility had not properly attached the padding to the frame.[380]

In *Chapman v State*,[381] the injured gymnast argued that he did not assume the risk that his school would fail to follow its own rule requiring four spotters for gymnastic activities. However, his argument was rejected because the four-spotter rule only applied during physical education class, and the plaintiff was injured while performing in an extracurricular activity.[382]

Contributory Negligence

Gymnasts whose unreasonable acts caused their injuries, even catastrophic ones, may have their recovery limited or barred by their contributory negligence.[383] Of course, the fact that a gymnast failed to perform a gymnastic exercise correctly is not dispositive of whether he or she was contributorily negligent.[384]

Child gymnasts are contributorily negligent when their actions fall below the standard of care of a child of like age, intelligence and experience.[385] In *Grant v Lake Oswego School District No 7*, a 12-year-old girl was held not to have been contributorily negligent as a matter of law for jumping on a springboard in an area with a low doorway beam.[386] The plaintiff was given no detailed instructions regarding the use of the springboard and this was her first use of it. Therefore, the court held that neither she nor a similar child with her background might have appreciated the danger in jumping in that area.[387]

---

378 *See* Kungle v Austin, 380 SW2d 354, 359 (Mo 1964).

379 *Id.*

380 *Id.*

381 6 Wash App 316, 492 P2d 607, 614 (1972).

382 *Id.*

383 *See* Harrison v Montgomery County Bd of Educ, 295 Md 442, 456 A2d 894 (1983); *see generally* Cohen, *Gymnastics Litigation: Meeting The Defenses*, 16 Trial 34 (Aug 1980); §9.04.

384 *See* Bellman v San Francisco High School Dist, 11 Cal 2d 576, 81 P2d 894, 897 (1938).

385 Grant v Lake Oswego School Dist No 7, 15 Or App 325, 515 P2d 947, 950 (1973); *see generally* §§9.04, 9.14, 9.16, 9.22.

386 Grant v Lake Oswego School Dist No 7, 15 Or App 325, 515 P2d 947, 950 (1973).

387 *Id.*

The doctrine of last clear chance places liability on the defendant, even though the plaintiff was contributorily negligent, where the defendant actually saw the plaintiff's peril, appreciated the danger, and still failed to act in a reasonable manner.[388] If the defendant did not realize the plaintiff's danger or had insufficient time to react, the doctrine is inapplicable.[389] Accordingly, where a physical education teacher was not cognizant that a student on a trampoline was in danger, a jury instruction on this issue was properly refused.[390]

§9.16 Hockey

Assumption of the Risk

Hockey players generally assume the known and appreciated risks of injury in that sport.[391] In *Everett v Bucky Warren Inc* the court held, as a matter of law, that a player assumed the risk of injury caused by playing with a hockey helmet which had gaps larger than the size of a puck.[392] The court reasoned that the obvious risk caused by the large gaps could support an inference that the player was aware of the risks and assumed them.[393]

However, players who are not aware of certain risks do not assume those risks.[394] For example, children who do not appreciate the risk of floor hockey because of their lack of intelligence, experience, and information, do not assume the unknown risks of this activity.[395]

Spectators at hockey games who are familiar with the risks of being hit by a puck may assume that risk.[396] In *Kennedy v Providence Hockey Club, Inc,*

---

388 *See* Chapman v State, 6 Wash App 316, 492 P2d 607, 610 (1972).

389 *Id.*

390 *Id.*

391 *See* Everett v Bucky Warren, Inc, 376 Mass 280, 380 NE2d 653, 659 (1978); *see generally* §§9.02, 9.03.

392 *Id.*

393 *Id.*

394 Berman v Philadelphia Bd of Educ, 456 A2d 545, 550 (Pa Super 1983).

395 *Id.*

396 *See* Tite v Omaha Coliseum Corp, 12 NW2d 90, 95 (Neb 1943); Ingersoll v Onondaga Hockey Club, 245 AD 137, 281 NYS 505, 508 (1935); Kennedy v Providence Hockey Club, Inc, 117 RI 70, 376 A2d 329, 333 (1977).
Most courts have held that spectators who were sitting in an unprotected area did not assume the risk of injury as a matter of law. Uline Ice, Inc v Sullivan, 187 F2d 82, 85-86 (DC Cir 1950); Shurman v Fresno Ice Rink, 91 Cal App 2d 469, 205 P2d 77, 81 (1949); Lemoine v Springfield Hockey Assn, 307 Mass 102, 29 NE2d 716, 718 (1940); Shanney v Boston Madison Square Garden Corp, 296 Mass 168, 5 NE2d 1, 2 (1936); Morris v Cleveland Hockey Club, 157 Ohio St 225, 105 NE2d 419, 426 (1952); James v Rhode Island Auditorium, Inc, 60 RI 405, 199 A 293, 298 (1938).

a long-time hockey fan who had attended numerous hockey games in person and was familiar with the danger of hockey pucks flying off the ring and into the seats, assumed the risk of being hit by the puck.[397] The court held that it was irrelevant that the only seats available when this fan purchased the tickets were in an area close to the arena floor.[398]

Contributory Negligence

Hockey players who act unreasonably may be guilty of contributory negligence.[399]

Child players are usually judged by what is reasonable for a similar child with the same background.[400] In *Berman v Philadelphia Board of Education*,[401] an 11-year-old floor hockey player was held not contributorily negligent in playing that sport. The plaintiff did not have an exceptional amount of experience playing this game, had not observed other injuries, and did not have a superior intellect which allowed him to perceive dangers that he did not observe.[402] Therefore, he did not realize the danger in playing floor hockey and, since the court held that a similar child also would not have realized the danger, he was not contributorily negligent.[403] Indeed, in this case the defendant failed to overcome the presumption that an 11-year-old child was incapable of negligence.[404]

§9.17   Horseback Riding

Assumption of the Risk

Several courts have held that horseback riders assume the reasonably foreseeable risks which are inherent in that sport.[405] Accordingly, a rider

---

The courts have reasoned that hockey is not well-known in this country and, therefore, the plaintiff should not be considered to have been aware of the risk of being hit by a puck. Uline Ice, Inc v Sullivan, 187 F2d 82, 85-86 (DC Cir 1950); Thurman v Ice Palace, 36 Cal App 2d 364, 97 P2d 999, 1001 (1939); Lemoine v Springfield Hockey Assn, 307 Mass 102, 29 NE2d 716, 718 (1940); James v Rhode Island Auditorium, Inc, 60 RI 405, 199 A 293, 298 (1938). However, those are old cases and hockey is better-known today.

[397] Kennedy v Providence Hockey Club, Inc, 117 RI 70, 376 A2d 329, 333 (1977).

[398] *Id.*

[399] *See generally* §9.04.

[400] *See generally* §§9.04, 9.14, 9.15, 9.22.

[401] 456 A2d 545, 549-50 (Pa Super Ct 1983).

[402] *Id.*

[403] *Id.*

[404] *Id* 549-50.

[405] *See* Hargrave v Wellman, 276 F2d 948, 951 (9th Cir 1960); Baar v Hoder, 482 P2d 386, 388 (Colo Ct App 1971); Liossis v Cavalry Riding Academy Co, 86 Ohio App 334, 87

who knew that a particular horse was dangerous assumed the risk in riding that horse.[406] In *Reynolds v Kenwood Riding Club*, a rider who knew she was unable to control her horse, and yet continued to ride after she had an opportunity to dismount, was held to have assumed the risk.[407] Indeed, even an inexperienced rider may assume the risk if the rider was told several times not to ride a "spirited" horse.[408]

Further, experienced riders may assume additional risks.[409] In *Daniel v Cambridge Mutual Fire Insurance Co*, the court held that an experienced rider who knew and appreciated the danger which can result when even a well-trained horse shies or rears, assumed the risk of injury from such an occurrence.[410]

Riders generally do not assume risks they do not understand and appreciate.[411] For example, they do not assume the risk of improper saddling where they have no knowledge that this has occurred.[412] One court held that a 12-year-old child with little experience as a rider did not realize and appreciate, at least not as a matter of law, the danger of urging his horse to go faster.[413]

Contributory Negligence

A horseback rider is contributorily negligent if his or her conduct falls below that of a reasonable person under the circumstances.[414] For example, a rider on a horse which exhibits unmanageable characteristics must take reasonable safety precautions, e.g., dismounting[415] In a different case, the

---

NE2d 266, 268, 41 Ohio Op 375 (1949); Alfonso v Market Facilities, Inc, 356 So 2d 86, 89 (La Ct App), *writ denied*, 357 So 2d 1169 (La 1978); Roots v Claremont Riding Academy, 20 AD2d 536, 245 NYS2d 172, 173 (1963), *affd without opinion*, 14 NY2d 827, 200 NE2d 457, 251 NYS2d 475 (1964); Lackey v Perry, 366 SW2d 91, 95 (Tex Civ App 1963).

[406] *See* La Hoste v Yaarab Mounted Patrol, Inc, 89 Ga App 397, 79 SE2d 570, 573 (1953).

[407] 59 Ohio App 453, 18 NE2d 612, 614 (1938).

[408] *See* Brooks v Mack, 222 Or 139, 352 P2d 474, 477 (1960).

[409] Daniel v Cambridge Mut Fire Ins Co, 368 So 2d 810, 814 (La Ct App), *writ denied*, 369 So 2d 1063 (La 1979).

[410] *Id.*

[411] *See* Liossis v Cavalry Riding Academy Co, 86 Ohio App 334, 87 NE2d 266, 268 (1949); Dee v Parish, 160 Tex 171, 327 SW2d 449, 452 (1959); Lackey v Perry, 366 SW2d 91, 95 (Tex Civ App 1963).

[412] *See* Liossis v Cavalry Riding Academy Co, 86 Ohio App 334, 87 NE2d 266, 268 (1949); Lackey v Perry, 366 SW2d 91, 95 (Tex Civ App 1963).

[413] *See* Dee v Parish, 160 Tex 171, 327 SW2d 449, 452 (1959).

[414] *See* Reeves v John A. Cooper Co, 304 F Supp 828, 834 (WD Ark 1969); Baty v Wolff, 162 Neb 1, 74 NW2d 917, 918 (1956); Willenbring v Borkenhagen, 29 Wis 2d 464, 139 NW2d 53 (1966).

[415] Baty v Wolff, 162 Neb 1, 74 NW2d 917, 918 (1956).

court held that a rider who pulled his horse out of line on a trail ride acted unreasonably and was contributorily negligent.[416]

One court held that an inexperienced rider was judged by the standard of an ordinary inexperienced rider.[417] However, an inexperienced horseback rider may be contributorily negligent in refusing to accept the services of a guide.[418] Indeed, the Wisconsin Supreme Court in *Willenbring v Borkenhagen* held that a 14-year-old girl, who had little experience riding horses, should have realized the danger of riding when, after she told the horseback riding facility that she wanted to ride without a guide, the facility disclaimed all liability.[419]

The fact that there are some inherent risks of horseback riding which all reasonable individuals should realize, e.g., that one may fall or get thrown off the horse, does not, for that reason alone, make all riders contributorily negligent.[420] Horseback riding facilities generally are still liable for injuries caused by their negligence.[421]

§9.18 Motorcycling

Motorcycling is a dangerous activity. In 1983, over 4,000 motorcyclists were killed in accidents.[422]

Assumption of the Risk

Motorcyclists assume the risk of injury from defective motorcycles where they have actual knowledge of the specific risk which caused the injury, appreciate the magnitude of that risk, and still use the motorcycle.[423] For example, one court held that a motorcyclist who was aware that a motorcycle was not equipped with crash bars, tubular steel bars which bolt to the motorcycle frame in front of the rider's knees, and was aware of the attendant

---

[416] *See generally* Reeves v John A. Cooper Co, 304 F Supp 828, 834 (WD Ark 1969).

[417] *See* Vaningan v Mueller, 208 Wis 527, 243 NW 419 (1932) (plaintiff was injured while attempting to stop a run-away horse).

[418] *See* Willenbring v Borkenhagen, 29 Wis 2d 464, 139 NW2d 53 (1966).

[419] *Id.* The dissent argued that the facility should have required a guide to go on every ride. *See id* 57 (Hallows, J, dissenting).

[420] *See generally* Christian v Elden, 107 NH 229, 221 A2d 784, 789 (1966).

[421] *See id; see also* §1.12.

[422] US Dept of Transportation, Fatal Accident Reporting System 1983, at ii. However, motorcycle fatalities have dropped about 17% from 1980 to 1983. *See id* i.

[423] *See* Cota v Harley Davidson, 141 Ariz 7, 684 P2d 888, 895 (App 1984); Hunt v Harley Davidson Motor Co, 1978-79 Prod Liab Rep (CCH) ¶8243, at 17,279 (Ga Ct App 1978).

dangers of not having this safety device but still used the motorcycle, assumed the risk of injury.[424]

Motorcyclists do not assume risks when they have only a general knowledge of the danger.[425] Accordingly, in *Cota v Harley Davidson* the court concluded that a motorcyclist's knowledge that: (1) it is easier to be injured on a motorcycle than in an automobile; (2) riding on the wrong side of the road is dangerous; and (3) if there is a hole in the gas tank, gas can spill out and ignite, did not justify an assumption of the risk jury instruction.[426] The defendant failed to prove that the motorcyclist knew and appreciated the specific risk of injury in that case—viz., that the motorcycle tank could be penetrated by the fairing bracket or mirror bracket—and yet still rode the motorcycle.[427] Absent proof that the motorcyclist knew of the specific defect, this defense was not applicable.[428]

Contributory Negligence

Motorcyclists who act unreasonably may have their claim for recovery extinguished or limited.[429] Unsurprisingly, motorcyclists traveling too fast under the circumstances have been found contributorily negligent.[430] Indeed, in *Perricone v DiBartolo*, an Illinois court held that a minor who raced a gas-powered minibike on a public sidewalk and acted oblivious to the known danger of nearby cars was contributorily negligent as a matter of law.[431]

A motorcyclist's violation of a statute may show that the motorcyclist acted unreasonably.[432] One court held that a motorcyclist who went 25 miles per

---

[424] *See* Hunt v Harley Davidson Motor Co, 1978-79 Prod Liab Rep (CCH) ¶8243, at 17,279 (Ga Ct App 1978).

[425] Cota v Harley Davidson, 141 Ariz 7, 684 P2d 888, 895 (Ct App 1984).

[426] *Id.*

[427] *Id.*

[428] *Id.*

[429] *See* Prichard v Veterans Cab Co, 63 Cal 2d 727, 408 P2d 360, 47 Cal Rptr 904, 906 (1965); Perricone v DiBartelo, 14 Ill App 3d 514, 302 NE2d 637, 641 (1973); Stevens v Salt Lake County, 25 Utah 2d 168, 478 P2d 496, 498 (1970); *see generally* Cutway v State, 89 AD2d 406, 456 NYS2d 539, 541 (1982) (plaintiff was operating an all-terrain vehicle).

Of course, where there is no evidence of defendant's negligence, then contributory negligence is not an issue. Pawlak v Brown, 430 So 2d 1345, 1352 (La Ct App 1983).

[430] *See* Prichard v Veterans Cab Co, 63 Cal 2d 727, 408 P2d 360, 47 Cal Rptr 904, 906 (1965); Perricone v DiBartelo, 14 Ill App 3d 514, 302 NE2d 637, 641 (1973); Brown v Yamaha Motor Corp, 38 Wash App 914, 691 P2d 577, 581 (1984) (plaintiff may also have improperly handled the motorcycle); *see generally* Cutway v State, 89 AD2d 406, 456 NYS2d 539, 541 (1982) (plaintiff was operating an all-terrain vehicle).

[431] 14 Ill App 3d 514, 302 NE2d 637, 641 (1973). The plaintiff also violated a city ordinance prohibiting driving a vehicle within a sidewalk area. *See id.*

[432] *See* Epling v United States, 453 F2d 327, 330 (9th Cir 1971).

A motorcyclist's violation of the speed laws is prima facie evidence that the motorcyclist

hour in a 5 miles per hour zone was contributorily negligent.[433] However, the violation of a statute is not contributory negligence unless there is a causal relationship between the violation and the accident.[434] For example, a motorcyclist who drove a motorcycle which had more horsepower than he had a license to operate was not contributorily negligent when this factor did not cause the injury-producing collision.[435]

Motorcyclists generally can assume that others will follow the traffic laws.[436] In *Simmons v Wexler*, the court held that a motorcyclist on a highway protected by stop signs may initially rely upon the fact that vehicles on the intersecting streets should not be driven into the rider's path.[437] Accordingly, it concluded that the lack of direct evidence as to whether the motorcyclist did or did not observe cars in the intersection was not, standing alone, evidence of the motorcyclist's contributory negligence.[438]

It is, of course, well-known that drinking and driving are a combustible combination. Therefore, a motorcyclist who has been drinking may be contributorily negligent.[439] In one case where a motorcycle left the pavement and crashed into a guardrail for no apparent reason related to the motorcycle, the defendant was allowed to introduce evidence of the plaintiff's intoxication.[440]

Motorcyclists must take reasonable precautions under existing weather conditions.[441] However, one court held that a motorcyclist who was not wearing a hat or goggles in a heavy rain was not contributorily negligent as a matter of law.[442]

A passenger on a motorcycle generally may rely upon the driver to monitor driving conditions.[443] Indeed, in one case, a passenger who failed to observe road conditions was found free of contributory negligence as a matter of law.[444]

---

was acting unreasonably. Gravley v Sea Gull Marine, Inc, 269 NW2d 896, 901 (Minn 1978).

[433] *Id.*

[434] Williams v Esaw, 214 Kan 658, 522 P2d 950, 953 (1974).

[435] 522 P2d at 954.

[436] Simmons v Wexler, 94 Cal App 3d 1007, 1013, 156 Cal Rptr 810 (1979).

[437] *Id.*

[438] *See id.*

[439] McInnes v Yamaha Motor Corp, 659 SW2d 704, 708 (Tex Ct App 1983).

[440] *Id.*

[441] *See generally* Moulton v Gaidmore Poultry Co, 100 NH 92, 120 A2d 135, 136 (1956).

[442] *Id.*

[443] Crowe v State Farm Mut Auto Ins Co, 416 So 2d 1376, 1382 (La Ct App 1982).

[444] *Id.*

Virtually all courts have held that a minor is held to the standard of care of an adult, not the lower standard of a child of similar age and experience, when operating a motorcycle,[445] motorbike,[446] motor scooter,[447] or motorized mini-bike[448] in determining whether the minor was contributorily negligent.[449] The courts have reasoned that driving a motorcycle or other motorized vehicle is an adult activity and an adult standard of conduct is required.[450] It is simply too dangerous for society to allow anyone to use such vehicles unless they can be operated with safety, and that requires an adult standard of care.[451]

Helmets

In the mid-1960s, under the Federal Highway Safety Act, the Secretary of Transportation conditioned the availability of certain highway funds on the existence of state helmet statutes.[452] As a result, by 1975 almost all states had passed such laws.[453] However, in 1976, the Secretary's power to condition federal funds on the existence of state helmet laws was withdrawn and some states began to repeal these laws.[454] The repeal has not been uniform and some states still require motorcyclists to wear protective headgear.[455]

---

[445] *See* Burns v Wheeler, 103 Ariz 525, 446 P2d 925, 929 (1968); Harrelson v Whitehead, 236 Ark 325, 365 SW2d 868, 869 (1963); Prichard v Veterans Cab Co, 63 Cal 2d 727, 408 P2d 360, 47 Cal Rptr 904, 907 (1965); Williams v Esaw, 214 Kan 658, 522 P2d 950, 959 (1974); Daniels v Evans, 107 NH 407, 224 A2d 63, 66 (1966).

[446] *See* Medina v McAllister, 202 So 2d 755, 757 (Fla 1967); Sheetz v Welch, 89 Ga App 749, 81 SE2d 319, 323-24 (1954); Davis v Waterman, 420 So 2d 1063, 1066 (Miss 1982); Adams v Lopez, 75 NM 503, 407 P2d 50, 52 (1965); Powell v Hartford Accident & Indem Co, 217 Tenn 503, 398 SW2d 727, 733 (1966); *but see* Hemmelgarn v Bailey, 61 Ohio L Abs 179, 104 NE2d 50, 52 (1950).

[447] *See* Medina v McAllister, 202 So 2d 755, 757 (Fla 1967); Powell v Hartford Accident & Indem Co, 217 Tenn 503, 398 SW2d 727, 731 (1966).

[448] *See* Perricone v DiBartolo, 14 Ill App 3d 514, 302 NE2d 637, 641 (1973).

[449] *See generally* §2.12.

[450] *See* Burns v Wheeler, 103 Ariz 525, 446 P2d 925, 929 (1968); Harrelson v Whitehead, 236 Ark 325, 365 SW2d 868, 869 (1963); Prichard v Veterans Cab Co, 63 Cal 2d 727, 408 P2d 360, 47 Cal Rptr 904, 907 (1965); Williams v Esaw, 214 Kan 658, 522 P2d 950, 959 (1974); Daniels v Evans, 107 NH 407, 224 A2d 63, 66 (1966).

[451] *See* Burns v Wheeler, 103 Ariz 525, 446 P2d 925, 929 (1968); Harrelson v Whitehead, 236 Ark 325, 365 SW2d 868, 869 (1963); Prichard v Veterans Cab Co, 63 Cal 2d 727, 408 P2d 360, 47 Cal Rptr 904, 907 (1965); Williams v Esaw, 214 Kan 658, 522 P2d 950, 959 (1974); Daniels v Evans, 107 NH 407, 224 A2d 63, 66 (1966).

[452] Dare v Soule, 674 P2d 960, 963 n 5 (Colo 1984).

[453] *Id.*

[454] *Id.*

[455] *See, e.g.,* Minn Stat §169.974 (1984) (persons under 18 years old); ND Cent Code §39-10.2-06 (1972) (persons under 18 years old).

A motorcyclist's failure to use a helmet rarely contributes to the cause of the accident.[456] Nonetheless, it may be a contributing cause to the severity of the plaintiff's injuries.[457] Indeed, in one study about 65 per cent of all people killed in motorcycle accidents were not wearing a helmet.[458] Therefore, a motorcyclist's failure to wear a helmet may be relevant to the quantum of damages recoverable from the defendant.[459]

However, in *Dare v Sobule*, the Colorado Supreme Court held that evidence of a motorcyclist's failure to wear a protective helmet is inadmissible to show his or her contributory negligence or to mitigate damages.[460] Indeed, it held that the plaintiff is entitled to a jury instruction stating that operating a motorcycle without wearing a helmet is not contributory negligence.[461]

The *Dare* court basically grounded its analysis on two points. First, a defendant should not obtain a windfall by not paying for all damages caused by his or her negligence.[462] Second, allowing this defense would result in a battle of experts as to what injuries would or would not have been prevented.[463]

Neither reason is persuasive. First, the essence of comparative negligence is that the negligence of both parties is compared and damages are allowed only for the proportionate amount of the damages caused by the defendant's actions or omissions. The court's analysis also fails because there is no a priori reason why the plaintiff should obtain a windfall by not having damages reduced by acts which aggravated his or her injuries. Second, there is no reason why a battle of experts in this area is any more disadvantageous than on any other issue. It is not unusual to have conflicting expert testimony in most cases, but this should not be seen as a reason to bar a defendant's experts.

There is authority that a plaintiff's failure to use a helmet is relevant evidence.[464] In *Halvorson v Voeller*, the North Dakota Supreme Court held that evidence of a motorcyclist's failure to wear a protective helmet is admissible to reduce the plaintiff's damages so long as there is competent testimony by a

---

456 Halvorson v Voeller, 336 NW2d 118, 119 (ND 1983).

457 *Id.*

458 *See* US Dept of Transportation, Fatal Accident Reporting System 1983, at 87.

459 Halvorson v Voeller, 336 NW2d 118, 119 (ND 1983); *see generally* Note, *Helmetless Motorcyclists—Easy Riders Facing Hard Facts: The Rise Of The Motorcycle Helmet Defense*, 41 Ohio St LJ 233 (1978).

460 674 P2d 960, 963 (Colo 1984).

461 *Id.* The court also held that it was error to admit evidence regarding the cyclist's failure to use a helmet even though the plaintiff did not timely object to this evidence. *Id* 963-64.

462 *Id.*

463 *Id.*

464 *See* Halvorson v Voeller, 336 NW2d 118, 120 (ND 1983).

qualified expert that the use of a helmet would have lessened the injuries the plaintiff sustained.[465] At least one state statute has a similar requirement.[466]

§9.19 Roller Skating

Assumption of the Risk

Most courts have held that roller skaters assume the obvious risks inherent in that activity.[467] This generally includes injuries from falling because of the lack of skill by the plaintiff or other skaters.[468]

However, roller skaters do not assume the risk of injury from the reckless actions of other patrons which should have been detected and controlled by the roller skating facility.[469] For example, in *Dobard v Skate Country, Inc*, the court held that the danger presented by wildly skating patrons is within the control of floor guards of the skating rink who have a duty to prevent such behavior.[470] Accordingly, a jury's determination that a skater did not assume the risk of injury of being hit by several other patrons who had been skating "wildly" for some time prior to the accident was affirmed.[471]

In addition, the risk of injury from dangerous conditions on the rink floor is usually not assumed.[472] However, skaters were held to have assumed this risk where they actually knew of the dangerous condition or the condition was so obvious that any testimony to the contrary was not credible.[473]

Contributory Negligence

Roller skaters who act unreasonably may have their recovery limited or

---

465 *Id* 120.

466 *See* Minn Stat §169.974(6) (1984).

467 *See* Benoit v Marvin, 120 Vt 201, 138 A2d 312, 316 (1958); Humbyrd v Spurlock, 345 SW2d 499, 503 (Mo Ct App 1981); Schamel v St Louis Arena Corp, 324 SW2d 375, 378 (Mo Ct App 1959); Dobard v Skate Country, Inc, 451 So 2d 1231, 1233 (La Ct App 1984); Blizzard v Fitzsimmons, 193 Miss 484, 10 So 2d 343, 344 (1942).

468 Schamel v St Louis Arena Corp, 324 SW2d 375, 378 (Mo Ct App 1959); *see also* Dobard v Skate Country, Inc, 451 So 2d 1231, 1233 (La Ct App 1984) (some bumping and jostling is an ordinary risk of roller skating).

469 *See* Thomas v Studio Amusements, Inc, 50 Cal App 2d 538, 123 P2d 552, 555 (1942); Dobard v Skate Country, Inc, 451 So 2d 1231, 1233 (La Ct App 1984); Schamel v St Louis Arena Corp, 324 SW2d 375, 378 (Mo Ct App 1959).

470 451 So 2d 1231, 1233 (La Ct App 1984).

471 *Id.*

472 *See* Benoit v Marvin, 120 Vt 201, 138 A2d 312, 316 (1958).

473 *See* Benoit v Marvin, 120 Vt 201, 138 A2d 312, 316 (1958); Dorry v Lafluer, 399 So 2d 559, 561 (La 1981).

eliminated.[474] Indeed, in several cases, skaters who fell were held to have been contributorily negligent.[475] In one such case, the court held that the skater's failure to check whether her skate was properly adjusted was contributory negligence.[476]

In some situations, even a skater's contributory negligence does not bar recovery.[477] In *Dorry v Lafluer*, the court held that a skater who continued skating even though he saw some puddles on the rink did not have his recovery limited because the defense of contributory negligence was inapplicable where the facility was strictly liable for the building's defects.[478]

§9.20 Snowmobiling

Assumption of the Risk

Generally, experienced snowmobilers who are aware of and understand the risks of that sport assume those risks.[479] In contrast, novice snowmobilers usually have been held not to have assumed the risk of injury because they were unaware of the risks.[480] This is true even where the risks were obvious to others, e.g., there were ice patches on the track.[481]

Passengers in a snowmobile usually do not assume the risk of injury caused by the operator's actions.[482] For example, in *Ujifusa v National Housewares, Inc*, a professional photographer who took pictures of a snowmobile did not assume the risk that the snowmobile operator would go over an obstacle rather than going around it.[483] Similarly, in *Olson v Hansen*, a passenger did not assume the risk of the operator's decision to traverse some hills, an action which increased the probability of tipping over, because she had no actual knowledge of the danger.[484]

---

474 Damer v State, 34 Misc 2d 363, 228 NYS2d 997, 999 (Ct Cl 1962).

475 *Id*; Fry v Alexander, 290 P2d 397, 399-400 (Okla 1955).

476 Fry v Alexander, 290 P2d 397, 399-400 (Okla 1955).

477 Dorry v Lafluer, 399 So 2d 559, 561 (La 1981).

478 *Id*.

479 *See generally* §§9.02, 9.03.

480 *See, e.g.*, Olson v Hansen, 299 Minn 39, 216 NW2d 124, 127 (1974); Ujifusa v National Housewares, Inc, 24 Utah 2d 219, 469 P2d 7, 9 (1970).

481 *See* Watson v Zanotti Motor Co, 219 Pa Super 96, 280 A2d 670, 672 (1971).

482 *See* Olson v Hansen, 299 Minn 39, 216 NW2d 124, 128 (1974); Ujifusa v National Housewares, Inc, 24 Utah 2d 219, 469 P2d 7, 8-9 (1970).

483 24 Utah 2d 219, 469 P2d 7, 8-9 (1970).

484 299 Minn 39, 216 NW2d 124, 128 (1974).

Contributory Negligence

Snowmobilers who act unreasonably may be contributorily negligent.[485] In several cases, experienced snowmobilers who were riding as passengers and who knew of the potential for injury, but failed to warn the driver of the danger, were held contributorily negligent.[486] In *Powell v Alaska Marine Equipment, Inc*,[487] the court held that the plaintiff, a passenger who was an experienced snowmobiler, could not recover where she was injured after the driver *nosed down* over a river bank.[488] The court held that the passenger, who knew of the river channel's location and knew the snowmobile was headed in that direction, acted unreasonably in failing to warn the driver of the existence and location of the channel.[489] In a different case, the court held that a plaintiff who was familiar with the risks caused by the negligent operation of a snowmobile, but failed to caution the careless driver about the driver's conduct, should have his damages reduced about 20 per cent for his unreasonable actions.[490]

The plaintiff is not contributorily negligent when he or she did not act unreasonably.[491] For example, a passenger in a snowmobile was not contributorily negligent when she followed the driver's instructions to lean in the same direction he did, even though this caused the snowmobile to roll over, because it was reasonable to follow the driver's directions.[492] In another case, a passenger was also not contributorily negligent where the driver jumped an obstacle because the passenger had no opportunity to take preventive action.[493] The passenger was seated behind the driver, could not see the obstacle, and was not warned of the jump.[494]

In *Watson v Zanotti Motor Co*, an individual with no prior snowmobile experience, who was injured while test driving a snowmobile, was not contributorily negligent as a matter of law where he did not know the track

---

485 *See* Powell v Alaska Marine Equip, Inc, 453 P2d 407 (Alaska 1969); Olson v Hansen, 299 Minn 39, 216 NW2d 124, 127 (1974); Isker v Gardner, 360 NW2d 468, 470 (Minn Ct App 1985).

486 *See* Powell v Alaska Marine Equip, Inc, 453 P2d 407 (Alaska 1969); Isker v Gardner, 360 NW2d 468, 470 (Minn Ct App 1985).

487 453 P2d 407 (Alaska 1969).

488 *Id* 408.

489 *Id.*

490 Isker v Gardner, 360 NW2d 468, 470 (Minn Ct App 1985).

491 *See* Olson v Hansen, 299 Minn 39, 216 NW2d 124, 128 (1974); Ujifusa v National Housewares, Inc, 24 Utah 2d 219, 469 P2d 7, 7-8 (1970).

492 *See* Olson v Hansen, 299 Minn 39, 216 NW2d 124, 128 (1974).

493 Ujifusa v National Housewares, Inc, 24 Utah 2d 219, 469 P2d 7, 7-8 (1970).

494 *Id.*

was dangerous and there was no visible evidence of danger.[495] Although the plaintiff might have been contributorily negligent in not looking out for his own safety, the court held that this was a question of fact.[496]

In general, the violation of a statute enacted for the protection of motorists is negligence per se.[497] However, the violation is excused if there is an emergency created by another party.[498] For example, in *Reed v AMF Western Tool, Inc,*[499] the plaintiff pursued a runaway snowmobile onto the highway in an attempt to stop it. Unfortunately, a lumber truck was traveling on the highway and it collided with the snowmobile, causing the plaintiff to be thrown into the side of the truck. The court concluded that the plaintiff was not contributorily negligent.[500] It was not unreasonable to race onto the highway without taking the time to ascertain whether it was safe to do so because in this emergency situation time was critical.[501]

§9.21 Snow Skiing

Assumption of the Risk

Several courts have held that a skier who is aware of the dangers of skiing and still engages in that activity assumes the risk of injury.[502] One commentator suggested three practical policy reasons for the assumption of the risk defense in skiing accident cases.[503] First, it would be impossible for ski resort operators to oversee the ability of every skier.[504] Second, fluctuations in snow and weather conditions make it impossible for area operators to keep trails consistently free from danger.[505] Third, the inherent risks in the sport are part of what makes skiing enjoyable.[506]

---

495 219 Pa Super 96, 280 A2d 670, 672 (1971).

496 *Id.*

497 Reed v AMF Western Tool, Inc, 431 F2d 345 (9th Cir 1970).

498 *Id.*

499 *Id.*

500 *Id* 348.

501 *Id.*

502 *See* Wright v Mt Mansfield Lift, 96 F Supp 786, 791 (D Vt 1951); Leopold v Okemo Mountain, Inc, 420 F Supp 781 (D Vt 1976): McDaniel v Dowell, 210 Cal App 2d 26, 36, 26 Cal Rptr 140 (1962); Note, *Ski Operators And Skiers,* 14 New Eng L Rev 260, 275 (1978) (dangers of tramway towers are obvious); *see also* Pa Cons Stat Ann tit 42, §7102 (1982); Vt Stat Ann tit 12, §1037 (Supp 1984) ("a person who takes part in any sport accepts as a matter of law the dangers that inhere therein insofar as they are obvious and necessary").

503 *See* Note, *Ski Operators and Skiers,* 14 New Eng L Rev 260, 262 (1978).

504 *Id.*

505 *Id.*

506 *Id.*

A traditional application of this defense occurred in *Wright v Mt Mansfield Lift*, where the court held that a skier who was injured when he hit a snow-covered stump suffered harm from an inherent danger of skiing.[507] Therefore, he could not recover from the ski facility.[508]

Indeed, the *Wright* court graphically stated the risks of skiing:

> Skiing is a sport; a sport that entices thousands of people; a sport that requires an ability on the part of the skier to handle himself or herself under various circumstances of grade, boundary, mid-trail obstructions, corners and varied conditions of the snow. Secondly, it requires good judgment on the part of the skier and recognition of the existing circumstances and conditions. Only the skier knows his own ability to cope with a certain piece of trail. Snow, ranging from powder to ice, can be of infinite kinds. Breakable crust may be encountered where soft snow is expected. Roots and rocks may be hidden under a thin cover. A single thin stubble of cut brush can trip a skier in the middle of a turn. Sticky snow may follow a fast running surface without warning. Skiing conditions may change quickly. What was a short time before a perfect surface with a soft cover on all bumps may fairly rapidly become filled with ruts, worn spots and other manner of skier created hazards.[509]

Similarly, in *Leopold v Okemo Mountain, Inc*, the court held that a wife's suit, as executrix of her husband's estate, for wrongful death was barred by her husband's assumption of the risk.[510] In that case the skier collided with unpadded towers on the trail and died. The court concluded that skiers assume all the obvious and necessary risks involved in that sport, and this included the danger that skiers may collide with a tower if they lose their control or concentration.[511] Indeed, the court noted that the hazards created by unpadded towers on a ski trail were "obvious and necessary"[512] because the danger could easily be observed. Therefore, if the skier believed that the trail or the towers presented risks which were too great, he should have chosen not to proceed.[513]

However, in several recent cases, the courts have held that skiers did not

---

[507] 96 F Supp 786, 791 (D Vt 1951).

[508] *Id.*

[509] *Id* 790-91.

[510] 420 F Supp 781 (D Vt 1976).

[511] *Id* 787.

[512] *Id* 786.

[513] *Id.*

assume specific unknown risks.[514] In 1978, the Vermont Supreme Court handed down its landmark ruling in *Sunday v Stratton Corp*, holding that a skier did not assume the risk of injury from a small bush which was concealed by loose snow on a novice trail.[515] The court reasoned that it is a matter of common knowledge that skiers fall, but this does not make every fall a danger inherent in the sport.[516] In that case, there was no evidence that the plaintiff knew of the existence of the undergrowth before his skis ran into it and, therefore, there should have been no jury instruction on assumption of risk.[517] Similarly, in *Rosen v LTV Recreational Development, Inc*, the court held that a skier did not assume the risk of catapulting into a metal pole after a collision with another skier because the plaintiff had no knowledge of the danger until the other skier made an unexpected turn.[518]

In one case, the defense counsel's failure to produce evidence that the plaintiff was aware of the specific risk of being hit by other skiers on the slopes, even when there was testimony that the plaintiff was aware of the inherent risks of skiing, was held sufficient to remove this defense from the case.[519]

The assumption of the risk defense has not been applied when a skier slipped on a dangerous pathway where the skier had no reasonably safe alternative.[520] In *Stearns v Sugarbush Valley Corp*,[521] a person fell on a path from the bar to a parking lot located at a ski facility. The court held that the facility had invited the public to come to its premises and, therefore, could not, after the accident, claim that its patrons came at their own risk,[522] at least where there was no reasonably available alternative route back to the parking lot. Similarly, in *Eisenhart v Loveland Skiing Corp*, the court held that a skier who slipped on a piece of ice on her way from a public restroom did not assume the risk of injury as a matter of law when she chose this restroom, which was surrounded by ice, because she believed that the other restroom was occupied.[523]

---

514 *See* Rosen v LTV Recreational Dev, Inc, 569 F2d 1117, 1121 (10th Cir 1978) (Colorado law); Sunday v Stratton Corp, 136 Vt 293, 390 A2d 398, 402 (1978).

515 136 Vt 293, 390 A2d 398, 402 (1978).

516 390 A2d at 403.

517 *Id* 404; *see also* Note, *Ski Operators and Skiers*, 14 New Eng L Rev 260, 263 (1978).

As a result of the *Sunday* decision, the Vermont legislature passed a statute that provided that participants assume the obvious risks in their sport. *See* Vt Stat Ann tit 12, §1037 (Supp 1984).

518 569 F2d 1117, 1121 (10th Cir 1978).

519 *See* Seidl v Trollhaugen, Inc, 305 Minn 506, 232 NW2d 236, 240-41 (1975).

520 *See* Eisenhart v Loveland Skiing Corp, 33 Colo App 120, 517 P2d 466, 468 (1973); Stearns v Sugarbush Valley Corp, 130 Vt 472, 296 A2d 220, 222 (1972).

521 130 Vt 472, 296 A2d 220, 222 (1972).

522 *Id*.

523 33 Colo App 120, 517 P2d 466, 468 (1973).

The doctrine of assumption of the risk usually has not been applied in cases involving ski lift accidents for two reasons.[524] First, in several cases, skiers were not aware of the danger because the danger was not obvious[525] or the skiers were novices.[526] Second, skiers have little real choice as to how they will get to the top of the ski slope and without a choice, their conduct cannot be considered voluntary.[527]

Statutes

Several states expressly provide that skiers assume the risk of ski injuries.[528] Some statutes specify that the risks assumed include injuries caused by, among other things:

1. Variations in terrain

2. Surface or subsurface snow or ice conditions

3. Bare spots, rocks, trees, or debris

4. Lift towers

5. Plainly marked snowmaking equipment[529]

Contributory Negligence

Skiers who act unreasonably under the circumstances may be held to have been contributorily negligent.[530] For example, skiers who skied at a fairly rapid speed and failed to observe the course being taken or nearby obstacles were contributorily negligent.[531] Similarly, passengers on a ski lift may be

---

[524] *See* Lisman, *Ski Injury Liability*, 43 U Colo L Rev 307, 310-11 (1972).

[525] *See* Arapahoe Basin, Inc v Fischer, 28 Colo App 580, 475 P2d 631, 633 (1970) (ski jacket sleeve got caught on a stud).

[526] *See* Summit County Dev Corp v Bagnoli, 166 Colo 27, 441 P2d 658, 661 (1968).

[527] Lisman, *Ski Injury Liability*, 43 U Colo L Rev 307, 310-11 (1972); *see generally* §9.03.

[528] *See, e.g.,* Idaho Code §6-1106 (Supp 1983); Me Rev Stat Ann tit 26, §488 (Supp 1982); Mont Code Ann §23-2-736 (1983) (this is true notwithstanding comparative negligence); Utah Code Ann §78-27-53 (Supp 1983); *see also* Alaska Stat §09.65.135(c) (1983); *see generally* Vt Stat Ann tit 12, §1037 (Supp 1984); **§1.21.**

[529] *See* Idaho Code §6-1106 (Supp 1983); Utah Code Ann §78-27-52 (Supp 1983); *see also* Alaska Stat 09.65.135(c) (1983).

[530] *See* Leopold v Okemo Mt, Inc, 420 F Supp 781, 787 (D Vt 1976); Allen v State, 110 NH 42, 260 A2d 454, 458 (1969); Kaufman v State, 11 Misc 2d 56, 172 NYS2d 276 (Ct Cl 1958).

[531] *See* Leopold v Okemo Mt, Inc, 420 F Supp 781, 787 (D Vt 1976).
Of course, the fact that a skier was moving with some degree of speed does not establish, by itself, contributory negligence. *See* Rosen v LTV Recreational Dev, Inc, 569 F2d 1117, 1123 (10th Cir 1978) (Colorado law).

considered contributorily negligent if they failed to anticipate the chair and, because they did not see it sooner, collided with it.[532]

In *Eisenhart v Loveland Skiing Corp*, a case discussed earlier in this section, the plaintiff slipped on a piece of ice on her way from a public restroom near a ski facility.[533] The court held that the skier was not contributorily negligent as a matter of law when she chose this restroom, which was surrounded by ice, because she believed that the other restroom was occupied.[534]

A plaintiff's actions during an emergency are judged by what is reasonable under those circumstances.[535] Therefore, a plaintiff who had less than three seconds to act to avoid being hit by a chair lift should be judged by how a reasonable person would act in that situation.[536]

The plaintiff's contributory negligence does not bar recovery if there is a later act of negligence by the defendant which proximately causes the injury.[537] In *Sabo v Breckenridge Lands, Inc*, the court held that even if a skier may have been contributorily negligent in getting into a chair lift, that did not preclude her action for damages where the operator failed to stop the lift quickly after he realized her predicament and, as a result, she was left in a dangling position 20 feet above the ground before she became exhausted and fell.[538]

§9.22 Swimming

Assumption of the Risk

Swimmers who are cognizant of the dangers of swimming and diving but who nevertheless engage in those activities generally have been held to have assumed the risk of injury.[539] The Supreme Court of Ohio recently held in *Benjamin v Deffet Rentals, Inc*,[540] that a boy who slipped on a swimming pool slide and, as a result, struck his head on the bottom of the pool, which rendered him a quadriplegic, had assumed the risk of injury as a matter of

---

532 *See* Allen v State, 110 NH 42, 260 A2d 454, 458 (1969).

533 33 Colo App 120, 517 P2d 466, 468 (1973).

534 *Id.*

535 *See* Allen v State, 110 NH 42, 260 A2d 454, 458 (1969).

536 *Id.*

537 Sabo v Breckenridge Lands, Inc, 255 F Supp 602, 606 (D Colo 1966).

538 *Id.*

539 *See* Stephens v Shelbyville Central Schools, 162 Ind App 229, 318 NE2d 590, 591-92 (1974); Richards v Marlow, 347 So 2d 281, 283 (La Ct App), *writ denied*, 350 So 2d 676 (La 1977); Benjamin v Deffet Rentals, Inc, 66 Ohio St 2d 86, 419 NE2d 883 (1981); Christman v Senyk, 34 Ohio Misc 47, 293 NE2d 126, 127 (1972); *see generally* Brody v Westmoor Beach & Blade Club, Inc, 524 P2d 1087, 1090 (Colo Ct App 1974) (question of fact whether a pool slide represented an obvious hazard which the participant assumed).

540 66 Ohio St 2d 86, 419 NE2d 883 (1981).

law. The court reasoned that the plaintiff, an experienced diver, assumed the risk because he was aware of the possibility of slipping on the slide but still used it.[541]

However, where there was no evidence that a swimmer had actual knowledge of the danger of swimming, this defense did not apply.[542] For example, a swimmer who did not know that the main drain of a swimming pool was uncovered and that this created a dangerous condition did not assume the risk that his arm would become lodged in the drain outlet.[543] A swimmer also did not assume the risk of injury from an unknown, latent danger in a water slide.[544]

Contributory Negligence

A swimmer is contributorily negligent if he or she fails to exercise reasonable care for personal safety.[545] Therefore, a swimmer may be contributorily negligent in ignoring obvious dangers.[546] For example, a boy who drowned while attempting to swim across a lake was found contributorily negligent because, although he fully realized the danger of the swim and had told one of his companions that "he couldn't make it"[547] before he began, he still made the misguided attempt. Similarly, a person who fell in a shower room adjacent to a pool because he failed to observe the obvious, slippery condition of the floor was held to have been contributorily negligent.[548]

The plaintiff may be contributorily negligent in taking other unreasonable actions. Swimmers who were warned not to swim because of the dangers, but did so anyway, may be contributorily negligent.[549] It may also be contributory negligence to eat before swimming because that action can induce

---

541 419 NE2d at 886. The plaintiff admitted away much of his case during his deposition. *See id.*

542 *See* Henry v Britt, 220 So 2d 917, 919 (Fla Dist Ct App 1969); Pfisterer v Grisham, 137 Ind App 565, 210 NE2d 75, 78-79 (1965); McDonald v Hanneson, 563 Or 612, 503 P2d 674, 676 (1972) (swimmer did not assume the risk that a tow rope would be dragged across a float).

543 *See* Henry v Britt, 220 So 2d 917, 919 (Fla Dist Ct App 1969).

544 *See* Pfisterer v Grisham, 137 Ind App 565, 210 NE2d 75, 78-79 (1965).

545 *See* Stephens v Shelbyville Central Schools, 162 Ind App 229, 318 NE2d 590, 591 (1974) (there was some evidence that the student was engaged in an underwater breath-holding contest and that he violated his teacher's instructions when he dived into the pool); Rigdon v Springdale Park, Inc, 551 SW2d 860, 862 (Mo Ct App 1977); McFarland v Grau, 305 SW2d 91, 101 (Mo Ct App 1957).

546 *See* Grimes v Hettinger, 566 SW2d 769, 773 (Ky Ct App 1978) (swimming in cloudy water).

547 *See* McFarland v Grau, 305 SW2d 91, 101 (Mo Ct App 1957).

548 *See* Tweedale v City of St Petersburg, 125 So 2d 920, 921 (Fla Dist Ct App 1961).

549 Fowler Real Estate Co v Ranke, 181 Colo 115, 507 P2d 854, 855 (1973); Hamilton v Turner, 273 So 2d 590, 593 (La Ct App 1973).

cramps.[550] In addition, in *Davis v Larue Enterprises, Inc*, a swimmer was found contributorily negligent as a matter of law because while he was under water, he removed his mouthpiece, swallowed some water, and then in a panic refused to accept a mouthpiece from a companion.[551]

Several courts have held that plaintiffs who dived into shallow water were not contributorily negligent where their actions were reasonable even though they failed to determine the true depth of water.[552] For example, in *Miller v United States*, a man was found not contributorily negligent in diving off a pier into shallow water at a lake because he took reasonable precautions before entering the water.[553] He spoke to people at the end of the pier who told him that the water was *fine*, he saw people in the lake who had various parts of their bodies covered with water and his dive was not a deep one.[554]

It has even been held that it is not contributory negligence to dive into a swimming pool when the diver could not see the bottom of the pool.[555] In *Rigdon v Springdale Park*, the court held that the murky water in a pool justified a swimmer's reliance upon the depth markings provided by the defendant; it did not impose a duty upon the swimmer to ascertain the true depth of the water.[556] Indeed, in that case there were no signs prohibiting diving at that spot chosen by the plaintiff and she was given no warnings that the water was not deep enough for diving.[557]

However, several courts have concluded that a diver's failure to ascertain the actual depth of the water before the dive is unreasonable.[558] In *Davis v United States*,[559] a college student, while diving at Devil's Kitchen Lake, a

---

[550] Fowler Real Estate Co v Ranke, 181 Colo 115, 507 P2d 854, 855 (1973).

[551] 146 Ga App 516, 246 SE2d 515, 515 (1978).

[552] *See* Miller v United States, 442 F Supp 555, 562 (ND Ill 1976), *aff'd*, 597 F2d 614, 617 (7th Cir 1979); Pleasant v Blue Mound Swim Club, 128 Ill App 2d 277, 262 NE2d 107, 113 (1970); Rigdon v Springdale Park, Inc, 551 SW2d 860, 864 (Mo Ct App 1977).

A patron at a commercial swimming pool is under no duty to make a critical examination of the facilities; the patron may rely, at least to some extent, upon the assumption that the pool owner would not invite the patron to use a dangerous facility. *See* Chrisler v Holiday Valley, Inc, 580 SW2d 309, 315 (Mo Ct App 1979); Rigdon v Springdale Park, Inc, 551 SW2d 860, 862 (Mo Ct App 1977).

[553] 442 F Supp 555, 562 (ND Ill 1976), *aff'd*, 597 F2d 614, 617 (7th Cir 1979).

[554] *Id.*

[555] *See* Rigdon v Springdale Park, Inc, 551 SW2d 860, 864 (Mo Ct App 1977).

[556] *Id* (marking indicated water was five feet deep).

[557] *Id.*

[558] *See* Davis v United States, 716 F2d 418, 428 (7th Cir 1983); Schiavoni v Honus Wagner Co, 396 F2d 757, 758 (3d Cir 1968) (dove into shallow end of pool); Kalm, Inc v Hawley, 406 SW2d 394 (Ky Ct App 1966); Caruso v Aetna Ins Co, 186 So 2d 851, 853-54 (La Ct App 1966).

[559] 716 F2d 418 (7th Cir 1983).

name which itself may have indicated some danger, hit his head against a subsurface rock, and was rendered a quadriplegic. The Seventh Circuit noted that diving into water headfirst, without knowing whether the water has sufficient depth to absorb the dive, is very dangerous.[560] Indeed, it held that diving from a shore of a lake that has not been marked as safe for diving, without having taken careful soundings of the depth of the lake, is negligence per se.[561] In this case, the plaintiff's actions in ascertaining the safety of diving, viz., he and his friends had not noticed any subsurface rocks in other nearby areas, were minimal.[562] Accordingly, the court held that the plaintiff's actions were not merely unreasonable, but wilful and wanton.[563]

Similarly, in *Kalm, Inc v Hawley*,[564] the court held that a motel guest who dove off the side of a pool and severely injured himself was contributorily negligent as a matter of law. The court concluded that it was completely unreasonable for the plaintiff to attempt a deep dive when he did not know the actual depth of the water and, therefore, also did not know whether the water had sufficient depth to accommodate the dive.[565] Accordingly, it reversed plaintiff's $150,000 jury verdict.

The reasonableness of the plaintiff's acts or omissions is judged by the conditions which existed at the time.[566] In one case, an experienced swimmer who entered very rough waters to attempt a rescue was not contributorily negligent as a matter of law because the decision to rescue had to be made without time for reasoned deliberation.[567]

A minor swimmer is usually held to the standard of care of a child of similar age, intelligence, and discretion under the same or similar conditions.[568] Accordingly, a minor may be guilty of contributory negligence where he or she has the knowledge and appreciation of the danger which could result form his or her acts or a similar child would have had that knowledge or appreciation.[569] However, a minor's mere knowledge that injury might result, without appreciation of the risk of injury to which the conduct exposed him

---

560 *Id* 428.

561 *Id.* The diver's ability to gauge the depth of the lake was hindered by the glare of the sun. *Id.*

562 *Id* 429.

563 *Id* 430.

564 406 SW2d 394 (Ky Ct App 1966).

565 *Id* 397.

566 *See* Baroco v Araserv, Inc, 621 F2d 189, 193-94 (5th Cir 1980).

567 *Id.*

568 *See* Carter v Boys' Club, 552 SW2d 327, 332 (Mo Ct App 1977); *see generally* §§9.04, 9.14, 9.15, 9.16.

569 Carter v Boys' Club, 552 SW2d 327, 332 (Mo Ct App 1977).

or her, is not contributory negligence.[570] This is because thoughtless conduct, impulsive action, and immature judgment are inherent in children.[571] For example, in *Carter v Boys' Club*, a 12-year-old boy who drowned at a club pool while he was learning to swim was not contributorily negligent because there was no direct evidence that the child had been warned of the danger of deep water.[572] Absent such a warning, 12-year-old children may not realize the dangers of swimming.

In *Shuman v Mashburn*, the court held that the determination of whether an intoxicated person acted with the appropriate standard of care is made without considering that he or she was intoxicated.[573] Accordingly, in that case a person who, while intoxicated, dove into a shallow pool was found to be contributorily negligent.[574]

A swimmer who does not act unreasonably is not contributorily negligent.[575] For example, a swimmer who neither knew nor should have known that it was dangerous to go near the main drain opening of a pool was not contributorily negligent in doing so.[576] Similarly, a swimmer who dove to the bottom of a pool, where his arm became caught in a pipe attached to a powerful suction pump without a screen, was not contributorily negligent because he did not act unreasonably.[577]

Even where the plaintiff is contributorily negligent, his or her action may not be barred if the defendant had the last clear chance to avoid the injury and did not do so.[578] The last clear chance doctrine has three major elements.[579] First, the plaintiff, by his or her own negligence, must have been placed in a position of peril from which the plaintiff could not extricate himself or herself.[580] Second, the defendant must have known of and appreciated the injured person's peril in time to avoid the injury.[581] Third, the defendant's failure to act to avoid the injury was negligence.[582]

---

[570] *Id.*

[571] *Id.*

[572] *See id* 332-33.

[573] *See* 137 Ga App 231, 223 SE2d 268, 271 (1976) (it was also held irrelevant that the defendant supplied the alcohol).

[574] *Id.*

[575] *See* Henry v Britt, 220 So 2d 917, 919 (Fla Dist Ct App 1969); Brown v United States, 99 F Supp 685, 687 (SD W Va 1951).

[576] *See* Henry v Britt, 220 So 2d 917, 919 (Fla Dist Ct App 1969).

[577] *See* Brown v United States, 99 F Supp 685, 687 (SD W Va 1951).

[578] Shuman v Mashburn, 137 Ga App 231, 223 SE2d 268, 272 (1976).

[579] *Id.*

[580] *Id.*

[581] *Id.*

[582] *Id.*

This doctrine does not apply where the defendant was powerless to take any action to eliminate the danger.[583] For example, a last clear chance jury instruction should not have been given in a case where there was no evidence that after a high school swimmer was in danger, his supervisors had time to do anything to avert the accident.[584]

Contributory negligence is usually not a defense to strict products liability claims.[585] Therefore, a plaintiff's careless use of a diving board would not bar recovery against the diving board manufacturer.[586] However, the defendant should prevail if the plaintiff discovered the defect, was aware of the danger, and then proceeded unreasonably to use the product.[587]

§9.23 Miscellaneous Recreational Activities

Basketball

Some physical contact is inevitable in basketball.[588] Therefore, it has been held that players assume the risk of a reasonable amount of such contact.[589]

In *McFatridge v Harlem Globetrotters* the court held that in deciding whether spectators at basketball games were contributorily negligent, baseball spectator decisions should not be used by analogy.[590] The court reasoned that in baseball, in contrast to basketball, the danger of being hit by a ball is much greater and it is common to have some screened sections.[591]

Billiards

A billiard player is not obligated to make a critical examination of the facilities.[592] He or she can assume that the proprietor will take

---

583 *Id* (the plaintiff had already dived into shallow water before the defendant realized the danger).

584 *See* Cox v Barnes, 469 SW2d 61, 64 (Ky Ct App 1971).

585 *See* Sheehan v Anthony Pools, 50 Md App 614, 440 A2d 1085, 1092 (1982), *aff'd*, 295 Md 285, 455 A2d 434, 441 (1983); *see also* §§7.02, 9.04; *but see* Belfrey v Anthony Pools, Inc, 80 Mich App 118, 262 NW2d 909, 911 (1977).

586 Sheehan v Anthony Pools, 50 Md App 614, 440 A2d 1085, 1092 (1982), *aff'd*, 295 Md 285, 455 A2d 434, 441 (1983).

587 *Id*.

588 *See* Albers v Independent School Dist No 1, 94 Idaho 342, 487 P2d 936, 939 (1971) (court also held there was no negligence as a matter of law).

589 *Id*.

590 69 NM 271, 365 P2d 918, 921-22 (1961).

591 *Id*.

592 Archote v Travelers Ins Co, 179 So 2d 658, 661 (La Ct App 1965).

reasonable precautions for the player's safety.[593] In *Archote v Travelers Insurance Co*,[594] a billiard player was injured when he used a cue stick, unaware it was broken, and took a hard shot. The cue stick broke, ramming the end of the stick about an inch and a half into his thumb. The court held that the player did not assume the risk merely because his frequent visits to this establishment and his general familiarity with the premises and conditions there revealed that this was not a "fine club."[595]

In *Moone v Smith*, the court held that a patron in a billiard hall was not contributorily negligent as a matter of law in failing to leave after observing a fight among several other drunken patrons.[596] The billiard player could rely on the facility to quell the disturbance.[597] This was true even though the playing of billiards was illegal at that time.[598]

One court held that a billiard player who was aware that an electric fan in a nearby area had no guard, but still placed his hand against it, was contributorily negligent.[599]

Boxing

Boxers may assume the risk of injury, even death, in a voluntary boxing match.[600]

Camping

Campers generally do not assume unknown risks.[601] In one case, campers did not assume the risk of being bitten by a bear because the park rangers at a national park told the campers that it was safe to sleep outside.[602]

Dancing

An acrobatic tap dancer who fell on a waxed floor assumed the risk of injury and was contributorily negligent because she knew the floor was

---

[593] *Id.*

[594] 179 So 2d 658 (La Ct App 1965).

[595] *Id* 660-61.

[596] 6 Ga App 649, 65 SE 712, 714 (1909).

[597] *Id.*

[598] Moone v Smith, 7 Ga App 675, 67 SE 836 (1909).

[599] *See* Cost v Fidler, 119 Ark 540, 178 SW 373 (1915).

[600] *See* McAdams v Windham, 208 Ala 492, 94 So 2d 742, 743 (1922); Daniel v Tower Trucking Co, 205 SC 333, 32 SE2d 5 (1943) (dicta).

[601] Claypool v United States, 98 F Supp 702, 704 (SD Cal 1951).

[602] *Id.*

dangerous but did not ask anyone to modify the condition of the floor, did not use proper shoes for dancing on such floors, and did not refuse to perform.[603]

Dune Buggy

In *Wagner v Hazelquist*, the passengers who were injured in a dune buggy which did not have seatbelts were held not to have assumed the risk or have been contributorily negligent as a matter of law.[604] The court noted that the passengers had not been on the dunes before and did not know what to expect.[605] Further, the cause of the accident, viz., falling into a depression, was completely unexpected.[606]

However, in *Walker v Hamby*, the court held that a person who voluntarily rode in a dune buggy—a vehicle with just a motor and a frame and no doors or body—for fun assumed the risk of injury as a matter of law when the vehicle, traveling over 40 miles per hour, fishtailed, and the passenger, with nothing to hang onto, fell out.[607]

Fireworks

In *Shelanie v National Fireworks Association*,[608] a 14-year-old boy was injured after lighting an aerial bomb. The court held that the plaintiff was contributorily negligent as a matter of law because it was unreasonable for anyone, even a reasonably prudent child of the same age, experience, and intelligence as the plaintiff, to light that object.[609]

However, the fact that a child violated a statute by exploding a cherry bomb is not evidence that the child was contributorily negligent per se.[610] The reasonableness of a child's actions is judged by how other, similar children would act.[611]

Go-Carts

In *Regan v City of Seattle*, the Washington Supreme Court held that a go-cart racer is barred from recovery where he voluntarily exposed himself

---

603 Eisenhower v United States, 327 F2d 663, 664 (2d Cir), *cert denied*, 377 US 991 (1964).

604 347 So 2d 1265, 1271 (La Ct App 1977).

605 *Id.*

606 *Id.*

607 503 SW2d 118, 123 (Tenn 1973).

608 487 SW2d 921, 923 (Ky Ct App 1972).

609 *Id.*

610 *See* Calkins v Albi, 163 Colo 370, 431 P2d 17, 22-23 (1967).

611 *Id.*

to a known and appreciated danger.[612] However, it was a question of fact in that case whether the racer knew that there was water on the track.[613]

Health Clubs

Individuals using health club facilities usually assume the obvious risks inherent in using those facilities.[614] For example, in *Gatti v World Wide Health Studios*, a person who slipped on a slippery surface on the steps in a steam room assumed that risk.[615]

A patron's failure to take reasonable precautions at a health club may be contributory negligence.[616] For example, a member of a health club who knew that the club's showers were usually dirty and slippery, but who failed to look down at conditions on the floor, was contributorily negligent as a matter of law.[617]

It is common knowledge that a person can increase the probability that he or she will not fall when exercising in a manner in which balance shifts by holding onto a support bar.[618] Accordingly, one court held that a person who, while exercising, failed to use a support bar when she shifted her balance was contributorily negligent.[619]

In *McKinley v Slenderella Systems*, the court held it was a jury question whether the plaintiff was contributorily negligent in allowing the club to continue to treat her after she complained of a sore back.[620]

Horse Racing

The courts have not reached consistent results regarding whether jockeys assume the risk of injury. In *Santiago v Clark*, the plaintiff, a jockey, was injured when another jockey in a thoroughbred race improperly cut him off.[621] The court held that horse racing is a sport posing "great peril" to its participants and its dangers are well-known to experienced jockeys.[622] Accordingly, the court held that the plaintiff assumed the risk of injury as

---

612 76 Wash 2d 501, 458 P2d 12, 16 (1969).

613 *Id.*

614 *See* Gatti v World Wide Health Studios, 323 So 2d 819, 822 (La Ct App 1975) (there also was negligence by the club operator).

615 *Id.*

616 House v European Health Spa, 269 SC 644, 239 SE2d 653, 655 (1977).

617 *Id.*

618 *See* Sharp v Higbee Co, 56 Ohio App 278, 10 NE2d 932, 934 (1936).

619 *Id.*

620 63 NJ Super 571, 165 A2d 207, 215 (1960).

621 444 F Supp 1077 (ND W Va 1978).

622 *Id* 1079.

a matter of law.[623] However, a different court held that the assumption of the risk defense may not be applicable where jockeys were required by a state racing commission to fulfill all racing engagements irrespective of the condition of the track.[624]

Ice Skating

The New Jersey Supreme Court held in *Meistrich v Casino Arena Attractions, Inc* that a skater may have been contributorily negligent because he noticed that his skates slipped on turns, yet he continued to skate.[625]

Jumping

In *Dibortolo v Metropolitan School District,*[626] a student hit a wall while attempting a vertical jump. The student had never performed a jump before the day of the injury, had no knowledge of the proper way to perform this exercise, and had no actual knowledge of the danger of this exercise.[627] Accordingly, the court held that it was a question of fact whether she assumed the risk or was contributorily negligent.[628]

Karate

In *Kuehner v Green*, the court held that the plaintiff, injured while engaged in a karate maneuver, could not recover because he subjectively recognized the danger of a karate takedown activity and yet voluntarily proceeded to participate in the face of such danger.[629]

Machete

A customer in a retail store does not usually assume the risk of being injured by a machete encased in a sheath because the customer cannot discover the sharpness of the blade until the protective sheath is removed.[630] Therefore, in one case, the court held that the customer did not assume

---

[623] *Id* 1079-80.

[624] *See* Martino v Park Jefferson Racing Assn, 315 NW2d 309, 314 (SD 1982).

[625] 31 NJ 44, 155 A2d 90, 92 (1959). The court held that assumption of the risk in that state was the same as contributory negligence. *See* 155 A2d at 96.

[626] 440 NE2d 506 (Ind Ct App 1982).

[627] *Id* 511-12.

[628] *Id.*

[629] 436 So 2d 78 (Fla 1983).

[630] *See* Davis v Gibson Prod Co, 505 SW2d 682, 692 (Tex Civ App 1973), *writ ref nre*, 513 SW2d 4 (Tex 1974).

the risk of injury unless the weapon had already been withdrawn from the sheath.[631]

Playground

One court held that a child assumes the risk of falling from monkey bars.[632]

Running

In *Williams v Cox Enterprises, Inc*, the court held that a Phi Beta Kappa graduate of Duke University who was aware of the danger of running in a 10,000-meter race on a day when the temperature exceeded 85 degrees and the humidity exceeded 90 per cent assumed the risk of injury from overheating and dehydration.[633]

There have been several cases where runners collided with objects in their path and were injured. In *Siau v Rapides Parish School Board*,[634] the plaintiff, a high school student, while running in an area he knew was not used for that purpose and after having been told to stop, collided with a javelin which was stuck in the ground. The court held that although the plaintiff was not required to keep his eyes glued to the pathway in front of him, he was required to observe whether his course was clear.[635] In *Wilkinson v Hartford Accident & Indemnity Co*,[636] a student running in an unsupervised relay race in a gymnasium collided with a glass panel. The court held that the student was not contributorily negligent even though he had been warned not to engage in such activities.[637] The student's actions were not unreasonable because he was unaware that the glass panel, made up of plate glass rather than safety glass, was unsafe.[638]

Soap Box Derby

One court held that a spectator at a soap box derby who attempted to stop a car which appeared headed for a collision was not contributorily negligent as a matter of law because it was reasonable to try to stop the impending accident.[639]

---

631 *Id.*

632 Miller v Board of Educ, 249 AD 738, 291 NYS 633, 634 (1936).

633 159 Ga App 333, 283 SE2d 367, 369 (1981).

634 264 So 2d 372, 375 (La Ct App), *writ denied*, 262 La 1148, 266 So 2d 440 (1972).

635 *Id.*

636 411 So 2d 22 (La 1982).

637 *Id* 24.

638 *Id.*

639 Cummings v General Motors Corp, 146 Conn 443, 151 A2d 884, 889 (1959) (also held plaintiff did not assume the risk as a matter of law).

Soccer

In *Nabozny v Barnhill*, a goalkeeper who, while in a crouch in the penalty area, was kicked in the head by an opposing player, was found not contributorily negligent as a matter of law.[640] The court reasoned that the goalkeeper had no reason to know that an opposing player would blatantly violate the rules prohibiting contact in the penalty area and, absent that knowledge, he did not unreasonably expose himself to danger.[641]

Table Tennis

In *Hoffman v Silbert*, the court held that an individual injured while playing table tennis when his arm hit a glass window located in the wall behind the playing table was contributorily negligent and assumed the risk as a matter of law.[642] The court noted the plaintiff had passed through that room many times and had played at least two games at that table.[643] Therefore, it reasoned that he observed or should have observed the window and its distance from the table.[644] The plaintiff's argument that he did not realize the location of the glass window at the time of the injury because he was totally engrossed in the game was rejected, apparently for the reason that the plaintiff's improper act was in having undertaken to play the game in a dangerous environment.[645]

Tennis

A tennis player who was told of the dangers of playing on a court with *bubbles* and gaps between the seams may have assumed the risk of playing on that defective surface.[646]

Water Skiing

One court held that a water skier assumes the normal risks incident to skiing behind a boat.[647] However, the skier does not assume the risk that the

---

640 31 Ill App 3d 212, 334 NE2d 258, 261 (1975). This case is also discussed in §2.16 (soccer).

641 *Id.*

642 24 AD2d 493, 261 NYS2d 494, 495 (1965).

643 *Id.*

644 *Id.*

645 *Id.*

646 *See* Heldman v Uniroyal, Inc, 53 Ohio App 2d 21, 371 NE2d 557, 556-57 (1977) (professional tennis player was held to have a high degree of knowledge of dangers of playing on a synthetic court).

647 *See* Harrop v Beckman, 15 Utah 2d 78, 387 P2d 554, 555 (1963).

operator of the boat will fail to keep a proper lookout.[648] In another case, the court held that a water skier was contributorily negligent in failing to obtain signals from the boat operator and in skiing in an area where other boats were racing.[649]

Wrestling

Most courts have held that spectators at wrestling matches do not assume, as a matter of law, the risk of being hit by a wrestler who was thrown out of the ring by another wrestler.[650] However, in *Pierce v Murnick*,[651] the court held that the plaintiff, a spectator who was sitting in the first row at a wrestling match and who had previously watched many wrestling matches in person and on television, knew or should have known that he could be injured by a wrestler who was knocked out of the ring and, therefore, was contributorily negligent in choosing a seat that close to the action.

---

[648] *Id.*

[649] *See* King v Testerman, 214 F Supp 335, 338 (ED Tenn 1963).

[650] *See* Silvia v Woodhouse, 356 Mass 119, 248 NE2d 260, 263 (1969); Dusckiewicz v Carter, 115 Vt 122, 52 A2d 788, 791 (1947); *but see* Langness v Ketonen, 42 Wash 394, 255 P2d 551, 557 (1953) (may be contributory negligence to walk too close to a wrestling ring).

[651] 265 NC 707, 145 SE2d 11, 13 (1965).

Exculpatory Agreements

10

§10.01 Introduction

It is common for operators of recreational facilities to attempt to limit their liability. This is usually done by requiring participants and spectators to execute statements that provide that they will not hold the operator responsible if they are injured while participating in or watching the specified recreational activity.

These statements are usually called releases, although they are also sometimes known as waivers, disclaimers of liability, or indemnity agreements.[1] Nonetheless, since they usually purport to eliminate the possibility of an individual suing the operator of the facility for an injury which has not yet occurred, they are more accurately considered covenants not to sue.[2]

---

[1] Technically, an indemnity provision attempts to shift the responsibility for payment of the damages to someone other than the negligent party, while an exculpatory clause purports to deny the injured party the right to recover damages from the person negligently causing the injuries. See O'Connell v Walt Disney World Co, 413 So 2d 444, 446 (Fla Dist Ct App 1982).

In some states, covenants not to sue and releases cannot be introduced into evidence in jury trials. See, e.g., Conn Gen Stat Ann §52-216a (West Supp 1982).

[2] See Del Santo v Bristol County Stadium, Inc, 273 F2d 605, 607 n 1 (1st Cir 1960); Cash v Street & Trail, Inc, 136 Ga App 462, 221 SE2d 640, 641 (1975).

However, if the agreement is a true indemnity arrangement, meaning that the injured individual still has a party to sue (although that defendant-tortfeasor may be able to be reimbursed by another party), in contrast to a covenant not to sue, which eliminates the injured individual's legal remedy, the courts have been more sympathetic to enforcing it. This

514

For convenience, these statements will be referred to here as exculpatory agreements.

The enforcement of exculpatory provisions reflects the conflict between the traditional principle of contract law that the parties can define their relationship as they wish and the traditional principle of tort law that an individual is responsible when his or her actions injure others.[3]

The result of this conflict is that exculpatory clauses generally will be enforced when the adult who executed one knew or should have known what rights were being waived and the exculpatory provision clearly covers the accident that occurred. Courts have been more willing to uphold exculpatory clauses regarding recreational activities than many other activities, e.g., medical procedures, because they are a more voluntary type of activity.[4] Although a few decisions have implied that exculpatory agreements executed by participants may be treated differently than those by spectators,[5] no disparate results are evident from a review of the actual decisions.

The courts have repeatedly stated that exculpatory provisions are looked upon with disfavor,[6] and these clauses are strictly construed against the party asserting their valadity.[7] There are two reasons for this. First, public policy attempts to limit the effect of these provisions since they limit an individual's responsibility for negligence.[8] Second, writings are usually construed against their drafter.[9] Accordingly, an exculpatory provision which referred to injuries from an automobile race did not apply when the plaintiff was injured while

---

is true even when the plaintiff indemnifies the defendant from losses resulting from negligent acts by both the defendant and the plaintiff, a result which is substantively indistinguishable from a covenant not to sue. *See, e.g.,* George R. Lane & Assoc v Thomasson, 156 Ga App 313, 274 SE2d 708, 711 (1980).

Some state statutes specifically provide that releases for injuries which have not yet occurred can be treated as covenants not to sue. *See* Ga Code §13-4-81 (1982).

3 *See* Arnold v Shawano County Agricultural Socy, 111 Wis 2d 203, 330 NW2d 773, 777 n 2 (1983): Merten v Nathan, 108 Wis 2d 205, 321 NW2d 173, 177 (1982).

4 Restatement (Second) of Contracts §195 reporter's note (1981).

5 *See* Beardslee v Blomberg, 70 AD2d 732, 416 NYS2d 855, 857 (1979); Celli v Sports Car Club of Am, Inc, 29 Cal App 3d 511, 105 Cal Rptr 904, 910 n 4 (1972).

6 *See* Ferrell v Southern Nev Off-Road Enthusiasts, Ltd, 147 Cal App 3d 309, 314, 195 Cal Rptr 90 (1983); O'Connell v Walt Disney World Co, 413 So 2d 444, 446 (Fla Dist Ct App 1982); Merten v Nathan, 108 Wis 2d 205, 321 NW2d 173, 176 (1982).

7 *See, e.g.,* Rosen v LTV Recreational Dev, Inc, 569 F2d 1117, 1122 (10th Cir 1978) (Colorado law); Diedrich v Wright, 550 F Supp 805, 808 (ND Ill 1982); Doyle v College, 403 A2d 1206, 1208 (Me 1979); Schlobohm v Spa Petite, Inc, 326 NW2d 920, 923 (Minn 1982); Zimmer v Mitchell & Ness, 253 Pa Super 474, 385 A2d 437, 439 (1978), *aff'd per curiam,* 490 Pa 428, 416 A2d 1010 (1980); Merten v Nathan, 108 Wis 2d 205, 321 NW2d 173, 176 (1982).

8 Geise v County of Niagara, 117 Misc 2d 470, 458 NYS2d 162, 165 (Sup Ct 1983).

9 *Id. See also* Restatement (Second) of Torts §496B comment d (1965).

preparing for a motorcycle race.[10] Courts should not, however, strain the words used in the exculpatory provision to render them inapplicable.[11]

To be valid, the words used in an exculpatory clause must be unambiguous and understandable.[12] The party being bound must not be compelled to "resort to a magnifying glass and lexicon."[13] Although this does not mean that only simple, monosyllabic language can be used,[14] it probably would be a good idea to attempt to limit the agreement to those type of words.

The title of the exculpatory agreement does not need to state what the agreement contains as long as the body clearly does.[15] Furthermore, there is generally no duty to explain the effect of an exculpatory provision.[16]

It must appear that the terms were brought home to the plaintiff. If the plaintiff did not know of the provision in the contract and a reasonable person in the same position would not have known of it, it is not binding and the agreement fails for want of mutual assent.[17] Accordingly, when the exculpatory clause is in the middle of the agreement and is not conspicuous, it is not enforceable.[18] Similarly, when these clauses are printed on tickets

---

10 Phibbs v Ray's Chevrolet Corp, 45 AD2d 897, 357 NYS2d 211, 212-13 (1974).

11 See Empress Health & Beauty Spa v Turner, 503 SW2d 188, 191 (Tenn 1973). See generally Thomas v Sports Car Club of Am, Inc, 386 So 2d 272, 273-74 (Fla Dist Ct App 1980) (plaintiff's argument that the exculpatory provision was limited to injuries which exceeded the limits on defendant's insurance policy was rejected because there was no evidence to support this allegation).

12 Ferrell v Southern Nev Off-Road Enthusiasts, Ltd, 147 Cal App 3d 309, 318, 195 Cal Rptr 90 (1983) ("An agreement. . . must be clear, explicit and comprehensible in each of its essential details"); O'Connell v Walt Disney World Co, 413 So 2d 444, 446 (Fla Dist Ct App 1982); Geise v County of Niagara, 117 Misc 2d 470, 458 NYS2d 162, 164 (Sup Ct 1983) ("clear and unequivocal language"); Gross v Sweet, 49 NY2d 102, 400 NE2d 306, 424 NYS2d 365, 368 (1979).

Poorly written exculpatory clauses may also violate state plain language legislation. See Conn Gen Stat Ann §§42-151 to -158 (West Supp 1982); Hawaii Rev Stat §§487A-1 to -4 (Supp 1982); NJ Stat Ann §§56:12-1 to -13 (West Supp 1981); NY Gen Oblig Law §5-702 (McKinney Supp 1982).

13 Gross v Sweet, 49 NY2d 102, 400 NE2d 306, 424 NYS2d 365, 368 (1979).

14 Id.

15 Zimmer v Mitchell & Ness, 253 Pa Super 474, 385 A2d 437, 439 (1978), aff'd per curiam, 490 Pa 428, 416 A2d 1010 (1980). In Ferrell v Southern Nev Off-Road Enthusiasts, Ltd, 147 Cal App 3d 309, 319, 195 Cal Rptr 90 (1983) the court did not enforce an exculpatory agreement which had the word release in the title, but did not have that word or other similar words such as remise, discharge, or waive in the body.

16 Kotary v Spencer Speedway, Inc, 47 AD2d 127, 365 NYS2d 87, 89 (1975).

17 W. Prosser, The Law of Torts §68, at 442 (4th ed 1971).

18 See Baker v City of Seattle, 79 Wash 2d 198, 484 P2d 405 (1971). See also Celli v Sports Car Club of Am, Inc, 29 Cal App 3d 511, 521, 105 Cal Rptr 904 (1972) (questions whether public policy permits enforcement of exculpatory provisions in less than six-point type). See also Putzer v Vic-Tanney-Flatbush, 20 AD2d 821, 248 NYS2d 836, 837 (1964) (question of fact whether exculpatory provision in fine print was enforceable).

or receipts,[19] they generally are considered so inconspicuous that they do not bar recovery, at least when the plaintiff was unaware of them. In contrast, a college-educated, experienced skier who had read the agreement and had signed similar releases before was bound.[20] Other individuals have also been held to the agreement when the form and the language in the exculpatory agreement were so conspicuous that there was no doubt that the individuals had knowingly signed them.[21]

The fact that a patron has not read the exculpatory provision is generally irrelevant, as long as there was an opportunity to do so.[22] However, this is only true in the absence of fraud, misrepresentation, or duress.[23]

Indeed, an individual may be bound without signing the agreement. In *Blide v Rainier Mountaineering, Inc*, the injured party only signed an application form and not an exculpatory agreement, although he acted as if he had signed the exculpatory agreement.[24] Therefore, he was held to the terms of the agreement. The result reached appears to be correct since oral contracts are generally valid. The plaintiff apparently did not argue that the only proper acceptance of the terms of the agreement was by a writing and, since there was none, that the agreement lacked mutual consent.

In *Merten v Nathan*, an exculpatory agreement that contained a false statement about a fact which was relevant to a reasonable person's decision to execute the agreement was not enforced.[25] In *Merten*, the Wisconsin Supreme Court held that an exculpatory provision signed by a plaintiff who took horse

---

19 *See* Hook v Lakeside Park Co, 142 Colo 277, 351 P2d 261, 268 (1960); Moore v Edwards, 384 Ill 535, 52 NE2d 216, 222 (1943); O'Brien v Freeman, 299 Mass 20, 11 NE2d 582, 582 (1937); Brennan v Ocean View Amusement Co, 289 Mass 326, 194 NE 911, 914 (1935); Kushner v McGinnis, 289 Mass 326, 194 NE 106, 108 (1935). *See generally* Russo v Range, Inc, 76 Ill App 3d 236, 395 NE2d 10, 13 (1979) (question of fact whether clause valid when it was on the reverse side of a ticket at an amusement park).

20 Garretson v United States, 456 F2d 1017, 1020 (9th Cir 1972) (Washington law).

21 LaFrenz v Lake Country Fair Bd, 172 Ind App 389, 360 NE2d 605, 609 (1977); Provence v Doolin, 91 Ill App 3d 271, 414 NE2d 786, 796 (1980) (dicta); Hewitt v Miller, 11 Wash App 72, 521 P2d 244, 247 (1974). Obviously, counsel called upon to draft an exculpatory agreement should review the agreements in the above-cited cases since those agreements have already received a judicial imprimatur.

22 *See* Palmquist v Mercer, 43 Cal 2d 92, 98, 272 P2d 26 (1954); Carrion v Smokey, Inc, 164 Ga App 790, 298 SE2d 585, 586 (1982); Lee v Alled Sports Assoc, 349 Mass 544, 209 NE2d 329, 332 (1965); Franzek v Calspan Corp, 78 AD2d 134, 434 NYS2d 288, 290 (1980).

23 *See* Gillespie v Papale, 541 F Supp 1042, 1045 (D Mass 1982); Lee v Allied Sports Assocs, 349 Mass 544, 209 NE2d 329 (1965); Theroux v Kedenburg Racing Assn, 50 Misc 2d 97, 269 NYS2d 789, 792 (Sup Ct 1965), *affd without opinion*, 28 AD2d 960, 282 NYS2d 930 (1967). *See generally* Erickson v Wagon Wheel Enter, Inc, 101 Ill App 2d 296, 242 NE2d 622, 626 (1968) (question of fact whether plaintiff knew he was signing a release).

24 30 Wash App 571, 636 P2d 492, 494 (1981).

25 108 Wis 2d 205, 321 NW2d 173 (1982).

riding lessons was not valid because it stated that the defendant did not have insurance when in fact the defendant was insured. The defendant did not have insurance when the exculpatory agreements were initially drafted but obtained insurance before the plaintiff signed the agreement. The *Merten* court held that the agreement should not be enforced because the probability of unfairness existed.[26]

An exculpatory provision was also held unenforceable when it was not supported by consideration.[27]

One landlord was able to eliminate its liability because of the plaintiff's breach of a lease agreement.[28] In *George R. Lane & Associates v Thomasson*,[29] a young child drowned in an apartment pool. The lease provided that the tenant would indemnify the landlord for all losses incurred by the tenant's failure to perform a covenant under the lease. In this case, the tenant violated the lease provision requiring the tenant to follow all landlord rules. The accident occurred when the tenant, contrary to explicit pool rules, was using the pool before it opened. The tenant also failed to supervise the child. Accordingly, the court held that the tenant had to indemnify the landlord; a result that extinguished the landlord's liability.[30]

The courts have not been receptive to arguments that exculpatory agreements should not be enforced on public policy grounds. Indeed, the courts have repeatedly held that exculpatory agreements for recreational activities are not contrary to public policy.[31] However, at least one state has a statute declaring

---

26 321 NW2d at 178.

27 Cohen v City of New York, 190 Misc 901, 75 NYS2d 846, 847 (Sup Ct 1947).

28 156 Ga App 313, 274 SE2d 708, 710-11 (1980).

29 *Id.*

30 *Id.*

31 *See* Rutter v Arlington Park Jockey Club, 510 F2d 1065, 1069 (7th Cir 1975) (race track) (Illinois law); Grbac v Reading Fair Co, 521 F Supp 1351, 1355 (WD Pa 1981), *affd*, 688 F2d 215 (3d Cir 1982) (automobile racing); Trumbower v Sports Car Club of Am, Inc, 428 F Supp 1113, 1118 (WD Okla 1976); Gore v TriCounty Raceway, Inc, 407 F Supp 489, 492 (MD Ala 1974) (automobile racing); Barker v Colorado Region-Sports Car Club of Am, Inc, 35 Colo App 73, 532 P2d 372, 377 (1974); Morrow v Auto Championship Racing Assn, 8 Ill App 3d 682, 291 NE2d 30, 33 (1972); Bers v Chicago Health Clubs, Inc, 11 Ill App 3d 590, 297 NE2d 360 (1973) (health club); Tope v Waterford Hills Road Racing Corp, 81 Mich App 591, 265 NW2d 761, 764 (1978) (automobile racing); French v Special Serv, Inc, 107 Ohio App 435, 159 NE2d 785, 788 (1958) (no public policy requires invalidation of exculpatory agreements signed by stock car race participants because "old cars are used, which are expected to be cracked up for the edification of a blood-thirsty public who attend merely to see accidents happen"); Hewitt v Miller, 11 Wash App 72, 521 P2d 244, 247 (1974) (scuba diving). *But cf* UCC §2-719 ("Limitation of consequential damages for injury to the person in the case of consumer goods is prima facie unconscionable. . .").

If the performance of the tortious act for which indemnification is claimed under the contract is only an undesired possibility in the performance of the contract and the contract does not tend to induce the act, the indemnification provision is valid. *See* Tope v Waterford Hills Road Racing Corp, 81 Mich App 591, 265 NW2d 761, 764 (1978) (allegedly negligent design of

exculpatory agreements to be unenforceable if a fee or other consideration were given to the operator of the recreational facility.[32]

Even when exculpatory provisions are on printed forms, are given on a take-it-or-leave-it basis, and relate to recreational services which may not be easily obtainable elsewhere, they have rarely been struck down as illegal adhesive contracts.[33] There are two reasons for this.

First, the courts have usually held that there is no disparity of bargaining strength. Since recreational activities are not essential services, individuals always have the viable option of refusing to sign the agreement and forgoing the activity.[34]

Second, recreational activities are usually considered to be private activities in which the government does not have a major interest in setting the limits of the parties' relationship.[35] This is in contrast to other activities, e.g., those involved in heavily regulated industries, where the government has an interest in allowing injured parties to be fully compensated. In this regard, a court's conclusion may depend on whether it focuses on the particular recreational activity at issue or on physical education in general. Although the government may have little interest in who bears the cost of injuries in one specific

---

guardrail in automobile racing accident). *See generally* Restatement of the Law of Contracts §572 (1932).

When a plaintiff's argument that the clause is invalid because it is against public policy is not raised in the trial court, it is considered by an appellate court to have been waived. *See* Thomas v Sports Car Club of Am, Inc, 386 So 2d 272, 274 (Fla Dist Ct App 1980).

[32] *See* NY Gen Oblig §5-326 (McKinney 1978). This statute has not been applied retroactively. *See* Johnson v Thruway Speedways, Inc, 63 AD2d 81, 407 NYS2d 81 (1978). Where an individual did not pay a fee or receive a ticket to toboggan, the New York statute did not apply; the individual's payment for refreshments was not a fee or other consideration. *See* Geise v County of Niagara, 117 Misc 2d 470, 458 NYS2d 162, 164 (Sup Ct 1983). For a discussion of consideration in a different statutory context, see **§5.18**.

[33] *See* Jones v Dressel, 623 P2d 370, 374-75 (Colo 1981); Williams v Cox Enters, Inc, 159 Ga App 333, 283 SE2d 367, 369 (1981); Schlessman v Henson, 83 Ill 2d 82, 413 NE2d 1252, 1254 (1980); LaFrenz v Lake Country Fair Bd, 172 Ind App 389, 360 NE2d 605, 608 (1977) (demolition derby); Schlobohm v Spa Petite, Inc, 326 NW2d 920, 924-25 (Minn 1982); Winterstein v Wilcom, 16 Md App 130, 293 A2d 821, 825 (1972). *But see* Trumbower v Sports Car Club of Am, Inc, 428 F Supp 1113, 1117 (WD Okla 1976) (question of fact).

[34] *See* Jones v Dressel, 623 P2d 370, 378 (Colo 1981); Williams v Cox Enter, Inc, 159 Ga App 333, 283 SE2d 367, 369 (1981) (rejected plaintiff's claims to the contrary as ludicrous); Kubisen v Chicago Health Clubs, 69 Ill App 3d 463, 388 NE2d 44, 46 (1979); Owen v Vic Tanny's Enter, 49 Ill App 2d 344, 199 NE2d 280, 282 (1964); Schlobohm v Spa Petite, Inc, 326 NW2d 920, 924-25 (Minn 1982).

[35] *See* Jones v Dressel, 623 P2d 370, 376-77 (Colo 1981) (skydiving) (the fact that there is governmental regulation is insufficient to change the result); Perry v Cosmopolitan Spa Intl, 641 SW2d 202, 213 (Tenn Ct App 1982) (health spa); Blide v Rainier Mountaineering, Inc, 30 Wash App 571, 636 P2d 492, 493 (1981) (mountaineering). *Cf* Tunkl v Regents of the Univ of Cal, 60 Cal 2d 92, 96, 383 P2d 441, 32 Cal Rptr 33 (1963) (exculpatory provisions will be enforced only when they do not affect the public interest).

recreational activity, it may have an interest in who bears the cost of athletic injuries in general.[36]

Even if the releases are unenforceable, they may be probative of the plaintiff's assumption of the risk.[37]

§10.02 Scope of Agreement

Most exculpatory clauses are worded very broadly. Nevertheless, such clauses will not bar claims which were not within the contemplation of the parties at the time the clause was executed.[38] Accordingly, when a spectator at an automobile race track was injured by a maintenance vehicle not involved in the actual race, it was a question of fact whether the exculpatory agreement signed by the spectator covered this type of injury.[39]

However, it is not necessary that the parties contemplate the precise occurrence which results in the injury. In adopting the broad language employed in the agreement, it seems reasonable to conclude that the parties contemplated the similarly broad range of accidents which could occur.[40] In addition, when a race car driver could produce no competent evidence that the exculpatory provision was only intended to cover claims over the car club's insurance policy limits, the provision was held to apply to all claims.[41]

A few courts have held that exculpatory provisions which waive *any claims* do not bar claims of negligence, unless negligence claims have also been specifically waived.[42] These decisions are analytically highly suspect. After

---

36 *Compare* Schlobohm v Spa Petite, Inc, 326 NW2d 920, 926 (Minn 1982) *with id* at 927 (Simonett, J, dissenting) *and* Leidy v Deseret Enter, Inc, 252 Pa Super 162, 381 A2d 164, 168 (1977).

37 *See* Celli v Sports Car Club of Am, Inc, 29 Cal App 3d 511, 521-22, 105 Cal Rptr 904 (1972); *see also* Gary v Party Time Co, Inc, 434 So 2d 338, 339 (Fla Dist Ct App 1983); Moss v Fortune, 207 Tenn 426, 340 SW2d 902, 903 (1960); *See generally* §§9.02, 9.03. *But see* Barker v Colorado Region-Sports Car Club of Am, Inc, 35 Colo App 73, 532 P2d 372, 378 (1974).

38 Arnold v Shawno County Agricultural Socy, 111 Wis 2d 203, 330 NW2d 773, 778 (1983) (question of fact whether negligent rescue is covered by release).

39 *See* Johnson v Thruway Speedways, Inc, 63 AD2d 204, 407 NYS2d 81, 83 (1978).

40 Schlessman v Henson, 83 Ill 2d 82, 413 NE2d 1252 (1980).

41 *See* Thomas v Sports Car Club of Am, Inc, 386 So 2d 272, 273-74 (Fla Dist Ct App 1980).

42 *See, e.g.,* Diedrich v Wright, 550 F Supp 805, 808 (ND Ill 1982); Sivaslian v Rawlins, 88 AD2d 703, 451 NYS2d 307, 309 (1982). *See also* Jones v Walt Disney World Co, 409 F Supp 526, 528 (WDNY 1976) (Florida law); Celli v Sports Car Club of Am, Inc, 29 Cal App 3d 511, 518-20, 105 Cal Rptr 904 (1972) (general language in exculpatory clause does not insulate defendant from active negligence); O'Connell v Walt Disney World Co, 413 So 2d 444, 447 (Fla Dist Ct App 1982); Doyle v College, 403 A2d 1206, 1208 (Me 1979); Hertzog v Harrison Island Shores, Inc, 21 AD2d 859, 257 NYS2d 164 (1964) (beach and yacht club membership). *See also* Restatement (Second) of Contracts §195 comment b (1981).

all, an agreement not to sue on any claims certainly seems to include claims for negligence. Nevertheless, the decisions may be supportable if a reasonable person standing in the place of the individual who agreed to the exculpatory clause did not understand that waiving any claims meant that claims for negligence were being waived.[43] Most courts, however, have concluded that negligence does not have to be specifically stated to bar recovery.[44]

There has been some question whether the exculpatory clause could apply to negligence which occurred prior to the execution of the agreement. In *Zimmer v Mitchell & Ness*,[45] the plaintiff signed an exculpatory provision before renting ski boots. He was subsequently injured and claimed that defendant was negligent in renting the ski boots without first testing and fitting the bindings. The plaintiff argued that the exculpatory provision could not bar claims of negligence which occurred before the agreement was signed. The court side-stepped this issue and held that, even if the defendant were negligent, the negligence occurred simultaneously with the injured party's acceptance of the rental agreement and the exculpatory clause barred the claim. A different court held that if the agreement waives all claims, it covers negligence which occurred before, as well as after, the agreement was executed.[46]

Some obligations cannot be contracted away under any circumstances. In *McCarthy v NASCAR*, the court held that an exculpatory provision was invalid when the state legislature had imposed a safety requirement on the defendant.[47] Although the general rule is acceptable, the facts in *McCarthy* may not have justified its application. The New Jersey legislature had provided that the Department of Law and Public Safety was to promulgate regulations for car races. The Department had prescribed various safety requirements but it had not, prior to the accident, required an inspection to see whether the cars

---

43 *See* Sivaslian v Rawlins, 88 AD2d 703, 451 NYS2d 307, 309 (1982) (plaintiff would need legal skill to realize that when he released *all manner of actions* he was giving up his right to sue for injuries arising out of defendant's negligence).

44 *See* Cash v Street & Trail, Inc, 136 Ga App 462, 221 SE2d 640, 642 (1975); Hine v Dayton Speedway Corp, 20 Ohio App 2d 185, 252 NE2d 648, 651 (1969) ("it is not necessary to use the word 'negligence' if the intent of the parties is expressed in clear and unequivocal terms"); Zimmer v Mitchell & Ness, 253 Pa Super 474, 385 A2d 437, 439 (1978), *affd per curiam*, 490 Pa 428, 416 A2d 1010 (1980); Hewitt v Miller, 11 Wash App 72, 521 P2d 244, 248 (1974). *See generally* Owen v Vic Tanny's Enter, 48 Ill App 2d 344, 199 NE2d 280, 281 (1964); Lee v Allied Sports Assocs, 349 Mass 544, 209 NE2d 329 (1965); Empress Health & Beauty Spa v Turner, 503 SW2d 188 (Tenn 1973); Moss v Fortune, 207 Tenn 426, 340 SW2d 902 (1960); Blide v Rainier Mountaineering, Inc, 30 Wash App 571, 636 P2d 492, 493 (1981).

45 253 Pa Super 474, 385 A2d 443, 440 (1978), *affd per curiam*, 490 Pa 428, 416 A2d 1010 (1980).

46 *See* Grbac v Reading Fair Co, 521 F Supp 1351, 1356 (WD Pa 1981), *affd*, 688 F2d 215 (3d Cir 1982).

47 48 NJ 539, 226 A2d 713, 715 (1967). *See generally* Winterstein v Wilcom, 6 Md App 130, 293 A2d 821, 825 (1972).

were in compliance with those requirements. The *McCarthy* court held that an inspection was clearly implicit in the prior regulations and, therefore, the defendant could not escape liability because of the exculpatory clause when it failed to inspect the plaintiff's car.

The courts and commentators have been virtually unanimous in holding that exculpatory clauses, no matter how they are worded, do not bar claims of an individual injured by gross negligence or by wilful, wanton, or intentional acts.[48]

This higher standard of culpability in many instances cannot be shown. For example, a flagman who temporarily threw himself to the floor of the starter's stand to protect himself from possible flying debris after an accident did not commit gross negligence even when his immediate failure to display a yellow flag may have lead to a second accident.[49] Furthermore, some courts have denied plaintiffs the opportunity to amend their pleadings to allege gross negligence when there was no evidence of it in the record.[50]

Parties not specifically identified in the exculpatory provision can still be covered as long as they can be identified by reference to other facts.[51] Accordingly, an agreement which stated that it covered all parties insured under a specifically named insurance policy, but did not state the names of those parties, was nonetheless enforceable by those individuals.[52] However, no matter how broad the agreement, it does not cover individuals who are not identified in some fashion.[53]

---

[48] Gillespie v Papale, 541 F Supp 1042, 1046 (D Mass 1982); Wade v Watson, 527 F Supp 1049, 1052 (ND Ga 1981); Barker v Colorado Region-Sports Car Club of Am, Inc, 35 Colo App 73, 532 P2d 372, 377 (1974); George R. Lane & Assoc v Thomasson, 156 Ga App 313, 274 SE2d 708, 710 (1980); Schlobohm v Spa Petite, Inc, 326 NW2d 920, 923 (Minn 1982); Gross v Sweet, 49 NY2d 102, 400 NE2d 306, 424 NYS2d 365, 367 (1979); Seymour v New Bremen Speedway, Inc, 31 Ohio App 2d 141, 287 NW2d 111, 116 (1971); Broderson v Rainer Natl Park Co, 187 Wash 399, 60 P2d 234, 237 (1936), *overruled on other grounds*, 79 Wash 2d 198, 484 P2d 405 (1971); W. Prosser, The Law of Torts §68, at 444-45 (4th ed 1971); 6A C. Corbin, Contracts §1472, at 596-97 (1962); Restatement (Second) of Contracts §195 (1981); Cal Civ Code §1668 (West 1973).

[49] Grbac v Reading Fair Co, 521 F Supp 1351, 1357-58 (WD Pa 1981), *affd*, 688 F2d 215 (3d Cir 1982).

[50] Grbac v Reading Fair Co, 521 F Supp 1351, 1357 (WD Pa 1981), *affd*, 688 F2d 215 (3d Cir 1982); Seymour v New Bremen Speedway, Inc, 31 Ohio App 2d 141, 287 NE2d 111, 116-17 (1971); *but see* Gillespie v Papale, 541 F Supp 1042, 1046-47 (D Mass 1982).

[51] *See* Kircos v Goodyear Tire & Rubber Co, 108 Mich App 781, 311 NW2d 139, 143 (1981) (agreement covered advertisers and participants); Arnold v Shawano County Agricultural Socy, 106 Wis 2d 464, 317 NW2d 161, 164 (1982), *affd*, 111 Wis 2d 203, 330 NW3d 773 (1983). *See also* Doster v CV Nalley, Inc, 95 Ga App 862, 99 SE2d 432, 435-56 (1957) (ambiguity regarding coverage).

[52] *See* Gillespie v Papale, 541 F Supp 1042, 1045 (D Mass 1982).

[53] Church v Seneca County Agricultural Socy, 41 AD2d 787, 341 NYS2d 45, 47-48 (1973), *affd without opinion*, 34 NY2d 571, 310 NE2d 541, 354 NYS2d 945 (1974).

§10.03 — Individuals Not Necessarily Bound

Minors

Exculpatory provisions are contracts which, like other contracts, are usually only enforceable when the parties have capacity to contract. The traditional rule is that minors can disaffirm their contracts unless they relate to the necessities of life. Since recreational activities are almost by definition not necessities of life, exculpatory provisions signed by minors are usually voidable by them.[54] This is usually true even when a minor misrepresented his or her age.[55]

To be effective, the disaffirmance must be done while the individual is still a minor or within a reasonable time after reaching majority.[56] There are no talismanic words or acts which must be stated or performed to prove that the contract is repudiated. Indeed, the filing of a lawsuit against the defendant is sufficient.[57]

In some instances, upon reaching majority an individual may ratify an exculpatory contract entered into while a minor. For example, an individual's use of recreational facilities after reaching the age of majority ratified a contract containing an exculpatory clause entered into in order to use those facilities while a minor.[58]

The courts have been virtually unanimous in holding that a minor's parents' execution of an exculpatory provision for their child is ineffective to bar the child's claims.[59] In fact, a parent's execution of an agreement on behalf of the minor does not even bar some claims by the parent. A parent's claim for loss of services resulting from the child's injury is derivative from the

---

[54] Del Santo v Bristol County Stadium, Inc, 273 F2d 605, 607 (1st Cir 1960) (Massachusetts law); Kotary v Spencer Speedway, Inc, 47 AD2d 127, 365 NYS2d 87, 90 (1975); Cunningham v State, 32 NYS2d 275, 278 (Ct Cl), *modified on other grounds*, 204 AD 811, 34 NYS2d 903 (1942); Celli v Sports Car Club of Am, Inc, 29 Cal App 3d 511, 517, 105 Cal Rptr 904 (1972).

[55] Del Santo v Bristol County Stadium, Inc, 273 F2d 605, 607 (1st Cir 1960) (Massachusetts law). *See generally* Annot, 29 ALR3d 1270 (1970).

[56] Del Santo v Bristol County Stadium, Inc, 273 F2d 605, 607-08 (1st Cir 1960) (five months after reaching age of majority is reasonable) (Massachusetts law); Celli v Sports Car Club of Am, Inc, 29 Cal App 3d 511, 517, 105 Cal Rptr 904 (1972).

[57] Del Santo v Bristol County Stadium, Inc, 273 F2d 605, 607 (1st Cir 1960) (Massachusetts law); Celli v Sports Car Club of Am, Inc, 29 Cal App 3d 511, 517, 105 Cal Rptr 904 (1972).

[58] Jones v Dressel, 623 P2d 370, 374 (Colo 1981).

[59] *See* Fedor v Mauwehu Council, 21 Conn Supp 38, 143 A2d 466, 467-68 (1958); Fitzgerald v Newark Morning Ledger Co, 111 NJ Super 104, 267 A2d 557, 558 (1970) (also refused to enforce a parent's indemnification provision); Santangelo v City of New York, 66 AD2d 880, 411 NYS2d 666, 667 (1978). *See generally* Jones v Dressel, 623 P2d 370, 372 n 1 (Colo 1981); Doyle v College, 403 A2d 1206, 1208 (Me 1979).

child's claim, and since the child's claim is not barred, neither is the parent's.[60]

Spouse's Claims

An individual usually cannot release the claims of another. Accordingly, most courts have held that an exculpatory clause signed by a patron at a recreational facility does not bar a spouse's claim for loss of consortium after the patron was injured.[61] However, there are a few decisions to the contrary.[62]

Relatives

A valid exculpatory provision bars a subsequent wrongful death action brought by the decedent's relatives.[63]

---

60 Santangelo v City of New York, 66 AD2d 880, 411 NYS2d 666, 667 (1978).

61 *See* Gillespie v Papale, 541 F Supp 1042, 1047 (D Mass 1982); Barker v Colorado Region-Sports Car Club of Am, Inc, 35 Colo App 73, 532 P2d 372, 378 (1974); Arnold v Shawano County Agricultural Socy, 111 Wis 2d 203, 330 NW2d 773, 779 (1983).

62 *See e.g.*, Winterstein v Wilcom, 16 Md App 130, 293 A2d 821, 828 (1972) (joint claim for loss of consortium barred); Ciofalo v Vic Tanney Gyms, Inc, 10 NY2d 294, 177 NE2d 925, 220 NYS2d 962, 963 (1961) (implied).

63 Grbac v Reading Fair Co, 688 F2d 215, 216-17 (3d Cir 1982); Wade v Watson, 527 F Supp 1049, 1052 (ND Ga 1981).

Cases

A

Aalco Mfg Co v City of Espanola, 95 NM 66, 618 P2d 1230 (1980) **§7.02**

Aaser v City of Charlotte, 265 NC 494, 144 SE2d 610 (1965) **§§8.01, 8.05**

Abbott v American Honda Motor Co, 682 SW2d 206 (Tenn Ct App 1984) **§§7.16, 7.17, 7.18, 9.04**

Abdin v Fischer, 374 So 2d 1379 (Fla 1979) **§§5.02, 5.05**

Acosta v Daughtry, 268 So 2d 416 (Fla Dist Ct App 1972) **§§9.04, 9.11**

Adamczyk v Zambelli, 25 Ill App 2d 121, 166 NE2d 93 (1960) **§3.01**

Adam Dante Corp v Sharpe, 483 SW2d 452 (Tex 1972) **§§1.10, 9.01**

Adamo Wrecking Co v United States, 434 US 275 (1978) **§1.07**

Adams v Lopez, 75 NM 503, 407 P2d 50 (1965) **§§2.12, 9.18**

Adams v Montana Power Co, 528 F2d 437 (9th Cir 1975) **§2.05**

Adams v United States, 239 F Supp 503 (ED Okla 1965) **§§3.15, 3.18**

Adamson v Hand, 93 Ga App 5, 90 SE2d 669 (1955) **§§1.02, 9.05**

Adie v Temple Mt Ski Area, Inc, 108 NH 480, 238 A2d 738 (1968) **§1.21**

Adkinson v Rossi Arms Co, 659 P2d 1236 (Alaska 1983) **§2.08**

Adler v Copeland, 105 So 2d 594 (Fla Dist Ct App 1958) **§6.06**

Aetna Casualty & Sur Co v Safeco, 103 Cal App 3d 694, 163 Cal Rptr 219 (1980) **§2.08**

Agans v Showalter, 92 Ill App 3d 939, 416 NE2d 397 (1981) **§§1.16, 2.17**

Agar v Canning, 54 WWR 302 (1965), *affd*, 55 WWR 384 (1966) **§2.17**

Agricultural Workers Mut Auto Ins Co v Baty, 517 SW2d 901 (Tex Civ App 1974) **§§2.02, 2.13**

Aimone v Walgreen's Co, 601 F Supp 507 (ND Ill 1985) **§§7.01, 7.22**

Akins v Glens Falls City School Dist, 53 NY2d 325, 424 NE2d 531, 441 NYS2d 644 (1981) **§8.03**

Akridge v Park Bowling Center, Inc, 401 SW2d 204 (Ark 1966) **§1.05**

Albers v Independent School Dist No 302, 94 Idaho 342, 487 P2d 936 (1971) **§§4.15, 4.19, 9.23**

Albert v State, 80 Misc 2d 105, 362 NYS2d 341 (Ct Cl 1974), *affd*, 51 AD2d 611, 378 NYS2d 125 (1976) **§§1.17, 1.18, 1.20**

Alden v Norwood Arena, 332 Mass 267, 124 NE2d 505 (1955) **§§8.02, 9.06**

C

Cessna v Coffeyville Racing Assn, 179 Kan 766, 298 P2d 265 (1956) **§8.02**

Champ v Butler County, 18 Pa D&C3d 282 (1981) **§5.06**

Chanaki v Walker, 114 NH 660, 327 A2d 610 (1974) **§§1.12, 1.13**

Chandler v Gately, 119 Ga App 513, 167 SE2d 697 (1969) **§1.14**

Chapman v City of Grosse Pointe, 385 F2d 962 (6th Cir 1967) **§2.05**

Chapman v Foggy, 59 Ill App 3d 552, 375 NE2d 865 (1978) **§§1.01, 1.16**

Chapman v State, 6 Wash App 316, 492 P2d 607 (1972) **§9.15**

Chapman v United States, 575 F2d 147 (7th Cir 1978) **§2.05**

Chappell v Dwyer, 611 SW2d 158 (Tex Civ App 1981) **§3.14**

Chappel v Franklin Pierce School Dist, 71 Wash 2d 17, 426 P2d 471 (1967) **§4.15**

Chase v Shasta Lake Union School Dist, 259 Cal App 2d 612, 66 Cal Rptr 517 (1968) **§9.03**

Chase v State Farm Mut Auto Ins Co, 131 Ariz 461, 641 P2d 1305 (Ct App 1982) **§§2.01, 2.11**

Chauvin v Atlas Ins Co, 166 So 2d 581 (La Ct App 1964) **§§6.04, 6.06, 6.09**

Childress v Continental Casualty Co, 461 F Supp 704 (ED La 1978), *affd per curiam*, 587 F2d 809 (5th Cir 1979) **§2.17**

Chimerofsky v School Dist No 63, 121 Ill App 2d 371, 257 NE2d 480 (1970) **§4.21**

Chittum v Evanston Fuel & Material Co, 92 Ill App 3d 188, 416 NE2d 5 (1980) **§6.13**

Chute v United States, 610 F2d 7 (1st Cir 1979) **§2.03**

Chrisler v Holiday Valley, Inc, 580 SW2d 309 (Mo Ct App 1979) **§§1.22, 9.22**

Christman v Senyk, 34 Ohio Misc 47, 293 NE2d 126 (1972) **§§9.17, 9.22**

Christensen v Potratz, 100 Idaho 352, 597 P2d 595 (1979) **§6.04**

Christian v Elden, 107 NH 229, 221 A2d 784 (1966) **§§1.12, 1.13**

Christians v Homestake Enters, Ltd, 97 Wis 2d 638, 294 NW2d 534 (1980), *revd on other grounds*, 101 Wis 2d 25, 303 NW2d 608 (1981) **§§5.01, 5.13**

Christman v Senyk, 34 Ohio Misc 47, 293 NE2d 126 (1972) **§§6.09, 6.16**

Christou v Arlington Park—Washington Park Race Tracks, Corp, 104 Ill App 3d 257, 432 NE2d 920 (1982) **§§8.01, 8.06**

Church v Seneca County Argricultural Socy, 41 AD2d 787, 341 NYS2d 45 (1973), *affd without opinion*, 34 NY2d 571, 310 NE2d 541, 354 NYS2d 945 (1974) **§10.02**

Churilla v School Dist, 105 Mich App 32, 306 NW2d 381 (1981) **§3.09**

Chute v United States, 610 F2d 7 (1st Cir 1979) **§3.13**

Cincinnati Gas & Elec Co v Abel, 533 F2d 1001 (6th Cir), *cert denied*, 429 US 858 (1976) **§2.07**

Ciofalo v Vic Tanney Gyms, Inc, 10 NY2d 294, 177 NE2d 925, 220 NYS2d 962 (1961) **§10.03**

Cirillo v City of Milwaukee, 34 Wis 2d 705, 150 NW2d 460 (1967) **§§4.08, 4.15, 9.01**

Citrano v Berkshire Mut Ins Co, 171 Conn 248, 368 A2d 54 (1976) **§2.13**

City of Anadarko v Swain, 42 Okla 741, 142 P 1104 (1914) **§6.02**

City of Houston v George, 479 SW2d 257 (Tex 1972) **§3.03**

City of Houston v Riggins, 586 SW2d 188 (Tex Civ App 1978) **§6.03**

City of Lampasas v Roberts, 398 SW2d 612 (Tex Civ App 1966) **§§3.14, 6.02**

City of Terre Haute v Webster, 112 Ind App 101, 40 NE2d 972 (1942) **§3.03**

E

G

H

I

J

L

N

O

Simpson v United States, 652 F2d 831 (9th Cir 1981) §§5.01, 5.02, 5.17

Sims v Etowah County Bd of Educ, 337 So 2d 1310 (Ala 1976) §§3.03, 4.01

Sindell v Abbott Labs, 26 Cal 3d 588, 163 Cal Rptr 132, 607 P2d 924 (1980) §7.11

Sioux City & P RR v Stout, 84 US (17 Wall) 657 (1874) §6.07

Sipari v Villa Olivia Country Club, 63 Ill App 3d 985, 380 NE2d 819 (1978) §§7.01, 7.02, 7.14, 9.14

Sivaslian v Rawlins, 88 AD2d 703, 451 NYS2d 307 (1982) §10.02

Skaggs v Junis, 27 Ill App 2d 251, 169 NE2d 684 (1960) §6.07

Small v Rockfeld, 66 NJ 231, 330 A2d 335 (1974) §2.03

Smith v Alexandria Arena, Inc, 294 F Supp 695 (ED Va 1969) §7.04

Smith v American Flyers, Inc, 540 P2d 1212 (Okla Ct App 1975) §§1.22, 1.24

Smith v Arbaugh's Restaurant, Inc, 469 F2d 97 (DC Cir 1972), cert denied, 412 US 939 (1973) §6.01

Smith v Ariens Co, 375 Mass 620, 377 NE2d 954 (1978) §§7.03, 7.19

Smith v Consolidated School Dist No 2, 408 SW2d 50 (Mo 1966) §§4.01, 4.05, 4.07, 4.08, 4.22

Smith v Crown-Zellerbach, Inc, 638 F2d 883 (5th Cir 1981) §5.19

Smith v Evans, 178 Kan 259, 284 P2d 1065 (1955) §6.07

Smith v Goldman, 53 Ill App 3d 362, 368 NE2d 1052 (1977) §§6.06, 6.11

Smith v Hustler, Inc, 514 F Supp 1265 (WD La 1981) §§2.05, 2.06, 3.12

Smith v Jung, 241 So 2d 874 (Fla Dist Ct App 1970) §§1.01, 1.22, 1.23

Smith v Maryland Casualty Co, 246 Md 485, 229 A2d 120 (1967) §7.02

Smith v Mutual Beneficial Health & Accident Assn, 175 Kan 68, 258 P2d 993 (1953) §2.17

Smith v Pabst, 233 Wis 489, 288 NW 780 (1939) §1.12

Smith v Scrap Disposal Corp, 96 Cal App 3d 525, 158 Cal Rptr 134 (1979) §§5.03, 5.07

Smith v State, 93 Idaho 795, 473 P2d 937 (1970) §3.02

Smith v United States, 383 F Supp 1076 (D Wyo 1974), affd on other grounds, 546 F2d 872 (10th Cir 1976) §§3.11, 5.06, 5.18, 6.02, 9.04

Smith v United States, 337 F2d 237 (9th Cir 1964) §§3.19, 9.04, 9.07

Snyder v Kramer, 94 AD2d 860, 463 NYS2d 591 (1983) §1.12

Soares v Lakeville Baseball Camp, Inc, 369 Mass 974, 343 NE2d 840 (1976) §1.06

Soule v Massachusetts Elec Co, 378 Mass 177, 390 NE2d 716 (1979) §6.07

Space v National RR Passenger Corp, 555 F Supp 163 (D Del 1983) §5.19

Spanel v Mounds View School Dist, 264 Minn 279, 118 NW2d 795 (1962) §4.01

Spiers v Lake Shore Enters, Inc, 210 So 2d 901 (La Ct App 1968) §§1.04, 1.05

Spillway Marina, Inc v United States, 445 F2d 876 (10th Cir 1971) §3.11

Spires v Goldberg, 26 Ga App 530, 106 SE 585 (1921) §1.07

Sports, Inc v Gilbert, 431 NE2d 534 (Ind Ct App 1982) §1.01

Spote v Aliota, 254 Wisc 403, 37 NW2d 31 (1949) §1.04

Spotto v Hayward Mfg Co, 2 Conn App 663, 482 A2d 91 (1984) §7.21

Stafford v Catholic Youth Org, 202 So 2d 333 (La Ct App), writ ref, 251 La 231, 203 So 2d 559 (1967) §§1.01, 4.05

Staley v Security Athletic Assn, 152 Colo 19, 380 P2d 53 (1963) §6.07

W

Y

Yania v Bigan, 397 Pa 316, 155 A2d 343 (1959) **§1.23**

Yearke v Zarcone, 57 AD2d 457, 395 NYS2d 322 (1977) **§7.01**

Yeater v Decatur Park Dist, 8 Ill App 3d 957, 290 NE2d 283 (1972) **§3.08**

Yerdon v Baldwinsville Academy & Cent School Dist, 50 AD2d 714, 374 NYS2d 877 (1975) **§4.09**

YMCA v Bailey, 107 Ga App 417, 130 SE2d 242 (1963) **§§1.22, 1.23**

Yogerst v Janish, 303 Minn 33, 226 NW2d 291 (1975) **§1.22**

Young v Robertshaw Controls Co, 560 F Supp 288 (NDNY 1983) **§7.01**

Young v Tide Craft, Inc, 270 SC 453, 242 SE2d 671 (1978) **§§7.08, 7.09**

Z

Zaepfel v City of Yonkers, 56 AD2d 867, 392 NYS2d 336 (1977) **§9.08**

Zahrte v Sturm Ruger & Co, 709 F2d 26 (9th Cir 1983) **§9.02**

Zalak v Carroll, 15 NY2d 753, 205 NE2d 313, 257 NYS2d 177 (1965) **§2.17**

Zambito v Southland Recreation Enters, Inc, 383 So 2d 989 (Fla Dist Ct App 1980) **§1.16**

Zamora v J. Korber & Co, 59 NM 33, 278 P2d 569 (1955) **§1.07**

Zawadzki v Taylor, 70 Mich App 545, 246 NW2d 161 (1976) **§3.10**

Zieman v World Amusement Serv Assn, 209 Iowa 1298, 228 NW 48 (1929) **§8.02**

Ziginow v Redford Jaycees, 133 Mich App 259, 349 NW2d 153 (1983) **§8.01**

Zimmer v Celebrities, Inc, 44 Colo App 515, 615 P2d 76 (1980) **§§1.01, 1.04, 1.05**

Zimmer v Mitchell & Ness, 253 Pa Super 474, 385 A2d 437 (1978), *affd per curiam*, 490 Pa 428, 416 A2d 1010 (1980) **§§10.01, 10.02**

Statutes

United States Code

1 USC §3 §2.07
14 USC §86 §3.13
15 USC §1261 §7.22
15 USC §2072(a) §§7.01, 7.22, 7.23
15 USC §§2301-2312 §7.04
15 USC §2308 §7.05
15 USC §2310(e) §7.05
16 USC §1 §3.15
18 USC §921 §7.12
18 USC §922 §1.07
28 USC §1331(1) §2.06
28 USC §1333 §2.06
28 USC §1333(1) §2.06
28 USC §1346 §3.11
28 USC §2671 §3.11
28 USC §2674 §§3.11, 5.06
28 USC §2678 §3.11
28 USC §2680 §3.06
33 USC §409 §3.13
33 USC §901 §1.08
42 USC §1983 §3.01
42 USC §1985 §3.01
46 USC §183(a) §2.07
46 USC §185 §2.07
46 USC §188 §2.07
46 USC §740 §2.05
46 USC §741 §3.12
46 USC §742 §3.12
46 USC §1451 §2.04

Uniform Commercial Code

§2-313 §§7.04, 7.05
§2-314 §§7.04, 7.05
§2-314(2)(c) §7.04
§2-315 §§7.04, 7.05
§2-316 §7.04
§2-318 §7.05
§2-607 §7.05
§2-607(3)(a) §7.05
§2-714(2) §7.05
§2-714(3) §7.05
§2-719 §10.01

State Statutes

Ala Code §7-2-318 (1984) §7.05
Ala Code §11-47-190 §3.04
Ala Code §11-47-192 §3.04
Ala Code §11-93-1 §3.04
Ala Code §11-93-2 §3.04
Ala Code §13A-11-57 (1982) §§1.07, 2.09
Ala Code §31-9-16 §3.04
Ala Code §35-15-1 §5.01
Ala Code §35-15-21 §5.19

Regulations

Authorities

Government Publications

Athletic Injuries and Deaths in Secondary Schools and Colleges, Natl Center for Educ Statistics, US Dept of Health, Education and Welfare (Nov 1979) §4.01

NY State Assembly Committee on Consumer Affairs and Protection, Amusement Parks: How Safe Are They? (Apr 1982) §1.02

US Consumer Prod Safety Commn, Natl Injury Information Clearinghouse, Prod Summary Report (Mar 28, 1984) §§1.02, 1.03, 1.04, 1.07, 1.08, 1.09, 1.10, 1.15, 1.16, 1.17, 1.22, 1.26, 2.10, 2.11, 2.12, 2.14, 2.15, 2.16, 4.21, 6.10, 6.11, 6.15, 6.16, 7.07, 7.11, 7.12, 7.13, 7.14, 7.15, 7.16, 7.19, 7.20, 7.21, 7.22, 7.23, 9.08, 9.13

US Consumer Prod Safety Commn, An Overview of the Consumer Prod Safety Commn's Involvement in Amusement Ride Safety (rev ed May 15, 1984) §1.02

US Department of Transportation, Boating Statistics 1983 (June 1984) §§2.03, 7.08

US Department of Transportation, Fatal Accident Reporting System 1983 §§9.08, 9.18

Wis Divn of Health, Dept of Health & Social Servs, Snowmobile Deaths By Age And Sex (1984) §7.19

Books

Benedict On Admiralty (7th ed 1983) §§2.06, 2.07

Blackstone, Commentaries (10th ed 1887) §3.02

Civil Actions Against State Government §§2.03, 3.02, 3.11, 6.1, 6.4, 6.11, 6.16, 6.17

C. Corbin, Contracts §10.02

K. Davis, Administrative Law of the Seventies (1976) §3.03

K. Davis, Administrative Law Treatise (1958) §3.02

E. Devitt & C. Blackmar, Federal Jury Practice And Instructions (3d ed 1977) §7.01

L. Frumer & M. Friedman, Products Liability (1984) §7.05

Gilmore & Black, The Law of Admiralty (1957) §2.07

Gilmore & Black, The Law of Admiralty (2d ed 1975) §2.07

F. Harper & F. James, The Law of
Torts (1956) §§6.01, 6.05, 6.07,
6.09

R. Horrow, *Sports Violence: The
Interaction Between Private Law
Making and the Criminal Law* (1980)
§2.17

L. Jayson, Handling Federal Tort
Claims §3.11

W. Keeton, D. Dobbs, R. Keeton &
D. Owen, Prosser And Keeton On
Torts (1984) §9.02

D. Merrihugh, The Esoteric Torts
(1980) §2.17

J. Page, The Law of Premises Liability
§§5.19, 6.07

1 F. Pollock & F. Maitland, The
History of English Law (2d ed 1968)
§3.02

Powell on Real Property (1981) §5.07

W. Prosser, The Law of Torts §§3.03,
4.16, 5.08, 6.02, 6.03, 6.05, 6.07,
6.08, 6.14, 10.01, 10.02

C. Sands, Statutes and Statutory
Construction (4th ed 1973) §5.19

J. White & R. Summers, Uniform
Commercial Code (1980) §§7.01,
7.02, 7.04, 7.05

Law Journals

Admiralty Jurisdiction, 13 J Maritime L
& Comm 537 (1982) §2.05

*Admiralty Jurisdiction And The
LMLA; The Maritime Lien On
Houseboats*, 14 USF L Rev 641
(1980) §2.05

Appleson, *Shaping Up Has Many New
Pitfalls*, Natl LJ, Oct 3, 1983, at 10,
col 2 §1.11

*Assualt And Battery—Liability For Injuries
Received In Athletic Contests*, 26 Mich
L Rev 322 (1927) §2.16

Atkinson, *Torts*, 22 Wayne L Rev 629
(1976) §5.07

Baker, *Federalism and the Eleventh
Amendment*, 48 U Colo L Rev 139
(1977) §3.01

Bardenwerper, *Snowmobile Litigation And
Insurance Coverage*, 13 For The Def
29 (1972) §2.14

Barrett, *Good Sports And Bad Lands: The
Application of Washington's Recreational
Use Statute Limiting Landowner
Liability*, 53 Wash L Rev 1 (1977)
§§5.01, 5.18

Beumler, *Liability In Professional Sports:
An Alternative To Violence*, 22 Ariz L
Rev 919 (1980) §7.13

Birnbaum, *Unmasking The Test For
Design Defect: From Negligence [To
Warranty] To Strict Liability To
Negligence*, 33 Vand L Rev 593
(1980) §§7.01, 7.03, 7.08

Black, *Admiralty Jurisdiction: Critique And
Suggestions*, 50 Colum L Rev 259
(1950) §2.05

Bohlen, *Voluntary Assumption Of Risk*, 20
Harv L Rev 14 (1960) §9.02

Borchard, *Governmental Liability in Tort*,
34 Yale LJ 1 (1924) §3.03

Calamari, *The Wake of Executive Jet -
A Major Wave or A Minor Ripple*, 4
Mar Law 52 (1979) §3.12

Carmilla & Dizal, *Foremost Insurance
Co v Richardson: If This Is Water, It
Must Be Admiralty*, 59 Wash L Rev 1
(1983) §2.05

Coben, *Motorcycle Helmets*, 19 Trial 62
(Nov 1983) §7.18

Cohen, *Gymnastics Litigation: Meeting
The Defenses*, 16 Trial 34 (Aug 1980)
§9.15

Comment, *Admissibility of Safety Codes,
Rules And Standards In Negligence
Cases*, 37 Tenn L Rev 581 (1970)
§1.24

Comment, *Assumption Of Risk And
Vicarious Liability In Personal Injury
Actions Brought By Professional Athletes*,
1980 Duke LJ 742 §§2.17, 9.03

Comment, *Automobiles—Family Purpose Doctrine*, 3 Vand L Rev 644 (1950) **§2.01**

Comment, *Duty of Owners and Occupiers of Land to Persons Entering The Premises: Should Pennsylvania Abandon The Common Law Approach*, 17 Duq L Rev 153 (1979) **§§6.01, 6.02, 6.03, 6.05**

Comment, *Federal Jurisdiction—Torts*, 11 Rut-Cam LJ 497 (1980) **§2.17**

Comment, *Finance Lessor Liability Under Section 402A Restatement (Second) Of Torts*, 7 Am J Trial Advoc 155 (1983) **§7.01**

Comment, *Liability of Texas Public Officials for Their Tortious Acts*, 16 Hous L Rev 100 (1978) **§4.15**

Comment, *Limitation Of Liability In Admiralty*, 19 Vill L Rev 721 (1965) **§2.07**

Comment, *Limiting Liability: Products Liability And A Statute Of Repose*, 32 Baylor L Rev 137 (1980) **§7.02**

Comment, *Negligence*, 1 Washburn LJ 316 (1961) **§§1.17, 1.20**

Comment, *Obviousness Of Product Dangers As A Bar To Recovery: Minnesota Apparently Adopts The Latent-Patent Doctrine*, 3 Wm Mitchell L Rev 241 (1977) **§7.01**

Comment, *Products Liability—Tort Reform: An Overview of Washington's New Act*, 17 Gonz L Rev 357 (1982) **§§7.01, 7.02**

Comment, *Sale Of Goods In Service-Predominated Transactions*, 37 Fordham L Rev 115 (1968) **§7.04**

Comment, *Sales-Service Hybrid Transactions: A Policy Approach*, 28 SW LJ 575 (1974) **§7.04**

Comment, *Snowmobiles—A Legislative Program*, 1972 Wis L Rev 477 **§2.14**

Comment, *Status of the Social Guest: A New Look*, 7 Wm & Mary L Rev 313 (1966) **§6.04**

Comment, *Survey Of Developments In North Carolina Law, 1977*, 56 NCL Rev 843 (1978) **§2.01**

Comment, *Survey Of Developments In North Carolina Law, 1977*, 56 NCL Rev 1145 (1978) **§2.04**

Comment, *The Common Law Tort Liability of Owners and Occupiers of Land*, 36 Md L Rev 816 (1977) **§6.02**

Comment, *The Outmoded Distinction Between Licensees and Invitees*, 22 Mo L Rev 186 (1957) **§6.01**

Comment, *Torts*, 37 Minn L Rev 317 (1962) **§2.03**

Comment, *Torts*, 20 Syracuse L Rev 823 (1969) **§2.11**

Comment, *Torts—Abolition of the Distinction Between Licensees and Invitees Entitles All Lawful Visitors To a Standard of Reasonable Care*, 8 Suffolk L Rev 795 (1974) **§6.01**

Comment, *Torts: Athlete States Cause Of Action For Injury During Professional Football Game*, 19 Washburn LJ 646 (1980) **§2.02**

Comment, *Violence In Professional Sports*, 1975 Wis L Rev 771 **§§2.02, 2.17**

Comment, *Wisconsin's Recreational Use Statute: A Critical Analysis*, 66 Marq L Rev 312 (1983) **§§5.01, 5.10**

D'Amato, *The "Bad Samaritan" Paradigm*, 70 NW UL Rev 798 (1975) **§6.16**

Davis, *Comparative Negligence, Comparative Contribution, And Equal Protection In The Trial And Settlement Of Multiple Defenses & Product Cases*, 10 Ind L Rev 831 (1977) **§9.04**

Diamond, *Dillon v. Legg Revisited: Toward A Unified Theory Of Compensating Bystanders And Relatives For Intangible Injuries*, 35 Hastings LJ 477 (1984) **§7.01**

Dickerson, *Products Liability: How Good Does A Product Have To Be?*, 42 Ind LJ 301 (1967) **§7.01**

Digges & Klein, *Comparative Fault In Maryland: The Time Has Come*, 41 Md L Rev 276 (1982) **§9.04**

Eddy, *Effects Of The Magnuson-Moss Act Upon Consumer Product Warranties*, 55 NCL Rev 835 (1977) **§7.05**

Fagen, *Ski Area Liability for Downhill Injuries*, 49 Ins Couns J 36 (1982) **§§1.17, 1.21**

Farnsworth, *Implied Warranties Of Quality In Non-Sale Cases*, 57 Colum L Rev 653 (1957) **§§7.04, 7.14**

Feinberg, *The Applicability Of A Comparative Negligence Defense In A Strict Products Liability Suit*, 42 Ins Couns J 39 (1975) **§§7.02, 9.04**

Field, *The Eleventh Amendment and Other Sovereign Immunity Doctrines: Part One*, 126 U Pa L Rev 155 (1978) **§3.01**

Fleming, *Forward: Comparative Negligence At Last—By Judicial Choice*, 64 Cal L Rev 236 (1976) **§9.04**

Frakt, *Recreational And Leisure Product Liability*, 1 J Prod L 5 (1982) **§7.01**

Franklin, *Vermont Requires Rescue*, 25 Stan L Rev 51 (1972) **§6.16**

Fraser, *Application Of Strict Tort Liability To The Leasing Industry: A Closer Look*, 34 Bus Law 605 (1979) **§7.01**

Fuller & Casner, *Municipal Tort Liability in Operation*, 54 Harv L Rev 437 (1941) **§3.03**

Gabrielsen & Olenn, *Swimming Pool Litigation: Educating For Safety*, 18 Trial 39 (Feb 1982) **§§1.22, 7.21**

Gargiulo, *Liability For Leaving A Firearm Accessible To Children*, 17 Clev-Marsh L Rev 472 (1968) **§2.08**

George, *Maritime Tort Jurisdiction: A Survey Of Developments From Executive Jet To Foremost Insurance Co v Richardson*, 24 S Tex LJ 511 (1983) **§2.05**

Gershon, *Torts*, 35 Mercer L Rev 291 (1983) **§5.05**

Gibbons, *The Eleventh Amendment and State Sovereign Immunity: A Reinterpretation*, 83 Colum L Rev 1889 (1983) **§3.01**

Gibson, *Violence In Professional Sports: A Proposal For Self-Regulation*, 3 COMM/ENT 425 (1981) **§§2.02, 2.17**

Goff, *Defective Firearms*, 20 Trial 36 (Nov 1984) **§§7.11, 7.12**

Greenhill & Murto, *Governmental Immunity*, 49 Tex L Rev 462 **§3.02**

Hagglund, *Ski Liability*, 32 Fedn Ins Q 223 (1982) **§§1.17, 1.20**

Halbrook, *Tort Liability For The Manufacture, Sale And Ownership Of Handguns?*, 6 Hamline L Rev 351 (1983) **§7.12**

Hall, *Sovereign Immunity and Reemergence of the Governmental/Proprietary Distinction: A Setback in Idaho's Governmental Liability Law*, 20 Idaho L Rev 197 (1984) **§§3.02, 3.03, 3.04, 3.07**

Hallowell & Meshbesher, *Sports Violence And The Criminal Law*, 13 Trial 29 (Jan 1977) **§2.17**

Harbison, *Family Responsibility In Tort*, 9 Vand L Rev 809 (1956) **§2.01**

Harley & Wasinger, *Governmental Immunity*, 16 Washburn LJ 12 (1976) **§3.03**

Harolds, *Limitation Of Liability And Its Application To Pleasure Boats*, 37 Temp LQ 423 (1964) **§2.07**

Harris & Schnepper, *Federal Tort Claims Act: Discretionary Function Exception Revisited*, 31 U Miami L Rev 161 (1976) **§3.11**

Hasten, *Comparative Liability Principles: Should They Now Apply To Strict Products Liability Actions In Ohio*, 14 U Tol L Rev 1151 (1983) **§§7.02, 9.04**

Hechter, *The Criminal Law And Violence In Sports*, 19 Crim LQ 425 (1976) **§2.17**

Hoffman, *Stacking Uninsured Motorist Coverage*, 26 For The Def 3 (Nov 1984) **§2.13**

Hollister, *Parent-Child Immunity: A Doctrine In Search Of Justification*, 50 Fordham L Rev 489 (1982) **§2.01**

Jaffe, *Suits Against Governments and Officers: Sovereign Immunity*, 77 Harv L Rev 1 (1963) **§3.02**

James, *Accident Liability Reconsidered: The Impact Of Liability Insurance*, 57 Yale LJ 549 (1948) **§2.01**

James, *Assumption Of Risk*, 61 Yale LJ 141 (1952) **§9.02**

James, *Assumption Of Risk: Unhappy Reincarnation*, 78 Yale LJ 185 (1968) **§9.02**

James, *Tort Liability of Occupiers of Land*, 63 Yale LJ 605 (1954) **§1.05**

James, *Tort Liability of Occupiers of Land: Duties Owed To Licensees and Invitees*, 63 Yale LJ 605 (1954) **§§1.04, 3.14, 6.02, 6.03, 6.04, 6.09**

James, *Tort Liability of Occupiers of Land: Duties Owed To Trespassers*, 63 Yale LJ 144 (1953) **§§6.05, 6.07**

Keeton, *Product Liability And The Meaning Of Defect*, 5 St Mary's LJ 30 (1973) **§§7.01, 7.03**

Knowles, *Landowners' Liability Towards Recreational Users*, 18 Idaho L Rev 59 (1982) **§§5.01, 5.06**

Lambert, *Tort Law And Participant Sports: The Line Between Vigor And Violence*, 4 J Contemp L 211 (1978) **§§2.01, 9.04**

Liebman, *Assault on the Citadel*, 4 Suffolk UL Rev 832 (1970) **§3.03**

Lipsig, *Tort Trends*, NYLJ 1 (July 27, 1984) **§3.15**

Lisman, *Ski Injury Liability*, 43 U Colo L Rev 307 (1972) **§§1.01, 1.17, 9.21**

Malone, *Torts*, 25 La L Rev 47 (1964) **§5.19**

Marshall, *An Obvious Wrong Does Not Make A Right: Manufacturers' Liability For Patently Dangerous Products*, 48 NYU L Rev 1066 (1973) **§7.01**

McCurdy, *Torts Between Parent And Child*, 5 Vill L Rev 521 (1960) **§2.01**

McCurdy, *Torts Between Persons In Domestic Relations*, 43 Harv L Rev 1030 (1930) **§2.01**

McGovern, *The Variety, Policy And Constitutionality Of Product Liability Statutes Of Repose*, 30 Am UL Rev 579 (1981) **§7.02**

Mikva, *Sovereign Immunity: In A Democracy The Emperor Has No Clothes*, 1966 U Ill LF 828 **§3.11**

Note, *Allowance Of Punitive Damage Awards In Product Liability Claims*, 6 Ga L Rev 613 (1972) **§7.02**

Note, *A New Beginning For the Attractive Nuisance Doctrine*, 34 Mercer L Rev 433 (1982) **§6.07**

Note, *A Shot At Stricter Controls: Strict Liability For Gun Manufacturers*, 15 Pac LJ 171 (1983) **§7.12**

Note, *Assumption Of Risk After Sunday v Stratton Corp*, 3 Vt L Rev 129 (1978) **§§1.17, 1.21**

Note, *Assumption Of Risk And Vicarious Liability In Personal Injury Actions Brought By Professional Athletes*, 1980 Duke LJ 742 **§2.01**

Note, *Automobiles-Agency-Family Purpose Doctrine*, 38 NCL Rev 249 (1960) **§2.01**

Note, *Beyond Good Samaritans and Moral Monsters: An Individualistic Justification of the General Legal Duty To Rescue*, 31 UCLA 252 (1983) **§6.16**

Note, *Compensating Injured Professional Athletes: The Mystique Of Sports Versus Traditional Tort Principles*, 55 NYU L Rev 971 (1980) **§§2.17, 9.03**

Note, *Consent In Criminal Law: Violence In Sports*, 75 Mich L Rev 148 (1976) **§2.17**

Note, *Contracts For Goods And Services And Article 2 Of The Uniform*

Commercial Code, 9 Rut-Cam LJ 303 (1978) §7.04

Note, *Contributory Negligence And Assumption Of Risk—The Case For Their Merger*, 56 Minn L Rev 47 (1971) §9.01

Note, *Economic Loss In Products Liability*, 66 Colum L Rev 917 (1966) §7.01

Note, *Handguns And Products Liability*, 97 Harv L Rev 1912 (1984) §§7.12, 7.22

Note, *Helmetless Motorcyclists - Easy Riders Facing Hard Facts; The Risk Of The Motorcycle Helmet Defense*, 41 Ohio St LJ 233 (1978) §9.18

Note, *Injuries Resulting From Nonintentional Acts In Organized Contact Sports: The Theories Of Recovery Available To The Injured Athlete*, 12 Ind L Rev 687 (1979) §§2.17, 7.13

Note, *Judicial Scrutiny Of Tortious Conduct In Professional Sports: Do Professional Athletes Assume The Risk Of Injuries Resulting From Rule Violations? Hackbart v Cincinnati Bengals*, 17 Cal WL Rev 149 (1980) §2.17

Note, *Landowners' Liability in New Jersey: The Limitation of Traditional Immunities*, 12 Rutgers L Rev 599 (1958) §6.01

Note, *Liability In Professional Sports: An Alternative To Violence*, 22 Ariz L Rev 919 (1980) §2.17

Note, *Local Government Sovereign Immunity: The Need For Reform*, 18 Wake Forest L Rev 43 (1982) §§3.02, 3.03, 3.04

Note, *Parental Immunity: California's Answer*, 8 Idaho L Rev 179 (1971) §2.01

Note, *Participant's Liability For Injury To A Fellow Participant In An Organized Athletic Event*, 53 Chi-Kent L Rev 97 (1976) §2.17

Note, *Professional Sports And Tort Liability: A Victory For The Intentionally Injured Player*, 1980 Det CL Rev 687 §§2.01, 2.17, 9.03

Note, *Product Liability Reform Proposals: The State Of The Art Defense*, 43 Alb L Rev 944 (1979) §7.03

Note, *School Liability for Athletic Injuries*, 21 Washburn LJ 315 (1982) §4.01

Note, *Second Collision Liability: A Critique Of Two Approaches To Plaintiff's Burden Of Proof*, 68 Iowa L Rev 811 (1983) §7.17

Note, *Ski Operators And Skiers*, 14 New Eng L Rev 260 (1978) §§1.17, 1.21, 9.21

Note, *The Applicability of Sovereign Immunity to Independent Public Authorities*, 74 Harv L Rev 714 (1961) §3.02

Note, *The "Booby" Trap: Does The Violent Nature Of Professional Football Vitiate The Doctrine Of Due Care In Participant Tort Litigation?*, 10 Conn L Rev 365 (1978) §2.17

Note, *The Demise Of The Parent-Child Tort Immunity*, 12 Willamette LJ 605 (1976) §2.01

Note, *The King Can Do Wrong - Maybe: Abolition of Court - Imposed Sovereign Immunity for Nondiscretionary Negligent Acts*, 3 Miss CL Rev 103 (1982) §3.03

Note, *The Minnesota Recreational Use Statute: A Preliminary Analysis*, 3 Wm Mitchell L Rev 117 (1977) §§5.01, 5.03, 5.10

Note, *The Minnesota Supreme Court 1963-1964*, 49 Minn L Rev 93 (1964) §3.19

Note, *The "Reasonable Parent" Standard*, 47 U Colo L Rev 795 (1976) §2.01

Note, *Tort Law*, 21 Duq L Rev 815 (1983) §§9.03, 9.13

Note, *Tort Liability And Recreational Use Of Land*, 28 Buffalo L Rev 767 (1979) §5.01

Note, *Tort Liability In Professional Sports*, 44 Alb L Rev 696 (1980) §§2.01, 2.02, 2.17, 9.03

Note, *Tort Liability In Professional Sports: Battle In The Sports Arena*, 57 Neb L Rev 1128 (1978) §2.17

Note, *Torts*, 42 Brooklyn L Rev 125 (1975) §§2.01, 2.17

Note, *Torts*, 31 SCL Rev 131 (1979) §3.14

Note, *Torts: Assumption Of Risk At Sports Car Event*, 10 Hastings LJ 344 (1959) §9.04

Note, *Torts-Assumption Of Risks—Golf Courses*, 14 Mercer L Rev 295 (1962) §9.14

Note, *Torts: Athlete States Cause Of Action For Injury During Professional Football Game*, 19 Washburn LJ 646 (1980) §2.17

Note, *Torts—Duty of Occupier to Social Guests*, 19 La L Rev 906 (1959) §6.04

Note, *Torts In Sports—Deterring Violence In Professional Athletics*, 48 Fordham L Rev 764 (1980) §§2.01, 2.02, 2.17

Note, *Torts: Negligence: Duty Of A Place Of Amusement To Protect Patrons Against Acts Of Third Persons*, 6 UCLA L Rev 494 (1959) §8.03

Note, *Torts—Statutes—Liability of Landowner To Persons Entering For Recreational Purposes*, 1964 Wis L Rev 705 §5.01

Note, *Utah's Inherent Risks Of Skiing Act*, 1980 Utah L Rev 355 (1980) §§1.17, 1.21

Olson, *Governmental Immunity From Tort Liability Two Decades Of Decline: 1959-1979*, 31 Baylor L Rev 485 (1979) §3.03

On Finding Civil Liability Between Professional Football Players: Hackbart v Cincinnati Bengals, Inc, 15 New Eng L Rev 741 (1980) §2.17

Owen, *Punitive Damages In Products Liability Litigation*, 74 Mich L Rev 1256 (1976) §§7.02, 7.18

Peck, *The Role Of The Courts And Legislatures In The Reform Of Tort Law*, 48 Minn L Rev 265 (1963) §§2.03, 2.12

Pelaez, *Ownership At Sea: Identifying Those Entitled To Limit Liability In The Admiralty*, 22 Duq L Rev 397 (1984) §2.07

Philo & Stine, *The Liability Path To Safer Helmets*, 13 Trial 38 (Jan 1977) §7.13

Pleasure Boating And Admiralty, 51 Cal L Rev 661 (1963) §2.07

Pleasure Boating Under Admiralty Jurisdiction: An Unwarranted Expansion Of Federal Authority, 12 Cap UL Rev 545 (1983) §2.05

Powers, *Distinguishing Between Products And Services In Strict Liability*, 62 NCL Rev 415 (1984) §§7.02, 7.10

Proehl, *Tort Liability of Teachers*, 12 Vand L Rev 723 (1959) §§3.03, 4.01, 4.08, 4.09, 4.11, 4.12, 4.15, 4.21, 9.03

Prosser, *The Assault Upon The Citadel (Strict Liability To The Consumer)*, 69 Yale LJ 1099 (1960) §7.01

Prosser, *The Fall Of The Citadel (Strict Liability To The Consumer)*, 50 Minn L Rev 791 (1966) §§7.01, 7.03, 7.04, 7.10

Prosser, *Trespassing Children*, 47 Cal L Rev 427 (1959) §6.07

Ranii, *Sports Violence Lawsuits Erupt*, Natl LJ, Feb 19, 1981, at 30 §2.17

Reel, *Dashing Through The Snow: Oregon And The Open Sleigh*, 3 Env L 74 (1973) §2.14

Robb, *A Practical Approach To Use Of State Of The Art Evidence In Strict Products Liability Cases*, 77 NW UL Rev 1 (1977) §7.03

Roberts & Thronson, *A New Perspective—Has Utah Entered The Twentieth Century in Tort Law?*, 1981 Utah L Rev 495 **§3.03**

Sales, *The Innocent Misrepresentation Doctrine: Strict Tort Liability Under Section 402B*, 16 Hous L Rev 239 (1979) **§7.06**

Scalf & Robinson, *Injuries Arising Out Of Amateur And Professional Sports: Viability Of The Assumption Of Risk Defense*, 27 Def LJ 419 (1978) **§§2.11, 9.03**

Schwartz, *Strict Liability And Comparative Negligence*, 42 Tenn L Rev 171 (1974) **§9.04**

Seasongood, *Municipal Corporations*, 22 Va L Rev 910 (1936) **§3.03**

Seitz, *Legal Responsibility Under Tort Law of School Personnel and School Districts As Regards Negligent Conduct Toward Pupils*, 15 Hastings LJ 495 (1964) **§§4.01, 4.08, 4.15**

Sherman, *Torts*, U Pitt L Rev 451 (1966) **§2.08**

Siegel, *Liability Of Manufacturers For The Negligent Design And Distribution Of Handguns*, 6 Hamline L Rev 321 (1983) **§7.12**

Stolz, *Pleasure Boating And Admiralty*, 51 Cal L Rev 661 (1963) **§§2.05, 2.07**

Swartz, *Leisure Time Product-Related Torts*, 1983 SMU Prod Liab Inst 5 (1983) **§§7.03, 7.21**

Swartz, *Toys-R-Dangerous*, 18 Trial 28 (Feb 1982) **§7.22**

Teret & Wintemute, *Handgun Injuries: The Epidemiologic Evidence For Assessing Legal Responsibility*, 6 Hamline L Rev 341 (1983) **§7.12**

Thornton, *The Eleventh Amendment: An Endangered Species*, 55 Ind LJ 293 (1980) **§3.01**

Thuillez, *Parental Nonsupervision*, 40 Alb L Rev 336 (1976) **§2.01**

Tort Law—Reckless Misconduct In Sports, 19 Duq L Rev 191 (1980) **§2.17**

Tort Liability For Players In Contact Sports, 45 UMKC L Rev 119 (1976) **§2.17**

Torts, 15 Gonz L Rev 867 (1980) **§§2.17, 9.03**

Torts - Assumption Of Risk, 12 Ga L Rev 380 (1978) **§2.17**

Torts - Participant In Athletic Competition States Cause Of Action For Injuries Against Other Participant, 42 Mo L Rev 347 (1977) **§2.17**

Tough to Tackle, 70 ABA J 32 (May 1984) **§§4.05, 4.12, 4.22**

Turley, *Manufacturers' And Suppliers' Liability To Handgun Victims*, 10 N Ky L Rev 41 (1982) **§7.12**

Turley & Harrison, *Strict Tort Liability Of Handgun Suppliers*, 6 Hamline L Rev 285 (1983) **§7.12**

Utah's Inherent Risks Of Skiing Act, 1980 Utah L Rev 355 **§9.02**

Vacca, *Teacher Malpractice*, 8 U Rich L Rev 447 (1974) **§§4.01, 4.08, 4.12, 4.15, 4.16**

Voelker, *The Application Of Comparative Negligence To Strict Products Liability*, 59 Chi-Kent L Rev 1043 (1983) **§§7.02, 9.04**

Volk & Cobbs, *Limitations Of Liability*, 51 Tul L Rev 953 (1977) **§2.07**

Wade, *On Product "Design Defects" And Their Actionability*, 33 Vand L Rev 551 (1980) **§§7.01, 7.03**

Wade, *On The Nature Of Strict Tort Liability For Products*, 44 Miss LJ 825 (1973) **§7.03**

Wade, *The Place Of Assumption Of Risk In The Law Of Negligence*, 22 La L Rev 5 (1961) **§9.02**

Weinrib, *The Case For A Duty To Rescue*, 90 Yale LJ 247 (1980) **§6.16**

Wells, *Liability Of Ski Area Operators*, 41 Den LJ 1 (1964) **§1.17**

Wilkens, *The Wrongful Death of Willie McCord*, 47 U Cin L Rev 591 (1978) **§§5.01, 5.06**

Wilkinson, *Sports Products Liability*, 17 Trial 58 (Nov 1981) **§7.01**

Woods, *Product Liability: Is Comparative Fault Winning The Day*, 36 Ark L Rev 360 (1983) **§§7.02, 9.04**

Woods, *The Trend Toward Comparative Fault*, 20 Trial 16 (Nov 1984) **§9.01**

Wunsch, *The Definition Of A Product For Purposes Of Section 402A*, 50 Ins Couns J 344 (1983) **§7.02**

Medical Journals

Barclay, *Equestrian Sports*, 240 JAMA 1893 (1978) **§1.12**

Brayna, *Blood Creative Kinase Isoenzyme BB In Boxers*, Lancet 1308 (Dec 11, 1982) **§4.22**

Clark, *Survey Reveals 476 Spinal Cord Injuries*, 5 Physician & Sportsmedicine 17 (1977) **§4.22**

Cooper, *Are Double Dual High School Wrestling Matches Advisable*, 236 JAMA 200 (1976) **§4.22**

Grossman, *Equestrian Injuries*, 240 JAMA 1881 (1978) **§1.12**

Hursch, *Food and Water Restriction in The Wrestler*, 241 JAMA 915 (1976) **§4.22**

Hussey, *Ice Hockies Injuries*, 236 JAMA 187 (1976) **§4.22**

Kaste, *Is Chronic Brain Damage in Boxing A Hazard of The Past*, Lancet 1186 (Nov 27, 1982) **§4.22**

Maroon, *"Burning Hands" In Football Spinal Cord Injuries*, 238 JAMA 2049 (1977) **§4.22**

Ross, *Boxers - Computed Tomography, EEG and Neurological Evaluation*, 249 JAMA 211 (1983) **§4.22**

Thornton, *Use of Diuretics For "Making Weight" In Sports Is Harmful Practice*, 236 JAMA 200 (1976) **§4.22**

Torg, *The National Football Head and Neck Injury Registry*, 241 JAMA 1477 (1979) **§4.22**

Opthalmologist Wins Hockey Safety Campaign, 238 JAMA 2591 (1977) **§4.22**

Yeager, *The Savage State Of Sports*, Physician & Sportsmedicine, 94 (May 1977) **§2.17**

Newspapers

Barrell & Shuster, USA Today, Mar 8, 1985, §C, at 1, col 3 **§7.20**

Bearak, *New Laws Combat An Old Problem: Drunk Boaters*, Los Angeles Times, July 30, 1984, at 6, col 1 **§§2.03, 2.04**

Gross, *State Of The Art: Still Alive And Well In New Jersey*, Legal Times, Sept 17, 1984, at 12 **§7.03**

Jackson, *School Districts Fear Suits Over Athletic Injuries*, LA Daily J, May 30, 1984, at 1, col 6 **§§4.01, 4.05, 4.12, 4.22**

Klein, *Fast Lanes: Bowling On TV*, Wall St J, Mar 23, 1983, at 19, col 1 **§1.04**

LA Daily J, Apr 27, 1983, at 1, col 5 **§§4.05, 4.13, 4.22**

Mortisuge, *Should Courts Be Refereeing Sports Fights*, Wall St J, Sept 1, 1982, at 19, col 3 **§2.17**

Scanlon, *Revving Up A Regulatory Merry-Go-Round*, Wall St J, July 14, 1984, at 24, col 4 **§7.07**

Schmalz, *Increasing Problem Of Drunken Boating Spurring New Laws*, NY Times, Sept 2, 1984, at 23, col 1 **§2.03, 9.09**

Sloane, *Homeowners' Insurance Is Revised*, NY Times, Dec 26, 1984, at 28, col 3 **§§2.01, 2.17**

Wolff, *Drunkenness: Ugly Pastime For Some Baseball Fans*, NY Times, June 16, 1985, at 23, col 5 **§8.03**

Miscellaneous

Council of State Governments, XXIV Suggested State Legislation (1965) **§5.01**

Metropolitan Life Ins Co, 60 Statistical Bulletin 5 (July-Sept 1979) **§4.22**

Mueller & Blyth, Natl Center for Catastrophic Sports Injury Research 1982-83 School Year **§§4.18, 4.19, 4.20, 4.22**

Mueller & Schindler, Annual Survey of Football Injury Research 1931-1983 **§§4.05, 4.22**

The Washington Area Bicyclist Assn, A Consumer's Guide To Bicycle Helmets (Apr 1984) **§9.08**

Index

G